MAGILL'S
LITERARY ANNUAL

1977

MAGILL'S
LITERARY ANNUAL
1977

*Essay-Reviews of 200 Outstanding Books
Published in the United States during 1976*

_____

*With an Annotated Categories Index
and a Listing of 1,100 Review Sources*

Edited by
FRANK N. MAGILL

SALEM PRESS
Englewood Cliffs

LIBRARY OF CONGRESS CATALOG CARD NUMBER: 77-99209

ISBN 0-89356-077-4

First Printing

PRINTED IN THE UNITED STATES OF AMERICA

LYNDON JOHNSON AND THE AMERICAN DREAM

Author: Doris Kearns (1943-   )
Publisher: Harper & Row Publishers (New York). 420 pp. $12.50
Type of work: Biography
Time: 1908-1973
Locale: The United States

A life of Lyndon Johnson in which psychological forces and institutional dynamics are interwoven to explain his successes and failures

       Principal personages:
         LYNDON B. JOHNSON
         REBEKAH BAINES JOHNSON, his mother
         SAM EALY JOHNSON, his father
         CLAUDIA TAYLOR (LADY BIRD) JOHNSON, his wife

Lyndon Johnson tried to persuade and finally pleaded with twenty-five-year-old Doris Kearns to help him write his memoirs. During the last months of his Presidency, when he was so disliked by many people that he rarely left the White House, he was convinced that his last chance would be with the historians. He was not very sanguine about how the historians would treat him, but he felt that he had to get his side of the story out. Though he had planned to write three volumes, his efforts resulted in only one book, *The Vantage Point: Perspective on the Presidency.* It was not a success, in spite of Kearns's efforts to get him to reveal himself, largely because, while LBJ was one of the greatest of storytellers, he was ineffective and artificial when dealing with unknown audiences.

Kearns was never asked to be an official biographer, but Johnson must have known that one day she would write a book about him. Long after he had lost interest in his own memoirs he continued to hold long, introspective talks with her. He said he revealed his innermost thoughts to her because she reminded him of his dead mother. One suspects, however, that he had chosen this Harvard intellectual as the instrument by which he could convey his story to the historians. She would be accepted by the thinkers he could not reach, and she could write the book he could not produce. It may be that he realized that even his vaunted persuasiveness could not totally overcome her professional integrity and that her book would contain criticism as well as praise and thus be more believable. Whatever his motivations, LBJ's conversations with Doris Kearns have resulted in the most significant book yet written about the Johnson years.

Since the primary material for the book is derived from the notes Kearns took during her conversations with Johnson, it dwells more on his thoughts and motivations than on the details of his career. He told her of his childhood, his dreams and his fears, so Kearns has attempted to provide a psychological interpretation of their impact on his personality and ambitions. One gets the impression that the author is never very comfortable in her role as a psychoanalyst. As a result, these efforts are the least convincing parts of the biography. The fact that LBJ was never seriously constrained by the truth while telling a story casts further doubt on the validity of the data on which the analysis is based.

Kearns is much more sure-footed when she draws on her professional background in analyzing the dynamics of the governmental institutions in which Johnson operated. In tracing his political career from congressional secretary through Director of the Texas National Youth Administration, member of the House of Representatives, Senator, Vice-President and finally President, the author uses Johnson as a case study to illustrate the characteristics of each position and to demonstrate how his talents and personality matched or clashed with the institutional environment. By use of this device, Kearns is able to expand this biography into a commentary on the interaction of leadership, institutional momentum, and the forces of history. She summarizes these observations in an "Author's Postscript," which in many ways is the most fascinating part of her book.

Psychologically, Johnson's personality and drives may have been formed in the tension between his father and mother. Rebekah Johnson was a melancholy woman who sought to compensate for an unhappy marriage and a father whose bright prospects were never realized and whose death destroyed her ambitions of being a great novelist by driving her son to seek outstanding intellectual and cultural achievements. She sought to manipulate him by granting or withholding her love in response to his behavior. As a result, he continually sought to perform good deeds and expected love in return. This found its highest expression in his "Great Society" programs, and his greatest disappointment resulted when the American people failed to express their love for him after he had given them so much.

His mother's demands for intellectual and cultural achievement were counterbalanced by a father who considered such pursuits unmanly. Sam Ealy Johnson was a crude, hard-drinking local politician. Much of Lyndon's vulgarity and interest in politics can be traced to the model his father provided. According to Kearns, the mismatch between his mother, who loved to discuss the "higher things," and a father whose idea of pleasure was to sit up half the night with his friends drinking beer and telling stories, created a great tension which prompted Johnson to seek to control his environment. Control of one's environment requires power, and his pursuit of power encompassed a wider and wider world as he moved up the political ladder.

The author also attributes Johnson's lifelong devotion to the politics of consensus to his early childhood experiences. She feels that the conflict between his parents gave him such a distaste for confrontation that he became the eternal compromiser during his political career. Of course, LBJ would explain this tactic quite rationally by pointing out that extremists never accomplish anything and that he was, above all else, a doer rather than a thinker. In this instance Johnson may be closer to the truth than his biographer, who was very much a part of the 1960's and shares the tendency of that generation to take moral stands rather than pursue practical alternatives.

In her analysis of the tactics Johnson used to attain his remarkable political successes, Kearns discovered a recurring pattern. His formula for success in most instances involved working harder and longer than any of his competitors. Since he was endowed with seemingly boundless energy, his capacity for work was prodigious. He apprenticed himself to the top man in whatever institution he found himself and showed great astuteness in discovering who the real leader was. By effectively serving his master he learned how to control the organization and, usually, quietly supplanted his mentor while continuing to maintain his friendship.

Johnson first demonstrated the effectiveness of this process while a student in college. He ingratiated himself with the college president after becoming an assistant to his secretary. Soon, even the faculty began to consider Lyndon the way to get the President's ear. He became the editor of the school's newspaper and carried out a successful four-year campaign to supplant the ruling student *clique* by organizing the disorganized outsiders. He used the skills he developed in college to attain success as the secretary to a wealthy Texas congressman and to develop his own political base as a representative of one of the New Deal agencies.

Many feel that Johnson attained his greatest success in Congress. He first got there by another often repeated trait, the ability to decide quickly and take action before his competitors. By declaring his candidacy for the seat of a deceased congressman from his district only a few days after the funeral, LBJ was able to discourage the widow from seeking to replace her husband. After his election, Johnson chose Sam Rayburn as his mentor and could probably have become a power in the House. He was able to obtain a choice committee assignment through Rayburn, but soon decided the Senate offered greater opportunities for his talents. The House was simply too large a body for him to use his one-on-one persuasion to its greatest effectiveness, and it was too committed to the principal of seniority for a young man in a hurry.

His first try for elective office revealed another curious quality. Johnson had a great need to control his environment, and elections, even in Texas, are not totally controllable. In many of his elections he seriously considered withdrawing at the last minute to escape the pain of confrontation and possible failure. He also became physically ill on the eve of several of the most crucial contests. Because of this tendency, Kearns feels that LBJ's decision not to run in 1968 was quite predictable.

The character of the United States Senate is not a static condition but varies with the personalities of the Senators and the forces of history at any given time. The Senate of the 1950's was an ideal milieu for LBJ, and he soon dominated it in a way that has rarely been duplicated. He apprenticed himself to Richard Russell, the most influential of the small group that dominated the body. When the opportunity arose, he sought the position of minority leader and had few rivals for the post because it entailed much work and little power. Johnson made a science of knowing what was important to each Senator and then trying to provide it, along with countless favors; thus he secured the gratitude of most of the members. His effectiveness was in the cloakroom rather than in debate. In fact, he discouraged debate because debate meant taking public positions, and that made compromise more difficult. Without compromise little legislation was possible. Thus, Johnson sought consensus through individual persuasion. He spoke of principles to the liberals, and mocked the liberals to the Southerners. He was able to get a majority to support a bill for opposing reasons. The Senate became more effective than it had been in decades, and Johnson's reputation grew. Kearns is quite critical of his methods because she feels the Senate should have been debating important issues and arousing the public. She feels Johnson thus sowed the seeds of his own destruction because the Senate was unable to regain its voice in time to ameliorate his Vietnamese policy. As majority leader he so weakened the system of checks and balances that it was unable to control him when he was President.

It seems clear that the Senate matched Johnson's needs and talents to a higher degree than any other post that he occupied. He ran an inept campaign for the Presidential nomination, partially because he assumed that Senators controlled the state delegations. He accepted the Vice-Presidential nomination because he thought he might use his apprenticeship method to attain the presidency. The constitutional system was stronger than LBJ's tactics, and he was no more successful in supplanting Kennedy than Seward had been in replacing Lincoln.

Johnson's Presidency is best remembered for the Great Society programs and the tragedy of the Vietnam War. His most successful accomplishment was the skillful transition he managed after the assassination. He was assisted in this by the Republicans, who gave him a landslide victory through their nomination of Barry Goldwater. For a few brief months Lyndon Johnson enjoyed the admiration of the American people that he craved so much.

Kearns attributes Johnson's success with the Great Society to three factors. One is the groundwork that Kennedy had laid and which Johnson exploited in the name of the martyred President. Another is the affluence which the country was then enjoying, which enabled it to afford benefits for the poor without taking anything from the rich. Finally, there was Johnson's legislative skill in steering this greatest of social welfare reform programs through Congress. Unfortunately, most of the programs failed to attain their goals because the Vietnam War occupied Johnson's attention and drained away the resources needed to sustain them.

The Vietnam War was Johnson's greatest failure, and it ultimately destroyed him. He did not understand foreign policy, viewing it in simplistic terms. He sought to have both guns and butter by lying to the American people. He knew the Great Society would be abandoned if the true extent of the cost of the war were known. Americans were accustomed to winning their wars, and in their frustration they turned on the manipulator in the White House.

Doris Kearns has written a good book. One of its major flaws is its failure to capture the pure pungency of LBJ; and it is also limited by being based too heavily on her conversations with Johnson. Nevertheless, her biography is a very sensitive and astute analysis of the man and of the institutions with which he was associated.

Alfred D. Sander

Sources for Further Study

Book World. May 30, 1976, p. F7.

Commentary. LXXII, August, 1976, p. 75.

Horn Book. LII, December, 1976, p. 652.

New Statesman. XCII, October 8, 1976, p. 484.

Spectator. CCXXXVII, October 16, 1976, p. 20.

Village Voice. XXI, March 29, 1976, p. 42.

Wall Street Journal. CLXXXVII, June 4, 1976, p. 10.

THE MAKING OF AN ASSASSIN
The Life of James Earl Ray

Author: George McMillan (1913-   )
Publisher: Little, Brown and Company (Boston). 318 pp. $8.95
Type of work: Biography
Time: 1928-1968
Locale: Southern United States

A psychosociological biography which concludes that James Earl Ray was the lone assassin of Martin Luther King, Jr.

> Principal personages:
> JAMES EARL RAY, the assassin of Martin Luther King, Jr.
> GEORGE "SPEEDY" RAY, his father
> LUCILLE "CEAL" RAY, his mother
> JACK RAY and
> JERRY RAY, his brothers
> CAROL RAY, his sister
> MARY "MOM" MAHER, his aunt
> EARL RAY, his uncle

In the past fifteen years, nearly a hundred books have been published that claim to answer the legal questions: who really killed President Kennedy, Martin Luther King, Robert Kennedy? If Lee Harvey Oswald, James Earl Ray, and Sirhan Sirhan killed them, did they act alone or were they part of a conspiracy? In *The Making of an Assassin*, George McMillan gives his answer to that question regarding one of the three killings: James Earl Ray was the lone assassin of Martin Luther King. Few books attempt to answer the sociological and psychological questions. McMillan poses and answers those questions as well. His task is to convince his readers—in 318 informally, ambiguously documented pages. With most reviewers, he succeeds.

McMillan once intended to subtitle Ray's biography "An American Life"; but that point, implicit on every page, was reiterated by most reviewers. If their noble slain leaders exemplify their aspirant qualities, Americans must accept the concept that their ignoble celebrities exemplify squalid aspects of the American character. While arguing no conspiracy in fact, McMillan argues a conspiracy of the spirit, between society and the psyches it helps to produce, a conspiracy that turns the American Dream into nightmare.

Few books examine American heroes and their destroyers closely enough. The man who dedicated himself to a simple solution was the complex product of a society that taught him to believe in simple, direct solutions to complex problems. McMillan, a freelance journalist, devoted eight years to investigating not only the facts but also the social and psychological processes that produced and perhaps begin to explain them. Ray did not act simply from a racism grounded in envy and spite. McMillan begins to explain the development of far more complex factors and how they combined to produce the one criminal racist in all America capable of acting out his version of the American Dream: to assassinate "The Big Nigger," enthrone George Wallace, and thus create a conservative society based on white supremacist religious, ethical, and economic principles.

McMillan goes to Ray's very genes to delineate prefigurations of Ray's enormous act. If blood tells, it told McMillan a great deal. He argues that Ray's great-grandfather was *probably* Ned Ray, hanged for participating in a mass murder in Montana in 1865. He meshes this exercise in genealogical detection with descriptions of the family (steeped in a long history of poverty, violence, crime) and the Missouri hometown environment that shaped Ray.

Ray's racist mentality was inculcated in a close-knit, lower-lower-class, semirural family. Ray was a loner, an outsider even within a family of loners and outsiders. What set him apart was his obviously superior intelligence (IQ 108) and a temper that even at seven frightened them all. McMillan says the sum of their lives was "sordid degradation and spiritual destitution," and quotes a county juvenile judge's summation: "They were a lousy outfit."

Ray's first teacher in Ewing, Missouri, characterized him on his report card as a violator of every rule, dishonest, seldom polite, and physically "repulsive." In that school, he was taught he was socially inferior but that Negroes were worse. Ray dragged Ewing with him down the Mississippi, from one "wretched and squalid" physical and "moral slum" to another—to Quincy (where "two blocks is a lifetime") and Alton, Illinois, St. Louis, to several Missouri prisons, to Memphis. He carried with him a defensive hatred of his own worst feature—weakness.

But he pitied the weakness of children. This Huck Finn who set out for the heart of darkness was also a Catcher in the Rye. He told Curtis, his partner in crime, that he wanted to rob enough money to build an orphanage for neglected children, and he would maintain it by robbing. He had a total lack of sympathy for suffering adults, because adults were the cause of suffering in children. As for women, they were all whores, useful for "hauling his ashes."

McMillan points out the absurdity of Ray's crimes, the sordidness of their settings, the inept violence and self-degradation of their commissions, the humiliation of his captures. Discharged from the army for "ineptness," he robbed a Kroger store in Chicago; chased by police, he fell through a basement window into a washtub. Another time, police captured him in a bathroom. He escaped from prison in a bread basket. And he carried out "the most important single act of his life . . . with his feet in the old, stained, rooming house" bathtub. Then bloodhounds found the escapee under soggy leaves. McMillan suspects that he wanted to get caught, to end the anger that infused his crime. Captured, he was strangely calm; incarcerated, he was a model prisoner, who dreamed intensely of a future of high crimes.

McMillan's tracing of the evolution of Ray's politics may strike the reader as a little forced, but no less fascinating, and true, at least metaphorically. As a child in Ewing, Ray had hated Roosevelt so much that he became the only Republican in Ewing. "Nazism can attract those who are emotionally fragmented, who want to believe it will make them whole." Indoctrinated by the unregenerate Nazi who worked with him in the tannery, Ray, at seventeen, "followed the Swastika to Germany like the Holy Grail." His hero-worship of Hitler suffered disillusionment when Ray was assigned as an MP to the Nuremburg trials in 1946. The weakness of the defeated German citizens in the ruined cities inspired his contempt. Ironically, he was locked in the stockade at Nuremburg for drunkenness.

During the televised army trials, he passionately supported Senator Joseph McCarthy and despised Eisenhower. Having concocted two schemes for assassinating President Kennedy, he felt contempt for Oswald's bungling. His conservatism found a leader in Goldwater. His individualism found expression in Ayn Rand's novel *Atlas Shrugged.* An escaped convict, he was a well-remembered hard worker in Wallace's campaign headquarters. After killing King, he planned to flee to Rhodesia.

Blacks became to Ray what Jews were to Hitler. He nurtured his hatred of Martin Luther King in "Jeff City," the federal penitentiary at Springfield, Missouri, "the roughest damned city in the country," " 'a medieval twilight zone.' " On television, he watched the civil rights leader rise in the early 1960's to national prominence and hero status. The upward mobility of blacks generally, from the late 1950's to 1968, and of their most believed in, though not always most powerful, leader, enraged this poor-white, smalltime criminal loser. Ironically, Ray never had much direct contact with blacks, not even in Jeff City, where they were brutally segregated. McMillan sees that factor as a further indication that Ray's hatred of blacks was a projection of self-hatred and hatred of his father and mother.

Ray found a father in a local opposite of his own, a cultured, mild man named Graves who might have made the difference had his teacher, Miss Tots, not already convinced him of Ray's absolute worthlessness. His tough uncle, Earl Ray, in prison at Ray's birth and most of the time thereafter, remained a father-figure who confirmed the perverse value of his worthlessness. The German with whom Ray worked as a teenager in a tannery in Alton became an intellectual father-figure; together, they worshiped the Führer.

As the oldest male child in the family, Ray, early in his life, was consciously given and consciously assumed the burden of making up for his father's lacks, of revenging his parents' disappointments, for he embodied their "hopes, fears, ideals and unspoken dreams." "He had the perilous task of linking his family and the world all over again." "He felt everybody had responsibilities," says his admiring little brother, Jerry. "Jimmy felt if you don't do your duty, it's not worth living." Later, he felt that he embodied the passions of thousands of people like himself. From J. Edgar Hoover and the FBI, to Governor Wallace (he established residency in Alabama so Wallace could pardon him if he got caught), to the citizens of Memphis and their police, Ray felt assured of spiritual complicity in an act only he had the "guts" to force from dream to reality.

Love is power, and as Ray grew up in Ewing without it, impotence and rage, compatible bedfellows, bred their likenesses rapidly, like cockroaches. Unable to see the democratic process as the way to realize the American dream of rags to riches, log cabin to White House, obscurity to celebrity, a nightmare minority has acted on the notion that to become a celebrity, one must simply kill a celebrity; to cease being a diminished person, obliterate a superperson. A self-conceived father-figure himself, Ray would slay the father-figure. As McMillan writes, there was "a conspiracy of the influences on Ray as an individual to lead him to make his decision." The murder of King was "an over-determined act." King's masculinity made him also an ideal father-figure, strong and loving. Killing King was "revenge for the withholding, un-loving aspects of both his actual parents." It was also suicide, an end to unbearably overwhelming emotions that rendered him inept.

McMillan's claim is that his book proves, in traditional sociological and psychological terms, that Ray, and Ray alone, was motivated to kill King; and that his book provides facts to show that the money Ray is known to have spent since his escape from Jeff City came not from sources who hired him to kill King but from his own resources as a "merchant" during years in prison. Some readers may find McMillan's methods as amateur sociologist and psychiatrist dubious, and even more may doubt the conclusiveness of the "evidence" he offers to support his lone assassin theory. But even in its inconclusiveness, to whatever degree, McMillan's book is valuable, for it provides readers with a basis for comparison and discussion.

The major weakness in McMillan's argument stems from the fact that, in amassing his "evidence," he placed too much reliance on unreliable people (some of whom he paid modest sums that the informants may not have considered modest). That officials in our time are not necessarily reliable either needs to be mentioned in passing. The moods, attitudes, allegiances of Ray's family and fellow con men are changeable and contradictory. In a *Life* magazine story of June 21, 1968, Jerry Ray, one of McMillan's key sources, said, "I know he wouldn't have put himself in a spot like that unless there was something in it for him." Doesn't that contradict McMillan's major claim—that Ray eked out in prison the money he spent to kill King out of profound psychological compulsions? It was Jerry who told McMillan that his brother was one of those self-styled Ku Klux Klansmen with pillowcases over their heads who beat and stabbed the newly integrated blacks at Jeff City. Investigations at the time showed Ray was not even in the area. It was Jerry, the family jester, who, McMillan admits, ridiculed, obscenely teased, and lied to Ray over the years.

McMillan often points out the unreliability of the notes Ray provided

William Bradford Huie for his book *He Slew the Dreamer,* but he seldom questions his own secondary sources, Ray's family and friends, on crucial issues. If
Ray brags of making a fool of Huie by creating a dashing international spy
named "Raoul" (simply another alter-ego, McMillan contends) as the man
who hired him, what assured McMillan (and what assures the reader of his
book) that the whole crew of liars similar to Ray aren't laughing at McMillan's
gullibility, aren't telling him what he wants to hear? McMillan often assures us
that he was always frank with his informants as to his purpose, as if that would
assure frank responses. Wouldn't McMillan's very honesty about his own
point of view make it easy for them to tailor their stories to his, their fantasies-
mixed-with-fact to his own?

   In response to questions about why Ray behaved as he did in the months
before the assassination, McMillan says, "What is wrong with those questions
is that they assume James Earl Ray was operating on rational lines." When the
subject behaves irrationally, the writer is freer to speculate, but then the reader
must reserve assent to his answers and conclusions. McMillan dismisses all
competing theories as fictions, lacking evidence. But even in the handling of
facts, a sense of fiction pervades McMillan's own approach. Denied access to
Ray, himself an arch-fantasist, McMillan observably conjures him up, with a
kind of conjectural voodoo. The result for some readers will be a mixture of
fact and fantasy that culminates in a metaphor for part of the truth, which, in
the absence of conclusive evidence, sustains one aspect of the appetite to
know.

David Madden

Sources for Further Study

Kirkus Reviews. XLIV, August 15, 1976, p. 947.
Library Journal. CI, September 1, 1976, p. 1791.
New York Times Book Review. October 31, 1976, p. 6.
Newsweek. LXXXVIII, October 25, 1976, p. 110.
Publisher's Weekly. CCX, August 23, 1976, p. 62.

A MAN CALLED INTREPID
The Secret War

Author: William S. Stevenson (1925-   )
Publisher: Harcourt Brace Jovanovich (New York). Illustrated. 486 pp. $12.95
Type of work: History and biography
Time: 1896-1962, with a concentration on the period 1933-1945
Locale: Great Britain, the United States, Germany, and other countries involved in the outbreak and course of World War II

A history of Anglo-American espionage activities during World War II and the role played by the masterspy who coordinated them

> *Principal personages:*
> SIR WILLIAM STEPHENSON (CODE NAME, INTREPID), head of British Security Coordination
> WILLIAM DONOVAN, head of the United States Office of Strategic Services (OSS)
> SIR WINSTON CHURCHILL, First Lord of the Admiralty, 1939-1940; Prime Minister of Great Britain, 1940-1945
> FRANKLIN DELANO ROOSEVELT, President of the United States, 1933-1945

William Stevenson's *A Man Called Intrepid: The Secret War* is the third book to appear in the last two years which deals with the subject of Anglo-American espionage activities during World War II. First, Frederick Winterbotham revealed in *The Ulta Secret* how the British intelligence service broke the German code. Subsequently, Anthony Cave Brown, in *Bodyguard of Lies,* told the story of how the Allies deceived the Germans and used complex intelligence tactics to launch the D-Day invasion on June 6, 1944.

In *A Man Called Intrepid,* Stevenson, a Canadian journalist, provides an exciting account of the career of Sir William S. Stephenson, the Canadian industrialist and scientist, who, at the direction of Prime Minister Winston S. Churchill and with the cooperation of President Franklin D. Roosevelt, established the nerve center of worldwide British intelligence operations in New York City in June, 1940. It was at this time that Churchill assigned Stephenson the code name "Intrepid." During the war, the author himself was involved in a special intelligence arrangement which brought him into contact with Stephenson. (Despite the similarity of their names, they are not related.) They became close friends, and some years after the war, Sir William provided his wartime colleague with his papers, which largely form the basis for *A Man Called Intrepid.*

In the foreword to the book, Sir William sets forth what he considers to be the reasons why his espionage activities and those of his many operatives should at last be revealed. First, he cites the need to pay tribute to those gallant men and women who risked and often gave their lives while carrying out covert operations on behalf of the Western Allies. Second, Sir William feels that such a book can dispel many of the myths and inaccurate accounts about key events in World War II and thus provide the basis for a reinterpretation of that conflict. Finally, he hopes that the story of his wartime activities may demonstrate the need which the democracies have for strong intelligence agencies. Although he regards intelligence gathering as an essential secret weapon for which safeguards against its abuse must be devised, he does not consider its existence as being incompatible with the principles of democracy.

The book, in its overall scope, reflects Sir William's stated reasons for its publication. The author discusses Stephenson's career as a fighter pilot in World War I and his role after the war as a member of the circle of scientists and former officers that Churchill put together to keep a watch on German weapon research. Stephenson's fears about Germany's threat to the peace were more than confirmed with Adolf Hitler's rise to power in 1933. Thereafter, as the author relates, Sir William went on to establish what amounted to a private intelligence service which fused with official British government espionage activities once World War II began. In addition to recounting Sir William's exploits during World War II, Stevenson focuses on many clandestine operations of other secret agents and officials who were part of Intrepid's organization. One such official was William Donovan, head of the famed American "Fighting 69th" Regiment in World War I and a longtime friend of Stephenson. Under his direction and training, Donovan set up what came to be known in 1942 as the United States Office of Strategic Services (OSS). The author's depiction throughout the book of the exploits of Intrepid and his associates is designed, in keeping with Sir William's comments in the foreword, to explain certain heretofore misunderstood events in the war and to point up the need for the democracies to maintain strong, vigilant intelligence operations.

Stevenson devotes considerable space in his book to Intrepid's role in setting up British intelligence operations in the United States during 1940. With the consent and cooperation of President Roosevelt, Intrepid chose New York City, specifically Rockefeller Center, as the headquarters of what came to be known as British Security Coordination (BSC). New York was selected because it was the commercial and communications center of the free world and because of its location outside the war zone. There, intelligence experts could work on specific problems in relative calm and dispatch their findings to London by code machines perfected by Intrepid's own team of inventors. Intrepid's mission was basically threefold. First and foremost, he was to serve as the intelligence intermediary in the collaboration between Churchill and Roosevelt. Prior to the entry of the United States into the war, Stephenson, as Churchill's personal envoy to the President, had instructions to persuade him to increase American military aid to Great Britain. Second, Intrepid's spy organization, in cooperation with the FBI, was to direct all Allied intelligence operations, including both counterespionage against Nazi fifth columns in the Americas and all forms of secret warfare in Nazi-occupied Europe. Finally, Intrepid's agency had the task of taking over the direction of British resistance in the event the Nazis invaded and occupied the United Kingdom. In his espionage activities on both sides of the Atlantic, Intrepid drew upon German secret reports which the British were gathering from a captured German Enigma code-decoding machine. Intrepid labeled all information drawn from this source as "Top secret Ultra." This information was so confidential that it was confided to only a small number of British leaders and also to President Roosevelt.

By far Stephenson's most important intelligence enterprise during World War II was his participation in the race for control of the first atomic bomb. This race, as far as his role in it was concerned, had two major objectives. First of all, the Germans would have to be prevented from taking delivery on shipments of deuterium oxide or "heavy water," as it was called, from the Norsk Hydro plant in Norway. This plant was the world's only commercial producer of heavy water, the use of which was essential for the control of an atomic reaction. Stephenson, the author points out, had learned that I. G. Farben, the German industrial colossus, not only sought Norsk Hydro's total output of heavy water but was a large investor in that atomic plant. The second objective was to bring from Copenhagen the Danish atomic scientist, Niels Bohr, who had already split the uranium atom in his laboratory. Intrepid identified these two objectives as being paramount during the winter of 1939-1940, in the period of the so-called "Phony War" prior to the German invasion of Norway and Denmark. Once the Nazis had occupied both countries in April, 1940, the need to realize these objectives as soon as possible became all the more apparent.

Stevenson devotes several fascinating though rather disjointed chapters to the efforts of Intrepid and his operatives to accomplish this twofold mission. Late in February, 1943, Norwegian demolition experts trained in Great Britain destroyed the Norsk Hydro plant. The Germans, however, restored full production there within a few months, whereupon the Allies mounted a series of bombing raids against the plant that proved to be a total failure. Finally, in February, 1944, a team of Norwegian saboteurs blew up a ferry which was hauling 5,000 pounds of heavy water on the first leg of its trip to Germany. This action was responsible for preventing the Germans from building an atomic bomb. Intrepid, meanwhile, had realized his second objective. In the fall of 1943, British agents spirited Niels Bohr out of Denmark, thence to England via Sweden, and finally to the United States, where he joined the Manhattan Project which was working on the atomic bomb. Stephenson thus made an important contribution to the efforts of the United States to explode the first nuclear device. In his last big espionage operation of the war, Intrepid was responsible for hiding Igor Gouzenko, the Russian cipher clerk, who defected in Ottawa, Canada, in September, 1945, and revealed the Russian spy-ring that stole secrets from the American atomic bomb project.

Intrepid, the author writes, was always "in the thick of a dozen battles." Indefatigable, he worked twenty hours each day of the war. Besides the atomic bomb enterprise, he supervised numerous other wartime operations as well, among them the assassination of Reinhard Heydrich, the *Reichsprotector* of Bohemia-Moravia. Czech agents, specially trained in one of Intrepid's facilities in Canada, carried out this mission in May, 1942. Its purpose was to instill hope and encourage resistance among the enslaved peoples throughout Nazi-occupied Europe and at the same time to eliminate one of the most powerful and ruthless leaders of the Third Reich. Throughout the war, more than 30,000 agents engaged in intelligence-gathering activities were linked to Intrepid's British Security Coordination. Interestingly, these agents included a number of people in the entertainment world, among them Greta Garbo, Noel Coward, and Leslie Howard, who was killed in 1943 when the Germans shot down his plane after they learned of a secret mission in which he was engaged. One other individual who worked closely with Intrepid was Ian Fleming. As the author of spy thrillers, he based the intrigues of his fictional character James Bond on his wartime espionage experiences and on those of Stephenson.

William Stevenson's *A Man Called Intrepid* is as valuable a story as it is exciting. It provides the solution to a number of mysteries in World War II, among them the full story of the plot against Heydrich. The book is also important for showing how deeply involved President Roosevelt was in supporting British intelligence operations in the United States prior to American entry into the war in December, 1941. Another strong point of the book is the excellent selection of photographs, showing, among other things, the German code-decoding machine, Enigma.

Otherwise, the book's effectiveness is marred by a number of flaws. For one, the author's writing style is frequently disjointed, muddled, and repetitive. This is illustrated in his discussion of how a British intelligence unit managed in 1939 to bring to England one of the German Enigma code-decoding machines which Polish agents had stolen from the Nazis. Stevenson's almost cryptic organization of the telling of this episode and others adds to the mysteries which his book is supposed to solve. The lack of sufficient and exact dates in the text is another source of distraction, although this problem is somewhat mitigated by a table of key dates. Stevenson's vagueness on dates also causes him to make a number of serious errors. Thus, at one point, he refers to Intrepid's first visit with President Roosevelt "in early spring of 1940." On that occasion, Stevenson writes, Intrepid informed Roosevelt about the guerilla warfare techniques which the British planned to use that would enable them to return to Europe. The Germans, however did not drive the British off the Continent until June, which was long after Stevenson's first meeting with Roosevelt. In another passage, Stevenson describes the Nazi reprisals that took place after the assassination of Reinhard Heydrich in 1941. He cites the destruction, with their inhabitants, of the villages of Lidice in Bohemia and Oradour-sur-Glane in France as examples of the German revenge taken on various communities throughout occupied Europe in the wake of Heydrich's death. Although this was the fate of Oradour-sur-Glane, it did not befall that village until June 10, 1944, two years to the day, coincidentally, after the tragedy of Lidice.

These shortcomings notwithstanding, *A Man Called Intrepid: The Secret War* does complement the two aforementioned studies related to it, *The Ultra Secret* and *Bodyguard of Lies.* Collectively, these books are significant for contributing to the reinterpretation of World War II, but the definitive study of espionage in that conflict remains to be written.

Edward P. Keleher

Sources for Further Study

America. CXXXIV, May 29, 1976, p. 482.
Book World. March 14, 1976, p. 9.
Contemporary Review. CCXXVIII, April, 1976, p. 223.
National Review. XXVIII, September 3, 1976, p. 964.
Spectator. CCXXXVI, April 10, 1976, p. 20.
Times Literary Supplement. May 28, 1976, p. 643
Wall Street Journal. CLXXXVII, May 6, 1976, p. 16.

THE MANLY-HEARTED WOMAN

Author: Frederick Manfred (1912-   )
Publisher: Crown Publishers (New York). 185 pp. $7.95
Type of work: Novel
Time: The early nineteenth century
Locale: Southwest Minnesota

A deeply symbolic tale of sacrifice for the good of the tribe by an Indian brave, and of the love which he inspires in an Indian woman

> *Principal characters:*
> FLAT WARCLUB, a young Dakota brave who has been directed by a vision to give his life in battle against the hostile Omaha tribe
> MANLY HEART, a young woman of a sister tribe, a bisexual
> PRETTYHEAD, Manly Heart's young "wife"

With the publication of *The Manly-Hearted Woman,* Frederick Manfred has returned to the world of the Plains Indians before the arrival in force of the white man, first depicted in his novel *Conquering Horse* (1959). Like that novel, and intended to be read as the first of his five-novel Buckskin Man series, *The Manly-Hearted Woman* describes the coming of age of a Yankton Dakota brave. It has some of the familiar strengths of Manfred's previous writing: a sharply defined sense of place, vivid appeals to the senses, and a profound sense of sympathy for his protagonists. It lacks, until the concluding battle scene, the striking depictions of action which are found in his other books: the fights with the white stallion in *Conquering Horse,* with the bear in *Lord Grizzly,* and with the puma in *Scarlet Plume.* It also lacks the suspense of Manfred's other books, perhaps because the author is attempting for the first time to achieve a psychological density in describing an Indian woman.

A relatively slight novel in terms of length, *The Manly-Hearted Woman* turns around the dramatic encounter of two comparative outcasts from sister tribes, each of whom might be described as the protagonist. The title character is one seldom if ever encountered in fiction about American Indians: a female bisexual. Having had two husbands, Manly Heart declares herself a man of the tribe; this declaration is accepted and Manly Heart is given Prettyhead as a "wife." Into their village and their lives then comes a young Yankton Dakota named Flat Warclub; he, though scorned in his own village for reasons not entirely clear, has been assured in a vision that his destiny is to die heroically in battle with the Omahas, who have ursurped his tribe's buffalo hunting ground.

There are technical problems of no small magnitude for a modern white American author who writes about an essentially vanished primitive culture. Not the least of these is character motivation. The Indians were animists, and as such intense symbolists; living *in* nature, as they did, and not merely close to it, every storm and sunset, every curled snake and darting lizard, was potentially a sign of divine favor or discontent. The problem for a modern writer and for his modern readers, who presumably do not share these beliefs, any more than they "believe" the Greek myths or the Icelandic eddas, is to bridge the distance between the characters' actions and the beliefs that prompt those actions. The actions are usually comprehensible to us—they may involve ritual mortification of the flesh to show sorrow or formal apologies to a deer one has just shot. The beliefs which prompt the actions are so distant from our industrial urban society, resting as they do on a mystical union with nature, that the modern reader is more likely to feel the curiosity of an anthropologist, observing strange customs and mores, than he is to feel intensely about the characters involved.

Manfred attempts—successfully, for the most part—to bridge the gap for us between a character's beliefs and his actions by entering into his mind and re-counting the dialogues he has with his "helper." Each Indian brave had a helper, some object that was secret to everyone else; for Flat Warclub it was a piece of stone fallen from the heavens, still warm when he found it. The helper is "wakan," or magic, an intermediary between the observed, tangible world, and that of the spirit. As it is represented in the novel, the helper talks to its owner, advises him, warns him, and interprets the actions and motivations of others for him. It might be said to be the equivalent of the devout Christian's conscience or of the artist's muse. In terms of the art of fictional narrative, the helper serves to explain what a character thinks and why he does what he does; it is useful for spiritual and psychological development in a way that is not available to other kinds of realistic fiction.

Because she has become in effect a man, Manly Heart also has a helper, a triangular piece of rock which she calls Point from the Clouds, a fit mate for Flat Warclub's helper, called Stone from the Clouds. Too many helpers may spoil the book, especially when we learn that the helpers get together, indepen-dent of their owners, to discuss mutual problems of interest. At any rate, Manly Heart, Prettyhead, and Flat Warclub are soon engaged in a peculiar, not-quite-fulfilled *ménage à trois:* because Flat Warclub is going to die for the village, after killing (according to his helper) seven of the enemy braves, he has requested and been granted the right to "talk" with any of the village maidens he chooses. This privilege corresponds nicely with a problem that has been worrying Manly Heart since Prettyhead came to live with her, a matter of weeks: how will they have children? The solution is obvious: invite Flat Warclub to "talk" with Prettyhead. The consummation is realized, at which time the watching Manly Heart realizes that she is indeed a woman, not a man, and offers herself to the spent Flat Warclub. He rejects her out of both decorum and fatigue, but later sees as he dies that she was more deserving of his attentions than the merely charming Prettyhead.

These complications are handled with dignity and good humor by Manfred; the joys of the flesh are celebrated by these fatalists with a fine sense of *carpe diem.* Inevitably, of course, the story ends with the death in battle of

Flat Warclub—ironically, though, as the result of an accident—and the last pages tell of Manly Heart's inconsolable grief and quick decline.

The Manly-Hearted Woman is Frederick Manfred's twentieth book. Because his works deal with the upper Midwest from Minnesota to the west of the Rocky Mountains, he is considered a "regionalist," a term that despite such regionalists as William Faulkner, Willa Carther, and John O'Hara, is a critical kiss of death. The heart of the publshing industry is in New York, along with the literary nerve centers for the nation, and Manfred has received far less than his due as a writer of stature. Within the growing body of writers, critics, and teachers interested in Western American literature, however, Manfred's achievement is widely recognized, as evidenced by the attention given his work at the Western Literature Association convention in October, 1977, held near Manfred's home in Sioux Falls, South Dakota.

Of particular interest with regard to *The Manly-Hearted Woman* are the aforementioned Buckskin Man novels. These five books are all currently in print (New American Library, Signet editions) and represent a panorama of the American West from the time just before the arrival of the white man in force—about 1800—to the 1890's. A common theme or attitude that runs through all these novels, and which is found in *The Manly-Hearted Woman* as well, has to do with the way the grand sweep and size of the land determine both the character of those who inhabit it and the stories which are told about those people, both white and Indian. Passions, emotions, joys, and griefs are all outsized, intensely dramatic if not melodramatic—there are few petty or small characters in Manfred's novels. The mode of Manfred's work is, accordingly, not so much fiction as it is romance; it follows the lines of romance explained by Richard Chase in his classic study, *The American Novel and Its Tradition.*

The American romance as discussed by Chase includes *Moby Dick* and *The Scarlet Letter.* Different though those books are from Manfred's, they share with them two qualities; idealism and moral didacticism. There is a recurrent argument in the Buckskin Man series that reflects these qualities, and which must be understood for *The Manly-Hearted Woman* to be appreciated. The argument is as follows: before anything, there was the land. The Indians lived in conformity with the land, drew their strength from it, were one with it. The Indian metaphors for the land are all feminine; those for the sky all masculine. The union of the sky and the land, especially during a storm with its thunder and lightning, was of the profoundest significance to the Indian (hence the importance of the stones which the protagonists in *The Manly-Hearted Woman* have as helpers). The white man, on the other hand, viewed the land as an antagonist, carrying with him in his intellectual baggage an assortment of ideas from John Calvin, Alexander Pope, Benjamin Franklin, Charles Darwin, Alfred, Lord Tennyson, and others. Nature was red in tooth and claw, there to be conquered. The white man thus scorned the Indians' symbolic interpretations of natural events as the grossest superstition—one need only read Francis Parkman's *The Oregon Trail* to see how the most intelligent, sensitive, and cultured traveler of his time, later to become a world-renowned historian, regarded the Indians' concept of visions. In a word, the white man came, saw, and conquered: he imposed his will on the land, and on the Indians who had reached a harmonious accommodation with it.

The novel which most forcefully depicts the Indian way of life as noble and fulfilling is *Conquering Horse*. Like Flat Warclub, Conquering Horse at the beginning of his story is a relative outcast, at least in his own mind, because he has not yet received a vision. He thus is known as No-name, a man without an identity. Ultimately, he achieves his goal, and the novel ends on a triumphant note.

The next novel according to the historical chronology, though the first of the series to be written, is *Lord Grizzly* (1954). *Lord Grizzly* is about Hugh Glass, a hunter in the 1820's with a fur-trading party who is mauled by a bear and left for dead by his friends. Hugh crawls to safety, a hundred miles on his hands and knees, dragging a broken leg, through hostile Indian territory. He survives his ordeal because he adapts to the land instead of fighting it—he is literally on his knees before it. And like the Indians, Hugh dreads the day when the prairies will be broken by the plow, though ironically he has done much to open the hostile land to settlers.

It is with the third novel in the Buckskin Man series that the tragedy of the American Indian begins. *Scarlet Plume* (1964) describes the Sioux uprisings of 1862 and the consequent brutal suppression of the Plains Indians as a whole. It is a captivity narrative of a kind extremely popular in the nineteenth century, the most famous example being Cooper's *The Last of the Mohicans*. It is also a precursor to *The Manly-Hearted Woman* in its depiction of a woman who loves an Indian brave, though in this case the woman is white. At the heart of the tragedy are the differing attitudes held by the Indian and the white man concerning the land; as a novel it is a harrowing experience, though unconvincing in its opposition of good Indians and detestable whites.

In the fourth and fifth novels of the series the whites have established their supremacy over the land, and blood-lust and insanity have become dominant. *King of Spades* (1966) is set in the Black Hills of South Dakota in 1876. It is a horrific retelling of the Oedipus story, not the most successful of Manfred's books but significant in terms of the general theme under consideration here: the crucial choice which the hero must make turns around a beautiful, unspoiled valley to which he is taken by a beautiful, unspoiled Indian maiden. He rejects both in order to plunder the valley for gold. The valley is ravaged and the hero is destroyed.

Finally, *Riders of Judgment* (1957) is about a time when the white men have taken total control over the land; it describes the famous range wars of Wyoming in the 1890's, in this case between the large and small cattle ranchers.

The protagonist, Cain Hammett, has much of the reverential feeling for the land that Conquering Horse, Scarlet Plume, and Hugh Glass have, but he is doomed and destroyed by the forces of industry represented by the large, and largely absentee, ranch owners. Thus those most distant from and least interested in the land have the most control over it.

The Buckskin Man novels, then, represent a hundred-year saga of deterioration, of steady estrangement from the land. Read in isolation, *The Manly-Hearted Woman* is a slight book compared to the earlier novels. But read in the context of the Buckskin Man series, *The Manly-Hearted Woman* is a return for Manfred to the primeval clarity of a way of life which had dignity and meaning for those who lived it.

Anthony Arthur

Sources for Further Study

America. CXXXV, November 13, 1976, p. 332.
Booklist. LXXII, January 15, 1976, p. 667.
Library Journal. CI, February 15, 1976, p. 636.
New York Times Book Review. May 23, 1976, p. 38.

MARRY ME
A Romance

Author: John Updike (1932-   )
Publisher: Alfred A. Knopf (New York). 303 pp. $7.95
Type of work: Novel
Time: 1962
Locale: A fictional Connecticut suburb called Greenwood, and Washington, D.C.

A novel about an adulterous love affair, realistic with touches of romantic fantasy, that is concerned with the conflicting claims of love, conscience, and religion

Principal characters:
> JERRY CONANT, a designer and animator of television commercials
> RUTH CONANT, his wife
> SALLY MATHIAS, a suburban Connecticut housewife who is having an affair with Jerry Conant
> RICHARD MATHIAS, her husband, who has had an affair with Ruth Conant

Marry Me, John Updike's eighth novel, is a love story, a social comedy, and an attempt at a serious treatment of sex and religion. It is written in Updike's usual luminous prose. Whether it is a successful novel is another question.

Jerry Conant and Sally Mathias are in love. Unfortunately, each is married to another person, and each has three children. They are having a passionate affair which involves sly telephone calls and secret rendezvous. To a certain extent, the joke is on them. Their respective spouses, Ruth Conant and Richard Mathias, have also had an affair, less serious, and now ended. This allows Updike to add a slight touch of irony to his story, the only effective use of irony in what seems to be at least partly a comedy of manners, but is also a novel told in a very earnest and straightforward manner. It also enables him to add a slightly different wrinkle to the, by now, in these times of the sexual revolution, overused situation of the two couples who are swapping partners. Updike does not avoid the cliché; he circles around it, and hackneyed situations and scenes are a part of the problems of this novel.

Jerry and Sally and Richard and Ruth live in a fictional Connecticut suburb called Greenwood. Like most of Updike's characters, they are members of the upper middle class. Jerry, a failed freelance magazine cartoonist, is now a designer and animator of television commercials. Jerry is afflicted with two obsessions: a love for Sally and a fear of dying. He is a fundamentalist Lutheran with great concern for his salvation; and both his fear of death and his fight to hold onto his faith amid an adulterous affair, often give him psychosomatic asthma. He is given to reading serious theology, which does little to relieve his mind. An outwardly likable person, he is inwardly childish and self-centered. As such, and as the novel's protagonist, he becomes another of its problems.

Ruth Conant, Jerry's wife, is the most sensible and mature person of the quartet. A former artist, she has settled for the life of a suburban housewife after marrying Jerry. They met at art school, and by the time we meet them, a mutual interest in art and their children seems to be about all they have in common. Ruth is the most sympathetic of the four; she may be the true heroine of the novel, but she does not have enough spunk to gain control of the situation.

Richard Mathias is a well-to-do business entrepreneur. He is coarse, a grossly outgoing womanizer, and his atheism is an obvious thematic counterpoint to Jerry's Christianity. About Sally Mathias there is little to say except that she is sexy, blonde, and almost wholly concerned with whatever makes Sally happy. Joanne, Jerry's daughter, fully describes Sally when she tells her father that Mrs. Mathias never pays attention to anybody else.

For reasons that are not clear, Updike has chosen to subtitle his novel "A Romance." *Marry Me* is not a romance in the usual sense of the term, but the exact opposite: a novel of everyday life with no heroic action which, with the exception of some soft-focused lovers' sentimentality and a somewhat dream-like ending, is told in realistic detail. The story is set in 1962, during the idealistic, optimistic Kennedy "Camelot" period, and this is apparently part of the basis for calling it a romance. However, except for the fact that Jerry is involved in the drawing and production of a series of thirty-second television commercials for the government—animated propaganda pieces espousing the cause of democracy in underdeveloped countries—there is little reference to the time period. Concerned only with their two-family marriage crisis, Updike's quartet shows no interest in the larger world about them. This indifference to other events, this almost total emphasis on the neurotic and emotional problems of four people, tends to give the novel an unfortunate and uncomfortable resemblance to daytime television drama. To the extent that this is a romance, it is a romance in the more mundane meaning of the term, as it is used in love-story movies and standard women's magazine fiction.

The novel opens with Jerry and Sally having an idyllic tryst on a beach. Updike is setting up his religious symbolism from the beginning, with Jerry and Sally as Adam and Eve figures, for he has them imagine themselves as ". . . the original man and woman."

But religion, for Jerry, is not symbolic at all; it is a reality. God and the prospect of heaven are very real to him, but this has done little to relieve his nagging fear of death. His inability to find stability in his religion has helped to lead him into a quest for solace in this extramarital affair. Though he still talks about religion a great deal, Jerry has substituted sexual satisfaction for spiritual solace, and with this observation Updike may have made a cogent comment on a considerable portion of modern society. Jerry's inward battle against death continues, nevertheless, and he explains to Sally that he is in a bind ". . . between death and death," meaning that life without her would be like death to him, but that he is afraid that leaving his family for her would be the same as denying God, and that by so doing he would lose his immortality. In another frame of mind, however, he can see the same problem from an almost opposite angle. He can see Sally as the symbol of his salvation, though in a more temporal vein. He tells Ruth, "Whenever I'm with her . . . I know I'm never going to die. Or if I know it, I don't mind it, somehow."

As that quotation indicates, the affair becomes known, though Sally and Jerry never learn the truth of the previous one between their spouses. The majority of the novel is about Jerry's attempt to make up his mind to leave his family and marry Sally, while the other three principals spend their time trying to get him to decide one way or the other. It is a decision that he cannot make. Jerry and Sally have a lovers' dream of running away, with her children, to a ranch in Wyoming—the typical modern suburbanite's fantasy of getting away to a place where life is more simple. Toward the end, it seems that they have finally made this break. But then we learn that we have been reading another daydream of Jerry's; he has apparently slipped into an almost total dreamworld in which he imagines that he can have his Sally and keep Ruth and the kids also.

Jerry's problem is not so much spiritual or sexual as a matter of immature self-centeredness and indecision. Updike surely knows this, and his novel carries some elements of comedy, but, on the whole, he seems to take Jerry seriously and to try to make him a sympathetic character. This he fails to do, for Jerry is a boor and ultimately boring. This causes a serious flaw to develop in Updike's carefully constructed parable—a flaw which tends to rend its philosophical tenets.

The fault is not in the writing. The famous Updike style is still in evidence. In his poetic mode, he can conjure up exactly the right image to convey the deep emotional reverberations that can hit one of his characters in the middle of what seems to be a small, surface moment. In his realistic mode, he can, like a good photographer, focus on the telling detail in the middle of life's general clutter. In one marvelous scene, which occurs early before the truth of the Jerry-Sally affair is out, Sally has sneaked to Washington for a rendezvous with Jerry, who is there for consultations about his series of commercials for the State Department. Now they must get back to New York, where she has left her car, and he is to meet Ruth. Stranded without reservations at National Airport, they can't get a flight, have trouble renting a car, meet a friend who suspects that something is going on, are hounded by a salesman who must get to Newark and follows them around hoping to share whatever ride they can find. This is the only scene in the novel in which the comedy really works; yet it is a sad kind of comedy, and it makes the reader, in spite of reservations about them, pull for the couple, want them to get out of this mess without having their secret discovered. By itself, this is a fine short story. One can imagine it as a great scene in one of Billy Wilder's sad screen comedies. With telling details and revealing dialogue, Updike manages, in this one section, to explore the whole situation, the entire thematic range of his novel. Thus even this scene works against the novel in that it makes much of the rest seem superfluous.

The standard criticism of Updike has long been that he writes brilliantly about matters of small substance. This is an oversimplification, and may even be entirely wrong. To be able to write as Updike can about ordinary people involved in ordinary situations in such subtle but substantial detail as to evoke their deepest fears, fancies, and needs, is to write with great substance and create art. When Updike fails, it is for the opposite reason given in the standard criticism. It is because he is writing with a fine style about matters of great importance, but does not have a story strong enough to bring his philosophical ideas down to earth in a concrete manner.

Updike has been attacking America's problem of sexual and religious scruples for some time now; he dealt with the same theme in his bestseller, *Couples,* and in his most recent previous novel, *A Month of Sundays,* about the debauched preacher, Tom Marshfield. He was beginning to wrestle with theology in print at least as far back as 1962 or 1963. His collection *Assorted Prose* contains reviews of books by Karl Barth and Paul Tillich published in those years. A year further back, Updike published a story called "Lifeguard," later collected in *Pigeon Feathers and Other Stories,* that contains most of the thematic concerns of *Marry Me.* It is a monologue by a divinity student who is a summer lifeguard, replete with symbolism about sin, salvation, and sex. In a half-dozen pages, Updike's lifeguard says almost as much about these subjects, and his ideas of their interconnection, as is transmitted in the three hundred pages of this novel; and the young lifeguard impresses one as being a more mature analyst of his own shaky perch that Jerry Conant.

The basic trouble here, however, is not repetition. The personal war with the demons of death and sin—sexual or otherwise—is important enough to bear constant repetition, as long as it is approached from a new angle, or bolstered by strong characters in a good story. To see a major talent writing seriously, rather than satirically, about religious conflict is refreshing in a time when most major writers create from a strict secular point of view. The trouble is that Updike has shown little imagination, as if he had, in previous work, gone as far as he can, or dares, with these ideas. The result is a banal story with weak characters; neither the lightweight people nor the ordinary situation can carry Updike's heavy theme.

William Boswell

Sources for Further Study

Atlantic. CCXXXVIII, November, 1976, p. 115.
Harper's Magazine. CCLIII, December, 1976, p. 80.
Nation. CCXXIII, October 30, 1976, p. 437.
New Republic. CLXXV, November 27, 1976, p. 22.
New York Times Book Review. October 31, 1976, p. 2.
Saturday Review. IV, November 13, 1976, p. 41.

MEDICAL NEMESIS
The Expropriation of Health

Author: Ivan D. Illich (1926-   )
Publisher: Pantheon Books (New York). 294 pp. $8.95
Type of work: Current affairs

An argument that the medical profession does not really heal, but rather that health is a function of an individual's environment

Ivan Illich claims that modern medicine has reached the stage where, in itself, it has become a major threat to health. Such a provocative theme is one in a series of books on the plight of modern man by Illich: *Celebration of Awareness* (1969), *Deschooling Society* (1971), *Tools for Conviviality* (1973), and *Energy and Equity* (1974).

In his foreword to the current work, Illich states not only that the medical establishment has become a major threat to health, but that it now affects all social relations. He further states that he will demonstrate that only a political program aimed at the limitation of professional management of health will enable people to recover their own powers for health care, and that such a program is integral to a society-wide criticism and restraint of the industrial mode of production.

The book is divided into four parts. The first three deal with three different types of iatrogenesis, or physician-originated disease, the clinical, social, and cultural. The fourth section deals with the political solution to the problem.

In the first section, on clinical iatrogenesis, Illich argues that improvement in the health of the human population has not come about through the efforts of physicians, but through changes in the human environment. Through extensive footnotes (pugnaciously defended in the foreword) he purports to demonstrate that most diseases were on the wane just as they were finally understood and thereafter "cured." He contends that the general improvement in the health of a population has not had any real relationship to the amount of health care available, but rather on such things as better awareness of sanitation on the part of the populace, coupled with improved environmental and nutritional factors. He raises many provocative questions, puts forth many intriguing generalizations, but fails to make a strong and logical case, despite his footnotes. *Medical Nemesis* is not cluttered with facts, for they are relegated to the fine print at the bottom of the page. This is not to say, however, that there is not the ring of truth to many of the generalizations, nor that the author has not researched his subject. His is a philosophical argument following from a basically humanistic concern for the individual and that individual's right to be human. It is this "civil" right that he sees violated, the increase in malpractice suits being symptomatic of the depersonalization of diagnosis and treatments that has changed medical care from an ethical practice to a purely technical and callous one. The second section of this first part, although headed "Defenseless Patients," is a restatement of the scope of the chapters to follow, in a remarkably similar construction to that of the foreword.

The second major part deals with social iatrogenesis, which is the level of iatrogenic disease at which the medical establishment sponsors sickness, reinforcing societal trends that would encourage people to become consumers of medicine. Such trends include creating ill-health by increasing stress or by multiplying disabling dependence. Illich is distressed that all "normal suffering" such as birth, sickness, and death have become occurrences to be dealt with by the establishment in a hospital rather than by the individual at home. Underlying this distress is the author's concern for the individual's loss of the ability to deal with these most human of experiences, and consequently the loss of part of his own humanity and ultimately his freedom and independence. Much of this message is over-elaborated upon however, by militant political rhetoric.

Illich is rightfully indignant over the proportion of the average man's budget which is now spent on the purchase of medical care, and peppers his discussion with much-needed statistics. The role of insurance coverage in the escalation of health care and particularly hospital costs is a telling one. Illich shows that such disproportionate costs are not confined to the United States alone, nor even to the other developed Western nations. In fact, he does a creditable job of proving that the same problem occurs in all countries, regardless of their level of development.

The pharmaceutical industry is another object of Illich's concern. Drugs today are much more powerful and much easier to get, but the directions for usage that used to accompany them for the enlightenment of the layman have now been replaced by a warning to see a physician. Even physicians often have limited understanding of possible side effects of drugs, according to Illich, but they are the least likely agents to bring about reform in the pharmaceutical business.

The recurrent theme here as in the first part is that selfcare on the part of the individual is best, and that less is always better when dealing with medicine and/or the medical professions. Illich gives numerous examples of simpler cultures that use the old standard folk remedies to good effect, implying that folk medicine is just as effective as modern industrialized medicine, and far less traumatic for the patient. His salient examples here are on the dehumanization of the birth and death processes. Although the political verbiage with which he laces his argument is distracting if not irrelevant, the basic idea is an appealing one, as long as one does not look beyond the simplest examples to situations with which folk medicine is not capable of coping.

The medicalization of disease prevention, Illich contends, is another aspect of social iatrogenesis, which tends to relieve the individual of his personal responsibility for his future and place that responsibility on the medical establishment. The hidden fallacy in this situation, he purports, is that when a physician is asked to examine someone, he will most likely feel more professional if he diagnoses an illness than if he does not. Often the tests to determine illness are themselves risky.

The rhetoric in which Illich envelopes his discussion of death in relation to social iatrogenesis nearly obscures his underlying true concern for the dignity of the dying. This concern, moreover, seems to be unrealistic. He blasts the medical establishment for the misuse of life-sustaining equipment, even after there is no hope of normal life, claiming that such misuse results in an undignified death. While this may be an acceptable example of the dubious usefulness of modern medicine in many circumstances, it is unrealistic to direct the same amount of wrath to the use of pain killers in situations where they might actually allow the dying patient relief and thereby some amount of dignity.

The third level of iatrogenesis is the cultural, in which, according to Illich, the medical establishment removes from the people the ability to suffer their own reality. He contends that the ability to suffer is uniquely human and that to deny a person suffering is to deny him true humanity. Pain is seen as part of the reality of the body, something with which to cope, rather than something that requires a cure. Illich is indignant that the Cartesian separation of body and soul could have evolved to a point where the sickness could be separated from the sufferer. Modern physicians, he claims, treat the illness but ignore the patient, robbing him of the acknowledgement of his suffering. They transform pain and death from existential challenges into technical problems, abolishing the ability for the individual to cope with reality. Persons who can deal with their own pain will more likely heal themselves than those who depend upon the medical establishment to resolve their problems for them

The extensive definition and history of the concept of pain which constitutes this area of the work is a philosophical essay which belies both the author's philosophical background and his theological beliefs. His insistence that the suffering of pain should be allowed as an opportunity for penance and purification is deeply rooted in his own Christian theological beliefs regardless of the supporting evidence that he interjects from other cultures to broaden theoretically his basis for the contention. An acceptance of the metaphysical nature of pain is crucial to the truly human experience, and the scientism that treats pain without considering its source denies that metaphysical aspect of human experience. Illich's argument is a radically humanistic and existential one, but one that seems somewhat incongruous juxtaposed against his militant/statistical rhetoric of the other chapters. One suspects that Illich had written an essay of compassion, an essay which decries mass society in many forms and glorifies the individual in all of his aspects, but was too afraid that such an essay, with its old-fashioned concern for persons and their personhood, might not sell unless clothed in cleverly constructed terms and political verbiage. Apparently, Illich is convinced that if you want to sell philosophy (or theology) in this secular age, it must be militant and controversial, or it will not be read. Lamentably, he is probably quite correct.

The final segment of the work is devoted to the politics of health. While the medical establishment receives the majority of his condemnation directly, Illich's principal target actually seems to be the materialistic society which allows and even encourages bureaucratic processes to erode the individual's intellectual and spiritual autonomy. He sees industrial expansion placing more and more responsibility for the individual's well-being in the hands of professional managers. Illich's proposed solution to the problem is radical, somewhat unlikely, and unrealistic in the context of modern society as he paints it. The solution as he sees it will not come from any housecleaning by the medical establishment itself, but through political action on the part of consumers. He proposes that individuals take responsibility for their own health care.

However, if all that the author has purported concerning the helplessness of modern man in the previous three sections is true, the vast majority of people will neither recognize their own dilemma nor find themselves with the tools necessary to carry out the transformation. Illich writes in the hope of awakening modern man to this predicament, but there is some doubt that a revolution of the size that he deems necessary could occur, for only those few individuals who have not been totally in step with society will be able to meet this existential challenge.

Illich seems to yearn romantically after a simpler, more golden age of pre-industrialized society where men were free to feel that whole range of human joys and pains. The fallacy here is that those in that idealistic setting yearned fervently for the alleviation of that same human pain, and consequently went about discovering things such as penicillin. Just as ancient man did not happily accept pain and death because it made him human, it is doubtful that Illich will find a throng of followers willing to accept them so that, by contrast, their joys and pleasures will be greater.

In the end, the only viable suggestion to emerge from the angry rhetoric of *Medical Nemesis* centers on a more responsible populace controlling doctors and hospitals, becoming as discerning—as consumers in the area of health care—as they should be in other areas.

Margaret S. Schoon

Sources for Further Study

America. CXXXV, September 25, 1976, p. 174.

Christian Century. XCIII, September 29, 1976, p. 818.

Commonweal. CIII, February 27, 1976, p. 153.

Critic. XXXV, Winter, 1976, p. 73.

New York Review of Books. XXIII, September 16, 1976, p. 3.

Village Voice. XXI, March 29, 1976, p. 42.

MEMOIRS

Author: Tennessee Williams (1914-   )
Publisher: Doubleday and Company (New York). 264 pp. $8.95
Type of work: Autobiography
Time: The twentieth century
Locale: St. Louis, New Orleans, New York, Rome

The internationally celebrated playwright's own autobiography, as outrageously frank and as unusual in form as his plays

Principal personages:
TENNESSEE WILLIAMS
MRS. EDWINA WILLIAMS, his mother
ROSE ISABEL WILLIAMS, his sister
THE REVEREND WALTER E. DAKIN, his grandfather
FRANK PHILIP MERLO, his most constant lover
AUDREY WOOD, his agent
IRENE SELZNICK, his producer
LADY ST. JUST,
ANNA MAGNANI, and
CARSON MCCULLERS, his friends
ELIA KAZAN, a director
MARGO JONES, a producer

Is Tennessee Williams' *Memoirs* an important contribution to the art of autobiography—one of the most interesting but least artful genres in the history of world literature—or is it simply another readable account of a life? The answer lies somewhere between. The uncannily conversational phrasing and tone of its style, with ingratiating, self-conscious, direct comment to the reader, and its deliberate anti-chronological structure, set Williams' memoirs off artistically among a few notable American autobiographies of recent decades. But the style, the structure, and the elements of Williams' life and times do not cohere effectively enough to make the book a work of art. Williams is not an important poet, and, while his short stories are almost as unusual and distinctive as Dylan Thomas', he is not a major contributor to the genre. But his plays are the work of a highly gifted artist. His few comments on his own plays and on writing in general suggest that he is a natural writer, a Dionysian who writes out of personal torments transformed into charged theatrical images. In his *Memoirs,* the Williams we have known sublimated, transmuted through imagined characters, mostly female, speaks directly to us, artlessly. The achievement is both more than we have come to expect from autobiographies, even those by imaginative writers, and less than we might have hoped from a man so deeply involved in theater for more than four decades.

No voice in American literature is more distinctly audible and alive on the printed page than Williams' in the *Memoirs.* He tells us about his early life, about his most intimate personal adventures and spiritual experiences, his travels, his writings, his friends, the agents, producers, directors, and actors with whom he has worked over the years, and the writers he has known. He tells us all the things we want to hear because Williams is preeminently an interesting person, a celebrity whose life has always promised to be as fascinating as those of his bizarre, tormented, unpredictable, doomed characters. But one also hopes and expects to hear insights about his life and about the people he has known and the craft of playwriting that he would seem uniquely able to offer. He seems to sense readers are waiting for such insights, and he delivers a few in response, rather routinely, on a level not much higher than Rex Reed's. He quite deliberately begs off talking about the mysteries of his craft. But there, as in other areas, readers may suspect he does not have anything of much depth to say anyway. One of the freedoms he allowed himself at the outset was the dubious freedom to tell his story effortlessly.

Williams' life before he earned sudden fame as the young author of the autobiographical, lyrical, innovative *The Glass Menagerie* was not as bizarre as one's knowledge of his characters might lead one to expect. The first eight years of his childhood in Mississippi were "the most joyously innocent" of his life. He was physically robust and energetic, and his Dakin grandparents provided him and his sister Rose (Laura in *The Glass Menagerie*) with an Edenic environment. The abrupt removal to St. Louis was a trauma from which in many ways neither Williams nor his sister recovered. For both, social humiliations and estrangement and physical and mental deterioration began there. His father, a boozing, woman-chasing shoe salesman, gave Williams' mother cause to suffer as only a Southern belle with obsessive pretensions can suffer. His soulful-looking sister made brave attempts to dress and live like a Southern debutante. He hardly mentions his brother. During his high school years, Williams spent most of his time with Rose. His first love was a girl named Hazel who was his best friend for many years. Williams' anecdotes and character sketches of his Dakin grandparents, of his mother and father, and of Hazel are the most moving in the book. And he tells us how each of them figures in many of his poems, stories, and plays. Throughout the book, the reader—or listener—is aware of the stark contrast between the life of the famous playwright, rich in experiences, and the plight of his sister, institutionalized most of her life. While they never experienced even a casual physical intimacy, "our love was, and is, the deepest in our lives."

Williams' attempts to show and to comment on the way events and people during his childhood, adolescence, and college years shaped his life and affected his writings are disappointingly halfhearted, but the events and the people themselves are interesting. Williams gives us material with which we may imagine the things that stimulated him to become a writer, but he merely tells us what he wrote, where, and when, and in the midst of what relationships. His life at the University of Missouri, where he was, unpredictably, a member of a fraternity, was rather routine. There he became more clearly aware of his homosexual tendencies, but he was also attracted to an oversexed

young woman. The first and only sexual experience he had with a woman occurred later at the University of Iowa—a sexual marathon that lasted over a
month. But when he met Kip in Cape Cod, he realized he would always love
"boys," and throughout the book, he often apologizes for his compulsive attempt to describe each encounter (there were literally hundreds) graphically.
Except for Frank Merlo, his companion for fourteen years, most of the affairs
blur into one rather mechanical procession, despite his attempts to assure us
that each was beautiful, memorable, though ineffable. Elsewhere, he has said
that the only woman he would have considered marrying was Anna Magnani,
herself a *heterosexual* dynamo. Wonderfully lustful, mischievous, depraved,
insatiable, Williams has lived his fantasies.

Despite a shyness that during one period of his youth made him blush
violently when his eyes met those of any person male or female, and the excru-
ciating loneliness that has plagued him all his life, Williams has known, lived
with, traveled with, and worked with legions of men and women. Although he
is probably one of the most disciplined, energetic, and diligent workers at his
craft—starting always with a swim and Balzacian black coffee—he seems to be
in constant motion. We move with him to Mexico, Italy, Sicily, Puerto Rico,
Cuba, Germany, England, Morocco, Thailand; he has lived in Mississippi, St.
Louis (which he dreads to revisit), Knoxville, Tennessee in the summers of his
childhood, Key West, New Orleans, and New York City. There is a certain
theatrical aura and desperation about the globe-trotting of a shy, lonely,
usually intoxicated or doped-up, ill celebrity, with his morose withdrawals and
social and professional rages and tantrums, sulks, and paranoia. One senses
that he has never had a fully committed lover or an unconditional friend in his
life, that all his relationships have been on the level of theatrical affections and
affectations, which, after all, generate their own intense reality. "Love . . . is
nearly always present on-stage when the play is imperiled."

One imagines this short, tidily built, pleasant-looking man, with his
resonant drawl, the grace of a swimmer in his loping walk, moving about
America and the world, pursuing business and bodily appetites and his relationships with lovers, friends, agents, producers, directors, and actors, always
on the verge of physical and mental collapse, which perhaps contributes to his
imaginative leaps and artistic gestations. We follow his relationship with his
agent Audrey Wood, from her nursing of a fledgling talent to her abandonment of a neurotic, famous playwright in decline, and we contrast Williams'
new agent, handsome Bill Barnes, with that powerful mother figure (we see
them in the photographs, too). Williams also gives us distinct impressions of
his producers: Lawrence Langner, Cheryl Crawford, David Merrick. Most important to him were Margo Jones and Irene Selznick. His plays have been
produced in a variety of theaters: many Broadway houses, the Margo Jones
Dallas Theater in the Round, the regional repertory Barter theater, the Spoleto
Festival theater, the Circle in the Square off-Broadway, the experimental New

Theater. Williams offers vignettes of the directors: Eddie Dowling, who also portrayed Tom in *The Glass Menagerie;* Margo Jones, Alan Schneider, José Quintero, Herbert Machiz, Harold Clurman, and the English directors Tony Richardson, Peter Glenville, and John Gielgud. The most powerful presence in Williams' theatrical life is Elia Kazan, one of the five "gentlemen" of the theater Williams lists. We are told very little about their famous, serious clashes. We learn nothing about the nature of reproducing, agenting, directing from the point of view of a fabulously successful playwright; everything is focused on Williams' personal relationships with these professional theater figures, or we are given a routine listing of who produced and directed what—facts without illumination, unrelated anecdotes. With each new play the reactions Williams was most eager to have were those of Audrey Wood, a mother figure, agenting his work, and Kazan, a father figure, directing it. The more reliant Williams was on them professionally, the more extreme his personal involvement, and we see how he drew them into his personal affairs, including his tempestuous homosexual wrangles and his physical and mental agonies.

Williams has also known some English and European film directors—Visconti, Zeffirelli, Jack Clayton. And he has worked with Joseph Losey on *Boom* and Kazan on the original screenplay, *Baby Doll,* and on film versions of some of his plays. But again, neither his vivid anecdotes about those directors nor his colorful comments on their work contributes to our understanding of the film medium to which most of his plays and some of his fiction (notably *The Roman Spring of Mrs. Stone*) have been adapted.

Though Williams was an actor briefly in college and acted in a recent play, *Small Craft Warnings,* he seems to have kept a certain distance from actors and actresses. He has made it a strict rule not to become sexually involved, not even casually, with actors in his plays. He tells us of his attraction to Marlon Brando and Donald Madden, and of his restraint. He has written plays for Brando, Madden, and Michael York. About Paul Newman, star of *Sweet Bird of Youth* we are told only that he is "terribly good." Williams gives us anecdotes about Laurette Taylor of *The Glass Menagerie,* Tallulah Bankhead of *A Streetcar Named Desire,* Helen Hayes of *The Glass Menagerie,* and Maureen Stapleton of *The Rose Tattoo.* Among other actresses who have been most crucially involved in his plays and/or films are Hermione Braddeley (for whom his admiration is enormous), Barbara Baxley, Miriam Hopkins, Ruth Ford, Anne Meacham, Julie Haydon, Jessica Tandy, and Vivien Leigh, as Blanche on stage and screen, Geraldine Page, Elizabeth Taylor (in *Boom, Suddenly Last Summer,* and *Cat on a Hot Tin Roof*). His tribute to Laurette Taylor is moving, but not particularly perceptive: "I am afraid it is one of the few close friendships I have ever had with a player . . . a whole career of writing for the theatre is rewarded enough by having created one good part for a great actress." He provides us with only a typical view of Tallulah Bankhead, who sometimes talked with him while sitting on the toilet. One looks in vain for some comment on Geraldine Page, famous for her portrayal of Amanda in *Summer and Smoke* and the Princess in *Sweet Bird of Youth*. His meeting with Garbo is interesting; his relationship with Diana Barrymore, who committed suicide a week after being refused the part of the Princess, is sad. Many of the actors and actresses who gave Williams' plays their special interpretation and aura came out of Lee Strasberg's Actors Studio, but Williams offers no meaningful analysis of that relationship.

Readers will quite reasonably expect to be told about Williams' associations with other writers, to gain some insight into their lives and works, if only tangentially, by inference. But Williams merely tells us interesting little stories. He is possibly the most put-down of famous writers. Dylan Thomas asked, "How does it feel to make all that Hollywood money?" Thornton Wilder, with a rather papal hauteur, put down *A Streetcar Named Desire*. Jean-Paul Sartre failed to show at one of Williams' parties. But Williams himself was rude to John Steinbeck and his wife, making a friendly call with Kazan. Introduced to André Malraux at a White House reception, he thought it cute that he had never heard of him. Williams, one gathers, is not a writer who explores the work of other writers; the ones he reads, one suspects, are his friends. He had pleasant brief encounters with E. M. Forster, Jean Cocteau, Sartre on a second occasion, and friendships with Yukio Mishima, the Japanese novelist who committed *hara-kiri*, and Françoise Sagan. His good friends among writers for long periods have been Christopher Isherwood, Jane and Paul Bowles, Carson McCullers, Gore Vidal, Truman Capote, and Donald Windham, and, among playwrights, William Inge. All those writers have in common many things in their lives (beyond the sexual) and work, but Williams never attempts to see a design that might in turn give him insight into the patterns of his own life. In the natural course of garrulous, rambling recall, he sparks a few insights, but they fade in the light of a recital of garish, transient events.

In writing about their lives, writers are often reluctant to attempt an analysis of common features and techniques in their work, but Williams is perhaps the most reticent. His judgments on other writers are simply that; he never attempts to share his understanding of their work. Chekhov's "*The Sea Gull* is the greatest of modern plays, with the possible exception of Brecht's *Mother Courage*." Lawrence was a "highly *simpatico* figure in my literary upbringing, but Chekhov takes precedence as an influence." Williams doubts the importance of influences, credits instead "my own solitary bent." Sartre's *Huis Clos* "appealed" to him, but he does not bother telling us why. Hart Crane is probably his favorite poet; Williams has read Crane's poems on Caedmon records; and he wants his bones dumped in the Caribbean near where Crane drowned himself. He inflates the genius of his friends, especially Jane Bowles, whom he ranks above Carson McCullers as "the greatest writer of our century in the English language." And in the category of astonishing judgments by famous writers, none can beat Williams' on Clayton's movie of *The Great*

Gatsby: "a film that even surpassed, I think, the novel by Scott Fitzgerald."
Nothing in the *Memoirs* is likely to suggest to the reader that Williams is capable of making valuable comments on his own work or the works of others. He is not a consciously self-trained writer. He is of that rare species of natural, intuitive writers whose impressions *work*. He tells us where and when (though sometimes vaguely) most of his plays, some of his stories and poems were written, and the relationships among them, and sometimes relates them to events, attitudes, and people in his life, but he traces no patterns, nor does one emerge. From Williams' *Memoirs*, students and scholars will learn very little that is new and useful.

One also expects from a man who has lived such a fascinating life and written some of the most sensitive and suggestive plays of our time some philosophical reflections. As if aware of those expectations, Williams dutifully treats the reader to some rather sentimental, platitudinous comments on religion, politics, death, love, and his own future. His plays are full of great one-liners; the theatrical context elevates what are really only sentimental asides into metaphors of universal significance. Like Blanche, he feels that "deliberate cruelty is the one unforgivable thing" (Williams has been cruel to people, but whether deliberately or not is ambiguous). Just as such lines work in the theater, they work to some degree here, because the magic of the book—and the *Memoirs* is a rare, if not ultimately unique performance—emanates from our sense of the presence of the man himself, the voice talking to us in the dark night of the soul where, as Fitzgerald said, it is always three o'clock in the morning. Williams often tells us the circumstances under which he is writing, over a two-year period, what he calls "this thing," written, at first, admittedly to make money, often literally in the early A.M., and most often in New York or New Orleans. Like many of his characters, mostly women, given to long arias that stop the action but elevate the sentiment, Williams talks, loquaciously, sometimes, as he does on television talk shows. But here the range of topics and moods is impressively wide; and even when he dwells on trivialities, or gives yet another account of his frail physical or precarious mental state, or tells of yet another one-night stand, with a marine or New Orleans female impersonator, or ticks off another opening night, this unique Southern talker holds us.

If no controlling conception or pattern gives shape to the meandering narrative, Williams' device of telling us what happened the day or night before the A.M. when he is writing a section of "this thing" is an effective pacing and rhythm device, if not an illuminating technique. We hear of his fears of playing Doc in *Small Craft Warnings* and doing symposia afterwards, the plans for producing *Out Cry*, and his dreams of the future, raising goats and geese on a little farm in Sicily. "Listening" to Williams' *Memoirs,* one feels that quality of something special and unusual which one feels watching his best plays, a quality not totally absent even from his mediocre works. This distinctive quality encompasses elements of the bizarre, the outrageous, the audacious, the comical, the farcical, the lyrical, the uniquely imaginative, and the unsettling.

The value of the *Memoirs,* then, must rest not on the depth of observation and insight about any of its elements, but on the *way* Williams talks to us about his life, his work, and the people he has known. This may be a limited achievement, but, within the genre of autobiography at least, it is an achievement nonetheless.

David Madden

Sources for Further Study

America. CXXXIV, January 10, 1976, p. 11.
National Review. XXVIII, April 16, 1976, p. 405.
New Leader. LIX, March 29, 1976, p. 18.
New Republic. CLXXIII, December 27, 1975, p. 31.
Spectator. CCXXXVII, November 20, 1976, p. 19.
Virginia Quarterly Review. LII, Spring, 1976, p. 42.
Yale Review. LXV, June, 1976, p. 587.

MERIDIAN

Author: Alice Walker (1944-   )
Publisher: Harcourt Brace Jovanovich (New York). 228 pp. $7.95
Type of work: Novel
Time: The 1960's and early 1970's
Locale: The Deep South and New York

A symbolic, penetrating analysis of the effects of guilt, hatred, and love in American society

Principal characters:
>MERIDIAN HILL, a sensitive, spiritual black girl in search of her own individuality
>TRUMAN HELD, a black artist and the man Meridian loves
>LYNNE, Truman's white wife

Alice Walker's latest novel, *Meridian,* is a fine, spiritual, insightful book. It is a book about social and individual change, and can rightfully be considered a book about revolution. For Walker presents the Civil Rights Movement of the 1960's, a social and political revolution which sought to elevate the status of blacks in American society, and uses it as an effective metaphor for spiritual renewal. The voter rights drive is a symbolic act. It symbolizes the conscious, deliberate movement of blacks away from passivity, acquiescence, and indifference. It further represents a vital step beyond the boundaries of all that blacks had ever known in the past to a sense of worth and power and hope and ultimate freedom. While the emphasis in the novel is placed on blacks and the necessity for them to take decisive action, the universal significance of its message is clear enough.

Also presented in the novel is the theme of individual revolution. The characters are forced through their personal experiences to face honestly their own guilt, anger, frustration, and hatred. In so doing, they come to understand one another and to assess their own worth. Finally, there is a kind of revolution against the past in the sense that the author is urging that certain negative traditional myths and beliefs be examined, understood for what they are worth, and discarded.

It is obvious that Walker believes these kinds of transformations are called for if there is to be any real freedom for American people, black or white. She wants us to be aware, to live fully conscious of our lives. The alternative is to continue to walk as if dazed or half asleep in the same old tracks of the past. It is to continue to impose useless, negative, and even destructive beliefs on one another until all genuine feeling is gone, and life in its fullest sense has no hope of being.

Against a rich tapestry woven of threads of the past and social unrest, the personal struggles of the main characters are highlighted. *Meridian* is basically the story of Meridian Hill, a sensitive, spiritual black girl who quietly fights to free herself from the smothering weight of her own ignorance, intolerable guilt, and self-hatred. Her guilt grows out of her lack of understanding and a series of incidents primarily associated with her mother, a rigid, angry woman who feels she has been betrayed in some way by marriage and her children. Because of her mother's attitude toward her, Meridian in her innocence believes she has stolen something of value from her mother simply by being born. When, in spite of her mother's urgings, she cannot bring herself to join the Church, her sense of guilt about failing her mother again is intensified. Later, out of a desperate sense of inadequacy, Meridian gives her own infant son away. This act further adds to her almost intolerable burden of guilt, and, in addition, causes her to despise herself. She believes she is a traitor, not only to her mother, whom she sees as the epitome of black motherhood, but to her ancestral slave mothers who had endured unbelievable agonies in order to keep their children with them.

Her relationships with men, such as they are, bring her no pleasure or feeling that she is loved. The men Meridian has known, including her husband whom she does not love and Truman whom she does, want her body but give little or no thought to her as a person. Eventually, they all leave her. Feeling rejected by her mother, used by men, and, because she is black, unacceptable in white society, she sets out to free herself from the life that so cruelly imprisons her.

The dawn of Meridian's awareness and subsequent freedom comes with her participation in the Civil Rights Movement. Prior to this time, Meridian had been a passive observer, much of the time caught up in fantasy in order to escape her pitiful existence. With the emergence of the Civil Rights effort and her ensuing wholehearted involvement in it, she begins to face reality for the first time. As a result, she begins to make choices for herself based on reality. She begins to change.

Meridian falls in love with Truman Held, a handsome, pretentious, self-centered young black man who is somewhat active in the movement. An intelligent young artist, Truman is nonetheless in many ways insensitive and superficial. He is unable to see the incongruousness of his preoccupation with spouting French phrases while wearing African dashikis and chasing northern white girls. His participation in the voter registration drive is prompted mainly by his desire to be considered *au courant*, rather than by any sense of commitment. Confounded by his own egotism, he underrates Meridian's love for him and fails to comprehend the real meaning of the Civil Rights effort. Whenever life appears to be coming too close, Truman "escapes" to New York, where the black man is allegedly free, and where he can lose himself in his art, the only world where he is in control.

Out of confusion and underlying anger at the injustices of the real world, Truman strikes out at women. He treats the white woman as a bitch-goddess, a scapegoat who has the sins of her race heaped high upon her head. Her punishment at his hands is sex without love or compassion. The black woman is praised. She is celebrated in poetry, sculpture, and paint. She is art, but seen in this light she is not human. Thus her punishment is more insidious.

It is only after his stormy marriage to Lynne, a liberal, white, middle-class exchange student from New York, and the death of their five-year-old daughter, who dies as the result of a brutal attack, that Truman moves toward some semblance of a mature understanding of himself and his life. He finds himself drawn back to Meridian time and again as if she were a magnet. This attraction is partly based on his awareness of Meridian's contempt for him; but more important, he half consciously knows that with her help and a sincere involvement on his part in the blacks' struggle he can find himself and indeed become a "true man." He travels through Southern communities with Meridian witnessing the personal torment in the lives of the people there. He begins to grasp what getting people to vote really means. He sees them act in the face of brutality, terror, even death in order to remake their lives for the better, in order to uphold their human dignity. Truman's newfound awareness causes him to decide to stay in the South. With that decision comes the promise of a new life for him.

For all of its hopefulness, *Meridian* is not a fairy tale; Alice Walker understands human nature too well for that. She knows the inherent human resistance to change which grows out of fear of the unknown or the misunderstood. Her novel grapples with probably the most devastating fear of all—the fear of facing the truth and living with it. It is this fear that overwhelms Lynne. She has lost everything: Truman, her daughter, her parents, and her place in white society. Through agonizing experiences, she has learned the truth about blacks and whites in America. Her idealism has been torn from her and discarded like so much trash. But Lynne cannot live with the truth that, as she sees it, hovers like doom all around her. So she arms herself with the remains of old, tired myths and fantasies such as choosing to see the South and its blacks as art: a pastoral scene with warm dark bodies against a lush green landscape. Her most damning fantasy, however, is the one that reveals her belief in the white goddess myth. Lynne refuses to relinquish her belief that as a white woman her body has special power over black men. She knows that this power is shabby and demeaning, but she holds desperately to it. She is unable to give it up even if it means a chance for something better; she cannot envision something better. Power is superiority. If Lynne is meant to symbolize white society, the symbol holds dreadful implications.

It is difficult to detect flaws in this inspiring novel. That is not to say that it is a perfect work, but simply that it is so genuine in its expression that its weaknesses, whatever they are, are greatly overshadowed by its beauty and emotional power. A feminist note can be detected from time to time, but the note is subtle and true and never mars the beauty of the novel's motif.

Walker's style is graceful and poetic. Even when she is describing scenes of mutilation and extreme suffering, she does so with exceptional sensitivity. She is an intensely concerned writer, and her serious tone reflects this concern. However, there are traces of humor that paradoxically give the reader some respite from the pain being revealed, yet, at the same time, underline that pain. Walker also makes use of satire and irony which she applies liberally, although not exclusively, to her male characters. Her use of irony serves to point out our fallacious beliefs about ourselves and others. In her advocacy of change, Walker employs a style that is satiric but sympathetic, poetic and poignant, graceful yet wrenching.

The title of the novel refers to the central character, but more than that, it points to the character as symbol. Meridian, as her name suggests, attracts and guides. The reader is drawn to her because there is much about his own spiritual plight that he shares with her; she symbolizes the individual's struggle to make sense out of his existence. In a sense, Meridian is an existential heroine. While we may face somewhat reluctantly our own feelings of isolation, unworthiness, and guilt as Meridian does, it is most gratifying to be able to witness her victory over them. We share in this victory and take heart. Alice Walker gives us a haunting depiction of what it means to create oneself out of time, effort, and pain in order to emerge triumphant in the knowledge of who one is and what it takes to truly live.

Joan S. Griffin

Sources for Further Study

Atlantic. CCXXXVII, June, 1976, p. 106.

National Observer. XV, July 17, 1976, p 17.

New York Times Book Review. May 23, 1976, p. 5.

New Yorker. LII, June 7, 1976, p. 133.

Newsweek. LXXXVII, May 31, 1976, p. 71.

Virginia Quarterly Review. LII, Autumn, 1976, p. 130.

Yale Review. LXVI, October, 1976, p. 146.

THE MIND-READER
New Poems by Richard Wilbur

Author: Richard Wilbur (1921-   )
Publisher: Harcourt Brace Jovanovich (New York). 67 pp. $6.95
Type of work: Poetry

The sixth collection of poems by one of America's best-known traditional poets

Richard Wilbur is one of the best poets of his generation, winner of both a National Book Award and a Pulitzer Prize. He has been well-known since his first book, *The Beautiful Changes,* appeared in 1947, yet it is difficult for him to get a wide hearing. The reason for this should be obvious by now. In the ongoing controversy between the redskins and the palefaces or, as Robert Lowell put it, raw poetry and cooked poetry, he is decidedly in favor of cooked verse. He has said himself that the strength of the genie comes of his being confined in a bottle; but this is an age when the bottle has been uncorked or, better, smashed to bits and pieces. Nor has Wilbur paid frequent court to the Social Muse or embraced the Tragic Vision of post-World War II poets. He has chosen to write in strict forms, for the most part, in a literary mode that is unfashionable—a course which, one must observe, requires a certain amount of courage.

Theodore Roethke once observed that Wilbur

> can look at a thing, and talk about it beautifully, can turn it over in his mind, and draw truths from a scene, easily and effortlessly (it would seem)—though his kind of writing requires the hardest kind of discipline, it must be remembered. Not a graceful mind—that's a mistake—but a mind of grace, an altogether different and higher thing.

This sums up succinctly the quality of the mind behind the poetry in *The Mind-Reader,* with its emphasis on looking, discipline, and grace. Wilbur has always been a poet primarily of the eye, one looking at the things of this world—and admittedly half-creating them at times. One is reminded that Wilbur's father was a painter and that the poet has written beautiful poems about painting and sculpture.

Of his new collection, his critics (and they are numerous) might say that here is the mixture as before, the same brilliant surface, impeccable rhythms, and skillful rhymes, but put in the service of themes that are less than urgent or overpowering. This is true, but only up to a point.

Wilbur, of course, has never been a Johnny-one-note; within his limitations he has always been capable of a dazzling variety of forms and themes, as this new collection attests. There are some developments in his recent work—though there is no fresh ground broken—and they need to be noted. Ten years ago it looked as though Wilbur's lines were loosening up, like those of almost all contemporary poets who began as strict formalists, such as Lowell and Roethke. But in *The Mind-Reader* there has been a drawing in, a tightening up of his forms, though he can break out of a quatrain when he needs to. In any case, he has seldom been tyrannized by his fixed patterns.

Wilbur also seems to have lost interest in the anti-poetic: one recalls his "Potato" or his memorable poem about a junk heap, a trendy theme of the 1950's. Except for "Children of the Darkness," a poem about fungi, few of his images are deliberately ugly; and even so, the rootless parasites are pronounced good in the end. This poem may be too long, but it is a brilliant *tour de force* nevertheless.

Also, at least for the time being, Wilbur has turned away from his famous animals. There is nothing in the present volume to recall *A Bestiary*—no toads, horses, or unicorns. For once, like Frost, Wilbur seems to be drawn more to trees and New England landscapes. And there are changes simply because Wilbur is older. He is, of course, no Archibald MacLeish brooding on death and writing about lost friends. But there is a poem here about his daughter who is growing up and learning to write herself. "A Wedding Toast" celebrates the marriage of his son:

> May you not lack for water,
> And may that water smack of Cana's wine.

But there is also a great deal that recalls the old Wilbur, and nowhere is there a decline in his art. There are three of four purely comic poems, though none quite so fine as "Pangloss' Song." "For the Student Strikers" is about the Vietnam War's impact on his college campus, which reminds us that Wilbur has written some powerful war poems; in fact, he began writing seriously when he was a soldier in Europe. "Teresa" and "Peter," a retelling of Peter's betrayal of Christ, serve to remind us that Wilbur might be classified as a religious poet. There are other poems that spring from his reading: a poem about Johnny Appleseed, "April 5, 1974," which relates Lewis Carroll and General Grant at Vicksburg to the Negro Rights movement. A number of these poems are "academic," but none of them are mere exercises. Only "Sleepless at Crown Point" might have been omitted.

Richard Wilbur is one of our best translators, and his translations of Molière's *The Misanthrope* and *Tartuffe* are well-known. The nine translations offered here, from the classical French and modern Russian, are not included to pad out a slim collection. Wilbur has a way of feeling his way into the poems he translates, always offering new renderings rather than mere translations. One feels that these are poems he might have written himself. Especially memorable are his modern treatments of Villon's "Ballade of Forgiveness" and Voltaire's "To Madame du Chatelet." De la Fontaine's often-translated "The Grasshopper and the Ant" is the kind of poem well-suited for Wilbur's brand of wit.

Wilbur's style in his latest poems is what we have become accustomed to. It is marked by grace, delicacy, wit, and a supple strength. There is always balance and control, never an awkward line or disruptive image. These poems are obviously well-wrought works of art, and the maker is proud of their polish. In fact, they are quintessential "cooked poems," just the type to enrage the defenders of the new naked poetry.

When all is said, it must be added that the poems in this volume are not all of a piece; they employ a variety of voices. A number are written in an elegant, fastidious style—though there is not much of the dandified diction of Wallace Stevens. The translation of De Bellay's "Happy the Man" is written in a plain, almost journalistic style. "A Black Birch in Winter" begins with a Frostian monosyllabic line: "You might not know this old tree by its bark," though he soon turns to the un-Frostlike diction of *striate, Lateran,* and *tesserae.* Wilbur obviously has not repudiated his old "literary" style; one still discovers here such "poetic" diction as "lewd espials" and "sanctuaried fanes."

Perhaps one final point needs to be made. A truculent note creeps into a few of these poems—as though Wilbur had suffered long enough from the barbs of his critics and now would like to strike back. For example, in "What's Good for the Soul Is Good for Sales," he lashes out at all confessional poets, who when "fictive music fails your lyre" write about Nixon, hangovers, or "God's death, the memory of your rockinghorse, /Entropy, housework, Buchenwald, divorce, . . ." One might sympathize with his impatience with the confessional school, but still point out that not all poems about Nixon or Buchenwald or divorce are written for the sake of fame or sales.

The same ungenerous note enters the conclusion of "Cottage Street, 1953." This poem is based on a true incident, according to the notes, in which Wilbur was invited to tea with Sylvia Plath and his mother-in-law. This was after Plath's first suicide attempt, and his role was that of the successful poet who might possibly cheer her up. In the end he notes that Sylvia went on to live another decade, outliving their hostess, "To state at last her brilliant negative / In poems free and helpless and unjust." No doubt it is too early for anyone to label Sylvia Plath's poems as "unjust" without seeming to be condescending.

The Mind-Reader, then, is not quite the mixture as before, though it includes no radical departures for the poet. Wilbur continues to celebrate the things his eye beholds, though he admits that he sings in a diminished world. If there are no poems here that seem to obsess the poet or haunt the reader (the title poem is the most ambitious, a superb dramatic monologue), there is still much of the very highest order. Richard Wilbur has rediscovered the language of praise in an age that is bleak and thorny, and he employs it in poems of rare imagination and felicity. Perhaps one should not ask for more.

Guy Owen

Sources for Further Study

America. CXXXV, August 21, 1976, p. 83.
Book World. July 25, 1976, p. G2.
Christian Science Monitor. LXVIII, October 13, 1976, p. 28.
Commonweal. CIII, September 10, 1976, p. 596.
New Republic. CLXXIV, June 5, 1976, p. 21.
Wall Street Journal. CLXXXVIII, July 7, 1976, p. 14.

MISS HERBERT
The Suburban Wife

Author: Christina Stead (1902-   )
Publisher: Random House (New York). 308 pp. $8.95
Type of work: Novel
Time: Approximately 1940 to the present
Locale: England

A novel about a modern young woman's struggle to integrate her sexual and intellectual drives and talents with her traditional views of what a woman should be

Principal characters:

ELEANOR HERBERT BRENT, a beautiful young woman who aspires to a literary career

HEINZ (HENRY) CHARLES, her husband, a fundraiser for an obscure religious society

RUSSELL AND DEBORAH, their children

DR. LINDA MACK AND MARKY, old school friends of Eleanor's

GEORGE AND MARGE BRENT, Eleanor's divorced brother and ex-sister-in-law

COPE AND BRONWYN PIGSNEY, members of London't literary circles

GEOFF QUAIDESON, a publisher

Christina Stead, an expatriate Australian who lived much of her life in England, published her first novel in 1934. Between that book and this, there are nine others, two of them recently reprinted in a revival of her major works. She has been called one of the most distinguished novelists writing in English; and Randall Jarrell, who wrote the introduction to the reissued novel *The Man Who Loved Children*, compared that work with *Moby Dick*. These facts notwithstanding, *Miss Herbert* is a novel with serious flaws.

Miss Herbert tells the story of Eleanor Herbert Brent, a tall, athletic beauty who is bright, ambitious, and energetic, yet who cannot escape a series of dreary fates. Set in postwar Britain, the novel spans more than thirty years of her tedious life and sees her in and out of several affairs, a bad marriage, and grueling periods of poverty, all without eliciting reader sympathy. This Stead accomplishes by drawing Eleanor as a silly, self-centered, narrowminded woman, given to flattering herself and badly misjudging others.

As a character, Eleanor appears as a paper figure pasted to a twentieth century urban landscape. She is obviously meant to be the modern woman ("the suburban housewife"), wrestling with drives, both intellectual and sexual, that seem to put her at odds with societal pressures. Yet neither the character nor the reason for the struggle becomes believable: the pressures seem to come from her own shallow mind, while the drives emanate from her imagination. The anticipated collision and reassessment of values never occurs because there is no protagonist and no antagonist; there is just Eleanor.

At times, the insipid banalities she spouts lead her, in apparently total innocence, to insult the person with whom she is conversing. Yet the insults have an exasperating habit of falling on deaf ears. One such case involves Marky, an old school friend who is living (unmarried) with Ivo, a foreign journalist in Paris. Eleanor tells the couple, "You, my dear ones, could never be so happy, shine and beam with happiness as you do, you darlings, in England, for in Paris these things are quite normal, but in dear old fusty England, people must be married. And even here, I suppose you are not received in society?" Marky and Ivo look at her and laugh good naturedly. Eleanor continues:

> "Oh my dears, but you do miss good company, it is a pity. On the train over, I met Mrs. Blanding-Forest, an artist. She did the whole Royal Family and she was most curious when I said I was going to stay with an artist in Paris. I said a woman artist, of course—only it was on the tip of my tongue to tell her where I was staying, but I thought it better not, in your situation."

Marky and Ivo do not react at all; the scene changes. Not only this scene, but several others like it, involve the defiance of traditional morality—a pastime that Eleanor has engaged in for years without ever admitting it to the rest of the world. Her hypocrisy irritates more so than her silliness.

We first meet Eleanor when she is in her twenties, young, beautiful, and confident. She is, we are told, different from her friends, for not only is she more beautiful than they, but she is an engaged woman. That particular status does not last long, however, as she breaks her engagement to devote her energies to a literary career. She is now young, beautiful, and free, and to these attributes we can add sensuous, for she begins her literary education by tasting the sordid life, first as a hotel maid, seducing and seduced by fellow employees and clientele; and then, living in a respectable women's residence, where she makes part of her living entertaining male students in her room, after first discussing philosophy with them.

Eleanor eventually falls in love with a man she refuses to marry because the feelings are too passionate ("I want fresh air in my marriage, not passion, love, the hand of fate . . ."), and she eventually marries a man she does not love. We are evidently meant to sympathize with Eleanor as a woman who can neither understand nor control the drives that shape her life. Her sensuality is an integral part of her personality, but so are her old-fashioned values, and she wavers constantly between her two selves. But instead of becoming a tragic, or even sympathetic figure, she becomes—from this point on—merely pathetic and irritating.

As the novel continues, we see Eleanor devoting herself singlemindedly to her marriage, just as she earlier devoted herself to experiencing life. But when the marriage finally ends in divorce, she is a broken woman, unable to comprehend her husband's infidelity. She declares herself a widow, forces her two young children into an awareness of their father's infamy, and embarks on a tedious series of attempts at making a living on the fringes of the London literary world. She becomes involved once more in a series of affairs (this time almost totally imaginary) with peculiar men (a homosexual, a voyeur, a Scottish farmer who does not know her at all but cherishes her for the editing job she has done on his manuscript). These men and others populate her fantasies for a decade or so while she and her children are living in abject poverty.

Eleanor at length comes to a resolution of the moral-sexual split in her personality only when she falls passionately in love once more—this time with her daughter's fiancé. The solution to this dilemma is, as we should by now expect, incredible. Stead describes it this way: ". . . then something strange happened. It was just as if someone lifted the top off her head for a moment and let air in so that part of her brain blew cold. . . ." When her daughter arrives home, Eleanor is in a beatific state. "I kept the rules," she announces, "but the rules didn't keep me. . . ."

It is difficult to reconcile how an established author can deal with what Eleanor would term "grisly reality" in such unrealistic terms. All the affairs in the novel are held tastefully offstage, and solutions to real dilemmas are absurdly simple. We get the impression that Stead is a woman of delicate sensibilities, much like her heroine—a moralist who knows more of the seamy side of life than she would ever admit.

Miss Herbert is a novel about a woman alone: a woman who believes in her abilities to succeed in whatever role she assumes and who ultimately fails at all of them. Whether or not Stead intended the book to be read as a "women's novel," given the subject matter it is impossible in this age to overlook that element. However, the truth is that Eleanor Herbert's repeated failures result not from the inequities of an unyielding society but from her own vacuous personality.

To give Christina Stead her due as a writer whose earlier works have won the respect of many critics, we must assume that delineation of plot, as well as the main character's hypocrisy and insipidity, are intentional facets of the portrait. Eleanor Herbert's character does in fact reflect both the dreariness and the ambiguity of modern English life. The country is moving toward socialism; the glorious Empire is no more; and life in London for a bright, educated woman who must somehow support herself and two children is tedious and difficult. Vaguely present in the book is evidence for a comparison between character and background, but Stead fails to marry the elements. She may have intentionally painted Eleanor drab and flat, but instead of elucidating the moral poverty of modern English life, she diminishes her major character.

The novel is very English, perhaps too English for the American reader; but it is not a novel about England. Time and place are strangely immaterial to Stead. The only precise reference to time that we are given is that Eleanor is fifty-five at the novel's end. But we are given no dates and no specific references to locate the action in a particular time; nor are we told the heroine's age at the outset of the story. References are made in the course of the novel to things that happened "after the war" or "during the war," but we do not know whether the war occurred during the time-frame of the novel or not. This is the more peculiar if we accept the argument that Eleanor's portrait is purposely flat as a reflection of her surroundings. What surroundings? A writer whose protagonist's successful characterization depends upon references to the decline of the British Empire from the late 1930's to the present does not write her novel without once mentioning a time period. Hence, we are forced to find either the characterization or the plotting flawed.

Stead is not a novice writer, nor are the themes in *Miss Herbert* unfamiliar to her. As in her earlier works, she makes us aware of the pressures and constrictions of a character's own needs in opposition to society. The tensions of family life have been a recurrent theme in her writing, as has the struggle of the individual in the city. Politics, too, are important: most of the interesting characters are represented as socialists or ex-communists trying to outlive a reputation for radicalism. But themes are useless unless the character who is pitted against them has a moderate amount of believability and nobility. Eleanor Herbert has neither. She is a flat character who has been instilled with no energy to rise above the clichéd landscape in which she has been placed.

Stead tackles a problem of interest to most twentieth century women, but her solution to her character's troublingly divided nature is no solution at all. The novel fails to provide either hope or elucidation.

Julie Barker

Sources for Further Study

Atlantic. CCXXXVIII, August, 1976, p. 87.
Best Sellers. XXXVI, October, 1976, p. 214.
New Republic. CLXXV, October 9, 1976, p. 38.
New York Times Book Review. June 13, 1976, p. 4.
New Yorker. LII, August 9, 1976, p. 74.
Saturday Review. III, July 10, 1976, p. 50.

MOSHE DAYAN
Story of My Life

Author: Moshe Dayan (1915-   )
Publisher: William Morrow (New York). Illustrated. 640 pp. $15.00
Type of work: Autobiography
Time: 1915-1976
Locale: Israel

The autobiography of Moshe Dayan with special emphasis on the military and govern mental roles Dayan played in Israel's War of Independence, the Sinai Campaign of 1956, Israel's Six Day War of 1967, and the Yom Kippur War of 1973

Principal personages:
MOSHE DAYAN
DAVID BEN-GURION, Israel's first Prime Minister
LEVI ESHKOL, Israel's Prime Minister, 1963-1969
GOLDA MEIR, Israel's Prime Minister, 1969-1974
YITZHAK RABIN, Israel's Prime Minister, 1974-1977

Moshe Dayan's autobiography, *Moshe Dayan: Story of My Life*, is interesting for what it includes and what it excludes. There is in this account little of the inner or private Moshe Dayan, for the book focuses on the man as a military leader and a member of Israel's various governments. While Dayan reveals little of his personal relationships even with his wives (divorced from Ruth in 1971; married to Rahel in 1973) and children, the book is important for the information it supplies on the history of Israel and Dayan's role in Israel's war of Independence, the Suez Crisis and the Sinai Campaign, the Six Day War, and the Yom Kippur War and its consequences.

The book begins with a description of Moshe Dayan's parents and childhood. Dayan was born and reared in a Kibbutz, and throughout his life maintained a fondness for farming and for the inhabitants of Kibbutzim (agricultural communities). He also acquired a respect for Arabs and especially for Bedouins that has remained with him throughout his life.

Dayan's earliest memorable experiences were of attempts of Jewish settlers in Palestine to protect themselves against Arab terrorism at a time when England, the Mandatory government, both prohibited the Jews from arming themselves in self-defense while at the same time refusing to protect Jewish settlements. Consequently, the Jews formed their own Jewish Settlement Police Force and the Haganah, the secret self-defense force of the Jews in Palestine. In 1929 at the age of fourteen Dayan joined the Haganah and in 1937 was assigned to regular defense and other duties which occupied him until the outbreak of World War II. In May, 1939, the British Government issued its White Paper on Palestine, which limited further Jewish immigration to Palestine for the subsequent five years (thereafter banning it altogether) and restricting the purchase by Jews of land in Palestine. The White Paper, which would guarantee that Jewish refugees from Nazi concentration and death camps during World War II could not escape to Palestine, caused a further deterioration of relations between the British Mandatory government and the Jewish settlers in Palestine. Nonetheless, Jews had little alternative but to support England during World War II, and Dayan participated in recruiting and training young Jewish settlers for the Haganah and to assist British military forces in the Middle East.

In serving as a part of an Australian military unit in 1941, Dayan participated in a military engagement in which he lost his left eye. Recovering, he returned to military duties, aiding the British and organizing the Haganah in Palestine and in other Arab countries to prevent such occurences as the 1941 massacre of some four hundred Jews in the Jewish section of Baghdad. The Haganah was also involved in facilitating clandestine immigration to Palestine of Jews from the Arab nations.

Dayan's autobiography jumps from mid-World War II to 1947. Curiously missing is any description of the Holocaust or its effects on Palestine, or the ingathering into Palestine after the war of Jews from Europe. Nor is there a description of the problems of settlement. These deficiencies underscore the nature of this autobiography as a description primarily of Israel's military history. Dayan returns to his story when, in November, 1947, the United Nations approved a partition resolution recognizing Israel's right to statehood. In refusing to accept the resolution, Palestinian Arabs and their supporters from various Arab nations began a war that raged intermittently against Jewish settlements and that eventually broadened into a full-scale war. Within hours of Israel's Declaration of Independence in May, 1948, the Arab armies of Lebanon, Syria, Iraq, Jordan, and Egypt (Saudi Arabia sent troops that fought under Egypt's direction) invaded Israel. Dayan's leadership abilities in this war resulted in his elevation from commander of the 89th commando battalion to commander of Jerusalem. That strategic position permitted Dayan to negotiate directly with King Abdulla of Jordan. Failing to defeat Israel, the Arab states signed peace treaties in the spring and summer of 1949.

With the conclusion of the war, Dayan's appointment as commander of Israel's Southern Command involved him significantly in supporting the development of settlements within his command. Dayan played an important role in assisting the government of Prime Minister David Ben-Gurion in encouraging settlement. As commander in these desert regions, Dayan also developed an interest, sustained throughout the remainder of his life, in archaeology. He eventually acquired a substantial collection of high quality items unearthed in his digs. Dayan's administration of the Southern Command was of sufficient skill and competence that promotion followed.

On December 7, 1952, Dayan became head of the Operations Branch of the General Staff and on December 6, 1953, he was elevated to Chief of Staff of the Israeli Armed Forces. In this position, he concentrated his efforts on improving the training and overall quality of Israel's armed forces. In November,

1955, the Soviet Union began supplying Egypt with massive quantities of arms. This alerted the Israeli General Staff to the possibility of a threat from Egypt and convinced the General Staff and the Israeli government to seek arms from abroad. While the United States refused to sell arms, France and England provided Israel with limited quantities of weapons. In addition to producing a Middle East arms race, the Soviet armaments provided Egypt's ruler, Gamal Abdel Nasser, with the confidence to nationalize the Suez Canal on July 16, 1956. The nationalization of the Canal convinced France to seek English and later Israeli cooperation to launch a joint invasion of Egypt to recover the Suez Canal and topple the government of Nasser.

Dayan eventually became part of the team negotiating with France and England to undertake an invasion of Egypt. Israel, in Dayan's view, hardly needed a justification for an invasion of Egypt, in the face of Egypt's blockade of the Straits of Tiran, terrorist activities launched from Egypt against Israel, Egyptian military preparation for an invasion of Israel, and Nasser's continuous statements of a state of war between Israel and Egypt. However, England and France still sought further justification for their invasion. Although in negotiating with the British and the French, Israel found the English particularly uncooperative, a strategy was finally developed for British and French entry into a war against Egypt. Israel would initiate military action against Egypt; France and England would then issue an ultimatum to Egypt and Israel demanding their withdrawal from the Suez Canal, and when it was rejected, they would then intervene to secure the Canal.

The Sinai Campaign began on October 29, 1956, as Israel began an invasion of the Sinai desert. The Sinai campaign has become a classic in military strategy. Eventually it involved Israel in four thrusts across the Sinai desert. In the first operation, Israeli paratroopers were dropped at the western end of the Sinai in position to seize two crucial passes, the Mitla Pass and the Gidi Pass. The paratroopers received support when armored and infantry forces linked with them at the end of a thrust directly west across the desert and toward the Egyptian city of Suez. Meanwhile another column was successful in crossing the desert from east to west on a line parallel to and north of the first thrust and toward the city of Ismailia. Two other columns completed Israel's seizure of the Sinai—one paralleling the Mediterranean coast and advancing from east to west across the desert toward Kantara on the Suez Canal, and the other moving directly south along the Gulf of Aqaba to seize Sharm el-Sheikh (support for this thrust came from troops dispatched from the vicinity of the Mitla Pass and moving southeast paralleling the Gulf of Suez until they joined the attackers of Sharm el-Sheikh). By November 5, Israel was in control of all of Sinai. Dayan and his military commanders and troops had performed brilliantly in seizing the initiative and overcoming the enormous advantage in Egyptian arms; but that military success did not result in a permanent resolution of Israel's problems in the Middle East and was somewhat offset by diplomatic activities.

The United States used all of its diplomatic resources to oppose the British-French-Israeli invasion and was successful in leading a campaign of public opinion around the world that put pressure on the combatants to end the war. In England there was great public resentment directed against Prime Minister Anthony Eden. Working through the United Nations, the United States obtained a U.N. General Assembly call for a ceasefire. Russia recalled her ambassador to Israel and later broke off diplomatic relations. In participating in the war, Israel had helped to secure freedom of Israeli shipping through the Straits of Tiran, an end to Egyptian-based terrorist raids, and an end to the threat of attack from Egyptian forces in the Sinai. On March 16 1957, Israel withdrew her forces from the Sinai in return for pledges from Nasser that Israel would be allowed free shipping through the Straits of Tiran and that Egypt would stop its support of terrorism.

At the end of the war, Dayan left the government to return to private life, but in 1959 he returned to government as Minister of Agriculture. In this position, he sought to improve agricultural development throughout Israel, while extending Israeli technical assistance to many of the less-developed countries of Sub-Sahara Africa. On July 16, 1963, David Ben-Gurion resigned as Prime Minister and was succeeded by Levi Eshkol. Sixteen months later, Dayan resigned his position in the Israeli government and again returned to private life.

Purely from the weight of autobiographical attention to periods of his life, it is clear that Dayan regards himself as a public man. While elaborating on the activities (particularly military activities) of the Israeli government while he was in office, little attention is given to his private concerns and interests while out of office. Thus, the period from his resignation in 1964 to the 1967 Six Day War represents a hiatus, and Dayan resumes his discussion of the history of Israel's military encounters in 1967.

On May 14, 1967, intelligence reports reached the Israeli government that Egypt, under Nasser, was moving large quantities of troops and equipment into the Sinai. On May 17, 1967, Egypt ousted the United Nations Emergency Force in the Sinai and along the Gaza Strip. On May 22, Egypt blockaded the Straits of Tiran to all shipping going to or coming from Israel. Four days later, Nasser publicly announced the Egyptian intention to destroy Israel. On May 30, Jordan's King Hussein placed his military forces under Egyptian command as did Iraq. Syria had, for the previous six months, been regularly shelling Israeli villages from the Golan Heights, along Israel's northern border. The Syrian government was also receiving large shipments of Russian arms, which troubled Israeli intelligence. Thus, by early June, 1967, Dayan indicated that Israel was threatened on all sides and a decision had to be made on whether Israel would wait to be attacked or launch a preemptive strike against the Arab nations.

The immediate response of Dayan (who was not in the Israeli government at the time) to the growing threat to Israel was to attempt to assess the situation and Israel's degree of preparedness by making a tour of the Southern Command. Dayan then offered some specific suggestions to military planners regarding Israeli objectives in the event of the outbreak of hostilities. On May 30, Dayan was offered the post of deputy prime minister in the government of Levi Eshkol. Dayan refused and began an effort to maneuver himself into a position that he preferred—the Defense portfolio. He received that position in a coalition government and soon began to evaluate military plans and objectives with the General Staff.

A decision was made to begin an attack on Egyptian air bases on June 5, 1967. The attack proved exceedingly successful and resulted in destroying the Egyptian air force. While Israel was attacking Egypt, the Syrian and Jordanian air forces, along with a few planes from Iraq, began an attack on Israel. Soon the Jordanian air force was destroyed, along with fifty percent of the Syrian air force and a number of Iraqi planes. At the start of the war, Israel controlled the skies. By June 8, Israel had taken control of all of the Sinai as far west as the west bank of the Suez Canal and Egypt was directing her UN representative to seek a ceasefire. In the meantime, Israel turned its attention to Jordan and Syria. By June 7, Israel had seized all of Jerusalem from Jordan and was in control of the West Bank of the Jordan River. The Israeli forces sought control of a part of the Golan Heights in order to prevent the shelling of Israeli settlements. By June 9, Israel had secured the line that Dayan sought as the goal of Israeli fighting. The Six Day War ended successfully for Israel with Israel in control of additional square miles of territory and new responsibilities in regard to the inhabitants of those territories.

Dayan was able to deal with the additional responsibilities in ways that enhanced relations between the Arabs and Jews. The barriers Jordan had erected to freedom of worship in Jerusalem were removed and Christians, Jews, and Arabs alike were admitted to worship in their respective holy places. Dayan himself was responsible for working out many of these arrangements. He facilitated communication between Jordan and Israel so that Jordanian Arabs could sell goods in Israel. Residents of the Gaza Strip were taken out of Palestinian refugee camps supported by the U.N. and were provided with housing, the requirements of living, and jobs in Israel, where they were soon able to climb out of the grinding poverty that had characterized them for the previous generation. This produced an economic revolution. Dayan encouraged the Arab administration of many of the towns of the West Bank. The Israeli government also provided health care and homes for Bedouins who wished them. Dayan's role was very significant in all of this, although satisfactory treatment of the Arabs did not end Israel's difficulties. The end of the Six Day War was followed by an intensification of terrorism, supported by Syria, Egypt, and, for a time, Jordan. That terrorism became international in scope.

As Minister of Defense, Dayan had to attempt to cope with growing terrorism as well as maintain defenses against Egypt and Syria, both of which continued a war of attrition against Israeli troops. Egypt only agreed to a complete ceasefire in the summer of 1970, almost three years after the Six Day War. The Dayan autobiography only briefly discusses the period from the 1967 war to the Yom Kippur War of 1973.

While Dayan's military and governmental career was largely successful prior to 1973, the Yom Kippur War proved to be a difficult and bloody confrontation for Israel, and heavy responsibility for this was placed on Dayan and the government headed by Golda Meir. Both eventually resigned their positions because of public blame. Dayan's description of the Yom Kippur War of 1973, therefore, differs from previous descriptions of Israel's military activities. Instead of accepting credit, as in previous wars, Dayan attributes responsibility for Israel's unpreparedness and military operations to members of the General Staff and to the military, and emphasizes the lack of Defense Ministry authority over military matters. In the Yom Kippur War, Israel was caught unprepared. The sophisticated missiles of the Arabs weakened Israel's air power and precluded destroying the Arab air forces as completely as in the Six Day War. The element of surprise and superiority of forces were of great advantage to Syria and Egypt at first.

Although attacks on Israel came across the Sinai and the Golan Heights, Israel concentrated on the Syrian attack first. The fighting began on October 6, 1973, as Israelis were celebrating Yom Kippur, the holiest day of the Jewish year. Syrians were first able to begin to push Israeli defense lines on the Golan back. By October 9, however, Israeli forces were on the offensive and finally pushed the Syrians back beyond the line established at the conclusion of the 1967 war. On the Southern front, the Egyptians had crossed the Suez Canal almost unopposed and were sending massive quantities of troops and armaments into the Sinai.

In the Sinai, Russian-made Egyptian missiles had a devastating effect on Israeli aircraft. Israeli pleas for military supplies from the United States were unavailing until it was clearly established that the Soviet Union was providing an airlift of supplies for the Arabs. Then the United States responded favorably to Israel's request for arms.

With military aid forthcoming and the Golan front stabilized, Israel began to push Egyptian forces back toward the Suez Canal. Eventually Egyptian forces were pushed back near the Canal and Israeli forces crossed the Canal to the East Bank, encircling and trapping the entire Egyptian Third Army. Given this pressure, President Anwar Sadat of Egypt announced a ceasefire on October 22. Syria accepted a ceasefire the next day.

Although the Yom Kippur War ended in victory for Israel, it was a troubled victory for the Israelis and produced considerable demoralization, but eventually it led to some agreement with Egypt. Negotiations were initiated through the efforts of United States Secretary of State Henry Kissinger that resulted in an Israeli withdrawal to a north-south line near the Gidi and Mitla

Passes, thereby permitting Egypt to reopen the Suez Canal. Dayan is convinced that Israel was forced to withdraw from the Canal because of pressure exerted as a consequence of the oil embargo of 1973. "The world was interested in oil, not justice. . . ." Dayan believes, however, that as a consequence of the war, Anwar Sadat modified the Egyptian "war policy" "into a peace policy." Therefore, Dayan sees hopeful signs for peace following the Yom Kippur War.

Although Dayan remains hopeful about the future, the Yom Kippur War resulted in his and Golda Meir's resignations from the Israeli government. Lack of preparedness and the loss of Israeli lives in the war produced a public clamor to oust the government. Yitzhak Rabin replaced Golda Meir as Prime Minister in 1974 and Dayan again returned to private life. The book, written in 1976, concluded shortly before the victory in 1977 Israeli elections of Menahem Begin and Dayan's return to power as Foreign Minister under the Begin government.

More than an autobiography, Moshe Dayan's book is a perceptive history of the military encounters of the modern State of Israel and a description of how deeply Dayan's own life is intertwined in that history.

Saul Lerner

Sources for Further Study

Christian Science Monitor. October 12, 1976, p. 38.
Economist. October 9, 1976, p. 125.
Los Angeles Times. October 4, 1976, *Books,* p. 9.
New Republic. CLXXV, November 27, 1976, p. 35.
New Statesman. XCII, September 17, 1976, p. 377.
New York Times Book Review. October 24, 1976, p. 4.
Spectator. CCXXXVII, September 18, 1976, p. 31.

MUSSOLINI'S ROMAN EMPIRE

Author: Denis Mack Smith (1920-   )
Publisher: The Viking Press (New York). 322 pp. $12.95
Type of work: History
Time: 1922-1943
Locale: Italy, other European countries bordering on the Mediterranean Sea, and Africa

An analysis of the foreign policy of a totalitarian state and the unsuccessful efforts of its leader to create an empire

> *Principal personages:*
> BENITO MUSSOLINI, Prime Minister and Fascist Dictator of Italy, 1922-1943
> ADOLF HITLER, Chancellor and Führer of Germany, 1933-1945
> GALEAZZO CIANO, Italian Minister of Foreign Affairs, 1936-1943; son-in-law of Mussolini
> PIETRO BADOGLIO, Chief of the Italian General Staff, 1925-1928 and 1933-1940, with the rank of Marshal; Governor of Libya, 1928-1933

Denis Mack Smith, a Fellow of All Souls College in Oxford, England, has established himself as a leading authority on Italian history, primarily on the basis of several of his books that deal with leading figures in the Risorgimento. His latest book, *Mussolini's Roman Empire,* concentrates, as the title suggests, on Fascist foreign policy. The theme of this book is how Benito Mussolini, as the Fascist dictator of Italy, deliberately steered his political movement into imperialism and a series of wars which eventuated in the prostration of his country. In writing this volume, Mack Smith begins with the assumption that the nature of Mussolini's career is better revealed by the political and military defeats for which Fascism was responsible than by how the movement began. Since the history of Italian Fascism is virtually synonymous with the rise and fall of Mussolini, the author pays particular attention to the character and personality of Il Duce throughout the book. Chronologically, the book covers three general periods, including the consolidation of Mussolini's dictatorship, 1922-1933; the establishment of the short-lived Fascist Empire and the alliance with Adolf Hitler, the Nazi dictator, 1933-1940; and Mussolini's participation in World War II, 1940-1943. In view of the yawning gap which existed in Fascist Italy between pretense and reality, Mack Smith places considerable emphasis throughout his study on the effectiveness and dangers of propaganda.

The architect of Fascist propaganda and ultimately its most tragic victim was of course Mussolini himself. Mack Smith depicts Mussolini as a violent, arrogant, and insensitive individual, for whom the possession of power was the highest virtue. Like other dictators in history, he could not tolerate having his authority or prescience called into question. This was not in keeping with what Mack Smith refers to as the "fascist style." On the contrary, Il Duce loved to convey the impression that he did not need expert advice on any subject, whether it was the type of equipment possessed by his army or some decision in foreign policy. Significantly, he regarded a successful foreign policy as the best way of strengthening his position at home. Mussolini's foreign policy, however, was mainly based on his bombastic and intimidating statements and the threat, if not the actual use, of his military forces. His genius as a propagandist in the conduct of his foreign policy served him well at least through the Munich crisis of 1938.

Thereafter, reality steadily caught up with Mussolini, whether he wanted to admit it or not. German power in Europe was clearly in the ascendancy, and Hitler generally avoided taking Mussolini into his confidence about Nazi plans for conquest. By this time, then, Italy had become the junior partner of the Berlin-Rome Axis. Mack Smith's description of Mussolini is particularly good in showing his agonized indecisiveness over the question of whether to participate in the war which Germany started in September, 1939. He had informed Hitler just a week before the Nazi invasion of Poland that Italy was ready to fight only if Germany would supply the munitions. This was Mussolini's way of saying that he would not be able to honor his alliance with Hitler, as formally concluded in the Pact of Steel just a few months before. Mussolini was anxious, Mack Smith notes, to conceal the fact that the Italian army was in worse condition than before World War I. Its limited resources had been dissipated in the conquest of Ethiopia in 1935-1936, and thereafter by Italy's military intervention on behalf of Francisco Franco in the Spanish Civil War. Mussolini also feared that if he maintained a status of neutrality, Germany might invade Italy, but that if he did not, the British might launch an attack against him. It was typical of Mussolini that, to save face and to avoid what to him was the odious term "neutrality," he coined the concept "non-belligerence." This expression gave him but passing comfort, for he did not consider Italy's nonparticipation in the war as being consistent with the "fascist style."

Yet it was only with considerable anxiety that he decided to enter the war, in June, 1940, by invading France at the moment when her troops were retreating before the advancing German columns in the north. He was still afraid to fight because his army was not yet ready, but, politically, he was afraid to stay out of the war any longer lest Italy be relegated to the status of a second-class power. Mack Smith points out that in the short French campaign Mussolini's propaganda machine was far more powerful than his war machine; thus, the Fascist press proclaimed to all who would listen that Italian intervention against France had been responsible for her surrender. As the war progressed, Mussolini's power of decision making, such as it was, continued to decline. His planning for the invasion of Greece in the fall of 1940 proved so inept that German troops had to rescue his forces soon after they had begun their attack, a situation which contributed to his increasing sense of depression and humiliation. Mack Smith believes that by the end of 1941, he was no longer capable of making rational judgments and indeed exhibited symptoms of minor derangement. From that time onward, Mussolini withdrew more and more into his own private illusions which his propaganda had created. Blaming and despising those around him, he refused to accept any responsibility for the collapse of his regime in 1943.

Mussolini's ineptitude in administering his Fascist state was amply illustrated by his choices for the positions of Minister of Foreign Affairs and Chief of General Staff. Count Galeazzo Ciano, his son-in-law, headed the foreign ministry from 1936 to 1943; Marshal Pietro Badoglio was Chief of General Staff from 1925 to 1928 and again from 1933 to 1940, after serving in the intervening period as Governor of Libya. Mack Smith paints a very unflattering portrait of both officials, regarding them as being totally unfit to carry out the responsibilities that would ordinarily be associated with the important positions which they held.

Ciano, the author observes, held his post solely because he was the Il Duce's son-in-law. He had but a limited knowledge of foreign policy and only a marginal influence in formulating it. The main functions, therefore, of this young and irresponsible minister were to protect his father-in-law from having to see foreign ambassadors and to execute any policy that Il Duce might choose. Ciano's major contribution as foreign minister was the establishment with Germany of the Berlin-Rome Axis in November, 1936. Otherwise, he projected an image that brought discredit on a none-too-creditable regime. Thus, he scandalized those present at the coronation of Pope Pius XII by strutting down the nave of St. Peter's Basilica giving the Fascist salute. Hitler was equally displeased with Ciano, referring to him as "that disgusting boy." The Germans were especially alarmed by his notorious inability to keep secrets, which was one reason why they seldom took Mussolini into their confidence. In fact, one of Ciano's female companions would immediately pass any important facts which he divulged to her to the British ambassador. In his personal habits, he went so far as to imitate Mussolini's mannerisms and even his handwriting. Mack Smith asserts that, despite what Ciano said later, at the time he held the post of foreign minister he wanted close ties with Nazi Germany and war with Great Britain. Though he was aware of the risks involved in such a policy, he did not question Mussolini's view that Germany would win the next war.

Marshal Pietro Badoglio was, in Mack Smith's estimation, almost as incompetent as Ciano. The duties of the position of Chief of General Staff to which Mussolini appointed Badoglio in 1925 were so ill-defined that one general boldly stated that the result of its creation might be the paralysis of the higher command. With Badoglio at the helm of the military establishment, this prophecy more than came true. Badoglio, in his capacity as military chief and Governor of Libya, found, like Ciano, that it was much easier to maintain

Mussolini's favor by flattering him than by presenting him with realistic opinions that ran counter to his own. It was to Badoglio's credit, Mack Smith points out, that he did counsel Mussolini against intervention in the Spanish Civil War because the military services were desperately in need of reorganization and recuperation after the campaign in Ethiopia. Mussolini, however, did not heed Badoglio's advice, and he protested no further. Rather, he was content to continue drawing his enormous salary for which he did very little work. Mack Smith notes that despite his position, he did not even bother to attend the main army maneuvers of 1937 or 1938; yet, in 1939, he expressed surprise at discovering that most artillery pieces were still horse-drawn. Nonetheless, Mussolini rewarded Badoglio's incompetence by naming him in 1937 as the Director of the National Council of Research, thus further exemplifying the primacy of mediocrity in all branches of the Fascist administration. Mussolini finally removed Badoglio as Chief of General Staff in December, 1940, using him as a scapegoat for the disastrous campaign in Greece.

By far the most fateful decision which Mussolini made in his quest for empire was his decision to join forces with Hitler. Initially, Mussolini and his fellow party members were repelled by the rising Nazi movement, especially by its racist doctrine which condemned the Jews while extolling the Germanic or Aryan race. Mack Smith observes that by 1933, however, the year that Hitler came to power in Germany, Il Duce's propaganda machine was also waxing racialist by proclaiming that Fascism alone could provide the spiritual values necessary to save white civilization from nonwhite races. Mussolini was simultaneously preoccupied in his speeches with great imperialist wars that might lead to the conquest of Ethiopia and the annexation of Corsica, Nice, Savoy, and Tunisia at the expense of France. Where rivalry with France was concerned, writes Mack Smith, Mussolini felt that as a matter of longterm policy there were good arguments for backing Nazi Germany, a country which also had revisionist aspirations. Mack Smith goes on to explain how the Nazi *Putsch* in Austria, in July, 1934, produced a severe strain on Italo-German relations, especially in view of Mussolini's guarantee of Austrian independence some months earlier. In the Stresa Conference of April, 1935, Italy, France, and Great Britain reaffirmed the independence of Austria. By that time, however, the Ethiopian crisis was beginning to loom on the horizon. Mussolini's invasion of that helpless country beginning in October, 1935, led to the collapse of good relations with France and Great Britain, and by late 1936 to his *rapprochement* with Hitler which became known as the Axis. Significantly, the Ethiopian War gave Mussolini an empire to boast about and the ensuing alliance with Nazi Germany held out prospects that Italy could enlarge this empire with Hitler's help. The realities of the situation proved entirely different. For in agreeing to sacrifice Austrian independence in the process of aligning himself with Hitler, Mussolini opened the floodgates of German expansion in eastern Europe which eventually led to World War II and his own destruction.

Mussolini's Roman Empire is a readable and comprehensive analysis of the history of Italian foreign policy in the Fascist era. The author is particularly adept in dissecting the glaring weaknessess of the Fascist state in general and of the military establishment in particular. He presents Mussolini, Ciano, and Badoglio to the reader as vain, hollow individuals, whose wild dreams of empire led to the ruination of their country. In writing this account, Mack Smith might have made more use of primary source material, but, as he states in the preface, the archives for departments of the Italian government for the 1930's are still largely inaccessible. Otherwise, he has thoroughly researched his study, as the bibliography of more than twenty pages indicates. Generally, though, too many reference citations are sprinkled throughout the text in places where they are not really necessary. Because the notes are located at the end of the book, the serious reader must constantly flip back to check the sources. Shortcomings such as these, however, do not unduly detract from the inherent value of Mack Smith's book.

Edward P. Keleher

Sources for Further Study

America. CXXXV, November 6, 1976, p. 306.
Christian Century. XCIII, September 29, 1976, p. 820.
Christian Science Monitor. LXVIII, July 8, 1976, p. 23.
History: Reviews of New Books. V, October, 1976, p. 18.
New Yorker. LII, July 12, 1976, p. 106.
Newsweek. XCII, September 24, 1976, p. 411.

NAPOLEON SYMPHONY

Author: Anthony Burgess (1917-   )
Publisher: Alfred A. Knopf (New York). 366 pp. $7.95
Type of work: Novel
Time: The early nineteenth century
Locale: France, Italy, Egypt and the Mediterranean, Eastern Europe, Elba, St. Helena

A *tragicomical fictional biography of Napoleon Bonaparte, constructed in the pattern of Beethoven's* Eroica *symphony*

Principal character:
NAPOLEON BONAPARTE, Emperor of France

When Beethoven began the *Eroica,* he dedicated it to the honor of Napoleon, but by the time he finished its composition, Napoleon had antagonized the composer by proclaiming himself Emperor, and the symphony was rededicated as a hymn to Prometheus.

In *Napoleon Symphony,* Anthony Burgess has once again proven his virtuosity by meticulously weaving a raucous biography of Napoleon Bonaparte within a structure parallel to Beethoven's third symphony. The novel is written in four sections, representing the four movements of the symphony, with an overture and a coda. The various themes that constitute Napoleon's life—his love for Josephine, his brilliance as a strategist, his political tyrannies, and his ruined life devolved into a heroic myth—are interwoven into the symphonic pattern.

The overture is handily paralleled by a scene of officials waiting with Josephine for Napoleon to arrive and begin the wedding ceremony and leads to the first movement with his arrival as he pronounces the word "Begin." The first movement of the symphony is *allegro con brio,* or brisk with animation. The exposition of the theme here covers the campaign in Italy, and the development is effected through the campaign in Egypt. The recapitulation comes with Napoleon's election as First Consul of France, and the coda ranges from the Duc d'Enghien's assassination attempt through the coronation.

The funeral march which encompasses the second movement of the symphony and is paralleled in the second section of the book presents as its main theme a recurring nonsense poem of heavily beating syllables. Just as the music for this movement is written in a minor key, so the emphasis in this section of the novel is on defeat.

Beethoven's third movement was truly revolutionary in that he substituted a *scherzo* for the traditional minuet. Technically, a scherzo is something of a lively musical joke, and for his joke, Burgess presents a hilarious Prometheus ballet. Additionally, one can almost see the defeat at Waterloo as a joke played on the over-confident Napoleon.

The fourth and final movement gives us variations on the theme of INTERFECIMUS NAPOLEONEM REGEM IMPERATOREM, the initials of which, INRI, are the same as those placed on Christ's cross during the crucifixion. The main theme of the final section centers around Napoleon's martyrdom as an exile and his death. The coda is an epistle to the reader written in heroic couplets.

In the presentation of this work, both its peculiar structure and its popular style, Burgess treads the thin line between the ridiculous and the sublime. His portrait of Napoleon vacillates between extremes, showing him to be a violent amalgam of the intellectual and the physical, a coarse, energetic, and charismatic man. The Napoleon who is presented to us has been reduced to life-size. We see not only his military brilliance and brash political aplomb, but his inability to realize the true consequences, in human terms, of his actions on the lives of others. In his coldblooded contemplation, for instance, of the most efficient way to kill four thousand prisoners (settling, tellingly, on gas chambers as the ideal method of the future, though he was forced to use bayonets), he is concerned purely with technique.

Burgess does a particularly good job of advising his audience as to the effect of many of these decisions on the soldiers in the front lines, including much of the violence and misery and dreariness of war from the foot soldier's point of view. The device he uses is a picaresque Everyman who crops up intermittently throughout the work to complain as he slogs through the mud or the desert or the snow at finding himself once more in untoward circumstances, the political consequences of which he does not understand. He is there to fight more out of loyalty to the Napoleonic myth than to his commander in chief's political dreams.

In one particularly chilling example of this dedication, the army's retreat from Russia is chronicled in part by a nameless member of the Corps of Engineers as he describes their efforts to build bridges over the Berezina River. They spend endless hours in icy water laying the foundation and losing several men to the current, and watch as the desperation of some of the army units and their lack of discipline ends in tragic consequences. Several groups attempt to use the bridge at the same time and succeed in drowning or trampling dozens of their number. One of the bridges collapses under the weight of heavy artillery, and the same tragic stampede occurs. This all-too-accurate depiction of the retreat and many other horrors of war throughout the book certainly balance any temptation to think of the campaigns in terms of glory.

One of the facets of Napoleon that is displayed to the reader, along with his larger-than-life public self, is his private self and many of his shortcomings. His passionate love for Josephine is coupled with his failure to understand her. His pride in his son by his second wife is tempered somewhat by his impatience when the toddler seems to enjoy knocking down his tin soldiers that represent the French army rather than those representing the enemy.

Napoleon seems somewhat warmer and more human whenever someone in his entourage says something that disturbs him. Because we are privy to his thoughts, we know that, coldblooded and egotistical though he sometimes can be, he is really much nicer than the shows of temper and forced public reactions would seem to indicate. Burgess hits a universally responsive chord, for we all have at some time felt a disparity between the way that others have perceived us, and our true natures as we know them to be.

Burgess offers the reader a sprinkling of historical gossip about Napoleon and his family, but he mainly seems content to display this complex character before us without much analysis or commentary. Nonetheless, Burgess' fondness for Napoleon is obvious. Ruthless and driving, supremely egotistical, Napoleon is still quite human in this portrait, and one cannot help but like him.

Other people have only brief parts to play in the novel; their characters are not really developed, nor need they be. Napoleon's wives, the other members of his family, the generals and politicians that complete his world are only defined in their relation to him, and in comparison, play only minor supporting roles. The only other major voice in the work is that of the nameless soldier from whom we learn the realities of life from time to time.

The work is not focused entirely on the horrors of war, however. Some of the turns of phrase are clever enough to evoke a chuckle and a few of the scenes are downright hilarious. One of the funniest moments occurs when Napoleon, at the head of the table for a family dinner just before he is proclaimed Emperor, attempts a serious discussion with all of the members of the family. His mother, brothers, sisters, and various in-laws are ranged around him in a tableau reminiscent of a dinner with a mafia don pontificating. As Napoleon begins to discuss the ramifications of his accession to the throne, their individual self-interest becomes more and more evident. Napoleon tries very hard to keep them to the topic at hand, since he is at the time without a direct heir, but their greediness for wealth and power focuses their attention on what their new titles are to be. Napoleon's temper finally flares when one of them voices a dislike for the Chicken Marengo that is being served for dinner, and Napoleon replies that it is already a historical dish and orders them to eat it, meanwhile lamenting their lack of respect for his new position and authority. The gentle irony here of course, is that he is brilliant in leading great armies, but cannot manage to lead a family discussion.

Throughout the work there echoes the theme of a mystical, irrational patriotism, exemplified in the German quest for the supremacy of the pure Aryan race, which Napoleon fails to understand just as he fails to understand many other abstract or unquantified concepts. His first confrontation with this abstract rather than personified loyalty comes when he interrogates a young German student as to his motivations when the student attempts to assassinate him. The mystical near-reverance for, say, sunset in the Black Forest that can only be felt by a true German according to the young man, is held up to Napoleon time and again as a shortcoming of all other peoples who cannot experience it, the French in particular. Napoleon's violent attempt to unify

Europe through military conquest for his personal aggrandizement almost marks the end of an era, as it provokes, to a great extent, the unification of the German princes against a common enemy. In this context Napoleon is something of an old-fashioned pragmatic monarchist rattling around in a vaguely republican shell.

Throughout the novel, Burgess dazzles us with his wealth of knowledge. As Napoleon travels from country to country in his extensive campaigns, Burgess is given the opportunity to dabble in the language and customs of each, making jokes, writing rhymes, and playing linguistic games. Musical allusions throughout the work are myriad. The choric voice is one example; Napoleon's declaration at the beginning of the work that the age of the minuet had been superseded by the age of the waltz (alluding to the new tempo of the time as well as to Beethoven's work) is another.

Burgess uses Joyce's stream of consciousness technique to good effect, bringing it to a popular level. Although he has written this novel in a fairly breezy style, part of the popular audience to whom it will no doubt appeal may often be lost in the vague allusions to historical events and politics. *Napoleon Symphony* is a high-class entertainment which takes its structural basis from the work of a great musician and its plot from the life of a great hero; and the two elements are deftly combined in the hands of a marvelously well-versed author.

Margaret S. Schoon

Sources for Further Study

The Times of London. May 1, 1976, p. 11.

A NEW AGE NOW BEGINS
A People's History of the American Revolution

Author: Page Smith (1917-   )
Publisher: McGraw-Hill Book Company (New York). 2 vols. 1,838 pp. $24.95
Type of work: Historical narrative
Time: 1764-1783
Locale: The American colonies and England

A detailed and vivid portrait of the battles, personalities, and mentalities that produced and effected the American Revolution

> *Principal personages:*
> GEORGE WASHINGTON (1732-1799), Commander in Chief of the American forces
> JOHN ADAMS (1735-1826), patriot leader and political philosopher
> THOMAS PAINE (1737-1809), British-American pamphleteer and philosopher
> FREDERICK NORTH, 2ND EARL OF GUILFORD (1732-1792), Chief Minister of England, 1770-1782
> GEORGE III (1738-1820), King of England

The American Revolution has a fair claim to being the single most important episode in American history; given this fact, the prospective student faces a strange neglect of the period by historians. It is hard to find any part of this nation's past which is not the subject of an eminent historian's general treatment at least once a decade. The Civil War, for example, has received at least half a dozen synthetic works in the past generation. If anything, the field is plagued by an overabundance of broad, introductory works. But to find a comprehensive history of the Revolutionary era, one must search back to the work of the English liberal George Otto Trevelyan, who published his four-volume series at the turn of the century. The absence of synthetic works is all the more surprising in this case, for the seventy years since Trevelyan's contribution have witnessed a remarkable series of monographs and interpretive essays which have dramatically altered our understanding of the Revolution and its causes. The subject has provoked profound disagreement among scholars, but their debates have been fought in skirmishes which have steadily avoided the main field. As a result, many new layers of historical insight have failed to break out of the academic environment and penetrate the traditional textbook accounts of the Revolutionary War.

Page Smith's massive account of the period is clearly an attempt to fill this gap. Although much of his work is interpretive, he is largely concerned with dispelling the myths about persons, battles, and events that have accumulated over the years. An enormous part of his writing is based on "eyewitness accounts" and other primary materials which have only become available in recent years. The scholarship of his volumes, combined with their scope, provide us with a view of the Revolution we have not been able to see before.

Such is the function of general histories; but Professor Smith has not permitted his work to be so typical or so easy to classify. He has experimented with history, and his work shows both the complexities and the ambiguities of an uncertain act of creation. These are immediately implied in the subtitle: *A People's History of the American Revolution.* One wonders at the use of the word "People's"; does this mean it is addressed to a broad reading audience, or is Smith implying that he views the Revolution as a populist phenomenon? The reader quickly perceives that Smith is implying both meanings.

One of the ongoing debates about the Revolution revolves around the issue of whether the break with England was genuinely a mass phenomenon, or a movement initiated and carried off by a wealthy and educated elite. In the twentieth century, the pendulum of consensus has tended to swing toward the latter view. Some historians have gone so far as to insist that the shift in power does not even merit the name of revolution, but resembled more closely the modern *coup d'etat.* Although the era was a profoundly important one for every stratum of society, and though the war had many bloody and uncontrolled moments, the episode as a whole was far more stable and coherent than most later revolutions. True, British authority was overthrown, and new governments were created in the colonies, but American society retained its old social structure, its religious diversity, and its distribution of wealth; most important, the colonial elite remained, for the most part, intact. Confiscation of property and violence against Loyalists were not extensive in comparison with the French Revolution or the English Civil War. These and other characteristics have made it quite plausible for scholars to argue that the Revolution was staged by a small and clever group of colonial leaders who had lost their patience with British meddling and regulation, and who used the weapon of mob violence to formalize their power in America, thus becoming the Founding Fathers. More recent studies have dampened the credibility of the position that patriot leaders cynically manipulated men and ideals for economic convenience, but continue to emphasize the critical role these leaders played in provoking and consummating the Revolution.

Though there is a competing tradition which assigns greater importance to the artisans and farmers of the colonies, the populist view has perhaps never been so aggressively stated as in Page Smith's volumes. Throughout his work, the pulse of popular feeling and movement is never far below the surface. Rather than making vague references to the "people" in this or that action, he attempts to define the actual groups involved in resistance, and often focuses on specific individuals, previously lost in historical oblivion. Though the leader of a particular Stamp Act mob may be relatively unimportant in himself, what he tells us about the nature and motivation of such groups makes him a fascinating personality. Smith does devote a great deal of attention to the more traditional heroes of the Revolution (most notably John Adams, the subject of an exhaustive biography by Smith). Yet still the reader feels that the age was greater than the individual persons, and that the Founding Fathers were simply the brilliant and dynamic crest of a grand, massive wave of genuinely revolutionary sentiment.

Interspersed with the work's flowing narrative, the author tries to create a specific theory to substantiate his populist view of the Revolution. Early in the first volume, after surveying the development of the English colonies, Smith summarizes in a chapter entitled, "What Then Is the American, the New Man?" (The original words are those of the French immigrant and Loyalist Jean de Crèvecoeur.) Like Crèvecoeur, Smith believes that the circumstances of the American colonies have combined to create a new breed of civilized man. He argues that the Protestant Reformation of the sixteenth century liberated new energies inside the minds of Europeans, energies which tended to push them in the pursuit of a new and unprecedented individualism. In Europe, these energies were stymied by the dead weight of European institutions: established churches, aristocracies, and dynastic kings. But in America, Smith argues, the English colonists were suddenly and unwittingly freed of these restraints, even in Puritan Massachusetts. The environment permitted the rapid development of a new sort of "consciousness," which led each person to find a new and very nonmedieval relationship between himself and the world, his ideas, and most of all, his fellow man. Inevitably, the attitudes and institutions which such a consciousness would engender had to conflict with those of the mother country.

Given his theoretical orientation, it is easy to understand Smith's populist stand on the political course of the Revolution. He believes that Adams' famous remark, that the Revolution took place "in the hearts and minds of the American people," and not on the battlefield, reveals an essential truth. The broad mass of Americans could maintain their loyalty to the British crown only so long as they did not perceive the essential difference that had sprung up between the two nations. Smith concludes that the passage of the Stamp Act was the most critical event of the whole era for it was then that the people were first alienated from the English government and first suspected the entire British attitude toward the colonies. From that point on, suspicion gradually grew into a certainty that the colonies would be "enslaved" if Americans did not stand up for their rights. British authority ceased to function effectively, argues Smith, and the patriot leaders assumed effective control of colonial government. From this point of view, Lexington and Concord represented the end, not the beginning, of the struggle for independence. A populace angry and determined enough to risk everything to rout a British force marching through the countryside was already, in effect, free.

Having intertwined his populist philosophy with the subject matter of the American Revolution, Smith uses an identical approach in dealing with his audience. Issued in the bicentennial year, *A New Age Now Begins* is clearly addressed to the general reader. This is most apparent in his style, Smith writes in a clear, direct narrative form, carrying his reader easily from one topic to the next and adding a flavorful atmosphere to the driest repetition of events. When necessary for dramatic purpose, he does not hesitate to insert historical dialogues of dubious authenticity.

In some ways, the casual and freewheeling style of the work is one of its best features. In his continual effort to make politics interesting, Smith gives the reader an unusual perspective on the course of events. In opening his account of the First Continental Congress, he avoids the traditional course of focusing on Philadelphia and recounting the arrivals of each group of delegates. Instead, he follows the journey of the Massachusetts delegation, tracing their concerns for the upcoming meetings and their reactions to the various political climates they pass through on their way to Pennsylvania. By continually bringing in the external environment—editorials, popular demonstrations, political thinkers, and English observers—the book provides a sense of the real dynamics of conflict and the excited confusion of the time.

It is clear that Smith is not simply trying to make his work readable. At the same time he is attacking the scholarly establishment, and his work is intended as a comment on the way Smith feels history should be written. In a bibliographical postscript, he scolds his fellow historians for their preoccupation with footnoting, and remarks that he has almost entirely dispensed with the writings of contemporary historians, focusing instead on the primary materials of the eighteenth century.

This thrust away from historical scholarship and toward a mass audience seems at many points to hurt the work. For example, Smith's theory of a new American consciousness has the advantage of making it possible to view the Revolution with some detachment. Obviously, neither the colonies nor England were "bad" or malicious; they simply viewed the same course of events very differently. Indeed, much of the time Smith seems to extend genuine sympathy to the British government and analyzes its dilemma. Too often, however, he succumbs to the temptation of making George III and Lord North the villains and the bold patriots the heroes. Smith also seems to pander to the popular taste in his attention to the exciting aspects of the Revolution. On a theoretical level, he plainly believes that the really important changes in the period were mental, that once American attitudes toward the British hardened, as they had by 1776, no number of British victories could prevent America from becoming independent. When faced with writing a narrative history, however, he devotes far more attention to military history than his theory warrants. His command of the material enables him to add just the right touch to his battle descriptions, whether it be an image of cannonballs exploding underwater, or a tender episode between the usually austere Washington and his staff. Nonetheless, one wonders at a man who assigns such importance to the American mind and yet writes more than one thousand pages on the battles of the war.

Through his lack of documentation, his inattention to the prevailing historical debates, and his neglect of consistent theoretical analysis in dealing with American institutions, Smith makes it unlikely that his work will receive the consideration it deserves from other historians. Yet one suspects that this will not bother Smith much. His primary concern is not that of the historian, but of the moralist. His two volumes are in many ways a massive effort to link the people of eighteenth century America with the Americans of today. After drawing the lessons of the Revolution, he suggests that similar lessons need to be relearned by modern man. His concluding chapter, "Novus Ordo Seculorum," is both a testimony to the achievement of the Revolution, but also a warning that yet another new age begins. Once again, he concludes, the American consciousness may innovate, free itself, and change the world.

Smith's vision is as intriguing as his work is enjoyable, but one is always bothered by a certain vagueness in his treatment. The author so enjoys asking provocative questions that he never pauses to give a complete answer. For all his talk of an American consciousness, Smith never adequately accounts for the fact that so many Americans remained, throughout the Revolution, either loyal to the British Crown or indifferent to the patriots' success. Even Crevecoeur, who understood and celebrated the new American man, shrunk at the prospect of Revolution and fled from the land he loved. Though Page Smith has written what in many ways is a remarkable work, his failure to plumb the full complexity of eighteenth century civilization renders his history unconvincing and his vision of the future merely curious.

Alfred D. Sander

Sources for Further Study

America. CXXXIV, May 1, 1976, p. 388.

Antioch Review. XXXIV, Summer, 1976, p. 495.

Christian Century. XCII, April 28, 1976, p. 421.

Journalism Quarterly. LIII, Summer, 1976, p. 368.

Nation. CCXXII, May 29, 1976, p. 664.

New York Times Book Review. February 22, 1976, p. 7.

Virginia Quarterly Review. LII, Autumn, 1976, p. 701.

NEW & COLLECTED POEMS, 1917-1976

Author: Archibald MacLeish (1892-   )
Publisher: Houghton Mifflin Company (Boston). 493 pp. $15.00; paperback $6.95
Type of work: Poetry

A new collection of works by one of America's finest poets, whose career spans over half a century

With his *New & Collected Poems,* Archibald MacLeish has capped a long career as one of America's finest poets and shown that he continues to address himself both to the world at large and to the inner man. This work, spanning fifty-nine years from 1917 to 1976, is a record of history-making events, of the purpose and function of poetry, and of the personal, intimate search for meaning which occurs in everyone's life, but which the poet alone is capable of expressing.

MacLeish, onetime lawyer, editor of *Fortune,* executive director of the Library of Congress, and Harvard professor, has made a significant contribution to the world of letters and influenced the shape and direction of poetry. Three times he has won the Pulitzer Prize. *Conquistador* (1932), which traces the journeys of Cortés, based on Bernál Díaz' *True History of the Conquest of Spain,* earned him the Prize, and is included in this book. For his *Collected Poems, 1917-1952* he won not only the Pulitzer Prize, but also the Bollingen Prize and the National Book Award. Finally, at the age of sixty-six, he captured the Pulitzer Prize in Drama for his highly successful play, *J.B.,* a modernization of the story of Job.

But what distinguishes MacLeish perhaps more than this succession of honors is his boldness, his willingness to defy even his own notions of what poetry should be. Readers of this work will detect the stunning about-face the poet underwent from the philosophy expressed in his 1926 *Streets in the Moon* to the outward-turning, socially aware poetic voice in *Public Speech,* which was published in 1936 and which marked a change in the poet's approach. "Ars Poetica," probably the most anthologized of MacLeish's poems, reflects the early influence of the Imagists, of Ezra Pound and T.S. Eliot. MacLeish met many of the criteria of the Imagist poets in those early years. The first of these, that a poem is primarily a work of art with no relation to anything but itself, is best expressed in those frequently quoted lines from "Ars poetica," that "A poem should not mean / But be." MacLeish took, and still takes, special care with intricate rhythms; he seems, too, to be trying to create a specific image and to be aiming for variety in subject matter. Some of the poems from *New Found Land,* which appear in this work and were first published in 1930, seem best to illustrate the immediacy, the clear recording by the poet's careful eye. "Cinema of a Man" is precisely what its name implies, a series of pictures, full of photographic detail, which move from place to place and yet, paradoxically, stay inexorably the same. The man is filmed in "the rue St. Jacques at the iron table," "by the canal," "in the light of the full moon," "with Ernest in the streets of Saragossa." The poem, lovely for its description, ultimately goes nowhere in the sense of a climax or a change. And yet its conclusion rises to symbol, juxtaposed as it is against a vision of Chicago:

> Those are the cranes above the Karun River
> They fly across the night their wings go over
> They cross Orion and the south star of the Wain
> A wave has broken in the sea beyond the coast of Spain.

Suddenly it seems that these separate moments in time fuse into a solidified and impenetrable unity. "You, Andrew Marvell," another frequently anthologized poem, is equally as inscrutable, as hard and gleaming as "Cinema of a Man." Such poems concern themselves with capturing a moment and shaping it into an object made for Art's sake alone.

Hints of the change in MacLeish's view of poetry begin to emerge in poems from *Frescoes for Mr. Rockefeller's City* (1933) and *Poems, 1924-1933*, reaching the culmination of such change in *Public Speech* (1936). MacLeish begins to speak to the essence of America and, increasingly, to her problems, both social and political. Injustice begins to matter to the poet, and when this occurs, the poems do, indeed, take on meaning. In "Burying Ground by the Ties," the poet pays tribute to the builders of America's railroads, the laborers poured thoughtlessly into our melting pot. His style and tone are livelier, more robust, in keeping with the pioneer heritage of a young, raw, heartless country.

> It was we did it: hunkies of our kind.
> It was we dug the caved-in holes for the cold water:
> It was we built the gully spurs and the freight sidings:
>
> Who would do it but we and the Irishmen bossing us?
> It was all foreign-born men there were in this country:
> It was Scotsmen, Englishmen, Chinese, Squareheads, Austrians . . .

The poet is aware of the irony behind their labor, "the trains going over us here in the dry hollows. . . ."

In "Invocation to the Social Muse," the poet is wavering between his earlier opinion of poetry's function and his growing social consciousness. He says, "There is nothing worse for our trade than to be in style." Wondering "Who recalls the address now of the Imagists?," he seems now to wrestle with the question, "Is it just to demand of us [poets] also to bear arms?" Apparently, by the time *Public Speeches* appeared, MacLeish seemed to have resolved his dilemma, to have come out on the side of relevance, of the poet's obligation "to mix in maneuvers" and thereby change the world. In "Speech to a Crowd," the voice is strident, the message optimistic. He says, "Tell yourselves the earth is yours to take!" In *America was Promises*, the poet is openly critical of "The Aristocracy of Wealth and Talents." They "bled" the people, "sold" them, and "lost" themselves in the process. In a polemical exhortation the poet says,

> Listen! Brothers! Generation!
> Listen! You have heard these words. Believe it!
> Believe the promises are theirs who take them!
> Believe unless we take them for ourselves
> Others will take them for the use of others!

In other later poems, MacLeish continues to use poetry to change the world, maintains the public voice. In *Colloquy for the States,* "The Young Dead Soldiers," "Brave New World," "The Black Day," "Acknowledgement," and "Liberty," the poet takes a position on history, on events timely and hardly universal. At times, the exhortation grows tiresome, the shocked dismay at the normal way of the world seems naïve. At times, too, MacLeish's message seems preachy and prosaic. In *Later Poems,* the brief "Theory of Poetry" illustrates the poet's flaw: he has come too far from Art and now openly scorns the contemplative intellect, the aesthetic standard which must be applied even to poetry which is very much of and in the world.

> Know the world by heart
> Or never know it!
> Let the pedant stand apart—
> Nothing he can name will show it:
> Also him of intellectual art.
> None know it
> Till they know the world by heart.
>
> Take heart then, poet!

Such a poem ignores the fusion of "intellect and emotion" for which Eliot praised the metaphysical poets. It illustrates the danger of its own message, that pure feeling, the "heart" alone, will not suffice to make good poems.

But despite his public awareness, MacLeish is capable of composing exquisite and highly personal poems. This collection contains twenty-seven new poems, the most appealing of which are the lyrical, compelling "Voyage to the Moon," and the poignant, utterly simple "The Old Gray Couple (1)." The impact of such a poem as "Hebrides" lies in its cadences, rhythms, and startling syntax. It is a deceptive poem, seeming so plain, yet reverberating endlessly in the reader's mind along after it has been read. The old couple have seen their "children and all gone off/ over the water"; they "talk as the old will do / and they nod and they smile." Finally, the poet's voice intrudes, making the point, but so gently it cannot bring pain:

> You can live too long in a life
> where the sons go off and the daughter
> off over sea and the wife
> watches the water.

These new poems show the poet still concerned for the world. In "Long Hot

Summer" he knows that "the cities are dying one by one / of the heat and the hate and the naked sun." "Night Watch in the City of Boston" reveals a yearning for men like Emerson and Thoreau, for "New England's prophets" who "answered thundering skies with their own thunder." The poet is aware of death, saying in "Conway Burying Ground," "Only the old know time. . . ." In a section entitled *Three Photographs*, the old man mourns the soldier brother dead in the war, reminisces about his daughter at age four with "white hair, black eyes, exquisite."

Certain of these new poems are less successful either because substance is lacking or because the quality of the verses is uneven. One wonders what the poet has in mind in such poems as "Definitions of Old Age," which veer perilously close to cliché and consist of infelicitous lines.

> Or put it in contemporary terms: the time
> when men resign from their committees,
> cancel their memberships, decline
> the chairmanship of the United Fund,
> buy a farm in Dorset or New Fane
> and still get up at seven every morning
> right on time for nothing left to do but
> sit and age
> and look up "dying" in the yellow pages.

Such a verse disappoints, not because it is a bad poem, but because the writer of those lines is also capable, very often, of a poem "palpable and mute / As a globed fruit."

Suzanne Britt Jordon

Sources for Further Study

Book World. June 20, 1976, p. L1.

Booklist. LXXIII, September 15, 1976, p. 119.

Choice. XIII, October, 1976, p. 982.

Library Journal. CI, September 15, 1976, p. 1862.

New York Times Book Review. October 3, 1976, p. 27.

THE NEW GOLDEN LAND
European Images of America from the Discoveries to the Present Time

Author: Hugh Honour (1927-   )
Publisher: Pantheon Books (New York). Illustrated. 300 pp. $20.00
Type of work: History
Time: 1492-1970
Locale: America

A pictorial history of European images of America from Columbus to the present time

Hugh Honour's *The New Golden Land* tells with words and visual images what the Europeans saw in America, from the first discoveries to the 1970's. They saw America as many things—an experiment, a refuge, a curiosity, a new Heaven, and a real Hell. A torrent of books has been written by hundreds of European visitors over the last 450 years. Libraries have been filled with travelers' accounts and studies of travelers' accounts, but few authors have attempted to study the European artist and his view of America. Honour, a prolific British art historian and author of *Horace Walpole, Chinoiserie, The Vision of Cathay,* and other works, is an urbane and literate writer, an intellectual who enjoys the broad sweep and the study of cultural contrasts and who has a profound grasp of his subject. This study has been done in conjunction with the Bicentennial exhibit "The European Vision of America," organized by Washington's National Gallery of Art, the Cleveland Museum of Art, and France's Reunion des Musees Nationaux.

Although only a few of these European artists were outstanding and only a few ever came to America, their works have had a lasting significance on how Europeans have viewed America. Goethe wrote "We see only what we know." The artist relying upon geographical lore and oral tradition has had great difficulty in separating fact from myth. The Europeans saw what they expected to see. This is not unique, for the mind needs to grasp the familiar and known in order to lessen the shock of the unknown and unfamiliar.

This book is basically a study of stereotypes. The first European painting of the New World was Jan Mostaert's *West Indian Landscape.* Here we see the Europocentric artist grappling with the need to comprehend America within the frame of the two central European traditions, classical and Judeo-Christian. The artist clearly misunderstood the oral description in depicting the fauna of the American Southwest, for this unusual landscape of Coronado's attack on a Zuni village includes animals which a Dutch farmer would recognize, as well as a parrot and a monkey. Further, the painting shows a garden-like setting of innocents being attacked by the more advanced Spaniards who, in this action, we condemn. The atrocities committed against the Indians were an issue of deep concern even before Coronado's 1540 campaign. Priests told of the massacres of entire tribes. In response to this horrendous issue, Mostaert's painting serves as an important historical depiction of

European impressions and concepts of America only fifty years after Columbus.

American Indians were placed by the European within the traditional Christian concepts of mankind. Based upon classical ideas about progress and human development, Europeans began to accept the fact that all peoples went through different stages of development. The appearance of these natives offered the Europeans an insight into their own ancestry. With this comparison, Europeans could view themselves in new ways. In viewing America, the Europeans were in part viewing themselves—their own golden past and their age of barbarism. Honour omits John White's drawings of Indians that were used to represent the Ancient Britons and which show "how that the Inhabitants of the great Bretannie have bin in times past as sauvage as those of Virginia."

Another skilled artist who came to America was Frans Post, who was commissioned to paint the official landscape for the Governor of Brazil, Count Maurits of Nassau. His "Sao Francisco River and Fort Maurice" is one of the finest works Post did while he was in Brazil. The painting offers a fresh, almost ethereal, world view. The unfamiliar flora and fauna in the picture, the large *opuntias* cactus, the amazing *capybara,* and the unlimited horizon must have left a lasting impression on the Europeans. However, once Post had returned to Europe, with its expectations and prejudices, his landscapes became exotic, the natives happy children, and the vegetation lavish and contrived.

Honour defines the European images as "bifocal vision"—an ambivalence of admiration and abhorrence. On one side the European artists represent America, as did Mostaert and White, as an Arcadian paradise populated by noble savages whose golden way of life was shattered by the *conquistadores.* These paintings parallel the words of Columbus and Las Casas and represent the newness and excitement of their first contacts. Here the European not only created the myth of the noble savage but also the anti-Spanish myth of the "black legend." This vision of America was often encouraged by the artist's deeper study of and greater relationship with the natives than by those who portrayed a more negative view.

On the other side, the European artist drew the Indians as brutal cannibals with blood and severed limbs as seen in the maps of Grynaeus and Homem and in the two Goya paintings of cannibals. From these and other paintings, the image of cannibalism made a lasting impression on the Europeans. The European fascination with anthropophagi in the New World was one of the predominant themes of European artists based upon their knowledge of classical literature and upon the accounts of John Mandeville's travels in Asia.

These descriptions of the barbarism and cannibalism of the land and natives paralleled the rapid decline in the American Indian tribes which had been brought about through conquest, exploitation, and disease. But this different view of America came about because changes were taking place within Europe as well, from the fifteenth century view that man was created in the image of God to one emphasizing the sinfulness of man in the sixteenth century.

The land in these misconceptions lost its happy and healthy image and became a place of evil, as seen in a Portuguese painter's representation of the New World as Inferno. With the devil witnessing the agonies of the damned, the Indians were sketched as children of the devil who torture and devour Catholic priests. Recent works of German and British artists such as David Hockney's view of California, *A Bigger Splash,* continue this sordid image of America.

Columbus created the initial misconceptions for the European artists of the New World as a land made up of European virtues and Oriental magnificence. Here, too, Biblical images abound. An Indian representing one of the three wise men may have been the first Indian to be presented in a European painting. But a land where new Adams and Eves walk naked and unembarrassed was soon to be transformed into a land of murder and mayhem. The question of nakedness was filled with differing views. The Catholic fathers believed that, after the Fall, man became ashamed of his body, and felt that to show one's body would be offensive to God. Yet in America there were children of God who did not blush at staring strangers. What was the reason for this difference between American and European man? The answer was that the power of the devil had clouded innate virtue, and this became the rationale for conquest and conversion.

Further violations of the European code of ethics besides cannibalism and nakedness were human sacrifice, communal ownership, and sexual promiscuity. For the European artists, this may in part have been a projection of their own repressed sexual desires on to the natives in their works, but these native acts were usually depicted with terror and contempt. However, rather than appearing unclean and degraded, the natives in these paintings seem to have no remorse, and to be thoroughly enjoying their sinning. And figures of ancient mien and perfect health which only Old Testament patriarchs had earlier possessed, posit an anomaly and paradox.

Fascinating images abound—innocent men and corrupt men, noble savages and wild men, statuesque buxom women and toga-draped American patriots. Americans who traveled in Europe were portrayed as if they were English gentlemen. But with the American Revolution there was a renewed awareness in Europe of, to quote Crèvecœur's popular phrase, "a new man, who acts upon new principles." The key person to be so represented was Benjamin Franklin, whose mission to France in the 1770's was to gain an American alliance with that nation. With his appearance on the Parisian scene, a number of paintings of Franklin were seen, such as those by Houdon and Nim, Fragonard's *Le Docteur Franklin Couronne par la liberte,* and *Au Genie de Franklin.* In fur cap and old coat with his happy, forthright visage, Franklin was portrayed as much for his quaintness as for the fact that, to quote Turgot, "he snatched the lightning from heaven and the scepter from tyranny." There was a great demand for his portrait, whether engraved, etched, carved, or painted on tea cups.

If no American was portrayed so often as Franklin, then no event was so closely noted as the American Revolution. The shot heard round the world, followed by the Declaration of Independence and the French-American alliance, strengthened the interest in things American. The Revolution itself was most important in creating for Europeans heroes and villains, symbols and legends. The European imagination dwelt upon the Minute Men, the Green Mountain Boys, the Swamp Fox, and George Washington. Houdon's marble statue of Washington is one of the best of the late eighteenth century. Images of the Revolutionary events were usually found in satirical prints and engravings which were often displayed in peepshows. One of these prints was Basset's *The Destruction of the Royal Statue in New York* which depicts the statue of George III being hauled down by American patriots. Another work, Dawe's *The Bostonians in Distress,* shows ten famished Bostonians in a cage being fed fish, an image which had become a symbol of slavery. The section titled *Libertas Americana* concludes with a Thomas Colley engraving, *The Reconciliation Between Britania and Her Daughter America,* in which the two countries embrace, Britannia saying "Be a good Girl and give me a Buss." America replies "Dear Mama say no more about it," while to the side Spain and France try to pull America out of Britannia's arms.

To see ourselves as others have seen us can be shocking and disconcerting, but after two hundred years, Americans should be able to weather the experience. This book is so complete and well-written that only a few criticisms are in order. Honour might have included the European conceptualization of culture and cultural relativism as applied to works of art. It would have been helpful had he estimated how the quality and numbers of these works of art compare with the works based upon African and Asian themes. The influence of Africa and the Pacific cultures upon Picasso and Gauguin are well-known, but why has native American art such as Aztec and Mayan had so little impact upon the European artists? Where in Europe was the interest in America most strongly felt? And why? What Europeans were especially interested in America—church leaders, scholars, traders? The author does not tell the reader what method he used to choose these art works—quality, availability, or random selection. Nevertheless, *The New Golden Land* is an excellent work which must surely rank as an important consequence of America's Bicentennial.

Richard A. Van Orman

Sources for Further Study

American Artist. XL, July, 1976, p. 12.
Burlington Magazine. CXVIII, July, 1976, p. 526.
History Today. XXVI, May, 1976, p. 342.
New Statesman. XCI, April 9, 1976, p. 473.
New York Review of Books. XXII, January 22, 1976, p. 11.
Spectator. CCXXXVI, May 1, 1976, p. 18.

A NEW LIFE OF ANTON CHEKHOV

Author: Ronald Hingley
Publisher: Alfred A. Knopf (New York). Illustrated. 352 pp. $12.50
Type of work: Biography
Time: 1860-1904
Locale: Russia, France, Germany, Italy

A well-documented, sensible, scholarly, and smoothly written account of Anton Chekhov's life

Principal personages:

ANTON CHEKHOV, Russian fiction writer and dramatist
PAUL CHEKHOV, his father, a grocer
YEVGENIYA CHEKHOV, his mother
MICHAEL CHEKHOV, his youngest brother
MARIYA CHEKHOV, his sister
D. V. GRIGOROVICH, an author and Chekhov's literary discoverer
A. S. SUVORIN, Chekhov's friend and sometime publisher
LYDIA AVILOV, memoirist and fiction writer who claimed Chekhov
   loved her
LYDIA YAVORSKY, an actress who was briefly Chekhov's mistress
OLGA KNIPPER, the actress who became Chekhov's wife, 1901-1904
LEO TOLSTOY, the Russian author and Chekhov's friend
VLADIMIR NEMIROVICH-DANCHENKO and
CONSTANTINE STANISLAVSKY, co-founders of the Moscow Art
   Theatre and friends of Chekhov

Ronald Hingley is a distinguished, Oxford-based scholar of Russian history and literature, with a special fondness for Chekhov. In 1950 he published a biographical and critical study of the Russian author, and he is editor and translator of *The Oxford Chekhov,* of which nine volumes have so far been issued. He thus comes equipped with enormous authority for writing this comprehensive, fully detailed but largely noncritical biography of one of Russia's most complex major writers. The result is an impressive achievement in literary scholarship: erudite, industrious, sensible, and gracefully written. It fails, however, to illuminate the nature of Chekhov's literary genius: partly because Hingley confines himself to a sparse number of literary judgments, but largely because Chekhov, in his life as in his art, insists upon remaining elusive.

Hingley has based his biography on the twenty-volume Russian edition of Chekhov's *Complete Works and Letters* (1944-1951), but serves his readers notice that an even more ambitious thirty-volume Russian publication is now in progress, to be published in Moscow from 1974 to the early 1980's. Whether this expanded *Works and Letters* will contain significant new material, one can only speculate; Hingley managed to read only its first two volumes as he polished his own study, discovering them in the University of North Carolina's library after having been denied them in the Soviet Union. The only certainty in Russian-generated Chekhov scholarship is the censor's continuing intervention. Chekhov's correspondence has been markedly mutilated, for reasons of prudery as much as politics; and Hingley, having discovered more deletions in the Soviet 1944-1951 edition than in the Tsarist 1912-16 edition, can only hope that the censors of the 1974-1982 edition will be more enlightened. Muscovite control of the Chekhovian archives is totally impregnable to Western researchers.

Anton Pavlovich Chekhov was born into a family of tradesmen on January 16, 1860, in the southern Russian port town of Taganrog, a stiflingly provincial place where he spent his first nineteen years. Chekhov often complained that Taganrog offered him and his siblings "nothing, absolutely nothing, new," and used the adjective "Taganrogish" for behavior he regarded as dull, boorish, squalid, or vulgar. Anton's father was a despotic grocer who terrorized his wife, five sons, and one daughter, overworked them, eventually went bankrupt, and had to flee town to escape his creditors. His mother was the soul of kindness, but too timid and deferential to protect her children against an abusive father who birched and clouted his offspring, ordered them to attend church services daily, but forbade them the luxury of play. "We felt like little convicts at hard labor," Chekhov wrote in an 1892 letter about his childhood— though he did manage to fish and swim, and to become a great practical joker and jester.

It is nonetheless crucial to note that Anton was deprived of an adequate portion of familial love in his formative years. He later recalled that, "So little affection came my way as a child that I treat caresses as something unfamiliar, and almost beyond my ken, now that I'm grown up. That's why I just can't show fondness for others, much as I'd like to." Hingley regards this self-analysis as "not entirely convincing," but offers no other competent explanation for what may be the central flaw in Chekhov's character: his marked tendency to avoid emotional (and with women, physical) intimacy with family, friends, and lovers.

Anton's Taganrog schooling stressed Greek and Latin syntax, encouraged spying to curb nonconformity, and enforced harsh discipline. Though his years as a pupil coincided with tremendous socioeconomic revolutionary ferment fomented by the writings of Bakunin, Herzen, Pisarev, and others, and culminating in the assassination of the Tsar in 1881, he was sheltered from these winds of modernity and showed no particular inclination, either in his youth or manhood, to espouse or oppose radical causes. Chekhov as a schoolboy preferred to inscribe comic anecdotes in his exercise-book, and read them to his classmates during the teacher's absence. He showed early signs of the poor health that would cost him his life at the age of forty-four: attacks of peritonitis, catarrh, malaria, hemorrhoids, migraine, and scotoma. His symptoms may well have indicated an early tubercular infection, with the bacillus aided in its assault on Chekhov's body by his hard boyhood regimen of schooling, church-going and shop-minding.

In July, 1876, the elder Chekhovs and all the children but Anton fled Taganrog for Moscow, leaving Anton to finish grammar-school and giving him a theme—dispossession—he was to feature in both *Three Sisters* and *The Cherry Orchard.* For three years the lad supported himself alone in his home town, burdened with economic worries but relieved of his tyrannical father. Astonishingly, Anton not only took care of his own needs but was able to send small sums to his family. He seems to have been born mature; even his occasional bouts of drinking, mimicry, play-acting, and dancing were subsumed to fastidious senses of order and responsibility that never deserted him.

In August, 1879, Anton joined his family in Moscow, to live there for the next twenty years. He set about a demanding five-year grind to become a physician, began his literary career in 1880 with comic sketches published in periodicals, and soon established himself as the *de facto* head of the Chekhov household. Chekhov later held his apprentice work in low esteem: of the forty-eight publications he had fathered from 1880-1882, he excluded every one from the "Collected Works" edition of 1899-1902.

Chekhov was enormously prolific in his early years as a writer (Hingley classifies all his pre-1888 work as "immature"). He wrote not only stories and short plays but sketches, story-sketches and sketch-stories, comic calendars and captions for cartoons, and even a detective novel, *The Shooting Party.* Hingley has counted 528 items as belonging to this apprenticeship period, in contrast to only sixty for the post-1888 "mature" period, though that lasted twice as long. When Chekhov reviewed his achievement for the ten-volume collected edition of 1899-1902, he excluded 342 of his early titles, calling them "my literary excrement," but only six of his later ones. The major source for Chekhov biographers is his enormous and often eloquent correspondence; the total number of his extant letters is estimated by Hingley as about 4,400, dated from the summer of 1875 to June 28, 1904, the day before his death.

In June, 1884, Chekhov passed his medical school examinations, and was to practice medicine sporadically during the remaining twenty years of his life, though always as a profession secondary to writing. He often claimed medicine for his "wife," literature for his "mistress"; but the mistress had little trouble supplanting the wife. Hingley assesses Chekhov's medical training as enabling him to become acquainted with people on diverse social levels, and as reinforcing his sane, sensible, pragmatic (or diagnostic) view of life. Chekhov often attested in his letters to the harmony of his two callings, claiming that familiarity with the scientific method had enriched his literary skills: "To the chemist nothing in this world is unclean. The writer must be as objective as the chemist."

In one respect, ironically, Chekhov's medical knowledge proved of no value: his care, or rather neglect, of his own health. As early as December, 1884, he suffered a serious attack of chest pains and blood-spitting; in October, 1888, he wrote of these bleedings and chronic coughing fits, but refused to characterize them as tubercular symptoms; hemorrhoids afflicted him with maddening torments, but he rejected a medical colleague's offer to remove them by an operation; gastritis, phlebitis, migraine headaches, dizzy spells, defective vision, heart palpitations—all these were frequent afflictions. No wonder that Chekhov complained, when he was thirty-three, "I'm well over thirty, and feel as if I was nearly forty. . . . I get out of bed and go to bed feeling as if I'd lost all interest in life." His brother Michael describes Anton as looking old, yellow, and pinched from 1895 on. In March, 1897, after having had a violent lung hemorrhage, Chekhov was examined by another physician and at last certified as tubercular. Tolstoy visited his bedside on March 28, and argued with him regarding problems of art and immortality. After Tolstoy's departure Chekhov had another severe hemorrhage.

How does one account for Chekhov's persistent denial of his tubercular symptoms? Hingley rather enigmatically states, "To ignore, consciously or unconsciously, what cannot be mended can sometimes be the highest form of wisdom." Chekhov, as the provider for his large and mainly improvident family, may have felt a powerful need to deny his own dependency, let alone mortality. Physicians, trained to sustain others, make notoriously poor patients themselves. It is hardly credible that Chekhov should have deluded himself about his tubercular symptoms; it is credible that he deluded others about the desperate state of his health.

Hingley devotes a great deal of attention to the remarkably scant attention Chekhov paid to women. In the 1890's, with Chekhov established as a highly eligible bachelor, many women sought him out, while he usually managed to avoid or evade them. A highly productive, hardworking writer, Chekhov both used his writing as a shield against amorous involvements and insisted that sexual energy (of which he had very little) bore no relation—except perhaps an inverted one—to creative energy (of which he had a ceaseless supply). He frequently linked artistic creativity with erotic self-denial: "If I was a landscape painter I'd lead an almost ascetic life. I'd have a woman once a year and eat once a day." Hingley points out that sensual, fleshly women in Chekhov's fiction and drama are almost invariably predatory, distasteful, and villainous, with Chekhov-the-author idealizing as romantically desirable pallid types with thin arms and flat breasts; yet Chekhov-the-man, when interested in women at all, preferred them robust, hearty, and earthy. While love is the dominant theme of Chekhov's mature work, it is almost never happily consummated love: he prefers to collapse illusions rather than fulfill hopes; to stress romantic frustration and forlorness rather than union and bliss.

Anton's only sister, Mariya, was devoted to him and kept house for him. He managed to detach her from three suitors, at least one of them a man she cared for, and whom she gave up when her beloved brother made clear his disapproval. Hingley rates this action as Chekhov's unkindest, motivated by his selfish desire to retain the sacrificial Mariya as his domestic servant. Mariya in her turn opposed his marriage to the actress Olga Knipper, agonizing over its possibly deleterious effect on his health. Chekhov and Knipper went ahead with the wedding, failing to give Mariya advance notice of it. She confided her deep hurt to her diary, but never to her brother's face.

Before his marriage at the age of forty-one Chekhov had only one incontestable mistress, the actress Lydia Yavorsky. Hingley fails to discover all-consuming passion in either party: Lydia wanted Chekhov to promote her theatrical ambitions, while he referred to her, somewhat condescendingly, as a "very kind woman and an actress who might have come to something if she hadn't been spoiled by her training." Hingley draws an understandable conclusion concerning the Chekhovian libido: "We are certainly entitled to deduce that he was somewhat undersexed." He goes on to raise a more disturbing problem: "Was Chekhov's reserve so profound that he found it difficult or impossible to establish intimate terms with anyone, man or woman, outside as well as inside the sexual sphere?" Like all preceding Chekhov biographers, Hingley begs off answering this most troubling of questions.

Olga Knipper was Chekhov's second certain mistress, then his wife for what were to be his last three years. She had taken drama lessons from Nemirovich-Danchenko, co-founder of the Moscow Art Theatre, and graduated into leading roles with his company, including Masha in *Three Sisters* and Lyuba Ranevskaya in *The Cherry Orchard.* Olga was Chekhov's opposite rather than duplicate: lusty to his asceticism, insecure and manic-depressive in contrast to his stable, steady, sensible temperament. By July, 1900, she was creeping into his Yalta bedroom at night, stepping on creaking stairs that awakened Anton's old mother and spinsterish sister. The forthright, determined Olga took the initiative in courting the evasive, elusive Anton. He was careful to stay in Yalta during the freezing half-year that Olga performed in Moscow; for good measure he kept his distance from her in the nonwintry months of August and September as well. But Olga persisted in pursuit, insisted on regularizing their relationship, and she had her way when they married on May 25, 1901. Yet Chekhov even thereafter retained his bachelor habits of separating from women as often as possible; that, plus his deteriorating health and Olga's career away from Yalta, caused them to live together, Hingley calculates, only half the time of their wedded life. One result of such a distant union is a Chekhov-Knipper correspondence of 1,300 pages. Even in matrimony Chekhov preferred his mistress, literature.

In June, 1904, Anton and Olga traveled to the German spa of Badenweiler, near the Black Forest, to attempt his cure. On June 29 he suffered a heart attack. On July 1 he died, first taking the time to explain to his wife that he was about to die, then draining a glass of champagne, turning calmly on to his left side, and passing away. Chekhov's corpse was delivered to Russia in a railway wagon labeled "Fresh Oysters"—an incongruous effect he would have loved to use in one of his stories.

Hingley's biography is the most informative and clearly organized study of Chekhov's life published to date. But it remains no more than a background study for his art. To get to know the subtlest of modern storytellers and dramatists, the writer capable of examining his characters' darkest despair with calm sympathy, gentle irony, and restrained affection, we need to encounter Chekhov's work directly. The only way to understand Chekhov is to read Chekhov.

Harry Brand

Sources for Further Study

Book World. June 27, 1976, p. G1.

Economist. CCLIX, May 22, 1976, p. 124.

National Observer. XV, July 24, 1976, p. 19.

National Review. XXVIII, August 20, 1976. p. 910.

New York Review of Books. June 10, 1976. p. 40.

Spectator. CCXXXVI, May 15, 1976, p. 21.

Times Literary Supplement. August 6, 1976, p. 988.

NEW LIVES

Survivors of the Holocaust Living in America

Author: Dorothy Rabinowitz (1935-   )
Publisher: Alfred A. Knopf (New York). 242 pp. $10.00
Type of work: Historical essay

A study based on interviews of representative survivors of the Nazi concentration camps

Principal personages:
LEON JOLSON, a successful businessman
ABE FLEIKER, a sales representative
STELLA, a housewife

The destruction of European Jewry during World War II continues to claim the world's moral attention. Unspeakably inhuman and staggeringly efficient, the Nazi murder machine remains a crushing indictment of the modern world. The Germans must struggle with the historical fact that they were the agents of the Holocaust, and the rest of the nations must struggle with the fact that the torture and killing was permitted to continue even after knowledge of it had spread throughout the world. This struggle, after more than thirty years since the last oven cooled, still turns on the simple question of basic comprehension. Many Germans still believe that the "concentration camp stories" are exaggerated, a kind of Jewish propaganda, and many other people throughout the world, whose objectivity is not clouded by repressed guilt, find it inconceivable that anything quite so barbarous could ever have happened.

But happen it did, as Lucy Dawidowicz in her monumental *The War Against the Jews, 1933-1945* (1975), has documented so powerfully. The data her book and other historical accounts provide have still to be interpreted by thinkers and writers in forms that will permit us to understand the meaning of the Holocaust emotionally as well as rationally; to find room in our reluctant imaginations for this overpowering evil, which demands a myth the old "Hell" cannot provide. Poets and novelists have made valiant efforts, but, on the whole, they have only approximated their subject. In his study of what he calls the "literature of atrocity," Lawrence L. Langer (*The Holocaust and the Literary Imagination,* 1975) puts it this way:

> Perhaps no one will ever clarify satisfactorily or portray completely . . . the Holocaust; it remains the unconquered Everest of our time, its dark mysteries summoning the intrepid literary spirit to mount its unassailable summit.

Dorothy Rabinowitz's *New Lives* is not in any obvious way a work of literature; not a novel, drama, or poem, it does not attempt to climb the Everest of literary creation. Neither is her book, like Dawidowicz's, an exhaustively researched and extensively documented work of historical scholarship. Perhaps the best way to describe *New Lives* is to call it an extended essay, a brilliant adaptation of the journalist's interview for the purpose of illuminating a state of mind far greater than the opinions or recollections of any one person. Dorothy Rabinowitz walks the lower slopes of the Everest of the Holocaust; she introduces us to survivors—weary, descending climbers who look back at their ordeal with tragic emotions. Their terrifying memories of the past provide an inescapable context for the hopes and fears they bring to the future. By distributing the portraits so that the reader is given a psychological as well as social range, Rabinowitz succeeds in conveying an impression of a generation and a community. If this impression does not exactly convey what Günter Grass has called "the quivering flesh of reality," it goes a long way toward removing the luxury so many have permitted themselves—the luxury of thinking of the Holocaust as a thing remote in space and time. The men and women who speak to us in this book are our neighbors, the parents of our school friends, people who sell us sewing machines and insurance. Through them we begin to comprehend.

A man to whom the author has assigned the name Leon Jolson takes to the spirit of American entrepreneurship with the same adroitness and bold enterprise that saved his life in the concentration camp. Rabinowitz suggests that his willingness to volunteer readily for labor details in the camps exemplified his general capacity to risk the unknown, to make "instant crucial decisions" that often meant the difference between life and death. Bold initiative enabled him to survive the Nazis but also gives him the self-confidence to strike out for himself as soon as he reaches America. He roams New York's garment industry and ingeniously matches sewing machines and hard-to-get parts. Knowing that postwar Europe would be in desperate need of sewing machinery, he dictates, in broken English, letters directed to European manufacturers to a public stenographer in a New York hotel. In Europe, they welcome his services, and in a relatively short time he is financially independent. Jolson's ability to succeed so quickly, let alone survive, can be explained, suggests Rabinowitz, by the fact that he had known success before the war, that he had been well educated by a wealthy and successful father. The point is well-taken, but the reader is left with the lingering feeling that more concentration camp inmates with Jolson's background and psychological characteristics succumbed to the Nazis than survived them; that luck, physical endurance, and faith were factors even more crucial than self-confidence.

Jolson is compared with Abe Fleiker, a man fourteen years younger, who, in contrast to Jolson, is repelled by the New York crowds which recall the "suffocation" of the camps where bodies were shelved with intolerable proximity. Fleiker settles in Kansas City, where he attends night school and makes friends. When the Korean War breaks out, he is drafted and despite his broken English assigned to the role of Troop Informational Education instructor. His commanding officers feel that Fleiker's survival of the death camps make him an example of human endurance and courage. When fear of combat grips the men during the grim winter days of 1952, Fleiker is heralded as an authority on survival; to the men of his company, uneducated boys from Kentucky and Arkansas, Fleiker is someone who has learned how to escape death. Although he is no less afraid than his comrades, Fleiker begins to accept the role thrust upon him: the veteran survivor. His reputation for toughness is enhanced by his acute sensitivity to the slightest anti-Semitic slur. He is always ready to challenge with his fists any insults aimed at Jews. This truculence continues after the army, and despite a relatively comfortable position as a sales representative for several furniture companies, Fleiker never loses his sense that something like the Holocaust could happen again, anywhere. His life is haunted by a memory from which he cannot escape. When the Germans had taken him from his mother, he was only thirteen and convinced that after a few months he would be reunited with her. But his mother knew it would be the last time they would ever see each other again. Fleiker insists, "That's what hurts. I never gave her credit, see, for knowing."

Rabinowitz sees this as the bond uniting all death camp survivors, the "refusal of delusions." Just as Fleiker cannot talk himself into believing it could not happen again, so in the heroic story of Stella, Rabinowitz dramatizes the strength that comes from confronting reality. Stella miraculously escapes from a labor camp in Poland and wanders through Germany posing as a gentile Pole. After incredible adventures, she marries another camp survivor and later, in America, discovers she has an incurable cancer. It is so far advanced that her doctors are unwilling to operate. But she has fought for life too long to stop fighting now. Finally, she finds a surgeon willing to operate. Against all odds, she survives. But her greatest triumph is her ability to go back to the camp where her sister took her place in the ovens; once there, she goes through the cathartic ritual of crawling into the oven and covering her clothes with the ashes of the martyrs. She returns, happy to be reunited with her husband, but strengthened by her reconfrontation with her irrevocable past.

Whether it is expressed in one survivor's inability to accept the idea of his daughter marrying a gentile or in Jolson's munificent donation toward the erection of a memorial in Israel to the Holocaust, the people in *New Lives* refuse to forget. Memory protects against delusion. In a world where delusion is great enough to permit war criminals the benefit of historical and even legal indulgence, personal memory preserves a collective human truth that almost makes the pain bearable.

Peter A. Brier

Sources for Further Study

Booklist. LXIII, November 1, 1976, p. 376.
New York Review of Books. XXIII, November 25, 1976, p. 20.
New York Times. CXXVI, November 1, 1976, p. 37.
New York Times Book Review. November 7, 1976, p. 14.
Publisher's Weekly. CCX, August 23, 1976, p. 64.
Saturday Review. IV, November 13, 1976, p. 41.

NEW POEMS

Author: Eugenio Montale
Translated from the Italian and with an Introduction by G. Singh, and with an essay
on *Xenia* by F. R. Leavis
Publisher: New Directions (New York). 124 pp. $7.95
Type of work: Poetry

Selected translations from Montale's two latest books of poems, Satura *(1971) and*
Diario del '71 e del '72 *(1973)*

When Eugenio Montale received the Nobel Prize for literature in 1975, the reaction on this side of the Atlantic was overwhelmingly in the vein of "Who?" Poets, unless they have exercised considerable international influence or have been superbly translated, do not tend to gain much recognition outside their own country. This has been particularly true of Italian poetry after the age of Dante and Petrarch. English-speaking readers, at least those acquainted with Baudelaire, Rilke, and Lorca, tend to have only the vaguest notions of Leopardi or Carducci. It is not then surprising that they should view Italy's greatest modern poet (though some would claim the title belongs to Ungaretti) as a rather obscure light on the literary horizon.

Montale is not an easy poet—to read, to translate, or to classify. In 1965, New Directions brought out a selection of his works with Italian texts facing translations by a variety of translators. Now the same publishers have given us a good choice of poems from Montale's two most recent collections, *Satura* (1971) and *Diario del '71 e del '72* (1973). This time the original poems are omitted, and the translations are all by G. Singh, Professor of Italian at the Queen's University of Belfast, and author of a book on Montale. Although the wisdom of omitting the Italian texts in the present volume is questionable, it is certain that this book, like its predecessor, constitutes an excellent introduction to Montale's work, one which should help the American reading public to understand why it deserves to be better known.

Many readers of Montale have approached him as a kind of Italian parallel to T. S. Eliot. Both began writing at a similar point in the histories of their respective literatures, and with similar concerns. Montale, like Eliot, reacted against the late Romantic excesses and the inflated literary language which prevailed in *fin de siècle* poetry. Gabriele d' Annunzio, the sensation in Italian letters at the turn of the century, seemed to poets of Montale's generation to have reached a deadend with his Nietzschean cult of the superman, his pagan sensuality, and his florid language. Learning (like Eliot) from the French poet Jules Laforgue to introduce irony and the vocabulary and rhythms of everyday speech into poetry, Montale nonetheless retained something of d' Annunzio's sensuous celebration of nature in his first book, *Ossi di seppia* (*Cuttlefish Bones,* 1925). Yet the very title indicates an attention to humble, nonpoetic objects, and the poems show him to be a master at evoking things, places, and persons which objectify emotions and ideas. Montale recognized his own preoccupation with Eliot's critical notion of the "objective corrrelative." Like Eliot, too, he has stressed the importance of literary tradition in the development of individual talent, and has evoked the spiritual "wasteland" of Western culture in the early twentieth century. Unlike Eliot, however, Montale has never developed a credo, remaining instead an independent artist, searching and questioning rather than proclaiming.

Since *Ossi di seppia*, Montale has published only two other volumes of poetry before those under review, *Le occasioni* (*The occasions*), which includes poems from 1928-1939, and *La bufera e altro* (*The Storm and Other Things*), poems from 1940-1956. He has never been a politically active writer, although some of his best-known poems were inspired by his anti-Fascist commitment. He is perhaps at his best as a love poet. In both volumes, the love poems written for "Clizia," an idealized lady who served as a kind of modern Beatrice, are among his finest.

It is with a two-part love poem entitled "Xenia," which Singh has included in its entirety, that *Satura* opens. Dedicated to the poet's wife, Drusilla Tanzi, who died in 1963, these poems portray a deep, mature affection and a simplicity of style which are quite different from those written for the exalted, distant Clizia. The Latin title means "gifts" or "votive offerings" and also recalls Goethe's and Schiller's satirical epigrams, *Xenien*. "Xenia" in *New Poems* is prefaced by a fine essay by F. R. Leavis. Leavis stresses Montale's difference from Eliot in these poems in his ability to portray "a direct simplicity of personal feeling." The style is conversational, direct, and yet contains a range of tones and material which are under the control of a master craftsman. The first poem is typical enough:

> Dear little Mosca,
> so they called you, I don't know why,
> this evening almost in the dark,
> while I was reading Deutero-Isaiah
> you reappeared beside me,
> but without your glasses,
> so that you could not see me,
> nor could I recognize you in the haze
> without that glitter.

To understand the images here and others which follow, we need Professor Singh's footnote, which informs us that Montale's wife's nickname, "Mosca," means "fly" in Italian. The first two lines of the original read literally "Dear little insect, whom they called *Mosca* I don't know why." Montale is fond of building on such word games, and they are inevitably (except for cognates) lost in translation. So are the numerous internal rhymes and assonances, and, in this case, the anaphora in the three lines before the last (non avevi . . ./non potevi . . ./ne potevo. . .) What does come across in the translation is the quick pace of the lines of varying length, and the homely scene and familiar tone which nonetheless condense a wealth of motifs. The pedantic "Deutero-Isaiah" appears ironic here, yet, like many of Montale's religious images, indicates the poet's search for something beyond what appears to be reality. So does the dead Mosca's quiet reappearance, "without glasses."

Professor Singh points out in his introduction that the only possible parallel to "Xenia" in English poetry are the poems that Thomas Hardy wrote on the death of his wife in 1912. The very similarity of theme makes evident the difference in technique and the specific Montalean quality of these poems. In Montale's verse there is no direct expression of longing or of passion, little sentimentality. Instead, the details of domestic life become "objective correlatives" for a plenitude of shared affection. Montale skillfully weds the lyrical to the everyday:

> Spring comes out at the pace of a mole.
> I shall hear you talk no more
> of the poisonous antibiotics,
> the rivet in your thighbone, or
> the patrimony that shrewd unnamed rat
> nibbled away.

The last poem of the first part of "Xenia" is at once a poetic and philosophical statement and a tribute to Mosca—quite different from the idealized tributes to "Clizia." Montale takes to task the critics of his lack of *engagement* with characteristic understated irony:

> They say that mine
> is a poetry of non-belonging.
> But if it was yours, it was someone's

The second half of "Xenia" contains amusing character sketches of some of Mosca's eccentric friends and recollections of the couple's travels together. One poem is about a rusty tin shoehorn they left behind in a hotel. Objects such as this often serve as talismans, crystallizers of emotions and memories, in Montale's poetry. The entire series ends with a poem on the destruction of some of Montale's belongings in the 1967 flood in Florence. The poet, too, feels "encrusted," but

> It isn't mud has besieged me, but the events
> of an incredible reality which was never believed.
> In the face of these my courage was the first
> of your gifts and perhaps you didn't know it.

The title of the entire 1971 collection, *Satura*, is a Latin word which Montale uses in its original sense of a mixture of various types of things as well as to indicate the satiric nature of many of the poems. Singh has selected poems representative of this variety. Some of the satiric poems are like sharp etchings of people and places. Montale is particularly fond of portraying turn-of-the-century relics (human and others) and decadent Venetian hotels. In one of these hotels we meet "the lover of bullfights and safaris," "Hemingway the bear."

> He's still in bed,
> from his hairy face only his eyes
> and the marks of eczema stand out.
> Two or three empty bottles of Merlot,
> avant-garde of the gallons that are to come.

Many of the *Satura* poems continue the "Xenia" theme of the poet's recollection of his dead wife. But these tend to be more abstract and impersonal than "Xenia," in tone, language, and images, as, for example is, the second stanza of "Ex Voto":

> It may well be
> that only distance and oblivion
> are real, that the dry leaf is
> more real than a green shoot. This
> and much more, may well be.

The Montalean combination of lyricism and colloquial irony is still there (though the translation does not render the latter quality in the last two lines, "Tanto e altro/ puo darsi o dirsi."). So is the sense of contact with the absent loved one, but the immediacy of the domestic detail and the sense of Mosca's individual personality is gone. While sometimes more accomplished technically, the poems on this theme outside of "Xenia" are on the whole less emotionally rich.

Philosophical and even theological concerns occupy Montale in many of the *Satura* poems. The poem entitled "History" makes clear the reason why Montale is not beloved by Marxist critics. For Montale, history contains neither pattern nor meaning, and is outside of human control. "History doesn't unravel/ like an unbroken chain of rings. . . . History doesn't teach/ anything that concerns us." Montale has stressed in other poems and essays that liberation for man, if it exists, is to be found outside of time, in moments of eternity. In the end, it is the individual, not the collective, which counts for him. A few "fish" manage to escape history's "trawl net" which scrapes the bottom of the sea. Yet the one who escapes does not necessarily find freedom: "He doesn't know he is out, no one told him./ The others in the bag think they/ are more free than he." God, if he exists, is in these poems as remote a force as history— the "great Abolished" or "the Other." Yet Montale seems to believe in supernatural forces which at times resemble Rilke's angels and at times are evidence of the eternal shining through, somewhat ironically, in the ephemeral. "I say/ that I've seen them more than once,/ . . . immortals who are invisible to others and perhaps unaware of their privilege,/ deities in jeans with rucksacks,/ priestesses in overcoats and sandals. . . ."

Skeptical toward politics and religion, Montale nonetheless retains a faith in the earthly and unearthly powers of human beings. He also retains a stubborn, humble belief in poetry. In the tradition of Mallarmé, he stresses that poetry is made with *words*, not fancy, expensive words but those which "recline on the backs/ of vouchers, on the margins— of lottery tickets,/ on wedding cards or those/ of condolence." Montale's great achievement has indeed been to "awaken" ordinary words, to make them resonate with both concreteness and suggestiveness.

The opening poem of Montale's last collection, the *Diaries of '71 and '72*, contains an ironic self-portrait of the poet:

> I too dreamt I'd be one day
> *mestre de gai saber*, but it was
> a vain hope. A dried up laurel
> doesn't put forth leaves even for the roast.
> With maladroit fingers I try to play
> on the celesta or the pestles of the vibraphone,
> but the music keeps receding. And anyway
> it wasn't the music of the spheres . . . What I knew
> was never gay nor wise nor celestial.

The ironic tone of these lines prevails in both the *Diaries*, making the poetry often somewhat cerebral, certainly less lyrical than Montale's earlier work, though there are echoes of "Xenia" in some of the poems.

The final poem of this volume, the short, sharp "To Conclude," is stylistically typical of Montale's latest poems and worth quoting in its entirety.

> I charge my descendants (if I have
> any) on the literary plane
> which is rather improbable, to make
> a big bonfire of all that concerns
> my life, my actions, my non-actions.
> I'm no Leopardi, I leave
> little behind me to be burnt,
> and it's already too much to live
> by percentages. I lived at the rate
> of five per cent; don't increase
> the dose. And yet
> it never rains but it pours.

The first three lines of the translation are rather awkward ("which" has no antecedent) but in the rest of it the broken rhythms, simple colloquial speech, and tone of resigned irony in the original come through. So do Montale's ideas that life is never really lived except in part and that what matters about a poet, finally, are his works and not his actions.

Any translator of poetry, especially of Italian, runs the risk of being called *traduttore-traditore*, and it is true that any translation, especially of work as dependent on linguistic skill and verbal nuance as Montale's, is in a sense inadequate. Still, it must be said that, with few exceptions, Singh has been successful in rendering Montale into English. His translations are more literal than daring—there is no point in comparing them with Robert Lowell's "imitations" of Montale, which are of another order. *New Poems* reads quite well as a volume of English verse, and Singh's introduction is informative and perceptive. The book should enable lovers of poetry who do not know Italian to take part in the creations of one of the major figures of contemporary world literature.

Mary Ann Witt

Sources for Further Study

Book World. June 13, 1976, p. M4.
Christian Science Monitor. LXVIII, September 27, 1976, p. 27.
Listener. XCVI, October 14, 1976, p. 484.
Nation. CCXXIII, October 9, 1976, p. 341.
Saturday Review. III, March 20, 1976, p. 26.

THE NEXT 200 YEARS
A Scenario for America and the World

Authors: Herman Kahn (1922-   ), William Brown, and Leon Martel
Publisher: William Morrow (New York). Illustrated. 241 pp. $8.95
Type of work: Current affairs

A prediction by the Hudson Institute of what life will be like during the next two hundred years

The Next 200 Years is a report of work at the Hudson Institute on long-range predictions of population growth, economic development, energy, raw materials, food, and environmental problems. The next two hundred years, in the view of Herman Kahn and his associates, will bring solutions to all of these issues. The current apocalyptic literature forecasting environmental crises looks to the immediate future and reflects an unjustified panic. The longer perspective of this book provides its authors with hope for the future. As such, this report of the Hudson Institute not only attempts to provide predictions for the future, but also takes issue with many current accounts of our present environmental crisis. Particular criticism is provided for Dennis Meadows' book, *The Limits to Growth* and Barry Commoner's *The Closing Circle*.

The thesis of the Hudson study is that

> 200 years ago almost everywhere human beings were comparatively few, poor and at the mercy of the forces of nature, and 200 years from now, we expect, almost everywhere they will be numerous, rich and in control of the forces of nature.

In 1976, America's bicentennial, America was midway between these alternatives. The authors anticipate that the future will permit almost all nations to develop large enterprises to solve their basic economic and social problems, and that industrial and technical improvement will make life's necessities readily available to all. The study refers to these characteristics as manifestations of "super- and post-industrial societies." Such a future will only be possible if economic growth continues. Prohibiting growth for the sake of the environment will leave the poor of the world forever in poverty and will result in an exacerbation of hostilities between the poor and the rich. The authors anticipate that economic growth if left alone will eventually slow to a low or no-growth rate.

Based on this perspective, population will continue to grow until it reaches a world level of about fifteen billion people. Population growth will not remain exponential as it presently is, although population increase will continue at a high rate for several generations before beginning to flatten out as a consequence of urbanization, affluence, improved health, birth control, and other factors.

The Kahn study identifies four basic interpretations of the future. The first is the neo-Malthusian that argues that in the future population will grow more rapidly than food supplies and result in starvation and catastrophe. The position of the guarded pessimist is somewhat more sanguine than that of the neo-Malthusian, but still is convinced of much famine and hardship for the future that will eventuate in disaster. The third position of the guarded optimist recognizes a future of hardship that will result in eventual success in bringing about a world of abundance. The "Technology-and-Growth enthusiast" anticipates the future with much optimism and expects success and abundance. The Kahn book maintains support of the third or fourth alternatives and contends that the future will be bright only if technology and industrial growth are permitted to continue uninhibited.

Because of the Hudson Institute assumption that the future will only be satisfactory through industrial and technological growth, all limited-growth or no-growth futures are rejected as are the works of those writers, such as Meadows and Commoner, who wish to place limits on industrial expansion. If growth is not curtailed, the Hudson study projects a future of abundance, a stable population in which most people "will do things for their own sake" and will dedicate their energies to game-playing and leisure activities, and in which the most important problem will be boredom. In short, the future of Kahn's book is distinctly utopian. All this is possible, Kahn argues, only if the current atmosphere of self-defeat, doubt, and desire to limit growth do not interfere. These ideas are worked out in detail as the authors discuss a series of specific problems.

In considering population growth, the Hudson study argues that an analysis of population growth patterns in perspective leads to the conclusion that exponential population rates are slowing as a result of rising living standards. The authors believe that developing nations are achieving and will soon attain higher living standards. The rising living standards will result from the impact of the industrial nations on the developing nations. The Western nations have been creating higher living standards for developing nations through the use of the labor and natural resources of the developing nations, by exporting technology, by providing examples of institutions and techniques, and by providing foreign aid. In other words, all of the exploitative aspects of historic colonialism are viewed by Kahn and his associates as productive of assisting the developing nations to improve the lives of their people. If the West continues its pattern of growth, it will literally pull the rest of the world to abundance with it.

Advocates of the "limits to growth" philosophy believe that continued growth is dangerous, that available resources and energy will be used up, and that future growth should be prohibited or curtailed. The Hudson Institute report disagrees with this view, arguing that the population rate will decline, thereby reducing the growth of demand, and the growth rate will automatically slow—without establishing limits. Moreover, once necessities are provided for all people, the demand for luxuries will moderate as people will come to revere genuine value and cease to be self-serving and greedy. The conclusion is utopian.

The Hudson Institute study is equally utopian when it addresses itself to energy. The oil crisis, brought about by the Middle East Organization of Petroleum Exporting Countries oil embargo of 1974 and the subsequent elevation of prices, is regarded in the Kahn volume as only temporary. The costs of energy have declined historically and this pattern will reassert itself. Thus the oil embargo will only induce people to use energy more efficiently. The nations of the world will attack the energy problem with vigor and will solve it. Three sources of energy are considered—short-range, intermediate-range, and long-range sources.

Short-range power sources include natural gas, oil, coal, and other nonrenewable sources. These will last for more than one hundred and fifty years, until the other sources of energy are in place. The most significant intermediate source cited is nuclear fission. Problems of wastes and lack of efficiency permit the development of this source only in the intermediate range. Taking advantage of short and intermediate range sources, a transition will occur to permanent or long-range power sources—solar energy, geothermal energy, wind power, nuclear fusion, and other sources. Moreover, efficiency will demand increasingly large generating facilities and cooperative efforts around the world. The authors conclude that the future will bring an abundance of low-cost energy so that the world will have ample power resources even for a population of fifteen to twenty billion.

As the Hudson study turns to a discussion of raw materials, the view is also optimistic. Rather than anticipating a shortage of raw materials in the future, the authors expect adequate resources, even as they project an increase of the need for raw materials in a factor of sixty. The problem that the authors see is not scarcity but maldistribution of raw materials, which they believe will be solved. Thus, raw materials will be available at the cost of extraction. In the near future, poorer nations will remain dependent on wealthier nations, but Kahn sees this as only temporary. Mutual dependence will bind the world of the future together in cooperative sharing of resources, as technology and industry will resolve all major problems of raw materials.

Contrary to neo-Malthusian views of population outstripping food supply the authors of the Hudson study anticipate that the future will bring an abundance of food and improvements both in the *per capita* amount of available food and in the quality of available food for each person. Conventional food production produced by present means will be adequate for a population of fifteen billion by the year 2176. Additionally, conventional foods produced nonconventionally and nonconventional foods produced nonconventionally will provide even greater yields and will more than adequately suffice for the population of the future. A great effort will be required to provide adequate supplies, but the technology and methods are and will be available to end the problem of human hunger forever.

The authors are not quite so confident about the world's initial ability to solve environmental problems. In the short range, the Hudson study acknowledges that cleaning up the environment will be expensive, but will be technically possible. The cost of such an effort will decrease in the future.

The book points to the environmental movement as drawing public attention to the environmental threat and creating barriers to the solution of the threat. However, environmentalists have been useful in identifying problems and in serving as a pressure group against the worst polluters. The Hudson study supports moderate environmental standards so long as they do not interfere with industrial growth. The failure of business to comply with environmental standards should not be punished because of their "struggles to comply," and "the losses they have already suffered may be punishment enough." This attitude is consistent with the thesis of the Hudson study throughout. The study supports growth over the environment, and environmentalism is stressed if it does not interfere with growth. Kahn contends that wealthier nations, such as the United States, should have higher water, air, noise, and radioactivity standards than poorer nations.

In the persisting debate over whether technology is a blessing or a threat, the Hudson study heavily supports the benefits of technology. The contention is that environmental pollution can be ended with a fairly small percentage of the Gross National Product and with a reliance on technology. Modifications in the internal combustion engine, improvement of electric power plants, and ending pollution problems all require technological solutions.

The Kahn book suggests that land-use policy should be based on categorizing all property into (1) pure and nonpollutible property; (2) residential, industrial, commercial, and farm property subject to pollution; and (3) "junk piles"—areas that could literally be destroyed at the will of business. Such a view of land-use would obviously fly in the face of the objectives of environmentalists. Could the nation afford such "junk piles?" Kahn indicates no interest in the impact of his "junk piles" on other surrounding categories of land utilization; he claims to provide in these suggestions the kind of compromise that will solve the environmental problems of the present.

An analysis of the environment in the long term convinces Kahn that technological progress cannot and should not be slowed, but in some cases should be accelerated. Efforts to halt such progress would require governmental repression. Moreover, if industrial and technical growth continues, most of the environmental problems will be solved. To the risks to health or of possible death from environmental hazards, the Hudson study contends that "there is nothing intrinsically immoral about society subjecting its citizens to this risk" when advantages outweigh disadvantages. Risks can and should be taken because technology might make them less risky in the future. The book does not reflect much concern with the increase of carbon dioxide in the atmosphere from the burning of fossil fuels, the uses of nitrogen fertilizers, dangers to the Ozone layer from supersonic jet planes, or experiments with recombinant DNA. Technology will provide answers for all of these problems, if growth continues. Environmentalists and moralists would disagree with the reasoning that supports these views.

The future that the Hudson study postulates is one in which "manipulative rationality" and "social engineering" will be applied to all human matters. Pragmatism, empiricism, manipulation, hedonism, and utilitarianism will be the values of the future and there will be a decline of concepts of the sacred and the morally traditional. In the future, scientific and technical knowledge will continue to increase along with affluence and leisure. On the economic side, industrialism will become worldwide and an integrated world economy will develop. The rate of economic growth will continue to accelerate to the mid-1980's and then begin to decline so that the four-hundred year curve of economic growth from 1776 to 2176, like the rate of population growth, will form an "S" curve.

On the personal side, the major problems of the future will involve adjustment to a life of leisure and success, avoidance of internal or external violence and hostility, and a feeling of *ennui.* The most difficult personal challenges will be emotional and psychological. While the major problems of population growth, energy, economic growth, raw materials, food supplies, environmental pollution, and the threat of thermonuclear war can, in the view of this book, eventually be overcome by technical and industrial growth, the psychological problems of the future may be more difficult to resolve, and hidden problems may arise which cannot be anticipated at present. The greatest unresolved problem of the future postindustrial world will be "Who will direct and manipulate, and to what ends?" in the words of Kahn. Expressed in more ancient language, this is really the problem of who will guard the guardians.

Kahn and his associates at the Hudson Institute are futurologists who are atempting to construct a model of the future. Their projections are based on their view of the present and its problems. Starting on the side of business and the corporate world, they attempt to construct a future that conforms to present corporate goals and objectives. These goals favor continued industrial growth and noninterference from environmentalists. If these goals and objectives are adopted, Kahn and his associates promise utopia in two hundred years. If the present goals of the business community are not adopted, doom and disaster loom ahead. Not only does their study reveal bias, but its interesting challenge to the environmentalists points to flaws in futurology as a discipline. In the hands of Kahn and his colleagues, the future becomes whatever the authors wish to say it will be and wish to advocate at present. The book is based on a value judgment, and conclusions logically follow once that judgment is adopted. The book is therefore less an accurate prediction than a defense of anti-environmentalism. Moreover, amid the epidemic of futurological studies in recent years, this book demonstrates that readers must beware of experts who, without proof, bend the future to support their present goals and prejudices. Predicting the future is easy. Turning those predictions into reality is much more difficult. The only thing that is certain is that the future will undoubtedly be different from what Kahn and his associates *or* the environmentalists predict.

Saul Lerner

Sources for Further Study

America. CXXXV, August 7, 1976, p. 61.
Best Sellers. XXXVI, September, 1976, p. 201.
Christian Science Monitor. LXVIII, July 13, 1976, p. 26.
Commentary. LXII, December, 1976, p. 85.
Critic. XXXV, Fall, 1976, p. 73.
New Yorker. LII, June 28, 1976, p. 91.

NIGHTMARE
The Underside of the Nixon Years

Author: J. Anthony Lukas (1933-   )
Publisher: The Viking Press (New York). 626 pp. $15.00
Type of work: Current affairs
Time: 1970-1976
Locale: Washington, D.C.; Key Biscayne, Florida; San Clemente, California

The attitudes as well as events that caused the downfall of Nixon are delineated in careful detail with succinct biographies of the persons who shaped those events

> *Principal personages:*
> RICHARD M. NIXON, President of the United States
> H. R. HALDEMAN, White House Chief of Staff
> JOHN D. ERLICHMAN, assistant to the President for domestic affairs
> JOHN W. DEAN III, counsel to the President
> JOHN MITCHELL, Attorney-General of the United States
> E. HOWARD HUNT, White House consultant on security problems in charge of the "Plumbers" operation
> G. GORDON LIDDY, a White House "Plumber"

During the height of the Watergate controversy, vast amounts of information, official and unofficial, reliable and unreliable, factual and conjectural, tumbled forth into the public view by way of the visual and printed media. J. Anthony Lukas was assigned by the *New York Times Magazine* first in April, 1973, and again in January, 1974, to sift through the excess of detail and distill it into a readable and accurate account. As a former member of the paper's Washington bureau, among many other assignments, Lukas had recorded the domestic turmoil of the previous decade, gaining the Pulitzer Prize and several other of journalism's top awards as a result. Each of his accounts of the unfolding story encompassed an entire issue of the magazine, and together they piqued his curiosity sufficiently for him to pursue the story on his own.

In this study of the Nixon years, Lukas weaves the various symptoms of a decadent political climate together with succinct and insightful profiles of the actors in the drama. The scope of the work covers more than only the Watergate era. Lukas believes that those explosive events were natural progressions evolving from the attitudes rooted in the earliest days of Nixon's political career. The uncovered events which were to bring about the resignation of President Nixon were the result of faults of character and perception on his part that radiated as an implicit attitude throughout his White House staff and into other political areas.

An obsession with the image of the event rather than its substance is the recurrent theme throughout the work. Nixon feels that his primary enemy is the press. Although early in his political career he exploited the press coverage of the Alger Hiss case to bring himself to the foreground in those hearings, Nixon's relationship with the press deteriorated during his tenure as Vice

President in the Eisenhower Administration, and fell to a new low during his campaign for the Presidency against John F. Kennedy in 1960. When he finally became President, he surrounded himself with aides who had extensive background in public relations, foremost among them H. R. Haldeman, the White House Chief of Staff, who had for years pursued a successful career with the mammoth J. Walter Thompson advertising agency before being tapped by Nixon to serve as the chief advance man for the 1960 campaign.

Lukas successfully proposes that it was this obsession with appearance and distrust of the media that led Nixon and his staff toward assuming that the news coverage of any event would be slanted so as to show the Administration at its worst. Using excerpts from the tapes made in the White House by Nixon, Lukas shows that the first reaction to an event, in particular to many events of marginal legality, was not whether it should or should not have occurred or whether or not it was legal, but how it would be depicted by the press and whether or not it would "sell" to the American people. These considerations focused the Administration's efforts on preventing the media from learning any facts that were not approved by the President or his men. Anything that might tarnish the President's image was suppressed, or a more "operative" version of the story was told in the hopes that it would be believed. Thus the importance of an event was subsumed in an effort to provide a plausible story for release to the public. A total distortion of reality grew out of this passion to reconstruct the "truth."

Although Lukas does not claim that Nixon's actions were entirely paranoic, nonetheless his portrayal of the man depicts evidence of such a problem. With such an attitude, it would be inevitable that one would perceive many individuals and groups as enemies. Lukas claims that Nixon's three primary enemies were the press, Daniel Ellsberg, and ultimately John Dean.

Lukas' assumption that the press was the primary enemy is indisputable. Richard Nixon had treated the press with something closely resembling contempt for many years. He felt it had unfairly favored John F. Kennedy in the Presidential campaign, and had otherwise been a detriment to his career. At one time Nixon even claimed that he taped Oval Office and other conversations so that the truth about the greatness of his Presidency would be preserved, being sure that the press would deny him his rightful place in history. The infamous Plumbers group was formed to stop leaks of information to the press that might be damaging to Nixon's reelection, although they ultimately were involved in many extralegal and illegal activities that were beyond the original intention of their formation.

Lucas places Ellsberg as the second enemy, although he probably was not so much a threat in and of himself, but as a member of the liberal, intellectual Eastern Establishment. It was Ellsberg's leak of the Pentagon Papers to the press that distressed Nixon and spurred the formation of the Plumbers. The burglary of the office of Dr. Fielding (Ellsberg's psychiatrist) was to be a means of obtaining information that would discredit Ellsberg in the public image; Lukas also sees the action as an ultimate manifestation of Nixon's deep distrust of all liberals, rather than solely a vendetta against Ellsberg.

John F. Kennedy, even more than the troublesome Ellsberg, personified to Nixon the liberal, monied, mannered Eastern Establishment of which he could never be a part. Moreoever, Nixon, having felt that Kennedy had been favored by the press during the 1960 campaign, held them equally in contempt because of it. Although many persons coming from a similar background were perceived as enemies to some degree, perhaps Nixon did not realize that he was perpetually battling an entire segment of the American culture, indeed a traditionally powerful segment in political circles. The majority of Nixon's aides, their staffs, Nixon's personal friends, and his early cabinet and other appointments were men from California, Florida, or elsewhere in the Southern "sun belt." They were primarily self-made men who were vigorous and possibly a little brash in their approach to others. Lukas rightly interprets the significance of their similarities as characteristics of people who could be "trusted."

Daniel Ellsberg, however, was an enemy, and it was in the pursuit of incriminating information against him that the Nixon staff brought into the everyday practice of politics techniques of foreign espionage that had previously not been regular components of the domestic political scene. The burglary of Dr. Fielding's office was a clearly illegal act, but in the climate of the White House at that time, any methods used by a President against those who seemed to be his enemies were above the law, as necessary adjuncts to the national security. Lukas delineates numerous cases of wiretapping of those not trusted by the President or his staff. The infamous "enemies list" also includes names of persons against whom investigations by other arms of government, notably the Internal Revenue Service, were used as weapons. Such investigations in themselves would not have been illegal, had the purpose of the information-gathering not been. Lukas has managed in this section of the book to incorporate many more instances of wrongdoing that were generally brought to the public's attention at the time.

The men of the liberal political establishment were even more difficult to compete against because they were in many instances monied, or had powerful acquaintances. Although Nixon had some powerful and monied friends, the power base and funding source for his campaigns for office was to be corporate contributions. Since outright corporate contributions of this type were not legal, Nixon's campaign staff and other friends devised ways in which to disguise the source of the money, or "launder" it. This illegal activity was perceived by those involved as essential to the national interest, for it would enable Nixon to compete in the political arena and ultimately win reelection. As Lukas amply describes, it was yet another segment of the Nixonian public-relations ethic against the popular and powerful intellectual liberals.

The majority of *Nightmare* is devoted to a careful description of the Committee to Re-elect the President (CREEP) and how its staff, hired for various and sundry duties, went about its primary task. Lukas is a faithful recorder of dates and places, but he does not fully succeed in clarifying the many parallel chronologies involved in their connected activities.

The profiles of the various persons involved in the staff activities, however, are major contributions to the work. In very succinct and clearly drawn portraits, the primary and less-than-primary personages are depicted in such a way that the reader is immediately aware of the attitudes and experiences that the newcomer brings to the narrative. The profiles are written as asides to the primary narrative, just as each person comes to the foreground in the events. Thus, Lukas provides for his readers important psychological characterizations just as they are pertinent for a thorough understanding of the unfolding events. Although these mini-biographies could have been more easily identified in the index, they remain a major asset.

Two such profiles are of E. Howard Hunt and G. Gordon Liddy. Hunt and Liddy were minor functionaries in an overall view of the Nixon White House and reelection campaign, but an understanding of the background which they brought to CREEP is essential if the reader is to understand how their illegal acts and foreign intelligence techniques could be perceived as excusable necessities toward Nixon's reelection. Their demand for financial support once they were caught is understandable considering their background, as is the development of a hush-money scheme that would eventually become a major credibility gap for the President.

The later months of the Nixon administration are depicted as desperate in attempts to mollify the press and to mold their accounts of the illegal activities that were coming to the fore. As the scandal edged close to the Oval Office, more and more former staff members were sacrificed to the prosecution for the good of the reelection. Nixon's battle was ultimately lost through the efforts of the most tangible of the President's enemies, John Dean. Dean's psychological profile is perhaps less thorough than it should be, but Lukas is careful to show exactly how and why Dean became a Nixon favorite and, equally, his decision not to volunteer as a scapegoat in the prosecutions that followed. Dean's subsequent account of Nixon's complicity, and the concomitant discovery on the part of the prosecutors of the White House tapes, provided the levers which pried the President out of office.

Nixon's final months in office were engulfed in bending reality in the hopes of a favorable press account. Lukas portrays the President as a gloomy and paranoid man who is finally nudged into resignation by his remaining staff, having lost contact with reality altogether.

J. Anthony Lukas has, in this exhaustive work, provided a powerful psychological portrait fully bolstered by facts and dates to explain, to a great degree, how the unprecedented Presidential resignation could have proceeded from a gradual distortion of reality. The basically chronological approach of the work is marred somewhat by too few reminders of which events are parallel and too many references to particular months without mention of the year. Often individuals or corporations enter the narrative without being fully identified. Although the direct quotations in the text are not footnoted, the ample documentation at the end of the work can also act as a guide to further research.

Margaret S. Schoon

Sources for Further Study

Atlantic. CCXXXVII, April, 1976, p. 114.

Commonweal. CIII, September 10, 1976, p. 598.

Current History. LXX, April, 1976, p. 179.

New York Review of Books. XXIII, June 24, 1976, p. 21.

New Yorker. LII, February 23, 1976, p. 114.

Newsweek. LXXXVII, February 9, 1976, p. 75.

Virginia Quarterly Review. LII, Autumn, 1976, p. 126.

NORMAN THOMAS
The Last Idealist

Author: W. A. Swanberg (1907-   )
Publisher: Charles Scribner's Sons (New York). 528 pp. $14.95
Type of work: Biography
Time: 1884-1968
Locale: The United States

A biography of Norman Thomas, who was the Socialist candidate for President of the United States six times

Principal personages:
NORMAN THOMAS
MRS. NORMAN THOMAS, his wife
EVAN THOMAS, his younger brother
FRANKLIN DELANO ROOSEVELT
ROGER BALDWIN, head of the American Civil Liberties Union
UPTON SINCLAIR, writer, reformer, and friend of Thomas

W. A. Swanberg's *Norman Thomas* is a loving tribute to America's favorite Socialist. In his half century of political involvement, Thomas bridged the separate worlds of socialism and capitalism. His socialism was American rather than European, Christian rather than Marxist, and democratic rather than totalitarian. A gadfly to the American conscience, always teaching, beseeching Americans in that resonant, booming voice of his like an Old Testament prophet, he was never frightening like Eugene Debs and was never prosecuted or persecuted. Where Debs had Americanized socialism for the laboring man, Thomas had Americanized socialism for the middle class.

Swanberg is one of America's most distinguished biographers. This is his ninth biography; other works include *Citizen Hearst, Pulitzer,* and the Pulitzer Prize-winning *Luce and His Empire.* A Midwesterner like Thomas, Swanberg first saw Thomas when he was a student at the University of Minnesota. Swanberg, a Socialist at the time, voted for Thomas in the 1932 election; he was so impressed by him at the time that he "may have got my vote even had he been a Bolshevist or Falangist."

Born in Marion, Ohio, in 1884, also the home town of Warren G. Harding, Thomas was the son and grandson of Presbyterian ministers. A sickly and shy child, he had several close calls with croup and scarlet fever. For a while he was a delivery boy for Harding's *Marion Daily Star.* He attended Bucknell for one year before transferring to Princeton, and in 1905 graduated from Princeton at the head of his class. After working in a New York City settlement house, he traveled in Europe, attended the Union Theological Seminary, and was ordained a Presbyterian minister in 1911. While pastor of the East Harlem Church, he became involved with the antiwar movement, becoming chairman of the Fellowship of Reconciliation and No-Conscription League. Strongly critical of America's declaration of war, he aided Roger Baldwin in founding the American Civil Liberties Union in 1917 to help conscientious objectors, one of whom was his younger brother Evan.

By 1918 Thomas had joined the Socialist Party and had left the Presbyterian pulpit. He served on the staff of the *Nation* for a year and then became a director of the League for International Democracy, the educational arm of the Socialist Party. His first political campaign was when he ran for governor of New York as a Socialist in 1924; in 1925 and 1929 he ran for mayor of New York City. With the death of Eugene Debs in 1926, Thomas became the leader of the Socialist Party. He would run for the Presidency six times, one more than Debs did, on the Socialist ticket between 1928 and 1948; his best race was in 1932, when he received over 800,000 votes. He supported the nationalization of basic industry, elimination of child labor, unemployment insurance, and old age pensions.

During the New Deal, while many people maintained that Roosevelt stole most of the Socialist platform, Thomas said that Roosevelt did not carry out the Socialist platform "unless he carried it out on a stretcher." He attacked Roosevelt for not supporting more reforms and for not nationalizing certain industries and the nation's resources. Thomas led the fight to condemn the inequities of the Agricultural Adjustment Act on Southern tenant farmers. The acreage reduction proposals removed thousands of cropper families from the farms, and what had once been a local scandal now became a national one. Thomas traveled to Arkansas and delivered some of his most dramatic speeches. At the town of Birdsong, a drunken mob of planters and sheriff's police attacked Thomas, kicked him off the speaker's platform and chased him out of town, yelling "We don't need no Gawd-damn Yankee Bastard to tell us what to do with our niggers." Thomas left the state further committed to encouraging the nation's sense of justice. He wrote a letter to Roosevelt emphasizing that the situation was the most dangerous he had ever seen. Getting no satisfaction from Roosevelt's lieutenants, Thomas visited the President, who rejected Thomas' plans for helping the croppers as unworkable, saying "Norman, I am a damned sight better politician than you are." "Well, certainly, Mr. President," Thomas replied. "You are on that side of the table and I'm on this."

Thomas was ambivalent toward the Soviet Union. He criticized Stalin's secret police and the show trials of the 1930's, but he asserted that the Soviet economic system was progressive. He was active in antiwar organizations in the late 1930's, speaking at the same rallies with Charles Lindbergh. Thomas believed that America's involvement in a war would damage the moral order both here and abroad. After Pearl Harbor, he supported the war effort although continuing to attack government policies such as the internment of 100,000 Japanese-Americans and the dropping of the atomic bombs. Thomas was removed from the leadership of the Socialist Party in 1950, but he continued to act as its conscience. Thomas's last years were spent in fighting for nuclear disarmament, international peace, and an end to the Vietnam War. He died in his sleep in a nursing home in December, 1968.

Part of Swanberg's success is his ability to capture his subject's character—his kindness, tolerance, intelligence, and charity. Filled with the facts of Thomas' personal and political life, the book is especially solid when dealing with his myriad involvements and with his last years. Although a strong admirer, Swanberg is aware of Thomas' weaknesses—his ambivalence, his temper, his overinvolvement in different causes. The picture of the times in which Thomas lived is the weakest part of the book; the man overshadows the stage on which he walked. Even his associates appear more like a chorus shouting praise or denunciation than real people. More information into the Socialist movement would perhaps have filled this noticeable void by offering more complete pictures of such important figures as Daniel Hoan, Morris Hillquit, and Henry Wallace. Although Swanberg accurately points out some of Thomas' political weaknesses which hastened the party's decline—his inability to be ruthless, to make deals, to be a political manager—his overall view of the decline of the Socialist party is still simplistic.

In the 1930's Thomas was unable to hold the Socialists together, and factional wars between the Old Guard, the Militants, and the Trotskyites brought the Party to its grave. Thomas and his supporters were middle-class, college-educated, native-born Americans—non-Marxists who wanted to liberate the Party from procrustean ideas and develop closer relationships with American labor. But during the worst years of the Depression, the Militants pushed for a revival of the class struggle and demanded that the party work for socialism "in our lifetime." The Militants were also working for a closer relationship with the Soviet Union. Torn by these issues, the Socialist party was unable to take advantage of its golden opportunity—the Depression. With sit-down strikes and violent labor demonstrations now more common, the Socialists were unable to make effective connections with the unemployed and radical labor unions. The party spent more time on educational programs than on courting the groups that could give them power. Socialism was becoming a nullity; it had become something resembling social reform. And reform during the depths of the Depression was not enough. Thomas was more effective as a purveyor of socialistic ideas in a college auditorium than in a labor hall.

Between 1928 and 1932 the Socialist party almost doubled its miniscule membership from 7,000 to 15,000; but those were also the days when Leon Trotsky called the Socialists a party of dentists and made the cutting remark that Thomas called himself a Socialist "as the result of a misunderstanding." It was labor's turn to Roosevelt and the New Deal that effectively ended the Party's chances for real power. By 1936 labor had jumped on the Roosevelt bandwagon, thereby removing the Socialist Party's main support. Thomas was unable to redirect union sentiment back to Socialism. His antiwar policies in the late 1930's furthered the alienation between workers and the Socialist

Party. John Dos Passos wrote, "I should think that becoming a socialist right now would have just the same effect on anybody as drinking a bottle of near-beer."

Thomas' acceptance by so many Americans was in part based upon his middle-class ideas. He was married to the same woman for thirty-eight years; he never smoked and seldom drank. His reading was not the *Daily Worker* but the *New York Times*. His radicalism was of the faintest hue. He aroused few fears except to those on the extreme right; his cause was reform rather than revolution. And if Thomas was not a great man he was a good man who believed that politics should be honest, sensible, and honorable. Few men have worked so hard, traveled so far, and fought against such odds as did Thomas. For fifty years he was right about more issues than any man of his time. Fighting for freedom in America during World War I, helping starving sharecroppers during the Depression, condemning the armaments race of the post-World War II era, and attacking the Vietnam War, his stamina was amazing. Until his death he still gave speeches that stirred audiences, even though they wondered how he could reach the podium with his crippling arthritis.

The Cold War years brought out Thomas' great strengths and a few of his weaknesses. His attack upon the Smith Act and his support for individual Communists was at some risk to himself. But as a Cold War liberal, he supported the Central Intelligence Agency's actions in Latin America, the North Atlantic Treaty Organization, the Marshall Plan, and the Korean War, and he believed in the guilt of Alger Hiss. His belief that Communism was a conspiracy led him to purge his old friend Elizabeth Gurley Flynn from the board of the ACLU. He supported loyalty oaths and believed Communists should not teach in the public schools. The Cold War phobia overcame even his support for basic civil liberties.

Swanberg mentions the contempt that Thomas felt for Joseph McCarthy but neglects to mention that Thomas had a role in launching the Wisconsin Senator's career. After McCarthy won the Republican senatorial primary in 1946, the Wisconsin chairman of the Communist Party endorsed the Democratic candidate. A few days later, Thomas came to the state and attacked the endorsement, adding that perhaps the Democratic candidate intended to accept the fellow traveler label. Later McCarthy, following Thomas' lead, used similar red-baiting statements in his campaign and won the election.

Thomas' ideas were perceptive if eclectic; he wrote dozens of articles and twenty books which show the influence of Walter Rauschenbusch and the Social Gospel movement upon him. But it was his charm, his energy, and his decency that attracted so many to his banner. He gave thousands of Americans an alternative to a perceived Twiddledum-Twiddledee two-party system. His ability to suffer defeat after defeat and come optimistically back for more was a characteristic that endeared him to his fellows and much of mainstream America. If any American politician had a right to be pessimistic, it was

Norman Thomas; the lack of funds, the constant attacks, and the numerous defeats would have demolished a weaker man, but if anything they gave him strength.

When Thomas died, columnist Murray Kempton wrote that there would always be "some lonely, unfashionable place where he would stand." Swanberg's book serves as a reminder that America has yet to find his equal today.

Richard Van Orman

Sources for Further Study

Book World. August 29, 1976, p. M2.

Library Journal. CI, October 15, 1976, p. 2168.

New York Times. November 24, 1976, p. 31.

Newsweek. LVIII, November 8, 1976, p. 103.

Progressive. XL, December, 1976, p. 54.

Wall Street Journal. CLXXXVIII, November 22, 1976, p. 20.

NOW PLAYING AT CANTERBURY

Author: Vance Bourjaily (1922-   )
Publisher: The Dial Press (New York). 518 pp. $10.00
Type of work: Novel
Time: 1972
Locale: State City and University in the Midwestern United States

A modern-day Canterbury Tales—*shorn of Chaucer's theological and moralistic overtones—in which the richness and variety of the human condition are celebrated on a note of irony*

> *Principal characters:*
> HENRY FENNELLON,
> MAGGIE TARO SHORT,
> DEBBIE DIETER HAAS,
> SATO MURASKAI,
> BILLY HOFFMAN,
> HUGHMORE SKEATS, IV,
> HERVE GANDENBERG AND JANET MARGESSON,
> DICK AUERBACH AND SIDNEY BENNETT (NÉE CINDY BENESCH AUERBACH),
> JOHN TEN MASON,
> BETH PAULUS,
> DAVID AND SUE RIDING,
> MARCEL ST. EDOUARD, and
> MIKE AND MONA SHAPEN, participants in the premier performance
>   of a new performing arts center

Vance Bourjaily says that the writing of *Now Playing at Canterbury* took the better part of twelve years, and the richly interwoven series of characters, subplots, motifs, and themes in the novel testify to his statement. He often echoes the techniques of both Chaucer and James Joyce in attempting to present the macrocosm in microcosm. While the title points to Chaucer, the first important writer in the English language, Bourjaily is one of the few modern writers besides Thomas Pynchon to really learn from the modern genius of the same language, James Joyce.

In Chaucer's *Canterbury Tales,* only two of the pilgrims' stories are totally autobiographical. The stories, which express wide differences of tone and attitudes toward life, are mainly told in traditional medieval genres which Chaucer has adapted and clothed in magic garments. In contrast, all of Bourjaily's characters tell autobiographical tales; the only totally fictional story is that of the opera libretto. Like Chaucer, Bourjaily includes an animal fable (Sidney's), but it, too, contains autobiographical meaning. Since the time is set in the latter half of the twentieth century and God is supposed to be dead, the nearest Bourjaily comes to a saint's legend or sermon is Mike's tale of the student demonstrations against the Vietnam War; his wife, Mona, is the only martyr present. Since love in Bourjaily's world cannot be considered as an extension of Divine love, it has to be analyzed on the human level only. The closest any of Bourjaily's "pilgrims" ever comes to the philosophy and theology always hovering in the background of Chaucer's tales is in Maury's discussions of the god, Fats. In place of a theological or moralistic background, Bourjaily substitutes a consistent attitude to life: "life, after all, is only one of those solemn comic strips we all love secretly, except that instead of a handsome doctor or soldier or meddling old woman to make sure it comes out all right we have natural irony, to make sure it comes out oddly." The consistency of this attitude is maintained in both the frame story and in the tales told by the characters, thus producing a much more limited range of attitudes to life than that evident in Chaucer.

Chaucer's use of the frame device, which brings people of diverse classes and background together for a pilgrimage to the tomb of St. Thomas à Beckett, is loosely followed for the structure of this novel. For Bourjaily, however, the martyr's cathedral is replaced by the performing arts center of a Midwestern State University and the pilgrims become those involved in its premier performance. There are other, smaller pilgrimages contained within this frame: two processions to the local bar; two to the Riding's old schoolhouse; and two to the local jail.

In contrast to Chaucer, Bourjaily develops the frame into a major story of its own. While Chaucer uses his Prologue and introductions merely to identify characters and bind the tales together, with only brief interactions among the pilgrims, Bourjaily does the opposite: his frame story and characters are more important than the main storyline. After Chapter Seventeen, the omniscient author is interrupted only twice by other narrators: Maggie Short, who relates the story of the cast party, and Fennellon, who gives an account of Mona's death. During the complication, crisis, and climax (opening night), where the "miracle" is achieved, no other character interrupts. In both the frame story and in the final anticlimactic stories of Maggie and Fennellon, as well as in the final words of the novel, the idea of life as a pilgrimage with an oddly ironic end is the major theme.

To some degree, the thematic emphasis on this view of life partially excuses the major flaws of the novel: the excessive use of novelty and gadgetry, such as the comic strip blurb version of Sato's life; the italicized inserts of the background of Sidney Bennett and Dick Auerbach into Skeats's story of his war experiences and odyssey to New York; and the Joycean play on language evident in Maury's segments. The Bennett-Auerbach and Skeats stories both lose impact from the interruptions. Although Maury's Joycean style of language seems appropriate to his vision of life, it obscures crucial insights into his experiences, which can only be ferreted out by a serious reader, and only after the account of the cast party. Sato's tale, told in comic strip blurbs, is meant to illustrate his and Debbie's love of games, but the device grows old very quickly. It is at its best during the Green Hornet-like sequence of his naïveté during his first job in San Francisco, in which he participates innocently in a first-class con game, ending with the obligatory cop chase and escape. But the style is inappropriate and distracting for the other major elements of the story: his relationship with his stepfather Oog, and Oog's with Sato's mother, "Limehouse Lady." It seems especially out of place in the brief anecdote of her internment in an Oriental prison camp and in her poignant assurances to Sato that Oog loves them although he will never return. The successful realization of her character comes in spite of, rather than because of, the author's presentation and style.

The most successful, strongest, and most memorable of Bourjaily's short stories follow the more traditional pattern of building suspense, few interruptions, and clear conflict and resolution, such as Dick's story of Duke Woerbel, his mad mother, and the killer cats; Debbie's of her two brothers' estrangement; Hoffman's of Janey Lee; Marcel's of incipient castration; John Ten's of the greatest race ever run; Mike's of the student protest "wars" against the Vietnam War; and Henry Fennellon's of Mona's death. All of these are finely told traditional short stories with common ironic themes.

As in all of Joyce's major works, there is an important group of recurring motifs and allusions in Bourjaily's stories that serve to underline themes and to hold the multiple plots together more tightly. The diverse literary allusions range from the poetry of Blake to the prose of Hemingway and Fitzgerald. The influence of the latter two is obvious in this book's subject matter and style: Mona and Mike's escape from the city and state police and the National Guard on the night of the student demonstrations against America's strike against Cambodia echoes Hemingway's Caporetto retreat, just as Mona's death echoes Catherine's and raises the same questions about the absurdity of the human condition. Fitzgerald's short stories about Southern women are likewise echoed and his style reflected in passages such as those describing Sato's attitude at the premier. One chapter, titled "Fitzgerald Attends My Fitzgerald Seminar" (a clever idea which unfortunately becomes boring even to teachers of literature) calls attention to Fitzgerald's influence on the American novel and on the professor's life.

Interlocking motifs of machines—cars, airplanes, buses, motorcycles, and so on—are always turning up in the lives of these modern pilgrims, emphasizing the importance of machines in modern life. They are often more a means of fleeing from, rather than going to, a place. John Ten's story of Cougar in "The Fastest Jeep in the World" comments on the connection between the modern obsession with machines and speed and the death wish.

Another recurring motif is that of war. Debbie's brothers, Fennellon, Sato, Oog, Short, Skeats, and "Pill" all served in World War II; Cougar had just returned from Korea; Maury Jackstone served in Korea. Mike and Mona Shapen serve in a civilian "war" against Vietnam; Mona is killed in the American bombing of Hanoi in December, 1972. Maury tells a fantasy of Castro, predicting in 1984 the disintegration of America from internal dissension. The violence, killing, and death in modern life, seen in many of the other stories, is underscored by the multiple references to wars.

In his analysis of human nature, Bourjaily, like Chaucer and Joyce, includes a wide variety of people. Missing, of course, are perfect figures, such as the Knight and the Parson—in keeping with the author's ironic vision. Idealists are always disillusioned in this pilgrimage. However, although no one is presented as perfect, one "holy warrior" comes close—Henry Fennellon. Several men are presented as basically good and admirable, though flawed: Hoffman, Maury Jackstone, Marcel St. Edouard, Sato, the Banjo Man, Mike Shapen, and Davey Riding. Of the women, Mona Shapen is most obviously idealized, but Sue Riding, Sato's mother, and Debbie Dieter Haas come alive as admirable individuals. There are some equally villainous characters of each sex also. Among the evil men are "Pill," Earl Ransom, Rocky, and Charles; the bad women, usually ambitious, are destructive "users": Sally Anne, Christine, Sidney Bennett, and Mary Virginia. Janet Margesson, the famous soprano, is presented as the most depraved in her usage of everyone, especially of Beth, to please her own desires. The rest of the characters fall in between these two extremes, neither as admirable as some nor as evil as others.

The relationships between such individuals are often flawed ones. Especially memorable and poignant is Debbie's story of Gottfried and Gerhardt, of Sato and Oog, and of Maury's friendship for Sue and Davey. Just as in Chaucer's "marriage group," the relationships between married couples gets a great deal of analysis; Davey Riding's solo analysis of what is happening to his marriage is especially tender and thoughtful. The sexual relationship itself is treated in the work in all available facets: a tender and fullfilling love scene between John Ten and Beth Paulus is followed almost immediately by a sexual orgy; there are multiple affairs and two rapes; lesbians and gays drift in occasionally. Many of the relationships are good ones that exhibit a true caring for and acceptance of others, some are exactly the opposite; but all faithfully mirror the richness, variety, and significance of human relationships and the ephemeral nature of the human condition. It is the person who recognizes both of the latter points who can accept life and loss with grace and continue, both optimistically and realistically, on the pilgrimage of life, the comic strip with an oddly ironic ending. Such persons can continue, to paraphrase Debbie Dieter Haas, to keep throwing everything they have at those "who sit in the sky." In this novel, Henry Fennellon, Billy Hoffman, and Maury Jackstone best represent such persons.

Short, the English professor, tells his students to "remember, the form itself, the novel as an American expression shaped to the times, wasn't all laid out for him [Fitzgerald] as it might be for one of you. It still had to be developed." Some of Bourjaily's earlier books seemed to assume that Hemingway and Fitzgerald completed the laying out of that form. In *Now Playing at Canterbury,* Bourjaily himself is genuinely moving out into new territory, attempting the development of a new form which will enable him to express the modern American experience. That he is not always successful is not surprising, considering the chaotic immensity of America's last twenty years of experience. And the artistic successes of the book far outweigh its failures. *Now Playing at Canterbury* may not be the "masterpiece" described on its dust jacket, but it is an excellent, interesting, and important work, deserving wide attention.

Ann E. Reynolds

Sources for Further Study

Atlantic. CCXXXVIII, October, 1976, p. 111.

Christian Century. XLIII, December 8, 1976, p. 1104.

National Observer. XV, September 18, 1976. p. 23.

New York Times Book Review. September 12, 1976, p. 3.

Newsweek. LXXXVIII, September 13, 1976, p. 81.

Saturday Review. III, September 18, 1976, p. 26.

Time. CVIII, September 13, 1976, p. 75.

OCTOBER LIGHT

Author: John Gardner (1933-)
Publisher: Alfred A. Knopf (New York). 434 pp. $10.00
Type of work: Novel
Time: The present
Locale: Prospect Mountain, Vermont

The complex story of the conflict between brother and sister, tradition and change, and the clash of opposing values

> *Principal characters:*
> JAMES PAGE, a Vermont farmer in his seventies
> SALLY PAGE ABBOTT, his older sister
> GINNY HICKS, his daughter
> LEWIS HICKS, his son-in-law

John Gardner, whose previous works have wedded fancy to fact and myth to metaphysics, offers such a union again in this, his new novel. In it, he combines the elements of the earlier works that earned him a literary reputation of considerable stature. The philosophical complexity and existential questioning of *The Sunlight Dialogues* appear here in full measure. Blended well into this new novel are also the literary skill, echoes, and knowledge of *The King's Indian,* his 1974 collection of short stories. Finally, the simple realism of *Nickel Mountain* finds its way into Gardner's new novel.

This novel, his eighth work, consolidates Gardner's reputation as a major writer. Having earned that reputation with works of wide diversity and undisputed merit, including *Resurrection* (his first novel), *The Wreckage of Agathon, Grendel, Jason and Medeia,* and the above-mentioned three, Gardner offers *October Light* as a measuring stick of his maturation as a writer and of the growth of his concept of fiction. The novel's eclectic assemblage of ideas and elements from earlier works—both his and those of others—is a testament to the sophistication of the work and the writer.

October Light is primarily concerned with the American character, with observing in detail its traits and characteristics. Gardner turns a simultaneously critical and sympathetic eye towards these traits, examining them each as separate entities and as integral parts of the whole. He examines the American sense of tradition, its emphasis on values, its sense of both equality and superiority, its belief in free enterprise and the freedom to amass wealth, its obstinacy, its belief in principle, and its belief in the morality of labor. Noting the conflicting nature of many of these traits, Gardner presents them, nonetheless, and the resulting paradoxes help imbue his characters with realism and credibility. In *October Light,* Gardner's characters are human above all, earning both our admiration and our pity.

On the simplest of terms, this novel concerns the relationship between James L. Page and his older sister, Sally Page Abbott. James, a widower of seventy-two, finds his life changed by the return of Sally to his house to live, a return made necessary by the exigencies of her financial situation. A firm believer in traditional values and a man of the most conservative political opinions, James finds the foundations of his beliefs shaken and the basis of his opinions challenged. This challenge to his way of life comes not so much from his sister as it does from the things she represents and the things of the world outside of James's home that she brings with her, most notably, television.

For James, television is both obscene and ungodly. It represents the temptation of the devil and the desires of the flesh. It encourages greed and violence. He sees TV game shows as blasphemy and high treason, and television dramas as an outrage against sense. He had told Sally in the beginning that she could come and live with him, but that she could not bring her television. Defying him, she brings it, and, finally, when he has been pushed to his limit, James loads his shotgun and shoots the television without warning.

Following the shooting of the television, he and Sally continue an argument for some three weeks—an argument growing out of their diametrically opposed ideas and out of their competing efforts to gain a certain provincial control over some element of their relationship. Finally, James again feels forced into an unalterable course of action. In a cold rage at what he considers the stupidity of Sally's opinions, he picks up a piece of firewood and, brandishing it like a club, chases her upstairs to her bedroom where he locks her in.

This is both the beginning of the novel and its basic conflict. Sally goes on strike, refusing to leave the bedroom to do any work, and James refuses to let her out of the bedroom. Sally's revolution against the *status quo* and James's obstinate defense of the system—although the system may in this case be no more than the way things have always been done on his farm—combine to give *October Light* its tension. This "war of the bowels," as James calls it—so named because it is a test of whether he gives in to his constipation before she gives in to the diarrhea caused by a diet of apples only—becomes allegory.

October Light, however, is more than merely this allegory with its moving, honest, and detailed observations of life in New England and of life for the elderly. It is also a most ambitious literary undertaking. Although the cast of characters of *October Light* is not as extensive as that in *The Sunlight Dialogues,* Gardner presents two entirely separate and unrelated casts of characters in this novel, as well as two unrelated plots occurring simultaneously. This duality lends strength and tension to the work, emphasizing and enlarging the meaning in one plot by employing a contrapuntal answer to it in the other.

Gardner introduces the second plot of the novel by having Sally find a badly worn paperback book of questionable quality, entitled *The Smugglers of Lost Souls' Rock,* in her room. Bored by being locked in her room and intrigued and titilated by the apparent tone of the novel, Sally begins reading it, finding herself caught up in the activities of a ring of marijuana smugglers, the attempted suicide of a character named Peter Wagner, the sexual promiscuity of the characters, and their endless questioning of existence and its meaning. Gardner insures that the reader not only knows that Sally is reading the novel, but that the reader also reads the novel with Sally. To do so, he presents both novels within the cover of the same volume, distinguishing between the two by changing typefaces.

The novel-within-the-novel, *The Smugglers of Lost Souls' Rock,* a story written by Gardner and his wife, becomes a reflection of the action occurring between James and Sally, though it is a reflection seen in a carnival mirror. The faces and the forms are gnarled, misshapen, extended, shrunk, expanded, and narrowed. This story seems to be several things, but Gardner will not permit it to assume any single identity. One of the characters, a rather cold-blooded black man, discusses existentialism and recites Shakespeare. Another, Dr. Alkahest, an eighty-year-old doctor confined to a wheel chair, who has acute sensitivity of hearing and smell, seeks only the exhilaration of sensual escape. Captain Fist is the carnival's freak. Revolting in appearance, he attempts to justify the amassing of wealth as necessary to the defense of the "American Way." World-weary, Peter Wagner seeks suicide and wrestles with sexism.

Gardner makes of this story-within-a-story a microcosm of society, a focused examination of a contained community. Through the actions of this group, Gardner forces the reader to examine the cornerstones of society, including law and justice, suggesting that, in the end, laws are not by necessity just.

More provocative than these ideas, however, is the possibility that "Lost Souls' Rock" is, in fact, James's idea of heaven. This idea is suggested by the descriptions Gardner uses for both. In describing James's conception of heaven, he writes of it as ". . . some shadowy mountain calling down to intuition, some fortress for the lost made second by second and destroyed and made again. . . ." Similarly, he describes, within the context of the novel, *The Smugglers of Lost Souls' Rock,* the island as rising ". . . like a black, partly fallen natural castle. . . ."

The connection is made stronger by James's idea of the Devil's temptations as being all dazzle and false hope, as false as the idea of ". . . escaping from the world of hard troubles and grief in a spaceship," and by the conclusion of the novel *The Smugglers of Lost Souls' Rock,* in which a flying saucer figures prominently.

This novel-within-a-novel becomes an allegory for, and an amplification of, the conflict between James and Sally, just as their conflict is, itself, an allegory for a much larger conflict. The greatest testament to Gardner's skill in constructing parallel plots which appear so diverse is that the stories, the characters, and the action of the conflict between James and Sally are all thoroughly believable and realistic. The meshing of the two stories is intricately done with the reader switching from one to the other without any forced or false shifting on the part of the author. Part of this is due to the fact that Gardner has arranged for portions of *The Smugglers of Lost Souls' Rock* to be missing, thereby forcing the reader back to the present conflict between brother and sister.

October Light is an ambitious undertaking and one that succeeds remarkably well. Gardner must be commended for his expansive concept of fiction and for his vigorous extension of previously established limits for the genre of the novel. But perhaps the greatest ingredients of his success are his attention to detail, his honest and sympathetic portrait of his characters, and his capable plotting. *October Light* is a fine novel, and John Gardner is, above all else, an incredibly compelling storyteller.

James R. Van Laan

Sources for Further Study

Best Sellers. XXXVI, April, 1976, p. 3.

Horn Book. LII, April, 1976, p. 154.

Los Angeles Times. December 19, *Books,* p. 1.

New York Times Book Review. November 16, 1976, p. 29.

Saturday Evening Post. CCXLVIII, May, 1976, p. 69.

School Library Journal. XXII, January, 1976, p. 57.

OF WOMAN BORN
Motherhood as Experience and Institution

Author: Adrienne Rich (1929-   )
Publisher: W. W. Norton and Company (New York). 318 pp. $8.95
Type of work: Psychological and historical study

A probing examination of how the experience of motherhood affected the poet's life, both as an individual woman and mother and as part of a social and historical institution

Mentioned briefly in Chapter I of this study by Adrienne Rich is a particularly grisly incident. In 1975, a mother of eight children decapitated the two youngest of her brood on the front lawn of their suburban home in broad daylight. According to later testimony in the case, the woman, though prone to depression, seemed a very loving mother, doting especially on her two youngest children. *Of Woman Born* concludes with a fuller discussion of this same event. This framing incident is more than an artistic device to bring the work full circle. Indeed, one could argue that the entire study is an attempt to make the reader understand why this suburban mother, later declared insane, committed the crime she did.

To accomplish this understanding, Rich ranges easily and unpedantically over a diverse range of human learning: economics, history, biology, literature, medicine, sociology, anthropology, archeology, religion, mythology, and genetics. More impressive, however, is Rich's adept integration of her own personal experience as a mother of three sons, as well as the experiences of other historical and contemporary women, with considerations of Engels, Simone de Beauvoir, Levi-Strauss, Freud, and others.

The result is an eminently readable, informed, and intelligent study. Simultaneously, *Of Woman Born* conveys a deeply personal vision and will undoubtedly become a major feminist document. This is no small accomplishment in a relatively short work which also represents Rich's first attempt at prose.

After twenty-five years as a poet, Adrienne Rich, presently considered a major contemporary poet, brings to her first prose work the most important qualities of her own poetry, and perhaps of all poetry: the economic and organic integration of personal experience and vision with those social forces, be they ethnic, political, religious, or other, which are perceived as dictating to the individual consciousness. Thus, the book has both an inner and outer structure. *Of Woman Born* has ample and accurate footnotes and bibliography. The objective, argumentative structure of the work is clear. Yet, these are all merely tools to convey and explain an intensely private experience.

The outer structure, or the book's major argument, could be stated as follows: Power has been systematically denied women. They have little autonomous control over their biological, mental, emotional, or economic fulfillment as human beings. Historically, cultures which normally practiced the murder by exposure of infant females are numerous. Paradoxically, however, the apex of this process occurs late in history, at the beginning of the industrial revolution, when woman's place became more than ever circumscribed to the rearing of children and the nurture and support of men. Prior to this, the home, rather than being an oversized playpen and hospitality station, was a cottage industry. Everything from soap to food to heirs was produced on the premises with the female having at least an equal participation in the production.

Second, this denial of female power happened because men were threatened by women. Rich speculates, with mythological justification, that women must be feared because they are the ultimate creators of life, and what they create they can also destroy. For this, among other reasons, men have been driven to envy female creativity and equally driven to control it, trivialize it, and even to deny it. From such an urge, witchhunts are instigated.

Or, if one is uncomfortable with the interpretation of myth, there are numerous sociological findings to consider. For instance, from time immemorial, it has been the custom of men to congregate in exclusive societies or clubs. This grouping is considered natural, even prestigious. To this day, the banding together of women, for whatever purpose, is subject at the least to ridicule and at the extreme to being considered an unnatural and subversive condition.

An interesting historical footnote illuminating the systematic degradation of female status had been the ouster of the traditional midwives in favor of the modern tool-oriented and male-dominated science of obstetrics. Rich concludes that if men cannot create life itself, they at least have tried to control ultimately the process of birth. She jumps to future conclusions about recent male-dominated experiments in cloning and test-tube life. The obvious question is, "What kind of women will men create?"

Third, the destructiveness toward women of this historical course is clear, argued and documented in sources other than Rich's book. She goes one step further by arguing that the resulting patriarchal world has torn asunder the potentially integrated human being, whether they be male or female. Male has become equated with rationality, and the aggressive creation of the physical and intellectual world; in other words, he is God's image. The female is equated with the intuitive, the passive, and the untutored animal instincts. Hardly God's image, she is merely the unclean and sinful vessel which tempts the upright, rational man to lower himself to her level. This view seems to permeate institutions and individuals.

Finally, in this unnatural division, the resulting patriarchy which controls power in our society ultimately distorts and even makes violent the most important of relationships between man and woman, mother and daughter, mother and son. This is the outer structure of the book, and it is argued compellingly.

The inner structure is an attempt to chronicle, observe, and explain the author's own experience both as an artist and as a mother of three before she was thirty. She tries to convey that dark mixture of anger, responsibility, guilt, frustration, overwhelming love, and schizophrenic behavior that follows from motherhood, or at least from motherhood as the society defines it. Just as her argument is measured and controlled, so is her examination of her own experience of maternal darkness objective and intelligent.

As Rich would be the first to point out, it is difficult and unfair to search for analogues for art produced by women. Male artists have set the standard. When she began as a poet, she notes that the contemporary female poet most lauded by male critics was Marianne Moore. She also notes that Moore never so much as touches on female sexuality. Indeed, through all of literature Rich searches for a true portrait of a woman. All such studies are drawn from male perceptions, and whether sympathetic or not, they are not true to her experience. In fact they are detrimental insofar as their inaccuracies create false expectations in the female reader.

Nonetheless an analogue for *Of Woman Born* does exist: Joyce's *A Portrait of the Artist as a Young Man.* The underlying impetus in the two works is identical. Both define the urgency felt by the artist to define himself and his vocation. The questions dealt with in both works are basically the same: "Why am I doing what I'm doing? What part of my destiny is subconsciously chosen for me by my childhood, by my ethnic past, by my time in history?"

For Joyce, the answer was largely couched in terms of his emotional and intellectual interaction with his Irish Catholic heritage. For Rich, the answer is feminism. As she says,

> I could only go on working as a writer if I could fuse the woman and the poet, the woman and the thinker. This book comes out of the double need to survive and to work; and I wrote it in part for the young woman I once was, divided between body and mind, wanting to give her the book she was seeking, a perspective which would clarify the past and open ways of thinking and changing the future.

Finally, the impulse behind *Of Woman Born* is the impulse of an artist of whatever sex. From Shakespeare through Shelley to Joyce and Rich, the artist by various means inevitably is impelled to explain personally and justify socially his art. Viewed in this context. Rich's work is truly sexless despite her deep commitment to feminism.

There are two immediately perceivable flaws in this work which must be dealt with if only because the work succeeds so well. First, Rich talks at length about anthropological findings which strongly intimate the existence of prehistorical societies which were matriarchal. These were societies in which women were the creators, not only of children but of art and religion. Pottery, for instance, is believed to have been a sacred art practiced only by females. For the sake of the argument, one wishes that the evidence from such societies was stronger, more documented, and thus more arguable. Unfortunately, of necessity, discussion of many prehistorical practices must be mainly speculative.

Second, there is one important discipline which Rich mentions not at all: the study of animal behavior. In fact, one would think that findings and speculations in this area would have a great bearing on her thesis. Yet, Rich omits any mention of the work of such scientists as Konrad Lorenz or Jane Goodall, to mention only two of the most prominent present practitioners. More and more in doubt of his own survival and more and more questioning his own behavior, especially in groups, man is looking for clues to the social systems of various animals. Lorenz's *On Aggression* is a prime example of the importance and interest generated by animal behaviorists. The social systems, bond formations, and defenses and role playing of greylag geese, baboons, or lions could have been used by Rich as important considerations in discussing the present and historical position of the human female.

Admittedly, arguments from man's observations of what animals do and do not do and why they do it, have historically been fraught with inaccuracies. Man has been too willing to see only what he wanted to see, and, in addition, he has viewed such observations as manifestations of God's will in its purest sense. Present researchers into animal behavior can hardly be considered sexist, however, and Rich's failure to acknowledge their findings, especially since she seems aware of so many other areas of investigation, leaves the reader with a suspicion: Does she fear that such findings would be damaging to her argument? It is certainly a debatable and controversial question and one which deserves treatment.

Finally, although *Of Woman Born* is a work of polemics and history, it is also a work of art. At the least, it fulfills Emerson's definition of genius: "To believe your own thought, to believe what is true for you in your private heart is true for all men,—that is genius." ("Self Reliance," 1841)

Omit the word "men" and substitute "women" and one has a very exact description of *Of Woman Born.*

Susan Karnes Passler

Sources for Further Study

Book World. November 14, 1976, p. L1.
National Observer. XV, November 13, 1976, p. 23.
New Republic. CLXXV, November 6, 1976, p. 28.
New York Review of Books. XXIII, September 30, 1976, p. 16.
New York Times Book Review. October 10, 1976, p. 3.
Newsweek. LXXXVIII, October 18, 1976, p. 106.
Saturday Review. IV, November 13, 1976, p. 28.

OIL POWER
The Rise and Imminent Fall of an American Empire

Author: Carl Solberg
Publisher: Mason/Charter (New York). 326 pp. $12.50
Type of work: History
Time: 1859-1976
Locale: The United States

A survey of the history of oil and the oil industry in the United States

Principal personages:
JOHN D. ROCKEFELLER, founder of the Standard Oil Company
HENRY FORD, founder of the Ford Motor Company
JAMES HOGG, Governor of Texas in 1900

Carl Solberg's book, *Oil Power: The Rise and Imminent Fall of an American Empire* is both a comprehensive survey of the oil industry from the middle of the nineteenth century to the present and a description of the impact of oil and the oil industry on American society and life. The book seeks to document the marvelous historic advantages conferred by oil and the fact that our oil is almost used up. The book also describes the power of oil in government, in our public life, in our private lives, and in the creation of our technological civilization. Finally, the author argues that the American oil empire is rapidly becoming a thing of the past. As Americans seek other energy sources, the power and influence of the oil empire will wane. The author's view of the future is based on an excellent and highly readable survey of the history of the oil industry.

The American oil industry began with Edwin L. Drake's success in drilling for and finding oil in Titusville, Pennsylvania, in October, 1859. Drake's success began an oil boom similar to the California gold rush. Since American law granted subsoil wealth to those who owned the surface soil, Drake's discovery convinced Pennsylvanians and other Americans to buy Pennsylvania land and begin drilling. The atmosphere was intoxicating. John D. Rockefeller imbibed and became committed to the prospect of building an oil empire. Rockefeller had started in the produce business in Ohio and had built a fairly substantial operation by 1863. However, he sold that business and began to concentrate on—indeed, become obsessed with—oil.

At first the oil industry focused on the development of kerosene, which was used in lamps. Rockefeller was no innovator. He adopted the good ideas and techniques of his competitors and through diligence and cost-saving attention to detail, outproduced and outsold them. His costs were invariably the lowest in the industry, and this permitted him to make profits in times of national prosperity or depression.

Rockefeller entered the oil business just as American industry was beginning an industrial boom at the end of the Civil War. Rockefeller could not have selected a more appropriate moment. His characteristics of shrewdness, audacity, and ruthlessness served him well in the late nineteenth century. In pursuing his oil business, Rockefeller went to the railroads and received concessions from them. Rockefeller and his associates were effective in dominating the Cleveland area. The railroad rebates that Rockefeller obtained permitted him to undersell all of his competitors from western Pennsylvania. By 1870 Standard Oil had the largest refinery in America. By his thirtieth birthday, Rockefeller was a leading industrialist in Cleveland. Now he began an effort to establish a monopoly by destroying all of his competitors through his domination of railroads. The legislature of Pennsylvania prevented Rockefeller from establishing the monopoly that he sought, but he had other ways to accomplish his objective. Eventually coming to dominate refineries in Pittsburgh, Philadelphia, and New York in the early 1870's, Rockefeller even found the Panic of 1873 helpful in inducing competitors to sell out to him. Next, in the 1870's, he began his involvement in the pipeline industry.

The Standard Oil Trust was created in 1882 to combine control over many Rockefeller enterprises. In this, Rockefeller set the pattern for trusts all over the United States. In 1889 the Standard Oil Company was reincorporated as a New Jersey corporation. By this time, Standard had come to dominate most of America's refinery industry. Standard then made arrangements with firms elsewhere in the world to divide up the world's petroleum markets and thereby permit Rockefeller to place his products in every state of the United States and almost everywhere in the world. Solberg flatly states, "What Rockefeller aspired to was nothing less than world conquest."

Much as Rockefeller might have sought such a goal, the public became increasingly troubled about Standard Oil and frequently protested Rockefeller's activities as journalists, politicians, and governmental officials began to publicize and investigate his methods. Henry Demarest Lloyd, Ida Tarbell, and the Populists turned their ire on Rockefeller and Standard, but in spite of investigations and the public outcry, Rockefeller's empire remained intact, until in 1911 the Supreme Court dissolved the trust. By the late 1890's, however, Rockefeller was reducing the scope of his personal participation in his company and after 1900 was confining ever more of his attention to his family and to a new passion—golf.

It was curious that Rockefeller would turn away from oil at just the time that it became an integral part of American life. This was accomplished by three related phenomena—the enormous increase in the supply of oil resulting from discoveries in Texas; the widespread use of the automobile, stimulating demand; and the growing recognition of the political importance of oil, resulting in the oil depletion allowance.

The initial development of oil in Texas was attributable to the activities of Governor James Hogg of Texas. He accomplished two things of importance in oil. First, he kept Rockefeller and Standard Oil out of Texas; and second, he and his cronies bought up lease after lease in Texas after oil was discovered.

Ultimately they owned a large part of the developing fields. Then Hogg and his associates allowed the Mellons into Texas and the Gulf Oil Corporation was founded. Other investors founded the Texas Company. From Texas, the oil companies moved on to Louisiana and Oklahoma and then began constructing a complex of pipelines that became the most profitable part of the industry. Eventually arrangements were made among Standard, Gulf, Texas, Royal Dutch Shell in California, and foreign refiners before World War I. The result was a transition from Standard monopoly to oligopoly among the refiners.

While the refiners were organizing their empire, the automobile was becoming oil's chief customer. By 1911 in the United States, gasoline sales were greater than kerosene sales. By 1913 improvements in cracking processes helped meet the growing demand for gasoline. Servicing automobiles and providing them with a regular supply of gasoline was accomplished through the development of service or gas stations. As automobiles became an ever-more significant part of America, oil became a matter of public concern. Questions of conservation of oil rose and by 1918 Congress approved an oil depletion allowance to enhance conservation. The major oil corporations began to reap financial rewards in reductions of taxes. The oil depletion allowance established a close alliance between the oil companies and the United States Government that was to become even more friendly during World War I. Consequently, the oil companies became importantly involved in making public policy.

The relationship between the oil companies and government also led to abuses, the most blatant example of which was the Teapot Dome scandal. During the Harding administration, government-oil industry collusion resulted in reversing some of the public land policies of Presidents Theodore Roosevelt, William Howard Taft, and Woodrow Wilson. Oil companies were allowed into naval reserves previously retained for security purposes. As significant as the controversy was, however, Solberg concludes that in the prosperous decade of the 1920's Teapot Dome was soon forgotten.

In the period of the 1920's and 1930's, American society was fundamentally altered by oil. The automobile and the airplane changed life in many ways. Henry Ford, by developing assembly-line techniques and progressively reducing the cost of his basic automobile, made Americans dependent on the car. In turn, Americans demanded a continental road system, based on highway users paying for the highways through a gasoline tax. This was followed by the development of a uniform system of highway numbering. The oil companies too had undergone change. Most of the major firms had moved into all aspects of production, manufacturing, and marketing; they had become integrated. Moreover, they negotiated into existence the international cartel that established prices around the world.

The oil companies found it easy to deal with the administration of Franklin

Roosevelt in the 1930's, as Roosevelt relied on Sam Rayburn, who supported oil interests. The Roosevelt Administration did not interfere with the oil industry which sought to reduce output to keep prices fairly stable in spite of major discoveries of oil in Texas and elsewhere. Meanwhile, in the late 1930's the United States was being involved in circumstances that would lead to the start of World War II. The success of the Allies during the war was, in Solberg's view, directly dependent on Allied control of most of the world's oil. The problem of the Axis powers was that they literally ran out of gas.

On the home front, gas rationing was accompanied by the construction of additional pipelines. The growing demand for oil turned the attention of the United States and Franklin Roosevelt to the government of Saudi Arabia. By the end of the war, the major American oil companies had made private arrangements with the oil Shiekdoms all over the Middle East. This provided the United States with ample supplies of oil, but made the United States dependent on the Middle East in the years after World War II.

The end of World War II saw a society progressively dependent on mobility and oil. The price of gasoline remained low; it was taxed and the taxes were used to build highways. The public highway system was supported by state, local, and federal governments which ignored public transportation. Urban and suburban development grew around the highway system and was based on the availability of oil. Suburbia was also heated with oil and natural gas as Americans made a major switch away from coal. Hence, post-World War II social history was a product of automobility.

The oil and the automobile industries were also responsible for major technological changes after World War II. Automobiles became larger and more luxurious as they became more and more accessory-laden. This required additional horsepower, as did the new interest in acceleration. High compression engines resulted, with the pollution problems that they ultimately created. Improvements in transportation and the national highway system brought about the growth of the trucking industry. Although more expensive and inefficient than railroads, they eventually undermined the railroad freight industry, just as airplanes, buses, and cars undermined passenger rail service. Hence, America's dependence on oil grew, facilitated by close cooperation between government and the oil industry. The alliance and the operations of the oil companies remained, as they do today, hidden from public scrutiny.

As Americans became more and more dependent on oil, offshore oil deposits were viewed greedily by the oil industry. The critical question relating to offshore oil was who owned or should own the property. That determination was made during the Eisenhower administration when it was decided that the states should control tideland oil within the three-mile limit and the federal government would control offshore oil beyond the three-mile limit. As the state and federal governments leased their offshore property to private development, oil rigs began to sprout along American shores. Leases became more and more valuable until, in the winter of 1969, a blowout took place off Santa Barbara, California. The resulting enormous damage led to confining offshore operations to the Gulf of Mexico. But the oil companies continued to pressure the government to authorize drilling elsewhere along the coasts— particularly in the light of the shortages in the 1970's.

Those shortages in the 1970's were directly related to America's involvement with Middle East oil since World War II. Soon after the war, American oil companies were involved in obtaining concessions in the Middle East oil fields. Such deals were made because American oil producers realized that American supplies were finite. Meanwhile, west European and Japanese industrial recovery from World War II was based heavily on Middle East oil. In 1956 thirty percent of Europe's energy came from the Middle East. Europe and Japan became vulnerable to manipulation by the Arab countries.

As the Middle East loomed larger and larger in the world economy, the United States government sought to secure these areas against Soviet domination. American involvement in Iran and the Eisenhower Doctrine of the 1950's were based on this concern. The Suez crisis of 1956 ended the British and French empires in the Middle East and Soviet penetration of the area was increased. However, in the decade following the Suez crisis, the oil companies retained control over Middle East reserves and their profits grew enormously.

By 1960, however, the Arab nations were becoming independent. In that year, Exxon slashed the posted price of oil. In response, an angry Saudi Arabia began activities leading to the formation of the Organization of Petroleum Exporting Countries, or OPEC—a cartel of eleven oil producers. While the impact of OPEC was not great at first, in 1969 Libya showed OPEC how to exert its authority. In that year Libya's ruler, Muammar Qaddafi, demanded and received an increase of oil payments to Libya; other Arab nations demanded and received similar increases in payment. OPEC now had the power and methods to control oil production in their countries and raise oil prices at will—and the major American companies supported their manipulation. By 1971, led by Saudi Arabia, OPEC countries demanded shares of the ownership of oil concessions. The oil companies were forced to agree to OPEC's demands and made arrangements whereby 51% of the ownership of production would be in Arab hands by 1983.

From exerting their newly acquired power, it was a short step to the oil embargo of 1973-1974. Traditionally the United States since World War II had never purchased more than six percent of its oil from the Middle East. At the urging of the oil companies, that purchase of oil had increased to eighteen percent in 1973 and made the United States vulnerable to Arab oil pressure and dramatic increases in prices. The Yom Kippur War in the Middle East in 1973 served as the pretext to raise oil prices and embargo oil. The Arab nations were able to use this weapon very effectively. As the Arab countries took over complete control of the oil companies, the system created by the oil companies to control world oil collapsed and was also taken over by the Arabs. In this context, the United States has increased rather than reduced its dependence on Middle East oil to almost fifty percent. In the four years since the oil embargo, oil prices have increased greatly and have generated economic crises around the world. Meanwhile, the oil companies have been able to maintain enormous profits for themselves. The same types of manufactured shortages and manipulation, according to Solberg, have been exerted by the oil and natural gas producers in regard to natural gas production. Thus, America's energy resources have undergone major changes in the last four years.

Having sketched the rise of oil power in the United States, Solberg turns in his last chapter to a description of the decline of that empire as he briefly traces the environmental and economic impact of America's high consumption economy. He indicates that the future holds two certainties—"The age of cheap oil is over, and there will be unavoidable pain and turmoil while the nation restructures its economy." Solberg contends that conversion to other energy sources would eventually end the grip of oil on America. Had the United States not depended so heavily on oil, however, that transition would have been easier. Solberg concludes his interesting account with a brief description of alternative sources of energy.

The Solberg book is a well-written, comprehensive survey of the oil industry and the way that it became an integral part of American life. The author sustains interest as he skillfully moves from political, to economic, to social history, to international relations, and to public policy. He effectively combines all of these disciplines in his wide-ranging study. *Oil Power* should be read by all who wish to understand the contemporary United States and the current energy crisis. The author has done a magnificent job of presenting a richly textured study and an intelligent analysis. This is an exciting and thought-provoking history.

Saul Lerner

Sources for Further Study

Choice. XIII, June, 1976, p. 568.

Christian Science Monitor. LXVIII, February 19, 1976, p. 23.

Library Journal. CI, January 15, 1976, p. 351.

Publisher's Weekly. CCVIII, December 1, 1975.

ON BEING BLUE
A Philosophical Inquiry

Author: William Gass (1924-   )
Publisher: David R. Godine (Boston). 91 pp. $10.00
Type of work: Literary criticism

A literal and metaphorical use of the color blue to analyze sex in literature, the nature of perception, and the writer's love of language

In this essay on sex in literature, William Gass contends that the color blue, like the idea of love (which he implies is the compulsion to saturate), invokes the tone and mood of a variety of subjects and meanings, for it is the color of the human impulse to meditate, appropriate, complete. Pointing out how popular blue is in the ordinary speech of frustration and awe as well as in literature, Gass elaborately describes both the blue-bound books of his boyhood and the "blue" photo of the nude girl he treasured at that period of his life. As he later alludes to Aristotle, Descartes, Schopenhauer, Berenson, and other philosophers to explore the nature of color and perception, Gass refers to writers such as Barth, Hawkes, Colette, and Flaubert to exemplify the best use of sex in literature.

The author begins by insisting that it is useless to depict sex directly in a literary work. In the first place, to describe sex detail by detail fails to include or produce the feelings that belong to it. Moreover, the closer a writer approaches sex, the less he sees of it, and so the less justice he can do to the feelings which make it an actual experience. At times a writer such as Henry Miller, presenting details through metaphors, will enlarge sex beyond its mechanical limits, but in general the writer must stand back from this subject to redeem it. Without this distance, he impairs his freedom to manipulate the design of his work, for he exaggerates a part at the expense of the whole, and is unable to interrupt or rearrange the part (for example, placing climax before stimulation) without seeming ridiculous.

As for words themselves, Gass explains that our vocabulary of sex reveals hostility and contempt. There are too few of these words to distinguish among the physical and emotional varieties of a given sexual act. The writers who use these words usually betray not only a hatred for what they mean and an impoverished imagination, but extraneous motives like profit or fear of seeming out of date. Gass inquires why sex cannot have the same verbal abundance which the word blue has to the extent that the things and conditions it refers to and the word itself are loved.

The good writer is better off approaching sex indirectly. In John Hawkes's *The Lime Twig,* for example, sex is only implied when the character Thick beats Margaret with a truncheon. Since the language of this scene relies on unadorned descriptions and understated similes, and extends to the room the victim and her assailant occupy, the meaning of the scene comes into existence as the verbal texture itself, and this is the new experience of the old subject the reader undergoes. Flaubert and Colette write with a similar objectivity and care, for it is, Gass concludes, the sound become image, "the flesh made word," that matter when one is writing about love.

The vital blue in things which such writing reveals also exists in the reader, though the "blue eye" of lust is often the mode of this energy he brings to the text, just as it is the mode an artist can paralyze his work in the service of. The photograph of the nude girl which Gass presents earlier in his essay illustrates these *a priori* expectations. The photographer produced an amateur work because he cared nothing for art, only for the money that lust would pay to see it. The viewer is a boy, however, whose inexperience treats sex as a mystery and thus raises the snapshot, including its unintentional details (such as the weed growing between the steps), to the status of an icon. The problem for the literature of sex, Gass assures us, is how to lure the blue already in the eye of the beholder into its best meanings, as the mature Gass tries to do by his re-creation of the photograph in *On Being Blue*.

As a writer, Gass admits that every other consideration in his essay leads to the love for language. The good writer knows that "Sex as a positive aesthetic quality" can only occur in a work where, as in Beckett's description of Molloy's dilemma of the stones, there is no euphemism, no awkward rhythm or pace, no monochromatic syntax, no waste of any kind.

In his anatomy of language, Gass contends that words have layers. When we swear, for example, we mean something other than what we literally say, we imply a hostility not contained in the words themselves, and we reveal through this implication a despotic nature. Moreover, words can state, suggest, or escape a meaning. Gass calls such an escape "utterance," and a writer is guilty of it when he cares not for words themselves but about what others might think of them or of him for writing them. Even the word blue can be used carelessly and disposably in this way. But blue is also a word we love, which is why we return over and over to the lists and reference works in which it occurs, and why we regard it highly, and use it extensively, as a symbol.

Philosophers may have traditionally treated color as merely an aspect of substance, but Gass argues that blue is an essence in itself, and as such has a meaning beyond shape (the distance a color goes before it vanishes) and form (the relation among the vertical and horizontal, the exterior and interior modes of shape). Blue is "the color of the interior life," and though it has an emotional range as various as the instances of earth, air, fire, and water which complement it, it is a recessive color, and ultimately lends itself less to arrival than pursuit, less to sexual climax than to the meditation after it.

To see is to distinguish and compare. To do this well, to write well, requires distance and concentration. If the writer's intelligence pays attention to its own biases, his feelings will not deceive him; sex will not enter his work as a superficial and damaged notion, but will come into being as verbal strategies which contain "knowing" and which induct the reader into the pleasure of using his own mind.

One must admire Gass for his practical and sensitive view of language, perception, and the relation of sex to both in literature. From a philosophical standpoint, his essay takes issue with science for its narrow view of phenomena, and with metaphysics for its overfastidious view of being. Based on a love for language mortified by the corruption of love itself in the art of the time, the aesthetic of his essay projects itself through the words Gass loves, the writers he esteems, and the style in which he writes about style itself.

For *On Being Blue* is first and last about the writer's love for words, and though it follows the structure of reasoned discourse, it also proceeds by resonant analogies which suggest that the theme of blue finally exists as the style in which it is presented. Indeed, as in his *In the Heart of the Heart of the Country*, where the language of place and event *is* the situation and feelings of the narrator, Gass convenes a "blue" dialect in *On Being Blue* to put the reader as much in the presence of being or "quality" as the beloved is by the sound of the lover.

Mark McCloskey

Sources for Further Study

Booklist. LXXIII, November 1, 1976, p. 382.
Christian Century. XCIII, November 24, 1976, p. 1061.
New Republic. CLXXV, October 9, 1976, p. 38.
New York Review of Books. XXIII, August 5, 1976, p. 36.
New York Times. CXXVI, October 4, 1976, p. 25.
Time. CVIII, November 15, 1976, p. 98.

ORDINARY PEOPLE

Author: Judith Guest
Publisher: The Viking Press (New York). 263 pp. $7.95
Type of work: Novel
Time: The present
Locale: A suburb of Chicago

A modern domestic novel portraying the turmoil and guilt an average suburban family experiences following the failed suicide attempt of their seventeen-year-old son

> *Principal characters:*
> CONRAD JARRETT, a seventeen-year-old boy recently discharged
> from a mental institution
> CALVIN JARRETT, his father
> BETH JARRETT, his mother
> DR. T. C. BERGER, Conrad's modern, unpredictable psychiatrist
> JEANNINE PRATT, Conrad's first formal date

Conrad Jarrett, unable to understand why he survived a boating accident in which his older brother Buck drowned, slits his wrists, spends eight months in a mental hospital and, as the novel opens, arrives home perhaps in only slightly better mental and emotional shape then when he left on a stretcher.

Judith Guest's first novel, *Ordinary People* is set in a Chicago suburb, Lake Forest, near Northwestern University. But the specific location is superfluous. It could be any suburban town, perhaps any family in modern America. Guest attempts to portray the turmoil and guilt an average suburban family experiences following the drowning death of their oldest son, Jordan (Buck) Jarrett, and the near suicide of their other son, Conrad. Conrad, seventeen-year-old A-student, member of the high school choir and swim team, and avid golfer, feels guilt for surviving the boating accident that claimed Buck's life, feels guilt for having lived, and so decides to die.

The novel deals not only with Conrad's year-long recovery through counseling and his eight-month hospital stay, but also with the disintegration of the family. As Conrad understands and deals with his feelings and accepts his limitations, his parents, unable any longer to understand or to communicate with each other, separate. In addition, as Conrad returns to Lake Forest and reenters the world he left—school, choir, swimming—he confronts the typical reaction of people who look at him askance, questioning his stability, looking at the scars left on his wrists.

Judith Guest, a forty-one-year-old suburban Minneapolis housewife-turned-novelist, submitted her unsolicited manuscript for *Ordinary People* to Viking Press, and after waiting more than a year was notified that it had been accepted for publication. For the first time in twenty-seven years Viking accepted an over-the-transom manuscript that lacked even a query letter. Once accepted, the book, which took three years to write, quickly made the bestseller list, was placed on several book-of-the-month club lists, and was sold to Robert Redford for a movie. Guest, a former Michiganite, received a degree in education from the University of Michigan, taught elementary school for three years, and worked briefly as a reporter for a newspaper. Her brief sojourn with the newspaper was her only writing experience; she had no formal training while attending the University.

Each of the ordinary people in the novel is plagued by guilt. Conrad, who goes to Dr. T. C. Berger, the unpredictable modern psychiatrist, twice a week to learn "to be more in control," blames himself for his brother's death. He believes that his guilt contaminates everyone with whom he comes in contact. Events pile up, seemingly providing Conrad with support for his theory concerning himself. Not only does Buck, the stronger, older, idolized brother drown while Conrad, the weaker one, endures the ocean storm, clinging to the overturned dismasted sailboat and surviving, but also while in the mental hospital months later a fellow patient commits suicide by burning himself to death. Again Conrad believes that evil surrounds him and contaminates others when, after his release, a girl whom he met while in the hospital asphyxiates herself several months after her release. Conrad becomes convinced, as these events pile up, that he infects everyone he comes in contact with. He believes "all connections with him result in failure. Loss. Evil."

The conflicts in the novel deal with guilt and its spread, especially among members of the Jarrett family, and with forgiveness. These conflicts are resolved when the protagonist recognizes, understands, and then sheds unnecessary guilt, realizing that punishment does not erase guilt, that depression is merely "reduction of feeling," and that feeling and the expression of it is better than taking refuge, by controlling feeling.

Conrad, during a large part of the novel, has no self-love. In fact, he barely has a self, so confused has his identity become with his brother Buck's. Buck was the idol whom he tried through their limited lifetime together to imitate even to the point of dying. As the reader learns through flashbacks about Conrad's constant attempt to be like Buck, he questions whether Buck's death was perhaps necessary for Conrad's life and identity to begin.

Conrad begins to acquire self-knowledge only after Karen, a teen-ager hospitalized and released at about the same time as Conrad, kills herself. Distraught with guilt, feeling as though he infected Karen, Conrad arrives at Berger's office, and after key questions, Conrad reveals the gap created by his brother's death and the guilt associated with Buck's drowning. And so it seems a new beginning is possible for Conrad, for he begins to achieve his own identity instead of living through his deceased brother.

Yet other conflicts exist, particularly with Conrad's parents, who share extensively the center of attention in the novel. Cal Jarrett, a forty-one-year-old tax attorney who takes pride in his ability to provide for his family, becomes obsessed with responsibility for, duty to, and protection of his son, an attitude which irritates his wife Beth. Cal believes he is guilty for Conrad's attempted suicide and thinks "it has to be his fault, because fault equals responsibility equals control equals eventual understanding." Beth, a thirty-nine-year-old socialite suburban housewife known for her perfectionist tendencies, wants family life to return to the old pattern of orderliness, vacations, golf, and tennis. She avoids stress situations, and so she avoids Conrad, whom she thinks hates her. Her avoidance, though, is also based on her inability to forgive. When Conrad attempted suicide she termed it a "vicious" thing. Yet as Conrad grows in understanding himself, he also grows in understanding his mother and her limited ability to love him or forgive him.

The author shows a keen insight into the psychological underpinning of the adolescent mind; her presentation of Conrad shows an ability to probe in descriptive detail the inner sanctions of the human mind. Even Conrad's father is fully developed. Orphaned in youth, he believes family unity is important, and he tries constantly to preserve the family, to fulfill what he deems his duty, to be in control of every situation, thus "protecting [himself] from further guilt." He too seeks Berger's assistance. Frustrated because he cannot control his family, Cal feels his son and wife are on opposite sides of the fence "and that both are drifting . . . while I stand there watching."

But Guest falls short in creating and developing Beth, her sole important female character. We never understand why she cannot handle emotional traumas, why she thinks Conrad hates her, or why she must desert her family; Guest's reasoning here is weak. As the mother of three sons herself, she understands the problems and the feelings of adolescent males, but perhaps she was too close to the character of Beth to be objective. Dr. T. C. Berger, Conrad's psychiatrist, is often overdone. He is the man with ready answers who offers coffee to his patients and often helps them and the reader with his quick wit. Guest wants him to be unpredictable in his counseling techniques, modern enough to be strange and likeable to the variety of patients he sees; but her effort here shows.

Nevertheless, Guest's dynamic development of Conrad, her ability to present his anxieties, his fears, his desires, and his hopes serves to compensate for the flaws in her characterization of Berger and Beth. Although the tone is serious throughout the novel, often the conversations between Dr. Berger and Conrad are humorous, altering the tone and offering the reader relief from the burden of guilt all members of the family experience.

Told from the omniscient point of view, with combined use of stream of consciousness, Guest examines in detail the inner thoughts of Conrad's and Cal's minds. Dreams and memories, which are often symbolic, emerge particularly well when Guest uses stream of consciousness. The author's use of the device emphasizes the workings of the human mind and certainly helps the reader understand the conscious and subconscious lives of Conrad and Cal. But because Guest moves in time, place, and character, we are often uncertain who the stream of consciousness speaker is; that is, we often must stop to determine whose thought is being revealed to us. Often it is Conrad, but frequently, and without notice, it shifts to Cal. Although such shifts confuse the reader and appear to be flaws in the novel, the reader becomes increasingly aware of the similarities between Conrad's personality and his father's; thus we begin to realize that perhaps Guest's motivation behind shifting the stream of consciousness narrator was meant to demonstrate this similarity.

One of the major points Guest stresses in *Ordinary People* is that each individual is a free agent, not responsible for the actions of other people. Conrad, after eight months in a mental hospital and another year of counseling, understands finally that Buck drowned because he lacked the physical endurance to hold on, that Karen, acting as an individual, although unstable, chose death over life, and finally that Beth's decision to leave was no reflection on him. Each individual exercised his right to choose, and blame is nonexistent; guilt, consequently, leads only to self-defeat and self-effacement, rather than growth and understanding. However, Guest also shows the problems in constantly maintaining self-control and control of others, rather than allowing feeling to surface and be expressed. And finally, she emphasizes the unnecessary pain endured in assigning blame for actions when in reality fault is nonexistent. The Jarrett family learns in the end that what happened to their lives was "nobody's fault."

But the ending seems too planned, too pat. Conrad's growth and gradual change is certainly credible; we expect him to change, develop, and grow in awareness. But Cal, who visits Berger only once, suddenly has all the answers, or, in his newfound awareness, sees that there are no answers.

This conventional domestic novel, flawed as it is in literary terms, shows keen sensitivity and is well worth reading. It reaches out to a varied audience but will be of particular interest to students, teachers, counselors, and parents, for it shows insight into the workings and malfunctions of the family unit.

Janet H. Hobbs

Sources for Further Study

America. CXXXV, August 21, 1976, p. 81.

Christian Science Monitor. August 5, 1976, p. 19.

New York Review of Books. XXIII, June 10, 1976, p. 8.

Newsweek. LXXXVIII, July 12, 1976, p. 71.

Saturday Review. III, May 15, 1976, p. 34.

Time. CVIII, July 19, 1976, p. 68.

Village Voice. XXI, July 19, 1976, p. 36.

ORSINIAN TALES

Author: Ursula K. Le Guin (1929-   )
Publisher: Harper & Row Publishers (New York). 179 pp. $7.95
Type of work: Short stories

A collection of nine realistic stories and two historical fantasies by the prominent science fiction author

Ursula K. Le Guin is one of the most highly praised authors of the past decade. Within science fiction circles, her name immediately enters discussions of the best writers in the field: her fellow professionals in the Science Fiction Writers Association have twice honored her work with the Nebula Award for the best novel of the year—for *The Left Hand of Darkness* in 1969 and *The Dispossessed* in 1974. But one wonders how well Le Guin is known outside the genre. In larger circles she is likely to be known as the recipient of the National Book Award for children's literature for the three novels of her Earthsea trilogy. But defining those three books—*A Wizard of Earthsea, The Tombs of Atuan,* and *The Farthest Shore*—strictly as children's literature is like saying that *Alice in Wonderland* or *The Lord of the Rings* are only children's books. In her five award-winning novels (not to mention a number of others), she has built up an immense reputation in two specialized fields, but one that is scarcely felt in the literary mainstream. It sometimes happens that a movie actor gives an especially fine portrayal, but the excellence of the work is recognized too late for the presentation of an Oscar for the role. Hence, the next year finds the actor being voted the award for a much inferior part, as a kind of compensation. It is hard to avoid the feeling that something of that sort has happened to bring *Orsinian Tales* a nomination for a National Book Award.

Orsinian Tales is a collection of eleven stories; their publication dates span Le Guin's career, from the earliest, "An die Musik," first published in 1961, to the latest, "The Barrow," reprinted from a 1976 issue of *The Magazine of Fantasy and Science Fiction.* Yet, although they cover by far the greatest part of her writing career, a set of short stories less characteristic of her work could not have been assembled. In fact, an award for *Orsinian Tales* would be a kind of insult, as if one were to ignore the south forty acres and judge a farmer's work by the potted plant in the living room.

To evaluate *Orsinian Tales,* one must begin with the fact that Le Guin is a writer of science fiction and fantasy; all nine of her novels fall into that category, as does the greater part of her shorter works. But a science fiction novel is not easier to write nor less capable of reaching the limits of art than any other kind; indeed, Le Guin is one of the writers who in recent years has done much to prove the truth of these assertions. For fifteen years she has been writing science fiction and fantasy that suffer not at all by comparison with the work of any other living writer. Her work therefore arouses an expectation in the reader who purchases a volume by Le Guin that he is buying science fiction. The publishers of *Orsinian Tales* contribute to the maintenance of this assumption by the book jacket description of the stories as set in "imaginary countries inhabited by imaginary people with real problems." The reader's chief surprise is likely to be the discovery that the setting of all but two of the stories is not fairy land, or Earth of the future, or some far planet, but central Europe from 1900 to the present.

Although the setting of the stories of *Orsinian Tales* is never stated, and one will not find the towns listed in an atlas, the insertion of a few words suffices to locate them in Hungary or Czechoslovakia or Rumania. The inhabitants spend *kroner*, for example; they revolt against Soviet dominance in 1956. At another point, some characters go to church, to Lutheran services. Ah, one thinks, perhaps Sudetenland Germans, but nothing else supports or contradicts this impression. The musical instruments played, as another example, are not those specific to a particular folk culture, and therefore, identifiable, but those common to the whole of the Western world—a guitar in one instance, a bass viol in another. But these are exceptional details; in general, the stories are not particularized enough to identify them more precisely, and here is one of the principal problems in the execution of the stories. By contrast, in *The Left Hand of Darkness,* the plot moves through two large countries, Karhide and Orgoreyn, on the world of Gethen; the two are as different as Sweden and Portugal. One need not be told that the action is located in one country or the other; the manners of the people, the customs, even the languages tell us where we are. Similarly for *The Dispossessed:* a rich and abundant detailing differentiates the moon of Anarres from the nation of A-Io on the planet Urras.

Similarly, Le Guin has always supplied generous detail in her fantasy and science fiction: the characters in those works, in settings so strange to us, come equipped with features, habits, quirks, and customs. The characters of *Orsinian Tales,* in mundane settings, are curiously faceless, although we know that one is big and has large hands, another is small and nervous, and so on. The reason for their lifelessness may be their lack of identifying detail, their interchangeability, so to speak, with one another or with someone living now. Nevertheless, the characters of *Orsinian Tales* are plausibly drawn. If some of them seem dull or humdrum, their personalities reflect the ordinary lives they lead or their desire to conceal some inner depth from the world. A character in "A Week in the Country" explains why he plays the bass viol rather than the cello, and the few words of his answer provide a Joycean epiphany, revealing his fate and that of any artist unlucky enough to live under an oppressive regime. What he says give us an insight not only into his character but into his society, an insight too seldom achieved in the collection.

If the characters of the collection are at least competently drawn, the plots are defficient. Like her settings, Le Guin's plots lack the virtues she has so often shown in her science fiction. Shakespeare knew that interior conflict was not enough; it must be plausibly joined with exterior conflict to show the full range of human behavior. Interior, or psychological, conflict alone gives us *Portnoy's Complaint;* exterior conflict or mere adventure alone gives us *The Three Musketeers.* But where the pressures and tensions outside the character reinforce or counter those inside, where the detective moves closer to the arrest as Raskolnikov moves closer to breakdown, we have *Crime and Punishment;* when a young prince edges to and from madness while his uncle plots his death, we have *Hamlet.* Le Guin shows the joining of these inside and outside worlds in her novels: for example, as Shevek in *The Dispossessed* comes to understand his own unique needs and desires, his individual quest occurs against a background of global famine, space trips from planet to planet, wars, and revolutions.

As an illustration of a plot mainly concerned with interior conflict, "Ile Forest" tells the story of a boy and a girl who are uncertain of their love for each other, and are not sure that marriage is right for them. Their parents or relatives doubt that the union will work, but are not adamant against it. Money is a problem, but not an insurmountable one. After some conversation together and some meditation apart, they decide the reward is worth the risk, and get married. Here, we would agree, the conflict is mental: the obstacles to be overcome are primarily in the characters' minds, and very little happens in the way of incident. But if the story had been placed between a pair of adventures, dominated by action, peopled by characters who also faced problems in the external world, the reader would have enjoyed a change of pace and a demonstration of the author's versatility. Instead, Le Guin uses the simpler, less interesting plotline of "Ile Forest" again in "Conversations at Night" and yet again in "Brothers and Sisters." Yet, when compared with "A Week in the Country," in which the love story is set against conflicts in the larger political world, the relative dullness and repetitiveness of the earlier three stories become apparent.

The last story in the book, "Imaginary Countries," perhaps provides both an explanation of the author's motive in the collection and a reason for its failure. Set in 1935, it is the story of a brief summer vacation that an aristocratic family takes at their country house. The characters all have rich and fulfilling lives of the mind to join to their very comfortable ones in the real world: the father, who barely appears on the edges of the story, is "Baron Severin Egideskar, holder of the Follen Chair of Medieval Studies at the University of Krasnoy." The children, on whom the story focuses, find their lives of the mind not in history but in the worlds of myth and fantasy. For the youngest, it is the fantasy of the bridges and tunnels he builds for his toy cars in the soft earth. His is a miniature model of the real world. The older children play at being Thor and Odin in a wood nearby; their reading gives detail to their mythological model. As C. S. Lewis remarks in another context, reading about the tree Yggdrasil makes ordinary trees seem a little magical.

If we take this story, with its suggestive title, as a key to the meaning of the collection as a whole, then the author is saying something very curious, something that, if it is true, runs counter to her purpose in her work as a whole, and even contradicts the meaning of the finest story in the collection. At the end of "Imaginary Countries," the family members speak with regret of their impending return to their regular pursuits. They wish they could remain with their imaginations at the summer house. But they pack up and return to the city at the end, and the author closes the story with the words, "all this happened a long time ago, nearly forty years ago; I do not know if it happens now, even in imaginary countries." But it does happen; it happens in the science fiction and fantasies of Ursula Le Guin, for one place. Those "weeks in the country" are still possible, always possible, so long as we have access to living and breathing worlds of the imagination, worlds that tell us things about ourselves that we can learn from no other source. As "An die Musik" tells us, the usefulness of music is that it has no use; our persistent desire for it teaches us that utility is not the highest value. As with music, so with fiction. Fantasy teaches us something that the naturalistic novel does not and cannot. It is not coincidence, nor merely a matter of their authors' respective skills, that *Alice in Wonderland* is alive while *Uncle Tom's Cabin* is dead. The Earthsea trilogy, *The Left Hand of Darkness*, and *The Dispossessed* show that Le Guin knows this, and her knowledge and imagination have combined to expand and deepen our lives in a way that a million soap operas never will. Those novels are the imaginary countries, not the stories of *Orsinian Tales;* it is their fantasy that will make them treasured when *Orsinian Tales* is forgotten.

Walter E. Meyers

Sources for Further Study

America. CXXXIV, February 7, 1976, p. 107.

Booklist. LXXIII, September 15, 1976, p. 122.

Kirkus Reviews. XLIV, August 15, 1976, p. 912.

Library Journal. CI, October 1, 1976, p. 2086.

New Republic. CLXXIV, February 7, 1976, p. 28.

Times Literary Supplement. July 30, 1976, p. 950.

THE PAINTER OF SIGNS

Author: R. K. Narayan (1906-   )
Publisher: The Viking Press (New York). 183 pp. $8.95
Type of work: Novel
Time: 1972
Locale: Malgudi, a fictional city in India

A short novel of the love affair of Raman and Daisy, two young modern Indians who must confront the social forces, cultural conflicts, and diverse lifestyles of traditional and modern India as they seek to fulfill their love for each other

> *Principal characters:*
> RAMAN, a painter of signs
> DAISY, the family-planning agent assigned to the Malgudi district
> LAXMI, Raman's aunt who reared him from infancy

This latest novel by R. K. Narayan narrates a moving tale of young lovers in a changing society. The social forces include not only traditional Indian customs and beliefs but also the European intellectual traditions and ideas which have been disseminated throughout India. In addition, the impact of Western civilization in its technological innovations and its zeal for efficiency is a force of major concern in the progress of the tale. But this is not primarily a social novel. It is rather the revelation of the impact that these multifarious forces have upon the psyches of the principal characters, a condition which gives a richness and depth to the characterizations and to the levels of meaning implied in the events of the story.

The major premise underlying *The Painter of Signs* must be the conviction that people are products of their training, and that they cannot disengage themselves from their past lessons so that they might think and act independently, even though such conditioned behavior leads to heartache and loneliness. The dispersal of Raman, Daisy, and Laxmi at the conclusion, each to go their separate ways to fulfill their roles as they have been taught, despite the deep love Laxmi feels for Raman, and the ardent attraction which Daisy and Raman feel for each other, surely represents the total triumph of behavioral psychology. Minor characters in the novel are similarly entrapped by the activities and viewpoints they espouse. A sense of rich, teeming, vigorous liveliness results from the interaction of these people with Raman, and, through him, with one another.

Daisy, Raman, his aunt, and indeed all the characters in this novel seem less to be decisive, dynamic persons than hapless victims of the social turmoil of India today. The elderly aunt, who has devoted her life to caring for the orphaned Raman, is the very embodiment of ancient, traditional values and practices. Her entire existence, an unvarying routine, consists of caring for Raman and the house, preparing traditional foods, and attending the evening services at the temple. So circumscribed a world cannot admit the totally Westernized Daisy, whom Raman wishes to bring into the household as his bride. The aunt's departure on her pilgrimage to find death beside the Ganges represents on the surface the sulking pettiness of an old woman angered at the prospect of giving place to a beautiful young bride. But viewing the act apart from the momentary provocation, it represents the tenacious hold of traditional ritual and religious belief in determining the course of life and death in India today, even as in the bygone centuries.

Daisy's atheism and indulgent indifference to religion (so long as religious traditions do not impinge upon her family-planning activities) represents the "liberated" viewpoint, one which the author plainly depicts as a minority opinion in his fictional Indian microcosm of Malgudi. Her militant espousal of social change, her rejection of traditional customs and values, her ascetic self-denial of any personal comforts, and her almost fanatic zeal in pursuing her family-planning goals, all reveal her as the thoroughly conditioned product of her early training by a missionary whom she quotes whenever Raman or others try to suggest to her that other values might have merit. Daisy's rejection of marriage to Raman in favor of family-planning work is entirely consistent with her training, and her strength of character is finally a kind of mindless automated behavior for which she has been programmed. She remains a very human and touching person in her lapses from her own behavioral goals. Her weeping, her seeking out of Raman after their first quarrel, her admission of her love for him, and her sexual responsiveness are all evidences of an underlying warmth and emotional nature that she cannot entirely suppress.

Raman, reared in a traditional Hindu household by his devout aunt, educated in a college stressing the emancipated beliefs of the age of enlightenment, and committed by his occupation to communication of information, is at the center of the vortex of the winds of change. Forced to communicate through painting the signs, he is troubled by his lack of conviction about what he communicates.

His lack of commitment is underscored by his longing to retire from his work to a farm, by his ascetic attempt to expunge sexual desires, by his troubled cynicism about producing signs in which he does not believe. Raman's training in Western logic and ideas of the enlightenment will not let him truly believe in the ancient Hindu gods, but neither will his emotional ties to his past and to his aunt let him totally reject the traditions of India and the Hindu religion. In his contacts with customers for his signs, he is similarly disturbed by the conflict between his need to satisfy his clients and his need to paint signs which aesthetically and intellectually satisfy him.

Raman's abandonment of his zeal for rationalism in any practical situation when insistence upon rational thought would alienate clients, townspeople, friends, or especially Daisy or Laxmi, reveals an ambivalence within him. He idealizes rational thought, but willingly foregoes his ideal in order to satisfy his deep emotional need to be accepted and loved by others. He reproaches himself for his timidity, but is in fact choosing an emotional value which is stronger within him than the intellectual one. Because of these conflicts, Raman is at the mercy of the decisions of others, including all the minor characters in the story.

A pragmatic, unexamined solution to the conflicts involved in the clash of cultures is embodied in the neighbors, who manage to couple sincere belief and reverence for tradition with a practical adaptation to modern conveniences and creature comforts.

It is this spectrum of attitudes and beliefs—and the clashes, compromises, and changes which inevitably must come about—which are the central theme of Narayan's novel. The tragedy of the romance is not only that Daisy and Raman must part, and that Laxmi and Raman will never see each other again, but it is also that the crucial human values of love, tenderness, tolerance, and sexual fulfillment are rejected in favor of commitment to a social goal on Daisy's part, and to a religious commitment on Laxmi's part.

The attitudes and convictions of Raman, Daisy, Laxmi and the neighbor with whom Laxmi is to travel represent a cross-section of those prevailing in India today. The conflicts of the characters are the conflicts of these apparently irreconcilable differences. If this were all, the novel would be an interesting fictional study of social changes. But the author establishes within each of his principal characters a conflict between the character's own values and his emotional needs. The conflict is particularly acute in Raman, who does not even have the intense polarization of beliefs which sustain Daisy and Laxmi in their decisions.

The love of Raman and Daisy is a strong physical attraction. Both resist it intellectually because it does not logically fit into their plans or their lifestyles. But both must finally succumb to its strength, and the impending intimacy of marriage forces a confrontation of the value systems Raman and Daisy represent. Daisy's coldness to traditional values and her commitment to social reform in the form of family planning are her dominant characteristics; she has been shaped by a missionary into a totally dedicated advocate of Western technology, propaganda, and values. She devotes her life to preventing life; not only is she a tireless propagandist and dispenser of devices for contraception, but she insists that she would reject any child which might by accident be born to her and Raman. Daisy is likewise unmoved by Raman's anguish over his aunt's departure and pilgrimage to death beside the Ganges. Daisy has rejected her Indian identity altogether. Even the name she has adopted is foreign. She represents the clinical, objective, efficient Western world—seeing India through Western eyes—determined to impose Western values, methodology, and efficiency upon a bemused and generally tolerant populace of Malgudi, and upon the love-stricken Raman as their lives become entwined.

But Raman, the central figure, through whose point of view the story unfolds, is a figure of lesser strength and lesser commitment because he is a creature of vastly greater complexity than either Laxmi or Daisy. Emotionally, he espouses things which are intellectually incompatible. As a self-proclaimed rationalist he is uncomfortable with his emotional involvements. He can act neither upon his convictions nor upon his reservations about the convictions of others which involve him.

Raman is the painter of signs. Hired by Daisy, his propaganda signs for family planning are by far his largest commercial contract. With Daisy, as with all his clients, he serves their needs in his work but lacks conviction about the messages he paints and posts. Signs are necessary, he feels, to communication. And yet he is troubled that he paints signs only to earn money, rather than to communicate the truth to people. And so he justifies his work by a fiercely stubborn commitment to the artistry of the lettering and the appropriate choice of colors. He can espouse no cause with conviction, and so he lacks the forcefulness and assurance of either his aunt or Daisy. His abortive attempt to rape Daisy—an attempt to assert his mastery over the situation through physical dominance—comes to naught because Daisy slips away while he hesitates in order to convince himself that he is doing the right thing. Daisy and the aunt, by contrast, pursue and fulfill their convictions unhesitatingly, even though this act means abandoning Raman and their home with him. Through them, East and West still contend for the allegiance of India. But Raman, a hybrid product of both cultures, cannot commit himself fully to either, and when he is left alone, he turns to that refuge of no commitment, The Boardless—so called because it is an inn where there is no sign to communicate any message at all.

In loading the characters with such strong symbolism that they come to border on caricature, Narayan diminishes the reader's sympathy for them. Raman is not ultimately tragic, but rather pitiful, and his retreat to anonymity represents the assertion of the author that the future of India—culturally, intellectually, and technologically—is most uncertain. The painter of signs, the young Indian intellectual, is not giving unequivocal direction to his nation because he cannot espouse any cause unequivocally himself.

Against the social, religious, and political conflicts which preoccupy the thoughts and interior monologues of the protagonist, the author juxtaposes the adamant facts of nature in its workings. Raman would be a completely controlled rationalist, but he is unable to suppress or even control his own sexual urges; Daisy, who would be the totally efficient supressor of births in India, continually receives statistics showing large population increases. Both are at the mercy of the weather, events, and their own impulses. Raman, realizing his own hypocrisy in aiding Daisy's family-planning work, finally is willing to abandon his intellectual idealism in order to establish a marriage with Daisy. He wants to keep his childhood home by the river, and to make his life with Daisy part of the traditional and accustomed community life. Daisy too is attracted to the river, a symbol of the placid working of nature throughout India.

But Daisy is willing to reject this when her duty to work calls.

Narayan brings to the reader through Raman's encounters with minor characters a vivid sense of the lives and the variety within a city in India today. His vignettes of minor personages in the situations of their daily routines are sharp, believable, and compassionate. The minor characters might well have become interesting major figures had the novel taken a different turn, or had a subplot been developed. The fictional city itself achieves an authenticity of its own through Narayan's deft pen. He conveys a sense of life and reality to Malgudi so that one may well accept it as a typical Indian city bustling with the daily life of real people.

Narayan writes with knowledge of the human soul. His characters, both male and female, have depth and complexity which give them strength and life. Though he writes with a constant compassion and fine benevolence toward his characters, he maintains an ironic distance which enables him to reveal absurdities and ironies at every turn of events. The tone is finally more pessimistic than tragic, more ironic than outraged, at the sadness of the outcome of the affair. It is a book which should outlast this season. Its characters live: their problems will also.

Betty Gawthrop

Sources for Further Study

Book World. July 11, 1976, p. E8.

Christian Science Monitor. LXVIII, July 14, 1976, p. 22.

National Observer. XV, August 14, 1976, p. 17.

New York Times Book Review. June 20, 1976, p. 6.

New Yorker. LII, July 5, 1976, p. 81.

Newsweek. LXXXVIII, July 4, 1976, p. 99.

THE PAST MASTERS
Politics and Politicians, 1906-1939

Author: Harold Macmillan (1894-   )
Publisher: Harper & Row Publishers (New York). Illustrated. 240 pp. $15.00
Type of work: History

Political memoirs of the author with observations and assessments of some of the major British politicians of the early twentieth century

Principal personages:
DAVID LLOYD GEORGE, British Prime Minister 1916-1922
JAMES RAMSAY MACDONALD, British Prime Minister 1924, 1929-1931, 1931-1935
STANLEY BALDWIN, British Prime Minister 1923-1924, 1924-1929, 1935-1937
NEVILLE CHAMBERLAIN, British Prime Minister 1937-1940
WINSTON CHURCHILL, British Prime Minister, 1940-1945

In this book, Harold Macmillan, himself a later British prime minister, offers his opinions and judgments on some of the men who preceded him in that high office, the men who were his own "masters" in the art of politics.

Although he was born into the prominent publishing family of The Macmillan Company, Harold Macmillan decided early in life to pursue a political career, to go to the House of Commons. He was much influenced in that decision by the opportunities he had as a young man to observe and listen to some of the leading men of the day. His family estate in Sussex adjoined that of Lord Robert Cecil, a Conservative party leader. John Morley, the Liberal, was a lawyer for The Macmillan Company. Lord James Bryce visited the family frequently, and H. H. Asquith invited young Harold to No. 10 Downing Street on two occasions. Through his acquaintance with such men, Macmillan became persuaded that the pursuit of political office would be an "honourable ambition."

The Great War of 1914-1918, however, disrupted all personal plans. Volunteering for King and country, Macmillan fought at the Somme, was severely wounded and invalided home. For many months he recuperated. Then he decided he would spend some time learning the family business; his political career was further postponed.

Not until 1924, at the age of thirty, did Macmillan return to his early ambition. In that year, standing as a Conservative, he won a seat in Commons from Stockton-on-Tees, an industrial constituency. As a young back-bencher, Macmillan had little influence and made little impact on the politics of Britain for quite some time. He gave few speeches and worked on committees where he did not attract much attention. Furthermore, by his own account, he was quite modest and self-effacing. But he observed, studied, and continued to learn the art of politics.

A major art in the British parliament was that of debating and speechmaking, and the "best parliamentary debater of his, or perhaps any day" was David Lloyd George. Macmillan first admired Lloyd George from a distance, and then more intimately when Lloyd George took an interest in the young man. A high point of their association came after Macmillan had presented a well-prepared but rather poorly delivered speech to the House. Lloyd George took Macmillan aside and offered him valuable advice on how to be a more effective orator. Macmillan does not say whether Lloyd George's recommendations made him into a better speaker, but he was most grateful for the advice. The author leaves no doubt that Lloyd George was the greatest of his political masters. To him, the Welshman was a genius; a "giant among pygmies." And he repeats the tribute that Winston Churchill delivered at Lloyd George's death: "when the English history of the twentieth century is written, it will be seen that the greater part of our fortunes in peace and war were shaped by this one man."

The next leader of whom Macmillan writes is James Ramsay MacDonald, who formed the first Labour government in 1924, and later headed a coalition called the National government. Macdonald appeared to Macmillan a complex figure: romantic, handsome, and vain—a perennial actor. It seemed to Macmillan that MacDonald's political philosophy most resembled the Christian Socialist tradition ("like my grandfather"). MacDonald was certainly not a Marxist as some of his associates were. MacDonald remains a political enigma: a "prince among men" to many of his followers, a double-dyed traitor to those who thought that personal ambition led him to ruin within the Labour Party.

A possible successor to MacDonald as leader of the Labour Party was Sir Oswald Mosley, a "man of ideas . . . a man of courage" in whom Macmillan found much to admire. But Mosley, disillusioned with the Labour Party, broke from it and attempted to found a so-called New Party. Macmillan, for a brief time, was nearly induced to join Mosley's New Party and work to bring greater social reform in Britain. However, when he realized that Mosley was changing the organization into a movement resembling Fascism, Macmillan could not follow in that direction. Nor, he believed, would the British people. Macmillan was, of course, proved right; Mosley and his movement were eventually disgraced. All the same, one wishes that Macmillan had devoted more of this book to the Mosley story, which he calls a tragedy of great talents and strength of character thrown away.

Then there was Stanley Baldwin. In the conventional view of the time, Stanley Baldwin is depicted as a solid, trustworthy, English squire, fond of the rural life and his garden, epitomized by the political slogan "Safety First." Macmillan detected another personality behind the stolid pipe-smoking face of Baldwin. He saw sensitivity, artistic appreciation, and impulsiveness which made Baldwin not at all the kind of man the public thought him to be, or the

Conservative Party publicity characterized him to be. Macmillan deplores Baldwin's frequent and often lengthy periods of indolence, his political drifting, and indecisiveness. Baldwin "was never quite sure that anybody was right, especially himself." On the other hand, he gives Baldwin high praise for saving Britain from possible disaster at the time of the General Strike of 1926.

Macmillan has very little praise for Baldwin's successor as Prime Minister, Neville Chamberlain. He does find that when Chamberlain was Minister of Health and then Chancellor of the Exchequer, he did excellent work. Had Chamberlain retired from politics in 1935, Macmillan thinks he would have been remembered as one of the most progressive and effective social reformers of his or any other time. But Chamberlain did not retire; he moved up to the premiership in 1937, and there followed the tragic years of Munich, appeasement, the British armaments crisis, and then the overturning of "peace in our time" which Chamberlain had so desperately sought. Macmillan quite obviously did not like Chamberlain as a person. He found him "lacking in warmth," "intellectually arrogant," "disagreeable," a man who knew he was right on every question, and perhaps most damning of all, Chamberlain was "unclubbable," not joining in the cameraderie of the Commons. It is somewhat surprising that a man with those personality traits could ever become leader of his party and prime minister. Macmillan does allow that all of the blame for the failures of the Chamberlain years must not fall on that ruined old man. The fault, he says, "lay . . . in ourselves—in Parliament and the democratic system itself."

The last political master of whom Macmillan writes is Winston Churchill. Books already published about Churchill are so numerous that Macmillan here limits himself to a short sketch of Churchill's career before 1940, and then some of his own personal memories of that remarkable man.

Like Lloyd George, Churchill offered advice and encouragement to the younger Macmillan from time to time. The Churchill estate, Chartwell, lay rather close to Macmillan's own home and, especially during the ten years when Churchill held no public office (1929-1939), the two men met often to discuss political affairs. Macmillan at the time was entirely involved in plans for the economic recovery and reconstruction of Britain, concerning which Churchill frequently offered his own recommendations and support. Those were Churchill's locust years, years of political impotence and frustration. The visits between the two men increased in frequency. Churchill's interest turned constantly to the need for British preparedness to confront the rise of Naziism in Germany. Macmillan shared that concern, but the government and the nation did not. It is Macmillan's belief that had Churchill's warning been heeded, and had Churchill, not Chamberlain, held the prime ministership after 1937, Britain would have had the strength and determination to call Hitler's bluff, and World War II would have been "unnecessary."

The latter chapers of *The Past Masters* are essays in which Macmillan presents his thoughts and observations on various political topics, including "The Whig Tradition," "Independent Members," and "Women in Politics." Of these, the essay on Whiggery, its history and principles, is especially illuminating; the essay on women in politics is less so.

In the final chapter, Macmillan speculates as to the future of Britain, and wonders whether Britain can again produce the sort of leaders she has in the past, men of the stature of Lloyd George or Churchill. He finds little reassurance of that at present, but extraordinary times often bring forth exceptional leaders. So he has faith (or hope) that Britain will survive, even prosper "if the moral urge and the idealism to which our predecessors could appeal can be brought into play."

The Past Masters strikes one as little more than a partial condensation of the author's multivolume autobiography, "The Winds of Change," with numerous illustrative photographs added. The photographs are very well-chosen, and constitute about one-third of the book. As to the narrative, Macmillan has attempted to blend sober history with personal recollections. This can be done, and has been done, well; but not in this book. About one hundred and fifty pages of narrative is simply too brief a space to do justice to either history or biography. Memories of events and individuals do give some useful insights, but too often characterizations seem merely derived from other observers. The writing is clear if rather pedestrian. Occasionally Macmillan repeats himself, but, in general, the account flows along quite smoothly.

The book's chief virtue is the reasonableness, fairness, and moderation Macmillan shows in assessing the politicians he has known. Perhaps he goes too far in his criticism of some leaders (Chamberlain), and not far enough in criticizing others (Lloyd George), but he is never malicious or vindictive.

The Past Masters offers little for the professional historian or political scientist. For the general reader it provides a short, if superficial, survey of a critical and dramatic period of British history.

James W. Pringle

Sources for Further Study

Book World. August 1, 1976, p. H10.
Books and Bookmen. XXI, December, 1975, p. 7.
Economist. CCLVII, November 1, 1975, p. 103.
History Today. XXV, December, 1975, p. 799.
Library Journal. CI, August, 1976, p. 1624.
New Yorker. LII, June 7, 1976, p. 138.
Virginia Quarterly Review. LII, Autumn, 1976, p. 114.

THE PEACOCK SPRING

Author: Rumer Godden (1907-   )
Publisher: The Viking Press (New York). 274 pp. $8.95
Type of work: Novel
Time: The present
Locale: New Delhi, India

A strongly plotted, sensitive novel of the coming of age of two English girls in India and of the confrontations inevitable between two different yet historically intertwined cultures

Principal characters:
>UNA GWITHIAM, a fifteen-year-old British schoolgirl
>HAL GWITHIAM, her twelve-year-old sister
>SIR EDWARD GWITHIAM, their father, a professional diplomat
>ALIX LAMONT, their tutor and Sir Edward's mistress, a beautiful Eurasian
>MRS. LAMONT, Alix's mother
>RAVI, a gardener and poet
>HEMANGO SHARMA, his friend, a medical student
>VIKRAM SINGH, a captain of the Indian cavalry

The plight of children caught in the hypocrisies of the adult world and their subsequent awakening to the painful truths of maturity and responsibility has almost always been the special subject matter of Rumer Godden's finely wrought novels. In *The Peacock Spring,* the author unites this theme with the contrasting cultures of East and West and the conflict of tradition with the progress of the modern political-industrial world. In a story more strongly plotted than many of her previous tales, Godden carries her characters and the reader through a series of emotional and intellectual conflicts which ultimately conclude in a manner both dramatic and resourceful. Godden has already written some fine books about India, of which the best known is *The River,* a short, moving novel about two girls growing up in a big house on the banks of a river in Bengal. In *The Peacock Spring,* she takes up much the same theme, but the plot here is much more elaborate, and she relies less on her remarkable ability to describe character and landscape. Although *The Peacock Spring* is perhaps not one of the author's best novels, it is nevertheless a wise, sensible, and finely crafted work.

Godden made her reputation with a series of exquisite novels written in a rare and gentle prose in which she seldom raised her voice above the muted note of understatement. She early proved her ability to write of sentiment and yet avoid the dangers of sentimentality, as well as her gift for portraying the pain and beauty of youth and its transition to maturity. In this, her first novel since *In This House of Brede* in 1969, she has produced a love story infused with both suspense and intrigue, yet has managed to maintain the evenness of tone and grace of style which are her trademark. Despite the modern trappings of the story, this is essentially an old-fashioned novel, and offers that particular satisfaction for the reader that only an old-fashioned novel can give.

Two teen-aged girls, Una and Hal Gwithiam, are withdrawn from an English boarding school and sent to India to join their diplomat father, who needs them as a respectable front for his Eurasian mistress, Alix Lamont, who is engaged as the girls' tutor. Lonely and unhappy, especially after her father marries Alix, Una, the older daughter, drifts into a love affair with a young Indian poet and becomes pregnant, while Hal becomes involved with a deposed rajah. Una loses her lover and suffers a miscarriage, and Hal is sent to America to live with her mother. On the bones of this story, Godden has created a wise and generous fabric that transcends nationality and age. Her vivid depiction of the India of garden parties and polo matches, poverty and primitive villages makes colorful reading, but nothing is drawn in merely for the sake of "local color." Each scene, each detail, adds to the symbolic and emotional impact of the novel.

If the British characters are somewhat stereotypical, the Indians are varied and believable: the charming, egoistic Ravi; the calculating Alix and her cheery, raffish mother; the servants with their shrewdness born of observing life from the background; and the formerly rich families now reduced to making-do in run-down palaces. The many and varied relationships are treated with sympathy and compassion. There is the affair between the girls' father, Edward, and Alix, difficult for them both because of propriety and because of Alix's fears and Edward's blindness. At the other extreme, there is the secret romance of the schoolgirl Una and the idealistic and selfish young poet, Ravi, a romance that burns brightly until confronted with the chill winds of reality. In the background, the brief relationship of Hal and Vikram Singh reveals the vulnerability of youth and the risks of thoughtless toying with the emotions of other people. Perhaps the most touching relationship is the unspoken love between the medical student, Hemango Sharma, and the poet Ravi; essentially onesided, this friendship ends with Hemango sacrificing much for Ravi and receiving in return only the satisfaction that he was able to help his friend. The relationship between Alix and her mother, of whom she is ashamed, is both humorous and painful, and underlaid with a poignance born of the vulnerability of human beings when confronted with the merciless power of society. The interactions of these characters are described with a compassion and tact rare in contemporary novels.

Technically, it is fascinating to observe Godden's device of alternating points of view in her narrative. By writing her novel in this way, she highlights the contrasting Asian and European attitudes which compose a large part of her theme. The reader learns of Ravi's deep convictions about the old Indian traditions and then of the far different beliefs and feelings of the Europeans and of the modernized attitudes of Hemango and Vikram Singh. Each individual is presented with an understanding that prevents any of them from being reduced to a caricature or a villain. If it is vital to Ravi that his poetry be

completely pure of Western influences, it is equally important to Hemango
that he learn all of the most modern Western medical techniques. Alix's
scheming is ultimately understood as being motivated by a terror of poverty
and of the early struggles she endured to escape it. Even the coldness of Ravi's
father and the gentle aloofness of his grandmother are explained in terms of
their cultural influences and beliefs. No character in the book, however minor,
fails to contribute to the understanding of the theme and to the overall pattern,
yet the author's technique is such that the novel never seems artificial or
contrived.

Two symbols which run through the book are the peacocks and the
"Monkey Man." The peacocks symbolize not only the exotic splendor of India,
but also the inherent sexuality of life in this tropical atmosphere. And beyond
this, Una discovers, when she watches the mating dance of the peacock, that
there is always the fact of the naked earth on which even the peacock must
walk. Una feels that she is the drab peahen who must be subservient to the
peacock, but she learns that the peacock must scratch in the dirt to find its dinner. Una's only memory of her first childhood visit to India is of the Monkey
Man, with his captive animal on a string made to perform for the amusement
of passersby. Now, as a young woman, when she sees the Monkey Man and his
wretched animal she no longer is charmed; now, she sees the pitifulness of the
monkey's plight, and she realizes that, in some way, everyone she knows—
including herself—is a monkey on a string, "playing to the drum." Perhaps the
emotional climax of the novel comes when Una sees two monkeys on strings
made to copulate to amuse an audience, and realizes that, in a sense, she and
Ravi were made to perform helplessly in public. The act which is beautiful and
holy in some circumstances can be made to be dirty and cruel under other conditions. The difference lies in free will, in the ability to make choices, and in
the wisdom to see those choices honestly.

Behind the action of the novel, but very much a part of the Indian setting, is
a new, internationally oriented world, symbolized by the United Nations
house in which Sir Edward and his daughters and his Eurasian mistress all
live. The great mansion, with its vast gardens and countless servants, is owned
and run by the United Nations as a guest house and temporary residence for
dignitaries from around the world. Citizens of many nations pass through its
doors, as guests and on business, illustrating the new closer relationships that
exist between countries in the second half of the twentieth century. But if the
relationships between nations are often difficult, those between individuals—
particularly between individuals of different nationalities—are no less difficult.
And, finally, there must always be areas in such relationships in which there
can be no perfect resolution; some differences must not only be accepted, but
must be seen as sacred.

The glow of vitality and the rare sensitivity of *The Peacock Spring* give the
novel a unique place in the works of Rumer Godden. The characters, with

their human weaknesses and individual brands of integrity, are fascinating, and the India around them saturates the tale with the beauty and drama of a nation and a world in transition. With *The Peacock Spring*, Godden has maintained her position as a distinguished craftsman and a novelist of wisdom and warmth.

Bruce D. Reeves

Sources for Further Study

Booklist. LXXII, January 1, 1976, p. 613.

Contemporary Review. CCXXVIII, January, 1976, p. 45.

Library Journal. CI, July, 1976, p. 1555.

Observer. November 23, 1976, p. 31.

Publisher's Weekly. CCIX, February 2, 1976, p. 89.

Times Literary Supplement. January 30, 1976, p. 100.

PLAGUES AND PEOPLES

Author: William H. McNeill (1917-   )
Publisher: Anchor Press/Doubleday (New York). 369 pp. $10.00
Type of work: History
Time: 100,000 B.C. to the present
Locale: The world

A study of the impact of infectious disease upon the development of mankind and the extent to which it has altered the course of human history

Plagues and Peoples stands as another significant contribution of William H. McNeill to a world view of history. McNeill, who is Robert A. Milliken Distinguished Service Professor of History at the University of Chicago, established his reputation as an authority on the totality of man's past in his celebrated book, *The Rise of the West: A History of the Human Community* (1963). Indeed, in *Plagues and Peoples,* McNeill uses the conceptual framework of *The Rise of the West* in referring to man's beginnings as a hunter, to the development of distinct but not entirely unrelated centers of civilization in Eurasia, and to the ultimate diffusion of civilization on a worldwide scale.

Having presented a sweeping picture of human history in *The Rise of the West*, McNeill attempts in his latest study to fit the nature of disease experience into that picture. The objective, then, of *Plagues and Peoples* is to explore the impact which infectious disease has had on mankind in ancient and modern times. As a world historian, McNeill examines the effect of indigenous disease on the ancient civilizations located in the Middle East, India, China, and the Mediterranean, and the disasters which resulted, where corroborating evidence exists, when these civilizations exchanged their diseases. Major disease exchanges of more recent history, including those which led to the introduction of the bubonic plague from the Mongol Empire into Europe and numerous diseases from Europe and Africa into the New World, comprise a major portion of the book. The closing chapter discusses the response of modern medicine to infectious disease. Throughout his study, McNeill makes parallel reference to what he calls microparasites and macroparasites. The microparasites are the foreign organisms within the body that cause disease. Macroparasites are human beings who in their various activities as builders of cities, oppressors of the poor, or military conquerors make possible those conditions in which microparasites can grow and spread the diseases associated with them from one people or civilization to another. Conceding that many of his suggestions are tentative, McNeill regards his book as a starting point for scholarly investigation by experts in numerous languages. Meantime, the author looks upon his study as a means of drawing to the attention of ordinary readers the existence of important gaps in older ideas about the story of man's past.

Working within the framework he established in *The Rise of the West*,

McNeill devotes the first two chapters of *Plagues and Peoples* to the relationship between disease and the origin and diffusion of human populations throughout much of the world. He speculates that *Homo sapiens*, who may have first evolved in Africa about 100,000 B.C., was originally a hunter, a macroparasite, who lived on the flesh of large game animals while killing off rival humanoid forms. Once early man moved from his original tropical environment with its numerous diseases and infections and began to push into the temperate zones, his health and vitality improved considerably. Consequently, by 10,000 B.C., human hunting groups occupied all the major land masses of the earth except Antarctica. By this same time, however, the large herds of game animals had long since begun to die out and man, in order to survive, was obliged to domesticate plants and animals, thereby laying the foundations of sedentary societies. Man was attracted, in particular, to the rich soil of the major river valleys in the Middle East (the Nile, the Tigris and Euphrates), India (the Indus and Ganges), and China (the Yellow River), and later to the Mediterranean coastlands. McNeill points out that in these densely populated areas, the transmission of disease parasites from person to person increased considerably with the passage of time as the sedentary communities in these four areas grew into civilizations. Hence, by about 500 B.C., each of the major civilized regions of Eurasia had developed its own unique variety of infections, person-to-person diseases. Within each region, the people built up an immunity to the diseases indigenous to it. McNeill thus attributes the territorial expansion of civilized peoples, in part, to the spread of their indigenous diseases to neighbors in adjacent sparsely populated areas who were unaccustomed to and unable to withstand such a vast array of infections.

McNeill contends—on the basis of very fragmentary and questionable evidence—that shortly after the beginning of the Christian era, the four divergent civilized disease pools, as he calls them, began to converge. The cause of this convergence was the increased trade between the Roman Empire, India, the Middle East, and China that was carried on by caravan and by ships plying the Indian Ocean. The author reasons that, in view of the great epidemics, perhaps smallpox and measles, which decimated the Roman and Chinese populations, infections must have been exchanged as well as goods. India and the Middle East, he states, seem to have escaped these epidemics. Interesting though these speculations are about the origin and nature of epidemics in Rome and China, they are largely just that in the absence of strong evidence.

McNeill is on somewhat firmer ground in discussing the advent of the bubonic plague in Europe in 542-543, during the reign of Emperor Justinian. He states that the bacillus of the plague, *Pasteurella pestis*, (isolated by disciples of Louis Pasteur only in 1894) was spread from an original focus in northeastern India-southwestern China or central Africa into the Mediterranean by ships that traversed the Indian Ocean and Red Sea. These ships were infested with the species of "black rats" which in turn were infested with the fleas that actually carried the bubonic bacillus into Mediterranean Europe. McNeill attributes the failure of Justinian's efforts to restore imperial unity to the Mediterranean world in good measure to the decline of imperial resources resulting from the plague. Although this factor cannot be entirely discounted, a more realistic explanation for the failure of Justinian's grandiose scheme of imperial reunification was the sheer enormity of the task whatever the status of his resources.

Europe's most disastrous encounter, however, with the bubonic plague came in the period 1346-1350, when the "Black Death," as it was called, swept over most of the Continent, killing about one-third of the population. McNeill holds that the establishment of the Mongol Empire between 1250 and 1350 with its incorporation of China, central Asia, and most of Russia led to the transfer of the *Pasteurella pestis* bacillus to the rodents of the Eurasian steppes for the first time. The infection must then have traveled the caravan routes of Asia before reaching the Crimea in 1346, where in that year it decimated the armies of a Mongol prince who, as a consequence, was compelled to break off the siege which he had laid to the Crimean trading city of Caffa. From there it was carried by the rather extensive shipping network of Europe to various ports on the Continent and then spread into the interior where it wreaked havoc on a population that had grown fairly dense by the fourteenth century. McNeill concedes that he is dealing in probabilities in showing how the bubonic plague eventually reached Europe at that time, but he is on stronger ground here than in his discussion of the spread of diseases in ancient times. The basis for his hypothesis is the documented pattern of the spread of bubonic plague in the nineteenth and twentieth centuries on a worldwide scale. McNeill points out that one of the results of the Black Death, aside from the great loss of life and its general disruption of feudal society, was that it discredited the rational theology of Thomas Aquinas in favor of a more mystical and personal relationship to God. While this view has some merit, it must be remembered that William of Ockham and Marsiglio of Padua had challenged Thomistic philosophy many years before the Black Death swept into Europe.

The author rounds out his discussion of the bubonic plague in Europe by offering several interesting hypotheses, which he labels as such, as to why in the years after 1346, some other diseases, such as leprosy (referring to the specific disease known today as Hansen's disease) apparently declined while tuberculosis seems to have increased. One theory which McNeill advances is that of changing patterns of disease competition. In short, any immunity built up toward the more mobile tuberculosis bacillus may also have provoked an immunity to the slower moving leprosy bacillus once it arrived in the host. At best, however, this is only a theory.

In his analysis of disease exchanges, McNeill devotes considerable attention to the disastrous impact which the diseases of Europe and Africa had on the native inhabitants of the New World when abruptly introduced there during the Age of Discovery and Exploration. Little is known, the author relates, about the level of disease experience among pre-Columbian American Indians, except that it seems to have been quite low in comparison to that of the peoples of Eurasia. McNeill offers as many hypotheses to explain the apparent absence of infections among the civilized Indians of the New World as he does to explain their presence among the peoples of the Old. Hence, when the Spanish conquistadores arrived in Mexico and Peru in the sixteenth century, the smallpox they brought with them decimated those Indian nations which initially tried to resist their advance. This explains why Cortez and Pizarro, respectively, were able to conquer the Aztecs and Incas with only a handful of men. More significantly, these disasters, compounded in quick succession by outbreaks of measles, influenza, and perhaps typhus, further explain why the Spanish were so successful in transferring their culture and language to the New World. McNeill attributes the mass conversion of the Indians to Christianity to the fact that the Christian God seemed to spare the white newcomers from the ravishes of disease which he unmercifully visited upon the native populations because they were not of the Christian Faith.

Diseases of African origin, especially malaria and yellow fever, also took their toll of those Indians and some European settlers who inhabited the tropical regions of the New World. The mosquito carriers of the malarial parasite entered the New World beginning probably in the sixteenth century on ships bringing slaves from Africa. There, McNeill explains, malaria had kept natives in the tropics culturally backward through the centuries. In the mid-seventeenth century, the influx of yellow fever, transferred from West Africa, resulted in major epidemics which killed off large numbers of tropical Indian populations that had escaped decimation by malaria. Thus, according to McNeill, the introduction of these tropical infections from Africa in combination with the influx of deadly European diseases resulted in almost the total destruction of the pre-existing American Indian populations, especially those living in the tropics.

Plagues and Peoples is a synthesis based largely upon speculation, hypothesis, and conjecture. To a considerable extent, McNeill has taken the documented history of modern disease as a model to explain how infections developed and spread among and between peoples in ancient, medieval, and early modern times. Many of his observations on diseases, especially those in antiquity, are so speculative as to be of very questionable value. Despite this shortcoming, indeed perhaps because of it, the book should attain the author's objective of providing what he refers to as "a target to shoot down." McNeill bases his study mainly on secondary sources as contained in the fifty-five pages of chapter notes at the end of the book. Although the author's style of writing is at times rather repetitive, *Plagues and Peoples* is a thoroughly engrossing, if controversial, book which provides the general reader with a good introduction to a world view of history by one of America's leading historians.

Edward P. Keleher

Sources for Further Study

Atlantic. CCXXXVIII, October, 1976, p. 115.

Book World. August 29, 1976, p. M1.

National Observer. XV, September 25, 1976, p. 21.

New York Review of Books. XXIII, September 30, 1976, p. 3.

New York Times. CXXVI, October 25, 1976, p. 27.

Progressive. XL, December, 1976, p. 58.

THE POET AS JOURNALIST
Life at The New Republic

Author: Reed Whittemore (1919-   )
Publisher: The New Republic Book Company (Washington, D.C.). 232 pp. $8.95
Type of work: Essay

A collection of essays, book reviews, and occasional pieces, most of which appeared first in The New Republic *from 1969 to 1973, by a distinguished American poet*

Whittemore's title betrays a certain *mauvaise honte*. That he is a poet of notable achievement—the author of six volumes of poetry and another two volumes comprising poems, stories, and essays—is a matter of record. Less widely understood for the record is the circumstance that, for four "interesting" years from 1969 to 1973, he also put his foot into journalism (as he describes the venture) to work as literary editor of *The New Republic*. Now, it is not unusual for poets to be journalists. Some of the supreme masters of the English tongue, among them Coleridge and Walt Whitman, not only dabbled in journalism during dreary stages of their writing careers; they were journalistic hacks. Other poets not entirely dependent upon piecework hacking to earn their major livelihood, nevertheless served for a while as part-time journalists, contributing essays, articles, or reviews to their publications. These more fortunate poets, from Dryden to T. S. Eliot, are usually described by the more polite term *essayists*. Yet in the popular imagination they too are tainted, as the dyer's hand marks his craft, by the ink of journalism.

Whittemore is particularly embarrassed by his brief business ties with *The New Republic* because Ezra Pound, one of his favorite pundits on matters poetical, once declared that journalists "had absolutely no minds of their own but functioned only to tell the public what the public wanted to hear." Poets, on the other hand, according to Pound, had the obligation "to tell the bloody public what it did not want to hear." In the main, Whittemore agrees with Pound. A self-designated "effete snob," Whittemore would like the poet to breathe the pure sublime of an atmosphere uncontaminated by commercial odors. But the world will not let poets remain pure. (Robert Penn Warren once made the same remark.) So this poet, an English professor for nearly thirty years, carries his hired message to the impure world, as journalist to mass reader, without ever forgetting in his secret heart that he is a poet also, with a higher duty to the business of fine discriminations.

Thus Whittemore is a kind of spy in the camp of the editorial office of *The New Republic*. Although fairly comfortable with the liberal—in recent years moderate-liberal—political policy of the magazine, he is actually a poetical anarchist, an Outsider in Colin Wilson's sense of the word, who cannot conform with perfect complacency to any social or political establishment, even a liberal one. Whittemore sees his job as that of unsettling opinions; whereas journalists are supposed to approach their public, supremely self-confident, to settle their opinions. Commissioned to write television commentaries under the pseudonym "Sedulus," the poet-spy uses his column to confound rather than comfort the masses. Of course, masses do not read *The New Republic;* educated, intelligent, mostly liberal subscribers do. Yet these sophisticated readers may at times think *en masse.* Whittemore, for his part, thinks as one— as a poet, in fact.

This collection of essays, critical pieces on TV and other topical subjects, and book reviews is distinguished, then, from the usual volume of its kind because of the poet's bias. At fifty-seven, Whittemore is still an anarchist of sensibility; opinionated, sharp of tongue, always a "solipsistic loner." Long acclaimed as an established poet—even as an Establishment poet, inasmuch as he was official poet for the Library of Congress in 1964—he belongs properly to the generation influenced by Pound and Eliot. Like his masters, he admires sound craftsmanship, intelligence, seriousness. And he hates work that is shabby, merely clever, or merely entertaining. His opinions are decidedly old-fashioned. An unreconstructed humanist, he approves of Erasmus but not Ho Chi Minh. An anarchist of sensibility, he praises hard, careful thinking; precision rather than effusion. To him most modern poets are superficial. Worse, they are lazy. Whittemore criticizes, as one would expect, the glibness of Alan Ginsberg (*Howl* "had the effect of a sort of natural disaster"). But Whittemore is equally severe with Kenneth Koch, who is "always on the edge of nonsense or frivolity, or of a bottomless pit of images, fancies, soft squirmy words." For an "old sense-monger" like Whittemore, the school of "New York Poets" of the 1960's deserves to be chastised as "boringly self-indulgent." He hates shoddy wares, cheap games. "The poets of my generation," he writes, "grew up reading—Eliot, Yeats, Pound, Stevens and so on." But the "poets who started the new poetry of the sixties—Ginsberg, Ferlinghetti, Corso and so on—are alike in their incapacity to live with the culture."

Because he cannot approve the ill-crafted verse produced today, Whittemore is the more a loner, cut off alike from the mass-mind and from the poetic enthusiasms of the younger generation. He is that rare personality: an anarchist of sensibility who opposes revolution. In "Checks & Balances: The Poet in the Bank" he confesses outright the damaging words: "I am not a revolutionary." Indeed, he would not fret if poets have to work for a living. T. S. Eliot, he contends, was not harmed by working in a bank. And Whittemore himself has apparently not been destroyed as a poet by earning his sustenance as a pedagogue (as he likes to call himself)—nor as a journalist. If poets had to work, they would understand more about the real world, or at least about the economics of that world. According to Whittemore, Ezra Pound did T. S. Eliot an injury by persuading his friend to leave the bank. Indeed, if Pound had clerked in a bank, he might have learned a few simple lessons about the laws of interest. The true revolutionary, Whittemore believes, is one who exercises his sensibility to make fine discriminations.

On the one hand the writer deplores popular poets like Bob Dylan, Rod McKuen, the Beatles, and their ilk, sentimentalists who are incapable of finely discriminating; on the other, he deplores revolutionary poets like Mayakovsky and Ho Chi Minh, who are incapable of clear thinking. To Whittemore, sensibility cannot be isolated from intelligence; and intelligence requires discipline. The trouble with Jack Kerouac and with many other writers of the 1960's, according to Whittemore, is that they could never discipline their private sensibilities. Instead of standing apart from the mass culture—"the Kulch," as he calls it—they became involved with it. Instead of disciplining their sensibilities, they merged with the common mass.

But Whittemore, lonely humanist and pedagogue, refuses to merge. He distrusts fads and modern fashions, grows "nostalgic for the old days of Beauty and Truth." At *The New Republic,* certainly one of the most intelligent of periodicals, he was uncomfortable and "unaccommodating." His true home, he believes, is in the English Department of some college or university, a place where new ideas clash with old, where at least one has time to think clearly, feel deeply, and discriminate finely. Some of Whittemore's most convincing essays concern this mythical place. In "English Department Ills (I)," he scorns a certain "Professor Simon O'Toole" (a pseudonym) for his failure of nerve. "O'Toole" earlier had argued in a scholarly paper that "American higher education is a low-grade farce." Whittemore counters that the fault in higher education lies not with its discipline, but with undisciplined pop-culture professors like "O'Toole." To Whittemore, the alternative to disciplined education is "Stuff"—a merging of poetry and vulgarity, of the mass mind with the finely perceptive. And the poet rejects the impurity of Stuff.

Yet in "Climbing the Wall" Whittemore confesses that he too has sometimes spread his perceptions thin. "I have written too much all my life—or at least written too much for print," he says, "because I have chosen the American commodity-way." This is the way of commerce, success, popularity. One part of Whittemore shyly resists the commodity-way. He would prefer to write for the few, the cultured elite. Yet journalism requires a mass audience. So does popularity. Whittemore writes,

> The modern young writer imagines that he is a tremendous powerhouse ready to emit juice spontaneously; and this image of the poet's or novelist's function fits beautifully with his capitalist, self-made-man projections—the poet as millionaire, the novelist as tycoon.

If these projections seem vaguely sinister, at least part of Whittemore is attracted to the seductiveness of power. As journalist he can speak with a mighty voice to the mass-audience. Yet, faithful to his anarchistic sensibility, he chooses to disturb rather than comfort his readers. As "Sedulus," he complains about pretentious culture shows, questions "the narrow focus of liberal criticism of TV," and finally questions the media at large. This criticism did not sit well with his editors. "Knee-jerk liberals had been a steady target for conservatives," he writes, "but what, I wanted to know, about knee-jerk reporters, liberal or conservative?" This sort of question was received less and less kindly in Mr. Harrison's office at *The New Republic.*

So, after serving four terms as a spy in the enemy's camp—a poet disguised as a journalist—Whittemore packed his books. His sensibility intact, now he was free again. The essays that he has collected for this volume—sharp, thoughtful, independent—are significant contributions to what Lionel Trilling once called "the liberal imagination." Taken as a whole, they resemble in sprightliness though not in originality E. M. Forster's *Two Cheers for Democracy.* Least impressive are the brief pieces on television, most of which have lost their topical appeal. But the essays on poetry and "the Kulch" express with precision, sanity, and good temper ideas that are permanent. Among the voices of the 1960's—many blatant with their self-advertisements, revolutionary poses, and hard sells—Whittemore's voice is the quiet one of reason, decency, and integrity. It is, finally, the voice of the poet.

Leslie B. Mittleman

Sources for Further Study

Book World. November 7, 1976, p. G4.
Booklist. LXXIII, September 1, 1976, p. 7.
Library Journal. CI, July, 1976, p. 1533.
New York Times Book Review. July 25, 1976, p. 6.
Village Voice. XXI, March 29, 1976, p. 45.

POETRY AND REPRESSION
Revisionism from Blake to Stevens

Author: Harold Bloom (1930-   )
Publisher: Yale University Press (New Haven) 293 pp. $11.95
Type of work: Literary criticism

The last in Bloom's tetralogy of books concerning antithetical criticism

Poetry and Repression: Revisionism from Blake to Stevens is painfully esoteric, which means that few but initiates of modern literary scholarship are likely to have the knowledge and stamina to gauge the significance of Harold Bloom's explorations. To outsiders, Bloom's erudition will seem numbing, as he eclectically gathers from a host of critical ancestors and employs lofty terminology to map and explain revisionism in post-Enlightenment poetry. Moreover, Bloom's grandiloquence is disturbing. For there is an inescapable sense that what is being created here, instead of a lucid explanation of great poetry, is another sect in the religion of literary criticism.

This is not to say that Bloom's achievement is not significant or that his critical approach does not reveal valuable insights from which poetic study may benefit. If poetry is anything, it is the expression of relationships, and *Poetry and Repression* seeks to penetrate poetic relationships at every turn and find in those relationships obscure workings of the poetic self, particularly the poetic self as manifested by *strong* poets of the post-Enlightenment: Blake, Wordsworth, Shelley, Keats, Tennyson, Browning, Yeats, Whitman, and Stevens. Viewing poetry in a broad sense, Bloom also discusses Freud, Nietzsche, and Emerson because, for Bloom, "a poetic text . . . is not a gathering of signs on a page, but is a psychic battlefield upon which authentic forces struggle for the only victory worth winning, the divinating triumph over oblivion." Opposed on this battlefield are the forces of anteriority and belatedness in a crucial struggle from which derives the concept of poetic repression, resulting in poetic revisionism. Bloom's previous books—*The Anxiety of Influence, A Map of Misreading, Kabbalah and Criticism*—prepare the ground for his discussions in *Poetry and Repression*. But it is in this last book that he attempts to show the usefulness of a peculiarly Kabbalistic interpretive model as he investigates what he calls the "dialectics of revisionism."

This investigation is wideranging and produces an incredibly complex critical apparatus. In Vico, Bloom finds "language . . . particularly poetic language, is always and necessarily a revision of previous language," so that every poet after the first must be a late arrival. All poets select some prior traces of the language of poetry and avoid others, since they must stand in the literary tradition but also seek to shape it. This selectivity is a result of repression, so, unavoidably, the poet's readings of his precursors are "misprisions," or creative misreadings from which he fashions his own modes of speaking. These misprisions can be seen, in a Freudian psychological sense, as defense mechanisms. Above all, the strong belated poet actively represses influences of his precursors to establish his own rhetorical stance and, in doing so, achieves a much greater goal; for, to Bloom, "rhetoric is also what Nietzsche saw it as being, a mode of interpretation that is the will's revulsion against time, the will's revenge, its vindication against the necessity of passing away."

Bloom characterizes the strong poet as a Gnostic—one who knows his subjectivity and self-consciously seeks freedom, specifically, "revisionary freedom of interpretation." Further he sees the Gnostic as "ancestor of all major Western revisionists."

Considering Gnosticism, Bloom ascertains that the closely related Kabbalah, especially doctrines of Isaac Luria, can serve as a model for poetic interpretation. That such models are necessary is a certainty for Bloom since "all reading is translation, and all attempts to communicate a reading seem to court reduction," a danger any critical pattern should strive to avoid. Because of the nature of post-Enlightenment poetry, its near identity with what Bloom has elsewhere called "the anxiety of influence," Bloom seeks "as interpretive model the most dialectical and negative of theologies that can be found." Because of "a dialectic of creation astonishingly close to revisionist poetics" and "a conceptual rhetoric ingeniously oriented towards defense," Kabbalah meets Bloom's needs. Particularly significant is Luria's story of "creation-by-catastrophe" which, according to Bloom, revises the *Zohar's* dialectics of creation to a regressive process: "creation by contraction, destruction and subsequent restitution." This correspondence between Kabbalistic signification and poetic repression Bloom further relates to the language of psychoanalysis, finding, "modes of aesthetic limitation can be called different degrees of sublimation." Bloom sees attainment of the sublime mode as the achievement of poets that allows them to prevail though they arrive late on the scene and must overcome the force of their precursors. Mapping the poem's process which leads to this attainment is what Bloom expects his interpretive model to make possible, and "different degrees of sublimation" become his revisionary ratios.

Unfortunately, Bloom's theory entails elaborate vocabulary with elaborate explanation to document the origins of the terms, establish the complex relationship between them, and justify their use. He follows Coleridge in using *clinamen* to identify "the beginnings of the defensive process" or the "trope-as-misreading, irony as dialectical alternation of images of presence and absence" which equals the Kabbalistic concept of breaking-of-the-vessels. Irony is seen as aesthetic limitation, which leads to an act of restitution. Following Mallarmé and Lacan, Bloom calls this second poetic act *tessura* "in its ancient, mystery-cult meaning of an antithetical completion, the device of recognition that fits together the broken parts of a vessel, to make a whole again." Discussing the relation of these two terms, Bloom claims (recognizing how possibly outrageous this may seem) that most significant poems of the last three centuries have as their opening movements the move from *clinamen* to *tessura*, from internalization to incomplete externalization. This incompleteness forces a movement of *kenosis*, or emptying out of divinity; the term is St. Paul's word for Christ's humbling of himself, and Bloom see *kenosis* subsuming metonymy and parallel Freudian defenses of regression, undoing, and isolating. Repression is subsumed by *daemonization* and usually occurs at the strong poem's crisis point. "As trope, poetic repression tends to appear as an exaggerated representation, the overthrow called hyperbole, with characteristic imagery of great heights and abysmal depths. Metaphor is subsumed by the revisionary ration *askesis*, a term chosen by Walter Pater from pre-Socratic usage, which represents "the dualistic imagery of inside against outside nature." This limitation of meaning gives way to a final poetic movement which Bloom names *apophrades*, selecting his term from Athenian mythology where the apophrades are the days when the dead return. In this revisionary ratio, a balance is often created between introjection and projection, between identification and casting out the forbidden. Bloom maintains that few strong poems fail to attempt introjecting what he calls earliness (a sense of original insight) while projecting belatedness (a following of influence) in their conclusions. In the ratio of apophrades a final poetic figuration, anciently called metalepsis or transumption, "becomes a total, final act of taking up a poetic stance in relation to anteriority, particularly to anteriority of poetic language, which means primarily the loved-and-feared poems of the precursors."

The central question which must be asked of Bloom is: does this approach clarify our understanding of the poetic process and resultant poems? In one sense the answer is probably yes. Bloom adroitly analyzes selected poems by selected poets to find relationship among them. His essential concept, that poets react to their predecessors and hope to establish a unique stance which will endure, is not difficult to comprehend. Critics have spoken of influence and allusion in poetry since the beginning of criticism. They have seen that poets are selective in using certain ideas while discarding others, and that chosen ideas appear in varied forms. But Bloom is a pioneer in the extent to which he seeks to stress influence and selectivity as central impulses which generate poetic expression. And he pioneers in the extent to which the poet's reaction in influence and his successful selectivity may be viewed as yardsticks measuring the significance of his poetry. Moreover, Bloom has pioneered in his development of a particular model and in recognizing that models are essential for understanding poetry. As he says in his essay on Wallace Stevens:

> The function of criticism at the present time, as I conceive it, is to find a middle way between the paths of demystification of meaning, and of recollection or restoration of meaning, or between limitation and representation. But the only aesthetic path between limitation and representation is substitution, and so all that criticism can hope to teach, whether to the common reader or to the poet, is a series of stronger modes of substitution.

But doubt concerning the value of Bloom's model has to center on his reliance on the complicated, jargon-ridden apparatus which he devises, for such a mechanism will, for most readers, seem to be obfuscation. The common reader Bloom mentions in the above passage is often unlikely to fathom what Bloom has to say.

Poetry and Repression is circuitous and plethoric, certainly an abomination against clear style. By his example, Bloom seems to suggest that reading criticism should be more difficult than reading poetry. Sentence construction is often tortuous. And lengthy digressions, interesting as they may be, often blunt the forward thrust of Bloom's essays. Allusions and direct references to precursor critics are necessary to development of his model, but the round-about ways in which Bloom introduces supportive material, combined with continual explanations of his organizational structure, often interfere with concise and direct understanding of his points. The reader may find himself lost in a labyrinth awaiting Bloom's return, only to espy the critic following another tangent.

Furthermore, Bloom's familiarity with his jargon allows him to brandish it repeatedly, revealing, at least, inconsideration for most potential readers. He refers to his interpretive model, as he uses it to analyze specific poems, as shorthand, but his shorthand requires complete familiarity not only with the terms themselves but with their origins and their complex relationships with other terms. Application of the terminology requires reading knowledge far broader than most readers are certain to have. One passage, mapping Wallace Steven's "The Snow Man," will indicate to what extent Bloom expects readers to follow him. Saying the poem "reveals itself as another version of the apotropaic litany that poetry has become," he continues to apply his pattern:

> This apparently least restitutive of poems moves also to heighten its initial synedouche of the beholder, to the hyperbole of pathos in the misery of the Shelleyan wind, on to the introjective metalepsis of the final "beholds," where the "nothing" that is there and the "nothing himself" of the beholder both are effectually equated with the greatest of American epiphanies: "I am nothing; I see all."

A firm grasp of all that Bloom has discussed prior to this passage makes the jargon accessible. But a question remains: is the point of analyzing poetry to apply such jargon?

Clearly Bloom sees as the province of critics a realm far removed from common, direct communication. Instead a ritual is developed to encode messages between initiates of esoteric caliber, with the resultant sense of elevation furthering the need to develop more complex models for display within the professional circles the critics negotiate. Because *Poetry and Repression* requires laborious reading by anyone, its audience is immediately limited. This statement suggests a direction literary scholarship has been heading for some time, and with some assurance it can be recognized that graduate students in English programs throughout the country, along with professors already entrenched in the inner circles, will be obliged to read and comment on Harold

Bloom's latest book. Other readers had best beware, for this is not a book written for every man.

Gary B. Blank

Sources for Further Study

Book Forum. II, Spring, 1976, p. 258.
Christian Century. XCIII, March 24, 1976, p. 292.
New Statesman. XCI, March 19, 1976, p. 364.
New York Times Book Review. March 14, 1976, p. 6.
New Yorker. LXIX, August 16, 1976, p. 14.
Times Literary Supplement. June 25, 1976, p. 775.

POLONAISE

Author: Piers Paul Read (1941-   )
Publisher: J. B. Lippincott Company (Philadelphia and New York). 347 pp. $10.00
Type of work: Novel
Time: The mid-1920's to 1958
Locale: Warsaw; Paris; Mulford, England

A novel of life, politics, and disillusionment with an overshadowing concern for definitions of love and happiness

> *Principal characters:*
> STEFAN KORNOWSKI, a writer and intellectual
> RACHEL ZAMOJSKA, his wife
> KRYSTYNA KORNOWSKI, his sister
> BRUNO KACZMAREK, a political idealist and Krystyna's husband
> TEOFIL KACZMAREK, son of Bruno and Krystyna
> ANNABEL BROOK, his wife
> LORD AND LADY DERWENT, her parents
> SIR JACK MARRYAT, her intended lover

By definition, a polonaise can be a slow, stately processional, almost a walk, set to moderate, 3/4-time music. *Polonaise,* by Piers Paul Read, is such a promenade, based upon a triple rhythm, a beat of love, God, and politics. This "triad" is carried over into the format of the novel, which has three parts, the first two of which are set mostly in Warsaw during the 1930's, while the last is set in Paris and Mulford, England, on the North Cornish coast, in 1958.

For his march through places and events, Read brings together a mixture of landless-but-titled Polish aristocrats, members of the landless-but-proud Polish proletariat, wealthy Polish Jews, French and English bourgeoisie, and super-wealthy English nobility. To accommodate all of these people—there are more than a half dozen central characters—the rhythm of the novel must be somewhat slow, although it is a slowness interspersed with jumps of time and city.

Part of the leisurely pace is caused by Stefan Kornowski, whose father, Count Stanislas Kornowski, is in the process of losing the family estate in Jezow by insisting upon a profligate lifestyle when the novel opens in the mid-1920's. By the summer of 1929, when Stefan is fifteen, the Count is bankrupt, and the bank will soon foreclose its mortgage on the estate. Such mundane troubles do not prevent Stefan from spending his summer vacation—from the Catholic lycée of St. Stanislas Kosta, in Warsaw—in a long internal monologue about "the loftiest riddles of our existence—its purpose, value, significance, etc."

It is this "Cartesian speculation" which first brings Stefan to the decision that there is no God and that his former religious beliefs were based strictly upon accidents of birth and geography. The fact that extended prayers to the Virgin of Czestochowa three years earlier had not prevented his mother's death helped him reach this decision, but his struggles with the pangs of puberty were the definitive factor in his conclusion. Unfortunately, his battles with biological maturation are entirely intellectual ones. The extended contemplation on the reactions of his body to the sight of his former childhood playmate, now a sweaty, well-endowed young lady who runs through the fields around the estate in a loose blouse, convinces Stefan there is no God.

That is, the earlier speculations had proved to him that he had a brain—"I think therefore I am"; the sight of Wanda with her sweating arms and legs physically proved he had a penis; the desire for food proved he had a stomach. But it is an intellectual analysis of physical reality, and such data do not lead him to God but to the absence of God. "I am therefore a sweaty-limbs-loving entity which is incompatible with a God-loving entity because the notion of God repudiates sweaty limbs and sweaty limbs laugh at the notion of God." Others in the novel come to the same realization about God, at least temporarily, but they do so on the basis of acts of cruelty seen in the society or for political reasons. But for Stefan, this realization is all the product of a cold, calculating intellectualizing; that is his chief problem, and Stefan's intellectualizing is a major problem of *Polonaise.*

After dallying with the law as a profession and with Communism as a political belief, Stefan decides to become a writer and begins a series of private-journal stories, as well as stories and plays for public consumption. By the late 1930's Stefan becomes the reigning literary light of Warsaw. He publishes a few *avant-garde* stories in Polish magazines and has two plays produced, thanks to the influence of his patroness.

Both plays are printed in the book; one takes up six pages, and the other covers about four. When they are performed, they are hailed by the critics as the new "theatre of brevity," just the thing the Warsaw society desires, since everyone knows that people in Poland go to the theater only for the eating and drinking which take place at the intermission and at the parties which follow. Certainly, Stefan's plays are brief. They might also be categorized as "theatre of the absurd," for they become another example of his intellectual gameplaying.

Of more interest than the little plays and short stories are the pornographic and/or violent vignettes Stefan writes in his journal, the most extreme of which have to do with the processes by which one can define love as more than an abstract, intellectual notion. The physical expressions of love, as performed by Stefan's admitted alter ego, Raymond de Tarterre, "urbane young Parisian," become increasingly sadistic as the novel progresses.

Love—and ecstasy—can only have final definition if Raymond manages to murder the love object with a knife. By being butchered in this way, for the sake of the ultimate sacrifice, the union of death and ecstasy, the young woman will joyfully and willingly "shriek blasphemies at the extremity of her pleasure and pain." So strongly does Stefan identify with the characters and the underlying concept of these grotesque fantasies, so debilitating an effect does his intellect have upon his reason, that he decides to kill the daughter of his patroness.

He is prevented from carrying out his kill-for-love program, at least this time. The fact that the obstacle to his plan is a prostitute, whom he saw several years before with a school friend and about whom he also has been dreaming for years, makes no more sense than his absurd little stories.

Perhaps Read wants to ridicule abstract art-for-art's-sake in its ultimate form when he has Stefan accept his own literary creation as a desirable goal which needs only his will power to make it an actuality. That Stefan feels such an act will make him a God—he who does not believe in God—and that by following his gross design, he will partake of the "Fruit of the Tree of Knowledge," is more absurd than Stefan's playlets and is as obscene as his journal entries.

When the emphasis of the novel moves away from art to politics, the emphasis on the characters changes, too. The political story of young Communists in Poland in the 1930's is built around Krystyna, Stefan's older sister, and her husband, Bruno.

With the financial collapse of the family estate, Krystyna and the deranged Count move to Warsaw to live with an aunt. Although it shocks her aristocratic uncles, Krystyna takes a job selling jewelry in the same shop where she disposes of her mother's gems to support the family. It is an appropriate time for a change in lifestyle and outlook, as major political changes also are taking place. In fact, much of the chronology of the first two sections of the novel is announced through Hitler's conquests in Germany and other parts of Europe and through changes in Party statements from Moscow.

Through Stefan, Krystyna meets Bruno Kaczmarek, a fellow student, who is active in the outlawed Polish Communist Party. Soon he converts Krystyna to Communism (and away from God) and marries her. They, along with Bruno's next convert, Stefan, become involved with secret Communist cell meetings, the distribution of secretly printed handbills, and the overall confusion caused by the changes in the official Party line, especially as Stalin conducts his purges of Trotskyites and other threatening sections of the Party.

It is here that Read shows his knowledge of the political history of the times. The changes in strategy which Bruno and Krystyna make, the dizzying role-reversals in good-guys and bad-guys, the faithful Party members who are called to Moscow with expectations of praise, only to find themselves arrested and executed as spies—all of these events and the intellectual, ideological games are very true to what happened in those turbulent days.

Regardless of the shifting attitudes and prejudices he must assume as a Party stalwart, Bruno is dedicated to the ideals of humanism as he can sift them from the constant flow of political verbage. As with many young idealists of the period, he subverts his own desires for security and family happiness to become a professional Party worker, at such a low salary that Krystyna must continue to work to support the family, which now includes a son, Teofil.

In many respects, Bruno serves as the balancing agent for the intellectual excesses of Stefan. When Stefan and Bruno are ordered by the Comintern to fight in the Spanish Civil War, Stefan deserts in Paris, before even joining the International Brigade, while Bruno rises to a position of authority and respect, such a position of authority and power, in fact, that he becomes a Party executioner, eliminating politically deviant soldiers. All the while, Bruno knows his actions are humanistically wrong, but he is an "atheist monk," whose only goal is to serve the official dogmas. Bruno becomes the figure whose strong intellect leads him to support a personally dangerous cause, while Stefan's intellect leads him only into erotic fantasies about sex and murder.

Stefan leaves his socialist ideals behind him in Paris as easily "as a reptile sheds its skin. He had not betrayed them; he had simply stepped out of them. . . ." Bruno abandons the Polish Communist Party when it collapses in the chaos caused by the nonagression pact signed by Hitler and Stalin, an agreement which immediately resulted in the division of Poland between the two countries.

On the other hand, morally, Stefan and Bruno are two ends of the same extreme continuum: one wishes to kill for love, the other does kill for politics. Stefan is prevented from completing his goal by coincidence; Bruno stops when he can no longer rationalize his actions; but both have death as their ultimate goal.

Prior to his withdrawal from the political scene, however, Stefan has one experience which presents another irony of misplaced allegiances. When he decides to make his art serve his beliefs, he presents a short story to the members of his cell for constructive criticism. In this polite but artistically degrading exchange, Piers Paul Read crystalizes the frustration faced by many writers of the 1930's, regardless of the country in which they lived. When, in Stefan's story, a young, valiant, activist worker succumbs to sexual temptation, Stefan is told he is guilty of a Trotskyite error and must change the plot. The story's intended readers are Polish workers, Catholic born and trained, and—according to the members of Stefan's cell—adulterous behavior of any kind would be unacceptable to the worker-readers. In line with accepted proletarian formulae of the day, Stefan is allowed to have the workers lose their strike, as such losses were thought to be beneficial in keeping the proletariat stirred up.

The problem with Stefan's story, and with most such formula writing of the 1930's, is that the workers for whom it is meant seldom read the magazine which prints the stories. Thus, Stefan—and all the others—suppressed their artistic talent for questionable reasons.

Apart from any shortcomings of character motivation one may discern in the novel, there is also the problem of the third section. All the characters of the first two parts except Stefan, Krystyna, and Teofil have been killed in the war. The three survivors are living in Paris, and it is 1958. If the first two-thirds of the novel can be viewed as a promenade, the last third appears to be a limping afterthought. The political timeclock denotes its progress now in terms of de Gaulle, Algiers, and the Fourth and Fifth French Republics, which is not quite the grand scale of Hitler, Stalin, and all points between.

Does it really matter that the reader is led through Teofil's courtship and marriage to a plain but fantastically wealthy English girl, when that courtship is such a pale shadow of the fiery lovings and leavings of his parents and uncle in Warsaw just twenty years earlier? Does it matter that Stefan finally has an opportunity to carry out his grand scheme, when the motivation and execution of the plan now are almost silly? *Polonaise* would be a much more stimulating novel if its author had left his characters in the fluctuating world of Europe in the throes of World War II. They had no solutions for the problems of the time, and they were imperfect—and thus very human—personalities involved in their dance. But by sounding this final refrain, by ending the dance and bringing up the lights in the grand ballroom, the dancers and the dance itself become much less interesting.

John C. Carlisle

Sources for Further Study

America. CXXXV, December 4, 1976, p. 404.

Booklist. LXXIII, October 1, 1976, p. 236.

New Statesman. XCII, November 19, 1976, p. 722.

New York Times. November 27, 1976, p. 21.

New York Times Book Review. November 28, 1976, p. 8.

Observer. November 14, 1976, p. 29.

Spectator. CCXXXVII, November 20, 1976, p. 22.

A PRINCE OF OUR DISORDER
The Life of T. E. Lawrence

Author: John E. Mack
Publisher: Little, Brown and Company (Boston). Illustrated. 561 pp. $15.00
Type of work: Biography
Time: 1888-1935
Locale: England, Arabia, and the Arabic portion of the Ottoman Empire

An analysis of the personality of T. E. Lawrence and of the sources of his genius and influence

> *Principal personages:*
> T. E. LAWRENCE, also known as John Hume Ross and T. E. Shaw; "Lawrence of Arabia"
> THOMAS ROBERT TIGHE CHAPMAN, later Thomas Lawrence, his father
> SARAH JUNNER LAWRENCE, his mother
> ARNOLD, ROBERT, AND WILLIAM LAWRENCE, his brothers
> HUSEIN, Sharif of Mecca

"Lawrence of Arabia"—the romantic images of desert warfare, of the young British "colonel" in Arab dress leading the tribes against the Turks of the Ottoman Empire, are all the sharper in contrast to the deadly, unromantic stalemate of trench warfare as World War I knew it. When Lowell Thomas' account appeared in 1924, the starting-point for widespread interest in Lawrence, the English-speaking world may have been ready for glamor and heroism; individual bravery and skill seemed antiquated and irrelevant, yet here such qualities were still alive and effective, and set in that especially "romantic" world of *The Arabian Nights,* Valentino's *The Sheik,* and *The Desert Song.*

The fifty-odd years since Thomas' book, and nearly sixty since the fighting in Arabia and Syria, have added complications to the story. If events and biographers have tried to reduce the cloud of legend, others have added to it. Lawrence's own books, especially *Seven Pillars of Wisdom,* reveal a great literary artist, but also a complex personality, and a story more profound than boyish adventure. After the blaze of glory, he sought obscurity in the Royal Air Force, then the Tanks Corps, then the Air Force again as an enlisted man, using the names of Ross and Shaw. He died—fittingly—in a crash on his motorcycle.

Politically, Lawrence and his campaign involved the British in the Arab world, and especially in promises of independent Arab states, or a single independent state. The difficulty of keeping that promise, in the light of British and French colonial ambitions, and of the promise of a "Jewish homeland" made by the British, are among the roots of today's Middle Eastern troubles. They put Lawrence into postwar diplomacy, and then into rejection. Romance gives way to questions of sordid reality; was British military and colonial strategy using Lawrence? Was Lawrence using the Arabs? Inevitably, or as nearly so as human affairs permit, the legend attracted de-mythologizers, or denigrators. Simple search for fact led to revelations: Lawrence was illegitimate, his father a landowning gentleman in Ireland, part of the Anglo-Irish Protestant "ascendancy," who left his wife for Sarah, the governess for the Chapman daughters. Lawrence was the second of their four sons.

One of the difficulties for biographers was that Lawrence himself, if not deceptive, was cryptic and evasive about much of his life. If various accounts circulated, he was himself in some ways responsible. To the cynicism of the later twentieth century, both the evasiveness and the search for obscurity could seem ways of retaining public attention.

The latest attempt to deal with Lawrence is by John E. Mack, a Harvard psychiatrist, and professionally more interested in Lawrence's personality than in narrative history or biography. Several things differentiate his work from much that is called "psycho-history." One, quite simply, is Mack's quality of writing. Another is his respect for *historical* knowledge, and therefore for the historical context, historical accuracy, and techniques of the critical historian. Perhaps most significant is that his subject-patient and his approach are unusual.

Lawrence was a man of unusual gifts, literary, military, and personal. He left a considerable amount of material in his books, miscellaneous writings, and letters, and much of it is introspective and analytical. Furthermore, friends, acquaintances, and comrades left accounts of their contacts with him, many of them insightful and articulate. (How many subjects have a long friendship and correspondence with George Bernard Shaw and his wife?) Some of these, and Lawrence's surviving brothers, were available for interviews with Mack. All of this partly makes up for the great difference between the psycho-historian and the analyst: the patient is not there on the couch. Another great difference is obvious—the object of analysis is the patient's knowledge, not the analyst's, save as the analyst's is necessary to the patient's. The object of the historian is the *reader's* understanding.

Mack seems throughout aware of these differences, and of the differences in method they suggest. He is insistent on the limits to which knowledge based on the surviving materials can go, and is careful not to transgress. Moreover, he lifts his study to a different level by setting as his object not merely the understanding of Lawrence's personality, but of the kind of personality which affects the course of history.

It is this approach, this question, which makes Mack's study especially important. The author does not claim any "great man" or "genius" theory; on the other hand, he does not accept the notion that individual character does not count. There is, as he sees it, a convergence of events to a point where this particular man can influence, even influence greatly, the further course of events. This is not mere adaptation to external reality; it means changing the reality, or at least altering its direction. Lawrence is to Mack a superb example; granted the course of events that brought on World War I, and the growth of weakness in the Ottoman Empire and of nationalism among its Arab subjects, it still was Lawrence, and Lawrence's personal combination of gifts and drives, that made the revolt what it was.

This is the path of the investigation, and the general lines are clear. The peculiar combination of illegitimacy and strong moral and religious principles on the part of Lawrence's parents are one line of explanation: Lawrence felt not only a sense of guilt, of differentness, but also an obligation to restore, to do penance. That the mother was the dominant influence here, Mack is sure, though he suggests that Lawrence's father was not the negligible figure Lawrence sometimes suggested.

Mack assumes both Lawrence's extraordinary intellect and his remarkable constitution. But just as what Lawrence did with his physical constitution is not reported—the arduous training, the testing of the body for endurance, feats of going without food or sleep—neither is his use of the intellect. Lawrence apparently never was satisfied with following the prescribed schooling, though he was capable of great effort to achieve what he wanted. A great fondness for medieval romance led Lawrence to an interest in Crusaders' castles, his Oxford thesis, and Middle Eastern archaeology. In the years just before World War I he worked with Sir Leonard Woolley at the excavation of Carchemish, the Hittite site. Mack believes it was one of Lawrence's happiest experiences; it was also remarkable training for the great adventure. He learned not only the Arabic language, but the topography and the folkways of the area as well.

The war was, of course, a central experience. Mack is not as clear about the military operations as he might be—perhaps he takes them for granted. Rather, the focus is on Lawrence's skill in dealing with the Arabs, and to some degree with fellow Britishers. He was never, apparently, an orthodox officer in dress or behavior. Mack stresses, against some of the denigrators, the evidence of both his courage and his tactical ability. The trauma of the experience at Dera'a, apparently homosexual rape by the Turkish governor, or troops (Mack seems to believe), or both, is a main theme of the rest of the book. Another abiding note is the reaction to the fighting itself, a mixture of exultation and revulsion.

That mixture carries over to the postwar struggle over the demands of Arab nationalism. Lawrence turned politician, with some limited success, and claimed he despised the whole business. Disappointment with the settlement, and disillusionment with his own government, led—in Mack's reading—to questioning the value of the war and of his own part in it. Again, a sense of guilt, as well as of anger and frustration, come through.

In a sense (with exceptions to be noted) Lawrence's public services ended here. The legend, however, was only beginning. Enlistment in the Royal Air Force as an ordinary airman was a sign of his retirement; the parallel to one of his medieval heroes entering the monastery is bound to occur. Yet—the question is also bound to raise itself—how many ordinary airmen corresponded with the Marshal of the RAF, with M.P.'s and newspaper editors?

If Mack does not explicitly raise the questions, his account certainly provides the material, and even the impetus, to ask. The "retirement" is the puzzle of the Lawrence legend, in one sense, and one of its strongest themes, in another. Mack's theory of Lawrence's drives—the desire to accomplish, to repay, and yet the feeling of unworthiness—affords explanation, and at the same time explains both the satisfaction Lawrence derived, and his continuing sense of frustration and inadequacy. Mack details the writing and rewriting, and even more the publishing, of *Seven Pillars of Wisdom*. The book was circulated only to a chosen few although there were subscription copies and copyright problems; here again is illustrated the tension between fame and obscurity.

Mack's evidence is that "Ross" and "Shaw" served well. His fellow-airmen and soldiers surely knew he was different. Some officers knew who he was; apparently the men, as a rule, did not. Whenever newsmen found out what he was doing and where, the post became the center of attention, usually unwelcome to commanders and other officers. Yet, by and large, he seems to have been on good terms with his "mates" and even, Mack repeatedly says with evidence, to have helped them individually. He was generous with his money, but even more with his time, introducing enlisted men to literature and music and concerning himself with their problems. It is this personal generosity and its effectiveness that Mack stresses. Lawrence's contacts, and later his book about his experience in the service, *The Mint*, brought about reforms in the treatment of enlisted men, perhaps trivial-seeming, but often important to the men themselves and unseen by command. He worked with success in the last years on air-rescue boats, of significance especially in the days of World War II.

But his great gift, in Mack's word, was as "enabler"—not merely encouraging others, or helping them, but really *enabling* them to exert their powers, whether the Arabs to rebel, or ill-educated airmen to read the classics.

Along with the generosity, Mack describes the difficulties of these years, the withdrawal, the flagellation, which he relates to the experience at Dera'a. Together they form the pieces of a character: but do we ever have more than mere pieces? Mack's account is nevertheless persuasive, for one reason because it is cautious and recognizes the limits of any such investigation.

Some questions arise that are left unanswered. For example, Mack does not explicitly deal with Lawrence as outsider—an Irishman (he himself insisted) in England, a boy cut off from his class (when class was important) by his parents' situation; an officer in Cairo headquarters not really part of that order. If these isolations created problems, they may also account for some of Lawrence's special abilities, such as his talent for dealing with Arabs or with men of other classes. Again, Mack deals with charges of falsehood, and insists that where Lawrence can be checked, as in accounts of raids in the desert, he is accurate and truthful. He does not really concern himself with the more difficult but more intriguing question: how much was the avoidance of publicity a way of attracting attention? One need not be a public relations expert to know that disguises and disappearances were sure to be bait to the newsmen. Nor need one be more than an armchair psychologist to accept that, whatever his conscious desire, Lawrence too may have expected and subconsciously wanted the results he obtained.

A Prince of Our Disorder is a rich and subtle book. The professional may fault Mack for contradictions, gaps in information, and important questions left unanswered. But the nonprofessional reader should find the treatment fascinating, persuasive, rewarding, and refreshingly free of jargon.

George J. Fleming

Sources for Further Study

America. CXXXIV, May 1, 1976, p. 386.
Atlantic. CCXXXVII, May, 1976, p. 111.
Best Sellers. XXXVI, June, 1976, p. 82.
Christian Science Monitor. LXVIII, May 5, 1976, p. 27.
Commonweal. CIII, December 3, 1976, p 791.
Critic. XXXV, Fall, 1976, p. 91.
Economist. CCLIX, May 15, 1976, p. 121.

THE RAIDER

Author: Jesse Hill Ford (1928-   )
Publisher: Little, Brown and Company (Boston). 468 pp. $10.00
Type of work: Novel
Time: The nineteenth century
Locale: Western Tennessee

> *A chronicle of one family on the Tennessee frontier in the years before and during the Civil War*

> *Principal characters:*
> ELIAS McCUTCHEON, a frontiersman
> JANE NAIL, his wife
> ISAAC AND WILLY, their sons
> SHOKOTEE, a rich Chickasaw, Jane's foster-father
> LEOLA, Jane's Indian nurse
> ELLEN ASHE, mistress of a neighboring plantation
> EDWARD, her son by Elias

Jesse Hill Ford's *The Raider* took a long time to write: eight years, including research and revision. It is, as he says, a simple story; it is not *Gone with the Wind,* nor was it meant to be. There is no grand cinematic climax, no immortal passion. Instead it is a family chronicle, its bare facts passed down the generations by word of mouth, and given flesh by the author, whose great care it has been to set the story forth in such a way as to keep faith with his forebears who lived it.

Hill has aimed to show that the Tennessee frontier was settled not by heroes and demi-gods but by mortals whose chief virtues were singlemindedness and perseverance and whose only wealth was their own strength spent without stint. They were a complex and a restless people, with vaulting dreams and feet of clay. Chief among them was Elias McCutcheon, who came to West Tennessee orphaned and bereft by a cholera epidemic, possessing only a dog, a horse, and a certain vision. *The Raider* is the story of how the character of the man and the conditions of his life combined to form first a great landholder, then a consummate soldier.

In the beginning of the novel, Elias is alone and loneliness and physical striving form the poles of his existence. Like Adam, his every act is pristine; his dog is called Dog, as if it were the first one in the world. This comparison with Adam cuts two ways, emphasizing Elias' moral isolation on the one hand, and on the other pointing up the fact that he inhabits no temperate bountiful garden but a winter-bound wilderness, hostile and demanding. Instead of God Almighty, he confronts Shokotee, a prosperous Chickasaw landowner and dispenser of all good things, in the shape of edibles, tools, and ultimately Elias' Eve, Jane. Elias and Jane couple in the fields and Elias' seed falls into the plowed earth; symbolically he weds the land, forming a mystical union. Not that he puts it that way to himself, being a plain man, roughly literate; still he remembers it, especially amid the griefs and terrors of the Civil War, like a talisman, a reason to labor and to fight. Godlike Elias is: in his work of creating a farm and a home, and in the gift of his person to his wife and his mistress Ellen Ashe. Yet the author humanizes his ancestor deftly: he is also capable of smacking his thumb with a hammer, of expounding fatheadedly the primacy of Christian dogma over Indian myth, of being manipulated by various females.

Elias and Jane represent two strains of civilization, one hard, analytic, and European, the other yielding, intuitive, and Indian. In a curious way the one culture, in supplanting the other, subsumes it, so that the resulting society shows elements of both, and indeed not always the best elements. The raider Sim Hornby, who, having robbed Elias, slices Jane's face in a wholly gratuitous act of savagery, is, pointedly, a half-breed. Jane is the premier example of the conjunction of two ways of life. An orphan whose family were long ago murdered by Indians, she is Shokotee's adopted child, calling him "Father" and his house "home." Her mix of Indian hardihood and European sense of duty makes her the ideal mate for Elias; it saves her life and her mind after her mutilation, and enables her to run the plantation during the war. Yet another example of the fusion of cultures occurs after the freebooters' attack, in which all the farms in the district are robbed, and the civilized Chickasaws under Shokotee's command and the settlers under Elias join forces. They stage the famous raid on the bandit stronghold called the Horse Pens. Employing a hybrid strategy of Indian-style ambush followed by regular volleys of musketry, infantry-fashion, the combined forces wipe out the robbers and plunder their stores, thus enriching themselves and bringing order to the district in one bold stroke. The raid transforms both Elias and the neighborhood. The settlers, previously feeling merely part of a scatter of clearings along the creeks, after the raid feel themselves part of a community, with a corporate self-respect and a communal moral standard. And Elias, before the raid merely one among many skilled and tireless hunters and farmers, emerges from the adventure a recognized strategist and leader of men, able to forge a mob into a weapon, and to compel men to exceed their normal capacities.

The raid on the Horse Pens has other, darker consequences, both public and private. For Elias, though it has meant material riches and social recognition, it also seems to put an end to his content. Jane's mutilation preys on his mind; he wonders guiltily if it is a punishment for his liaison with Ellen Ashe. Jane's withdrawal from their former intimacy drives him more and more into Ellen's arms, but prosperity has changed even this comfort: he feels less easy in her fine house than he had in her rough cabin in the midst of its stump field. Paralleling the change in Elias' life, the economic and social life of the district undergoes pervasive mutation as a result of the Horse Pens raid: the settlers now own slaves.

The labor of slaves transforms the clearings into plantations, and diversified farming gives way to the singleminded cultivation of cotton. Cotton works miracles, and the region becomes rich. Though fundamentally opposed to slavery in principle, Elias finds himself profiting from it nonetheless. Between them, cotton and slavery breach the green walls of the forest that isolate the Western frontier, and bring it into the arena of conflict between North and South.

Two events signal the end of the Garden-of-Eden period of settlement, a time when, whatever misfortune might befall, the moral questions confronting men and women had straightforward answers and virtue was rewarded daily in a satisfying material way. The first of these events is the death of Dog, Elias' companion in the wilderness. Dog dies of wounds received in a fight with a bear, a she-bear that would scarcely have winded him in his prime. Thus at a stroke Elias is cut off from the time when his course ran clear and clean before him, in the noon of his youth and hope. Soon afterward the second event takes place: a wolf bites his dog Chutt, who later turns rabid and bites every animal on the plantation. One by one, the mules and cattle, the horses, hogs, and geese go mad and die, tearing their own flesh. This happens at the beginning of the section of the book entitled "The Wolf"; the rest of the section details the spread of Confederate sentiment in the district. War fever seizes the minds of people of all conditions, with the same impartiality as the hydrophobia among the animals, and with equally dire results. Even Elias, who has all along felt that he did wrong in owning slaves, and who furthermore harbors a strong conviction of the sacredness of the Union, is drawn in. When all his neighbors form a company of mounted rifles and apply to him to lead them, he succumbs to the pressure of their old bond. His sons, Edward Ashe and Willy, raised on stories of the Horse Pens raid, view the war as a rite of passage. For the failed planter Dutt Callister, the madness takes a different shape: the war offers both a chance to sink the shame of his bankruptcy and an opportunity to put distance between himself and his large and exigent family. Others, like Shokotee's son Pettecasockee and the old artilleryman Jasper Coon, join up out of loyalty to Elias. So the infection spreads, and the fate of the South is sealed.

From the beginning, Elias and his little command thrive on combat. Accustomed from boyhood to the use of firearms and to hunting on foot and horseback, the mounted rifles come ready-trained to the fray. As the war continues, the unit and its commander become more and more expert and inventive at their adopted *metier*. Gradually they suffer a sea-change; they are no longer farmers gone to war, but soldiers pure and simple. Putting aside rhetoric and principle, they take Jane's simple injunction "Kill as many as you can" for motto. They also take whatever they need of the goods and services of civilians, regardless of sympathy; they destroy the railroad and the steam packet, and burn the cotton warehouses. Like a rabid creature tearing itself, they maul the very soil and populace they took up arms to protect. Thus the rabid-wolf metaphor is fulfilled.

The rabies plague as a metaphor for the disastrous war is a device typical of this work, one that fits its pleasing modesty of tone. Frequently, a momentous event is preceded by, and seemingly foreshadowed by, a similar happening on a smaller scale. For example, the raid on the Horse Pens follows a successful campaign to kill out marauding bears; Willy's death seems to be presaged by a curious accident in which his horse is killed; Elias' grey cat deserts the brigade just as the South's fortunes falter. In this way, without seeming to claim a transcendent fate for the McCutcheon family, the author manages to relate their vicissitudes both to the natural world and to the life of the nation.

Hill uses a different technique in making clear his moral stance, however unemphatic, on the issue of slavery. It is clear that from several points of view the institution of slavery was directly responsible for the corruption of a fundamentally strong emergent society. Slavery elevated men who could not by their own efforts have commanded notice or respect, such as the Poe brothers and Dutt Callister. It permitted the development of a class whose common pursuits made them ideal soldiers, so good at their work that soldiering could come to seem an end in itself, and all civilians its legitimate victims. It made feasible a one-crop boom-or-bust economy without the flexibility either to regulate or to repair itself. And it encouraged a self-justifying habit of mind which militated against a proper grasp of economic and political realities. It is hardly to be expected that an author would depict his own family as a microcosm of a diseased society, yet that is what Hill has done, understandingly, forgivingly, yet with unswerving firmness. The great virtue of the work is that it maintains this conviction without sounding either abject or shrill.

Apart from the artlessness of the tale and the superb delineation of character, *The Raider* pleases by its myriad details of frontier and plantation life, in which Hill's meticulous research is evident. Facts of farm and army life, once common as mud, nowadays as exotic as the moon's dark half, bestrew the narrative. The cradle hung from the rafters, the sand hearth of Elias' cabin, the proper shaving-soap for a gentleman to take to war, the proper stowage of a soldier's toothbrush and tin cup all are worked into the matrix of the story in such a way as to give the reader access to a way of life that is past. Perhaps the most interesting set of details are those showing the complicated relations among the three races. On the face of things, it seems that whites regarded Indians on a plane equal with themselves, while blacks were beyond the pale entirely, which explains the horror that greets Edward Ashe's running away with the slave Betsy. The Chickasaws also kept African slaves, nor is there evidence that they were regarded differently from the servants of the whites. Yet Ellen Ashe, in a temper, taunts Jane with her putative Indian blood, which seems to indicate toleration if not active prejudice. More teasing still, while all the white people are revolted by Edward Ashe's passion for Betsy, Shokotee is not; instead, he seems highly amused. In fact, his smile of wicked wisdom might serve as a quietus on all questions of race, both in this fine novel and in the world at large.

Jan Kennedy Foster

Sources for Further Study

Best Sellers. XXXV, December, 1975, p. 273.

Booklist. LXXII, January 1, 1976, p. 613.

National Observer. XV, January 24, 1976, p. 19.

New York Times Book Review. May 16, 1976, p. 37.

Virginia Quarterly Review. LII, Autumn, 1976, p. 130.

RATNER'S STAR

Author: Don DeLillo
Publisher: Alfred A. Knopf (New York). 438 pp. $10.00
Type of work: Novel
Time: The present
Locale: The United States and an unidentified location, probably in the South Pacific

The satirical and often frightening view of a scientific community involved in the development of increasingly abstract and increasingly useless mathematical and astrological projects centering around the decoding of a message from space

Principal characters:
> BILLY TWILLIG, a fourteen-year-old Nobel Prize winner
> ROBERT HOPPER SOFTLY, Billy's friend and mentor
> HENRIK ENDOR, a mathematician and astrophysicist
> CYRIL KYRIAKOS, a transitional logician
> ELUX TROXL, a conglomerate director
> ORANG MOHOLE, twice winner of the Cheops Feely Medal
> SHAZAR LAZARUS RATNER, an astronomer-turned-mystic

To say that there is a plot in Don DeLillo's *Ratner's Star* is to say that $2 + 2 = 4$ and $5 + 3 = 8$, but that does not tell much. That is, the real importance of a mathematical formula lies as much in the manipulation of it as it does in the abstract sense of the computation itself. Thus it is with *Ratner's Star;* the plot—if, indeed, such a formal literary term may be applied to the bizarre and often grotesque behavior of the characters—exists only as a thin line onto which DeLillo may attach his anecdotes. The storyline concerns a group of scientists in a think tank who attempt to decode and to respond to a message from outer space. Dangling from this often frayed thread are multiple subplots, often unresolved, which allow DeLillo to joke-with-and-about, to poke-fun-at-and-ridicule science, abstract intellectualism, and corporate conglomerates.

In fact, "Bi-Levelism"—a philosophical viewpoint which LoQuardo, an abstract-mathematician-turned-computer-programmer, defines as a system that allows one to "talk with an appearance of truth *and* falsity about all things"—can serve as the operative mode for the entire novel, as DeLillo describes the serious (perhaps tragic) and the comic (perhaps burlesque) aspects of life at Field Experiment Number One.

Supposedly, Field Experiment Number One (which is never presented in the book in its acronym form) is designed to overcome national differences, which pure science should be above, and to bring about a unity of mankind, "a planetary community," which will "look beyond science." DeLillo never says just what is "beyond science," but, by implication, it might be a higher form of humanism. The opposite outcome, however, is more often the case, as the projects undertaken by the scientists do not look beyond humanistic concerns—indeed, seem to have little cognizance of any human side at all.

Not all the scientists are caricatures, evil geniuses lost in a statistical fairyland of their own making. Olin Nyquist, an astral engineer, first mentions a recurring image of the novel, that of "an overarching symmetry." He becomes concerned with the problems of physics and metaphysics. In the end there seems to be something about the universe which defies measurement, which does not lend itself to neat definitions. Even if it is not really a "totally harmonious picture of the world system," the human condition seems to need something to perpetuate "our childlike trust in structural balance."

If there is a totally innocent scientist in the novel, it must be Henrik Endor, mathematician and astrophysicist, who apparently has found the meaning of the message. Rather than destroy the symmetry or upset the balance which his translation might cause, Endor has taken up residence about ten miles east of the scientific complex, where he lives in a large hole, eating insects and worms and talking to no one. Endor is the most grotesque major figure in the novel, with his beard full of maggots and his torn clothing. Using a bent clothes hanger and his fingernails, he is digging a tunnel, a hole in a hole, towards the center of the earth. In addition, many of the scientists, the human beings who are programming the computers and developing the hypotheses, worry about mysticism, or the lack of it, in their lives.

Billy Twillig, a fourteen-year-old mathematical genius on loan from the Center for the Refinement of Ideational Structures, who was given a Nobel Prize for the development of a "zorg . . . a kind of number," has recurring dreams about death. Cyril Kyriakos, a transitional logician, has as his primary function the chairing of a committee which is attempting to define the word "science"—a project which has already produced five hundred pages, but no agreements; Kyriakos feels the definition must include a reference to the "terror of death," which he perceives as "the ultimate horrifying vision of objective inquiry." Skip Wismer, a NASA consultant, defines death as a turning inside out, "an unknotting of consciousness in a space of n dimensions," which certainly is a nonobjective, nonquantifiable way of describing the phenomenon.

This level of mystical intellectual process exists with the highly scientific, "history-has-no-worthwhile-statements-to-make-to-us" level in other persons as well. Ratner, for whom the star is named, and who has abandoned abstract mathematics for the strict codes and rules of Orthodox Judaism, tells Billy that "g-dash-d" could exist anywhere in the universe, since the universe is a system which "works on the theory of opposites. To see what it looks like outside the universe, you have to go into a trance or two." Orang Mohole, whose "mohole totality theory" explains the Big Bang origin of the universe, finally concedes that during the first one thousandth of a second of the Big Bang, there developed certain "relativistic forces" which no one understands, so far.

The problem with this value-oriented level of the novel, this "yes" portion of a "yes-no" binary system, is the DeLillo is perhaps too capable a word-monger. There is nothing wrong with verbal fluency, but in this case it may not be right, either. The comments relating to religion or art or the space-time continuum, all of them valid, all of them interesting, even exciting, are virtually hidden deep inside a convoluted, jargon-filled style.

Without doubt, on the comic level of his approach, DeLillo occasionally does become carried away with his own abilities, especially when it comes to names for some of the characters: Robert Hopper Softly, who, in his sexual relations with the lady journalist, Jean Sweet Venable, does anything but that; Mimsy Mope Grimmer, the resident expert on infantile sexuality; Elux Troxl, the conglomerate director, and his bodyguard-enforcer, Grbk.

The epitome of DeLillo's word games comes with Viverrine Gentian, an old lady Billy sits beside one day, from whom he fears "sour odors" will arise; Viverrine also is strikingly good-looking for her advanced age. If one plays around with the name for a while, one finds: "gentian," a striking, late-blooming, autumn (the advanced season?) wildflower (preserved for posterity in Bryant's "To a Fringed Gentian"); "viverrine," a family of small carnivores, including the civet cat, which produces a thick musky-odored substance used for perfumes. This is definitely the "no" of the binary, for it is burlesque, and low burlesque, at that.

However, in a satiric vein, DeLillo effectively castigates the stupidity of the super-intellectuals who create a new formula or a new number theory (like the zorg), whose only measure of validity is "the beauty it possesses, the deft strength of [the] mathematical reasoning." Even Billy admits zorgs are useless and cannot be used for anything except mathematics; "in other words," he says, "they don't apply."

The problem which Kyriakos' committee is having in completing its definition provides DeLillo the opportunity to ridicule the committee system, and it is a picture which anyone who is involved in any kind of institutional bureaucracy can appreciate. Almost everyone can accept a definition of science as a systematic, objective investigation of nature which is supported by observation, identification, and repetition. The definition committee's problem is how to account scientifically for such things as "venerated emblems, sandpaintings, legend-telling, ceremonial chants and so on." No one wants to take a stand to point out that the value to mankind of an icon or a Gregorian chant is not in its ability to be exactly replicated or counted or categorized; its value is aesthetic and emotional. The best way to destroy the inherent value of such artifacts of humanism is to attempt to codify and to sterilize them.

Billy Twillig's major function at Field Experiment Number One is to decipher the message which seems to have come from Ratner's Star, but Softly finally tells Billy that it makes no difference whether the message is decoded or not. The value of the message is not its content, but that it allows Softly to develop Logicon, a universal, mathematical language which will be used to send mankind's reply back into space.

When it is determined that the message was sent millions of years ago and that it did not come from space but simply was detoured through space, Softly defends his creation by saying his "task is to frame a reply . . . it doesn't matter what the reply is." In fact, to send an actual message to actual message-senders would be "to miss the point of the whole thing." In other words, my mind is made up, so don't bother me with the facts!

Such mind-over-practicality or intellect-over-sense is also found in Cyril Kyriakos, who practiced a unique form of birth control. He postulated that he could sever the psychic link between his logical, intellectual processes and his biological processes. That is, he determined that if he willed a denial of a "localized point" to his reproductive cells, they would just sit there doing nothing. When his wife became pregnant, it did not mean there was anything wrong with the theory, just that there had been a minor malfunction.

There is also in *Ratner's Star* a certain element of science fiction, of abstraction carried to extremes in the giant computer, Space Brain. Although it was originally constructed with the smallest crystals known and weighed only fifty pounds, it had outgrown its data-storing capacities, and additional storage facilities had to be provided. Since the additions were quite sophisticated, Space Brain helped with the physical, structural computations and was, therefore, "self-designed," at least in part. With the additional storage capacity, Space Brain collected data from the radio antennae surrounding the complex, converted it into electrical impulses, "stylized" the impulses into simulations of "observed and probable phenomena," and created its own "computer universe." Whether such a universe is really out there or not is unimportant; the important fact is that the computer has created a complete, stylized system.

The final parody DeLillo presents is that of big business in the form of Elux Troxl. When Troxl's scheme for controlling the value of all the world's monies by controlling all the computer time in the world fails, he changes the name of his multi-national financial giant to ACRONYM and does effect a corner on the market for bat guano. Billy's neighborhood words-of-wisdom from his childhood are appropriate here: "Keep believing it, shit-for-brains."

Yet, the most devastating comment DeLillo makes, the twist of the knife he has jabbed into the scientific body, comes at the end of the novel when the decoded message proves to be prophetic. The tight little dehumanized world of Field Experiment Number One (if not, in fact, the entire world) ends, not with a bang, but with a shriek. Abstract science fails Billy and Softly; they become maniacal animals, with Softly deep in the earth in Endor's tunnel, clawing with his hands over Endor's now decomposing body, trying to reach—who knows, or cares, where or what?

Ultimately, *Ratner's Star* is a tragedy and/or a farce; it functions in both worlds. It can be taken for the gigantic put-down it is as DeLillo plays his linguistic games while flexing his verbal muscles. Or it can be seen as a frightening portrayal of what could happen in a society where "logic" is a word with only its mathematical meaning left, a world in which Space Brain, the binary computer, with its 0-1, yes-no capabilities can answer questions which cannot be programmed into it until it designs a new problem board for itself.

John C. Carlisle

Sources for Further Study

Atlantic. CCXXXVIII, August, 1976, p. 86.
Book World. June 13, 1976, p. M3.
Booklist. LXXIII, October 1, 1976, p. 233.
New York Times. May 27, 1976, p. 33.
Newsweek. LXXXVII, June 7, 1976, p. 90.
Time. CVII, June 7, 1976, p. 84.

REAL LOSSES, IMAGINARY GAINS

Author: Wright Morris (1910-   )
Publisher: Harper & Row Publishers (New York). 186 pp. $8.95
Type of work: Short stories

Thirteen stories crafted in various styles, on a wide range of themes, displaying the author's usual array of astonishing characters and situations

Not counting anthologies of his work, this volume is Wright Morris' twenty-fifth book. Best known, perhaps, for such works as *The Field of Vision, Love Among the Cannibals,* and *Fire Sermon,* he has always worked diligently and well throughout a long career which has seen some of the juicier prizes carried off by lesser talents. Wright Morris continues in excellence. The man's gift is amazing. It is not mere energy; it is an outrageously, excruciatingly powerful precision of vision bound to an equivalent, commensurate ability to express, to convey that which he sees, feels, so deeply *needs* to share with us. He comes closer to sharing the whole range of human emotion and situation than any other American writer today. He is restless. He experiments constantly in methods of creating mood, character, and theme. The stories always surprise, sometimes shock, always reveal something memorable. He is fearless. He takes on the knottiest, the most enigmatic problems of our time and treats them in such a way as to make us affirm our humanity, sometimes to go away chastened, at other times to be encouraged, and always to be more conscious of our better possibilities.

So, the writer is amazing; he truly gets better as he gets older. How suitable to his cranky spirit. How wonderfully perverse and refreshing that seems in our century of youth worship. Moreover, one of the traits which most endears Morris to his admirers is his craftsmanship-within-tenacity. He is a professional, a writers' writer who is also the delight of the close reader. Never somehow having received the full recognition he deserves, he has continued observing life and reporting it in his inimitable way. He is honest; therefore he may at times seem merciless, but he relates the doings of humankind wide-eyed, sometimes in horror, sometimes in amusement, nearly always, though, in love, awe, or concern. He cares for this mystery, this pain and joy we call life. Every story in this collection aches with mingled pity and pride for humanity's meager strengths. In the volume's title story, Morris says of the gentle Aunt Winona, "She was at once serene, vulnerable, and unshakable. The appalling facts of this world existed to be forgiven. In her presence I was subject to fevers of faith, fits of stark belief." The description might well suggest his own artistic stance and effect.

The stories range widely across time and geography, and they vary remarkably in tone and style. The dates at the end of each story show that most of them were written in the late 1960's and early 1970's. The earliest one, "The Ram in the Thicket," which first appeared in *Harper's Bazaar* in 1948, is so poignantly universal in theme—the effect on his parents of the loss of a son to war—so timeless that it has probably been included here as a caustic reminder to contemporary readers that the pain of loss in war is not limited to Vietnam. The power of the story derives from its being determinedly about loss, whenever and wherever that loss occurs—not about topicality or region.

The most recent story—"The Cat's Meow," dated 1975—shows a tempered Morris, a man taking some temporary comfort in mellowness while at the same time not fully trusting it. The story is funny but tough, drawing its humor from inevitable reality, filled with gratitude for gifts of love and companionship and talent, yet at the same time sure of the knowledge of their inevitable loss. The narrator, Morgan, a writer, reveals the tentative quality of this plateau in his life as he describes his reliance on the settled regularity of things such as his cat's need to be let out at night: "He had relied on that meow, as he did his wife's breathing. If for any reason she checked that breathing, in order to listen to something, he was awake in an instant." The gifts are thus savored more fully, more poignantly because of the consciousness of their very finiteness. It is interesting to note, between these two stories, how Morris has moved, has refined through the times, always more surely isolating essentials in his treatments. He is thus to cut through the confusion of a period as confusing to most writers as was the decade of the 1960's, say, and wring out of it finally some parcel of good sense, feelings, and understandings which transcend mere time.

Geographically, Morris still seems most at home writing about the great, empty plains of this country. He seems to both hate and love a landscape reminiscent of a Georgia O'Keefe painting. He describes with loving care the deep-well-induced oases of small Nebraska or Missouri or Texas towns with their depots, their trees supporting tireswings, their picket fences, their houses, ". . . both crushed and supported by huge bushes of lilacs," or with a ". . . runaround porch that is tilted like a ship's deck." His eyes note with precision how "In the fall the yard is so bright with leaves . . . it's painful to look at," and he sees the ". . . cleared spot at the back hard as blacktop, where the trash and the leaves are burned." That is a landscape Morris shares with Inge and Tarkington, and he knows it to perfection. But he does not stop there. The settings for these stories range from New York to California, from Austria to Spain. Morris loves his roots, but he is determined to thrust beyond regionalism.

In the story, "In Another Country," for instance, he explores the idea of regionalism as a shortcoming to human understanding. An American tourist, romantically seduced into spending his honeymoon in Spain because of his having read Hemingway, has an encounter with a Spaniard. The result is a demonstration of the possible silliness, the narrowness of which both men, both nationalities, are capable through reliance on their prejudices. It is a witty, ascerbic story, saying in a new way much about the old confrontation between American eagerness and European *ennui.* Wherever he is writing about, Morris paints the scene deftly, economically, with just enough paint, just the exact pigments. In Texas, for instance, ". . . the daylight came slowly along the tracks. Nothing but space seemed to be out there. . . . The sky went up like a wall and the world seemed to end." In California, "He didn't like it. . . . Nothing had its own place. Hardly any of the corners were square. All through the Sunday morning service he could hear the plastic propellers spinning at the corner gas station, and the loud bang when they checked the oil and slammed down the hood." In Spain, "The slopes of the mountains were green right up to where the granite shimmered like a sunning lizard." And the city of Vienna in that singular year of 1939, ". . . was like a shabby, unaired museum full of aging attendants and apprehensive tourists, where . . . men and women . . . lived with dreams already buried. Vienna was not music. . . . The odor of fear was stronger than . . . incense."

Morris is capable of a wide variety and subtlety of tones of voice, and he demonstrates many of them in these stories. Most of the stories are told by an omniscient narrator, and a few—notably the first story and the last in this collection—are couched in the first person. Through his selection of images and dictional choices, through what he emphasizes, and even through what he determines to leave out, Morris reveals two major tones which are more easily analyzed. In love with the world, he must obviously deal with the pain it often metes out. In anger, some of these stories strike unrelentingly at life's seemingly absurd cruelties, sardonically lashing at nature's mercilessness, man's squalor and meanness, satirizing the inevitable waste and loss. In the story, "The Safe Place," for instance, a military man, a fifty-three-year-old colonel, is struck down on a city street by a pie truck, and later, looks from his hospital window ". . . to examine the teeming life in the streets. What he saw, however, was no surprise to him. To an old army man it was just another bloody battlefield. . . . Every day he read the uproar made in the press about the horrors of war. . . . Every moment he could see a life more horrible in the streets. Dangers more unjust, risks more uncalculated, and barracks that were more intolerable. . . . Sirens moaned through the streets like specters, every night." The cruelest irony in this story is that this old man, not interested in living, recovers. He has his wife send appropriate flowers for the death of an embittered young man with whom he has shared a room, untouched to the last by the young man's zealous craze for life even as the doctors slowly amputate his limbs.

But Morris is too filled with life, too much in love with our heartbeats, to remain angry or disillusioned all the time. While never lapsing into sentimentality, and knowing life is never easy, he does at times become more mellow, more affirmative and amused in his keen examination of living. Again, he does this through deliberate selection and stressing of incidents and images. The mask of the writer here is never one of outright laughter; it is more a quiet, oftentimes rueful grin—at others and at self. There is always in this less sardonic tone an element of pathos, a touch of awe at the enormous mystery unfolding, at the gradual losses, at the illusions of gains. It is as if the conditions of existence demand that lies be told, so the writer elects to tell beautiful ones with just enough lie to help, just as much truth as can be tolerated. These lies are better than the nothingness of despair which tempts darkly from the other side of experience. So, Morris fights darkness by creating, when he can, when he needs, a defiantly transcendent resolution—consciously temporary, bound beautifully to lose—but, being spun out of his spirit, providing as much comfort and promise as any *honest* writer can. In the title story, for instance, Morris's narrator mentions several eccentricities of his otherwise beloved Aunt Winona which, in his youthful pseudosophistication, he viewed with condescending humor. Among these unusual habits is her refusal to use any but well-water. On visits to this aunt's decaying house, the narrator's wife has ". . . seen things swimming" in the glasses. He has ". . . searched it for some sign of polliwogs." After the aunt's death, the narrator recalls her description of herself when once he hugged her: "There's nothing much to me, is there?" And he realizes his loss—what he calls the ". . . full knowledge" of his loss. The last line in the story surges resiliently, however, away from sadness, resisting the pain of recalling how once she was the object of gentle ridicule, celebrating now in more mature knowledge of loss, *all* our human peculiarities: "I weigh [my loss] each time I lift a glass of water and note its temperature, its color, and what it is that swims I can no longer see." Equally stubbornly, Morris pulls himself and us out of despair, too, at the end of the long and painful story—a memory of the turn-of-the-century—"A Fight Between a White Boy and a Black Boy in the Dusk of a Fall Afternoon in Omaha, Nebraska." After describing the futility and stupidity of the long, long fight, Morris slides up the scale to point out that now the scene of the fight has disappeared and is now the site of a highway cloverleaf which ". . . saves driving time. . . . Omaha is no longer the gateway to the West, but the plains remain, according to one traveler, a place where his wife still sleeps in the seat while he drives through the night." The past—whether beautiful or hideous—wears away. The present is our only comfort. Morris superbly defines those ephemeral moments, worth clinging to, which the imagination creates.

Morris is such a persuasive storyteller, and his use of prose style is so apt, that his innovations sometimes escape attention. He is always crisp and precise in his structures, fashioning sentences like the facets of jewels to reflect in various directions. Most of his writing seems at first simple, leanly uncluttered, and straightforward. This is a deception. On close reading, only the unclutteredness remains. Morris' mind is too rich for simplicity alone. He has mastered such devices of texturing and enriching his stories' possibilities as the montage or truncated dialogue, in which the reader is often confused—and creatively so—into strange discoveries of character by never knowing fully which characters are saying what. The writer also places unconscious ambiguities in characters' speeches. Sometimes this is wordplay, sometimes it is a misunderstanding which is richer than the understanding might have been. Another method he often uses is to lead the reader into believing the story is about one character and then suddenly to shift the focus, most tellingly, onto another character. This device has the effect of keeping one off balance and vulnerable. In the light of Morris' themes of loss and imagination, this feeling of vulnerability is a very realistic position to be forced into.

Another device Morris uses is the omniscient authorial insert to register an aside of different perspective, to make observations which do not occur to the characters in the story. Occasionally, too, he becomes downright surreal in his use of ellipses; he stringently deletes or delays any exposition of the obvious, thereby forcing the reader to pull the pieces of the puzzle together as best he can. "Magic," for example, is as inscrutable as a nightmare; yet it is a mark of Morris' stylistic daring and yarnspinning skill that he knows how to keep us riveted to this story even when it is so confusingly unreal, and has so bizarre a set of circumstances for its vehicle.

A major component of Morris' style is the excitement he achieves through the audacity of his surprises in plot. There are no complacent pages in his work; he has more to say that he can get out. And what he has to say is arresting in its depth and quality. He hooks us, then outrageously pushes us to the edges of disbelief, then with a stroke makes us *sure* of belief in the possibilities of what he describes. He is having fun with the writing *and* with the way he knows we will be reading. One example is in the dark, stark story, "The Rites of Spring," in which an orphaned boy is torn from his home and carted by an old man, a distant relative, to Texas. There he sits in a buggy witnessing, in mingled horror and pleasure, a hog-killing more like a coven's rites than the preparing of food. We are astonished, skeptical, then convinced finally of the aptness of the last scene in which the boy hangs himself—perhaps inadvertently, we cannot be sure—using two huge rope-suspended hams as the counterweights to swing him up, spinning. The final image is of the boy's and hog's sacrificed faces ". . . exchanging secretive smiles" in the emerging dawn.

Morris can be astonishing, frightening, viscerally challenging. His stories reflect a man passionately alive, superbly gifted in language, angry at the harsh brevity of beauty, and   finally inspired by the gift· of experience, whatever its form. *Real Losses, Imaginary Gains* is a masterful collection from an American master.

Thomas N. Walters

Sources for Further Study

Booklist. LXXII, June 15, 1976, p. 1452.
Choice. XIII, November, 1976, p. 1138.
Christian Science Monitor. August 23, 1976, p. 23.
Saturday Review. III, August 21, 1976, p. 41.
Sewanee Review. LXXXV, January, 1977, p. 126.

RED WOLVES AND BLACK BEARS

Author: Edward Hoagland
Publisher: Random House (New York). 273 pp. $8.95
Type of work: Essays

A series of essays dealing with animals, nature, and man's relation to both

Edward Hoagland represents himself as a quiet sort of person, of less interest to his readers than the subjects he writes about. The outrageous energy of Norman Mailer is not his, nor the peacock flummery of Tom Wolfe. A loner at prep school and at Harvard, he now travels alone to the far reaches of northern Minnesota and southern Texas to write about bears and wolves, and he has not stirred up any great fusses since he began writing novels and short stories after graduating from Harvard in 1954. But a man who routinely sits on a mountaintop calling to wolves with a hand-cranked Army surplus siren should be watched—or at least read—as one of the true individualists left on the continent.

Hoagland's chosen subjects are themselves uncommon; he notes with wry amusement that magazine editors trying to keep their readers up on "ecological" topics have only a small stable of writers to call on. There is not much of a tradition, little background of history or literature for modern writers interested in animals and their habitats to backstop their work; it must, in a sense, therefore be more "original" than observations on politics, history, or personalities. Hoagland is one of a few writers, the others being John McPhee, Edward Abbey, and Peter Matthiessen, to make national reputations for themselves as authorities on animals and, though he dislikes the word, ecology.

His work requires him to be in the field a good deal, and Hoagland seems to spend comparatively little time in his Manhattan apartment or at his house in Vermont. The nineteen essays in *Red Wolves and Black Bears* are the results of his travels on various magazine assignments (including *Sports Illustrated, The Village Voice, The Saturday Review, Harper's,* and *The New York Times Book Review*) from 1972 through 1975. The two longest essays, "Bears, Bears, Bears" and "Lament the Red Wolf," constitute between them nearly one-third of the total length of the volume, and there are several more, though briefer, essays on nature subjects. Close to one half of the book, though, consists of comments on the current literary establishment, on the nature of survival in the city today, on heroes, on dogs, and on coping with hard times. Hoagland suggests that the essays be read in the order they are presented, and it does seem clear that though the subjects are varied there is indeed a pattern to his book that gives it a coherence and unity.

In what might seem to the outsider a curious reversal of form, Hoagland turned from writing novels to essays in 1959. The pattern, however, is not unfamiliar, the line between fact and fiction having been blurred at least since Truman Capote's *In Cold Blood* in the early 1960's—a study of two murderers which he called, notoriously, a nonfiction novel. Today novelists routinely write essays (Mailer, Didion, Wilfred Sheed), and every reporter, movie star, and ex-felon seems to write a novel. Because life has become so outlandishly melodramatic, what with the assassinations of the 1960's, Vietnam, ghetto riots, and Watergate, mere fiction seems to pale by comparison. Echoing Mr. Gradgrind of Dicken's *Hard Times,* today "facts are wanted"—hence the movement in so many instances of a novelist toward nonfiction, and of the wide popular appeal of journalistic novels which have no merit except presumably privileged information once available to the author.

Even more significant is the loss of security the novelist once felt assured of, even if he had to wait until he was dead for recognition. Quality would tell in art eventually, and journalism, even in its best form, was transient by definition. But there is no longer any assurance of enduring for posterity, Hoagland says, for novelists and short-story writers: standards of judgment change too quickly, and the world itself seems unlikely to continue without blowing itself up.

Hoagland's reasons for switching forms, however, are probably somewhat different. For one thing, his style fits the essay better than it does the novel; it is comfortable, easy, and friendly yet not presumptuous, very fine in relatively short stretches. The longer pieces, though invariably interesting, tend to be repetitive and to lack the kind of dramatic structure and intensity that one would like in a novel. Moreover, Hoagland's cast of mind is not combative or hortatory; he is not particularly concerned to win over converts to his way of thinking. He thinks of the essay as a form "rooted in middle-class civility," one which presumes a set of shared assumptions between reader and writer. The reader is attending out of choice, and he is willing to make an effort, if it is called for, to meet the writer halfway—one might recall the origin in this connection of the word "essay" in the verb, "to try."

There is a still more important reason for Hoagland's choice of the essay form: the novel in the last generation, since World War II, has become the vehicle almost solely of irony and *angst.* "It's a destructive time," Hoagland says. The world is in a sorry state, and fictional heroes are either rebels or victims, dangling men in a landscape of nightmare. In the face of despair, however, Hoagland is unfashionably upbeat: bad attitudes can be changed for the better by one or two dedicated people; there are more things to be enthusiastic about than to cry over; life is at least acceptable.

But more than acceptable, life is good, and we only think it is bad because losing part of it—friends, family, pets—is so painful. It is a matter of balance between opposites, as is implied by the title of his book, *Red Wolves and Black Bears.* Wolves, we learn from Hoagland, are like people in society—they are social animals who establish conventions of manners in order to get along with one another. Bears, on the other hand, are of interest to most of us because they are "lumbering, churlish, and individual." Their anatomy resembles ours, and their "piggishness and sleepiness and unsociability with each other," Hoagland implies, also are all too familiar to each of us. The author's detailed descriptions of black bears and red wolves and of the men who study them are the substrata on which the other essays rest. Contained within them is the resolution to the apparent paradox noted by Hoagland: how can he live in the city and in the wild at the same time? The answer is that he, like all of us, is a compound of the wolf's sociability and the bear's reclusiveness. Studying them, he is studying himself; reading about wolves and bears, we are reading about ourselves.

Hoagland's attitude towards animals, accordingly, is that of an interested but unsentimental amateur; he is more interested in the people who devote their lives to studying the animals than he is in the animals themselves— Glynn Riley and his wolves and Lynn Rogers and his bears in particular. These men, and others such as the ninety-one-year-old ex-wolfer (wolf hunter) from Texas, are nineteenth century anachronisms: strong, self-reliant, solitary, like the mountain men and trappers of a time long past, and yet possessing a sense of reverence for nature that finds expression in deeds rather than in words. Hoagland sees it as his task to provide the words to explain these inarticulate but valuable men.

Optimism, energy, curiosity, and reverence for the inherent pattern of existence are themselves hallmarks of nineteenth century American transcendentalism, and there are many suggestions of Emerson and Thoreau in Hoagland's essays. The fascination with fact and details, for example, which is so prominent in Thoreau's *Walden,* is also present here. We learn that there is a mouse that points his nose to the sky and howls like a wolf; that the black bear concludes its year, before falling asleep for the coldest months, by putting a seal of licked fur and pine needles across its anus; that the Karankawa Indians, a vanished Gulf Coast tribe, used alligator grease to ward off mosquitoes; and that there were sixteen million deer in the United States in 1970, compared to 500,000 in 1910.

The ability of both animals and men to adapt to changing circumstances and even to triumph, as in the case of the deer, is a recurring theme in Hoagland, and an important reason for his Emersonian optimism. Initially one is taken aback by the Pollyanna quality of Hoagland's enthusiasm for life—one may doubt that the wolf is truly "amused" by the anatomy of the deer, or that the rabbit is enjoying himself setting "puzzles" while it runs from the dogs. But optimism is a matter of perspective: evolution for Hoagland is not "some process of drowning beings clutching at straws" for the transient privilege of momentary survival—it is "a matter of days well-lived, chameleon strength, zappy sex, . . . the whole fun of busy brain cells." What is remarkable is how *few* people die in accidents or get cancer or are murdered. If Hoagland lived in Los Angeles, he would look at the freeways with their millions of cars, each one with hundreds of fragile parts and many driven by grumpy, tired, foolish people, and he would note how astonishing it is that the system works so well, not that it is occasionally congested or hazardous.

Order and pattern imply hierarchy, both in the transcendentalists and in Hoagland, and much of Hoagland's nature writing deals with the hierarchies established in the wild—the relative amounts of territory claimed, rights of precedence in mating, and the like. It is the exceptional animal that Hoagland is drawn to most—the cannibal mouse, a cannibal from "verve," not necessity, the lone newt that survived in a forgotten terrarium, radiating exuberant good health as he prowls among the bodies of his fellow newts, and the fiendishly clever Martha, a red wolf who eluded all hunters for years, and who when caught proved to be a male—heroic individuals all, these creatures stand out from the common herd.

Similarly, in writing about subjects outside of nature Hoagland is drawn to the unusual, the eccentric, and the heroic. The "low-water man," for instance: a portly grandfather of seventy who likes to dive from forty-foot ladders into playpools filled with twelve inches of water. He survives by landing on his belly, and his ultimate goal is to land in a pool entirely empty of water. Gunther Gebel-Williams, the animal trainer, and the trapeze artist who went on to do her dangerous act the same day a horse bit off her finger, are still able to inspire Hoagland's boyish admiration. We are in sore need of heroes, Hoagland says, and he writes with nostalgic insight about the New York Yankees of the 1940's. The astronauts, brave and skilled though they are, do not excite the imagination as much as a "great, raunchy individualist explorer" like Cortez.

As noted earlier, Hoagland's essays reward, as the author suggests, a consecutive reading, because a pattern is apparent. The pattern, it seems, is that of an emerging portrait of American society in the last stages of bearishness—churlish, unsociable, potentially and actively violent, an America in which the names of Haldeman and Ehrlichman, John Mitchell, Elliot Gould, Jimmy Connors, and Howard Hughes are household words. But already many of these have left the scene; and one is struck, reading this selection of essays by an avowed optimist, how drab and sullen we were as a people so recently, and how much the mood has changed for the better.

Anthony Arthur

Sources for Further Study

Book World. May 16, 1976, p. 62.

New York Times. CXXV, July 7, 1976, p. 31.

Newsweek. LXXXVII, May 10, 1976, p. 108.

Publisher's Weekly. CCIX, March 22, 1976, p. 40.

Saturday Review. III, May 29, 1976, p. 35.

Time. CVII, May 3, 1976, p. 72.

REELING

Author: Pauline Kael (1919-   )
Publisher: Little, Brown and Company (Boston). 497 pp. $12.95
Type of work: Cinema criticism

A wide-ranging collection of reviews of films produced during the period between September, 1972, and May, 1975, written in Kael's usual pungent style

Pauline Kael, the *New Yorker's* movie critic, is a front row humanist, her eight hundred enimitable reviews in one hand, hot buttered popcorn in the other. On the one hand, she upholds the dead-center aesthetic standards of Western culture, and on the other, she tries to keep unmuddied the mainstream of social and moral values in popular culture. Robert Brustein, one of America's most astute and hard-to-please theater reviewers, said of Kael in *The New York Times,* "An intellectual who is not afraid of sensation, she is probably more in tune with the popular audience than any other serious American reviewer." A Los Angeles reviewer said that while her judgments are unusually well-informed, she endeavors to "connect performance with life." Out of the tradition of Robert Warshow, Graham Greene, Otis Ferguson, and Dwight Macdonald, she writes reviews "so audacious and passionate" said a Chicago reviewer, "that critics across the country lined up to dispute or discuss them." Her direct, personal voice once suggested the first hero of film criticism, James Agee, whose greatness Kael attributed, in her first book, to his use of "the full range of intelligence and intuition, rather than relying on formulas." Her genius has reached beyond Agee now, beyond her contemporaries John Simon and Stanley Kauffmann, the quality of whose work comes closest to her own.

Kael has been raising Cain in the swamps of Hollywood since she began reviewing in 1953. From the beginning, she has tried to affect audiences directly. She ran the Berkeley Cinema Guild, showing American and foreign classics, and her famous program notes on 280 of those movies are included in her second book, *Kiss Kiss Bang Bang.* From San Francisco, she broadcast reviews in the 1950's and 1960's; and in her published reviews, one hears her direct speaking voice clearly. Even the titles of her collections suggest that movie-going is primarily a sensual, personal experience for her: *I Lost It at the Movies* (1966), *Kiss Kiss Bang Bang* (1968), *Going Steady* (1971), *Deeper into Movies* (1973), and *Reeling* (1976). And her controversial essay in *The Citizen Kane Book* (1971) is called "Raising Kane." The company she keeps changes over the years. Most of the pieces (articles more than reviews) in the debut volume appeared in small circulation film and literary publications and built her reputation; the slick, mass-circulation magazines published most of the work in the second collection; in 1968, she found a home at the *New Yorker,* and the next three collections contain, except for two pieces, reviews from that magazine.

That Kael has structured her past three collections chronologically makes sense, for her reviews are always grounded in the immediacy of going to the movies in the context of the times. The present volume covers the period from September 30, 1972 to May 12, 1975, during which she reviewed 137 American and foreign movies—trendy block-busters, the disaster flicks, the black ventures, the last of the counter-culture hypes, along with the major works of cinematic art; *Reeling* also includes reviews of *The Fred Astaire & Ginger Rogers Book* and of Mailer's perverse study of Marilyn Monroe, and a long piece on the bleak future of the movies.

Reeling is too long—more than five hundred pages, with a thirty-one-page index—to afford a start-to-finish reading experience. Reading all that lush, tough rhetoric would be like watching six *Nashvilles* in succession. One might read, as impulse directs, reviews of those movies one saw in that period, then sample reviews of movies one wishes one had seen. The book thereafter becomes a magnificent reference volume, a time-capsule telling the way we were in those transitional years.

In her Foreword, Kael reminds us of the nature of movies, their ability to "overwhelm us," "arouse special, private, hidden feelings," their "erotic potential," their basic sensuality. We don't say we like movies, we say we "love" them. Theater audiences maintain a degree of control that is lost at the movies, where we experience sensations tribally—even those who have learned to discriminate, to think for themselves, to refuse to be led blindly. Whether we like or dislike current movies, we *feel* them in such a way that *thinking* about them is difficult. "The greater sensory impact of films in recent years— the acceleration in violence and in shock-editing" result in "marvelous entertainment" that creates a major problem: "they can be effective on shameless levels." The critic's problem is to convince people "that a shallow, primitive work can give them a terrific kick." A critic cannot fight the effects of *The Exorcist*, for instance, "because it functions below the conscious level." *Airport 1975* "is processed schlock, and it's really beneath a level at which movie criticism might serve a function."

Even the titles of Kael's reviews shape our attitudes. "Sex in the Head," "Round up the Usual Suspects," "Out of Tragedy, Suds," "New Thresholds, New Anatomies" (from a poem by Hart Crane), "Back to the Ouija Board," and "the Darned." Kael starts with a kiss kiss or a bang bang, praise or attack, and her Philip Marlowe voice—image-laden, witty, long-spinning convoluted sentences relieved by slangy, wisecracking, staccato declarative strokes—holds us to the climactic finish. Opening her review of *Sounder* (the first in the book), Kael raises the question of praise and attack: "It's easy to say why you think a movie is bad, but elements of embarrassment sneak into praise." She opens her review of *Nashville* in the language of praise: "Is there such a thing as an orgy for movie lovers—but an orgy without excess?" Having called it a "radical, evolutionary leap," she closes with: "*Nashville* is the funniest epic vision of America ever to reach the screen.

Opening on the attack, she hooks the reader's attention: "The theories of R. D. Laing, the poet of schizophrenic despair, have such theatrical flash that they must have hit John Cassavetes smack in the eye" (*A Woman Under the Influence*). Or, having made a judgment of taste, "the realism here is very offensive," she leaves the reader with a contemptuous wisecrack: "*The Towering Inferno* has opened just in time to capture the Dumb Whore Award of 1974." A few weeks later, she turned that crack around to damn a pretentious foreign film. First, she attacked it with her rapier wit: "*Stavisky* has been made as if vitality would be sin against art. . . . Resnais surrounds the women in this movie with so many baskets of white hothouse flowers that his ideal feminine position must be rigor mortis. . . . I realized I wasn't paying any attention to the dialogue, because the posters on the wall were more alive than the people. . . . *Stavisky* is an icy, high-minded white-telephone movie." Then she ends with an attack on the director, Resnais: "There isn't a whole man at work in this movie; if he thought he was whoring, he might warm up enough to be human."

Part of the compulsion to read Kael is to experience her wit as it praises or attacks. Charlie, the gangster in *Mean Streets,* "is so frightened of burning, he's burning already." *Shampoo* is about sexual bondage, "the bondage of the universal itch among a group primed to scratch." Blatty, author of *The Exorcist*, is "like the pulp authors who provide flip-page sex . . . he provided flip-page torture." *Airport* demonstrated that "in Hollywood, cynicism and incompetence are natural bedfellows—one covering up for the other—but this time they've pulled the covers right over their heads, and they're both laid bare."

The movies Kael praises most highly from the 1972-1975 period are *Last Tango in Paris, Mean Streets, Shampoo, Nashville,* and *The Godfather II.* Regarding *Last Tango in Paris,* she writes that the film "made the strongest impression on me in almost twenty years of reviewing." She was right in saying that audiences would have trouble totally resolving their feelings about "the sex scenes and the social attitudes in this film." But she was wrong in predicting that people would argue about this movie "for as long as there are movies."

Kael attacks pompousness, pretentiousness, fakery, and distortion of values. In "Notes on Black Movies," she exposes the vile fakery of violent movies that vent black hatred of "honky," while making their white producers rich. Reviewing *The Day of the Locust,* the snobbery of white liberals is her target. With a wisecrack, she notes the film's "peewee Watergate analogy." In his novel, Nathanael West "expects you to identify with his comic horror" over the plight of his "suffering grotesques." "When you're young you're very vulnerable to West's highbrow-Christ attitude," but when you reread him years later "you're shocked by the elitist snobbery you once felt flattered to share."

With a single phrase, she attacks a similar distortion in *The Day of the Dolphin*: "It's an ugly-souled, manipulative movie." Some social-breakthrough movies distort their concepts with a commercial ending. *Alice Doesn't Live Here Anymore* "contradicts the logic of its own story" by giving Alice "a dream prince." Kael's style is stitched with slangy expressions, such as "loused up," and with effective use of profanity. Kris Kristofferson in *Alice Doesn't Live Here Anymore* is a "Big Daddy Santa Claus, he's the greatest goddam pillow in the world."

The electric center of Kael's reviews is her concern for the way movies affect us, starting with herself. To Houseman's performance as the professor in *The Paper Chase*, she brought an autobiographical experience: after seeing a play he directed when she was a chid, she threw up. She admits she is impressionable, but "just not as proud of it as some people are." Speaking of *The Last Detail*, she says, "you can feel the director trying to get a certain emotional effect, and he gets it all right (an effect I hate anyway), but he's also heavy and clumsy about getting it (which makes me even more aware of how I hate it)." But she responded to the "exploding effects" of *The Godfather II*. "I began to feel that the film was expanding in my head like a soft bullet." She usually looks away from violence in routine movies, but *The Godfather*'s Tolstoian greatness demanded she see the worst. "One scarcely has the emotional resources to deal with the experience of this film." On the other hand, she found *Some Call It Loving* unwatchable. When she does have a profound experience, she wants others to "have the pleasure of discovery that I had." *Sounder* "works directly on our feelings the way film poets do."

Because she is so in touch with her own sensations, Kael can read the dynamics of audience response. She contrasts the reaction of white audiences to the current cynical movies with their response to the positive black *The Autobiography of Miss Jane Pittman*. "While white audiences can laugh together at the same things—mainly evidence of American stupidity and rot—there's nothing positive that they share." Another alien group charms them, too—the *Mafiosi*. Was the audience of *The Godfather* "envying them those close family ties and the vitality of their lawlessness . . . their having gotten used to a sense of sin?" *American Graffiti* was one of those movies that young audiences like to say is the story of their lives, but Kael claims they are demeaning and trivial. The adolescents are stereotypes "who exist to be laughed at." Kael wonders for whom was it "just like that?" "Not for women, not for blacks or Orientals or Puerto Ricans, not for homosexuals, not for the poor. Only for white middle-class boys whose memories have turned into pop." She thinks audiences are looking for a certain kind of shallowness that *Don't Look Now* manages to transcend. She expects some people to ask, "What's wrong with shallow?" *The Exorcist* is shallow, but in asking to be taken seriously it is ludicrous. Fortunately, the audience that faints watching that hoax and cheers the head-cracking in *Walking Tall* is savvy enough to hiss *Airport* fakery and groan at the dialogue in *The Towering Inferno.*

It is Kael's preoccupation with an analysis of the affective aspects of movies as they relate to her and to the audience that is her most distinctive contribution to film criticism. Our shared love of movies enables us to respond to the "copious associations" with movies of the past in the background of *Last Tango in Paris.* Movies "are as active" in Bertolucci "as direct experience." *Mean Streets* "has its own unsettling, episodic rhythm and a high-charged emotional range that is dizzyingly sensual." Kael points out universal sensory experiences that unite the audience. When Miss Jane Pittman takes that long walk to the whites-only drinking fountain in front of the courthouse, "all of us in the audience can taste the good water." She points out delayed effects: "Nicholas Roeg employs fast, almost subliminal imagery in . . . *Don't Look Now*, and his entire splintering style works subliminally . . . one may come out of the theater still seeing shock cuts and feeling slightly dissociated." She also notes more obvious effects. Mel Brooks's *Young Frankenstein* is "a film to go to when your rhythm is slowed down and you're too tired to think. . . . You can go to see it when you can barely keep your eyes open, and come out feeling relaxed and recharged." One cries reasonable tears watching parts of *Nashville*, and when Barbara Jean sings, there is "an absolutely ecstatic moment." But Kael can see "the ultimate in modern show-biz sentimentality" in the pseudo-hip *Lenny*, a movie about the totally unsentimental, amoral comedian Lenny Bruce. Some films, whether commercial or serious, leave little impression. Such a movie is *The Day of the Locust.* "Having no emotional center, the film leaves little impression—only a chill."

This emphasis on the affective would place her too close to the pure aesthetic theories of Susan Sontag, whom Kael sees as her polar opposite, were it not for her constant effort to mesh those observations with both general and immediate historical, political, social, and moral concerns. This collection is especially interesting for her comments on blacks in recent movies and on the stark chauvinism of Hollywood's approach to or neglect of women in all aspects of movie-making. Distorted or corrupt moral feeling or thinking and simpleminded morality never escape her notice.

In discussing the personal and public effects of movies, Kael focuses on the director. She generally praises Altman, Bertolucci, Copolla, Malle, Scorsese, and Roeg, and generally finds fault with George Roy Hill, William Friedkin, Fellini, Resnais, James Bridges, Bergman, Antonioni. She gives lucid descriptions of the ways directors employ their techniques to send us "reeling." She is very knowledgeable about the craft of the designer, the composer, the cinematographer, the editor, and the screenwriter. And she captures in a few sentences the essence of actors and actresses, their special moments in each film, their audience appeal. In this volume, Marlon Brando, Paul Newman, Robert Redford, George C. Scott, Ellen Burstyn, Marilyn Monroe, Cecily Tyson, Gena Rowlands, and Julie Christie attract most of her attention.

As she analyzes her responses and the audience's to new movies, she often offers parallel discussions of other movies, directors, or actors to praise or attack by comparison. Jean Renoir is the director-as-film-poet she most often invokes. She also sets up parallels with works in other media—painting, music, theater, literature. For instance, she refers to Kafka and Borges, but discusses Dylan Thomas and Nathanael West at length. But her love-hate for Norman Mailer, who crops up in the other two recent books, seems a little obsessive. She finds or forces numerous occasions to refer to or digress about him; she does an extended "number" on him in her review of his book on Marilyn Monroe.

Kael often includes a piquant bit of trade gossip or behind the scenes information in her reviews. The movies she reviewed in the first two years of the current period led her to write the famous long piece "On the Future of the Movies," and the films in the year thereafter bear out her doleful prophecies. The despair is even blacker now than in August 1974. "The system doesn't work anymore, and it's not going to." Thus spake Pauline Kael. We will hear from her again

David Madden

Sources for Further Study

Book World. April 11, 1976, p. 2.

Journalism Quarterly. LIII, Autumn, 1976, p. 582.

New York Times Book Review. April 4, 1976, p. 1.

New Yorker. LII, December 13, 1976, p. 162.

Newsweek. LXXXVII, June 21, 1976, p. 76.

Village Voice. XXI, May 3, 1976, p. 48.

REFLECTIONS ON LANGUAGE

Author: Noam Chomsky (1928-   )
Publisher: Pantheon Books (New York). 269 pp. $10.00
Type of work: Linguistics

Chomsky's current views on linguistic theory and its relation to the problems of human knowledge

Reflections on Language is a reworking of two formulations of Noam Chomsky's current research in linguistics, the first and larger part being an elaboration of the 1975 Whidden Lectures delivered at McMaster University in Hamilton, Ontario, and the second part being a revision of an essay printed elsewhere on the same general questions. Both parts show the broad outline and some details of what might be called the MIT school of linguistics, in the form their theories have taken from about 1973 to the present.

The book is presented as a nontechnical outline of Chomsky's views, but if the reader understands "nontechnical" to mean something like Desmond Morris' *The Naked Ape* or Julius Fast's *Body Lanuage,* he will be baffled by *Reflections on Language.* The book demands at least an acquaintance with the work of philosophers and linguists over the last generation; it does not compromise on that demand. Chomsky's style is severe to the point of being forbidding; he presumes the reader's familiarity with many technical terms that the non-specialist is unlikely to know, and his use of stipulated abbreviations cumulates through the second part until some paragraphs read like parodies of the very worst of academic styles. The conscientious reader who wishes to supplement what the book presents by reading the referenced works will frequently be stymied: roughly a quarter of the cited studies, including several crucial to Chomsky's arguments, will be unavailable in even the most magnificently appointed university libraries. These include references to many works forthcoming at the time of the book's publication, to more than a dozen MIT dissertations, and to a score of unpublished papers, obtainable only by writing to the author. But the reader may take some small comfort from the fact that even fulltime linguists share the difficulty of finding out exactly what is being done at Cambridge, Massachusetts.

But if *Reflections on Language* is not a popular book in the publisher's meaning of the word, it is nonetheless an important one. It presents both linguistic and philosophic arguments, the linguistic ones dealing with a major change in Chomsky's theory of language, and the more general philosophic ones discussing the importance of transformational-generative theories in solving problems of human knowledge.

The specialized linguistic arguments deal with what information is available to the hearer of a sentence (in an idealized situation) when that sentence is understood. In works published in 1955 and 1965, Chomsky outlined and elaborated a theory that postulated a three-part division of human language faculties. For convenience we may call these three the syntactic component, the semantic component, and the phonological component. It should be mentioned at the outset that all three are abstractions, parts of a theoretical formulation intended to account for human linguistic ability. Whether these components correspond to brain structure or activities of any kind is another question, a question to which neurophysiology can at present give no answers. In any case, the production of a sentence (so the early theory goes) begins in the syntactic component, which is itself divided into parts. One part is a set of rules that produces a kind of labeled parsing, or *phrase-structure*. These rules, which are said to *generate* a phrase-structure, are of the form S → NP PP; the example here may be read as "a sentence is composed of a noun phrase (the subject) and a predicate phrase (the complete predicate of traditional grammar)." The phrase-structure rules incorporate, generally, the analysis of sentences of a traditional formal grammar. A second part of the syntactic component is the lexicon, a dictionary-like compilation that supplies lexical material to be attached to the phrase-structure at appropriate places. With many simplifications, an output of the syntactic component can be represented, for example, as (1):

(1) $[_S [_{NP} John] [_{PP} [_{AUX} past] [_{VP} [_V see] [_{NP} Sam]]]]$

The labeled bracketings provide information about the category and relationship of each item supplied by the lexicon: thus S labels the whole structure as a sentence; PP stands for "predicate phrase," as explained above; AUX, or "auxiliary," in this case contains only the marker for past tense, but for another sentence might contain auxiliary verbs or markers of aspect; VP, or "verb phrase," groups the verb (V) *see* with any modifiers it may have; NP identifies *John* and *Sam* as noun phrases. The functions of the two noun phrases as subject and direct object are defined by their positions in the bracketing.

A third part of the syntactic component, the transformational rules, changes the phrase-structures in specified ways. In general, transformations add, delete, or rearrange material in the phrase-structure. Suppose the passive transformation is applied to example (1); the result is phrase-structure (2):

(2) $[_S [_{NP} Sam] [_{pp} [_{AUX} past be participle] [_{VP} [_V see] [_{NP} by John]]]]$

In the standard transformational theory we are talking about, the two phrase-markers (1) and (2) are then operated on by the other two components: phrase-marker (1) plus a record of the transformations it undergoes (in this case, the passive) is interpreted by the semantic component. The semantic component identifies the parts of the structure that are to be associated with concepts such as *agent*, the performer of an action, *patient*, receiver of an action, and so on, and gives a reading of the meaning of the sentence. Phrase-marker (2) is acted on by the phonological component, a set of rules that will determine the pronunciation of the words, place stress where appropriate, and so on. The phonological component will determine how the sentence is spoken.

Phrase-structure (1) is what has often been termed the *deep structure* of the sentence, and (2) the *surface structure.* The general thrust of the early versions of the theory was that the deep structure provided semantic information and the surface structure phonological information. In the late 1960's this theory came under attack by some linguists who, to their break with standard transformational theory, called their theory "generative semantics." Aiming at simplifying the model, they argued that the syntactic component was superfluous, that transformations mapped structures of the semantic component directly into the structures of the phonological component. While the controversy is unlikely to increase the pulse rate of the man in the street, it is an important question, with consequences for the theory as a whole.

Chomsky's present position, set forth in *Reflections on Language,* agrees with the main changes advocated in these attacks: namely, that all information needed for the semantic interpretation of sentences is present in the surface structure. His contribution to the present version of the theory is the addition of what he calls a *trace.* Note that apart from inserting *be* and a past participle marker, the main function of the passive transformation was to move the two noun phrases (the phrase-structures are repeated here without bracketing):

(1) John past see Sam

(2) Sam past be participle see by John

The passive transformation moved *Sam,* the direct object of what would without the transformation become "John saw Sam," to the position of subject in (2), which will eventually become "Sam was seen by John." It likewise moves *John* from its position as subject of (1) to the new position of subject in (2), which will eventually become "Sam was seen by John." It likewise moves *John* from its position as subject of (1) to the new position in the *by*-phrase of (2). It would be a great simplification of the theory if all transformations could be characterized as instructions to move a noun phrase, and Chomsky aims at that goal. But when a noun phrase is moved in the *Reflections* model, it leaves in the surface structure produced a "trace" of its former position. We may think of the trace as an abstract element in the phrase-structure that marks the former position of the noun phrase. The semantic component will contain rules of interpretation that use these traces to discover the transformations the structure has undergone; important information about the meaning of the sentence is thereby brought forward into the surface structure. With the trace theory, Chomsky sees no difference between his position and that of the generative semanticists, the authors of the original criticisms of the standard theory. Whether this change, the notion of traces, is a significant one, or simply a different way of saying what Chomsky maintained in 1965, is a matter for debate. It might well be argued that the traces are simply covert ways of bringing deep structure information into surface structures, and therefore no real change from his earlier position, but that contention is a subject for the professional journals.

Less controversial but more interesting to the general reader is the second main contention of *Reflections on Language*, the implications of the theory of transformational grammar for the idea of the mind, and problems of how humans come to learn and know things.

A central part of all of Chomsky's work has been the insistence that a human is not born as a *tabula rasa*, acquiring all knowledge and abilities in the framework of a behaviorist system of stimuli and responses. It is important to remember that the behaviorist approach was virtually unchallenged in linguistics, psychology, anthropology, and even philosophy before Chomsky began his work in the 1950's. Now the situation is almost completely reversed. The doctrine of innate ideas holds the field, and Skinnerian behaviorism finds fewer and fewer defenders with each passing year. For example, in 1960 the philosopher W. V. O. Quine accounted for language learning totally in terms of a behaviorist theory of stimulus and response; now, although he disagrees with large parts of Chomsky's thinking, Quine accepts the notion of innate linguistic structures. Chomsky believes (and argues persuasively) that the human being is born equipped with a kind of universal grammar. The word *grammar* is used here in a special sense: it means a device that allows the infant to devise grammars of particular languages from the speech data that he is confronted with, and to evaluate the particular grammars produced in terms of a general restriction on what is possible and impossible in human languages. The attribution of this innate ability was a change in scientific thought of brilliant originality, of the highest importance in fields as diverse as biology and philosophy.

Chomsky in *Reflections on Language* considers the implications of innateness in fields other than language. He argues that language learning is not part of a general learning capacity (he doubts that any such general capacity exists) but rather a special genetically transmitted ability to interpret experience in particular ways. If we have a rich and complex inborn system for processing linguistic data, may we not have other equally sophisticated innate systems for processing the other data of experience? That we do have such systems is supported by the complex and otherwise inexplicable abilities we have in other fields, say, the ability to categorize objects in a common-sense way. Chomsky's example is the simplest he can find, the ability to determine whether or not something counts as a "physical object." To be considered a physical object, apparently, some part of experience must have continuity in space and time. The Colosseum is a "thing," but the Colosseum together with the stones that used to be a part of it and are now in some other Roman building, are not a thing. Second, to count as a physical object, we apply the notion of wholeness or function; thus, although it has continuity in space and time, the north half of the Colosseum is not a "thing." Finally, considerations of human intent come into play: a collection of objects can count as a thing if we are aware of a purposeful construction: Chomsky's examples here are, on the one hand, a picket fence or a Calder mobile, which count as "physical objects," but not, on the other hand, the leaves on a tree, although they may be more intrinsically connected than the parts of the first two examples.

As Chomsky puts it, "A study of human judgments concerning essential and accidental properties may give considerable insight into the cognitive structures that are being employed, and perhaps beyond, into the nature of human cognitive capacity and the range of structures that are naturally constructed by the mind." Questions as far-reaching as these could not even be raised under behaviorist strictures that limited the kinds of theories that could be formulated.

It is clear why Chomsky considers linguistics a branch of human psychology. Linguistics since his rise to prominence has resumed its place among those disciplines that deal directly with the powers and activities of the mind. If the behaviorism of the first half of this century comes to be seen as a curious aberration in the history of human thought, it will be primarily because of the work of Noam Chomsky.

Walter E. Meyers

Sources for Further Study

Books and Bookmen. XXI, June, 1976, p. 55.
Christian Century. XCIII, May 12, 1976, p. 466.
Economist. CCLVIII, March 27, 1976, p. 116.
Harvard Educational Review. XLVI, November, 1976, p. 645.
Spectator. CCXXXVI, March 6, 1976, p. 25.

REPRESENTATIONS
Essays on Literature and Society

Author: Steven Marcus
Publisher: Random House (New York). 331 pp. $12.95
Type of work: Literary essays

Sixteen essays on a variety of topics which attempt to bring the methods of the so-called cognitive disciplines to bear on imaginative literature or to apply formal literary analysis to supposedly nonliterary texts

Steven Marcus, a professor at Columbia University and an editor of *Partisan Review,* has done more than collect his scattered essays; his previous accomplishments, larger and more sustained efforts, have created a market for an inclusive collection of his essays, but *Representations* establishes quite another reason for its existence. Quietly, unassumingly, the book calls for a revolution in literary criticism and in the social sciences. Unlike such writers as George Steiner, who point out the social and humanistic failings of specific types of criticism, Marcus shows the need for revolution by positive means: he indicates what his methods may achieve.

When he assesses criticism and critics, as he does in "Three Obsessed Critics," he proves devastatingly inclusive. Hugh Kenner, Maxwell Geismar, and Harry Levin take almost equal punishment; Kenner speaks from the right, Geismar from the left, and "Levin is at the center, the dead center." This essay is wholly atypical, though the critical excesses Marcus catalogues reflect cultural deviancy elsewhere apparent in his essays.

"Three Obsessed Critics" takes us back to 1958, and its inclusion here suggests that Marcus has not recanted. As different as Kenner, Geismar, and Levin are socially, politically, and methodologically, their books which Marcus examines share one quality. "they are all excessive and extravagant." The books reveal "unbalancing commitment" to distorting points of view. Marcus' use of the word "unbalancing" suggests his chief critical virtue: he seeks balance.

The import of Marcus' essays and his brief Introduction is unmistakable: he wants to bring together the formal part of literary criticism with the part that is referential. He wants to read literary—and nonliterary—documents in ways that allow their form to reveal something real about their meanings—perhaps, in some cases, more than their authors would gladly admit. He wants form liberated from the ties to historical conventions on the one hand, and from the "merely" aesthetic on the other hand. In the last sentence of his Introduction, Marcus admits his desire to reassert and sustain the literary scholar's claim to intellectual seriousness.

But the world at large will not concede such seriousness so long as criticism engages in meaningless tasks, or conceals its meaning in jargon, or expatiates on the beauties of mechanical accomplishments either nonexistent or not observes many of the stripes and bruises it has lately suffered. Too often humorless and self-important, criticism has tended, in the present century at least, to forget that literature "refers to, refracts, and is part of" a real world. Equally often, the social scientist and social critic have tended to put forward theoretical constructs as if *they* represented reality. In such an intellectual world, actual institutions and human practices appear illusory, even capricious. One need not mention here the enormity of psychology's and psychiatry's claims in this respect.

A determined, even-handed application of the ideas Marcus advocates could resolve much of the conflict between the "practical" and "theoretical" disciplines. Never does Marcus deny the value of formal and theoretical approaches; in literary criticism, he himself practices the formal approach, by which he means those activities devoted to the "internal and quasi-autonomous structures." All he asks is that formalist activities take note of the referential part of criticism and literature; he recommends the tools of the social scientist to the formalist critic.

As Marcus admits in his Introduction, his own tendency to view imaginative literature in the light of analytical methods borrowed from cognitive disciplines has become more obvious in recent years. Nevertheless, earlier essays in *Representations* seem unified with the later ones by virtue of Marcus' preoccupations with what he calls the "imagination of society." That imagination works in poets and novelists as well as in other kinds of writers, all of whom bring "preconceptions" of what they are writing about to their supposedly systematic and cognitive analyses. Marcus calls attention to the disparity between what social scientists and psychologists *think* they mean and their "representations" or "imaginations" of society. Marcus applies a double set of tools in order to discover how society imagines itself.

Throughout, Marcus uses the word "representations" to mean fictions. His use of that word does not imply lack of respect for literary or so-called nonliterary productions. He simply argues that nonliterary documents yield new and unexpected meanings when they are read with the skills of the literary critic. Furthermore, the literary creation, because it comments on an external world, also represents a valid way of knowing that world. Marcus seeks "meanings" possibly more valid than the ones the artist or the "investigator" thought he was expressing.

Even Sigmund Freud (as Marcus shows in a close analysis of Freud's first great case history) sometimes confuses his role of psychoanalyst with his roles of assertive manipulator of someone else's life story and objective recorder. Marcus' title—"Freud and Dora: Story, History, Case History"—proves suggestive. Does the order ascend or descend? Marcus establishes that Freud often employed in his case histories what we normally call "literary strategies" and was deeply conscious of himself as artificer and as character in Dora's story.

Still, Marcus does not fault the psychologist, the social historian, or the social scientist who gets into the act and allows his personality to color, even dominate, the ostensibly objective narrative and analysis. Marcus does not impose such judgmental strictures; he assumes that human agents bring human tendencies to their labors. He also assumes that "literary art" reveals truth precisely because its methods are so seductive. That seductiveness, which prevents the most straightforward account from being wholly inartistic, requires literary analysis to determine the exact truth revealed.

No matter whether his topic is Freud, the climbing of Mt. Everest, the novels of Faulkner or George Eliot, or recent psychological experiments, Marcus reveals social forces and assumptions at work. He uses two books, for instance, to compare the spirit of two expeditions to climb Mt. Everest; through them, he shows important changes in the British National Spirit. Sir John Hunt (*The Conquest of Everest*, 1954) records the team-effort of an engineering feat designed to prove England's "greatness," while Apsley Cherry-Garrard's *The Worst Journey in the World* narrates an adventure undertaken by individuals for purely personal reasons. The changes in the British spirit do not appear to be for the better.

Practically everything literary or semi-literary proves grist for Marcus' mill. The Irish famine of the 1840's, and the published accounts of its ravages, prompt him to an essay on "Hunger and Ideology." Yale University experiments involving imposition of electrical shock as "incentive" to learn provide the starting point for an essay on "Authority and Obedience." Marcus expresses horror at Stanley Milgram's duping his volunteer subjects into revealing downright brutal willingness to "punish" their fellow humans. He expresses equal horror at Milgram's abandoning any semblance of objectivity when confronted by the shocking extent to which those subjects accepted authority without concern for their victims' pain. Marcus' chief interest, however, was to contrast the ingenuity of experimental models and data with the paucity, even poverty, of Milgram's analytical powers. The great pioneer figures in the social and psychoanalytical sciences, writes Marcus, formulated their "great explanatory systems" with the help of "relatively little data." Furthermore, those pioneers (Marcus names Hegel and Marx, Freud and Durkheim) wrote informed, if not always graceful, prose.

Social scientists and psychologists, according to Marcus, tend to take "theoretical constructions and systematic contrivances" from the natural sciences and apply them mechanically, "without reflection and without understanding," to social behavior. Implicitly, though Marcus never says as much, this kind of mindless transfer of method from one discipline to another brings to mind the English transfer of military and engineering skills to what used to be an individual endeavor. The result is the conquest of Everest but the loss of individual and national perspective. Logistical expertise neither proves England's greatness, nor the stamina and courage of the mountain climbers.

In an essay about Evelyn Waugh, Marcus implies another, and equally elaborate, transfer. Whatever Waugh's shortcomings as a "serious writer," Marcus finds him a genuine entertainer still able to make the "living connection between speech and traditional prose." American writers, on the other hand, seem to pattern their prose after voices wholly unrelated to themselves as human beings. Strife between speech and writing, Marcus says, is a "condition of our democracy" and it constricts nearly all our writers. American writers, then, in an overstatement of Marcus' case, substitute literary rhythms for the speech rhythms of life.

Hence, by including them in his book, Marcus links mountain climbing, psychological experimentation, and prose writing. The circumstances of the modern world and our "imaginations" of that world have allowed, or required, application of borrowed systems, extrinsic skills and competencies to activities deriving from personal, natural sources. Marcus speaks of the latter-day efficient and systematic approach to mountain climbing as "Americanized." Until very lately, Americans have universally prided themselves on their efficiency of production and elimination of the "human element."

An example of Marcus' style of literary criticism is the essay "Literature and Social Theory: Starting in with George Eliot" shows how that great moralist flawed her first published fiction ("The Sad Fortunes of the Reverend Amos Barton") through inability to treat directly the workings of sexual passion. Eliot's—and her society's—ambivalence toward passion colored all her works; she sensed the double function of passion as destroyer and preserver, but hid her narrative clues so cunningly that even Marcus sought for years before understanding her meaning. Furthermore, Eliot's ambivalence led her to frequent juxtaposition of class struggles with the conflicts of passion—or, to be more exact, it led her to treat one phenomenon in terms of the other. Although his work on Eliot allows Marcus to use all the skills of close reading and structural/textural analysis, one never suspects him of *mere* formal analysis. He generalizes from the particular and early work to the larger, more nearly mature ones in order to discover something more about the writer's relationship to the outside world. Other literary essays in the book reveal a similar aim.

"Snopes Revisited" (1957) examines the formal structure and authorial strategies of Faulkner's *The Town* in the light of what Marcus calls Faulkner's intense implication "with the fate of his culture." Doing so allows Marcus rightly to see *The Town* as Faulkner's movement back to the literary values which immortalized him. In "Sinclair Lewis," Marcus begins with Mark Schorer's 1961 biography of Lewis; surveying the writer's life and works, he judges Lewis wholly characteristic of a "culture which continues to express its vital principles almost exclusively through self-destructive contradictions." He finds Lewis himself and his life "an utterly dismaying vision." What first looked like a book review becomes a critique of an entire culture; the formal and the referential come together.

In "Stalky & Co.," Marcus does for England and for Kipling what he has done for America and her Nobel novelist. In examining Kipling's view of the boy's school as a hard-knocks training ground for military service in the British Empire, Marcus observes the passing of the Empire and, perhaps, the passing of boyhood as Kipling celebrates it. Above all, Kipling's book allows Marcus to pause over the intangibles which existed in "Stalky & Co.," but which Marcus calls "old, obsolete words." He enumerates such words as truth, honor, courage, self-sacrifice, and heroism.

The reader who judges Marcus no more than a doomsday prophet has missed the point. Marcus does not lament the passing of the "good old days" so much as he turns our heads back toward recognition that literature of all sorts reflects the kinds of societies we inhabit. Perhaps that literature does more; perhaps it obliges us to recognize what we may overlook in our everyday lives. "Madness, Literature, and Society" dramatizes the point most shockingly. The two-part essay ostensibly treats two recent books on madness—Milton Rokeach's *The Three Christs of Ypsilanti* (1964) and Michel Foucault's *Madness and Civilization: A History of Insanity in the Age of Reason* (1965). Rokeach studied three hopelessly deluded madmen, each of whom considered himself to be Christ. Marcus discovers in the transcripts of their tape-recorded utterances a direct parallel not only with the content but also with the verbal manner of much that is considered distinguished in modern literature. Even the "mad" situations imagined by the "three Christs" paralleled plot situations of poems, stories, and plays. Analyzing the verbal qualities of the madmen's utterances revealed formal similarities with works which seem to regard language as imprisoning, not expressive.

Though Marcus denies any wish to throw open the doors of Bedlam, he does not miss the opportunity to observe the social phenomenon of our culture's definition and treatment of madness. Further, and this point seems vital, society's increasing failure to accommodate eccentric behavior bears an ironic relationship to the resemblance in "very form and shape" of society and "the condition it keeps locking away." Although Marcus claims that Rokeach's book makes clear the relationship between madness and society, he argues that literature has been saying exactly the same thing "for the last two hundred years in a thousand different ways."

Pursuing the subject of madness and society as it emerges from Foucault's *Madness and Civilization,* Marcus shows that the study of madness is necessarily a study also of reason and its limitations. Accepting Foucault's assessment that the great nineteenth and twentieth century systems have failed to keep their promises, Marcus nevertheless finds hope. He admits that we live today in a "post-everything" world—"post-modern, post-history, post-sociology, post-psychology"; rejection of the Systems of the past, however, leaves everything potential. Contemporary man may either blow up his world, or he may replace the failed systems with viable ones. Our age, Marcus affirms, remains "aware of how much it still has to fall back on."

Representations, though not the sustained effort Marcus has produced previously, establishes the full extent of his curiosity and erudition, his thoroughness, and his tolerance. His consistent denial of hollowed-out specialization indicates the breadth of his humanism. Drawing these essays from what amounts to a lifetime of intellectual endeavor assures the reader of the book's sane, nonprogrammatic intention. *Representations* shows a mind in process, a broadening out—not a closing in. To heed this book's spirit and to seek to apply its methods could begin a return to something like health for contemporary culture.

Leon V. Driskell

Sources for Further Study

Booklist. LXXII, February 15, 1976, p. 831.

Choice. XIII, April, 1976, p. 216.

Library Journal. C, December 15, 1975, p. 2325.

New Republic. CLXXV, November 27, 1976, p. 31.

New York Times Book Review. March 21, 1976, p. 7.

Times Literary Supplement. October 22, 1976, p. 1323.

RESPONSES
Prose Pieces, 1953-1976

Author: Richard Wilbur (1921-   )
Publisher: Harcourt Brace Jovanovich (New York). 238 pp. $10.00
Type of work: Literary criticism

Useful essays on poetry and poets, including Wilbur himself, in a style and from attitudes congruent with the author's celebrated poems

Witty, sometimes pedantic but always perceptive and useful, these sixteen essays, written over a quarter of a century, enable the reader of Richard Wilbur's poetry to hear his humanistic concerns spoken in prose. One turns from the poetry for the first time to the prose, wondering what the author will sound like. Calling these essays "some prose by-products of a poet's life," and making "no ingenious claims of unity for this book," the arrangement being chronological except for two earliest pieces at the end, Wilbur says, "If the contents somehow hang together for the reader, I hope it will be because the voice, though changing with age and occasion, seems that of one person with certain persistent concerns and a mind largely his own." He achieves that effect.

In the preface, Wilbur observes that "poets sometimes write verses in answer to a request or expectation, but most poems are wholly uncalled for." That is true of his own poetry. But among his accumulated prose pieces, he found almost nothing he was not asked to write. Except for introductions to his translations of three verse-comedies by Molière, these pieces are responses "to invitations to give a lecture or speech, contribute to a symposium, compose a broadcast, introduce a work, interpret an author, or help mark an anniversary." One is a commencement address, given at Washington University. Through examinations of poems by Dickinson, Whitman, Frost, Poe, Shakespeare, Housman, Burns, and himself, Wilbur has talked and written about the nature, the practice, the meaning, and the interaction of poetry.

At Harvard in the late 1940's, Wilbur gave a seminar on Poe. He almost finished a book on Poe, discarded it, but wrote several other pieces, the three least accessible of which he includes in *Responses* (a principle of selection he employed when two essays deal with the same material). By including three on the same subject, he deliberately risked disproportion because "I regard my decodings of Poe with a frank satisfaction. They seem to me original and true, and the best excuse for this collection." He spaces them throughout the book. The first is his introductory essay to Poe in Perry Miller's college text *Major Writers of America* (1962), "a brief but comprehensive statement of my approach to Poe's life and works."

In summing up Poe's vision of and response to the cosmos, Wilbur reveals to readers of his own poetry an affinity for the American poet whose life and material were romantic but whose method was classicist. "The one true response to the creation, then, is to take an imaginative delight in its beauty and harmony, seen and unseen." Having told us the story of Poe's life, Wilbur embarks upon a long, brilliant analysis of "Ligeia" that

> would be disproportionate were the story not so central to Poe's thought, so characteristic of his method, and so much an index of his symbolism, that it opens up the fiction in general. The typical Poe story is, in its action, an allegory of dream experience: it occurs within the mind of the poet; the characters are not distinct personalities, but principles or faculties of the poet's divided nature; the steps of the action correspond to the successive states of a mind moving into sleep; and the end of the action is the end of a dream.

Wilbur applies the dream theory to his long and even more perceptive discussion of Poe's only finished novel, *The Narrative of Arthur Gordon Pym*. This essay introduced a new edition published in 1973. Defending the work despite its obvious faults, Wilbur argues that Poe achieved a "coherent allegory throughout; and that what Poe took from his many sources, forgetting, for the moment, his borrowings for mere authenticity's sake—is made to coalesce, especially at the close, into a powerful vision which is Poe's and nobody else's." Echoing the earlier essay, Wilbur concludes that "on the literal plane, then, Pym initiates very little action and is nearly—perhaps wholly—free of blood guilt. Yet on the plane of dream allegory and vision, Pym's obviously *must* be the imagination that drives and determines the narrative. . . ." Wilbur delineates convincingly the many ways in which "*Pym* is latently a spiritual quest."

Of his book reviews, Wilbur includes only one—a cursory overview of Poe criticism that "presumes by the way to expose one of Poe's deepest-laid plots." (Wilbur provides explanatory headnotes for eacn of his pieces.) Wilbur's contribution to Poe criticism is to show that all his detective fiction, especially "The Murders in the Rue Morgue," have "an allegorical stratum." Detective Dupin, "Though sometimes depicted as a reasoner," is "the embodiment of an idea, strongly urged in *Eureka* and elsewhere, that poetic intuition is a supralogical faculty, infallible in nature, which includes and obviates analytical genius." Dupin's logic is "really intuition in disguise." "There is a decided duplicity, then, in Poe's presentation of Dupin." Wilbur's conception of Dupin anticipates his analysis of Pym. "The implication is that the mastermind Dupin, who can intuitively 'fathom' all the other characters . . . is to be seen including them all—that the other 'persons' of the tale are to be taken allegorically as elements of one person, whereof Dupin is the presiding faculty." And so Dupin "uses his genius to detect and restrain the brute in himself, thus exorcising the fiend." Those who know the poetry of Wilbur, about whom Randall Jarrell said, "he obsessively sees, and shows, the bright underside of every dark thing," may wonder whether his interest in Poe's paradoxical vision and method may not be his way of detecting and restraining, if not exorcising, the Poe fiend in himself.

But the Wilbur who is best known to readers of poetry and to himself is the one who can unblushingly include a commencement address in a collection of literary essays. "A Speech at a Ceremony" is as much about the kind of academic, formalist poetry of which Wilbur is the most accomplished practitioner as any of his other essays. He sees the commencement address as "an extremely difficult form" (this is his third) "demanding in respect of clarity, animation, appropriateness, and wide pertinence. . . ." The parallel with his poetry is delightfully obvious. "The function of any ceremony is to enable one to feel some appropriate emotion decisively . . . to punctuate our lives with what look like significant choices and deliberate changes, and to hide from us the extent to which we are aimless and passive. . . . We are engaged in something corporate, something collective." Wilbur argues here what his poems often exemplify—our "need, at times, of the benign coercion of ceremony." Responses to places, too, may take shape as poems do. "Regarding Places" is his introduction to *A Sense of Place,* a collection of paintings and texts by American landscape artists, edited for The Friends of the Earth. Events in nature are so often occasions for his poems that many critics compare him with Frost, who might have felt a shock of recognition had he read Wilbur's definition of "place": "a fusion of human and natural order, and a peculiar window on the whole."

Three other essays, widely spaced, deal more directly with the nature and practice of poetry. In "Poetry and Happiness," Wilbur shows poets (Whitman, Hopkins, Roethke, and Williams, for example) happily fulfilling the primitive desire, "so radical to poetry . . . to lay claim to as much of the world as possible through uttering the names of things," making "an inventory of external reality." Another impulse to poetry, seen in Emily Dickinson, Robert Lowell, and Elizabeth Bishop, is to discover, clarify, embody, and project the self. But poets must also have "a sufficient cultural heart from which to write." Wilbur, more than most of his contemporaries, is acutely aware of this dilemma: that "where art does not arise from and nourish a vital sense of community, it is little more than an incitement to schizophrenia." To demonstrate an integrated poetic sensibility at work, Wilbur analyzes Robert Frost's "Birches," "doubtless the best-loved American poem of this century," showing ways in which it "converses" with Shelley's *Adonais.* "Frost's poem does justice to world, to self, to literary tradition, and to a culture" (New England). "It is happy in all the ways in which a poem can be happy."

Wilbur's experience teaches him that the thing that calls each artist to his art is not encounters with life's diffuse occasions but with art itself. Astonished, artists want "to make something like *that.*" "Art is provoked by art." In "Poetry's Debt to Poetry," Wilbur, whose own poetry is replete with academic allusions, quickly dispenses with arguments against his theme, citing Yeats's exhortation "that the soul which would sing must study monuments of its own magnificence." Epigraphs, Eliot's and Crane's, for instance, acknowledge such debts, as do quotations within the body of a poem. "Open admissions of poetic indebtedness are attractive and useful; they remind us that art is ultimately a loose collective enterprise, and they tell something of the particular writer by exposing his affinities." Most imitators of Dylan Thomas and several of Roethke's imitations, especially of Yeats, are negative examples. Wilbur is fascinated by the phenomenon of the wildly unlikely influence, as that of Winthrop Mackworth Praed's poem "The Vicar" on Edwin Arlington Robinson's poems, or Edward Lear's decorous, submerged parodies of poems by Thomas Moore, Tennyson, and Poe. As an example of "a rare kind of imitative poetry," Wilbur examines Auden's "Their Lonely Getters" as an attempt to "write a Frost poem on a Frost subject." And Frost's "Stopping by Woods on a Snowy Evening" "converses with a poem by Beddoes" ("The Phantom-Wooer"), "declines its invitation, and pays its beauty the tribute of resistance." Wilbur labors lovingly to convince us that "the courteous conversing of one poem with another is artistic response at its best."

In 1948, Wilbur was invited to react to addresses by Louise Bogan and William Carlos Williams given at a "lively conference on poetic form" at Bard College. His "brash article," "The Bottles Become New, Too" draws on Baudelaire, quoted by Bogan: "When poets put new wine in old bottles, the bottles become new, too." Responding to Williams' attack on traditional poetics, Wilbur observes that

> the tendency of poems to feed on other poems (we sometimes call this "writing in the Tradition") is only one aspect of the really great and frequent failing of poetry: its weakness for autonomy, its wish to inhabit the world which it creates, its larval self-satisfaction, its pleasure in manufacturing hermetic prisms.

That is a direct attack on the kind of poetry Williams preferred. "No poetry can have any strength unless it continually bashes itself against the reality of things." But "the relation between an artist and reality is always an oblique one. . . . If you respect the reality of the world, you know that you can approach that reality only by indirect means."

Critics, and even his many admirers, have faulted Wilbur for cleaving too strictly to these early-stated formal concepts, such as:

> Paradoxically it is respect for reality which makes a necessity of artifice. Poetry's prime weapon is words, used for the naming, comparison, and contrast of things. Its auxiliary weapons are rhythms, formal patterns, and rhymes. . . . There is no way of noticing certain subtleties and stresses and variations unless there is a norm, an apparent regular structure, from which divergences are made.

The poet's imperative is not to surrender to traditional forms, but to take them over, as Wilbur has. Wilbur applies all these attitudes and concepts in his general discussions and specific explications of poems by Shakespeare, Burns, Dickinson, Whitman, Housman, Frost, and himself.

Wilbur deals with traditional approaches to Shakespeare's *Venus and Adonis,* admits its obvious faults, but praises its "elaborate inventiveness, its rhetorical dexterity, its technical *éclat*," its "artful variety"—all of which make it "an ostentatious poetic performance." *The Rape of Lucrece* is "more obtrusively artificial." He characterizes "The Phoenix and the Turtle" as a "strange and masterly metaphysical poem."

One of the finest essays in the collection is "Sumptuous Destitution," delivered as a speech at Amherst College celebrating the Dickinson bicentennial in 1959. Wilbur sees Dickinson's poetry "as an effort to cope with her sense of privation . . . she was deprived of an orthodox and steady religious faith . . . of love . . . of literary recognition." "An unsteady congregation of one," she questioned "god about the economy of His creation." In her poems, she achieved compensation through renunciation. She magnified by desire everything of which she was deprived, making possession of anything by appetite impossible. Written out of such dilemmas, her poetry reveals an "articulate faithfulness to inner and outer truth" and an "insistence on maximum consciousness" that achieve "not an avoidance of life but an eccentric mastery of it."

Compared with the empathetic essay on Dickinson, Wilbur's piece on Whitman is slight. Also of questionable lasting importance are the introductions to Wilbur's translations of three of Molière's verse comedies: *The Misanthrope* (1955), *Tartuffe* (1963), and *The School for Wives* (1971).

Some readers may return again and again, though, to the explications of Housman's often misread "Epitaph on an Army of Mercenaries," of Burns's "A Red, Red Rose" ("Explaining the Obvious"), and Frost's little-discussed "The Gum-Gatherer." Those essays are not only fresh, useful, close readings of the poems, but they offer general insights into the way writing and reading poetry work. In the Housman essay we see two characteristics of Wilbur's method in most of these essays as well as in his own poetry: the use of ordinary, everyday experiences and of allusions to imaginative works of the past to elucidate our understanding of the creative process and of the way we may perceive it.

"On My Own Work" is Wilbur's response to a request that he discuss his own writing and the current condition of poetry "in a manner suitable for broadcast by the Voice of America," that he "touch upon the relations of art to culture, ideology, and the state." As we have seen, Wilbur responds to such clear-cut invitations with a total awareness of the occasion. "Poetry is sterile unless it arises from a sense of community or, at least, from the hope of community." He notes that one of the changes in his work has been "a partial shift from the ironic meditative lyric toward the dramatic poem" and quotes and discusses "A Baroque Wall-Fountain in the Villa Sciarra," which Randall Jarrell called "one of the most nearly perfect poems any American has written," to illustrate the first and "Two Voices in a Meadow" to illustrate the second mode. Wilbur still believes what John Crowe Ransom and his teachers taught him: that "the most adequate and convincing poetry is that which accommodates mixed feelings, clashing ideas, and incongruous images." Having quoted a third poem, "Love Calls Us to the Things of This World," Wilbur sums up the persistent concerns in his poetry, above all

> the proper relation between the tangible world and the intuitions of the spirit. . . . What poetry does with ideas is to redeem them from abstraction and submerge them in sensibility; it embodies them in persons and things and surrounds them with a weather of feeling; it thereby tests the ability of any ideas to consort with human nature in its contemporary condition.

Elegant, fastidious, graceful, delicate, charming, attractive, appealing, engaging—commentaries on Wilbur's ten volumes of prize-winning poems are studded with such words. And these: funny, witty, beautiful, playful, sensuous, vigorous, exuberant, cautious, tolerant, ironic, paradoxical, ambiguous, meditative, intelligent, clever, skillful, sophisticated, anti-romantic, "classic," allusive. Such words, used by both admirers and critics of his poetry, apply to his prose as well. With "a passion for acceptance" and a profound belief in the power of imagination to rival and enhance reality, Richard Wilbur reconciles contraries in "a world shimmering with reciprocity," striving to achieve balance. "For some of us unity is still a virtue."

David Madden

Sources for Further Study

America. CXXXVI, April 16, 1977, p. 362.
Christian Science Monitor. LXIX, March 2, 1977, p. 23.
Kirkus Reviews. XLIV, September 15, 1976, p. 1078.
Library Journal. CI, October 1, 1976, p. 2066.
New York Times Book Review. October 24, 1976, p. 6.
Publisher's Weekly. CCX, September 20, 1976, p. 69.

ROOSEVELT AND CHURCHILL, 1939-1941
The Partnership That Saved the West

Author: Joseph P. Lash (1909-   )
Publisher: W. W. Norton and Company (New York). Illustrated. 528 pp. $12.95
Type of work: Narrative history and biography
Time: December, 1905-January, 1942, with a concentration on the period September 11, 1939-January 1, 1942
Locale: Washington, D.C., London, and the countries involved in World War II

A study of the personalities of President Franklin D. Roosevelt and Prime Minister Winston Churchill, and of the development of their alliance against Germany, Japan, and Italy early in World War II

> *Principal personages:*
> FRANKLIN DELANO ROOSEVELT, President of the United States, 1933-1945
> SIR WINSTON LEONARD SPENCER CHURCHILL, First Lord of the Admiralty, 1939-1940; Prime Minister of Great Britain, 1940-1945
> HARRY LLOYD HOPKINS, personal adviser to Roosevelt and administrator of the Lend-Lease program
> ADOLF HITLER, Chancellor and Führer of Germany, 1933-1945

Joseph P. Lash, the author of the award-winning book *Eleanor and Franklin,* now adds *Roosevelt and Churchill, 1939-1941: The Partnership That Saved the West* to the several books he has written on major figures of the administration of Franklin Delano Roosevelt. Through his activities in the American Youth Congress in the 1930's, the author developed a close personal friendship with Eleanor Roosevelt. Because of that friendship, he was frequently a guest during the war years at the White House, where he came to know President Roosevelt himself. Lash has combined his knowledge of the Roosevelts gained at firsthand with the recently opened Roosevelt-Churchill correspondence and declassified documents from the British government's wartime files to produce a sweeping portrait of the two great leaders who forged the Anglo-American alliance against the Nazi dictator, Adolf Hitler.

Indeed, Lash's twofold objective in writing *Roosevelt and Churchill* is to develop a better understanding of the character traits of what he regards as two enormously egocentric men in order to learn what attracted them to each other, and to show how their mutual affection literally altered the course of history. To more effectively achieve this objective, Lash employs the narrative style of writing that makes considerable, though judicious, use of anecdotal material. A good story, as well as good history, thus emerges in which there are four general areas of concentration. The most important of these is, of course, the comparisons which Lash offers at various points throughout the book between the backgrounds and personalities of Franklin Delano Roosevelt and Winston Churchill. Otherwise, the book focuses on what may be defined as three major periods in the formation of an Anglo-American alliance. These include the early contacts between Roosevelt and Churchill from September, 1939, to the latter's appointment as Prime Minister in May, 1940; the genesis of the alliance from the fall of France in June, 1940, to the Japanese attack on Pearl Harbor on December 7, 1941; and the short span of time from the formal entry of the United States into World War II and the conclusion of an alliance with Great Britain as sealed in the Declaration of the United Nations of January 1, 1942. Lash, in fact, was present on that day at the White House on the occasion of the signing of the Declaration by Roosevelt, Churchill, and the representatives of China and the Soviet Union. The author opens his book with a vivid description of this historic event and recalls that when the signatures had been affixed to the document, there was a sense that Hitler's doom had been sealed.

The comparisons which Lash draws between Roosevelt and Churchill generally reveal more similarities of character than differences. Both men emerge in the book as charismatic personalities who had the ability to infuse those around them with their own optimism, energy, and sense of purpose. This dynamism helped to compensate for the fact that neither leader was a very good administrator on a day-by-day basis. In wielding their authority, Roosevelt and Churchill, unlike Hitler or Mussolini, always had respect for the people whom they governed. They sensed what people desired, and they had the ability to mobilize public opinion in support of actions which they deemed vital to the national interest. Lash, in a specific reference to Roosevelt, cites the President's success in obtaining public support for the programs he wanted from the Congress as a central feature of his greatness. To a considerable extent, the ability of Roosevelt and Churchill to shape public opinion in their favor was based upon their skill in public speaking. Roosevelt had to master this skill in order to have men do his bidding; for Churchill, public speaking, in Lash's view, was a compulsive manifestation of his personality. Churchill, especially, had a love for language and was an artist in choosing just the right word or phrase to drive home the idea he wanted to convey to his listeners. This love also embraced literary composition, to which his multivolume histories of the world wars and the English-speaking peoples so magnificently attest. In sum, both men were endowed with magnetic personalities that attracted people to them, Churchill by his rich imagination and instinct, Roosevelt by a keen sensitivity to men and their dreams. Ultimately, it was their attraction for each other which contributed, in the words of the book's subtitle, to "the partnership that saved the West."

There were, however, as Lash points out, a number of singular differences in their personalities. Churchill was the more impetuous of the two, while Roosevelt, because of polio, had long since learned the virtue of patience in dealing with others. As a child, the President had also learned how to hide his innermost feelings and purposes in an effort to protect himself from a very possessive mother. Churchill, on the contrary, allowed his passions to well to the surface and, in fact, took pleasure in revealing himself to others. On occasion, Churchill was subject to fits of depression; Roosevelt was called the "gay cavalier" by those who knew him. Lash observes that to the world of 1940 Churchill embodied the old order and did so magnificently. Roosevelt, by contrast, represented the new age that was dawning.

The roots of the close relationship between Roosevelt and Churchill can be traced to the dark days of September, 1938, when Hitler was demanding that Czechoslovakia cede the German-speaking Sudetenland to Germany. Roosevelt, Lash writes, informed British Prime Minister Neville Chamberlain that he was willing to support, though not initiate, a blockade of Germany should Great Britain be forced into war over the Sudetenland question. Chamberlain, bent on appeasing Hitler's demands, never responded personally to Roosevelt's offer of assistance. Hence, a year later, when war did finally break out with the German invasion of Poland, it was not surprising that a concerned Roosevelt did not contact Chamberlain. Instead, on September 11, 1939, as the German panzers knifed toward Warsaw, Roosevelt addressed a letter to Winston Churchill, long the staunch opponent of appeasement, who now held the position of First Lord of the Admiralty (civilian head of the British navy) in Chamberlain's cabinet. After referring to the similar naval positions each held during World War I, Roosevelt urged Churchill to keep in touch with him personally on anything that he wanted him to know about. This gesture, Lash states, considerably bolstered Churchill's position in government. During the so-called "Phony War," the six months between Hitler's destruction of Poland and his invasion of the Scandinavian countries in April, 1940, Roosevelt generally held Churchill in high esteem. The President's high opinion of Churchill, writes the author, plummeted with Hitler's successful landing in Norway, because the mistakes of the British Navy in failing to prevent this operation rested to some extent on the First Lord. Ironically, it was this disaster which helped to bring down the Chamberlain government. Churchill took over as Prime Minister on May 10, the day that Hitler launched his assault on Western Europe. Within six weeks the Nazis had overrun the Low Countries and France. It was the gravity of these events which prompted Roosevelt to run for a third term as President, an episode to which Lash devotes a most informative chapter. Churchill redeemed himself completely in Roosevelt's eyes when on June 18, 1940, he gave before the House of Commons a magnificent oration in which he resolved that his countrymen would fight on alone in the impending Battle of Britain.

So impressed was Roosevelt by Churchill's speech and by the British action of July 3, in sinking or capturing a major part of the French fleet, that he now resolved to provide as much military aid as possible to Great Britain, consistent with the official neutral status of the United States. During the ensuing eighteen months, as Lash explains in considerable detail, the President embarked on a course which led his country ever closer to open involvement in the war. Roosevelt's first major step in this direction was the conclusion of the Destroyer-Base Agreement of September 2, 1940, whereby in exchange for the transfer of fifty destroyers to Great Britain, the United States would receive ninety-nine-year leases of British bases in the Western Hemisphere. In this and other measures which Roosevelt took to aid Great Britain, he frequently aroused the animosity of the isolationists, a difficulty which Churchill often failed to appreciate. Nonetheless, British requests for aid continued to mount as the Battle of Britain continued. Roosevelt responded to these requests in late December, 1940, by proposing that the United States become "an arsenal of democracy" by "lending or leasing" war supplies to Great Britain. Lash, in a chapter entitled "Two Prima Donnas" paints a vivid contrast between Roosevelt's pride in his new idea for aiding Great Britain and the blasé manner in which Churchill received it. By this time, so many misunderstandings had developed between the two leaders on the role that the United States was playing that Roosevelt decided to send Harry Hopkins, his special adviser, to London in January, 1941, in an effort to restore a friendlier relationship between them. Lash devotes considerable attention to the significance of Hopkins' journey. Not only did Hopkins repair the troubled relations between Roosevelt and Churchill, but he also gave assurances to the Prime Minister that the Congress would pass the pending lend-lease legislation. When in March, 1941, the "Lend-Lease Act" became law, Hopkins was named the administrator of the program created by it.

Lash, in the balance of his book, shows how the United States steadily approached the brink of war during 1941. In July, important steps in this direction included Roosevelt's occupation of Iceland to relieve the British garrison there, and his decision to freeze all Japanese assets, which, in practical terms, meant an embargo on oil shipments to Japan. Hopkins, during the same month, journeyed again to London, where he completed the arrangements for the first wartime conference between Churchill and Roosevelt, to be held in August on board British and American warships anchored off Argentia, Newfoundland. In Lash's view, the significance of the so-called Atlantic Charter which emerged from this conference was that it carried the implication of America's armed intervention sufficient to ensure the realization of the declaration's postwar aims, one of which was "the final destruction of the Nazi tyranny." As the relations of the United States with Germany and Japan now sharply deteriorated, Roosevelt secured a sweeping revision of the Neutrality Act from Congress, in order to provide more effective aid to Great Britain. The Japanese attack on Pearl Harbor on December 7, followed four days later by Hitler's declaration of war on the United States, now completed the Anglo-American alliance between Roosevelt and Churchill as formally sealed in their joint declaration of January 1, 1942.

Joseph P. Lash, in his *Roosevelt and Churchill*, has made a significant contribution to the literature on World War II. A master of the narrative style of writing, Lash combines the gripping drama of a good story with sound historical scholarship. He is thus able to analyze the characters of Roosevelt and Churchill and their special relationship, while providing the reader with a detailed account of the development of the wartime alliance between the United States and the United Kingdom. Although Lash is personally attracted to the dynamism of the two leaders, he is by no means given over to hero worship in either case; indeed, he is quick to point out their flaws when he encounters them. His discussion of the growth of the Anglo-American alliance would have been more effective, however, had he consistently supplied exact dates for the major events which he describes. Otherwise, the book demonstrates Lash's talents as a painstaking researcher. In addition to using the Roosevelt papers in the Hyde Park Library and British government documents, the author has pored over the memoirs of the leading participants in the events he has portrayed and has utilized edited collections of documents relating to the foreign relations of the United States and Nazi Germany. The massively detailed index further enhances the value of the book.

Edward P. Keleher

Sources for Further Study

Book World. August 29, 1976, p. M1.

Booklist. LXXIII, November 15, 1976, p. 446.

National Observer. XV, December 18, 1976, p. 19

New York Times Book Review. October 24, 1976, p. 3.

New Yorker. LII, October 18, 1976, p. 187.

Saturday Review. IV, October 30, 1976, p. 40.

ROOTS

Author: Alex Haley
Publisher: Doubleday and Company (New York). 587 pp. $12.50
Type of work: Novel
Time: The eighteenth century to the present
Locale: The Gambia River, Africa, and the upper American South

A highly popular novel based on the black experience in America from earliest times which nurtures the desire for black identity

> *Principal characters:*
> KUNTA KINTE, "The African"
> BELL, his wife
> KIZZY, their daughter
> THE FIDDLER, a slave
> TOM LEA, a planter and cockfighter
> CHICKEN GEORGE, a son of Kizzy and Tom Lea
> MATILDA, his wife
> TOM MURRAY, their son, a blacksmith

The appearance of Alex Haley's *Roots* in 1976 was an event evocative of the publication of Mrs. Stowe's *Uncle Tom's Cabin* over a century ago. Both were novels describing the black experience in America and both quickly attained a level of public notice far beyond that warranted by their literary value. Both *Uncle Tom's Cabin* and *Roots* were avidly read, debated, and dramatized, one on the stage, one on television. Each shaped the mind of white America, but *Roots* also carried a particular message to blacks.

The timeliness of Haley's *Roots,* like Mrs. Stowe's "little book that caused the great war," has been central to its popular success. Issued at the end of the modern Civil Rights Movement at a time of strong black consciousness, *Roots* has become a symbol of the search for a black identity. It reminds the nation of the continuing struggle for equality, but it also signals the entrance of many black Americans into bourgeois affluence. It has inaugurated a popular pursuit of black genealogy that has directed the nation's librarians and archivists toward neglected plantation journals and musty county records.

Alex Haley, patiently telling and retelling his story to a hundred media interviewers, has been transformed into an American *griot.* This patently decent man learned the writer's craft during a career in the Coast Guard, and following his retirement, became a successful journalist. He wrote numerous magazine interviews and articles, and his powerful *Autobiography of Malcolm X* enriched black literature. The income from these activities and a *Reader's Digest* condensation of *Roots,* with other support from publishers, enabled Haley to spend over a decade writing his masterwork. Frequent travels to African and American ancestral homes consumed much time and money, but the results justified the effort. Alex Haley is now popularly regarded as a major custodian of the Afro-American heritage, and *Roots* is considered a highly evocative epitome of the black experience, viewed from the microcosm of one family.

Haley's ancestral chronology begins with the birth of his primary character, Kunta Kinte, "the African." The details of eighteenth century life along the Gambia River, the "Kamby Bolongo" of the Haley family oral tradition, are presented with accuracy and understanding. Haley draws an attractive picture of the molding of Kunta from birth to young manhood; the reader is fascinated by the customs and rituals of the Mandinka of Juffure. In dramatizing the interaction of boy and culture, Haley clarifies our understanding of African ways. Reality has finally reached a generation of Americans nurtured on Hollywood backlot jungles populated with childish Africans dependent on the white misfit Tarzan. A popular look at traditional Africa, a land of family, honor, and duty, is long overdue. Black Americans in particular, who have pondered their African roots, are captivated by Haley's picture of tribal life in a riverside village.

Haley's graphic descriptions of the ugliness of slavecatching and the coffled march to the African coast are shocking, but pale before his pictures of the brutality of the barracoon and the middle passage. Haley memorably describes life aboard a slave ship, alternately becalmed and storm-wracked and transformed into a floating hell of suppressed fury and rampant disease. How can humans so mistreat one another, asks our era, the parent of Buchenwald, the Vietnamese war, and the present government of Uganda? Haley answers this in some of his best passages, contrasting the misery and rage of hundreds of chained Africans against a callous white crew, riddled with lust, hatred, and fear.

The less revolting but infinitely more terrible process of enslavement in America is unveiled as Kunta Kinte is "broken," not so much by force—though beatings and worse are frequent—as by his awful lack of alternatives. Shorn even of his name, the African becomes "Toby" at his master's whim. Discovering that his culture is so thoroughly suppressed by whites that even blacks fear his ways and words, Toby grudgingly accepts the loss of his home, family, and freedom, and is given in exchange a travesty of American language and culture. He learns the few hundred English words issued by slaveowners, revolving about obedience, labor, and existence, and becomes, finally, "Massa's" obedient donkey. Only after the completion of this grand theft does Toby marry and found an American family that will pass through generations before its cultural and educational level will equal that stolen from Kunta Kinte.

The birth to Toby and his wife Bell of Kizzy Waller, an American with a surreptitiously African "Christian" name, launches the family into decades of profitless toil, good and bad masters, sales and separations. Haley convincingly describes birth, life, and death under the Damoclean sword of slavery and the daily horror of existence under the will of an uncontrollable "Massa." Yet in this adversity and misery in the concentration camp called slavery, the family not only survives, but grows strong. The desire for liberty, nurtured by the

American Revolution, grows into a demand from stronger men and women. Their aspirations are bared in the blighted attempts of the Fiddler to purchase his freedom, Bell's furtive newspaper reading, the trials and eventual seizure of freedom by the unforgettable Chicken George, and the wisdom and strength of Tom Murray, who practices the traditional metalcraft of the Kinte men. The postwar migration of the family under its black Moses, Chicken George, to the promised land in Tennessee has a clear symbolism for a race of Bible readers, and their settlement in Henning, a new, hardscrabble settlement, promises a bright future. Tom, warned by local whites that he cannot open a shop except as an employee of a white, successfully circumvents their will with a portable smithy, but learns that freedom has not replaced slavery. A new order of racist white supremacy has emerged, and the pilgrimage continues.

Roots' strengths are real: it is essentially an American success story. Its humanized chronology of black America from Africa to the present provides a synopsis of the rise from kidnaping and deculturization toward American respectability and comfort. Read in conjunction with the works of Kenneth Stampp, John Hope Franklin, or other recent scholars, and the narratives and autobiographies of slaves and ex-slaves, *Roots* offers clear insights into the black experience. It amplifies a growing American interest in the nation's history, and reinforces the Afro-American's parallel quest for identity through his cultural, geographical, and family origins.

Roots is not perfect. The reader's interest is maintained through extensive and taut dialogue, but overwritten passages are not infrequent. Historical errors abound (including antebellum pillared mansions and vast cotton fields in pre-Revolutionery Virginia, and references to states not yet founded). Its cursory sweep through recent history indicates that Haley's more recent forebears, busily smithing, farming, learning, and teaching, are simply less interesting. They were neither Africans nor slaves, but "us," and several factual and interesting but perfunctory chapters, tracing the story from Reconstruction to the present, confirm the fact that *Roots'* dramatic unity ends with the family's arrival in Tennessee.

Critics have attacked both the accuracy of the Haley family recollections and the author's historical reconstructions. Was Juffure really an unspoiled African village or a busy trading station, frequented by the coastal business community? Did the *griot* of Juffure tell Haley only what he wished to hear? Did Haley merely magnify shadowy family legends into a pseudohistory of black America for the millions? These frequently posed questions are irrelevant: *Roots* is a novel, and Haley was perfectly free to tell his tale as he wished. *Roots* is a brilliantly creative infusion of family lore with studies of Africa and antebellum America that may not approach the detailed historicity of Kenneth Roberts, but certainly transcends the believability of some "Bicentennial" effusions.

The television version of *Roots*—and its subsequent sale to the schools and libraries of America as an educational film—is a matter that cannot be ignored here. Broadcast to tens of millions in a weeklong production during early 1977, *Roots* touched the national mind and conscience. Unfortunately the staging of *Roots* suffered from the evils that afflicted *Uncle Tom's Cabin*; an overly melodramatic approach, casting that replaced negative black stereotypes with equally unreal white ones, historical anomalies, and a marketing approach that suggested that *Roots* was "social studies." The message is clear: *Roots* is a novel and the play is drama. The reader should evaluate *Roots* on its literary, not its teledramatic, merits.

Lance Trusty

Sources for Further Study

Atlantic. CCXXVIII, December, 1976, p. 116.

Christian Science Monitor. LXVIII, November 24, 1976, p. 812.

Commentary. LXII, December, 1976, p. 70.

Harper's Magazine. CCLIII, November, 1976, p. 104.

Los Angeles Times. October 10, 1976, Books, p. 1.

New York Review of Books. XXIII, November 11, 1976, p. 3.

New York Times Book Review. September 26, 1976, p. 1.

Newsweek. LXXXVIII, September 27, 1976, p. 94.

THE RUSSIANS

Author: Hedrick Smith (1933-   )
Publisher: Quadrangle/The New York Times Book Company (New York). 527 pp.
   $12.50
Type of work: Current affairs
Time: 1971-1974
Locale: The Soviet Union

   A portrait of the character of the Russian people and the various facets of Russian life under the Soviet regime

   Principal personages:
      ALEKSANDR SOLZHENITSYN, Soviet writer and dissident
      ANDREI SAKHAROV, Soviet physicist and dissident
      ROY MEDVEDEV, Soviet historian and dissident
      LEONID ILICH BREZHNEV, First Secretary of the Communist Party
      JOSEPH STALIN, former Dictator of the U.S.S.R.
      VLADIMIR ILICH LENIN (ULIANOV), former Dictator of Soviet Russia

   Hedrick Smith, the co-author of *The Pentagon Papers,* won the 1974 Pulitzer Prize for his coverage of the Soviet Union as the Moscow Bureau Chief for *The New York Times.* In his latest book, *The Russians,* Smith has put the essence of that coverage into a revealing and absorbing account of contemporary Soviet life and institutions. Smith's purpose in writing the book is to convey to his American readers those details of the life of the Russians which illuminate their character as a people and which define the society and times in which they live. Beyond simply recording his impressions, Smith has attempted to analyze the meaning of his experiences and of what the Russians told him about themselves and their way of life.

   The author divides his study into three areas of concentration: "The People," "The System," and "Issues." In Part One, "The People," Smith explores the status of women, the nature of the educational system, the restlessness of Russian youth, the privileged position of the Soviet leaders, and the personality traits of the Russian people as a whole. Part Two, "The System," provides an analysis of rural and industrial life in the U.S.S.R., the Soviet leadership, and the character of Soviet patriotism. Part Three, "Issues," deals with cultural, intellectual, and religious life and examines, among other things, the nature of dissent in present-day Russia.

   In the lengthy Introduction to his book, Smith related a number of stories and anecdotes which illustrate the nature of the relationship between Russians and foreigners and the untiring, and frequently ludicrous, efforts of the Soviet authorities to keep them from making any contacts not authorized by the state. Foreigners who travel to Russia for brief visits are usually escorted about in tour groups or delegations by guides and interpreters who keep a watchful eye on them from the time they enter the country until the time they depart. Smith observes that when he went to Russia, he was skeptical of such tales until an

Intourist guide confided to him that all guides are required to report to the KGB (secret police) any foreigners who stray from the group, speak Russian, or have Russian friends or relatives whom they attempt to contact. This particular guide even went so far as to show Smith the room off the lobby of the Intourist Hotel where KGB officers received reports from the guides. Another way in which the Soviet authorities separate their citizens from foreigners is to provide the latter who go to Russia as residents with separate housing. Smith notes that he and his family, like nearly all diplomats, businessmen, and journalists who work in Moscow, were assigned to an apartment building, one of half a dozen foreign ghettos around the city, which the Soviet government reserves exclusively for foreign residents. The building in which the Smiths resided was separated from an adjacent apartment complex where Russians lived by a ten-foot-high concrete wall, the single gateway to which was guarded twenty-four hours a day by uniformed policemen who worked for the KGB. Because of this and countless other barriers which the Soviet authorities literally erect, very few foreigners, the author points out, make a serious and sustained effort to meet and befriend Russians other than through their designated official contacts. Smith, as his book amply demonstrates, was more successful than most foreigners in getting close to the Russians and in making friends among them.

His ability, despite all the barriers, to develop a closeness to and understanding of the Russians is particularly illustrated throughout the first part of his book, "The People," in which he discusses the Russians by socioeconomic standing, sex, age group, and as a people *sui generis*. In examining Soviet society, Smith brings out the wide socioeconomic gulf which exists in a supposedly classless society between the privileged ruling class and the broad masses of the population. This contrast is especially evident in the shopping habits and in the dwellings of the two classes. Thus, members of the Communist Party Central Committee staff and their families are conveyed in chauffeur-driven polished black Volga sedans to a building in Moscow identified as "The Bureau of Passes." Here and at other similar sites, the party elite, or what one Soviet journalist acidly called "our Communist nobility," can shop for quality merchandise or food delicacies without having to encounter the usual harassments that confront ordinary citizens, including chronic shortages, rude service, and that classic Russian institution—the queue. Smith writes that in Russia, shopping for the average person is like a year-round Christmas rush, with the Soviet housewife generally spending two hours in line, seven days a week. People queue up to buy goods that are in extremely short supply, or to register for such goods as automobiles that will take eighteen months for actual delivery. Another major difference between the lifestyle of high Communist officials and that of the masses is to be found in their dwellings. The party elite, including first party secretary Leonid Brezhnev, all have their comfortable homes or *dachas* outside Moscow. These generally large mansions, often with several acres of land, present a sharp contrast to the cramped, poorly constructed apartments of many Soviet citizens. Most Muscovites, Smith observes, deride the lifestyle of the Communist party bosses as a mockery of Marxist ideals.

Elsewhere in this section of the book, Smith examines some of the contradictions that surface in the character of the Russian people as a whole and in various groups of the population. Foreigners who confront Russians in public generally find them to be cold and impersonal. In their private lives, by contrast, they are extremely warm, cheerful, and very hospitable. One of the roots, Smith explains, of the dichotomy in the Russian character is to be found in the authoritarian environment in which they live from cradle to grave. The Russians are the greatest of role-players, adopting two very different codes of behavior for their public and private lives. In one, they are taciturn, careful, and hypocritical as they hold their thoughts and feelings in check, while in the other, they are honest, open, and passionate in their relationship with those whom they feel they can trust. Smith also discovers contradictions in the status of Soviet women and youth. He points out that in spite of the declared Communist commitment to female equality, a strong tradition of male chauvinism in Russian life remains clearly unmitigated. As for the youth, they exhibit, despite their indoctrination and conformist training in the schools, a feeling of alienation from the system much as did their American counterparts during the 1960's. A Communist party journalist sums up the attitude of Russian young people toward the system when he is quoted by Smith as saying that the young person "acts as if ideology were irrelevant."

Smith, in discussing the system from which Russian youth feel alienated, devotes considerable attention in Part Two of his study to the nature of Soviet leadership and power. Most Russians, he finds, have a great admiration for bigness and power, be it huge Kremlins, cannons, and churchbells under the czars; or huge dams, missiles, and atom smashers under the Communists. Many people, interestingly enough, are very nostalgic about the "good old days" under Joseph Stalin because of the strong leadership which he provided. They contrast the apparent order of that period with the sloppy management in industry and agriculture and the lax behavior of youth which prevail at present under Brezhnev. These latter-day admirers of Stalin choose to set aside in their own minds—without completely forgetting—the great purges and sufferings for which he was responsible; instead, they point to the Stalinist era as the time when the Soviet power was firmly established. If Stalin symbolizes the substance of Soviet power and authority, Lenin, who is glorified at every turn, provides the basis for the legitimacy of that power and authority. Ironically, although the average Russian has unquestioning respect for authority, his tactic is to look for a loophole or hope that an official's inefficiency will somehow enable him to get by. These loopholes, Smith comments, proliferate in direct proportion to the proliferation of rules and regulations, thus providing Russians with many opportunities to mitigate the stern order of public life.

This sternness is nowhere more evident than in· the Soviet regime's repression of dissent and in the plight of the country's three leading dissidents, Aleksandr Solzhenitsyn, Andrei Sakharov, and Roy Medvedev. Smith, in the concluding section of his book, provides a most engrossing portrait of each of these men, citing the differences in their personalities and in the ideas of their dissent. Solzhenitsyn and Sakharov present the sharpest contrast, the former rough, confident, and outgoing; the latter more vulnerable, shy, and reticent. As one of the fathers of the Soviet hydrogen bomb and a full member of the Academy of Sciences at the unheard-of age of thirty-two, Sakharov could have lived out his life as a highly privileged member of the Soviet elite. He chose, instead, to speak out against the arms race and to urge, among other things, the convergence of the socialist and capitalist systems. His call for liberal reforms in the Soviet government has struck fear into the Kremlin leaders, lest his criticism undercut the legitimacy and *raison d' être* of the Communist Party When Solzhenitsyn issued his attack on the Soviet system, Sakharov discovered that they had many different views. Sakharov, in the pattern of nineteenth century Russian intellectual tradition, was more of a Westernizer in his reform ideas. He was dismayed at Solzhenitsyn's Slavophile aspersions on the West and his isolationist retreat into a kind of Great Russian nationalism which precluded global cooperation on the major world problems of hunger, health, and the environment. Whatever their differences, the Soviet government put increasing restrictions on both individuals, going so far as to exile Solzhenitsyn from the country in 1974.

By contrast with both Sakharov and Solzhenitsyn, Roy Medvedev, the author writes, "is the personification of the cool dissident [who] has always maintained the sober, dispassionate stance of the thoughtful, armchair reformer." Medvedev, unlike Solzhenitsyn and Sakharov, has avoided making direct attacks on the Communist Party or the Soviet system, confining his criticisms instead to what he calls Neo-Stalinist "deformations." As a consequence, the government has not harassed him nearly as much as the other two dissidents. Smith describes Medvedev as a pragmatist, a gradualist who envisions reform slowly evolving within the Soviet system. Thus in two or three generations, he foresees the Soviet Union evolving toward a multiparty system. In Medvedev's view, the reforms will be initiated from above but in response to pressures from an alliance between the best of the intelligentsia and the most progressive individuals within the government itself. According to Smith, the whole temper of Medvedev's dissent differs from that of Solzhenitsyn and Sakharov. Medvedev's patience and willingness to allow reform to evolve differs completely from the demands of Solzhenitsyn and Sakharov for immediate change. He rejects the religious Russophilism of Solzhenitsyn as unrealistic in the modern age where religion seemingly cannot attract enough bride. The aunt's departure on her pilgrimage to find death beside the Ganges represents on the surface the sulking pettiness of an old woman angered at the prospect of giving place to a beautiful young bride. But viewing the act apart from the momentary provocation, it represents the tenacious hold of traditional ritual and religious belief in determining the course of life and death in India today, even as in the bygone centuries.

Daisy's atheism and indulgent indifference to religion (so long as religious traditions do not impinge upon her family-planning activities) represents the "liberated" viewpoint, one which the author plainly depicts as a minority opinion in his fictional Indian microcosm of Malgudi. Her militant espousal of social change, her rejection of traditional customs and values, her ascetic self-denial of any personal comforts, and her almost fanatic zeal in pursuing her family-planning goals, all reveal her as the thoroughly conditioned product of her early training by a missionary whom she quotes whenever Raman or others try to suggest to her that other values might have merit. Daisy's rejection of marriage to Raman in favor of family-planning work is entirely consistent with her training, and her strength of character is finally a kind of mindless automated behavior for which she has been programmed. She remains a very human and touching person in her lapses from her own behavioral goals. Her weeping, her seeking out of Raman after their first quarrel, her admission of her love for him, and her sexual responsiveness are all evidences of an underlying warmth and emotional nature that she cannot entirely suppress.

Raman, reared in a traditional Hindu household by his devout aunt, educated in a college stressing the emancipated beliefs of the age of enlightenment, and committed by his occupation to communication of information, is at the center of the vortex of the winds of change. Forced to communicate through painting the signs, he is troubled by his lack of conviction about what he communicates.

His lack of commitment is underscored by his longing to retire from his work to a farm, by his ascetic attempt to expunge sexual desires, by his troubled cynicism about producing signs in which he does not believe. Raman's training in Western logic and ideas of the enlightenment will not let him truly believe in the ancient Hindu gods, but neither will his emotional ties to his past and to his aunt let him totally reject the traditions of India and the Hindu religion. In his contacts with customers for his signs, he is similarly disturbed by the conflict between his need to satisfy his clients and his need to paint signs which aesthetically and intellectually satisfy him.

Raman's abandonment of his zeal for rationalism in any practical situation when insistence upon rational thought would alienate clients, townspeople, friends, or especially Daisy or Laxmi, reveals an ambivalence within him. He idealizes rational thought, but willingly foregoes his ideal in order to satisfy his deep emotional need to be accepted and loved by others. He reproaches himself for his timidity, but is in fact choosing an emotional value which is stronger within him than the intellectual one. Because of these conflicts, Raman is at the mercy of the decisions of others, including all the minor characters in the story.

A pragmatic, unexamined solution to the conflicts involved in the clash of cultures is embodied in the neighbors, who manage to couple sincere belief and reverence for tradition with a practical adaptation to modern conveniences and creature comforts.

It is this spectrum of attitudes and beliefs—and the clashes, compromises, and changes which inevitably must come about—which are the central theme of Narayan's novel. The tragedy of the romance is not only that Daisy and Raman must part, and that Laxmi and Raman will never see each other again, but it is also that the crucial human values of love, tenderness, tolerance, and sexual fulfillment are rejected in favor of commitment to a social goal on Daisy's part, and to a religious commitment on Laxmi's part.

The attitudes and convictions of Raman, Daisy, Laxmi and the neighbor with whom Laxmi is to travel represent a cross-section of those prevailing in India today. The conflicts of the characters are the conflicts of these apparently irreconcilable differences. If this were all, the novel would be an interesting fictional study of social changes. But the author establishes within each of his principal characters a conflict between the character's own values and his emotional needs. The conflict is particularly acute in Raman, who does not even have the intense polarization of beliefs which sustain Daisy and Laxmi in their decisions.

The love of Raman and Daisy is a strong physical attraction. Both resist it intellectually because it does not logically fit into their plans or their lifestyles. But both must finally succumb to its strength, and the impending intimacy of marriage forces a confrontation of the value systems Raman and Daisy represent. Daisy's coldness to traditional values and her commitment to social reform in the form of family planning are her dominant characteristics; she has been shaped by a missionary into a totally dedicated advocate of Western technology, propaganda, and values. She devotes her life to preventing life; not only is she a tireless propagandist and dispenser of devices for contraception, but she insists that she would reject any child which might by accident be born to her and Raman. Daisy is likewise unmoved by Raman's anguish over his aunt's departure and pilgrimage to death beside the Ganges. Daisy has rejected her Indian identity altogether. Even the name she has adopted is foreign. She represents the clinical, objective, efficient Western world—seeing India through Western eyes—determined to impose Western values, methodology, and efficiency upon a bemused and generally tolerant populace of Malgudi, and upon the love-stricken Raman as their lives become entwined.

But Raman, the central figure, through whose point of view the story unfolds, is a figure of lesser strength and lesser commitment because he is a creature of vastly greater complexity than either Laxmi or Daisy. Emotionally, he espouses things which are intellectually incompatible. As a self-proclaimed rationalist he is uncomfortable with his emotional involvements. He can act neither upon his convictions nor upon his reservations about the convictions of others which involve him.

Raman is the painter of signs. Hired by Daisy, his propaganda signs for family planning are by far his largest commercial contract. With Daisy, as with all his clients, he serves their needs in his work but lacks conviction about the messages he paints and posts. Signs are necessary, he feels, to communication. And yet he is troubled that he paints signs only to earn money, rather than to communicate the truth to people. And so he justifies his work by a fiercely stubborn commitment to the artistry of the lettering and the appropriate choice of colors. He can espouse no cause with conviction, and so he lacks the forcefulness and assurance of either his aunt or Daisy. His abortive attempt to rape Daisy—an attempt to assert his mastery over the situation through physical dominance—comes to naught because Daisy slips away while he hesitates in order to convince himself that he is doing the right thing. Daisy and the aunt, by contrast, pursue and fulfill their convictions unhesitatingly, even though this act means abandoning Raman and their home with him. Through them, East and West still contend for the allegiance of India. But Raman, a hybrid product of both cultures, cannot commit himself fully to either, and when he is left alone, he turns to that refuge of no commitment, The Boardless—so called because it is an inn where there is no sign to communicate any message at all.

In loading the characters with such strong symbolism that they come to border on caricature, Narayan diminishes the reader's sympathy for them. Raman is not ultimately tragic, but rather pitiful, and his retreat to anonymity represents the assertion of the author that the future of India—culturally, intellectually, and technologically—is most uncertain. The painter of signs, the young Indian intellectual, is not giving unequivocal direction to his nation because he cannot espouse any cause unequivocally himself.

Against the social, religious, and political conflicts which preoccupy the thoughts and interior monologues of the protagonist, the author juxtaposes the adamant facts of nature in its workings. Raman would be a completely controlled rationalist, but he is unable to suppress or even control his own sexual urges; Daisy, who would be the totally efficient supressor of births in India, continually receives statistics showing large population increases. Both are at the mercy of the weather, events, and their own impulses. Raman, realizing his own hypocrisy in aiding Daisy's family-planning work, finally is willing to abandon his intellectual idealism in order to establish a marriage with Daisy. He wants to keep his childhood home by the river, and to make his life with Daisy part of the traditional and accustomed community life. Daisy too is attracted to the river, a symbol of the placid working of nature throughout India. But Daisy is willing to reject this when her duty to work calls.

Narayan brings to the reader through Raman's encounters with minor characters a vivid sense of the lives and the variety within a city in India today. His vignettes of minor personages in the situations of their daily routines are sharp, believable, and compassionate. The minor characters might well have become interesting major figures had the novel taken a different turn, or had a subplot been developed. The fictional city itself achieves an authenticity of its own through Narayan's deft pen. He conveys a sense of life and reality to Malgudi so that one may well accept it as a typical Indian city bustling with the daily life of real people.

Narayan writes with knowledge of the human soul. His characters, both male and female, have depth and complexity which give them strength and life. Though he writes with a constant compassion and fine benevolence toward his characters, he maintains an ironic distance which enables him to reveal absurdities and ironies at every turn of events. The tone is finally more pessimistic than tragic, more ironic than outraged, at the sadness of the outcome of the affair. It is a book which should outlast this season. Its characters live: their problems will also.

Betty Gawthrop

Sources for Further Study

America. CXXXIV, May 1, 1976, p. 395.

Commonweal. CIII, June 18, 1976, p. 406.

Harper's Magazine. CCLII, March, 1976, p. 112.

New Yorker. LII, April 1, 1976, p. 141.

Newsweek. LXXXVII, January 19, 1976, p. 71.

Spectator. CCXXXVI, June 5, 1976, p. 9.

Time. CVII, May 10, 1976, p. 84.

Virginia Quarterly Review. LII, Summer, 1976, p. 88.

SCOUNDREL TIME

Author: Lillian Hellman (1905-   )
Introduction by Garry Wills
Publisher: Little, Brown and Company (Boston). 155 pp. $7.95
Type of work: Memoir
Time: The 1940's and 1950's
Locale: New York, Washington, London, Connecticut, Italy

A brief account of Lillian Hellman's confrontation with the House Committee on Un-American Activities, what led up to her subpoena, and the impact of Senator McCarthy's witchhunt on her life and career

Principal personages:
LILLIAN HELLMAN, the author
DASHIELL HAMMETT, her common-law husband, author of detective
    novels
JOSEPH RAUH, her lawyer

Scoundrel Time is the third volume of Lillian Hellman's memoirs, having been preceded by *An Unfinished Woman* and *Pentimento: A Book of Portraits.* Both of the previous books were popular and critical successes; however, her aims have shifted here, and the scope of the present book is much narrower than that of the earlier volumes. In some ways, it is also less successful.

Hellman states her intention in the first paragraph:

> I have tried twice before to write about what has come to be known as the McCarthy period but I didn't much like what I wrote. My reasons for not being able to write about my part in this sad, comic, miserable time of our history were simple to me, although some people thought I had avoided it for mysterious reasons. There was no mystery. I had strange hangups and they are always hard to explain. Now I tell myself that if I face them, maybe I can manage.

And later:

> But I don't want to write about any historical conclusions—it isn't my game. I tell myself that this third time out, if I stick to what I know, what happened to me, and a few others, I have a chance to write my own history of the time.

Hellman's declared aim, then, is to set down *her* part in the McCarthy investigations—and since she was the first witness to defy the House Un-American Activities Committee, her role was of some importance. In addition, she is at pains to point out the parallels with Watergate. Richard Nixon came to power with Senator McCarthy in the Cold War period of Red-baiting; at the same time the FBI and CIA perfected their techniques for invading the lives of American dissidents. Nixon's role is pointed up; for example, there are two pictures of him and only one of McCarthy in the book. In other words, Hellman believes that Nixon's corrupt rule and the horrors of Watergate are a direct and inevitable result of the McCarthy witch-hunting of the 1950's.

When Hellman received her subpoena on February 21, 1952, she was the most important literary figure to be summoned before the HUAC, the author of half a dozen Broadway successes, including *The Little Foxes, The Children's Hour* and *The Autumn Garden.* Although she had been identified as a Communist by the screenwriter Martin Berkeley (she had never met him), she had never joined the party. However, she had long been associated with Dashiell Hammett, who became a Communist in the late 1930's. She had attended meetings with him and her name had appeared on various petitions and lists of sponsors. After Hammett went to jail in 1951, it was only a matter of time before the author's inevitable subpoena.

With her attorney, Joseph Rauh, she worked out a strategy that proved successful. She was reluctant to take the Fifth Amendment and was quite willing to reveal fully her political activities—so long as she was not asked to name others. In her famous letter to Chairman John Wood, she set the limits of what she was willing to discuss:

> I am prepared to waive the privilege against self-incrimination and to tell you anything you wish to know about my views or actions if your Committee will agree to refrain from asking me to name other people. If the Committee is unwilling to give this assurance, I will be forced to plead the privilege of the Fifth Amendment at the hearing.

When Hellman appeared before the HUAC on May 21, the Committee refused to grant her request and she was forced to take the Fifth. During her argument with Chairman Wood, he made the mistake of ordering her letter put into the record for clarification. At this point, her lawyer distributed mimeographed copies of the letter to the press. Shortly thereafter a voice from the press section rang out: "Thank God somebody finally had the guts to do it." Lillian Hellman had not won, but at least she had achieved a moral victory. She was praised in the press and the HUAC was embarrassed. She was the first person of importance to defy the Committee, and thereafter others adopted her strategy of what came to be called "the diminished Fifth."

Things went badly for Hellman for ten years after her appearance before the HUAC. Of course, she was blacklisted in Hollywood and could not get work there. When she did get a low-paying job for Alexander Korda, she had difficulty getting a visa. Once in Italy, she was hounded by the CIA and told falsely that Senator McCarthy planned to summon her before his Committee. In the end all her work and mental torture came to nothing; Korda went bankrupt and the film was shelved.

One of the most poignant sections of *Scoundrel Time* deals with the sale of her farm in Westchester, where she and Hammett had made a good life for themselves and the people working for them. The IRS had a lien against all of Hammett's earnings, so he spent the last ten years of his life without any income. Hellman was reduced to secretly working half-time in a dress shop. And, finally, there was the death of Hammett (Hellman has written movingly of this earlier in her memoirs). Since she has set out to tell the truth unsparingly, she records briefly a shabby love affair—if it can be called that. It is interesting enough, but not really significant to the present "history."

After a decade, Hellman finally had a new success on Broadway, *Toys in the Attic,* and ultimately was accepted again and poor no more. She concludes:

> I have written here that I have recovered. I mean it only in a worldly sense because I do not believe in recovery. The past, with its pleasures, its rewards, its foolishness, its punishments, is there for each of us forever, and it should be.

Hellman writes with controlled indignation about Senator McCarthy and his "boys"—though she seems unable to face up to saying much about them. To her the real "villains" of this shoddy era are the American intellectuals and liberals who stood by and let McCarthy come to power and ruin people, like Dashiel Hammett, without a word of protest. It is a dubious thesis, at best, but her assertion is that intellectuals like Lionel Trilling are more to blame than the witnesses who betrayed each other before the HUAC. (See Diana Trilling's reply to Hellman in *We Must March, My Darlings,* 1977.)

Although this is her third attempt to tell her story, Hellman still has some difficulty with the material. No doubt it is still painful for her to dredge up and confront such bitter memories. In any case, her organization is quirky, sometimes annoying and confusing. There is too much leaping back and forth in time—though she skillfully builds to the climax of her hour and twenty minutes before the HUAC. In her search for the truth, Hellman has not relied entirely on her memory; she makes use of her diary and scattered notes made at the time. She has also interviewed a few of the people involved—her lawyers, for example—to check her facts. And, of course, she has had access to the records of the Committee, which she found unreliable.

Although Hellman writes coolly and often with an edgy humor, she is still angry about what happened to her and Hammett, and rightly so. Perhaps she can be forgiven if she writes at times with a barely controlled malice; in fact, in a few instances she reminds one of Hemingway paying off old scores in *A Moveable Feast.* Among those who come in for her scorn are Clare Boothe Luce; Clifford Odets and Elia Kazan, both of whom were friendly witnesses; J. Edgar Hoover and Clyde Tolson ("a nasty pair"); and the editors of *Partisan Review* and *Commentary.* There is a marvelous anecdote about Henry Wallace, for whom she campaigned in his presidential bid. (He gave her a fifty pound bag of manure as a going away present when she sold her farm.)

Perhaps one should note, too, a few questions that need clearing up. It is unfortunate that the Internal Revenue Service cut off Hammett's income during his last ten years. But how and why did he shave on his taxes so long—and for how many dollars? There are also similar questions about Hellman's problems with income taxes. Also, Hellman must have known that many blacklisted screenwriters, such as Dalton Trumbo, continued their careers in Hollywood by making use of pseudonyms. Did she consider this alternative?

Finally, why did she wait so long to resume her career as a dramatist after her subpoena? And there are other questions left dangling.

Perhaps it is unfortunate that Garry Wills was chosen to write a lengthy introduction setting Hellman's memoirs in a historical context. (Was this merely to pad out a slender book?) Wills and Hellman are poles apart politically, and it is difficult to see how he could approve of her political activities. In any case, he disagrees with the author on a number of important points, blaming President Truman for the witch-hunts and not McCarthy. He also contends that McCarthy and Nixon were sincere in their cause, while Hellman writes them off as opportunistic liars. Wills also adds his own names to the list of liberal "enemies," among them Dwight McDonald and Mary McCarthy.

In the final analysis, *Scoundrel Time* seems in some ways self-serving and opportunistic. More damaging, it might have been cooked up and padded out to ride the wave of current Watergate and I-hate-Nixon bestsellers. Although it has been widely praised for its precision, restraint, and honesty, what importance it has is as a curious piece of minor history. Its literary value nowhere equals Hellman's *An Unfinished Woman* or *Pentimento*.

Guy Owen

Sources for Further Study

Christian Science Monitor. May 17, 1976, p. 23.
New York Review of Books. XXIII, June 10, 1976, p. 22.
New York Times Book Review. April 25, 1976, p. 1.
Newsweek. LXXXVII, April 17, 1976, p. 96.
Saturday Review. III, April 17, 1976, p. 28.
Time. CVII, May 10, 1976, p. 83.

SEARCHING FOR THE OX

Author: Louis Simpson (1923-   )
Publisher: William Morrow and Company (New York). 93 pp. $5.95
Type of work: Poetry

A collection of recent poetry dealing with the author's considerations of life, meaning, and literature

Searching for the Ox, Louis Simpson's latest collection of poetry, is a quiet, reflective, and introspective work. Divided into four sections, its divisions roughly equate the growth and development of Simpson as man and writer. The first two sections, "Venus in the Tropics" and "The Company of Flesh and Blood," concern the life of a boy and young man. Simpson, in his preface to this collection, suggests that the poems in these two sections are largely autobiographical. The poems in the third section, "Searching for the Ox," are directed at what Simpson calls "a way of life." They focus on the development of thoughts and ideas, of creativity and meditation. In the metaphor of the growth of man and writer, this section is the emergence from adolescence of the man as writer, and the emergence of thought from feeling and passion.

The final section of this collection is entitled "Further Adventures of the Letter I," the title of which is a continuation of the title of Simpson's previous poetry collection, *Adventures of the Letter I.* It is directed towards the ideas, thoughts, and experiences that grew out of Simpson's life as a writer. If the first three sections represented adolescence and the emergence of adulthood, perhaps this final section represents that quiet period of life when one may reflect on one's life and life work.

The author of numerous works, Simpson was awarded the Pulitzer Prize for his collection of poetry, *At the End of the Open Road.* In addition to this collection, he has written five others, this present collection being the seventh in the complete line of his poetry. The other collections are *The Arrivestes: Poems 1940-1949, Good News of Death and Other Poems, A Dream of Governors, Selected Poems,* and *Adventures of the Letter I.* Although his greatest recognition is for his poetry, Simpson is also a prose writer of considerable distinction. He has published five other works: *James Hogg: A Critical Study; Riverside Drive, An Introduction to Poetry; North of Jamaica;* and his critically acclaimed work, *Three on the Tower: The Lives and Works of Ezra Pound, T. S. Eliot and William Carlos Williams.*

Pursuing the idea that the collection is divided into four sections, each representing a stage in the development of man and writer, the placement of the title poem as the last poem in the third section becomes particularly significant. If the final section does, indeed, represent the stage in life when one may reflect on youth and early adulthood, then the poem "Searching for the Ox" becomes a bridge between the development of ideas and creativity and the reflection on them.

The poem, divided into five sections, opens with a description of a young girl suffering from schizophrenia in a mental hospital where a friend of the speaker works. It continues from this point to a conclusion of the first section with the image of a balloon being driven by its leaking air from one side of a swimming pool to the other, unable to escape its confining boundaries. The second section concerns science and technology and uses as its symbol the launching of the first manned mission to the moon. The third section introduces a concern with the past, while the fourth continues this theme, beginning with a quotation from Constantine Cavafy, the modern Greek poet. The fifth and final section opens with a consideration of Eastern philosophy and concludes with a final—both in position and in tone—three-line statement. The image of the ox provides for a strange series of considerations, some of these being, of course, a castrated bull, a beast of burden domesticated by man, and, perhaps, one of the gods whose limbs have fallen that Simpson refers to in the poem.

The poem taken as a whole opens with a speaker pursuing the "ox" through the personal ruminations of schizophrenia, the ephemeral, and the introspective. For the speaker, there is something in the darkness of the sea at night that rises to the surface but which disappears again before it is seen, and like this something, the speaker at dusk has stood outside and watched life continue in a shadowy way on the inside, feeling always apart. Simpson shows us the apartness, the introspective and the ephemeral aspects of this section with the image of the balloon mentioned earlier. The balloon, which is changing, dying, even as the escaping air forces it around the swimming pool, can never escape its confines, just as in this stage, the speaker cannot escape the boundaries of his own introversion.

In the second section, the speaker looks for meaning in the highly specialized and precise language of science, engineering, or law. He sees these special fields and vocabularies as a separate and equal branch of the path toward knowledge, but in the end, he is forced to conclude that he fears this knowledge. It is too much like the Latin of priests to peasants; it bears no resemblance to reality and, thus, has no meaning.

In the third section, as Simpson writes, "The search for the ox continues." Here, the speaker begins to look beyond and behind him, focusing his attention first on Osaka, then on a friend who now lives in Italy, and, finally, on the ruins and temples of the past. But even in the consideration of antiquity as a source for meaning, the speaker is without success. All he can finally do is conclude that had Hannibal not paused, leading to his defeat, there would still be a certain disorder in the world, suggested by the recurrence of the water image, and a certain vitality of thought.

"As you have wasted your life here in this corner/ you have ruined it all over the world," the quotation from Cavafy, opens the fourth section with a consideration of meaning as found in the sensual, physical, and sexual. The selection of Cavafy as a reference for the poem suggests a tragic sensuality and, conversely, a sensual tragedy about this search for the "ox." The section ends with doors down the street near the harbor opening and closing all night and Eros Peridromos going sleepless until dawn and running around close at hand.

Finally, in the fifth section, the speaker returns to the self, to introspection, to find the "ox." This time, he attempts to do so by following the way of Eastern philosophy which emphasizes meditation and the renouncing of reality and the material. This, too, fails for the speaker, for it only makes him more aware of the world around him and of the information gained from his senses. Now, the speaker says, he seems to understand what "the artist," Cavafy, meant. Every piece of information is clearly seen and understood; every idea begins to assume meaning by the combination of its pieces of information. The speaker now finds his "ox," tames it, and leads it home. Then, the speaker and the "ox" disappear, leaving only the moon and its cool light. In the final analysis, Simpson writes, "There is only earth:/ in winter ladened with snow,/ in summer covered with leaves."

In the winter of man's age, Simpson seems to suggest, there is no information to be used to find meaning, for meaning has disappeared with death, its importance suddenly dissipating. In the summer of man's life, there are so many pieces of information to be put together to form meaning that youth and meaning are covered by information and, thus, lie hidden.

Searching for the Ox is Simpson's search for meaning in poetry and in life. It is a quiet and thoughtful book, full of personal ruminations and memories. It is a book of important questions and conclusions. Louis Simpson is a poet for whom the ordinary becomes the special and for whom the separate becomes the whole. Simpson is a poet of remarkable control, economy, and quiet discovery.

James R. Van Laan

Sources for Further Study

America. CXXXV, October 2, 1976, p. 215.
American Poetry Review. V, July, 1976, p. 42.
Booklist. XXXVI, July, 1976, p. 130.
Library Journal. CI, October 1, 1976, p. 2069.
New York Times Book Review. May 9, 1976, p. 4.

THE SECRET CONVERSATIONS OF HENRY KISSINGER
Step-by-Step Diplomacy in the Middle East

Author: Matti Golan (1938-   )
Translated from the Hebrew by Ruth Geyra Stern and Sol Stern
Publisher: Quadrangle/The New York Times Book Company (New York). 280 pp.
$8.95
Type of work: Current affairs
Time: October 5, 1973 - September 2, 1975
Locale: Washington, New York, Cairo, Damascus, Jerusalem

An exposé of Secretary of State Kissinger's diplomatic maneuvering during and after the Yom Kippur War of 1973

Principal personages:
United States:
  HENRY KISSINGER, Secretary of State
  JOSEPH SISCO, has assistant
  RICHARD M. NIXON, President
  GERALD FORD, President
Israel:
  GOLDA MEIR, Prime Minister
  ITZAK RABIN, Prime Minister
  MOSHE DAYAN, Defense Minister
  YIGAL ALLON, Deputy Prime Minister
  ABBA EBAN, Foreign Minister
  YOSEF TEKOAH, United Nations Ambassador
  SIMCHA DINITZ, Ambassador to the United States
  ABARON YARIV, direct negotiator with Egypt at Kilometer 101
Arab States:
  ANWAR SADAT, Egyptian Prime Minister
  ISMAIL FAHMY, Sadat's special envoy
  ABDEL GHANY EL-GAMASY, direct negotiator with Israel at Kilometer 101
  HAFEZ ASSAD, President of Syria

Highly respected by his fellow journalists in Israel, Matti Golan has written a controversial account of the circumstances surrounding the diplomatic background of the war between the Arabs and Israel in 1973—the conflict that has come to be known as the Yom Kippur War. It began with a surprise attack across the canal by Egyptian forces on October 5, which marked the holiest day in the Jewish calendar (Yom Kippur) and supplied an opportune time to catch the enemy unaware; it was finally resolved on September 2, 1975, when Israel accepted the final terms of an agreement which involved the United States in surveillance of two strategic passes in the Sinai desert. Although ceasefires were achieved between Israel and the Egyptian and Syrian forces within a month of the outbreak of the conflict, a fierce diplomatic struggle between Secretary of State Kissinger and all the parties involved lasted for two years. It is that diplomatic struggle, which in fact began the day the war broke out, which Matti Golan records. What makes his book so controversial is its command of the most minute details of what were supposed to be top-secret meetings and discussions coupled with an unrelenting exposé of Israeli diplomatic blunders and of what Golan himself calls "Kissinger's perfidy." The Israeli censor and government took a dim view of Golan's access to so much privileged information and reluctantly released the book only after a four-month delay.

What will disturb the general reader, and may be one reason why Israel finally felt the book would not be taken too seriously, is the absence of any verifiable sources for most of Golan's revelations. Journalists must protect the identities of their sources, particularly when the issues are as sensitive as they were in this case. But such a policy can detract from the validity of the journalist's findings. Golan's reputation for accuracy and rectitude helped sustain the book in Israel where he was well-known, but the international reader cannot help but lament the lack of hard documentation. When journalism cannot achieve the impact that comes from proof, it is often tempted to settle for the sensation aroused by hearsay. In fairness to Golan, it must be said that his straightforward and even understated presentation of all the "facts" does lend weight to his credibility. Many will be persuaded that he has written a cold and grim book about things as they are.

Could the war have been averted? Golan seems to think that a good chance of stopping it, or at least postponing it, was lost in the fourteen hours preceding the outbreak. Israeli intelligence misinterpreted the true significance of the military buildup on the Egyptian side of the canal, and by the time Prime Minister Golda Meir knew that Egypt was indeed planning to attack, she and her Defense Minister Moshe Dayan had decided that in order to maintain their friendship with the United States, a preemptive strike was out of the question in any case. What they did not know at the time was that even if a preemptive strike had been called for, the Israeli ground and air forces would not have been able to launch such a strike in time. But Golan feels that Israel's failure to explore certain diplomatic initiatives in those fleeting hours was even less excusable than her lack of military preparation. Had Foreign Minister Abba Eban been contacted immediately in New York, where he happened to have been at the time, he would have been able to reach Kissinger, who was also in the city. Kissinger, in turn, could have contacted the Russians and Arabs and transmitted Israel's warning of a preemptive strike. Stripped of the "surprise element," the Egyptian-Syrian attack could very well have dissipated under Russian pressure. Eban, however, knew nothing of the impending attack because Golda Meir had left express instructions that he was to be the "last person to be informed of anything important." Her hostility to Eban caused her to conduct all serious business solely with her protégé, Ambassador Simcha Dinitz. His *charge d'affaires* was in possession of the news, but since he had been instructed by Dinitz that all communications should be "directly with the prime minister's office" it did not even occur to him to contact his true boss, Foreign Minister Eban, the one man who could have moved Kissinger to immediate action.

Once the war began, Israel's desperate need for supplies (there was even a shortage of winter underwear) gave Kissinger the opportunity to change the *status quo* in the Middle East. Whereas he could have been Israel's savior in the hours before the war started, he now became, according to Golan, a force for Israel's containment in the name of what Kissinger felt were ultimately the best interests of the United States. By making Israel wait until the last possible moment for her supplies, he made it possible for the Egyptians to stabilize their presence on the eastern side of the canal. Such a development, felt Kissinger, would not destroy Israel, but it would improve United States relations with the Arabs, thereby offsetting another oil embargo; and it would preserve *détente* with the Soviet Union. To accomplish this end Kissinger stalled Dinitz, whose vulnerable ego he had stroked ever since this junior diplomat had come to Washington, and secretly urged the Russian Ambassador, Dobrynin, to urge his government to exert influence on Egypt and Syria for a ceasefire; just as the United States was holding back supplies from its ally, Israel, the Soviets should hold back supplies from the Arabs. Dobrynin fed Kissinger promises of the Soviet Union's willingness to cooperate, while, in fact, the Russians did everything to encourage the Arabs forward. So, says Golan, just as Kissinger "seduced" Dinitz, Dobrynin "seduced" Kissinger.

By October 10, it was clear to both American and Israeli intelligence that the Soviets were airlifting massive amounts of supplies to Cairo and Damascus. On the same day the Soviet Union put three of its airborne divisions in Eastern Europe on alert. Although Kissinger later maintained that this was the moment that he realized the true course of Russian intentions and decided not to hold back the desperately needed supplies any longer, the record shows that it took Golda Meir's direct appeal to President Nixon on Friday, October 12, to release the sixty-seven transport planes to Israel. Kissinger's problem, insists Golan, was not, as rumor had it, with a Pentagon reluctant to send Israel her supplies, but with Kissinger's own unwillingness to confront the blatant disregard of *détente* by the Russians. The Secretary of State had difficulty in facing the possibility that *détente*—the grand diplomatic scheme of his own making and design, *his* solution to the Cold War—could prove meaningless in an international crisis. The supplies arrived barely in time to avoid a major defeat for Israel, which, as Golan insists, would have resulted in the Soviet Union's becoming "the dominant, permanent influence in the Arab countries." Kissinger was playing it too close for comfort.

Nevertheless, Kissinger's basic purpose in curtailing Israel was realized. She repulsed the enemy with a counterattack (on October 16), during which a small force succeeded in a brilliant and audacious crossing of the canal. By October 22, this spearhead had become an occupying force. In addition, Sadat's entire Third Army was surrounded by Israeli forces in the southern

Sinai. But despite all these accomplishments, Israel had not succeeded in dislodging the Egyptians from their firm foothold on the eastern bank of the Suez Canal. This constituted a mini-victory for Egypt, and Kissinger was determined to exploit it for improving United States-Arab relations.

Before landing in Israel on October 22, a few hours after the United Nations Security Council had adopted an American-Soviet proposal for a ceasefire, Kissinger had stopped in the Soviet Union. It was there that he had gotten the Russians to agree to a ceasefire in place; although, claimed the Secretary of State, they had originally demanded that Israel return to the pre-Six Day War borders of June 4, 1967 before the ceasefire should take effect. But Israeli successes in the field after October 16 obviously dictated a situation which forced the Russians to settle for a ceasefire in place, and when Kissinger arrived in Israel and tried to take credit for this favorable development, Eban reminded him that Israeli soldiering and not his diplomacy had made the Russians bend. Israeli citizens welcomed Kissinger at the airport and cheered him as the representative of the country that had helped save their own. But Golda Meir and her cabinet had other ideas. Why had he not contacted them about his ceasefire agreement with the Russians? If Israel had been properly informed of Kissinger's intentions in Moscow, then she would have sped up her military activities. Only the clever stalling of Yosef Tekoah, Israel's Ambassador to the United Nations, had prevented the ceasefire from taking effect before Israel had consolidated its gains. Why did Kissinger not at least send some warning signals? Because, said the Secretary of State with a perfectly straight face, the Russians engaged in electronic jamming of the communications system in his special plane and in the United States embassy. Prime Minister Meir would not believe this. How could he communicate with his own President so many times? And if he was able to relay a message on the ceasefire agreement to the British, why was it impossible to relay a message to Tel-Aviv? Kissinger, says Golan, "was not willing to go into details."

As Kissinger took up the reins of his famous shuttle-diplomacy after the ceasefire was arranged, Israel insisted on direct negotiations between official representatives of Egypt and Israel. Kissinger did not think Egypt was ready for this, but Sadat consented immediately. Golan feels that Kissinger repeatedly underestimated Israel's bargaining powers. When the question of Israel's control of the relief corridor to the trapped Third Army came up, Kissinger felt that Egypt should control it. "What would they use in further negotiations?" asked the Israelis. When Sadat agreed to Israeli control of the corridor, Israel was strengthened in her conviction that she must avoid making categorical concessions or risk the loss of the bargaining power essential to her survival. Kissinger bullied the Israelis with threats to the effect that the United States would not go to war to deliver the Third Army to Israel; that the Russians would force a corridor if the Israelis did not permit one. Kissinger was repeatedly annoyed with what he felt was Israeli parochialism. Israel did not see the "global picture." Golan counters by noting that Kissinger refused to consider the fact that Israel *did* see the global picture but drew different conclusions for its own policy. Kissinger's insistence on the international context of the Israeli-Arab dispute drove him to urge that Israeli-Egyptian negotiations be moved to Geneva, but Golan is convinced that if Yariv and Gamasy, the direct negotiators at Kilometer 101, had been given the chance, they might well have been able to reach the same agreement on their own that "Kissinger arranged with so much fanfare months later."

If Kissinger was not really needed in the Sinai, he was indispensable in Syria where there was not even the remotest possibility of direct negotiations. But this time the Israelis were prepared. They knew they would be forced to give up the city of El Quneitra, so at first they insisted on only giving up part of it. The ensuing shuttles exhausted Kissinger, and when he finally got his way, the Israelis were satisfied that they had not been forced to give up more. Perhaps the most interesting information Golan imparts about Israel's attitudes toward giving up occupied lands is the part that Moshe Dayan has played. This military man, with his reputation for being a "hawk," was reconciled to giving up El Quneitra from the beginning, just as he, rather surprisingly, is on record for advocating an Israeli withdrawal to the Mitla and Gidi passes in the Sinai. It seems that he would have preferred such a line as more defensible at the end of the Six Day War.

Because Prime Minister Rabin was politically unable to pursue a peace settlement with Jordan, who had remained neutral in the Yom Kippur War, Kissinger pursued further talks with Egypt which eventually resulted in further Israeli withdrawals with almost no diplomatic gains for Israel. Kissinger did commit an American team of observers to the passes in the Sinai which form the present border.

In his closing pages Golan argues that Kissinger's interim agreements do not deal with the real issues separating Israel and the Arabs and therefore do not provide a "new structure for peace." It is an objective but harsh judgment. Peace in the Middle East may never result from any binding resolutions, but rather from an extended period and climate of nonbelligerence. Until that climate is established, even makeshift umbrellas of the sort Kissinger was good at making serve their purpose. But if Golan is telling us the truth about Kissinger's diplomatic methods, many of his admirers will come to understand why Kissinger was, after all, in many significant ways Nixon's man.

Peter A. Brier

Sources for Further Study

America. CXXXIV, May 1, 1976, p. 396.
Book World. April 25, 1976, p. G7.
Guardian Weekly. CXIV, May 9, 1976, p. 18.
Journalism Quarterly. LIII, Autumn, 1976, p. 572.
New York Times Book Review. May 30, 1976, p. 2.
Publisher's Weekly. CIX, February 16, 1976, p. 85.

SELECTED POEMS

Author: Austin Clarke (1896-1974)
Edited and with an Introduction by Thomas Kinsella
Publisher: Wake Forest University Press (Winston-Salem, North Carolina). 207 pp.
  $12.50; paperback $6.95
Type of work: Poetry

  A volume by the Irish poet with notes by the author on his own poems

Austin Clarke is not well-known in America; few Irish poets after William Butler Yeats are. Perhaps Yeats casts too long a shadow in Irish verse, or perhaps the peculiarly local characteristics of much Irish poetry create too much distance between most American readers and the poets. At least in the case of Austin Clarke, this may be a major reason for relative anonymity in this country. Thomas Kinsella observes in his introduction to Clarke's *Selected Poems,* "it is as though Clarke courted obscurity. For a considerable part of his publishing life, it was his custom to issue tiny pamphlet editions of his work from a private press, making no attempt to distribute them beyond a few book shops in Dublin." Definitely Clarke's range of interests is narrow, which implies a sense of limited audience. Consequently, even his best poems are likely to prove unappealing to many readers, who might find the work antique in places. But Clarke's poems vividly present a sense of modern Ireland, with a detailed locality far more realistic on the whole than the romantic image depicted by Yeats. For this reason, if for no other, Clarke deserves greater attention from a wider reading public.

Liam Miller, at the Dolman press in Dublin, has sought to gain that wider audience for Clarke, publishing the poet's work through an extended program. Shortly after Clarke's death in 1974, his *Collected Poems* appeared, a book of close to six-hundred pages, subsequently printed in three paperback volumes. Now, with the *Selected Poems,* a more manageable grouping of the poet's better poems may receive attention, especially from readers interested in the Irish poetic tradition as it emerges after Yeats.

At times one is delighted with this book. When a wealth of details sheathes keen and lucid satire or reveals a ribald narrative, it is with pleasure that readers will follow Clarke's rambling lines of thought. At other times, however, details and ramblings are distractions leading to frustration, a sense that something is missing or, worse, that too much has been included. While this volume is an attempt to present Clarke's work at its best, even the best must be judged as uneven, with flawed poems alongside strong and entertaining poems. When Clarke becomes the satirist, he is penetrating. When he investigates sexuality, his poems are dynamic, full of vigorous humor that transport the reader to mythopoetic realms where humanity is measured by its passionate embrace of carnal love. These are not constant traits in his poetry, however, and his development to poetic power is slow in coming.

Certainly the early Clarke was mired in tradition and the Irish locale. Poems from *Pilgrimage and Other Poems* (1929) have historical and legendary bases. Irish place names are abundant, and references to particular events give the reader cause to refer to notes, both Clarke's and Kinsella's. As with the early Yeats, Clarke shrouds his early poems in romantic mystery and the mist of old Ireland, being driven by indomitable urges to recapture what twentieth century Ireland sees slipping away. Characteristic of these poems is "The Young Woman of Beare" which creates a legendary figure, though Clarke tells us in a note that "the episodes of this allegory are fanciful." She is the wanton temptress, the woman disdained by decent Irish folk:

> I am the dark temptation
> Men know—and shining orders
> Of clergy have condemned me.
> I fear, alone, that lords
> Of diocese are coped
> With gold, their staven hands
> Upraised again to save
> All those I have corrupted:
> I fear, lost and too late
> The prelates of the church.

Strikingly sensual passages evoke the image of a woman envied by others as she enjoys sexual pleasure and reaps monetary reward from the likes of a "big booted captain." She can enjoy "what is allowed in Marriage," but hear the murmurs of men and women as they return from devotions. Ever-present piety remains a dim backdrop that colors her speculation. Clarke's juxtaposition of sexual liberty and righteous behavior is not unique to this poem.

Throughout his early work there is frequent reference to the dominance Catholicism exerts in Ireland; conflict between strict dicta and libertine urges frequently pushes the voices in these poems to rebellion. It is clear that Clarke prefers the chance of possible damnation to celibacy. Furthermore, he recognizes and abhors the pain the church judgmentally inflicts, the anguish in those who violate moral codes but still feel their pressures. Poingnantly, "Her Voice Could Not Be Softer" registers this pain:

> Suddenly in the dark wood
> She turned from my arms and cried
> As if her soul were lost,
> And O too late I knew,
> Although the blame was mine,
> Her voice could not be softer
> When she told it in confession.

Other poems from *Night and Morning* (1938) are particularly heavy with dissatisfaction and wrestling to find freedom. Some satirize the deadening effect of religion as a replacement for life. Some glimpse a release from all this.

Such conflicts hampered Clarke, as did too-close allegiance to historical modes. Dissatisfaction with his work may have caused him to avoid poetry for a time; other concerns also interfered to draw him away. In any case, it was not until 1955 that he published another volume of verse. Significantly, with *Ancient Lights* the religious grappling in the poetry is lessened, indicating that questioning on matters of conscience was resolved to a great extent. A satirical tone with outright antagonism toward Church influence results. "St. Christopher," a poem from *Too Great A Vine* (1957), ends with the penetrating question:

> Fabulist, can an ill state
> Like ours, carry so great
> A Church upon its back?

Clarke's answer, a defiant no, resounds.

But even as conflict is resolved, new problems, evident in poems from *Flight to Africa,* enter the poet's work. Tangled wording, too-frequent rambling to record details, numerous and often obscure allusions to Irish literary and political history—all confront the reader with difficulties, sometimes insurmountable. Often, with new energy, a force not apparent in earlier poems, Clarke experiments with subject matter and technique. At time rhyme is too conscious, but at other times, especially in the shorter poems, rhyme lends joviality to content and creates an air reminiscent of Yeats in the "Crazy Jane" poems. "Our Dumb Friends" presents a hilarious image of canine sex-life, with the hilarity heightened by the use of rhyme. Almost avoiding rhyme, an experiment with technique produces quite a different mood and image in "Japanese Print" where the reader recognizes an intense visual experience; quiet embedded in Oriental aesthetics is created by sparse detail, an effect Clarke rarely attempts. In contrast, poems such as "Son of the Books" are catalogs where rhyme only emphasizes plodding details. In another vein, "Cypress Grove" exhibits Clarke's penchant for description, providing more details than the reader can possibly encompass as he follows the flight of a raven only to find the poet commenting on the loss of an elegant past through ravages of urban development. Rambling as he does, Clarke never fails to provide vivid images, though connections between these images are occasionally difficult to fathom, and rhyme may prove distracting.

Positive applications for Clarke's rambling, rhyming, and meticulous attention to detail are most readily seen in "Mnemosyne Lay in Dust" (1966), a sustained narrative of an amnesiac's sojourn in St. Patrick's Hospital, an institution for the insane. Maurice Devane is the central character to whom the inhabitants and administrators of this lunatic asylum were revealed. Clarke varies structure and tone with delightful results as Maurice observes his fellow inmates at their imbecilic occupations; hints of satire and ribald humor are woven throughout the narrative.

"Mnemosyne Lay in Dust" is Clarke at his best to this point in his career. What precedes the narrative in the *Selected Poems* lacks the sustaining force and usually lacks the ease of movement with which the reader is carried toward Devane's sudden release from St. Patrick's and the loss of memory. In "Mnemosyne Lay in Dust" there is cause for meticulous detail, and rhyme fits easily into the absurd context without the sense of strain evident in earlier poems. What follows "Mnemosyne Lay in Dust" shows a continued sense of ease, though there are occasional signs of earlier troubles reappearing.

The outstanding features of the later poetry are Clarke's ribald treatment of sex as he recasts tales from Greek and Irish mythology, and his clear wish that poetry be entertaining. Satire is still a vital element in some poems, Irish social comment still has its place, and Clarke cannot refrain from rambling, but all these aspects are subsumed by a definite lightheartedness missing from the earlier work. Even where wordplay is a bit strained, as with "In the Rocky Glen," the poem's vivid impact is heightened by such rhymes:

> How could I have guessed
> I would be the guest
> Of the god, that his missile would glow
> Once more in the country of Wicklow
> As I lay in bed,
> Bow-twanged, ready,
> That soon with Molly beside
> Me, ache would be mollified?

Two other explicit sexual poems, "Phallomeda" and "Amor Augustus Domi," show the sharply contrasting methods with which Clarke treats this subject.

But of poems treating sex, "Tiresias" is, without a doubt, Clarke's finest achievement. In the poem, based on a passage from Ovid's *Metamorphoses*, the seer is asked by Jove to:

> speak now and be fearless.
> Did you enjoy in the consummatory moments of lovemaking
> Greater bliss as woman or man?

Tiresias, after prompting, recounts his experiences, his affairs with women and men as man and woman, but the initial question is never answered. What is revealed is the complex bounty of human relationships, the entwining affairs of the heart and history as perceived by Tiresias. Clarke captures the flavors of past and present, exploring the strange mythological event with a modern perspective, giving the old tale new meaning in an emotional and sensual revision of ancient symbols. Vivid images, lucid diction, and occasional satiric turns energize the poem, creating a lasting impression of the seer's humanity.

This devotion to man's humanity is, finally, what makes Clarke's later work succeed. Men seek entertainment, and in the current era sexuality plays an increasingly large role in men's entertainments. Clarke's resolution of early conflict with the Church depended on bursting ingrained, repressive attitudes toward sexuality that he saw limiting him and his society. The result of that bursting is entertainment able to represent sexuality as a natural by-product of humanity, poetry that explores the jovial aspects of life, that presents the creative urge at its purest level but in contexts of ancient origins and modes.

If at times Clarke's modes seem anachronistic to current readers, if at times he seems to be "a garrulous rambling old Irishman," he will certainly, at other times, provide enjoyment in the Swiftian vein where ribald humor and essential detail excite the imaginative fancy. Though the *Selected Poems* will frustrate and disappoint some readers, particularly in its early selections, it will surely provide ample opportunity for readers to laugh at the jest of life once Clarke takes up the representation of that jest as his major concern. To be sure, there are many shadows in this work, places where light is blocked by rough edges protruding in the poetry, but where Clarke successfully follows the beam of laughter, his illuminations will show the bright landscape into which Irish poetic tradition has emerged.

Gary B. Blank

Sources for Further Study

New York Times Book Review. September 19, 1976, p. 6.
Saturday Review. IV, October 2, 1976, p. 36.

SELECTED POEMS

Author: Robert Lowell (1917-   )
Publisher: Farrar, Straus and Giroux (New York). 252 pp. $12.50
Type of work: Poetry

One of America's great poets traces the universal twentieth century movement from youthful religious ecstasy, through dead hopes, to middle-aged resignation

Robert Lowell in *Selected Poems* seems to be telling the classic tale of the lost, twentieth century *persona*. The sequence and pattern of the poems trace the movement from youthful religious preoccupations and rejection of familial ties, through deciphering of the past, fresh insights on childhood, love affairs, renewal of family ties, and, finally, resignation. Lowell is most convincing when he stays close to home. Home in his affluent world of upper-crust New England may be a summer cottage in Maine or the citified Boston of rigid tradition and regular cocktail hours. What the poet seems to lack is raw feeling, immersed as he is in the rarefied regions of highboys, family heirlooms, and proper reserve. He is busily trying to find it, to release a passionate temperament which contrasts with the New England setting. Such tasteful propriety may have led the poet to the obsession with God which is particularly evident in the early poems, but which resurfaces regularly throughout his life.

In 1940 Lowell converted to Roman Catholicism from his Protestant heritage. The mystical, inflamed language of the poems in *Lord Weary's Castle* or *The Mills of the Kavanaughs* contrasts sharply with the country-club atmosphere in *Life Studies*. In "Colloquy in Black Rock" the speaker agonizes, writhes under his religious obsession. His "skipping heart" is covered with "dust," perhaps the dust of the past, the oppressive weight of generations. He speaks of the martyre, Stephen, "broken down to blood," envisions Christ on the "black water." His heart, which beats "faster, faster" is reacting with passion, evoking the tone and ecstasy of Hopkins' poetry. The speaker seems to envy, even crave, such martyrdom. In "Mr. Edwards and the Spider" the poet asks, "What are we in the hands of the great God?" Other poems in *Lord Weary's Castle* show the same religious fire, as do various poems in *The Mills of the Kavanaughs*. Such poems examine the evils of the city as in "Where the Rainbow Ends," or present a curious jumbling of Christianity, paganism, and the burden of the past which weighs heavily both on New England and on the poet himself, as in "Falling Asleep over the Aeneid." The poet is torn between these influences and shows the schism by writing of an old man who has missed the morning services in the Concord church and dreams instead of Dido, "the ghost of Pallas," and the "elephants of Carthage." The density of images and seeming contortions of syntax reveal the depth of the poet's agony and the extent of religious comfort he desires. The early poems of Lowell seem, at the moment that their *persona* struggles to break through to God, to retreat into rigid form and an entanglement of words, as in "Mother Marie Therese":

                                                        . . . Christ enticed
          Her heart that fluttered, while she whipped her hounds
          Into the quicksands of her manor grounds,
          A lordly child, her habit fleur-de-lys'd—
          There she dismounted, sick; with little heed,
          Surrendered. Like Proserpina, who fell
          Six months a year from earth to flower in hell. . . .

Other sections of the book are successful for the degree to which Lowell deals with things he knows. The highly personal character of such poems and the shift in emphasis from religious preoccupations are refreshing. In *Life Studies,* he abandons the strained rhymes and rhythms to say what he means about his past and the awesome responsibility of being a Massachusetts Lowell and a Winslow. In later collections, among them *Nineteen Thirties, Mexico, For Lizzie and Harriet,* and *The Dolphin,* he returns to a set pattern of sporadic rhyming and sonnet-like verses to supply the telling detail, the revealing quote, the mannerisms, gestures, ways of his childhood, and adult milieu. In "My Last Afternoon with Uncle Devereux Winslow," perhaps the best poem in the entire collection, he captures the essence of the family hearth in a new and sprightly free verse pattern. Immediacy, whimsy, wit, melancholy are all here; scenes are sketched in quickly, easily:

          Up in the air
          by the lakeview window in the billiards-room,
          lurid in the doldrums of the sunset hour,
          my Great Aunt Sarah
          was learning *Samson and Delilah.*
          She thundered on the keyboard of her dummy piano,
          with gauze curtains like a boudoir table,
          accordianlike yet soundless.

Aunt Sarah has "risen like the phoenix / from her bed of troublesome snacks and Tauchnitz classics." What makes such poems succeed is the realization that this is his Aunt Sarah and, simultaneously, *everybody's* Aunt Sarah. The time, the place, the occupation retrieve a moment which nudges the memory of the reader like the melody of an old song.

Other poems, such as "Dunbarton," "Grandparents," and "Commander Lowell," similarly catch the complexity of feeling for members of Lowell's family whom he tried to understand and somehow to define. His father, a caricature of the conventional Naval commander, not at all "serious," showing up on the golf course "wearing a blue serge and numbly cut white ducks . . . ," is a buffoon, a charming phony pretending to be authentic. His life is a relentless decline marked by his being reduced to humming "Anchors Aweigh" in the bathtub. The memory of the poet's grandfather in "Grandparents" is one of tenderness and affection:

Never again
to walk there, chalk our cues,
insist on shooting for us both.
Grandpa! Have me, hold me, cherish me!
Tears smut my fingers. There
half my life-lease later,
I hold an *Illustrated London News*—;
disloyal still,
I doodle handlebar
mustaches on the last Russian Czar.

A little poem, "For Sale," is deceptively rewarding, capturing in its brevity
the lonely feeling death gives to his mother and the sensation she experiences
of being mildly surprised to still be here, trapped on this earth.

Empty, open, intimate,
its town-house furniture
had an on tiptoe air
of waiting for the mover
on the heels of the undertaker.
Ready, afraid
of living alone till eighty,
Mother mooned in a window,
as if she had stayed on a train
one stop past her destination.

In *For Lizzie and Harriet,* middle-aged hopelessness sets in; as the speaker
says in "Dear Sorrow," "It's our nerve and ideologies die first." *For the Union
Dead* likewise treats death and love's loss. Aching, the speaker addresses his
wife in "The Old Flame":

Poor ghost, old love, speak
with your old voice
of flaming insight
that kept us awake all night.

He has learned that "a father's no shield / for his child." "The Public Garden"
is "dying" where "all's alive." In "Myopia: a Night" the poet regrets, "At fifty
we're so fragile, / a feather. . . ." "Night Sweat" probably best conveys the
angst of the slipping, sliding journey into dead hopes and old age. Here, Lowell writes powerfully of his child and his wife, whose "lightness alters everything":

But the downward glide
and bias of existing wrings us dry—
always inside me is the child who died,
always inside me is his will to die—
one universe, one body . . . in this urn
the animal night sweats of the spirit burn.

He concludes on a prayerful note.

> . . . if I cannot clear
> the surface of these troubled waters here,
> absolve me, help me, Dear Heart, as you bear
> this world's dead weight and cycle on your back.

In *Mexico,* we find the poet in another of those stages through which men must go when death first assumes real, menacing contours. He is "fifty, humbled with the years' gold garbage . . ." and she is "some sweet, uncertain age, say twenty-seven." Having decided that history is "what you cannot touch," he goes "South of Boston" to "Midwinter in Cuernavaca" to experience raw emotion and passion. Mexico, far from Boston's oppressive tradition, conjures up images of life, vigor, heat, and sensuality, and supplies carefree anonymity. With masterful selection of detail, Lowell in "Mexico" evokes a season of sensuality in a series of rich sensual images. The mood of pleasure and abandon are here:

> I've waited, I think, a lifetime for this walk.
> The white powder slides out beneath our feet,
> the sterile white salt of purity; even
> your puffed lace blouse is salt. The red brick glides;
> bread baked for dinner never to be served. . . .
> When you left, I thought of you each hour of the day,
> each minute of the hour, each second of the minute.

In the poet's search for meaning, the answers which he earlier sought from God comes finally from himself in *The Dolphin.* The occasional petulance with the way the world and he are going evolves into a more sensitive, more inward-turning acceptance of what things have to be. Lizzie, the wife, suggests playfully, "Why don't you lose yourself and write a play about the fall of Japan?" They have come through, though not necessarily together, and are "humanly low." The mermaid, who represents the "insatiable fiction of desire," is put at last in her place, which is to say, in careful perspective. In "Mermaid," a note of common sense (or is it hopelessness?) signals a new maturity and perhaps a fuller, sturdier facing of life.

> I've searched the rough black ocean for you,
> and saw the turbulence drop dead for you,
> always lovely, even for those who had you,
> Rough Slitherer in your grotto of haphazard.
> I lack manhood to finish the fishing trip.
> Glad to escape beguilement and the storm,
> I thank the ocean that hides the fearful mermaid—
> like God, I almost doubt if you exist.

On his "irregular and uncertain flight to art," Lowell is perhaps weakest in the poems from *History.* This group of poems about various literary and historical figures are less successful because Lowell has ranged too far afield from his home bases. By trying to do so much, they do little, coming across as sketchily executed treatises rather than poems. He does not make us care for these figures. The subject, not the poem, becomes the thing. Technically, he is forced to rely heavily on ellipses to accommodate short phrases which will sum up necessary facts and characteristics. The too-frequent tendency to point a moral may well seem to many readers to deny the first function of poetry, which is, traditionally, to delight. Dialogue seems essential to insure understanding of the poems, but this too detracts rather than enhances. "Marcus Cato 95-42 B.C." demonstrates the poet's dilemma in trying to handle such material.

> As a boy he was brought to Sulla's villa, The Tombs,
> saw people come in as men, and leave as heads.
> "Why hasn't someone killed him?" he asked. They answered,
> "Men fear Sulla even more than they hate him."
> He asked for a sword, and wasn't invited back . . .
> He drowned Plato in wine all night with his friends,
> gambled his life in the forum, was stoned like Paul,
> and went on talking till soldiers saved the State. . . .

At the conclusion of the poem, we get a moral to complete the history lesson. Neither prose nor poetry, these pieces leave us uncomfortable and unsure of what our reactions to them should be.

The vitality, insight, and wit of Lowell's autobiographical and confessional poems leave no doubt of his prowess as one of America's finest poets. The technical intricacy of form is both an asset and deterrent, to the extent that the form controls and simultaneously prevents the reader from entering as fully as he might into the emotional level of the poetry. But if one is willing to spend time with Lowell, one will be rewarded with many poems which appeal to universal human senses and sensibilities, especially those which emanate from the heart. To Lowell's credit, he knows wherein he fails. In "Reading Myself" he sums up:

> Like thousands, I took just pride and more than just,
> struck matches that brought my blood to a boil;
> I memorized the tricks to set the river on fire—
> somehow never wrote something to go back to.

Suzanne Britt Jordan

Sources for Further Study

Book World. July 4, 1976, p. H7.

Commonweal. CIII, December 3, 1976, p. 792.

New Leader. LIX, October 25, 1976, p. 15.

New York Review of Books. XXIII, October 28, 1976, p. 3.

Newsweek. LXXXVIII, September 6, 1976, p. 63.

Saturday Review. III, June 12, 1976, p. 39.

SELECTED STORIES

Author: Nadine Gordimer (1923-   )
Publisher: The Viking Press (New York). 381 pp. $10.00
Type of work: Short stories
Time: The twentieth century
Locale: South Africa, Tanganyika, Zambia

A selection of stories from five volumes, published between 1952 and 1971, by one of South Africa's leading writers of fiction

For more than thirty years Nadine Gordimer has been writing and publishing short stories (many of them appearing first in English or American magazines and later in book form), and they have been greeted with increasing acclaim as representing some of the finest work being done in the genre of the modern short story. *Selected Stories* contains thirty-one stories which Gordimer has chosen from five earlier volumes: *The Soft Voice of the Serpent* (1952), *Six Feet of the Country* (1956), *Friday's Footprint* (1960), *Not for Publication* (1965), and *Livingston's Companions* (1971). In a brief introduction, Gordimer comments on the writer's need for solitude combined with a simultaneous empathy with other people and a detachment from them. "The tension between standing apart and being involved," she says, "that is what makes a writer." In this selection of her stories, with their varying points of view and with shifts from author-as-narrator in most of the stories to first-person narration in several, one is struck by Gordimer's closeness of observation, her wit and brilliance of style, her skill in presenting many characters of several ethnic backgrounds, and her usually firm control over her fictional materials.

Since Miss Gordimer (in private life Mrs. Reinhold Cassirer) is a native of South Africa and has lived there for more than fifty years, it is not surprising that most of her stories concern race relations in one way or another. Yet she does not confine herself to racial themes, though they are present in many stories. Even when her stories contain characters of more than one race, as most of them do, she is usually more concerned with human sympathy and love (or the lack of it) than with skin color or social status. The earlier stories were written before the movement for independence of the native or black majority and other nonwhite groups in South Africa's multiracial population. Several of the later stories, written after the mid 1950's, give glimpses of the efforts made by the "coloreds" of various skin hues and ethnic heritage and by white liberals and sympathizers in the South African struggle against the political system of apartheid. Under this system nonwhites are segregated in varying ways and degrees from whites so that the politics and the social structure of the country may continue to be controlled by a white minority government. American readers of Gordimer's stories need some knowledge of how apartheid operates, especially in regard to the segregating of blacks in slumlike "locations" on the outer edges of cities like Johannesburg, South Africa's largest city. The blacks (also called natives or Africans in many of the stories) work for and among whites in the daytime but are expected to return to their locations at night unless they have special passes which they must be ready to show to authorities upon request. The government strongly disapproves of social mixing of whites and nonwhites, and unauthorized whites found in black locations are subject to arrest. Older American readers of Gordimer's stories, particularly those who live or have lived in the South, will often be reminded of the many restrictions, sometimes state-legalized but more frequently enforced by local custom, which were placed upon American blacks until recent years. A major difference is that American blacks were, and in most cities and other political entities still are, a minority, whereas the South African blacks are a large majority of the total population. The continuance of apartheid in South Africa is complicated by the presence of a large number of Indians (a group originally brought in as a source of cheap labor) and by many other nonwhites who for convenience are all termed "colored" because of their mixed ethnic heritage, some of them being light-skinned enough to pass for white, as they do upon occasion.

As Robert F. Haugh has pointed out in his perceptive study of Nadine Gordimer's stories and novels, her short fiction derives in content, form, and technique (while still retaining its own originality) from such earlier authors as Anton Chekhov, Katherine Mansfield, James Joyce, Guy de Maupassant, Joseph Conrad, and Stephen Crane, and from her American contemporary J. D. Salinger, whom she greatly admires. Gordimer usually develops her stories to suggest or emphasize mood, theme, character, or tone rather than dramatic action or plot. The stories and sometimes the titles hint at meanings and leave unanswered questions. In "Is There Nowhere Else Where We Can Meet?" a young white woman meets a ragged black on a woods path, struggles to keep him from stealing her handbag and parcel, then runs away, and at last asks herself, "What did I fight for? Why didn't I give him the money and let him go?" In "The Catch" a young white couple on a seaside vacation see, admire, and later become friendly with an Indian fisherman ("They almost forgot he *was* an Indian") whose prize salmon the husband photographs first with his prettily smiling wife and then with the proud fisherman. Later, driving with three white urban friends of their own class, they offer a ride to the fisherman who, having vainly tried to sell his salmon, is now walking home with his heavy burden. He stows it in the car trunk and takes an offered seat next to the wife, who becomes inwardly resentful because the others silently leave her to talk with the Indian. After he has been let out at a turn in the road, the girl asks, "What on earth can he do with the great smelly fish now?" All five then break into hysterical laughter and the girl asks a final question, "What have I said?" In both stories the reader is left to draw a meaning from the questions as well as from all that has preceded them.

One of the best of the early stories is "The Train from Rhodesia." The train stops at a small station, and native artists show for sale to the passengers many carved wooden animals. A young white woman becomes interested in a beautifully carved lion offered by an old man but thinks it too expensive. When her husband offers three shillings and sixpence she says, "No, leave it." As the train is starting, the old man calls "One-and-six," the husband tosses the coins, gets the flung lion in return, and then cannot understand his wife's anger at him. She sits silent:

> One-and-six for the wood and the carving and the sinews of the legs and the switch of the tail. The mouth open like that and the teeth. The black tongue rolling like a wave. The mane round the neck. To give one-and-six for that. The heat of shame mounted through her legs and body. . . .

In her silent brooding she not only feels shame for the injustice to the black artist but also a sense of alienation from her young husband who has laughed and rejoiced at his clever bargaining.

Gordimer's sympathies lie more with the nonwhites than with those of her own race in her stories. The white housewife who narrates "Ah, Woe Is Me" is enough interested in the welfare of her former black servant Sarah (whose "Ah, woe is me" is a remembered refrain) to ask Sarah's daughter Janet about her mother. But when she learns that Janet has had to leave school in order to care for her ailing, overweight mother who can no longer walk, the white woman's compassion goes no farther than giving Janet an old dress and skirt, five shillings for her mother, and, finally, her handkerchief for the weeping girl to blow her nose into. Jennifer Tetzel is a young white woman in "Which New Era Would That Be?" who prides herself on her progressivism in associating with nonwhites like the mulatto Jake Alexander and his variously colored friends. Gordimer apparently has as low an opinion of Jennifer as does Jake, who, after Jennifer's departure from his New Era print shop, kicks aside the chair she has sat in. Ella Plaistow, in the ironically titled "Happy Event," is a witness when her native servant Lena is tried for having wrapped her newborn baby in one of Ella's nightgowns and then disposed of it in a discarded paraffin tin. Ella is more disturbed by the memory of the way the magistrate embarrassed her with his questions ("He made such a *fool* of me. . . .") than she is concerned about the plight of Lena.

The contrast of the whites and the nonwhites may seen a little too pat in some of the stories where the author's intent is to satirize the whites' self-centeredness or callousness while implying the nonwhites' need for sympathy, love, and understanding. The colored men and women are not sentimentalized and made heroic, though, or treated as mere pathetic victims. They are believable whether they appear as major or minor characters.

The prevailing tone in *Selected Stories* is serious, but occasionally there is a bit of comedy, as in "Abroad" when Manie Swemmer, a South African white, visits his son in Lusaka, the capital of Zambia (formerly Northern Rhodesia), thirty years after Manie helped construct some buildings there. Because of an independence anniversary celebration, the city is crowded and the only hotel room he can get is one which he must share with an Indian. Returning from a jolly bar party, Manie finds that his haughty Indian roommate has locked him out. Assigned to another room, one with four beds (". . . don't put me in with an African, now, man!"), Manie selects the cleanest-looking bed in the empty room and, almost giggling, drives "the rusty bolt home across the door."

Two of Gordimer's later stories, "Livingstone's Companions" and "Africa Emergent," offer a notable contrast in treatment. In the first, a cynical English journalist, ironically named Church, grumpily sets out on an assignment for his London editor to write a story to be used in connection with the centenary of the famous search for the supposedly lost Dr. David Livingstone. Church takes along a copy of Livingstone's last *Journals* to read for background information for his article. An hour-and-a-half plane ride covers territory that Livingstone needed ten months to traverse. Church continues by car to a resort hotel by a great lake. He wishes to see the graves of Livingstone's five companions who were buried near the hotel. Failing at first to find the graves, he observes and briefly becomes a part of the hotel life, a mixture of sport, drink, and sex. Before leaving he finally discovers the graves on a little hill and near them the grave of the hotel manager's first husband, a suicide. The story closes with a sentence that seems almost an echo from Conrad's *Heart of Darkness:*

> They all looked back, these dead companions, to the lake that Carl Church . . . had had silent behind him all the way up; the lake that, from here, was seen to stretch much farther than one could tell, down there on the shore or at the hotel: stretching still—even from up here—as far as one could see, flat and shining, a long way up Africa.

The lake is used as a symbol of Africa eternal, and Gordimer includes in the first half of the story several excerpts from Livingstone's *Journals* to contrast the devout and compassionate Livingstone, grieving for his dead companions but believing in their future resurrection, with the trivial and ephemeral life at the hotel and the attempts of its occupants to escape boredom.

A very different, and distinctly inferior, story is "Africa Emergent," narrated by a white South African who was formerly a student activist helping the country's blacks and their colored friends emerge from their deprived condition. Explaining as if to critics of apartheid who live in faraway lands such as England or America, he reveals himself now as one who has learned by experience that it is much safer to let the blacks do their own emerging. Some of them may be police spies ready to report illegal white actions. "There's only one way for a [black] man," he says, "to prove himself as far as we're concerned: he must be in prison." And that's where an acquaintance of his is now. "He's proved himself, hasn't he?" The satire is slathered on with a heavy brush and the narrator seems a cartoon character meant to be despised by the reader.

Gordimer has such lapses of creation in her weaker stories. The best of her stories, however, and there are many excellent ones in *Selected Stories,* deserve a permanent place in modern short fiction from the second half of our century.

Henderson Kincheloe

Sources for Further Study

Harper's Magazine. CCLII, April, 1976, p. 101.
Los Angeles Times. May 2, 1976, *Books,* p. 11.
Nation. CCXXIII, August 28, 1976, p. 149.
New York Review of Books. XXIII, July 15, 1976, p. 43.
New York Times Book Review. April 18, 1976, p. 7.
Newsweek. LXXXVII, April 19, 1976, p. 90E.

THE SHADOW OF THE WINTER PALACE
Russia's Drift to Revolution, 1825-1917

Author: Edward Crankshaw (1909-   )
Publisher: The Viking Press (New York). Illustrated. 429 pp. $12.95
Type of work: History
Time: 1825-1917
Locale: Russia

A history of Russia's tsars for almost a century preceding the revolution of 1917, and an examination of how each of their reigns helped prepare the way for the eventual Bolshevik takeover of power

Principal personages:
NICHOLAS I OF ROMANOV, Tsar of Russia, 1825-1855
ALEXANDER II OF ROMANOV, Tsar of Russia, 1855-1881
ALEXANDER III OF ROMANOV, Tsar of Russia, 1881-1894
NICHOLAS II OF ROMANOV, Tsar of Russia, 1894-1917
COUNT SERGEI YULEVICH WITTE, architect of Russia's industrial revolution and Prime Minister of Russia, 1905-1906
VLADIMIR ILYICH LENIN, major Marxist revolutionary and leader of the Bolshevik revolution

The Shadow of the Winter Palace is a lucid account of the decline and fall of the Romanov dynasty. Edward Crankshaw, whose personal experience with Russia goes back to his service on the British Military Mission in Russia during World War II and who has written extensively about Soviet Russia, addresses himself to nearly a century of eventful Russian history that culminated in the cataclysmic Bolshevik revolution. It is a fascinating and highly dramatic story, which opens with the abortive "Decembrist" revolt staged by officers of the Imperial Army and some liberal civilians who conspired to overthrow the autocracy on December 14, 1825, the first day of the reign of Tsar Nicholas I.

Although it failed miserably, the insurrection was a momentous event in Russian history. For the first time a genuine political movement sought to abolish the autocracy itself and establish a republican system. The beginning of the Decembrist movement reached back to the immediate post-Napoleonic period. A number of highly placed officers, the scions of prominent aristocratic families, formed the Union of Salvation in St. Petersburg. Its objectives were the abolition of serfdom and the establishment of a constitutional government. Palace *coups* and uprisings had occurred before, but they were never directed against the institution of the autocracy. The prevailing Russian view through the centuries was that only the autocratic power of the Tsar made possible the creation, continuation, and growth of empire. Any concession to constitutionalism or particular rights was considered a threat to Russian greatness. The requirements of empire not merely excused, they sanctified autocracy. The autocracy became a fundamental principle of national life and the moral order of society. Of course, royal absolutism and rule by divine right were not restricted to Russia. However, the overwhelming dominance of the Russian autocrat was not matched by European monarchs; if some of them had come close in the past, they certainly did not in the nineteenth century. The fatal consequence was, ultimately, that nobody was truly responsible in the whole of the vast empire. Everything was up to the will of the Tsar, but because the Tsar was everything, he was nothing. The doomed challenge of the Decembrists marked the beginning of a tremendous process, ending in the convulsions touched off by the Communists.

Nicholas I was determined to preserve the *status quo*. He wanted order and symmetry. The military with its rigid chain of command and perfect obedience was the visible expression of this harmony, under which everyone knew his place. It was to be the model to which civilian society must aspire. Crankshaw provides an interesting character study of this monarch, who ruled over a land of slaves. A man nearly devoured by self-pity, with a streak of sadism and more than a touch of paranoia, inhabited the vast Winter Palace. A characteristic institution was the Tsar's Personal Chancellery. It consisted of various sections, of which the Third was the most important. The Third Section was concerned with internal security; it kept track of any subversive ideas and institutions. The secret police became a powerful instrument of the ruler, eventually to be used far more effectively by the leaders of Soviet Russia. As Crankshaw's work reveals, it is one example of some of the fundamental features of modern Russia carried over from the past.

Despite the activities of the Third Section—the acute censorship, the close supervision of the schools and universities, the prohibition of foreign travel, and the official propaganda under the slogan, "orthodoxy, autocracy, nationality"—there were formidable disruptive forces at work against which the government was all but helpless. These were the problems emanating from the institution of serfdom, industrialization, and the growth of the intelligentsia. The preservation of the *status quo* became a fixed idea for Nicholas. He envisioned himself as the champion of the old order for all of Europe. In the end it was his foreign policy, not the internal social tensions and the activities of numerous members of the intelligentsia, that made reform inescapable. Nicholas had moved against Persia and Turkey with relative immunity, he waged successful campaigns in the Caucasus, he totally subjugated rebellious Poland, he even was able to play his self-appointed role as "gendarme of Europe" by helping Austria subdue rebellious Hungary. However, when in 1853 he again wanted to bring the Turkish Sultan to heel, he precipitated the catastrophic Crimean War. Nicholas saw himself as a crusader for Christianity, while Britain and France were guilty of the infamy of fighting for the Crescent. Crankshaw vividly describes the fiasco. The ineptitudes on both sides were horrendous. In the end, the Allies achieved what they set out to do; the Russians failed absolutely. After the fall of the Crimean fortress Sevastopol in 1855, the Russians had no choice but to surrender.

Meanwhile, Nicholas had died and Alexander II had become Tsar. It was this humiliating defeat in the Crimea which opened the way to impressive political and economic changes. For this was more than a military defeat—a whole social system had come to grief. Alexander II prepared a break with the past. Soon after the Treaty of Paris in 1856, he indicated his intention to free the serfs. A long and bitter struggle ensued between the abolitionists and their opponents. There were more than forty-eight million serfs on the eve of emancipation in 1861, half private and half state peasants. Together with their families they amounted to about four-fifths of the total population. As Crankshaw notes, it is hard to imagine the scale of the undertaking, the liberation of a nation of slaves. Seen in general perspective, the accompanying violence could perhaps even be considered moderate, yet it led to a new generation of revolutionary martyrs to languish in prison or Siberian exile. On the whole, the peasants' lot did not improve materially; they actually received less land than they had utilized in pre-emancipation times.

The reforms of the early years of the reign of Alexander II were the high water mark of the Russian autocracy as a creative force. Alexander opposed vehemently the idea of a national assembly; he alone was to be the source of all reforms. The remaining fifty years were essentially a holding action, while all sorts of forces were alive and gaining strength. The intellectual ferment erupted into and in turn was fed by novels. Particularly in the works of the greatest writers of the period—Ivan Turgenev, Fyodor Dostoevski, and Leo Tolstoy—the full force of the Populist themes was dominant. The radical and revolutionary aspirations found expression in such movements as "People's Freedom," endorsing a deliberate policy of assassination. A wave of terrorism was unleashed, culminating in the assassination of Alexander II in March, 1881. Although small in number, the terrorists had a tremendous impact. Crankshaw suggests, a bit speculatively, that the rebels enjoyed considerable sympathy among the populace. Still, the *coup* did not generate an upheaval. The terrorists' appeal to Alexander III to create a national assembly, in return for which terrorism would be suspended, was ignored. The response of the new Tsar was severely reactionary and repressive. His succession denoted a new phase for Imperial Russia. In Crankshaw's words, it constituted the peace of the graveyard and the end of all serious reforms from above.

However, industrialization reached the take-off stage under Alexander III and flourished, although to a considerable extent at the expense of agriculture. Under the energetic leadership of Sergei Witte, an outstanding organizer and negotiator, all branches of Russian industry and production showed a remarkable upsurge in the 1890's. Witte became the Tsar's most powerful minister and made the industrial development of Russia his foremost aim; among his achievements was the construction of the Trans-Siberian Railroad. During this period Russia's rate of growth far outstripped that of every other country. Of course, an important accompaniment of this development was the sudden and gigantic growth of the urban working class. The introduction of Marxism into Russia thus became a significant element, for which George Plekhanov, more than anyone else, was responsible. Plekhanov condemned as pointless the policy of individual assassination. Through his influence, small Marxist groups of workers and intellectuals came into being; one of these was joined by Vladimir Ilyich Ulyanov, later known as Lenin.

When Alexander III died in 1894, Nicholas II became the next and last Tsar. The picture of Nicholas presented by Crankshaw is one of a man who lacked all sense of purpose, whose impact was almost wholly negative. He was a weak, shy, and inept person, totally unable to cope with the developing circumstances. The modest expectations of popular participation in the affairs of internal government were turned away by him as "senseless dreams." In foreign affairs, tensions with Japan were intensifying, as the Trans-Siberian Railroad had pulled Russia into the competitive imperialism of the Far East. In February, 1904, the Japanese mounted a surprise attack on Port Arthur. Nicholas II, terribly prejudiced against the Japanese and woefully underestimating their ability, expected it to be a short and victorious war, which might even serve the useful purpose of stemming the rising tide of revolution. He had reason to be alarmed by the radicalization of all sections of Russian society that had taken on more and more extreme forms. Strikes and violent expressions of peasant discontent gave birth to a more radical version of the Populist groups, the Social-Revolutionary Party. However, the war with Japan was a disaster; Russia suffered a series of crushing defeats. First the Pacific fleet and then the Atlantic fleet, sent to the Far East for relief, were totally destroyed or captured. To compound the blow to the autocracy, the pride of the remaining Black Sea fleet, the *Potemkin*, became the cockpit of a mutiny and—later—the very symbol of revolution.

The revolutionary turbulence came to a pitch as a result of the tragic "Bloody Sunday" of January, 1905, when masses of unarmed, hymn-singing petitioners were shot down as they approached the Winter Palace. This outrage was the spark that set alight the flame of revolution. By the end of that month nearly half a million workers were on strike. Professional groups joined in and terrorism flared up again; events came about so swiftly and spontaneously that even the professional revolutionaries were taken by surprise. These developments resulted in two important events in October, 1905. The Tsar, recognizing the need for a strong and able man, appointed Witte prime minister. Witte saw the predicament of the autocracy and extracted from Nicholas II the famous October Manifesto, effecting a limited constitutional monarchy.

The second important event was the creation of the St. Petersburg Soviet, the progenitor of all soviets and the headquarters of revolution. Alas, the first of these events came too late, the second too soon. By 1906 the revolutionary elite were either in prison, in Siberia, or in European exile. The year had shown the astonishing resilience of the regime. The first Duma convened. The State Council, the upper chamber, consisted half of Crown nominees and half of elected members, representing the wealthier and professional classes. The State Duma was a purely elected lower chamber; it was a rigged assembly with little genuine competence. The Tsar's ministers had virtually no responsibility to it. Still, the creation of the Duma had generated a party system, and high hopes for a change for the better were held. The speakers burst forth with flaming demands, but the autocracy, having survived and sufficiently recovered, refused all cooperation with the Duma. Revolutionary activity subsided temporarily, gradually gaining momentum again after 1912. When World War I broke out, the dynasty had lost too much of its prestige to act as a rallying-point. The devastating military disasters inflicted by the German forces with casualties reaching unprecedented totals, the corruption and incompetence of the military leadership, and the unimaginable human suffering, at last spelled the end of Imperial Russia.

Edward Crankshaw's narrative is an elegantly written mixture of dynastic, military, diplomatic, economic, and social history. It is somewhat lacking in analytical astuteness, pardonable for a work intended to be a popular history. In developing his theme of Russia's drift to revolution, Crankshaw makes many insightful and poignant observations. He succeeds in bringing to light and life a period of Russia full of astounding and tragic paradoxes.

Manfred Grote

Sources for Further Study

Atlantic. CCXXXVIII, September, 1976, p. 99.

Economist. CCLX, September 11, 1976, p. 108.

History Today. XXVI, September, 1976, p. 617.

National Observer. XV, October 2, 1976, p. 21.

New Yorker. LII, October 4, 1976, p. 156.

Newsweek. LXXXV, August 16, 1976, p. 81.

Saturday Review. III, September 4, 1976, p. 42.

SIMPLE JUSTICE

The History of *Brown v. Board of Education* and Black America's Struggle for Equality

Author: Richard Kluger (1934-   )
Publisher: Alfred A. Knopf (New York). 823 pp. $15.95
Type of work: History

A study of the events, personalities, and human drama surrounding the 1954 Supreme Court decision Brown v. Board of Education *that desegregated schools and altered the history of the United States*

This book is more than a history of *Brown v. Board of Education* of Topeka. More importantly, it is a history of black America's century-long struggle for equality under law. It is a story of human drama, of social forces of the past colliding with those of the present, of determined people who in the face of intimidation, threats, and fear, refused to accept defeat along the legal path to the Supreme Court and final showdown.

Richard Kluger is not a formally trained historian; he began this seven-year study as a novelist and editor. Yet his work reveals the scholarship, detailed research, thoroughness, and accuracy of the professional historian. His ability to blend history, law, sociology, and humanity in his book is superb.

Kluger divides his work into three parts. Part One offers a wide-ranging historical background describing how American blacks reached their position in a segregated society. Several hundred pages are spent chronologizing events from the Declaration of Independence, through Reconstruction, to *Plessy v. Ferguson.* Kluger has the courage to be obvious. From the beginning he argues that the Declaration of Independence was marred by hypocrisy—all men were not equal if black.

Kluger conducts an all-inclusive analysis of the events, strategy, and personnel involved in the five landmark cases collectively known as *Brown v. Board of Education.* Beginning with the Reverend Joseph Albert DeLaine, Kluger tells the story of unheralded heroes. DeLaine led the first crucial fight for educational equality in Clarendon County, South Carolina. He was subsequently fired from his position as a school teacher, threatened with bodily harm, sued, convicted, and driven out of the state, all because he sought equal protection of the law for his three children. It is in telling the story of the struggle for human dignity that Kluger is at his compassionate best.

From Clarendon County the author moves to Prince Edward County, Virginia; Topeka, Kansas; Wilmington, Delaware; and Washington, D.C., where he records the events and presents the plaintiffs who braved violence and reprisals to be heard in court. Kluger refuses to allow reader complacency; he makes the reader a participant. The collective biases, the unsavory attitudes of Americans are a major theme in this work.

Kluger is not satisfied with tracing the historical background to the Brown case; he feels that the court decision cannot be understood unless a reader is familiar with previous litigation. More than one hundred cases are presented in a progression of severely crucial desegregation lawsuits, among them the Brown case. In the process the reader is given a short course in Constitutional law with copious quotes from civil rights cases.

Here too is a glimpse of the early rise of a black middle class centered in a black legal establishment. Sprung from Howard University Law School were a group of black intellectuals who led, relentlessly, the cumulative advance of the law to the Supreme Court and the Brown decision. Commanded by Thurgood Marshall, the group included such excellent lawyers as William Hastie, Robert Carter, and James Nabrit. Kluger has detailed character sketches of these men and others, lawyers, judges, and plaintiffs, who played a part in defining the rights of blacks in the years preceding 1954.

Finally, Kluger documents Supreme Court hearings on the five cases of *Brown v. Board of Education.* He reexamines and re-creates the months of research and interpretation by both sides, the arguments before the Court, the series of meetings and legal negotiations culminating in the unanimous decision that "separate educational facilities are inherently unequal."

Kluger's delineation of Chief Justice Warren's role is masterful. Warren's skillful handling of the questioning and argument and his conduct of the deliberations account more than anything else, in Kluger's view, for the Court's unanimous verdict. Any simplistic belief that what happened was inevitable is shattered. Kluger contends that the judicial unanimity necessary for any moral impact was unachievable until Earl Warren's fortuitous ascension to the Chief Justiceship. Indeed, he refers to Justice Warren as "Superchief." Kluger probably gives Justice Warren too much credit for the unanimous decision in the Brown case. Each justice renders a decision in isolation, separately from that of the other justices. That a decision is unanimous may be more the result of arguments heard, legal precedents, previous litigation, and individual research and interpretations than any impact by a Chief Justice, skillful though he may be.

Kluger makes the reader experience the awe of standing before the Supreme Court bench. Yet, to his credit, he reveals the hidden agitation of the justices, each of whom felt human emotion and reason pulling them in a direction contrary to legal precedent. This work may be the most revealing source of the disagreements, biases, and personal convictions of the 1954 Supreme Court judges.

Certainly the Brown decision was one whose time had come. Kluger's may be the definitive history of that case. This collage of facts, events, institutions, and people may never be duplicated. The single most glaring omission to an otherwise masterful work is the absence of footnotes documenting sources.

C. W. Harper

Sources for Further Study

America. CXXXIV, May 15, 1976, p. 434.
Atlantic. CCXXXVII, February, 1976, p. 109.
Christian Century. XCIII, June 9, 1976, p. 572.
Guardian Weekly. CXIV, February 15, 1976, p. 18.
National Observer. XV, February 7, 1976, p. 21.
Political Science Quarterly. XCI, Fall, 1976, p. 516.
Time. CVII, February 9, 1976, p. 82.

SINGIN' AND SWINGIN' AND GETTIN' MERRY LIKE CHRISTMAS

Author: Maya Angelou (1928-   )
Publisher: Random House (New York). 269 pp. $8.95
Type of work: Autobiography
Time: The 1950's
Locale: San Francisco, New York, Europe, and the Middle East

The third volume in the autobiographical saga of an extraordinary black American woman whose adventures in various professions and milieus give penetrating glimpses into black American life in the 1950's

Principal personages:
MAYA ANGELOU, the narrator, a young dancer, singer, and actress
CLYDE, later known as Guy, her illegitimate son
VIVIAN BAXTER, her mother, an astute businesswoman
IVONNE BROADNAX, her closest friend
TOSH, her husband for two years, a Greek-American

The third volume of Maya Angelou's autobiography continues many of the themes and the exuberant writing found in the first two, *I Know Why the Caged Bird Sings* (1969) and *Gather Together in My Name* (1974). So remarkable is her tale and so arrestingly is it presented that Angelou has actually become more famous since writing her autobiography—unlike those celebrities (especially sports or entertainment figures) whose already-achieved fame prompts them to engage in life-writing. Actress, dancer, producer, Angelou was little known to the white establishment until in 1969 *I Know Why the Caged Bird Sings* showed her to be an important new writer. Since that time she has published two more volumes of her autobiography and two books of poetry, written several plays, adapted several more, and worked in television as well as in opera and on Broadway. She recently appeared in the production of *Roots* for television and has been an interviewer on the public television series, *Assignment America*.

But it is her prose reminiscences of her early life that have established her place in American life and letters: *I Know Why the Caged Bird Sings* has become a classic of the "development genre" of the adolescent's education and search for identity, in the great tradition of *A Portrait of the Artist as a Young Man, Huckleberry Finn, Black Boy,* and *The Catcher in the Rye.* The work tells of its protagonist's childhood and adolescence in rural Stamps, Arkansas; St. Louis; and San Francisco, in the 1930's and 1940's. Reared successively by an awesomely religious grandmother (on her father's side) and then by her strong, beautiful mother, Angelou resonantly describes the black rural South during the Depression, the wealthier black sections of St. Louis, and the ghettos of San Francisco during World War II, as well as her own education (which included being raped by her stepfather at age eight). The book ends with the birth of her illegitimate son when she is sixteen. *Gather Together in My Name* continues the saga as Maya and Clyde eke out an existence; Maya works variously as a cook, a prostitute, and a madam, and learns about the horrors of heroin in the black community.

Running through the first two volumes of her autobiography are two parallel but sometimes contrasting themes of Angelou's life: the black gospel tradition instilled by her upbringing in the CME Church and personified by her grandmother ("Momma"); and the black blues or urban street tradition derived from the city eduation she gains in the Midwest and West and personified by her mother. These motifs recur in *Singin' and Swingin' and Gettin' Merry like Christmas.* Although Angelou's grandmother does not appear in person in this volume and dies while Angelou is hospitalized for appendicitis, her memory and influence are pervasive. When her young son Clyde is embarrassed at the ranting of a street preacher, Angelou realizes guiltily that the black religious tradition so important in her own early years is not being carried on. She begins teaching Clyde Bible stories and later assuages her own longing by attending a black charismatic church in San Francisco.

These details suggest the tension between the religious motif and the blues motif, which occupies more space in this volume. It is this urban street tradition that Angelou usually turns to in continuing to work out her own identity. She cultivates the kind of special savvy that makes her suspicious of a job offer from a white woman in the record store; that ultimately causes the breakup of her marriage to Tosh the Greek; that makes her deal honestly with customers while the only black B-girl in a North Beach, San Francisco, strip joint; that lends poignancy to her adventures with black American exiles in Paris.

Much of this volume is taken up with Angelou's adventures as the primary dancer in the touring company of *Porgy and Bess* in the 1950's. She gets her start in the North Beach burlesque house, and, because she dances and does *not* strip and explains to customers that the champagne drinks they buy for her are 7-Up, she is noticed by the chic coffee house crowd. She is "adopted" by the whites at "The Purple Onion" and begins a successful season as a calypso singer, followed by the then-unknown Phyllis Diller. It is at "The Purple Onion" that Angelou gets her name, taken from her married Greek name, Angelos. "Maya" was her brother's way of referring to her when a child, "mya sister." While at "The Purple Onion" she auditions for and gains a place in a Broadway musical but accepts instead the role of Ruby in *Porgy and Bess.* The all-black cast travels throughout Europe and the Middle East, often performing in areas where American blacks had never been—Yugoslavia, Egypt, Israel.

Memorable scenes, in terms of both politics and race, are described exuberantly by Angelou, as she finds uneducated Yugoslavs in Zagreb who know Paul Robeson's rendition of "Deep River," or marvels on landing in Alexandria at seeing for the first time dark-skinned peoples whose ancestors are the same as her own. She chronicles the tumultuous receptions the company gets at La Scala, in Paris, in Athens. And she includes wonderful anecdotes about herself and various cast members. In Yugoslavia, for example, most of the females were physically pursued by love-sick Yugoslavs—to their hotel rooms, outside the theater, on the street—and sent flowers, candy, and messages. Maya's own "romance" with the persistent "Mr. Julian" is hilariously detailed. When he claims in broken English that he cannot live without her and that he is sending her his heart, Angelou wonders how literally to understand this passionate Easterner. The heart appears in her dressing-room, a glass-encrusted bread-dough creation, complete with instruction in three languages, "Do not eat." In Cairo, to cite another adventure, several of the women decide to have their hair straightened, in order not to have to use hot combs. Angelou hurriedly leaves the luxurious beauty parlor when the chemicals begin to burn her scalp, but the others endure and have beautiful bouffant hairstyles—for about a week, until their hair falls out. For the rest of the tour, most of the women in the cast are forced to wear wigs. Angelou has other encounters in Europe, meeting some of the famous black expatriots, such as Bricktop in Rome, and performs her calypso at night clubs on Paris' Left Bank, welcomed as an exotic personage and treated differently from the more frequently encountered blacks from French Africa.

It is her plaguing sense of guilt over the "abandonment" of her son that sends Angelou back to San Francisco, where she fights psychological depression, deals with Clyde's psychosomatic skin rash, and finally begins a new career singing and dancing on the club circuit, this time taking Clyde with her. Like the other two volumes of her autobiography, this book thus ends on a beginning of sorts, just as *I Know Why the Caged Bird Sings* had concluded with the birth of Clyde.

Singin' and Swingin' and Gettin' Merry like Christmas gives us a statement and a glimpse into the life of a strong black woman, but the revelations about her racial and sexual identity are not as strong as they might be. In fact, this a much more "public" book than her other two volumes, less revealing and interesting in the sense that there is diminished introspection on the narrator's part. Questions are raised in the reader's mind that Angelou does not treat: How does Clyde respond to his lack of a father, both before and after Angelou's marriage? Where does Angelou fit into the beginnings of the Civil Rights movement? How did she react to the McCarthyism of the early 1950's? What were her reactions to the various political regimes visited on tour? What are her inner feelings about men and marriage, after the breakup of her own? What is her attitude toward being black and female by the end of the volume? Her brother Bailey, so important in her life in the previous volumes, is barely mentioned, and her father is not mentioned at all. More than these, however, the reader wonders about the underlying reasons for her marriage to Tosh, and the real reasons for its failure. And finally, why is she so opposed to bringing Clyde on the tour with the company: is it really a fear of the homosexuality of the males on the tour, as she states at one time?

The position of the black woman in the women's movement in the United States is a fascinating one, not yet carefully delineated or chronicled. Angelou's works are often used in women's studies courses since she is a strong black feminist. This work could give us a good deal of insight into the early adult life of a strong black woman at a period in American history (the 1950's) when the feminist movement was at its lowest ebb. Angelou's most explicit statements on the subject come as she is discussing her failing marriage and her loss of independence and identity. But there is so much that is omitted, so little inwardness, that, curiously, this autobiography is in danger of becoming that mere recital of meetings with the rich and famous that lesser autobiographies often are. Angelou readers await with interest the fourth installment of this fascinating inner and outer life.

Margaret McFadden-Gerber

Sources for Further Study

Booklist. LXXIII, September 15, 1976, p. 107.
Kirkus Reviews. XLIV, August 1, 1976, p. 864.
Library Journal. CI, September 1, 1976, p. 1763.
National Observer. XV, October 2, 1976, p. 21.
Publisher's Weekly. CCX, August 9, 1976, p. 74.
Saturday Review. IV, October 30, 1976, p. 46.

SINGULARITIES
Essays on the Theater 1964-1974

Author: John Simon (1925-   )
Publisher: Random House (New York). 239 pp. $12.95
Type of work: Essays

A collection of thirty-five witty and insightful essays on the theater, written in Simon's inimitable style

Like the film criticism of Pauline Kael, John Simon's theater criticism is in itself a dramatic event, and Simon is center stage. It is his "language as gesture" we hear and watch, and his reasoning is the action that develops. He tells us that *Singularities* has no "overarching theme other than *Theater* and, implicitly, the personality of the critic-essayist." The two epithets most often hurled at him, or admiringly applied to him, are "elitist" and "acerbic." Mingled, those two qualities are the ambience of the collection. He tells us we must "start thinking of theater as a high, perhaps even aristocratic and unpopular art." "On Being an Elitist Critic" is the subject of the introduction to one of his books. He suffers fools viciously and is intolerant of any work that falls short of excellence. Critical wrath as an expression of genuine anger is no vice, he declares. Jacques Barzun praises him for the splendid violence of his arguments. Simon has often declared that a critic must be an artist, a teacher, and a philosopher who writes as well as any other artist. Criticism is a work of art that is significant while being entertaining. Criticism by consensus is fallacious. Objective, constructive, or destructive criticism is impossible.

It may be useful to know what background helped to produce this approach. Born in Yugoslavia, Simon came to the United States in 1941 when he was sixteen. He went to school in England and studied comparative literature with Harry Levin at Harvard; he was taught at Harvard, M. I. T., and Bard College. All genres were represented in his first collection, *Acid Test* (1963), which concluded with a section on other critics. He has served as drama critic for *Commonweal, The New Leader, Hudson Review,* and *New York* magazine. He has also been film critic for *Esquire, The New Leader,* and *New York. Private Screenings* (1967), *Movies into Film* (1971), and *Ingmar Bergman Directs* (1972) are his books on movies. Circulation for the publications for which he has written columns regularly is too limited for his criticism to have had the effect our culture needs.

In *Singularities* Simon has collected most of the pieces on the theater written over the decade 1964-1974. They are not reviews or critiques but essays, he insists. For his reviews of the same period, one may consult *Uneasy Stages* (1976). To persuade the reader that "single works are illuminated by juxtaposition," that "themes and developments emerge" to reveal the critic's "cumulative achievement," Simon structures this collection of short pieces, some very short indeed, quite cleverly, focusing our attention with one-page introductions on "Appreciations," "Proposals," "Definitions," "Fulminations," "Appraisals," and "Convictions."

The epigraph is a puzzler. "No two on earth in one thing can agree,/ All have some darling singularity" (Charles Churchill, from *The Apology*, 1761). If Simon, who sees little singularity in the theater today, has a "singularity" among other critics, few of his subjects will find him "darling." He approves of few of the plays, books, and people he dissects; most of his subjects fail to achieve the high classical standards he imposes. The first "popular misconception" Simon clears up for us is the one that assumes critics would rather be nasty than nice. To prove his gall is not unmitigated, he opens with "Appreciations" of three playwrights who have two things in common: their plays are classics and they are dead.

Ibsen is the playwright most often cited as a touchstone of excellence in these essays. Simon demonstrates his exegetical acumen in essays on *Peer Gynt* and *The Wild Duck;* peeling the layers of their complexity as if they were onions, he demolishes "charges" made against them over the years. He examines the construction and satirical meaning of *Peer Gynt*, its techniques of imagery, ambiguity, counterpart, symbolism, and character revelation. *The Wild Duck* is offered as another proof that Ibsen, who is too often confused with the Ibsenites, is not simply a bourgeois realist, a polemist, lacking in beauty. Simon convincingly shows the play to be "original yet universal, poetic yet witty, savage yet humane, symbolic yet earthy," but his answer to the question, Why, then, is it not a beloved and popular masterpiece? is perhaps too facile: it lacks a hero and love interest.

Simon can think of no greater loss to world drama than the death at twenty-three of the genius Georg Büchner, author of *Woyzeck* and *Danton's Death*. He defends *Danton's Death*, too, against various objections. One of its achievements is the way the poetic style corresponds to "the acrid, bittersweet, and finally wormwoodlike laughter that is the true subject, the dramatic vision" of the play. When justifiable occasions for praise arise, Simon's enthusiasm is boundless. *Woyzeck* and *Danton's Death* anticipate "the essential elements of realism, poetic realism, naturalism, impressionism, expressionism, *Sachlichkeit* and magic realism . . . black humor and the theater of the absurd." The piece on *Cyrano de Bergerac* is the first of several two- and three-pagers. It is "not a great play, merely a perfect one"—pure theater. Another negligible bit that does not illuminate by juxtaposition is the comment on the exhibition *The Theater of Max Reinhardt*. He was a "ham of genius," "an impure artist," "whose achievements were ambiguous."

Having contended that "constructive criticism" is mythical, Simon offers the closest thing in "Proposals." Lower prices and bigger stars are his facetious answers to the urgent question, "Can Drama Be Saved?" Drama is "doomed to slow, lingering extinction . . . unless the public acquires some taste, educa-

tion and culture, which is easily the most utopian of all my suggestions."
Neither television nor the movies can help us "Toward the Conquest of Inner
Space." Living gestures and words in the theater "can penetrate deeper than
any lens ever will." Here Simon reiterates a proposal he makes often:
American theater needs vast national, state, and private endowment to promote a genuine theatrical culture of "civilized minorities." Just as important is
the need for a crash program to develop directors. The three last directors of
stature—Elia Kazan, William Ball, and Mike Nichols—have as many weaknesses as strengths, and Kazan and Nichols have gone over to film, along with
the new directors of talent. One of Simon's most eloquent and pertinent proposals is for a revival of old one-acters by great playwrights. "Should Albee
Have Said 'No Thanks'?" to the Pulitzer Prize, that "unnecessary evil," is not
one of the questions likely to be asked throughout the duration of this book's
usefulness. Simon's answer, Yes, is of limited interest. More interesting is his
"Advice to the Hatelorn," whose letters outnumber those of his fans five to
one. Simon poses the question, Who "is more likely to be right: the critic or the
irate complainer?" He rejects the democratic answer that "everyone's opinion
about theater is as good as anyone else's."

The essays in "Definitions" attempt "to make clear to the readers from what
bases my criticism proceeds." People are always telling critics what their attitudes toward the theater, where they see so many "brutally horrible" plays
and productions, should be. To those who insist that the critic must love the
theater, Simon says, "Who loves well, chastises well." He attempts a definition
of a very difficult concept in "What Is Taste?" In other pieces, he defines two
types of critics; the difference between realism and reality; and the word
"theater." The key essay in this section is "Is This the Right Way to Rebel?"
wherein Simon reminds us that "to a given artist, 'realism' means the conveying of what he understands by reality." Confusion arises in the double use of
the term "realism" to praise or deride. Simon provides a useful distinction
between "realism," which "tries to live up to the decent, solid citizen's view of
what is true and real," and "reality," which "tries to satisfy an individual
author's vision of a reality behind the everyday reality." Realistic theater is
essentially journalistic; the theater of reality is humanistic. Grotowski and
Richard Schechner are false prophets of a new theater of reality, argues
Simon, in one of his strongest essays.

Not surprisingly, the section called "Fulminations" is the longest, but
Simon insists that that may say more about the true nature of the theater than
of Simon himself. The most frequent occasions for the famous Simon invective
are the assaults that come from the new theater. He charges that most of us are
"sectarians and victims of the Cult of the New." The causes of this greed for
the new are boredom, a misunderstanding of the nature of art, and snobbery.
"Overabundance of money in hands short on culture and taste" facilitates the
killing speed with which we consume what is "New, Newer, Newest." For

those seeking a solution, Simon recommends consumption of tough, resisting criticism, especially from conservatives who may balance the pronouncements and incitements of the dominant radicals. He fulminates against Richard Schechner for promoting Events, Activities, and Happenings, "anarchy, anti-art, non-art," products of "an age in which both reason and feelings are suspect—or simply lacking."

As gadfly, Simon provides sobering perspectives on manifestations of the experimental impulse in the new theater. Robert Wilson's celebrated twelve-hour epic *The Life and Times of Joseph Stalin* is excoriated in "How Many Ostriches Can Dance on a Pinhead?" Simon is not one of those who sees as the work of a genius the pictorialness, dream-like images, "drug fantasies," protracted repetition, accumulation of fragments, artificially combined images, and interchangeable characters and events in this play. Nor is he likely to share the concepts Jan Kott advances in *Shakespeare Our Contemporary* or respond warmly to his *Theater Notebook 1947-1967,* in which the "born enthusiast" for the experimental theater and reinterpretations of the theater of the past expresses only "one adverse criticism" in 268 pages. In three pages crammed with adverse comment, Simon dispenses with Kott, "Theatrical Disorder of the Day," but to dismantle "Grotowski's Grotesqueries" requires seventeen pages of vituperative genius. Simon subjected himself to three "confrontations" staged by Jerzy Grotowski, founder and director of the Polish Laboratory Theater in New York. "Dumbfounded" at first by the "infantilism and coarseness" of the works, Simon recovers enough to observe coolly that "a little reflection will show that all this . . . is nonsense," that the "symbol-mongering" is "facile," the "repulsiveness" studied, the shock self-indulgent, the "outrageous excess . . . ambiguous in effect and limited in efficacy," the mystical spontaneity suspect when one recalls that all Grotowski's plays are rehearsed four hundred times.

Simon's fulminations do not leave the commercial theater unscathed. He detests the "Lovable Little People" packaged in dishonest Broadway entertainments, and campy "trivial, banal, mendacious and stupid" musical revivals like *No, No, Nanette* force him to ask another of his questions, "Should Shubert Alley Be Renamed Memory Lane?" Another acid-etched title sums up his estimate of Joseph Papp's free gift to the people, The New York Shakespeare Festival: "Mugging the Bard in Central Park."

Against arguments to the contrary, Simon insists that the theater is a branch of literature. Better to stage a play in the theater of the imagination than never to see it at all or, as so often happens with classics, to see it poorly done. "Appraisals" consists of reviews of published plays. He both defends and attacks Hochhutch's *The Deputy,* concluding that it is a "valid tragedy: not great, but good." What played well, even for Simon, in Peter Brook's production of Peter Weiss's *Marat/Sade* "neither moves nor moves us" on the page. For Simon, Robert Lowell's *The Old Glory* is merely further proof of his contention that "truly poetic" plays cannot be written today. One of the slightest pieces in the collection is Simon's review of Eugene Ionesco's *Fragments of a Journal.* More substantial is his praising-damning appraisal of British theater critic Kenneth Tynan's own collection of pieces, the quality of which rises and falls like a "roller-coaster."

"Convictions," the title of the concluding section, might well, of course, have been the title of the entire book—"Singular Convictions" perhaps. Simon is convinced that an actress' physical beauty is as important as her acting ability; that charm in an actor is "indefinable but indispensable"; that both white and black reviewers should review both white and black plays; that professionalism is superior to method acting; that there is no such thing as too-personal criticism; and that criticism itself suffers from the lack of a common language.

John Simon's essays are of crucial importance to the health of the theater for three major reasons: he has an exalted conception of the function of language in the theater and in criticism; he fearlessly explores taboo areas of discussion; and his essays demonstrate or argue at times overtly, at times implicitly, for excellence in the art of criticism itself.

The plays of Ibsen, Rostand, and Bückner soared on words. "The stage today has fallen victim to the general mistrust, dislike and recession of the word—the word which in all theaters but the most recent was equal in importance with movement or action." Between death screams and deathly silence—"the agony of the word." Even a "good" play, *The Deputy,* fails the word. "Must the Rest Be Silence?" Simon asks us.

Attacking the style of critics like Kott, Simon is on firm ground, for his own style is quite fine. Wit is its most distinguishing characteristic. "Night after night" the New York Shakespeare Festival "sells out—not its seats, which are gratis, but its artistic standards, which, if any, are gratuitous." He cannot resist punning on the name of the producer, Papp, who feeds his audiences "pap." Here is a more labored pun: "In fact, *Cyrano* can be said to finish ahead of many more ambitious efforts by a nose, a long nose." It is on the new theater that Simon sharpens his wit. The aim of Happenings is "worse than barking up the wrong tree; it is trying to bark a nonexistent tree into being." "I was most enlightened by Mr. Schechner's conclusion that the New Theater 'directly explores the inanimate human being.' This should make it of great interest to any audience consisting of inanimate human beings."

Among the taboo questions to which Simon dares address himself are these: "Shall color barriers be abolished everywhere but in criticism? Shall the ghetto mentality be perpetuated in the theater? . . . my answer is a resounding no." Some people argue that only blacks should review black plays, because whites cannot understand the black experience, and the criteria of white theater are too rigorous for this developing drama. Simon regards both arguments as being equally "patronizing, parochial and reprehensible." So he feels bound to point out that by no criteria is Papp's use of black actors in Shakespeare's plays appropriate. Some readers may question Simon's glancing references to homosexuals in the theater, and his uncharitable references to the inarticulateness and disheveled appearance of the young. Protests against his sexist contention that actresses he calls ugly.—Sandy Dennis, Sada Thompson, Zohra Lampert, Liza Minelli, Barbra Streisand—should be denied star status have been registered with the offender himself. Maureen Stapleton as Odets' *The Country Girl* is most cruelly abused. Nor does he spare directors—Grotowski is grotesque in Simon's description. A critic cannot get too personal about an actor's body or talent, Simon demonstrably believes.

Running those risks may have dubious value, but many readers will be glad to see him approach the rocky coasts of taste. Developing one's taste is a "slow, experimental process" to which the critic devotes more time than most people. His taste is revealed in a "pervasive sensitivity" expressed in discriminating language. The selective function of taste prevents him from becoming enthusiastic about many plays. Resisting the taste of one's time and milieu, often dictated by money, is "precisely the critic's duty." Almost alone among critics in keeping the term "art" alive in our language, he refers to it or defines it in nearly every essay.

Simon's daring is most singular when he attacks other critics. Elitist though he is, he goes by no gentlemen's understanding. Of the twenty-seven critics and reviewers named or discussed, some more than once, throughout the collection, Simon speaks well of Stark Young and only a few others. He notes two types of critics: New Chaps or Scouts on the frontiers of the new theater, and Old Boys or Curators of the theater of the past—and "to hell" with mere reviewers. His frequent comments on Walter Kerr suggest disdain at best, but he attacks in detail Richard Gilman's analysis of Grotowski's concepts of theater. "Clive Barnes in the *Times* danced his famous eggshell minuet" is one of his kinder remarks. With some fellow-feeling, he compares his own negative review of Rip Torn's acting with Robert Brustein's. His most sustained criticism of a critic is his review of *Tynan Right and Left,* in the first half of the opening paragraph of which he seeds the clouds of praise only to deluge Tynan with "appalling—modish, irresponsible, insensitive, ill-considered . . . ill-written" in the second half. Simon chastises Tynan for his arrogance, but shares his contempt for Broadway audiences, enjoys his "coruscating sentences," and notes his "supreme aptitude for parody and persiflage."

Simon justly bemoans the American public's failure to understand what criticism is, for every American feels himself qualified to pass judgment. He reminds us often that criticism is neither a business, in which the customer is assumed always right and endowed with the right to demand the critic "be summarily sacked," nor a science using instruments of precise measurement, but "the art of cultivating one's taste, of reasoning well in behalf of that taste, and writing . . . well about it." It is "the art of persuasion, civilized polemic . . .

inspired debate. It is founded on intelligence, sensitivity, experience and concern. It evolves in the critical consciousness through an endless process of comparing and contrasting, sifting and evaluating." He argues a need for "critics with high enough standards to squash Broadway if it is necessary."

David Madden

Sources for Further Study

Booklist. LXXII, February 15, 1976, p. 830.

Choice. XIII, June, 1976, p. 534.

Commonweal. CIII, April 23, 1976, p. 280.

Library Journal. CI, January 15, 1976, p. 358.

New York Times Book Review. January 4, 1976, p. 1.

SLAPSTICK: OR, LONESOME NO MORE!

Author: Kurt Vonnegut (1922-)
Publisher: Delacorte Press/Seymour Lawrence (New York). 243 pp. $7.95
Type of work: Novel
Time: The indefinite future
Locale: Manhattan Island

A satirical portrait of human life in the aftermath of the politics of our times

Principal characters:
> DR. WILBUR DAFFODIL-11 SWAIN, the final President of the United States
> ELIZA MELLON SWAIN, his dizygotic twin sister
> VERA CHIPMUND-5 ZAPPA, Swain's nearest neighbor
> MELODY ORIOLE-2 VON PETERSWALD, Swain's sixteen-year-old granddaughter
> ISADORE RASPBERRY-19 COHEN, Melody's lover
> STEWART ORIOLE-2 MOTT, the King of Michigan

Readers of Vonnegut have come to expect his verbal end-punctuation—"So it goes," "And so on"—by which he avoids arbitrary closure with the insistent implication that all closure is an arbitrary imposition by human beings on a reality that is obliviously continuous. The narrator of *Slapstick*, Vonnegut's eighth novel, calls the accumulation of "Hi ho's" that syncopate the story "a kind of senile hiccup. I have lived too long." If *Slapstick* itself is not a "senile hiccup," it is at least the senescent guffaw of a jaded satirist at the downswing of his emotional pendulum. That pendulum, in his earlier novels, takes us from bleak optimism to giddy pessimism, as Vonnegut focuses his satirical lens either on catastrophic human deeds (as in *Slaughterhouse-Five* or *Cat's Cradle*) or on humanity's absurd self-images (*The Sirens of Titan* and also *Cat's Cradle*). At the end of his last novel before *Slapstick*, *Breakfast of Champions*, Vonnegut turned his focus upon himself, to look and laugh at the satirist's self-concept as no more immune from life's absurdity than that of anyone else. The discovery that the artist's function is a futile one is, in retrospect, the inevitable result of Vonnegut's very methodical madness. It was implied as early as *The Sirens of Titan* (1961), in the lieutenant-colonel's realization "that he was not only a victim of outrageous fortune, but one of outrageous fortune's cruelest agents as well."

Slapstick continues the inward-turning self-examination. Its long autobiographical prologue points to the center of Vonnegut's comic satirical vision—an accessible vision that has made him, like Aristophanes and Jonathan Swift, one of those rare prophets who are listened to seriously by a large following in their own lifetimes. And Vonnegut is read precisely because he denies his own seriousness. The center of his vision is a kind of existential hysteria through which his characters recognize the abysmal gap between the degree of seriousness with which human beings take themselves and their own activities, and the degree of routine dishonesty they subject themselves to in the process. His vision is attractive because, laughing at the dishonesty, he recognizes its necessity as a coping mechanism against the emptiness within. And his writing is appealing because he freely admits that his emptiness is no less nor greater than ours. The human terror of existential solitude is something we can share only by laughing through our fears.

Vonnegut's satirical art, both in theme and in style, is the recognition and revelation of the limited. Humanity, he feels, gets itself in trouble every time it pretends to limitlessness. "I find it natural," Vonnegut writes in the prologue, "to discuss life without ever mentioning love." Yet both the prologue and the novel are centered on a close relationship, between Vonnegut and his brother and sister in the former, between Wilbur Daffodil-11 Swain and his sister Eliza in the latter. The apparent contradiction, as is usual in literature, dissolves into an informing paradox. Vonnegut does not believe in love; he does believe in hugging. He does not believe in brotherhood, but does believe in relatives. He shuns and distrusts all abstract generalizations, insisting on those few particulars that feel good to him. And *Slapstick,* he writes, "is about what life *feels* like to me"—recalling E. E. Cummings' declaration that "feeling is first."

In mock-parody of Faulkner's solemn Nobel Prize address, Vonnegut says that his novel is "about desolated cities and spiritual cannibalism and incest and loneliness and lovelessness and death, and so on." The bizarre, barren world which Wilbur inhabits is precisely the result of humanity's insistence on grand generalizations. Even among the ruins of a country depopulated by Albanian flu and The Green Death, of a planet whose gravity has become unpredictable and whose sky is bright yellow (and with no TV), well-meaning survivors have established a fanatic cult of "the kidnapped Jesus Christ" and are constantly darting their heads over their shoulders in hopes of spotting Him. In the midst of chaos, the narrator-satirist is writing the epitaph to this world, addressed "To whom it may concern," the invocation Vonnegut feels "should be used by religious skeptics as a prelude to their nightly prayers." The irony of the invocation is two-edged since universal impotency has precluded future readers, and no one on Manhattan Island, where Wilbur lives as "King of the Candlesticks," can either read or write.

From this irony we see the personal ramifications of the satirist's public stance: the vacillation between his humane determination to reveal and mend the scars in the moral fabric of society and the simultaneous recognition of the futility of the attempt. As Vonnegut identifies with the narrator he portrays himself as a latterday Cassandra who sees everything and is believed by no one. Even worse, Vonnegut understands that being believed is not enough. Action must follow belief. But the satirist must remain content with causing us to recognize our follies, and maybe laugh at them, as we continue destroying ourselves through them while he looks on in horror, trying to hold his clown's smile in place. Vonnegut aptly compares his own "grotesque, situational poetry" to the "slapstick film comedies" of Laurel and Hardy, to whom the novel is dedicated. "There are all these tests of my limited agility and intelligence. They go on and on. The fundamental joke with Laurel and Hardy, it seems to me, was that they did their best with every test." Handling a limited situation, a sharply circumscribed scene, with maximum wit and good humor is what Vonnegut calls "bargaining in good faith with destiny."

His sense of destiny ("zah-mah-ki-bo," as he calls it in the Bokononist religion of *Cat's Cradle*) is what separates Vonnegut's satirical voice from its existentialist echoes of Camus, Sartre, and Kafka. These writers, too, present life and the universe as absurd, without order or reason. But Vonnegut laughs at the situation and lacks the existentialists' grimness and intellectual despair which are themselves denials of the ultimate absurdity they propose. Like Joseph K. in *The Trial*, Vonnegut's narrators feel that something greater than man exists against which human beings are helpless. But like Arthur C. Clarke, Vonnegut has no idea what that something might be. As with Camus' Dr. Rieux in *The Plague*, the denial of rational order and logical causality leads to atheism ("The Church of God the Utterly Indifferent," in *The Sirens of Titan*): God cannot be the source of order or reason if none exists. Man himself, therefore, must be the ultimate value. That is the conclusion reached in the religion of Bokonon, in which "just man" matters, nothing else (the conclusion of Sartre's *The Flies*).

But Vonnegut extends the argument. He is not interested in "humanity," another useless and distracting generalization. Only the individual matters, the lonesome individual. If society can be useful at all, then, it is useful only insofar as it can do something to make the individual less lonesome, or at least more comfortable with his solitude. So Wilbur Swain's Presidential campaign is based on Vonnegut's remark in the prologue. "Human beings need all the relatives they can get—as possible donors or receivers not necessarily of love, but of common decency." Swain's slogan is "Lonesome No More," and he promises "a utopian scheme" of artificial extended families by which all persons with the same middle names would be relatives. After Swain's election, a computer in Washington, powered by burning the papers of Nixon, Grant, and Harding, assigns everyone in the United States a new middle name and number (flower, fruit, nut, vegetable, mollusk, gem, and the like, followed by a number from one to twenty). Those with the same middle name are cousins, with the same number *and* name are brothers. The system is successful. "I realized," Swain says as he resells the Louisiana Purchase to the King of Michigan for one dollar (on credit), "that nations could never acknowledge their own wars as tragedies, but that families not only could but had to. Bully for them!"

Readers of Vonnegut's earlier works will recognize the artificial families as "granfalloons," and sense a direct contradiction to the tenets of Bokononism. A granfalloon is an accidental, superficial affinity (such as being from Indiana, or having graduated from Cornell), as opposed to a real relationship ("karass") like the one between Wilbur and his neanderthaloid sister Eliza. The contradiction is there, and not to be explained away. For those few who see with the one-eyed vision of the satirist, the prophet, or the priest, only a narcissistic, incestuous, symbiotic relationship with another seer is intelligent. For those who do not—the vast majority—the granfalloons are preferable to no relationships at all. If you must live with lies, Vonnegut argues, as early as *Cat's Cradle* (1963), at least "live by the foma [harmless untruths] that make you brave and kind and healthy and happy."

The sick one is the one who sees. Like Dostoevski's Grand Inquisitor, on an Aristophanic comedic level, Wilbur Daffodil-11 Swain, dependent on the euphoric drug tri-benzo-Deportamil he takes for his Tourette's disease (whose sufferers involuntarily speak obscenities and make insulting gestures no matter where they are), deprived of his beloved Eliza because of the machinations of miniature Chinese who take her to Mars, embarrassed by unpredictable and impotent erections caused by the earth's erratic gravity, having spoken through a clay tube attached to a lunch-bucket to "the turkey farm" (the spirits of the dead) and having found things are even worse for them, scribbles an account of the melodramatic, tragicomic whimpering finale of "the human race." What keeps the satirist going in such a futile endeavor is only this: his technique. Each telegraphic paragraph is a stunt, a walkon scene in a comedy of unquestioned duration. In each paragraph, Vonnegut does the best he can to make a laugh, bargaining in good faith with destiny. The structure of the novel, and of his continuing satirical vision, is the structure of slapstick: one thing at a time until you get them with you, everybody together, forgetting themselves, in common laughter.

Kenneth John Atchity

Sources for Further Study

Book World. August 29, 1976, p. M1.

Choice. XIII, November, 1976, p. 1140.

New Republic. CLXXV, September 25, 1976, p. 40.

New York Review of Books. XXIII, November 25, 1976, p. 29.

New York Times Book Review. October 3, 1976, p. 3.

Times Literary Supplement. November 5, 1976, p. 1385.

SOCIOLOGY AS AN ART FORM

Author: Robert A. Nisbet
Publisher: Oxford University Press (New York). 145 pp. $8.95
Type of work: Social study

An argument for the essential unity of the arts and sciences, using the field of sociology as its principal source of evidence

The appearance of *Sociology as an Art Form* at this juncture in Robert
Nisbet's career comes as something of a surprise. What most of his readers,
both enthusiasts and detractors, doubtlesssly anticipated was an elaboration
and defense of the much-discussed *Twilight of Authority,* published in 1975.
Sociology as an Art Form not only eschews such an apologetic task, it promises
to embroil Nisbet in an entirely different kind of argument.

In the earlier work Nisbet had applied to contemporary society the analytic
perspective he has carefully worked out over the last thirty-five years. This
exercise yielded singularly pessimistic results. Inspired by such conservative
social philosophers and sociologists as Burke, Tocqueville, Durkheim, Toennies, and Proudhon, Nisbet decried the state's emergence as the central fact of
modern existence. In Nisbet's eyes, the state (including the American state)
has become an omnipotent power, slowly eviscerating those lesser authorities
that would, in a more organic social order, vie for man's loyalty. What impels
Western societies towards ever-enhanced state sovereignty is neither the demands of war nor the quest for more orderly industrial development. Important as these imperatives are, Nisbet regards them as secondary causal elements. Of truly fundamental importance is the ideal of social egalitarianism
which has tantalized and even obsessed many Western intellectuals for more
than two centuries. For Nisbet, Rousseau's *Social Contract* presents the
essential dynamic: the intense fellowship and dignified equality of the ancient
polis can be achieved under modern conditions when individuals transfer
totally all their rights to the body politic. Nisbet accuses contemporary intellectuals of unconsciously fostering this exact dynamic by their too-exclusive
concern for social justice interpreted as greater equality of conditions. Their
egalitarian ideology invites the state to penetrate and subvert lesser social
bodies—family, political party, university, local school, church, service organizations. Nisbet sees these intermediate authorities as dangerously weak,
insufficiently powerful to resist the state or provide the individual with secure
community. The natural hierarchical structure which gives them strength
crumbles under endless "affirmative action" demands from government bu-
reaucrats. The West is therefore in decline: the ominous twilight is the shadow
cast by Leviathan.

Despite the apparent dissimilarity of the two books, it helps immensely to
know something about *Twilight of Authority* when reading *Sociology as an Art
Form.* For while the latter may not be a defense of the former, it does in effect
constitute a justification of the *method* both of *Twilight of Authority* and a

much earlier statement of Nisbet's views, the famous *Quest for Community* (1953). In both works, Nisbet approaches contemporary issues obliquely, via the history of social and political thought. This strategy is not dictated by an antiquarian impulse. Rather, like the followers of Leo Strauss and Eric Voegelin, Nisbet tends to view social philosophy (and sociology) as dominated by prophets and seers, persons of enormous vision who find themselves captivated by a problem so portentous and fascinating that it wrests from them great and complex intellectual *creations*. One always needs to consult these original creations before tackling contemporary literature on the subject, for they often synopsize with brilliant compaction the critical elements of the problem. Moreover, the extraordinarily powerful images they present (one thinks immediately of Marx's *Manifesto*) may radically affect how the problem is understood ever after. Thus, in Nisbet's view, to study properly the morphology of revolution, one should not begin by consulting bibliographical pages in the *American Political Science Review*. Rather he must work with Machiavelli's *Discourses* or Burke's *Reflections on the Revolution in France*.

The assumption which generates Nisbet's method is obviously a controversial one. We are not inclined to evaluate the efforts of Marx, Weber, Tawney, Simmell, or Tocqueville using the standard of *creativity*. That Toennies or Durkheim should be regarded as *artists* strikes us as odd and perhaps even disrespectful. In *Sociology as an Art Form* Nisbet attempts to account for these reactions and show that they ultimately stem from a defective understanding of both science and art. Ironically, some of the very figures who are responsible for our present confusion—Descartes, Marx, Comte, Durkheim—were themselves perfect embodiments of that harmonization of art and science which Nisbet wishes to have restored.

Two well-entrenched ideas have interacted to produce the present sharp differentiation between science and art. From Bacon, Descartes, Comte, and a host of nineteenth century exponents of scientism, there has emerged the doctrine that correct *method* is the principal source of significant advances in our knowledge of the world. Nisbet disputes this claim, urging that neat sets of instructions on "problem-setting," "theory-building," and inductive strategy-formation do not produce the sort of breakthrough made by great scientists. Citing testimony from both scientists and historians of science (Kepler, Rabinowitch, Libby, Kuhn, Bronowski, Koestler), Nisbet argues that passionate curiousity, random image-play, dreams, and idle wondering are the true sources of scientific progress. The application of vigorous methods by which to verify primal insights is very much a secondary, albeit crucial, activity.

Nisbet thus begs us to distinguish between the "logic of discovery" and the "logic of demonstration." The first is a logic essentially beyond our comprehension. Fundamental discoveries cannot be commanded—the Muse accepts only prayers and her answers are registered first in the unconscious.

The second is a logic which, if taken to be the key to scientific insight, yields only barren exercises. Without powerful insights to work with, the logic of demonstration results in meticulous verifications of frivolous claims, tidy solutions to mere puzzles.

If the identification of science with method has served to obscure its intuitive, and creative inner essence, the equating of art with mere expressiveness prevents us from appreciating the scientific impulse in the arts. Relying heavily on such estheticians as Herbert Read and Etienne Gilson, Nisbet claims that the artists' most fundamental search is for the illumination of reality. The artist explores the unknown. Nisbet finds it instructive that the word "theory" comes from the same Greek root as the word "theater," and he tends to view novels, poetry, and paintings as ventures in which the artist discloses—often in concentrated and disguised ways—something essential about man, nature, or society. Far from merely "projecting" what he feels, or servilely embodying accepted religious or philosophic ideas, the serious artist engages in a sort of basic research. Both artist and scientist have truth as their object.

His general perspective established, Nisbet proceeds to illustrate and defend it by examining a discipline which from its inception has displayed an almost obsessive desire to be "scientific": sociology. The book's chapter titles nicely reveal Nisbet's tactic: "Themes and Styles," "Sociological Landscapes," "Sociological Portraits," "The Problem of Motion." He wishes to show in some detail that concepts derived from literary studies, the plastic arts, and esthetic theory can assist one to "look beneath the layer of theory, idea, concept and empirical study that first meets the eye in the study of sociology."

Nisbet also is concerned to reveal the cognitive priority of painting, music, and literature; in other words, he believes that sociological systems and studies have tended only to corroborate what was revealed first in an artistic context. His conviction here is strengthened by his reading of Eliade, Jung, Chomsky, and Levi-Strauss. In the book's most impressive sections, Nisbet shows how sociologists have worked with primal metaphors—growth, geneology, mechanism—without fully recognizing the power of such metaphors to canalize thought. Sociologists have thus insisted on endowing societies with the characteristics of plants and animals: social *change* becomes "development"; economies "grow"; societies manifest "pathologies." Or they have discovered adaptive "mechanisms," or, more recently, "systems" and "sub-systems." For Nisbet, the ultimate source of such primal metaphors is the mythic consciousness, which in artists is heightened and cultivated.

Given the impressive boldness of Nisbet's ideas, it is surprising to find how relatively unconcerned he is either to support them carefully or to measure their full implications. In "Sociological Landscapes," Nisbet reviews in a rather mechanical way the "vision" of the masses, power, industrial life, and metropolis which "emerges" from the works of nineteenth century artists and sociologists. His strategy is similar in the chapter entitled "Sociological Portraits." Aware that Marx, Weber, Durkheim, and others did not regard themselves as engaged in portraiture, Nisbet nevertheless insists that one can find in their works the precise equivalent of literary and artistic portraits. Sociological writing provides us with powerful "images" of the bourgeois, the worker, · the bureaucrat, and the intellectual—images which have had enormous influence on our ways of reacting to individuals who occupy these social roles. Nisbet then reviews the elements comprising these images, noting the correspondence between literary, sociological, and artistic "versions" of the images.

In all this, Nisbet is conscious that different sociologists frequently produced alternative portraits—Weber's capitalist "looks" more spiritually driven than does Marx's. Moreover, he knows that social historians have often found both literary *and* sociological portraits to be little more than caricatures. By these facts Nisbet is unperturbed:

> Never mind, in sum, that capitalism in practice has borne little relationship to the systems so eloquently described by Marx. We live in a world of ideas, and ideas, stereotypes, images have far greater directive forces in our lives, generally, than do the conditions they are supposed to reflect.

What therefore seems to matter most to Nisbet is eloquence, vividness, and power in the presentation of sociological theory and fact. His main concern here, and in the remainder of the book, seems to be to insist that sociological writing can astonish, and arouse, and move the reader—can have genuinely literary qualities.

If this is Nisbet's real point, there will be few to disagree with him. Indeed, almost everyone who reads recent sociological writings longs for a new Marx or Tocqueville or Veblen. But Nisbet has also maintained that the goal of both artists and scientists is truth or "reality." If this is the case, one must ask how one knows when a work of art has gotten at the truth. Is the truth-test of a social novel like *The Grapes of Wrath* the intensity of our feelings of outrage, pity, admiration? Surely not, for we know that such feelings can be aroused by purely imaginary as well as obviously distorted works. Because Nisbet fails to take up the question of what constitutes the "logic of demonstration" in the arts, he leaves his readers unsure about what it means to say that sociology is an art form.

Nisbet's final chapter, "The Rust of Progress," adds to the reader's suspicions that the author is far fonder of the image than its truth-value. Here he returns to the pessimism of *Twilight of Authority* by reviewing the analyses of sociologists such as Tocqueville and Durkheim, who saw in Western individualism a fatal solvent of the social bond. By choosing just the right quotes and embellishing them with his own often grandiloquent style, Nisbet succeeds in producing another of his Spenglerian lamentations. The book abruptly closes with the famous, but now trite, lines from the first stanza of Yeats's "Second Coming." That Nisbet omits an analytic conclusion secures our impression that he loves the bittersweet image of a decaying Western social order so much that not even reality will tear him from it.

Leslie E. Gerber

Sources for Further Study

Booklist. LXXIII, October 1, 1976, p. 221.
Kirkus Review. XLIV, August 1, 1976, p. 890.
Library Journal. CI, October 1, 1976, p. 2078.
New York Times. September 29, 1976, p. 35.
New York Times Book Review. October 31, 1976, p. 27.

SOMEWHERE IS SUCH A KINGDOM
Poems 1952-1971

Author: Geoffrey Hill (1932-   )
Publisher: Houghton Mifflin Company (Boston). 130 pp. $6.95
Type of work: Poetry

The first American edition of Geoffrey Hill's poetry, containing three earlier collections published in the United Kingdom in 1959, 1968, and 1971

Somewhere is Such a Kingdom allows American readers to follow, in one volume, the complete poetic work of an earnest, important young Englishman who is at once immersed in the tradition of English poetry and wholly original. Hill's three works, all of them slight in bulk, have earned for him critical acclaim, and election, at age forty, as a Fellow of the Royal Society of Literature. The earliest poems here date back to the poet's twentieth year, and the most recent represent his work on the brink of forty.

For the Unfallen, originally published in 1959, contains twenty-nine poems, several of them long ones. *King Log* (1968) offers only seventeen poems, and *Mercian Hymns* (1971) consists of thirty one-page poems. Whatever poetic virtues Hill has, he is not prolific. His earning such high critical regard on the basis of so few poems suggests that precision and compactness are among his chief virtues.

No matter where one begins to read *Somewhere Is Such a Kingdom*—beginning at the first page is a good idea—these poems will terrify and delight. They are strong fare, not recommended for the reader who seeks easy answers or uplift. A strong vein of Christian orthodoxy informs them all, but even Hill's orthodoxy is calculated to disrupt the merely normative Christian circle. His gods are gods of blood, and the Mysteries of the Faith keep coming back to disturbingly real, disquietingly bloody events. His view of things is strictly Augustinian and unlikely to appear Christian at all to a world caught up in a soft blur of distinctions.

Hill's poems are anything but occasional or topical. One welcomes the collection of poems lacking confessionals, poems written on a friend's birthday, or poems vaguely revealing the poet's satisfaction or dissatisfaction with public events. The eighty-six poems here tell us practically nothing about Hill; nor do they tell us the circumstances and daily tedium of the years of his life. One gets no sense, for instance, of the dissolution of the British Empire during Hill's lifetime. Nor does one hear of the comings and goings of the Royalty, the Prime Ministers, or the various social/political leaders who have affected the national destiny. One hears nothing of Gandhi, nothing of the Beatles.

The earliest poems in Hill's book were written in 1952. The poet was twenty; World War II had been over for seven years. Nevertheless, Auschwitz looms large in Hill's work; human suffering matters to him. Missing are those social observations a Stevie Smith delights in, those recollections of times past dear to John Betjeman. A Donald Davies, older and perhaps wiser, takes time to look at manners and morals, but Hill's concerns take in all times. In Hill's poems, even Auschwitz lacks grandeur; it is not unique, merely recent. Other poems cite Auschwitz' equals in horror, though their action occurred at early, relatively unprogressive periods of our collective history. "Funeral Music" in *King Log* celebrates multiple beheadings and shows us "reddish ice" tinging the reeds. "Then tell me, love," says Hill, "How that should comfort us—or anyone/ Dragged half-unnerved out of this worldly place,/ Crying to the end 'I have not finished.' "

For Hill, man is at once the "connoisseur of blood" and "the smitten man." History tells it all, and Hill is too objective to claim special suffering for himself and his contemporaries. The personal intrudes into Hill's work scarcely at all, though one must finally judge him a very private poet. Privacy, however, suggests neither self-indulgence nor obscurity. Hill's privacy arises from concern with internal quests, self-imposed riddles. He shares his preoccupations with writers and philosophers of many ages, and his work at once confirms the urgency of his quest and its futility. Hill takes his epigraph from the *Leviathan* of Thomas Hobbes. The seventeenth century philosopher and mathematician speaks of man's mind running "from place to place, and time to time" seeking "what he hath lost." Hill recognizes that he, and modern man, have lost something; his poems document his effort to isolate "where and when" that special something was lost.

Above all else, Hill's poetry achieves the degree of generalization possible for the writer steeped in experience. He achieves his generalization not by denying the local and immediate, but by placing it next to the exotic and antique. Though Harold Bloom chooses to compare Hill and his work to Blake, one could as well demand comparison with the great Augustans, those writers likely to admire Shakespeare not for creating Romans but for reminding them of men. Hill shares other qualities with the Augustans. He delights in language precisely and sparely used, and he delights in wit—though never at the expense of meaning.

Such precision as Hill's ends up baffling. Where nothing is left over, nothing is extra, the very elegance of utterance suggests something more, something not grasped. The something is mystery. The hint of mystery sends the reader back to the lines, the words, the images. The words and images in Hill's first two books seem so tightly controlled as to be impacted; the lines operate within so rigorous a logic that they seem frozen, static. One marvels at their subtle interlockings, but recognizes that they might as well be carved in stone. Their elegance tends to close the reader out, but exclusion still allows emotional response.

In his early books, *For the Unfallen* and *King Log,* images startle because their language strains plausibility, and they seem, at once, wholly arbitrary and devastatingly innocent. A poem in *For the Unfallen,* for instance, concludes with a section called "The Martyrdom of Saint Sebastian," in which the martyr is described as "naked, as if for swimming." This circumstantially wrongheaded observation lends pathos to the death, which the saint catches "in a little flutter/ Of plain arrows." The notion of the sufferer "catching" his death throws the reader wholly off guard. The adjectives "little" and "plain" hint at death's dimunition because of the homeliness of the agents. Such perceptions remind one of the traditional rendering of Sebastian's martyrdom, while expressing everything in oddly childlike terms. The event becomes, at once, familiar and strange.

The longish poem, "Of Commerce and Society," contains "Variations of a Theme," of which Sebastian's death is a part. In the poem's structure, Hill charts things to come in his latest, most distinctive, and most difficult work— *Mercian Hymns.* The earlier poem forces the reader to abandon his normally linear time and accept a world of all-at-once. The title of the first section of the early poem achieves the kind of anachronism Hill attempts to "explain" in the 1971 book; the title is "The Apostles: Versailles, 1919." In the same section, he introduces the poem's unifying motif—the sea—replete with contemporary and mythic implications. The last line speaks of the sea creaking "with worked vessels," thus allowing recall of the Gospel's fishermen as well as the commercial ships of the present.

Recurring sea imagery unifies "Of Commerce and Society," but Hill's timeframe will not be still. One section is called "The Death of Shelley"; the next alludes to Auschwitz; and the next is about the sinking of the Titanic and alludes to Babel. The final section, introducing Sebastian "naked as if for swimming," bears two subtitles: "Homage to Henry James" and the biblical quotation "But then face to face." The poem convinces that time need not be sequential and linear.

Time's persistence and pervasiveness account for much that initially confuses in *Mercian Hymns.* What the poet knows or imagines is present, and in *Mercian Hymns* Hill chooses to imagine England's West Midlands as they were in the eighth century and as they are now; presiding over the short, direct-discourse prose poems is King Offa, who—as Hill tells us—reigned over Mercia from 757 to 796. In what seems an explicit comment, Hill identifies Offa with the "presiding genius of the West Midlands." The long poem may appear a hodge-podge of then and now, but the poet's sense of economy insures inclusion of elements from both times likely to endure in the imagination. In some very real ways, Hill is Offa, and the poem contains his most personal statements to date. His obvious research, accompanied by notes to the poem, provides needed distance.

A boy growing up lives in these poems, and he lives simultaneously with the man the boy becomes and the questing poet the man becomes. Offa never quite *lives* in the poem, but he emerges as an important presence. The poems shift from third-person to first-person and back again; their terse narrative gathers authority from poem to poem, and Offa seems indeed a spirit, a presiding genius, through whom somebody speaks. The poem's landscape shifts, too; sometimes, the medieval is all we see, then the schoolyard and cloakrooms intrude and the bonfires made of beer crates. These intrusions remind one that the poem's consciousness is a poet who has grown up with the twentieth century. Legendary elements (yew and holly), archaic words and names demonstrate how the past persists in the boy/poet's imagination.

In *Mercian Hymns,* Hill continues the questions raised in his earlier works, but for all his distancing, he has come a step closer to the immediate and has affirmed anew the truth of the imagination. In his Introduction to *Somewhere Is Such a Kingdom,* Harold Bloom predicts that the poet will return in later verse to "the tighter mode" of his earlier volumes.

Such a turning back seems unlikely, for Geoffrey Hill has found the Kingdom announced in his book title. *Mercian Hymns,* as Bloom recognizes, is about the poet and what he knows, either from tradition or direct experience. What Bloom regards as the "tighter mode" of the earlier books demands of the poet a discursiveness, an object-orientation which seems downright didactic compared to the accomplishment of the most recent book.

Bloom's Introduction dismisses Hill's "mostly American" influences as "merely extrinsic," preferring to regard Hill as a poet "wrestling with the mighty dead." Nevertheless, those American influences are there in number; Hill acknowledges them freely. His book title comes from John Crowe Ransom, and his long poem "Of Commerce and Society" opens with six lines quoted from Allen Tate. How extrinsic these influences are remains open to debate; influences upon idiom, diction, and syntax, and upon one's sense of the medium itself, tend to shape one's poetic sensibility too. Poems are not ideas; treating them as such is Bloom's heresy.

Bloom's list of the "mighty dead," though clearly those poets continue to shape poetic utterances, seems exclusive for all the wrong reasons. Why is it better that a twentieth century writer show Blake's influence than, say, Ransom's or Tate's? Bloom also detects "visionary intensities" in Hill and attributes them to Richard Eberhart's influence; those intensities might well be Hill's own, though Hill's subject matter and versification sometimes allow glimpses of poets as different as Hopkins and Auden. Invoking these poets scarcely aids appreciation or comprehension of Hill's work; neither does Bloom's reiteration of Blake as the starting-point for practically everything. Bloom's Introduction may reveal more of the critic's preoccupations than the poet's.

Bloom's Introduction will not help Hill secure the widespread audience his work deserves. Despite his importance, Hill is unlikely, at least during his lifetime, to be more than a poet's poet, or a classroom poet—and that mostly on his side of the Atlantic. Bloom, moreover, has obfuscated Hill's importance by thrusting him, prematurely, into a largely academic range of meaning. The poet's struggle with tradition represents the poet's problem, not the reader's. What Bloom regards as central to Hill's technique and meaning produces a yawn among undergraduates.

Hill's true strength arises from his commitment, both obvious and poignant, to life and the living. What Bloom calls his "strong poetry" serves to express Hill's pity and fear for the human race in its march through horror after horror. Not for a moment does Hill suggest that suffering and death are the worst man may suffer, but, like the greatest of his predecessors, he hurts with humanity and seeks to discover that pain and death may mean something.

In his first book and first poem, "Genesis," Hill recites the six days of Creation. On the fifth day, God turned again "To flesh and blood and the blood's pain," for, as Hill writes, "There is no bloodless myth will stand." In "God's Little Mountain," he is unable to stand the "winnowing eyes" of angels and falls and finds the world again. Finally, though a poem named "Holy Thursday" clearly intends an allusion to Blake, Hill's poem allows the discovery that "our constant myth and terror" becomes gentle when we risk enough.

King Log opens with a poem called "Ovid in the Third Reich," yet another reference to the horrors of 1939-1945. Significantly, "God/Is distant, difficult" and the poet has learned one thing: "not to look down/So much upon the damned." He recognizes that they "harmonize strangely with the divine/Love." One of Hill's longest poems in that book ("Funeral Music," ostensibly for three noblemen beheaded in the fifteenth century) affirms belief in "Abandonment, since it is what I have." The poem's final section asks how the sameness of human experience ("all echoes are the same/In such eternity") should comfort us.

From the beginning, Hill's poems have suggested the "consumption" of poetry as the consumption of sacrificial flesh ("Annunciations," for instance, in King Log). Another of the fine poems in that book, "The Songbook of Sebastian Arrurruz," ends with the protagonist caressing propriety "with odd words," enjoying abstinence "in a vocation/Of now-almost-meaningless despair." Here, then, are others of Hill's genuine horrors—the Word unspoken, the life half-lived.

Hill's American publishers have done him and their readers a disservice in printing *Mercian Hymns* without the epigraph which appeared in the original British edition of the poem. Perhaps Hill withdrew the epigraph himself, or approved its withdrawal, but that seems unlikely from a poet as punctilious about his work's printed form as Hill seems to be. (Hill appended a note to *King Log* in which he expressed active dislike for one of his earlier poems and described publication of the revised poem as "a necessary penitential exercise.")

Harold Bloom's Introduction to *Somewhere Is Such a Kingdom* alludes to the epigraph of *Mercian Hymns* and its significance, without observing that the book he is introducing *omits* that epigraph. The omission—which saved a page—weakens the book, though perhaps it does not damage the poem as a poem. Bloom writes that the epigraph "analogizes" Hill's conduct "as private person" and Offa's "conduct of government." The epigraph does more and less than Bloom says.

The epigraph is attributed to C.H. Sisson, poet and essayist. The single paragraph places the conduct of government and of private persons on the same foundation, but distinguishes between government's methods as having all the difference of a "man acting on behalf of himself" from one "acting on behalf of many." The present publicly recognizes only the method, thus evading "the more difficult part of the subject, which relates to ends." Inclusion of Sisson's statement calls attention to a difficulty "no less ours than it was our ancestors'." It also suggests that contemporary concern with procedures and methods may blind the individual or the society to the *ends* those methods serve.

The last four poems in *Mercian Hymns* treat "The Death of Offa," though none dramatizes, or narrates, that death explicitly. The last poem tells us that he appeared "to walk toward us," then vanished, leaving behind "coins for his lodging, and traces of/ red mud." Geoffrey Hill, Offa, and Everyman still must pay their dues, rendering unto Caesar, but they leave behind progeny, artifacts, and humus. As in the early poems, Hill still tries to "demonstrate Jehovah's touchy methods"; he and Offa are connoisseurs of blood, the smitten men, and he knows still that "At times it seems not common to explain."

Leon V. Driskell

Sources for Further Study

Christian Science Monitor. LXVIII, February 11, 1976, p. 23.

Nation. CCXXI, December 6, 1975, p. 600.

New Republic. CLXXIII, November 29, 1975, p. 25.

New York Review of Books. XXII, January 22, 1976, p. 3.

Poetry. CXXVIII, July, 1976, p. 232.

Sewanee Review. LXXXIV, July, 1976, p. R96.

Yale Review. LXV, March, 1976, p. 425.

SPANDAU
The Secret Diaries

Author: Albert Speer (1905-   )
Translated from the German by Richard and Clara Winston
Publishers: The Macmillan Company (New York). Illustrated. 463 pp. $13.95
Type of work: Diary
Time: October 1, 1946 - October 1, 1966
Locale: Palace of Justice, Nuremberg, and Spandau Prison, West Berlin

The reflections of a convicted criminal on the daily routine of imprisonment and on his past deeds which brought him there

Principal personages:
> ALBERT SPEER, Reich Minister for Armaments and War Production in Nazi Germany, sentenced at the Nuremberg Trials for war crimes
> ADOLF HITLER, Dictator of Germany and Leader of the National Socialist German Workers' Party
> RUDOLF HESS, Deputy Leader of the National Socialist German Workers' Party, sentenced at the Nuremberg Trials for war crimes

Albert Speer, the gifted architect who directed Nazi Germany's wartime economy as Minister for Armaments and War Production, has written the most exhaustive and reliable memoirs of any of the leaders of the Third Reich. The first volume, *Inside the Third Reich* (1970), covers the period of Speer's life down to October 1, 1946, the date of his sentencing at Nuremberg for war crimes. At exactly this point, Speer begins the second volume of his memoirs, *Spandau: The Secret Diaries,* which covers the twenty years that he was confined, mainly in Spandau prison in West Berlin. While serving his sentence, Speer secretly compiled numerous biographical and diary notes, writing on everything from cardboard to toilet tissue, in an attempt to cope physically and intellectually with life in a cell. Smuggled out of Spandau with the help of sympathetic guards, the notes—more than twenty thousand pages of them— were kept for him by relatives. Following his release from Spandau on October 1, 1966, Speer spent several years reworking this raw material into two volumes of memoirs, both of which have been given excellent English translations by Richard and Clara Winston.

Spandau: The Secret Diaries, in its purpose and scope, shows how one man came to grips with himself—both as a prisoner and as a close associate of Adolf Hitler. Speer's purpose in writing *Spandau* was to give form and substance, in his words, "to years empty of content." He divides his book into twenty chapters, one for each year of his sentence, reflecting in this way the monotony of prison life. The book itself, however, is anything but monotonous to read because of its dual scope. In the first line, Speer effectively demonstrates the psychological impact which the daily prison routine had on his six fellow prisoners, including Rudolf Hess, onetime deputy leader of the Nazi Party, the naval chiefs Erich Raeder and Karl Dönitz, youth leader Baldur von Schirach, the diplomat Constantin von Neurath, and Walter Funk, economics minister. More interesting than Speer's account of the drudgery of prison life for himself and his comrades are his periodic and frequently lengthy flashbacks to the Nazi era. Through these flashbacks, Speer manages to supplement his vivid portraits of Adolf Hitler and other leading Nazis which he previously set forth in *Inside the Third Reich.*

Speer, in the opening chapter of his diaries, relates a number of interesting events which occurred during the first year of his sentence. Together with his six fellow prisoners, Speer was initially confined to the prison of the Palace of Justice in Nuremberg where the trials were held. On the night of October 15-16, 1946, two weeks after the Allied judges handed down their decisions against the Nazi defendants, the capital sentences were carried out. Particularly absorbing are Speer's brief character sketches of the condemned prisoners and the tense atmosphere which prevailed in the Nuremberg prison on the night they were executed. The other prisoners, including Speer, remained in Nuremberg until July 18, 1947, when they were transferred to Spandau prison in Berlin. The flight from Nuremberg to Berlin, Speer notes, gave a decided lift to his spirits, for he was able to observe that, despite the destruction which the Allied bombers had rained down upon Germany, the process of rebuilding had already begun. Upon the arrival of the prisoners at Spandau, Speer recounts how the guards made it a point of telling them that the tattered clothing which they were given had formerly been worn by the inmates of Nazi concentration camps. Assigned number five as his official identification, Speer settled down to the monotonous routine of prison life, characterized among other things by the monthly rotation of the prison guard and administration among the Russians, Americans, British, and French, in that order. To alleviate the boredom of prison life, Speer devoted much of his time in his first year at Spandau, and in those that followed, to such activities as drawing architectural sketches (he had done none since 1942), working in the garden, which he eventually landscaped completely, and musing in his secretly written notes about the roles that he and other Nazi leaders played in the Third Reich.

The formal diaries which later emerged from these notes consist largely of a collection of anecdotes on the leading personalities of Nazi Germany. Speer's accounts of the feuds between such party stalwarts as the blustering Luftwaffe chief, Hermann Göring; the deceptive propaganda minister, Paul Joseph Goebbels; and the degenerate Jew-baiter, Julius Streicher, add currency to the view held by most historians that the supposedly monolithic Third Reich was in fact an aggregate of administrative principalities ruled by incessantly quarreling barons. These conflicts, as Speer's diaries show, continued among the inmates of Spandau prison. Frequently, against the backdrop of the depressing atmosphere of prison life, the inmates, including Speer, would quarrel, make up, only to quarrel again over remarks made among themselves about one another's personality traits or their roles in the Nazi regime. By and large, Speer depicts his fellow prisoners as broken individuals, with little strength of character, who had lost all purpose in life.

Among the six convicts who were imprisoned with him, Speer regards Rudolf Hess as the most eccentric. Famous for his wartime flight to Scotland in May, 1941, Hess received a life sentence at the Nuremberg Trials. Speer's entries over the years indicate that he had as much trouble as anyone in trying to figure out whether Hess's perennial stomach cramps and losses of memory were genuine. Hess did state at one point, according to Speer's entry of November 20, 1946, that his loss of memory was faked. Nonetheless, Hess did revert to this condition, real or otherwise, from time to time in the years that followed. Irritated at his antics on one occasion, Speer notes that being a prisoner was perhaps the role destined for Hess, who could now play the martyr and the buffoon so as to fulfill the two sides of his personality. Speer, however, is not entirely critical of Hess. In his entry of January 28, 1949, he expresses admiration over the fact that Hess took the necessary steps at the end of 1938 to have the corrupt Julius Streicher removed from his party functions. Speer's entries during the closing years of his sentence show a genuine sorrow for Hess, who grew increasingly depressed over the fact that as of October 1, 1966, he would be the only Nazi inmate who remained in Spandau prison.

At frequent intervals in his diaries, Speer reflects upon his association with Adolf Hitler. Indeed, in the diary entry of October 2, 1946, the second day of his sentence, Speer ponders the fact that just fifteen years before, he had heard Hitler speak for the first time. Speer avows in this entry that in subsequently casting his lot with Hitler, he did so not out of a quest for political power but rather for the opportunity to become a great architect. Still, he acknowledges the guilt of carrying out Hitler's wartime orders as armaments minister, though his expression of that guilt is detached and devoid of emotion. In his capacity as Hitler's personal architect who would build lasting monuments to the Third Reich and as a technocrat who administered Germany's wartime armament production, Speer spent much time with Hitler. He thus records in his diaries some very engrossing observations about his chief, especially on the following subjects: the drive to the East and the idea of world conquest; the Jewish question; and the Führer's mania for destruction, especially as the war drew to a close. In discussing Hitler's position on these subjects, Speer reveals his own opinion about them and about Hitler himself.

Speer explains that in Hitler's invasion of Russia, the idea of world conquest was, of course, paramount. Hitler reflected on his imperial plans, writes Speer, in a conference which they held in August, 1942, at his headquarters in the Ukraine. This was the period in which the German army was rolling rapidly toward Astrakan and the oil fields of Baku. After the anticipated fall of the Soviet Union, Hitler boasted that his troops would advance from the Caucasus to the borders of India, a thrust which would precipitate the collapse of the British Empire. As far as the conquered Soviet territories were concerned, he expressed his aim of filling the vast Russian spaces with one hundred million Germans. In the process of Germanizing Russia, Hitler intended to launch an extensive building program, including fortified peasant villages and heavy industries, both of which would be tied together with a vast network of new railways and *Autobahnen*. Almost wistfully, Speer relates in his entry of July 21, 1950, that this building program would have kept him occupied for the rest of his life. His excitement about Hitler's plans in the East is further reflected in an entry three years earlier, in which he states that in the opening years of the war, he felt as though he was part of a European crusade which was moving against Asia.

If Speer, as late as 1950, could identify with Hitler on many of his plans for the East, several of his entries in late December, 1946, express in retrospect his horror about the way Hitler calmly spoke of the need to exterminate the Jews. Speer regrets that, although he had no knowledge of the killing of the Jews, he failed to challenge Hitler on his attitude toward them. He further regrets that on the eve of World War II, in which Hitler had promised to annihilate the Jewish race, he thought not of the endless misfortunes it would mean for everyone, but only of the grandeur of the historical hour. Speer shows how Hitler's stored-up resentment against the Jews intensified as the war took a turn for the worse toward the end of 1942. By this time, Speer states that he fully realized how essential the figure of the Jew was to Hitler—as an object not only of hatred but also of escape from the increasingly bad news from the battle fronts. In the summer of 1943, Hitler vowed that he would avenge upon the Jews the lives of those lost at that time in the Allied air raids on Hamburg. Speer observes that if he had listened more carefully, it surely would have dawned upon him that Hitler was making such remarks in order to justify mass killings which had already been planned. Writing in his diaries in August, 1960, he states that at the time he served Hitler, he considered the Führer's anti-Semitism "a somewhat vulgar incidental, a hangover from his days in Vienna." Now that Hitler's true intentions had come to light in the postwar years, Speer expresses regrets at having served in a regime whose main objective was devoted to an extermination program.

As further evidence of Hitler's hatred, Speer cites his mania for destruction which intensified as the war neared its end. He ordered that plans must be completed for the construction of a four-engine long-range jet bomber which would turn the skyscrapers of New York City into gigantic burning torches. On another occasion, he promised never to surrender, vowing that no German city would be left in the enemy's hands until it was a heap of ruins. Speer criticizes his fellow inmates for taking as soldierly virtue what in reality was merely

Hitler's callousness at the prospect of total destruction. If the Führer appeared to them as a sort of Frederick the Great, writes Speer, to him Hitler was only Attila.

If *Spandau: The Secret Diaries* reveals much about the basis for Speer's change of attitude toward Hitler, it also sheds considerable light on the nature of his sense of guilt. Speer appears in his diaries as a man who feels that he is superior to his fellow inmates because he honestly and openly acknowledged his share of the guilt for the crimes of the Hitler regime. Yet, his expression of guilt throughout his diaries lacks any real sense of remorse; he even questions his motives for insisting on his guilt. In his entry of October 2, 1946, he suspects that vanity and boasting may have been involved in his forthright admission of guilt before the court in Nuremberg. He notes further, in the entry of January 24, 1947, that Göring accused him of incriminating himself in order to win sympathy from the court. Speer's most telling revelation on the nature of his guilt is to be found in his entry of July 28, 1949. On this occasion he asks himself whether, in admitting his guilt at the Nuremberg Trials and in the years thereafter, he was simply conforming to the spirit of the postwar times which expressed shock and revulsion at the crimes of the Hitler regime. While claiming that his feeling of guilt at Nuremberg was entirely sincere, he expresses the wish that he could have felt this guilt in 1942. This admission is the most tragic one that Speer makes in the entire book.

Edward P. Keleher

Sources for Further Study

America. CXXXIV, May 8, 1976, p. 413.

Economist. CCLVIII, March 20, 1976, p. 113.

Nation. CCXXII, March 27, 1976, p. 378.

National Review. XXVIII, May 28, 1976, p. 571.

New Yorker. LII, April 19, 1976, p. 129.

Time. CVII, February 23, 1976, p. 63.

THE SPECTATOR BIRD

Author: Wallace Stegner (1909-   )
Publisher: Doubleday and Company (New York). 214 pp. $6.95
Type of work: Novel
Time: The present, with recurrent flashbacks to twenty years earlier
Locale: The California coast above San Francisco, and Copenhagen, Denmark

A realistic account of how, despite being without ancestors or descendants, tradition or place in the world, and despite the bitter realization that he has lived his life as a spectator, an old man achieves belated acceptance of himself and of his wife's faithful companionship

> Principal characters:
> JOE ALLSTON, a retired literary agent
> RUTH, his wife
> ASTRID WREDEL-KRARUP, a beautiful Danish Countess

The Spectator Bird is a powerful, important work. Because of its themes of aging and identity, it is destined to become even more influential as we move further into this century.

Wallace Stegner's previous novel, *Angle of Repose*, earned a Pulitzer Prize. He has written some twenty other books, including an influential conservationist, nonfiction work, *The Sound of Mountain Water*. He is perhaps best known still for his monumental novel of an American family and its dreams, *The Big Rock Candy Mountain*, or for his accurate depiction of love's pain in the novel, *All the Little Live Things*. Whether in fiction or nonfiction, Stegner has consistently demonstrated craftsmanlike ability to carry large concerns, tell large and difficult stories, make cogent observations on a wide range of life experiences. His importance lies not only in his energetic and unrelenting investigation of human motives and actions, but also in his considerable talent at arresting readers' attentions and telling them spellbinding tales about themselves and their neighbors.

Stegner has never retreated from a tough subject; instead, he has confronted, head-on, the two most difficult decades for fiction writers to grasp in this century. In the 1960's, which many writers found it expedient to slip away from into writing about the past, or biography, or mysticism-fantasy-occultism-escape, he lowered his lance and charged. What he charged, of course, was the tragically distorted emotional landscape of mid-Vietnam War America. The topics were frighteningly complex: the dissolution of the family, accelerating erosion of marital bonds, meaningless sexual permissiveness, political, social, educational and religious chaos, the dying environment. All these he treated, and he worked, too, on a pet theme, the angry, apocalyptic differences between young and old, black and white, people. There was no escape into the nostalgia of the Depression years for Stegner. The problems of the day were his meat. Some of his conclusions were not modish or popular for the acid-rock, guru-haunted, "it-it-feels-good-do-it" mentality of that period. But Stegner was not blindly attacking the times or youth. In many ways, he stood alone in his equilibrium, excoriating alike the silly balloons of mind-lessly, desperately "with-it" kids *and* the repressions longed for by the angrily confused, hurt "over 30's" and "senior citizens." Inexorably, he made those who would read him, young or old, look at how stupid and vain, cruel and wasteful we were being, and his novels offered some leanly won, old-fashioned humanistic remedies for the problems. He depicted characters as having to learn first of tolerance, then of acceptance, then of respect, then, if possible, of love and faith. Along the way, he suggested, it would not hurt to return to and improve upon the out-of-favor skills of listening and of helping, doing both with some modicum of courtesy and empathy. Stegner's novels have all been pleas for good sense, modulation, union. His gift, however, is that he deals *creatively* with the immediate, the important. He converts reality into art by emphasizing and crafting the drama of life itself mainly through strict adherence to accuracy of observation and thoughtful depiction of the natural drama of human problems.

The protagonist in *The Spectator Bird* is one of Stegner's most compelling characters. Joe Allston, a seventy-year-old former literary agent, is not enjoy-ing his well-off California retirement. In what his society considers a kind of twilight Eden, Joe and his wife, Ruth, live supposedly quiet, comfortable lives. But Joe is not quiet or comfortable. He rails and rages at television, students, land developers, writers, everything—including himself, and even at times his patient wife. Joe is intelligent and articulate, has enough insight to make himself convolutedly more miserable when he realizes he is indulging in self-pity. He knows it, but finds himself powerless to achieve another form of resistance to two foes his retirement makes it impossible any longer to avoid: his lack of identity, and his painfully advancing age.

Joe estimates himself to be a nonperson. He feels he has no foundations. He never knew his father. He goads himself with sparse memories only of the em-barrassment his Danish immigrant mother caused him:

> Everything in the New World that she tied her hopes to, including me, gave way. I spent my childhood and youth being ashamed of her accent, her clumsiness, her squarehead name, her menial jobs. It used to shrivel me to put down, in the space marked Mother's Maiden Name, Ingeborg Heegaard. I never discovered until she was dead that she was a saint, and that realization, with all the self-loathing that came with it, put me into a tailspin. . . .

Joe is thus emotionally cut off from his past. Additionally, he tortures himself with memories of his failure as a father to his own child. He comes back again and again to the scars of two decades before when he thinks of his only son:

> . . . Curtis, who had been nothing but anguish from the time he was breech-born, fell from or let go of his surfboard on the beach at La Jolla. He died an over-age beach bum, evad-ing to the last any obligation to become what his mother and I tried to make or help him be, and like my mother's, his death lay down accusingly at my door. He was my only descendant, as she was my only ancestor, and I failed both.

So, Joe is equally bereft of roots or any extension into the future. Moreover, Joe realizes that he has had no control whatever over these events, or any others, in his life. Powerless, it seems to him, except to make tragic mistakes, he has drifted in a current, ". . . gone downstream like a stick, getting hung up in eddies and getting flushed out again, only half understanding what he floated past, and understanding less with every year." Even the surface good fortune of an employment which has provided materially well, he now knows required no talent. It was all luck and he feels guilt for that. Indeed, he feels tainted to have lived off the talents of others.

All this painful introspection is compounded again and again by his growing consciousness of age. Joe will forget himself a moment, sitting, talking, then stand—thirty years younger in his mind—only to be arthritically, brutally reminded of his irreversibly deteriorating joints. And the pills his doctor prescribes do not deal with his real pain. Joe is frightened and disgusted, too, by the increasing frequency of the deaths of friends. He sees himself surrounded by decay, death, disease. And he is angry, does "not go gentle." He cannot accept the approaching end of things with the calm and—to him—clichéd sweetness which his wife seems to possess. Joe has found life empty; now he finds the end of it equally devoid of any affirmative point. His only solace is his own sardonic, wise-cracking, kid-it-before-it-kills-you stance. Unfortunately, his wife and friends are even further alienated by this mechanism, and Joe is caught in an untenable position he has no choice but to occupy. Even when he contemplates suicide, he mocks himself: "I have put away a bottle of pills, as who hasn't, but nobody can guarantee that when the time comes he will have the wit to take them, or even remember where he hid them." This, suggests Stegner, is modern man, either cut off from basic realities, or fearful of them, afloat, alone in an ever faster-moving sea, a tide bumping and cluttered with detritus which was supposed to make life wonderful but did not. Even worse, this is modern man grown old without grace or sense of accomplishment. Like the worst aspects of modernity, Joe is not truly part of any flock. He is an isolated observer. Outside the V-shaped flight of ritual, natural direction, Joe envies and despises those in the flight. He despises his envy and sneers at himself now as "the spectator bird."

What brings Joe's frustration to a climactic point is his realization that his advanced age has betrayed him even through its failure to relieve him— through what he calls the "grandfather clause"—of the memory of an old, disruptive passion. He discovers that, at seventy, he can still stump angrily away from Ruth through the dark of a rainy night, his cheeks stinging with tears for a chance at love lost twenty years earlier.

In California, Joe gleans what he can from grumping. He muses, gardens, picks at his past; Ruth visits and entertains "old" people, is caught up in civic affairs. To occupy his time, Ruth encourages Joe to write a book—the sort of thing he calls "my life among the literary." To placate her, he thumbs through his journals, knowing he will never write the book. It is all an unspoken charade.

Into this delicately balanced situation comes a postal card out of the past—a note from the Countess Astrid Wredel-Krarup, in whose home Ruth and Joe had lived several months during their journey to get away from the reminders of their son's death. Joe had rationalized their traveling to Denmark by suggesting he might visit there his mother's old village of Bregninge. Typical of Joe, he was cynical about his motives in doing this, since he was not sure he really wanted to find any roots after all. He and Ruth had developed a sincere and touching friendship with their hostess, the Countess Wredel-Krarup, her mysterious problems taking them outside their own sadness for the first time since their son's death.

The first hint of just how powerful an impact on their lives the Countess had is given when Joe keeps the postal card secret from Ruth. Inevitably, however, she senses that what he now reads among his papers is something more disturbing and important than he has encountered there before. Her probing results in his sharing the card with her, and in his confession to her that he had kept, secret from her, a very personal detailed journal during their Denmark stay. Now, because of the card, like lifting the bandage from a wound, he has begun to read that journal. Though it is dark and heavy with remorse, pain, confusion, even horrifying knowledge, Ruth insists that he read it aloud to her—that they share this pain together. Joe reads his journal to her. It becomes *their* journal.

Thus Stegner has provided himself with a remarkably effective framework for his method of rendering and texturing his story. Through this flashback device, we see Joe and Ruth in their present, and we see them in their past. We move back and forth not only in time, but also between cultures. We learn much that is personally linked to Joe and also much that is generally linked to the times and settings which Joe experiences. It is a marvelous device, as Stegner develops it, for giving us one of the most perceptive, brutally honest, and informative profiles of a man, his wife, his country, and his time.

As the story develops on its two levels, Joe and Ruth relive those curiously exhilarating yet puzzling days they spent in Denmark talking, traveling, and learning with their friend, the Countess. They live again, too, the dark turn of the learning, for in a hypnotically complex twist of events, Joe learns that the Countess knew of his mother, indeed knew why and how his mother was able to emigrate alone at age sixteen, penniless. They learn, as well, why no one speaks to the Countess at the opera or on the streets. There is her quisling husband, who has abandoned her, and other sad and sordid truths to be learned about the Countess's family; Ruth and Joe learn them. The sky of their retreat turns dark with Scandinavian night. Horrified, they learn of Astrid's scientist father's eerily objective experiments in incestuous human breeding. She bitterly tells them of her half-siblings who are listed in the family "stud book."

They learn that despite both her parents' suicides, resulting from the notoriety of these practices, Astrid's brother, Count Eigil Rødding, actively continues the work of his father. Before he knows all this, Joe, the troubled but relatively naïve American, meets the Count, the bored, moody, superbly intelligent and totally autocratic European, in a strange sort of comic-saga tennis match. Joe barely manages to hold his own in this battle between old and new worlds, one combatant with an ancient family line, the other thinking that he needs a heritage.

Through this dark theme of incest, Stegner seems to be suggesting that the many Americans like Joe should not be depressed at their rootlessness, their lack of discernible family line. Rather, they should see their "mongrel" blood lines as more natural, and as certainly more conducive to freedom. The distinction is clear: Count Rødding's incestuous experiments have improved nothing and are emotionally bankrupt. Such a clearly known, coldly controlled heritage as Astrid possesses has only produced evil.

Eventually Joe is attracted to Astrid as much, it seems, by her dignity-within-tragedy as by her beauty. In a powerfully restrained scene, Joe kisses her, though they both know they can never have each other. Joe and Ruth return to America and proceed for the next twenty years to avoid acknowledging what happened to them in Denmark. Significantly, something else more powerful happens to them in the comfortable bedroom of their old age as Joe reads his naked confessions aloud to Ruth. They are both hurt and frightened deeply. They talk of Denmark for the first time. They hurt each other. Then they help each other to heal, are drawn closer together—not in passionate love but in companionship. Joe realizes that he has been more blessed then he knew in the woman who is his wife. And he learns he loves and has loved her more than he knew. It is a harsh lesson, tender knowledge that comes to this white-haired Adam and his Eve in their stormy Eden. But the knowledge is not too late; they have each other. For a while longer yet.

Aside from his obvious prowess as a weaver of contemporary plots, Stegner's most striking gifts are his sure grasp of telling details and his ability to create memorable characters with an economy of description. Joe first sees the Countess, for instance, as ". . . sometimes earthy as the stableman's daughter . . . she noticed Ruth's shoes and cried out, 'Oh, those tiny American feet'. . . . She has a smile that would melt glass . . . a true Dane: her cheeks glow in the rain like shined apples." Usually, the details which are so sharply etched on Stegner's pages function first as images, then reflect deeper possibilities. Notice, for instance, these seemingly offhand observations on the first page of *The Spectator Bird:* "From my study I can watch wrens and bush tits in the live oak outside. The wrens are nesting in a hole for the fifth straight year and are very busy. . . . They are surly and aggressive, and I wonder why I, who seem to be as testy as the wrens, much prefer the sociable bush tits." And, in another of Joe's morbid ruminations on death, the images function on two levels: "One of these days the pump will quit, or the sugar in the gas tank will kill the engine in a puff of smelly smoke, or the pipes will burst, or the long undernourished brain will begin to show signs of its starvation." Finally, Joe summarizes his predicament: "I really *am* getting old. It comes as a shock to realize that I am just killing time till time gets around to killing me."

In his methods of characterization, Stegner is peerless. He can detect the exact moment or posture or tone in which to reveal a person. For instance, he shows us Ruth at the moment she surmises Joe is troubled by his papers, asks him what he's reading, sees through his demurrer that the journal is merely dull recollections of their journey. Stegner shows her lying in bed holding the cat, Catarrh, on her stomach as she says in her soft Bryn Mawr whisper, " 'I was watching you while you read it. . . .' The look she was bending on me . . . was troubled and troubling, steady, undisguised by any of the games we play. She wasn't sparring, or joking . . . 'Joe', she said, 'Why *not* aloud? Why not together?' " It is a poignant moment. Ruth's own loneliness and her bravery in beginning the painful process of healing through honest confrontation is a memorable scene and firmly establishes her among Stegner's finest portraits of women, of whom he writes with much admiration and considerable awe.

In a book filled with memorable characters, one who best illustrates Stegner's remarkable love of people—their resilience, their colorations, their subtleties—is Joe's physician, Dr. Ben Alexander. Ben, seventy-nine, who squires pretty women around in a top-down convertible, and is writing a book on old age as a time of liberation, gives "youngster" Joe some advice:

> ". . . For God's sake don't go thinking yourself into any God damned wheel chair!" He reversed his cane and thumped me for emphasis on the breastbone and almost knocked me down.
>
> "What the hell *is* that, a shillelagh?"
>
> "Haven't I shown you that?" He held it up. To the shaft, which looked like cherry wood, had been fastened this big bone, obviously the ball of the ball and socket joint of some large animal. . . .
>
> "That's my hip joint," Ben said, "When I broke my hip, and they had me in the operating room. . . I said to the surgeon . . . "Doctor save me that joint, I want it." I'd walked on it for seventy-nine years and I damn well wanted to go *on* walking on it.

It is a mark of Stegner's ability to establish character economically that Ruth, who speaks less than anyone in the book, and who is shown doing fewer things than practically anyone else, remains vividly in one's mind after the book is finished.

Challenging in its structure, *The Spectator Bird* is a vigorously inventive and restlessly seeking, probing work. It is brave in taking on the life-questioning dilemma of old age. It is ambitious in its themes and philosophy. It is honest in its resolution. Stegner's satisfying ability to limn our times is surely one of our most precious natural resources. We know ourselves better for his looking for us. In this novel he has important things to say, and he says them with stylistic sureness and mature power.

Thomas N. Walters

Sources for Further Study

Atlantic. CCXXXVII, June, 1976, p. 105.
Best Sellers. XXXVI, October, 1976, p. 214.
Booklist. LXXII, April 15, 1976, p. 1166.
Christian Science Monitor. LXVIII, June 23, 1976, p. 23.
National Observer. XV, July 10, 1976, p. 17.
New Yorker. LII, June 21, 1976, p. 118.
Saturday Review. III, May 15, 1976, p. 34.
Time. CVIII, July 12, 1976, p. 65.

SPEEDBOAT

Author: Renata Adler (1938-   )
Publisher: Random House (New York). 178 pp. $7.95
Type of work: Novel
Time: The 1950's, 1960's, and early 1970's
Locale: Mainly New York City, with side trips to Mississippi, Biafra, Vietnam, Egypt, Paris, Zurich, England, Venice, Washington, D.C., and the islands of the Mediterranean and Caribbean

An unconventional novel which combines realism with absurdity while examining the problems and pressures of mid-twentieth century urban life

> *Principal characters:*
> JEN FAIN, the narrator, a reporter and film critic for a New York tabloid newspaper
> ALDO, a writer, one of Jen's lovers
> WILL, a lawyer, another of Jen's lovers
> JIM, a political campaign director, another of Jen's lovers

This interesting and original first novel by an accomplished journalist and film critic is not conventional in form. It has no plot or story as such, though it does, in moving backward and forward in time, come to a kind of indecisive climax. It is not concerned with character development or revelation, though we gradually learn a great deal about the narrator, the only person whom the novel attempts to present in any depth or detail.

The narrator is Jen Fain, a thirty-five-year-old woman journalist who works for a New York tabloid newspaper. She has also worked at a public library and university infirmary, written promotional material for a foundation, and been a film critic and a speechwriter for a political candidate. She has taught classes on film theory and history at the city university.

Since this novel does not tell a story in the conventional sense, Jen Fain is not the average storytelling narrator. True to her occupation, she is a reporter, an observer. One of the arresting things about this fascinating book is that it reads as if written from both a limited and an omniscient viewpoint. This is a sensitive reporter's notebook, a random collection of conversations and confessions, anecdotes and aphorisms; it is a scrapbook made of fragments from the life and times of a sophisticated, urban American from the 1950's to the early 1970's. Some of these incidents, observations, and philosophical asides are interconnected and some are not, but the general effect is one of discontinuity. Some incidents have definite significance, while others seem to be shaggy-dog stories that, whatever their intention, lead the reader up a blind alley.

Most of the vignettes are from the firsthand experience of their reporter, but they are usually presented in an impersonal, reportorial manner. Thus we learn the aforementioned facts about Jen Fain, as well as other information, by indirection, almost by accident, by means of an extra line or autobiographical aside injected into one of her observations. The observations usually turn out to be witty or sad or satiric or ironic or absurd, or sometimes all of these, despite their straightforward rendition.

With the occasional exception of an intentional satiric gibe, the objective stance of the good reporter is held. The irony and absurdity are inherent in the material itself, and in the author's skillful use of it. Never do we catch Adler stretching her notes, straining for an effect. The individual incidents are often ludicrous, but always believable—even those that are hard to fit into any general context. The same original, skillful tone that Adler has used to make her report seem both personal and omniscient has also enabled her to write a novel that seems realistic in each of its short sections, and yet, in final effect, is a mixture of realism and absurdity. Perhaps Bruce Jay Friedman was right in answering critics who attempted to categorize him as a black humorist or writer of the absurd by claiming that he was no such thing. Friedman's contention was that he writes realism, and that if it comes out absurd it is because the times and society in which he lives are often more than a little crazy. Adler confirms Friedman's point in *Speedboat*.

Here are some of the other things that we learn about Jen Fain: she was educated at a progressive private school and an Eastern woman's college, going on to graduate studies in Paris and England, taking special courses in clinical psychology and anthropology in order to understand better the origins and nature of the society in which she lives. She has slept, or is sleeping—as the book flits about among the past two decades with no consistency in time progression—with at least four men: Adam, a graduate student of political science; Aldo, a writer with whom she has been having an off-and-on affair as far back as her graduate school days in England; Will, a lawyer for the foundation for which she writes requests for grants; and, most recently, Jim, the campaign director for the politician for whom she has been writing speeches.

These men are shadowy figures. No sustained attempt is made to give them any presence or personality. They exist only as names, and, as is the case with most of the remaining cast of even less-mentioned minor characters, only as first names. We learn of Jen's relationships with these men in the usual indirect manner, as she makes notes or records anecdotes about school days, the foundation job, the political campaign. There is no fashionable, explicit sex in the book, just as the novel is not explicit about anything else except the ironies and absurdities of life in the overpopulated urban centers that exist in the middle of the twentieth century.

These people are only lightly sketched because it is not important, for the purpose of the novel, that we know much about them. The purpose of *Speedboat* is not to portray people, but the society in which they are trying to live with some sense of purpose and dignity. Jen Fain, as Adler's observer, does briefly examine a large number of people, but no individuals to any consistent or concentrated extent; and she looks at people in the context of how they relate to the society in which they live. She often looks at them with disapproval, but usually in a gently satiric mood, rather than one of disgust. It is obvious that she likes most people in spite of their failings, and is addicted to neither cynicism nor rose-colored glasses. It is because Adler thinks that people, as individuals, are important that she deliberately subdues her characters in order to make the surroundings and atmosphere in which they are trying to survive stand out. As a postscript to one of her better short scenes, in which the occupants of Jen's brownstone spill out their varied neuroses to one another against a background of sirens in the street, Adler has Jen reflect, "When I wonder what it is that we are doing—in this brownstone, on this block, with this paper—the truth is probably that we are fighting for our lives."

It is important that we know the things we have recounted about Jen Fain because she is, in effect and intention, the book. The society being pictured is seen through her eyes, and translated through her mind and sensibility. Reared in a New England mill town, Jen has now become an authentic New Yorker, and this is very much a New York book. Where else but in New York would people walk by without a second glance while a man licks the sole of a woman's shoe? Where else but in New York would another man be injured by a flying suicide leaper? It remains a New York book, in its own particular mode of ironic sophistication, despite geographical side trips, as it follows the wanderings of Jen Fain's academic and journalistic career to such diverse locations as Mississippi and Malta, Biafra and Ben Tre, Egypt, Paris, Zurich, England, Venice, and Washington D.C. The real setting of this novel, however, is not New York, the place that Jen calls home. Neither is it any of those other cities, nor the islands of the Caribbean and Mediterranean that she likes to visit on vacations or between jobs, nor any of the Civil Rights or Vietnam battlegrounds of the 1960's that she visits as a journalist. The real setting is the sensibility of Jen Fain, and her abbreviated impressions of these places during recent times. It is worth the time to get to know Jen. Her eyes are sharp; her brain is alert; her sensibility is acute. Best of all—and this is also unfashionable—she manages to remain something of an optimist, in her own ironic fashion, despite all that she has seen.

Jen observes and, in her own roundabout way, speaks for the careful, conservative generation that grew up in the 1950's. It is a generation that was warned, and that took the warnings seriously, but that was still no better prepared for the profusion of minor factors that would complicate its collective adult life (television, tapes, the Xerox, changing sexual roles and standards, jet travel, drugs, educational upheaval, and psychiatry), than it was for the earth-shaking events (the Civil Rights movement, the Vietnam war, space travel, and widespread political corruption). It is a time of revolutionary change that Jen's generation has inherited, a time in which "The camel . . . was passing, with great difficulty, through the eye of the needle"; a time in which history is passing at speedboat velocity, and those who do not huddle low in their seats can get thrown backward or be broken.

Because of all this, Jen's generation is the victim of what she, at one point, calls "dislocations." Many, having grown up in a country climate, are also dislocated in the city, with its crime, congestion, and confusion. But Jen is too honest to blame the time in which she lives and the forces of history for all the problems she sees. She admits, for example, that she and her friends are in the cities by choice. They are there because they want to be in the center of the action.

In fact, Jen can be tough on herself and her contemporaries in spite of, or perhaps because of, her objectivity. She is appalled at the slackening of standards at the university, and by the virtual illiteracy of many of her students. She is at her satiric best in describing the silly faculty politics as her Drama and Cinema Department squabbles with the Art Department over jurisdiction of a course called Space on Film, with the English Department over a playwriting course, with the Department of Germanistics and Philology which, because of some odd politics in the past, had gained control of the courses on Ibsen and Strindberg. Jen wonders if a newly formed Women's Studies Division might not just stage a *coup* and take over everything. Jen is good at what might now be called the Edwin Newman Game: describing how the misuse and overuse of some words and phrases, and the coinage of silly new ones, has resulted in a language pollution problem.

Renata Adler has succeeded in writing an original, insightful novel about a rootless, urban society. Because of its form, or lack of form, *Speedboat* invites comparison with the French New Novel and the work of her fellow Americans who have been influenced by that school. But Adler's is a realistic and very human book, whereas most of the work of this group tends toward fantasy, surrealism, and an almost anti-human position. Her style and form are innovative and incisive. Written in disjointed sections as it is, this unusual novel will discourage some readers, but those who persist with a slow and careful reading will be rewarded.

In what may be the key aphorism in a book filled with quotable lines, Jen says, "I think sanity, however, is the most profound moral option of our time." Renata Adler has opted for sanity, and it is her considerable accomplishment to have written a very sane book about a society that often seems absurd.

William Boswell

Sources for Further Study

Atlantic. CCXXXVIII, October, 1976, p. 112.

Book World. October 24, 1976, p. F5.

Harper's Magazine. CCLIII, November, 1976, p. 90.

National Observer. XV, December 14, 1976, p. 21.

New York Times Book Review. September 26, 1976, p. 6.

Newsweek. LXVIII, October 11, 1976, p. 107.

Time. CVIII, October 11, 1976, p. 37.

SPENCER HOLST STORIES

Author: Spencer Holst
Publisher: Horizon Press (New York). 128 pp. $6.95
Type of work: Short stories

Nineteen stories and sixty-four "Beginnings" about the exotic and unpredictable in the ordinary and about the artist's ability to reveal them in his work

The notion of the artist as a sacred figure has made a fair amount of Western literature since the nineteenth century seem forced, hysterical, and self-centered. Spencer Holst's stories belong in the tradition of this notion, but they regard the artist and the creative process without the psychological overstatement one might expect. The writer to Holst is indeed a magician, and ordinary creatures, things, and events are magical. The writer accepts this phenomenon, as a child might agree that a mountain can cast a shadow on the moon, or as an adult might concede that the history of baseball is holy. Parable, satire, and parody are possible in Holst's work because the delight in the unpredictable and wondrous which the writer shares with the child is enriched by the moral sense which defines maturity. In a style free of self-congratulation, Holst's stories oppose the tyranny and paranoia in our view of nature, man, and art, and reveal that being is random and that this quality is the source of those transformations which we call magic and ought to revere. Transformation, in fact, is the essential point and procedure of Holst's book, and it shows up in his use of animals, in his belief in the unpredictable, and in his presentation of the "magician" and his audience.

Animals often arrive in Holst's stories as magic events. Among "64 Beginnings," we find the first ostrich which ever flew, plants transforming themselves into birds, and a gang of "baby Galapagos tortoises" approaching the narrator in the livingroom of a New England mansion with the word "memento" engraved on their shells. Animal transformations also occur in literary parodies. In *The Case of the Giant Rat of Sumatra,* Sherlock Holmes and Dr. Watson are presented as Conan Doyle's cats and fiction as a way of transforming the unstated into the stated. The story *The Frog* changes the frog into a drug addict, the prince into an Italian opportunist, and the princess into a teen-ager who abhors "junkies." Besides turning animals into humans and back again, Holst invests animals with human, and human with animal, properties. The parrot in *The Lovers* acquires a human fidelity and trust, and the youth in the story the bearing and skill of an animal.

The unpredictable or random complements the transformations in Holst's stories. *Finders Keepers* suggests that moral occasions depend on the unforeseen. By chance the narrator in this story finds a large sum of money belonging to the family whose garbage he collects. During a bestial search through the city dump, the father, corrupted by disappointment, forgets and attacks the narrator when the latter tries to return the money, and later the whole family dies of diseases contracted from the garbage. Coincidence has turned industry into greed, a good deed into a mistake, and a garbage collector into a rich man.

Such is the transformation of ordinary details into an extraordinary sequence in *The Prime Minister's Grandfather* (where the Canadian Prime Minister, looking through the periscope of a submarine, mistakes a playful walrus for his own grandfather) and in *The Blazing Blue Footprint* (where several Dutch youths paint an enlargement of Winston Churchill's baby-footprint on the Cliffs of Dover), that it is clear Holst delights in the unpredictable. His "64 Beginnings" relies on it. After a flood a ring appears on the outside of a bathtub; the fat puppeteer washes dishes in the dark; angry peasants bombard Paris with cucumbers from Piper Cubs; Poe acquires a new biography in which he becomes a thriving hedonist; the hangman shoots his prisoner and hangs himself; the yellow cabs convene around their garage as it burns and sound their horns in mourning.

As the unpredictable is the fun of transformation, so death is the sorrow of it. *The Cat Who Owned an Apartment* shows us a man so caught up in the transformation of sound into lovely music that he fails to hear the approach of his murderer, and *The Green Gardenia*—perhaps written with Poe's *Ligeia* in mind, even down to the shriek at the end—presents a funeral organist who wallows in the elaborate trappings and music which death occasions. He wants to transform death into beauty and save beauty (the gardenia) from death. But his impossible task isolates him, and fatigue, the harbinger of death, slowly turns him into something as ugly as the corpse of the fat man he had disdained.

The intrusion of death is the closest Holst comes to treating transformation as a dilemma. He is more interested in those who transform. These are the magicians in their various guises, and one of them is the con-man in *A Balkan Entertainment: The Man Behind the Scene.* He has stolen everything important there is to steal, and then, transforming the New Testament parable, he steals the treasures a second time by disappearing with them on his prize camel through the eye of a needle. The magician in *Real Magic* (which seems to be a version of the miracle of the loaves and fishes) creates many pairs of gloves out of one pair. The writer himself is a magician who can reconstruct history as well as literature. The insight of *The Scotch Story* is that Scotch whiskey might well have been invented in the absurd way the story pretends it was, for nothing, not even a material fact, is frozen in Holst's world. This includes the artist. *Doubletalk French,* a story in which an American painter and a French actor who speak each other's language without knowing what they're saying come to inhabit the same body, emphasizes that the artist's identity is liquid enough to assume other identities.

Concerning the writer's medium, Holst uses *The Hunger of the Magicians* to say that after centuries of vanity and gloom, language will disclose the magic in the world and return reverence to it. In this prophetic vein, *The Institute for the Foul Ball* maintains that the true artist, understanding the roots of his art and revering its monuments, will cashier its superficial customs and conduct its renewal with skill, imagination, and humility.

Beyond the magician and his means, there is his audience, and Holst tends to take a moral view of it. For example, the audience of greedy chieftans and unimaginative experts in *A Balkan Entertainment* is taught that treasure belongs to transformation, not to stasis. *The Typewriter Repairman* manipulates its main character to suggest the audience as supporter and interpreter, and to show that the second function can destroy the first. The repairman, sentimentalizing the creative act, does not see that the image for it is the terrarium where the writer maintains trees and animals as they are, reducing only their size, working on the reader's eyes like a playful optometrist. Committed to his trite notion of the artist as a dreamer and degenerate, the repairman mistakes a fungicide for opium, and smokes it while he sits at the author's typewriter to compose "the truth." The fungicide, a mixture of "Japanese snuff" and "powdered anthracite coal," is exotic enough in itself, but the repairman is too benighted to appreciate this. His arrogance turns him into the envious judge who types "BORGES IS BETTER," and when he breathes carbon monoxide from the water pipe and a truck runs over his fingertips, we see not only a sentence carried out but an image of the reader's self-betrayal as the writer's advocate.

To transform the reader's eye—which is to say his view of things—is the aim of Holst's style. Though it occasionally (in *The Green Gardenia,* for example) strains to convince us how childlike he is (something a real child would not have to do), it generally conceals the work that has gone into it. The transformations it shapes are unlabored and tonic, the characters which inhabit it are known simply by what they do and see and by where they are, and the morally apt exaggerations of the beast fable and the satirical legend which it draws upon are hilarious. Last, Holst's work resembles with its brevity and surreal images, and advances with its attention to characterization, motivation, and climax, the modern prose-poem.

If literary history means anything, one must credit Holst for his belief that the art of fiction has a future impelled by a momentous past; and if imagination means anything, one must thank him for a vision of the world more accurate and delightful than the cold mind of our age is likely to encourage.

Mark McCloskey

Sources for Further Study

Booklist. LXXII, June 15, 1976, p. 1451.
Christian Science Monitor. LXVI, August 2, 1976, p. 30.
New York Times Book Review. April 4, 1976, p. 8.
Publisher's Weekly. CCIX, February 9, 1976, p. 92.

STRIKING THE EARTH

Author: John Woods (1926-   )
Publisher: Indiana University Press (Bloomington). 93 pp. $6.95
Type of work: Poetry

> *The sixth collection by a poet of singular honesty, depth, and range*

A growing audience recognizes John Woods as one of the finest poets in America. With the publication in 1972 of his *Turning to Look Back: Poems, 1955-1970,* he made available many poems which had long been out of print, and which, for various reasons bound up in the mysteries of contemporary poetic reputation, had received the recognition they deserved from a relatively small number of readers. That book presented the work of a poet rooted in the vast flatness of the Middle West, movingly perceptive of time's patient ravages, and gifted with an imagination tuned to what an unusually bright author of jacket copy has called "the ominous potentialities of ordinary objects."

Woods's language is apparently straightforward; his techniques are apparently low-key and direct; there are few prosodic or typographical spectacles. And yet, the poems are rewardingly difficult, composed of confident lines containing unusual juxtapositions of image and phrase, like these lines from "Everyone Born in 1926":

> Everyone born in 1926 has tried too hard.
> Our grandparents occupy the ancient snows.
> Our parents buy houses with ramps,
> and are prepared to look Florida in the face.
> We forget what they taught us of use.

Gnomic utterance is nothing new, of course, and the country is overrun with poets who lean toward surrealism, or toward observation that singles out disturbingly peculiar features of the ordinary. The chief difference between Woods and most of these practitioners is that Woods has a deeper knowledge of this approach and its potential effects. He is aware that he is often close to utterance that would be merely silly if it were taken at face value with absolute humorlessness, and so his excellent sense of humor is always alert to opportunities for the right measure of self-mockery, irony, or outright gag writing. His poems are therefore resilient and inclusive in their vision to an extremely rare degree.

Striking the Earth is divided into three sections, chiefly concerned, respectively, with the evocation of weirdness in daily living, love, and reminiscence and satire. The first section begins with the title poem, a meditation arising from a conceit:

> As we strike the earth with our bodies,
> for we are always falling, and standing up,
> and falling again, though you call it dancing,
> or walking, or flying, there is the sound of stone
> coming to rest in quarries, the last spray of sand,
> as we knock on earth's sullen, historical face.

"The sound of stone/ coming to rest in quarries" is the sound of cessation, of death. The poem proceeds to elaborate on the act of love as a mode of striking the earth, and therefore as a way of rehearsing for death; it then draws a metaphor of war as natural upheaval, like a flood; it then concludes with a series of startling images of death and decay: white horses pulling a box, a fingerprint on a flower, sinking "into its/ dizzying spiral," a bruise on an apple, and, finally.

> Names that burned, that kissed deeply
> to the brain stem, that owned the Tartar plain
> from the high fur saddles, weather on stones,
> coming to rest in quarries.

It is easy to say that all natural processes are interconnected, that human life and death are small parts of an enormous, coherent scheme. It is much more difficult to suggest this notion persuasively, or to encourage the reader to imagine that the whole scheme might somehow be apprehensible. But because of his strength of conviction, and his gift for selecting the telling detail, Woods's "Striking the Earth" makes just such a contribution to our imaginative lives.

Most of the other poems in Part One of this collection are further explorations of the causal relationships that may lie unseen between apparently unrelated events; or they are extensions of apparently arbitrary observations, arrived at by the (apparently) chance association of two words, like "Bone Flicker" or "Pore Nightmares." These are risky poems; the tactic of weird association has been fashionable for a long time, and has produced some amazing results, but the danger is that one such poem may be not very different, essentially, from another. Woods clearly has let the phrases gather meaning for him, so that his meditations ride convincingly on the inner logic of the propositions. Their effect, finally, is to make us wonder why we have not ourselves noticed these phenomena.

Though Part Two of *Striking the Earth* is concerned mainly with love, it is tied to the first part by a continuing series of images for vision and the eye. In Part One, the eye is variously used to give us our humanity, to become a token of our potential for something supernatural, and as the vehicle for various metaphors, as in "Light Behind the Eye": "Old treelimb burning/ its red, eyewatering eye/ against the night eyes/ and saber mouths."

In Part Two, eight of the fourteen poems contain the word *eye*; but the emphasis it receives is somewhat muted, and it becomes instead of an avenue for vision, an external feature, often unseeing—a way of suggesting blank opacity:

> Sometimes she wears dense churchcloth,
> and from it, one breast
> opens its deep eye.

The tensions between Part One and Part Two, reflected in their different treatments of the word *eye*, arise from a belief that emerges as the two sections are compared. In the first section, the speaker looks outward, but through an eye conditioned by his inner distinctiveness; what he sees, he sees uniquely. Uniqueness makes encounters between two people—lovers, friends—both rewarding and difficult, so that in the second section, the eye becomes a symbol of the Other's ultimate inaccessibility.

And yet the poems do not sound bitter or pessimistic about such encounters; they celebrate love, if sometimes wistfully; but they strongly suggest that love is somehow possible, that mere sexual encounters are inevitable and often wasteful, and that enduring intimacy between two people is worth the struggle involved in preserving it. In short, the poems celebrate traditional values. The last poem in the section, "The Unexpected Light," makes a humorously surreal comparison of the casual encounter and more nearly permanent intimacy:

> When we hold someone close, does a face
> kiss a face, or does a wallet slide
> into a purse, ID's tenderly flattened
> against ID's?

In an extension of this grotesque metaphor, the questions continue, inquiring whether a sudden light in the room would reveal people, or a pair of featureless, vaguely outlined mannequins equipped with sexual organs; and whether "the literature/ which is squeezed out of the action" cries out like the first creatures to emerge from primordial liquid on their way to becoming reptiles, birds, insects; and whether the more precisely featured faces in the wallets declare eternal love. The questions are rhetorical, of course, but the effect of the images is haunting, and more suggestive of emptiness and futility than some more celebrated poems on the subject of adultery. The "unexpected light" is the light of truth, whether it be "a bloom of lightning" or a late headlight through the motel window. For all its inventiveness of image, Woods's love poetry is rooted in a conservative tradition.

Part Three of this collection does not at first seem like a further affirmation of tradition and the poet's respect for it, but it does in fact come to that. On first reading it casually, one is struck with the sudden outbursts of humorous narrative, reminiscent of old men sitting around a stove in a country store, wondering what the world is coming to. The most outrageous of these poems is "For Prevention of Disease Only," which begins with a pun-infested note about "truly American myths." It is a sequence of three incredibly hoary jokes, one about emergency defecation, one about the farmer's daughter, and one about a man who hurts only when he laughs. They are remarkably long; we have heard their punchlines before; and yet they are very funny, proving that, as Pope said with somewhat different expectations, what counts is how you say it. The inattentive reader of this section will be grateful for the humor, and will conclude that all of these poems have been placed at the end of the book to lighten the load a bit. Read in this way, the poems give pleasure, but their full significance, and therefore the unity of the collection, remain undetected.

Like the title of *Turning to Look Back,* these poems give us a sense of where Woods has been, and suggest ways of entering more deeply into the privacies of the earlier poems in the book. "J. B. Woods' Son, John," "Everyone Born in 1926," "Making Money," "Father's Voice," and "Auction Day" are all strongly evocative of a nearly rural life in the 1930's. Woods has always looked back at that life with a moving and honest mixture of gratitude and distaste. This is not nostalgia; this is a strong, sure sense of a past, and the ways in which it mattered. "Auction Day," superficially among the oddest of the poems mentioned above, is a sequence of fragments, some of them bits of old blues songs or fraternity ribaldry, some of them brief but telling snatches of overheard conversation. It is difficult to say definitively what brings all these fragments together; they could be spoken by various types that gather at a country auction; some of them could even be pieces of poems Woods never finished, and is now ready to put on the block. But taken as a group, they speak for a way of life it is worth trying to remember—even if the remembering gets clouded by the imagination, as it does in the concluding fragment, a list of items to be auctioned. It begins with flawless authenticity, and ends with a brilliant imaginative leap:

> Depression glass, handmade barrels,
> genuine oil paintings, cultivators,
> a Massey-Ferguson tractor, '48 Ford
> made into a pickup, milk cans,
> mule harness, ice picks, 30 bales
> of hay, crutches, featherbed,
> an aunt who rocks forever, an uncle
> who thinks he's going to live
> with Billy in Florida.

It is funny, of course. But it is also haunting, convincing, too close for comfort.

In five poems—"Handshake," "To LeRoi Jones," "To the Chairperson of the *Sonnets*," "You Can't Eat Poetry," and "Fox Light," Woods writes openly and directly about poetry—something all poets do at one time or another, though all reviewers, for some reason, scold them for it. But in "To LeRoi Jones," or "Handshake" (dedicated to James Wright), Woods tells the truth about why he writes some of the things he writes, and he does so without self-indulgence.

Striking the Earth is not as fully absorbing as *Turning to Look Back,* but how could it be? In the retrospective collection, there is a span of fifteen years, over which an important poet deepened his voice and honed his technique. In this more recent work, however, there is a strong trace of new boldness of imagination, along with the honest resourcefulness that has been Woods's hallmark for years.

Henry Taylor

Sources for Further Study

Booklist. LXXIII, September 15, 1976, p. 119.
Choice. XIII, November, 1976, p. 1141.
Library Journal. CI, July, 1976, p. 1535.

STRONG OPINIONS

Author: Vladimir Nabokov (1899-1977)
Publisher: McGraw-Hill Book Company (New York). 335 pp. $8.95
Type of work: Interviews, letters, articles

A collection of interviews, letters to the editor, and articles, compiled and collected by the author and reflecting his lifelong interest in matters of art, literature, and life

Strong Opinions by Vladimir Nabokov is just that. A collection of interviews, articles, and letters to the editor, this book offers a glimpse—almost as revealing as the author's autobiography, *Speak, Memory*—of Nabokov, the writer, the man, the lepidopterist. Through the works included, we see the wit, the style, the anger, and, at times, the almost peevishness of the author.

To say that Nabokov was a man of stature in the literary world is to be incredibly meiotic. Nabokov, who wrote thirty books during his lifetime, is perhaps best-known for his novels *Invitation to a Beheading, Laughter in the Dark, Pale Fire, Ada,* and, of course, *Lolita.* He is considered by many to be the consummate stylist and craftsman of the twentieth century. So much impact have his works had, in fact, that through them he has introduced a number of words into the English vocabulary, not least among which is "nymphet."

Nabokov, however, was much more than merely a man of letters, as his interviews, letters, and articles indicate. He was equally at home creating chess problems, collecting and studying butterflies, or translating works of Russian literature into English. He was largely apolitical, but he passionately opposed dictatorships and the Communist regime of the Soviet Union. His appetites ranged from novels and short stories to butterflies and chess; his dislikes included radios and piped music. A scholar, translator, scientist, and author, Nabokov's life was remarkably symmetrical in some ways—living in Russia for the first twenty years of his life, leaving soon after the Russian Revolution of 1917; in Germany for twenty years as an *émigré* until he fled Hitler's rise to power in 1939; in America for twenty years until 1959; and finally in Switzerland for eighteen years until his death in July, 1977. He was comfortable in any of these countries, and was equally at ease with their languages, particularly Russian and English.

Strong Opinions offers a better glimpse of the author, perhaps, than would a collection of his letters compiled after his death. It does so because it has been selected and arranged by the author and because it has a focus that a posthumous collection of letters seldom does. One must also say, however, that there is an obvious bias due to the author's control of the contents, but this seems a relatively minor problem. What is much more important is the glimpse into the man himself through interviews for the leading periodicals of the day, for recognized radio and television networks worldwide, and through letters and articles to many outstanding periodicals.

Divided into three sections—interviews, letters, and articles—the collection opens with twenty-two interviews having appeared in such periodicals as *Playboy, Life, The Paris Review, Vogue,* and *The New York Times,* or having been recorded for broadcast on such networks as BBC Television, Swiss Broadcast or the Bayerischer Rundfunk. In the preface to this collection, Nabokov informs the reader that he never gives verbal interviews; all interviews must be done by a method in which the interviewer sends Nabokov a set of written questions which are answered in written form, returned to the interviewer, and finally followed by the interviewer's sending Nabokov a copy of the final form of the interview which Nabokov then edits, corrects, emends, and approves. He does so, he says, because he is constantly rewriting his verbal responses while speaking them. Thus, the reader sees not a spontaneous conversation as he expects, but rather a deliberate and considered literary document. This is both advantageous in that it assures complete accuracy of statement and annoying in that interviews are often effective because of what they reveal beneath the studied surface.

Nabokov, who mastered literature as an art in both Russian and in English, includes in this collection an article for the *Saturday Review* entitled "Inspiration." This piece is one of the highlights of the book. In it Nabokov describes his process of inspiration and creation and offers some conclusions on the nature of inspiration in general. Throughout *Strong Opinions,* Nabokov provides the reader with rare pleasures such as this. Though many of the interviews are repetitious, there are moments in each of them that more than justify their inclusion, whether it is Nabokov describing a dream-process and explaining the basis for dreams in a counter-Freudian way, or reminiscing about the writing of the screenplay for *Lolita.* To see through the criticism of Alfred Appel, Jr., the cinematic, comedic, and slapstick nature of some passages of Nabokov's work is almost priceless. To learn through Nabokov's recollections of his lectures at Cornell that Gregor in Kafka's "Metamorphosis" is not a cockroach at all but a dung beetle of the scarab type is beyond value.

Strong Opinions abounds with these strong opinions, these recollections, these pronouncements on literature, on contemporary society, and on art. In them, the reader sees the whole man, the body of flesh beneath the cloak of the author. This is the book's value and this is why it will be of immeasurable interest to the student of Nabokov. Critics will find their wrists smarting from a sharp crack of the author's ruler, Freudians will find themselves buried beneath the avalanche of the author's impatience, erring scholars will find themselves knocked off their feet with a sure roll of a verbal bowling ball, and shortsighted, closedminded, and uninsightful reviewers will find themselves suffering from literate and witty bee stings from an authorial insect remarkably like a butterfly. No one has ever said that Vladimir Nabokov was not highly opinionated; *Strong Opinions* proves that no one probably ever will. It does prove that the impact that this author has had on literature will continue to be felt after his death, not only in his novels, but also in his thoughts and his public statements. For this reason alone, *Strong Opinions* is an invaluable addition to the bookshelves of Nabokovian volumes.

James R. Van Laan

Sources for Further Study

Atlantic. CCXXXIII, January, 1974, p. 3.

Kirkus Reviews. XLI, October 1, 1973, p. 1143.

New York Review of Books. XXI, November 28, 1974, p. 3.

New York Times Book Review. November 11, 1973, p. 36.

Observer. May 12, 1974, p. 36.

SUNFLOWER SPLENDOR
Three Thousand Years of Chinese Poetry

Editors: Wu-chi Liu and Irving Yucheng Lo
Publisher: Indiana University Press (Bloomington, London). 630 pp. $17.50
Type of work: Poetry

A chronologically ordered and representative selection of about a thousand poems, ranging from pre-Confucian to Mao Tse-tung

Too often in America, Chinese poetry has been allowed to mince forward, immaculately bound, exquisitely printed and illustrated—but somehow precious. The product of Western literati, such books reveal little more than the poetic sensibilities of their translators. Indeed, the so-called translators often work from earlier English versions of the same poems, and without deep study of Chinese culture, much less language, they "render" the poems. Their rendering invariably involves a kind of latter-day Imagism, and demands attenuation of lines in the pious conviction that brevity makes poetry. The products thus created intend to be enigmatic, but are more often merely confusing. Brevity, sharp juxtapositions, and plenty of plum blossoms—these are the qualities Western readers have been led to associate with Chinese poetry. But soy sauce doesn't make a Chinese meal, and plum blossoms—no matter how attenuated the lines—do not make Chinese poetry.

Sunflower Splendor—a large book, quite unlike the slim volumes—now provides another sense of Chinese poetry. A beautiful but no-nonsense book, *Sunflower Splendor: Three Thousand Years of Chinese Poetry* explores the scope of China's literary history and demonstrates variety and vitality of poetic expression. This book is a meal, a banquet, a month's provender compared to the usual Chinese fortune cookie.

Professor Irving Yucheng Lo's Introduction spells out the dominant themes of Chinese poems, and the selections amply, richly illustrate those themes. The reader will find martial poems, incantatory poems, meditative poems, poems dedicated to the stern Confucian moral principles, and love poems. The reader will doubtless find his favorite Chinese poets—Li Po (701-762), for instance, is generously represented—but he will also find new favorites.

Lo and his collaborator Professor Wu-chi Liu allow the diversity of the tradition to emerge from the texts as rendered by translators with varied backgrounds and voices, but they do not allow the translator's personal taste to govern those texts. The Preface and Introduction combine to convince the reader that scholarship informs all the texts; in most cases, that scholarship has also produced enjoyable poems, probably as true to their originals as can be achieved in English.

Both editors of *Sunflower Splendor* enjoy mixed cultural awareness: Chinese by birth and heritage, they have earned advanced degrees in English and understand the structures of both languages. They and their translators sometimes provide a specifically European equivalent of an Eastern concept, rather than to use a term which requires explanation in a note. In one poem, for instance, the River Styx replaces a slightly more difficult and foreign idea. The editors also refuse to waste words proclaiming the "impossibility of translation," though the Introduction says enough about linguistic and cultural differences between East and West to make clear that translations, at best, are equivalent experiences, not duplicates.

Rarely do the poems in *Sunflower Splendor* confuse; when they do, the cause is rarely an addiction to some stylistic peculiarity. Inconsistencies of punctuation among translators cause most of the confusion. Because English readers depend upon subject-verb units to determine rhythm, poems which omit either component need to use punctuation to indicate how units relate to each other.

The Preface reveals that three readers have confirmed the accuracy of all translations and that most poems have passed the test of larger but still select audiences' scrutiny. Such measures prevent idiosyncratic renderings, and they assure that translations will retain the musical quality inherent in Chinese poems. Even the nonspecialist will observe the retention of these and other qualities (including rhyme, alliteration, and assonance). Happily, the editors have omitted the usual tedious notes explaining how the translations capture the qualities of their originals. For a large and comprehensive anthology, *Sunflower Splendor* proves remarkably free of editorial obstructions. Notes appear rarely; they never presume to "interpret" the poem.

Lo's Introduction, though brief, surveys Chinese literary history and says enough about Chinese language and culture to underline thematic differences. (In China, love poems are rarer than poems celebrating friendship, and the love poems generally exercise more restraint than do Western ones.) Lo also manages to indicate what Chinese poetry has in common with poetry of all times, all places. The ancient Chinese ideal of combining self-expression with teaching in poetry parallels precisely Horace's *dulce et utile* dictum reiterated by poets and critics through the ages. Pope's *Essay on Criticism* (1711) stands as a particularly memorable statement of the ideal.

The title *Sunflower Splendor* (taken from Conrad Aiken's "Letter from Li Po") suggests the editors' concern with poetry's essence and the almost miraculous transmutation of daily experience into the ineffable. Selected lines from Aiken's poem serve as epigraph to *Sunflower Splendor,* and inform, particularly for the reader familiar with Li Po, the Introduction's claim that the concrete in poetry almost always reveals a more "lofty intention." Lo quotes the nineteenth century critic Thomas De Quincey to give substance to those lofty intentions: poetry restores the "ideals of justice, of hope, of truth, of mercy, of retribution." What De Quincey said of Homer, Sophocles, and Shakespeare, Lo applies to Chinese poetry.

The editors of *Sunflower Splendor,* working with more than fifty scholar-translators, have aimed at excellence of translation and inclusiveness of coverage. They seek to represent all major genres and periods of Chinese poetry and, within each, to represent "the chief exponent of the major schools." Such inclusiveness tends to reduce the book to a text or a reference work. Serious readers of poetry will agree that Chinese literature deserves publication in English in books other than period or individual author collections, but the editorial goal of *Sunflower Splendor* smacks of the historian's effort to "cover material" even at the cost of focus.

Sunflower Splendor does lack focus, which is especially unfortunate since the Western reader needs help to find direction in so many hundreds of poems. *Sunflower Splendor,* while scrupulous about poems, poets, and periods, lacks a principle of ordering more meaningful than strict chronology. Chapter titles tease the reader who lacks information about Chinese culture. The book overpowers the reader quickly, and the result is satiation. The reader begins to wonder what specific qualities (in Chinese or English) justify a particular poem, very much like others he has just read.

Three thousand years of poetry *must* mean something or *tend* to mean one kind of thing more than others. Still, neither selection nor placement of poems tends to support any more concrete thesis than the general belief that Chinese poetry remains important. Selections and omissions and the resulting emphasis qualifies that thesis; the editors hint that Chinese poetry *used* to be important. An early Chinese poet wrote that he wanted to "reflect and transmit the old/so that its splendor will last a thousand ages." The editors of *Sunflower Splendor* operate from a similar motive. Their classicist stance seems appropriate, but their book needs a counterforce, some further elaboration of the recent past; and the "recent past" in this case means the past six hundred years.

The editors confess in their Preface that they have had to cut by about a third the book they intended. Their final proportions dramatize their classical position. Finding no "major figures" in the last six hundred years, they have all but erased that period. Poems from the Ming (1368-1644), Ch'ing (1644-1911), and the Republic (1912-   ) require but sixty-three of the book's 522 pages of poems. The title of the final chapter manages, rather grandly, to ignore the existence since 1949 of the People's Republic of China, and only nineteen pages are allowed to poets alive during the twentieth century.

Lo's Introduction denies that Chinese poetry has been the province of a special class or group of people; he writes also that "the broad class of people trained in writing poetry included many women." Nevertheless, nearly all the poets in the collection took the proper examinations to qualify for governmental service and all but four of the 137 were men. (Oddly, Hsin Ch'i-chi, a woman about whom Lo has written a book, does not appear; but one woman, who had the distinction of at least being nominated for governmental service, makes up for that omission.) Anonymous poems, including those in the ancient *Shih Ching,* reflect social levels other than the bureaucratic.

Lo's anti-modern bias comes out in what he has to say about several twentieth century writers, Huang Tsun-hsein (1848-1905), Lia Ya-tzu (1887-

1958), and Wang Kuo-wei (1887-1927). He sees them painfully aware of the modern temper, of China's political weakness, and of their "estrangement from modern society." Poems like Wang Kuo-wei's "To Try To Find" poorly illustrate this wasteland judgment; that poem takes a toughminded, wry attitude toward the imponderables poets continue to ponder. No period in Chinese or any other history lacks poems painfully aware of their age's temper.

Representing any national poetry over a three-thousand-year span obliges an editor to regard mere centuries as negligible, and it may tempt that editor to skim over larger blocks. Still, the nonspecialist may be excused for wanting to know more about China's poetry after 1368, and in particular more about poetry after China became actively involved with the Western world. Even more, the reader living in the final quarter of the twentieth century and observing the growing power of the People's Republic of China may be excused for having a more than passing interest in what Chinese writers today are thinking. Chairman's Mao's poems, which end *Sunflower Splendor,* reveal what was once the "official" temper of the People's Republic, but those poems no longer speak for China's leadership or population. Mao is dead, and the government has rapidly achieved stability after his death. These facts and the facts of American withdrawal from Vietnam and increased Chinese belligerence toward American diplomacy late in 1977 deny China's political weakness.

Mao urged young Chinese not to emulate his example in writing classical poetry; perhaps they have taken his advice, but one wonders what, if anything, Chinese poets are writing now. Mao's poems in *Sunflower Splendor* strike revolutionary notes, both overtly and in their insistence that one must live in the present and ignore the past. Mao's view is ultimately anti-classicist. If contemporary scholarship does not find a progression of a lively classical tradition into China's present, it should indicate what has displaced that tradition.

One of China's earliest poems, taken from the *Shih Ching,* includes the line, "With ancient people did all this rightly begin." The poem alludes to the ancient origins of ritual and poetic celebration, of which many poems in the *Shih Ching* are examples. The *Shih Ching,* which took shape between the twelfth and seventh centuries before Christ, provides a beautiful example of poetry's antiquity, but because poetry began with ancient people seems poor reason to suggest it ends there.

Liu and Lo have done a great service in extending the types and quantity of Chinese poetry available in good translation; their book was out of stock by the summer of 1977, indicating a ready market for Chinese poetry. To suggest that the book would be better with fewer poems, and ordered to show some progression or regression, does not diminish its accomplishment.

Leon V. Driskell

Sources for Further Study

Booklist. LXXII, April 15, 1976, p. 1164.

Choice. XIII, April, 1976, p. 232.

Christian Science Monitor. LXVIII, January 16, 1976, p. 30.

Library Journal. CI, March 1, 1976, p. 721.

New York Times Book Review. December 21, 1975, p. 1.

Virginia Quarterly Review. LII, Spring, 1976, p. 48.

THE SURVIVOR
An Anatomy of Life in the Death Camps

Author: Terrence Des Pres
Publisher: Oxford University Press (New York). 218 pp. $10.00
Type of work: Psychological study

A sensitive exploration of how and why people responded as they did to the experience of imprisonment in Nazi concentration camps

From our positions within comfortable lives, we have difficulty understanding that for those who have come through terrifyingly dangerous ordeals "mere survival" is not so "mere"; for them "survival" equals existence, without qualifications, without the cultural trappings that for individuals in more normal circumstances elevate life to pleasurable levels. In *The Survivor: An Anatomy of Life in the Death Camps*, Terrence Des Pres examines existence in the state of extended extremity to clarify our understanding of how groups and individuals have responded and what the implications of their responses might be.

He begins by discussing the concept of survival as it appears in the literature of such writers as Camus, Malamud, and Solzhenitsyn. In doing so, he delineates a significant difference between the main figure in survival literature and our traditional concept of the hero:

> If by heroism we mean the dramatic defiance of superior individuals, then the age of heroism is gone. If we have in mind glory and grand gesture, the survivor is not a hero. He or she is anyone who manages to stay alive in body and spirit, enduring dread and hopelessness without the loss of will to carry on in human ways.

Another important difference separates the two types: *survivors* would choose another fate from that of living in an imperiled condition; they do not actively choose to place their lives on the line. However, unlike traditional heroes, that is where they remain until forces beyond their control release them.

Sustaining many survivors is what Des Pres calls the "will to bear witness." As a result, a wealth of literature documenting experiences in Nazi and Soviet concentration camps is available. To this Des Pres turns from the "ideal lucidity of fiction" in order to represent the nature of the survivors' testimony and to place this testimony in a proper perspective. He quotes often from numerous personal accounts, finding at every turn that when "confronting radical evil, men and women instinctively feel the desire to call, to warn, to communicate their shock." Survivors feel compelled to make the truth known, to dispel the pervading illusion that man is humane enough to forego atrocity, and to a very great extent, this can be understood as a survival technique or mission generating purpose in victims with no other hope or direction.

The documentary results are seen by Des Pres as "group portraits, in which the writer's personal experience is representative and used to provide perspective on the common plight." Des Pres reacts strongly to the idea that the survivor feels required to "justify his own survival in the face of others' deaths," an idea referred to as "survival guilt." He maintains such an idea is entirely negative and would have to develop after the experience, when in reality most survivors began their accounting long before release from the camps, many during the early stages of imprisonment. Further, account after account underscores the survivors' desire to speak for their fellow prisoners and impress upon a basically skeptical world "objective conditions of evil" which dominated the entire population of the camps in insistent ways. The survivors' point is to involve us directly: "in the literature of survival we find an image of things so grim, so heartbreaking, so starkly unbearable, that inevitably the survivor's scream begins to be our own."

Reading the numerous excerpts from these books, we can hardly fail to react in horror, aghast at the filth and degradation to which human beings were systematically subjected. Des Pres argues convincingly against a pervasive view that prisoners reverted to "infantile behavior" in the Nazi death camps. He says, "Here, as in general from the psychoanalytical point of view, context is not considered. The fact that the survivor's situation was itself abnormal is simply ignored." Bruno Bettelheim, in particular, comes under fire for advancing the case for "infantilism." Clearly the record as compiled by the bulk of camp survivors creates the most abnormal of contexts, and we must agree with Des Pres that prisoners "were the deliberate targets of excremental assault. Defilement was a constant threat, a condition of life from day to day, and at any moment it was liable to take abruptly vicious and sometimes fatal forms." For killing souls, humiliation and debasement were effective tools employed by the SS because resulting disgust and self-loathing among the prisoners could have only negative effects on their ability to endure; excremental assault aimed at depressing morale, destroying self-esteem, eliminating respect for one another. In addition, Des Pres suggests that when the prisoners appeared less human it was easier for the SS to do their job: killing bodies.

To counter this methodical assault, prisoners sought fundamental ways to maintain dignity: "washing, if only in a ritual sense—and quite apart from reasons of health—was something prisoners needed to do. They found it necessary to survival, odd as that may seem, and those who stopped soon died." Within the exceedingly abnormal conditions of the extermination camps, where essential bodily functions were denied or made nearly impossible to perform, the seeming fixation with maintaining some semblance of cleanliness appears entirely normal. Without taking into consideration the abnormality of conditions, psychoanalysis of the survivors' actions distorts perception of those actions; it denies the dignity of man in extremity, viewing him as a character continually controlled by his nightmares.

Des Pres presents the "nightmare" of the death camps with frequent passages from firsthand accounts, which create an indelible image of horror.

But Des Pres's inclusion of such passages is far from gratuitous, for he seeks to reveal essential information. For example, at one point he uses a striking group of excerpts as he identifies the phenomenon of *"initial collapse."* He also illustrates why newcomers to the camps had the highest death rate: "prisoners 'died soon' from a complex of conditions and forces which nothing in the world of their lives had prepared them to face or even imagine." He notes that prisoners found themselves within the "dream of Hell," an actualization of that "which for millennia had haunted the Western consciousness."

From this shock of recognition every survivor managed to turn, through a process of healing, toward "a capacity for realism, impersonal and without the least illusion, a realism which one survivor has called 'the inhuman frankness of Auschwitz.' " In this turn Des Pres sees great significance, a valuable clue to the function of intelligence in the state of extremity, where "the survivor's will to go on is illogical, irrational, stupid with another wisdom." Rather than dwelling on odds for survival, human intelligence must "make the most of each day's opportunity for getting through that day." Ultimately, Des Pres surmises, "life is existence laboring to sustain itself, repairing, defending, healing."

Sustaining life in the camps demanded cooperative action, and one point Des Pres makes abundantly clear: "prisoners in the concentration camps helped each other." The term *organize* was used in reference to every activity imaginable, especially activities deemed illegal by camp authorities: organizing depended on teamwork, and every prisoner had to make crucial decisions about sharing, about acting to help others, about whether to attempt the effort of survival alone or in helpless company. Deciding to survive in company, most prisoners give evidence to an important observation Des Pres makes: "that the need *to* help is as basic as the need *for* help, a fact which points to the radically social nature of life in extremity." Order prevailed in the camps despite the popular assumption that all was chaos. Certainly the period of initial collapse was real, but it passed. More generally, hysteria gave way to realism, so that an elementary kind of order based on spontaneous involvement in one anothers' lives prevailed. Giving and receiving were fundamental responses to circumstance; and a basic truth the biological sciences reveal was borne out: life depends on systems.

All this runs counter to Bruno Bettelheim's application of a psychoanalytical model to the concentration-camp experience, and Des Pres continually calls Bettelheim's objective in *The Informed Heart,* to compare the survivor's experience with the predicament of modern man in "mass society," invalid because our lives do not hinge on life or death. In general, Des Pres finds that Bettelheim's claims are not substantiated in the bulk of testimony by survivors, particularly that of Eugen Kogon, a member of the underground from the beginning to the end of Buchenwald, where Bettelheim was imprisoned for a relatively short time early in the camp's history.

Behaviorism also comes under fire for its failure to represent adequately camp behavior, for "like the psychoanalytical approach, behaviorism does not take into account the duality of action in extremity." By assuming environment is all-powerful and the human self is a function of its world, behaviorism sees man as a victim. Des Pres asserts that, in a sense, the camps were a kind of experiment, perhaps the closest thing to a perfect Skinner Box: negative reinforcers being pain and death, positive reinforcers being food and life. But he notes, almost defiantly, that survivors are proof the experiment failed.

As such, survivors evidence a biological rather than psychological phenomenon. By passing *through* Hell, they have negated "the single belief, as old as our Western culture, that human bondage can be transcended only in death." As a result, they give new value to life, a new meaning to the phrase "mere survival." Having confronted the Hell archetype's embodiment, survivors allow us to see that "the archetypes of doom are, if not cancelled, at least less powerful in their authority over our perceptions." Man *will* sustain his existence because of his biological capacity to do so, and not because of a psychic transcendence through physical death. Driven to extremity, the human individual falls back upon biological controls which underlie all his actions.

Conditions in the death camps necessitated certain behavior traceable to our ancient beginnings when all human existence was dominated by the essential problem of surviving in a totally hostile environment, when the human being was no more than a biological gamble. Des Pres asserts that the basic characteristics which sustain life in extremity also define us as human:

> . . . we may . . . speculate that through long periods of extremity, survival depends on life literally—life, that is, as the biologists see it, not as a state or condition but as a set of activities evolved through time in successful response to crisis, the sole purpose of which is to keep going.

From his extensive evidence, Des Pres finds that men and women "tend to preserve themselves in ways recognizably human" even within horribly dehumanizing conditions. Further, the contention that behavior is "biologically determined" assumes several principles considered by the biological sciences to be "facts of life": (1) almost all behavior directly or indirectly serves the general cause of survival; (2) particular patterns of behavior are the outcome of millions of years of trial-and-error experience passed down through the organism's genes; (3) primary behavior is innately inherited "life experience" of each line of descent; and (4) these facts apply to man as surely as they do to all other life forms.

That man cannot escape his biological makeup is, ultimately, his saving characteristic. Civilization, the accumulation of culture, tends to sheath man's primal nature, allows him to forget his origins and, to a very great extent, weakens his resistance to the pressures presented by extreme circumstances. But when normal conditions are stripped away, when life is reduced to absolute necessity devoid of cultural trappings, man as an organism governed by his biological experience is revealed. Des Pres suggests with certainty that a large part of man's biological nature is social:

> . . . the depth and durability of man's social nature may be gauged by the fact that conditions in the concentration camps were designed to turn prisoners against each other; but that in a multitude of ways, men and women persisted in social acts.

Again, this can best be understood in the context of biology, for "man is the culmination of a tendency toward social organization which appears everywhere in the biosphere." This tendency should be recognized as an essential survival technique when we consider that "protracted death-threat is the condition which brings social instincts to their strongest pitch. . . . The more threat from without, the more 'solidarity' from within." Moreover, although survivors might undergo drastic immediate adjustments to maintain existence, their efforts are mainly to "keep themselves *fundamentally* unchanged by the pressures to which they respond."

What emerges, finally, from *The Survivor* is a heartening view of man. Despite the vivid accounts of atrocity, the brutal images of prisoners undergoing demoralizing and destructive treatment, Des Pres draws conclusions about the stamina of man as an organism, the stamina to maintain his humanness in the face of overwhelming assault, stamina derived from the experience of human life as it has incorporated fundamental social knowledge within its biological evolution. *The Survivor: An Anatomy of Life in the Death Camps* is an assertion that the human condition is not the condition of a victim but of a survivor acting with total realism to sustain the fabric of human existence.

Gary B. Blank

Sources for Further Study

Best Sellers. XXXVI, June, 1976, p. 92.

Book World. March 21, 1976, p. 1.

Commonweal. CIII, May 21, 1976, p. 344.

Economist. CCLIX, April 17, 1976, p. 108.

New York Review of Books. XXIII, March 4, 1976, p. 19.

Spectator. CCXXXVI, April 24, 1976, p. 24.

Virginia Quarterly Review. LII, Summer, 1976, p. 90.

THE TAKEOVER

Author: Muriel Spark (1918-   )
Publisher: The Viking Press (New York). 266 pp. $8.95
Type of work: Novel
Time: 1972-1975
Locale: Nemi, Italy

A novel of the values and social interaction of the rich in contemporary Italy

> Principal characters:
> MAGGIE RADCLIFFE, an American heiress
> HUBERT MALLINDAINE, her once close friend who has since lost her favor
> BERTO, her new, aristocratic husband
> LAURO MORETTI, her enterprising servant

Muriel Spark's *The Takeover,* the author's fourteenth novel, is a fine and subtle rendition in novel form of the witty comedy of manners whose tradition began during the Restoration period of the late seventeenth century. The tradition has surfaced in drama several times since then throughout literary history, each time with a fresh perspective underscoring several basic ideas. Its counterpart in novel form, never really disappearing, yet at some times more successful than at others, shares the same premises: the affectations of an elite social group are both characteristic and valid material for satire; satire and the ambience in the novel's setting are to be emphasized over the significance of plot; and life is seen through a comic realism that focuses on the social situation, often with a slightly cynical slant.

Spark has selected a perfect backdrop for these various purposes to converge: contemporary Italy of 1972-1975. *The Takeover* slips in nicely with more somber Italian cinematic counterparts commenting on Italian upper class lifestyles of the same time, for example, Wertmuller's *Swept Away* and Visconti's *Un gruppo di famiglia in interno.* This is a period of tremendous political and sociological upheavals and reversals, witnessing, among other severe changes, the plunge in value of the lira as well as the ushering in and triumph of Italy's own form of Communism. As Spark states, ". . . a complete mutation of our means of nourishment had already come into being where the concept of money and property were concerned, a complete mutation not merely to be defined as a collapse of the capitalist system, or a global recession, but such a sea-change in the nature of reality as could not have been envisaged by Karl Marx or Sigmund Freud."

Yet, unlike other artistic interpretations of Italy's transformations in the first half of this decade, Spark's novel does not center strictly on the Italian upper class. The central figure is Maggie, an American whose wealth extends beyond comprehension. Clustered around her is an international assortment of the privileged who are equally culpable of her monied callousness. Therefore, the novel is not limited to being a mere study of Italian misfortune or

American crassness—it is instead a story of the complexities of maneuvering the rules of rich living in such a way that the inevitable clashes with the rules governing the rest of society are less than devastating.

Maggie has bought several parcels of land in mythically entrenched Nemi, not far from Rome. Two existing structures have been carefully renovated and remodeled; on the third piece of property Maggie has constructed a large villa to the specifications of one Hubert Mallindaine (some say that he has altered the last five letters of his name in order to make his claimed direct lineage from the goddess Diana less obvious), an individual who figures heavily, yet not intimately, in Maggie's past. Maggie's affections have recently turned. She has married a wealthy Italian who now urges her to evict Hubert from her property since he has refused not only to vacate civilly, but also to pay rent for the time he has occupied the house. Hubert has nested himself down firmly and comfortably pulled the complexities of Italian law around himself as protection. Furthermore, Maggie's husband, the Marchese Adalberto di Tullio-Friole, discourages Maggie from attempting to evict Hubert through the court system for fear of creating a scandal for which his family would suffer greatly. What follows is a series of events on the parts of others to exploit Maggie's vulnerability while she, in the meanwhile, attempts to reclaim her house through existing *sotto tavola* methods.

It is through this strange and contorted network of conventionalities that Spark most skillfully executes her satire on manners, propriety, and other accepted codes of conduct of the wealthy classes. The wealth of Maggie and her familiars forces them to maintain a certain self-protective distance from the rest of society, who occupy lower positions on the social scale. Lauro, one of Maggie's servants recently lured from Hubert and his dwindling resources, however, provides a perfect buffer between these distinctions for one such as Maggie who wishes to maintain the distance but who knows she must keep an open line of communication if she is to utilize successfully the system's shadiness to regain her absconded properties. Consequently, Lauro performs the duties of butler with impeccable precision, waiting patiently behind half-open doors to attend to any need of his employers. Yet, at the same time, he is willing and able to assume the role of surreptitious lover for Maggie and any number of women when the occasion arises.

But Lauro also demonstrates the difficulties and contradictions inherent in the ideologies of the present-day Italian working class. Although Italy's Communism is not only viable but in many cases successful and quite beneficial, it seems that its true defining characteristics have not been able to solidify in the minds of Italy's intelligentsia without confusion. Considerable contradiction exists: intellectuals and workers cry for fair wages, equality, and dissolution of Italy's wealth; but more often than coincidence will allow, these same people scramble for the outward appearances of the idle rich—jaded social affectations, fine cars, showpiece homes where whispers disturb nothing, and expensive clothes worn less than a season.

Lauro embodies these contradictions. First of all, he is a servant of working class origins. But second, he is revered by other members of his class since he has had the experience not only of observing how the wealthy class lives, but of living roughly the same lifestyle they do with the same expectations. The mark of success in serving the wealthy class is being able to expect nothing but exquisite service of oneself for one's employers, as well as being accustomed to expecting equally superb surroundings in food, lodging, climate, and diversion. Lauro has assimilated these values not only into his work ethic but also into his personal repertoire. As a result, his fiancée's family's preparations for the wedding with their attention to every last detail of nicety revolts him: "In the world Lauro knew, there was silence in between the talk, and afterwards music and space, and nobody talked of the food at all; they took the good food for granted and if the men discussed wines or the women certain dishes, it was all like a subject that you study in a university like art history or wildlife."

If there are any fools in Spark's novel, they are fools only because they lack enterprise and are incapable of manipulating the existing structure to their own purposes. The social-legal-political structure as a whole is impossible; but to someone who is able to compare the structure to his own designs point by point, it is a useful tool toward a desired goal. Only two characters appear to fit this description, but it only appears so because their own system has manipulated the entire world to its own end for centuries. These characters are the two American Jesuit priests, Father Cuthbert Plaice and Father Gerard Harvey. The two scurry about on the outskirts of the story completely absorbed either in their own personal ends or in the sheer delight of enjoying the visible results of the unseen intrigue that lies within. Although Father Gerard ostensibly is involved in his research into the "ancient ecological cults," both are actually quite free to dally in virtually anything that strikes their fancy. They do not have to learn how to comprehend and manipulate the system; they have been duping the world for centuries.

But Fathers Cuthbert and Gerard function in the novel in ways similar to Lauro, who bridges the gap between the working classes and the idle rich classes. The fathers with their dauntless enthusiasm for anything that succeeds in keeping them amused bridge the gap between the yoking demands of the Catholic religion, which still manages to keep a vice grip on Italy despite recent social and political progress, and the opportunistic cult of the Friends of Diana proselytized by Hubert Mallindaine.

Hubert believes that the greatness of his religion depends on the fact that it is somehow older, simpler, and consequently more true than that which is offered by other religions available today. His actual belief in what he is doing is unquestionable. But regardless of its origins and its unfettered existence, his cult of Diana, too, has succumbed to the corruption which characterizes other religions. This is so because Hubert himself is corrupt, and Hubert is corrupt because he is obliged to live in a precarious society in which only those who are capable of a discreet corruption survive.

Corruption is the key word to understanding the machinations of contemporary society epitomized by Italy, the same Italy which epitomized all the beauty, art, culture and idealism of the world in the past. But just as one finds it necessary to redefine the boundaries and concepts of Communism when one discusses it in relation to Italy, so must one learn to redefine the term "corruption." The corruption here is not based on malice or immorality or even amorality. Instead, it is an actual necessity since it is the same corruption that permeates and in a sense gives shape to the entire culture. And just as fish cannot be taught with patient understanding to exist out of water, neither can an individual exist in this epitomized culture without the adaptive mechanism of an inherent corruption in his character.

Hubert succeeds in living in and with this corruption for several years. Although he eventually loses control over his position in this society, he never actually succumbs because he possesses the survival mechanism. Lauro, pouting though he is over minor setbacks, succeeds beautifully since he not only understands the mechanism, but he also lives, breathes, and exudes it. With the exception of careless Coco, only Maggie comes close to actually being destroyed by this aspect of her society. But she experiences her near-miss precisely because she has allowed her money to isolate her from recognizing what the machinations of that society are.

Initially, she contented herself with extramarital affairs and slick avoidances of bothersome conventions, claiming her right to ignoring the norm by virtue of her wealth—she had never been exposed to convention and therefore could not be expected to conform to it. However, when she suddenly realizes one day that she has nearly lost every penny she once had, she at the same time realizes that she is in danger of losing that protective device that prevents the necessity of learning convention. Her solution to this perplexing dilemma is simple; she exposes herself just enough, like a shy girl sampling the water at the shore, to learn what conventions might help her regain what society's corruption is about to take from her. And what she extracts from this experience is simple: it is corruption itself.

So, by the close of the novel, each of the primary characters has not only experienced but also wielded corruption to one degree or another; each has achieved his goal to various extents. Order, however inequitable that order once was, has been restored once each of the characters has been purged in the cleansing bath of corruption. There is a contorted form of justice to this resolution. It is a justice because each character exits with essentially the same properties he rightfully entered with (Maggie's property, which had never been purchased through legal means, has been restored to the rightful owners only in turn to be inherited by cunning and clever Lauro) and no one is punished. Punishment has been avoided because the scales of justice were able to return to their rightful position without the intervention of police or law. Consequently, even Coco's kidnaping and ransom bespeak of justice without punishment, since all that is necessary for him to do to be sprung from captivity is to pay the ransom to his abductors, from whom the ransom money was stolen in the first place. The drama has ended, resolution is imminent, and the proverbial "happy ending" is inevitable.

Bonnie Fraser

Sources for Further Study

America. CXXXV, October 2, 1976, p. 196.

Atlantic. CCXXXVIII, November, 1976, p. 116.

Critic. XXXV, Winter, 1976, p. 88.

New Statesman. XCI, June 4, 1976, p. 746.

New Yorker. LII, November 29, 1976, p. 166.

New York Review of Books. XXIII, November 11, 1976, p. 30.

Times Literary Supplement. June 4, 1976, p. 665.

TERRA NOSTRA

Author: Carlos Fuentes (1928-   )
Translated from the Spanish by Margaret Sayers Peden
Publisher: Farrar, Straus and Giroux (New York). 778 pp. $15.00
Type of work: Novel
Time: Primarily the sixteenth century, but with important action in the first and twentieth centuries
Locale: Spain, the Netherlands, Mexico, Italy, Palestine, France

A fictionalized history of Spanish and Spanish-American cultures as examples of the dialectical and cyclical patterns of human history in general

> *Principal characters:*
> FELIPE, King of Spain
> ISABEL, his wife, Queen of Spain
> JOANNA REGINA, his mother
> GUZMAN, his secretary
> THE BASTARDS, his three brothers
> POLLO PHOIBEE, a man in Paris
> CELESTINA, a peasant girl, painter, and witch
> TIBERIUS CAESAR, Emperor of Rome

Terra Nostra by Carlos Fuentes is an epic novel about Spain, Spanish America, and the world. The setting, though localized in the Escorial of sixteenth century Spain, constantly shifts from place to place and period to period. The novel opens in Paris in the year 1999, then moves to sixteenth century Spain, where the major action unfolds despite the frequent shifts to other times and places, such as pre-Columbian Mexico, and the Italy and Palestine of Tiberius Caesar. Interestingly, these times and places are not strictly those of history, for in this novel we encounter a Spain ruled by the Hapsburg, Felipe (ostensibly Philip II), and Isabel (Elizabeth) Tudor; we also find that the New World has yet to be discovered despite the "late date." By manipulating history in this way, Fuentes examines its many possibilities— what might have been. If events had taken alternate courses, if men had made different decisions, if circumstances had been substantially different, what would have happened? Yet Fuentes is not so much interested in what would have happened, as he is in the historical process itself. In *Terra Nostra* we find the Hegelian process of thesis and antithesis followed by synthesis, but this pattern is not progressive; it is merely repetitious. In particulars—characters, events, places—history offers innumerable possibilities, but in its general pattern, it does not change.

When the action first shifts to Spain, Felipe's subjects are completing the Escorial, his huge palace which is also a mausoleum. To Felipe this palace represents the unity he has brought to Spain and the Christian world. Having achieved this unity, Felipe yearns for death and his reward in the afterlife. Actually, he yearns to be taken out of the changing world and placed into an unchanging heaven because he fears that before he dies the religious and national unity he has created will be destroyed. However, his greatest fear, fueled by the very heresies he has suppressed, is that his concept of an unchanging heaven may be false. This fear becomes obsessive when Felipe climbs a staircase leading out of his private chapel, and looks into a hand mirror he is carrying. As he ascends the stairs, he watches his image age step by step until he views his own corpse; however, not until he climbs farther up does he become truly frightened. Indeed he is terrified, when instead of seeing himself in heaven, he sees himself reborn as a wolf, and hunted by his own descendants. Thus, Fuentes, through the techniques of magical realism, develops the idea that personal history moves in cycles similar to those of history in general.

As a young man Felipe had discussed with a group of idealistic young people the possibility of a new world where freedom and variety would flourish. Although he shared the pleasures of free love and discourse with this group, he deeply disagreed with their ideals. Finally he revealed his authoritarian nature when he crushed a Protestant rebellion in Flanders, and defeated the forces of freedom and multiplicity that threatened his concept of order and unity. However, Fuentes makes it clear that the forces of multiplicity are rising from within the very unity of Felipe's world (the thesis producing its antithesis). Within his very palace, the forces of anarchy are embodied in his own mother and his own wife. His mother, Joanna the Mad Lady (historically the grandmother of Philip II), wanders from city to city with her entourage bearing the embalmed body of her late husband. His wife, Isabel, lives in the only luxurious chamber within the austere palace that is slowly driving her insane. Both these women suffer from the rigid world view of their husbands; both reflect the growing discontent felt by the workers, the townsmen, and the lesser nobles, including Felipe's secretary, Guzman.

Into this situation Fuentes introduces three archetypal characters—the Pilgrim, Don Juan, and the Idiot Prince—each with a red cross on his back and six toes on each foot. These extremely complex characters provide the links between the main plot and the subplots, between the novel's different times and places; in a sense they are not characters at all, but roles that may be played by specific individuals in specific times. These characters encompass the many desirable as well as undesirable possibilities of individual personalities and actions that constantly recur in history. But these possibilities are just that—possibilities. Because they often contradict one another, in any one period only a few possible personalities and actions can actually become real. Once they do, however, their reality is challenged by the many possibilities that have not been realized; these challenges must naturally arise from within the existing order, otherwise they remain purely imaginary. Thus, we have the thesis and its antithesis, the unity of reality versus the multiplicity of other possibilities, Felipe's world versus that of the rebels. Since the Pilgrim, Don Juan, and the Idiot Prince turn out to be Felipe's bastard brothers and Felipe has no son, Guzman, Isabel, and the Mad Lady each see the possibility of placing his own favorite on the throne.

Just as this threat to the unity of Felipe's kingdom arises, his entire world is challenged by the news of the discovery of a new world. He receives the news from the Pilgrim who at this point encompasses the role of Columbus. The Pilgrim recounts his journey to the New World, to Mexico, and as he does this, we find him encompassing the roles of Cortes and the mythic Quetzalcoatl and Tezcatlipoca. When the Pilgrim arrives in Mexico he is accepted as the god of freedom and peace who has returned from the east to reclaim his kingdom. Quetzalcoatl is the antithesis of Tezcatlipoca, a violent and tyrannical god, and the Pilgrim is pleased to find that he will bring good to Mexico. However, the Pilgrim soon finds that he is actually a synthesis of the good and evil gods. Because of the magic of this mysterious land, he had forgotten his destructive role as Cortes. Having violated his own ideals of freedom and peace, the Pilgrim must again turn his kingdom over to Tezcatlipoca, the authoritarian god who clearly resembles Felipe. The historical cycle is complete, but there has been no progress. Multiplicity and unity, freedom and rigidity, good and evil, though continually in conflict, are inextricably bound in Spain, in Spanish America, and in the individual.

The discovery of the New World with its pagan ways, the arrival of pretenders to Felipe's throne, and finally the threat of mass rebellion due to the oppressive monarchy, demoralize the King. The unity he created is being destroyed; he secludes himself in his palace and devotes himself to prayer and religious doubts. At last the rebellion explodes. The forces of multiplicity, Jews, Moors, heretics, and workers, inspired by the Pilgrim and led by Guzman, break into the palace and destroy Felipe's power, but they are betrayed from within. Guzman, seeing Felipe's power broken, takes command of the King's forces and crushes the rebellion, thus establishing a new "bureaucratic" unity with Felipe as a figurehead. Guzman then proceeds to the New World where he imposes Spanish rule. The cycle is again completed. But the forces of multiplicity will trouble Felipe again, for Isabel Tudor has fled back to England where she will seek the destruction of Spain.

After the rebellion Felipe discovers two strange bottles left by his bastard brothers. Inside one he finds a scroll that concerns the last days of Tiberius Caesar; inside the other he discovers an account of a strange war in a jungle. These two subplots, like the Pilgrim's tale of Mexico, echo the major theme: like Felipe and Tezcatlipoca, Tiberius heads a unified empire threatened on all sides by dissent. Felipe understands the narrative concerning Rome, but he can make nothing of the second scroll, for that scroll reveals the future: a strange jungle war is being waged by Mexican rebels against the United States, the twentieth century empire. A third bottle which Felipe never sees contains a scroll narrating his own story. The three bottled scrolls, like the three Bastards, are devices used by Fuentes to link the different sections of the novel. The three scrolls are histories which, when viewed together by an astute observer, reveal the general pattern of history, a cyclical pattern of never-ending conflict. This pattern is rarely perceived by the participants in the particular events because they think of themselves as unique since they have forgotten the past and do not know the future. While Felipe and Tiberius are unique possibilities realized by history, they are also specific manifestations of a more general type represented by Tezcatlipoca and the Pilgrim. It would seem, then, that they as well as the rebels are determined by history to act out certain roles in the cyclical pattern. The inability of either the forces of unity or those of multiplicity to win a permanent victory, does not cause despair and halt the cycle because succeeding generations forget the past and resurrect old ideals. Felipe's greatest fear, that he will be reborn, arises because he suspects the truth. Having discussed the problem as a youth, having doubted his own religion, and having read the scrolls, Felipe becomes suspicious, but through an act of will he maintains his ideal of a final unity. Nevertheless, in death he must face the truth: he becomes a wolf wandering through the Valley of the Fallen in twentieth century Spain.

Terra Nostra ends where it began, in Paris in 1999. Pollo Phoibee, who witnesses the decline of Paris at the beginning of the novel, now looks out on a nearly dead world. In an effort to control overpopulation, authoritarian governments have allowed starvation and disease and ordered mass executions. The resulting ecological disaster has caused the virtual extinction of humanity. Only Pollo and Celestina remain. Celestina, named after Rojas' famed procuress, is another of Fuentes' archetypal characters. Like the Bastards, she is a "generalized" character who appears in specific forms throughout the novel. As a maiden dressed as a page, she meets the Pilgrim in Spain; as a Mexican goddess, she meets him in the New World; and as a painter, she meets Pollo in Paris. Each time she offers guidance and hope by helping them learn from the past. Her tattooed lips, like the bottled scrolls, reveal the cyclical pattern of history. She helps the Pilgrim remember parts of his past, and finally she helps Pollo recall his entire past—that he is the Pilgrim, and as such has had a variety of past lives. Yet, in spite of the number of possible lives he has experienced, he has always followed the circular pattern of betraying his own freedom as soon as he gains it. Celestina offers him the chance to escape the pattern completely. By remembering the past as a whole, by recalling the cyclical pattern of history, one can escape it and hopefully reach the millennium. Like Rojas' procuress, Celestina offers man a chance to achieve what he most desires, a chance to escape rigidity and to love others freely. In the final scene Pollo and Celestina become a new Adam and Eve, but as they mate, they fuse into a new humanity whose differences are accepted, a humanity that can live in harmony. Fuentes realizes that only a drastic mutation in the evolution of human history will make this possible; however, he accepts the chance of such a mutation as sufficient cause for optimism. Nevertheless, we can only wonder if the "new" pattern established by Pollo and Celestina is not merely another synthesis containing the seeds of its own destruction.

In the construction of *Terra Nostra* itself, Fuentes tries to show that multiplicity can exist within a harmonious whole. He discards, as an example of rigidity, the idea that a novel must be tightly unified. We have already seen that he shatters time, space, and action. However, he also causes a disruption of language with his unorthodox punctuation and shifting point of view, and uses such literary figures as Don Quijote and Don Juan Tenorio, or such historical figures as Sor Juana Inés de la Cruz, Carlota and Maximilian, and Francisco Franco, in unique ways. *Terra Nostra* is a much more complex novel than the foregoing interpretation may seem to have implied. As a result, the novel is extremely rich, an epic in every sense of the word. Yet, Fuentes pays a price for this emphasis on variety. The final impression left by the novel is one of confusion, rather than harmony: images clash, action and characters overlap, and communication breaks down. Although there is definitely a major theme which runs through and unifies the work, that theme is often obscured by secondary ideas; this is especially unfortunate because the novel is very long and does not encourage a second reading. However, the novel's greatest problem concerns characterization: despite the multitude of characters, not one of them is a fully integrated person. Because of Fuentes' stress on archetypes, his characters lack individuality, and the novel as a whole completely lacks psychological depth. Consequently, *Terra Nostra* challenges the intellect, but leaves the emotions unmoved.

John R. Chávez

Sources for Further Study

Book World. October 24, 1976, p. F1.
Christian Science Monitor. LXVIII, November 17, 1976, p. 18.
Guardian Weekly. CXV, November 14, 1976, p. 18.
New Republic. CLXXVI, April 9, 1977, p. 30.
New York Times Book Review. November 7, 1976, p. 3.
Newsweek. LXXXVIII, November 1, 1976, p. 84.
Saturday Review. IV, October 30, 1976, p. 38.

A TEXAS TRILOGY

Author: Preston Jones (1936-   )
Publisher: Hill and Wang (New York). 338 pp. $15.00
Type of work: Drama
Time: 1953, 1962
Locale: Bradleyville, Texas

Three serious comedies about the desperate loneliness and lack of fulfillment in three people of two generations over three decades in a small West Texas town

The Last Meeting of the Knights of the White Magnolia

Principal characters:

RAMSEY-EYES BLANKENSHIP, the black custodian of the Cattleman's Hotel

RUFE PHELPS, a refinery worker

OLIN POTTS, a cotton farmer

RED GROVER, the owner of a small bar

L. D. ALEXANDER, the manager of A.B.C. Supermarket

COLONEL J. C. KINKAID, a retired U.S. Army Colonel and owner of Cattleman's Hotel

SKIP HAMPTON, a Texaco service station attendant

LONNIE ROY MCNEIL, a pipe fitter at Silver City

MILO CRAWFORD, a clerk at Bradleyville Grain & Feed

Lu Ann Hampton Laverty Oberlander

Principal characters:

LU ANN HAMPTON

SKIP HAMPTON, her brother

CLAUDINE HAMPTON, her mother, a nurse

BILLY BOB WORTMAN, Lu Ann's boyfriend

DALE LAVERTY, Skip's army buddy, a truck driver who becomes Lu Ann's husband

CORKY OBERLANDER, a dirt inspector

MILO CRAWFORD

CHARMAINE, Lu Ann's teen-age daughter by Laverty

The Oldest Living Graduate

Principal characters:

COLONEL J. C. KINKAID, the oldest living graduate of Mirabeau B. Lamar Military Academy

FLOYD KINKAID, his son

MAUREEN KINKAID, Floyd's wife

CLARENCE SICKENGER, Floyd's business partner

MARTHA ANN SICKENGER, Clarence's wife

MIKE TREMAINE, a hired hand

MAJOR LEROY W. KETCHUM, Commandant of the military academy

CADET WHOPPER TURNBULL, a student at the academy

CLAUDINE HAMPTON, a practical nurse

As with everything else in Texas, when you fail, you fail big, especially in the small town that superhighways have bypassed. The lower-middle-class citizens of Bradleyville fail emotionally, intellectually, and spiritually partly because they have failed materially; the upper-class citizens fail partly because they have *succeeded* materially. It is the smallness of the town, its social and cultural scope, that breeds a smallness in the citizens—that isolates, limits, and stunts them. *A Texas Trilogy* is about the failure and loneliness of people whose dreams of glory have rendered them sterile and stagnant.

Born and reared in Albuquerque, Jones graduated from the University of New Mexico in 1960 and joined the Dallas Theater Center's professional company as an actor in 1962, and also became one of its directors. Practical experience has taught him what works in the theater. The plays in *A Texas Trilogy* are actor's plays. But the paradox is that much more theatrically adept plays have been written by playwrights who have come no closer to the stage than a seat in the second balcony. These plays work, they play, but they have a crude simplicity and an overall amateurish aura about them that is apparent not in ineffective moments (those are few), but from moment to moment. The audience is thinking, these stereotyped, predictable characters, this cliché-ridden dialogue, these simple situations, this commonplace realism, this great bulk, should not work, but it *is* working. *A Texas Trilogy* is "dynamite theater." Jones's solid background in the theater and his audacious amateurishness may account for this happy fluke.

This play is exactly what pretentious anglophile New York theater needs to put it in touch with its own deepseated provincialism. But under the easy rubric of "regionalism," it spurned this once-in-a-generation opportunity. Outside New York, reviewers could unself-consciously rejoice, hailing the trilogy as a work as "satisfying" as *Death of a Salesman* and Jones as the most promising new playwright since Tennessee Williams and Arthur Miller relevant choices, for these plays generate continuity with the kind of theater the 1940's and 1950's produced, the theater of William Inge, Richard N. Nash, Clifford Odets. But sophistication is not so easily dethroned, especially with a British critic, Clive Barnes of the *New York Times*, holding the scepter. The epithet "regional" became the trilogy's epitaph, as if plays set in New York City or any other "foreign" place more truly expressed the American experience. Despite its only, but pervasive fault, its amateurish superficiality, the trilogy is authentic theater, and Jack Kroll of *Newsweek* had the courage to risk revealing the hick in himself by saying, "The enthusiastic . . . reaction to the complete trilogy suggests that Jones is that rare thing, a truly popular playwright who communicates directly and clearly with his audience."

Except for Lu Ann, the characters are not particularly interesting or memorable in themselves, even though the eccentric Colonel is strongly focused. Audiences will not think of them as they thought of Willie Loman and Blanche DuBois, nor do Jones's characters speak as memorably as Miller's and Williams'. But the trilogy is distinguished from the works of those playwrights by its remarkable pace. Unencumbered by the complexity of past history and present psychological anguish, Jones's characters move across three decades in a theatrical time that is amazingly swift. With the artistic and commercially successful dramas of Miller and Williams, *A Texas Trilogy*—at least the first two plays—has this in common: dynamic, memorable images that are purely theatrical, that endow simple action, stereotyped characters, and colloquial speech with dramatic immediacy and a sense of significance that derives as much from the nature of the theatrical experience as from an authentic and moving depiction of the way we live.

The theatrical image that generates energy in *The Last Meeting of the Knights of the White Magnolia* is the meeting room on the third floor of the Cattleman's Hotel, a flea-bag relic of bygone prosperity. We see a cross, made of light bulbs, that will light up gaudily in Act II and go berserk, flashing off and on erratically, like the fitful hopes and animosities of the Knights themselves. The cross hangs behind a podium bearing a fading magnolia, between two filthy flags, "The Stars and Bars" and "Lone Star." We see an old trunk; we will watch the Knights take their initiation hats out of it. On the walls we see old grimy banners representing the sun, the moon, and the west wind. As the curtain rises, we wonder what is about to happen in this peculiar setting. We also see a wheelchair and wonder how it will fit into the scene. This image, then, arouses expectations that only the theater can satisfy.

The dramatic tension between our response to the theatrical image and our rejection of theatrical clichés begins when we see Ramsey-Eyes, "an old black man in very old clothes," sweeping the floor "listlessly," singing "Red River Valley." How many plays begin with the use of a cleaning person as a class-contrast character? And it is a virtual certainty that such plays will end with that character's dismissive comment on the action that has transpired. The first Knights to enter are Rufe Phelps, wearing a baseball cap, and Olin Potts, wearing a straw hat. We start, then, with a mixture of the exotically familiar and the trite.

As Rufe and Olin dispute childishly over who did or did not cheat in the game of horseshoes they have just left, and as they draw Red Grover and Ramsey-Eyes into their wrangling, the formulatic dialogue is almost monosyllabic, having the effect of enhancing the theatrical visuals, instead of competing with them, as often happens in the theater. Setting, characters, and speech comprise a single expression of small-town emptiness and monotony.

The image that gives cohesion and theatrical energy to the second play, *Lu Ann Hampton Laverty Oberlander*, is a character image: the simply and lucidly articulated image of Lu Ann, who changes from a pretty high school cheerleader who dreams of a glamorous life away from Bradleyville in Act I, to a brash, sexy beautician, a divorcée who enjoys a drink and a little TV after work in Act II, to an attractive, work-worn middle-aged woman, divorced a second time, who is burdened with a rebellious teen-aged daughter, a derelict, alcoholic brother, an invalid mother, and painfully nostalgic memories of a few moments of small-town glory in Act III. Watching her physical transformation is a moving theatrical experience.

Enhancing that focus on character change over three decades is the succession of men, act by act, in Lu Ann's life: from Billy Bob Wortman, football hero, to Dale Laverty, World War II hero, to Corky Oberlander, charming highway inspector. Reminding her and the audience of the Lu Ann of Act I, Jones brings Billy Bob back in Act III; he is a successful preacher in another town. The settings, too, augment the physical objectification of Lu Ann's emotional deterioration: we see her on the eve of her graduation picnic in "a small frame house in a small frame town"; we see her in Red's bar, where her pathetic brother Skip slit his own throat the night before; in Act III, we see her again in the same frame house as in Act I. The nature of the theater has the power to render such images immediately overwhelming and forever memorable.

In *The Last Meeting of the Knights of the White Magnolia,* all the characters were almost equally important. The Colonel and Skip demanded special attention. In *Lu Ann Hampton Laverty Oberlander,* Skip is the second most important character, and his disintegration parallels Lu Ann's. Ten years before the Knights' last meeting, we see him already drinking and dreaming, like a brother in a Eugene O'Neill play; a year after the last meeting, we hear, graphically, of his suicide attempt in the bar (Red, Rufe, Olin, and Milo are also carried over to this play); ten years later, we see Skip totally dependent on his sister, ridiculed by his niece, and sickened by his doomed mother. There are echoes of Skip in the third play. In the aging of these characters—in shifting time perspectives—we experience a theatrical sense of time that becomes almost palpable.

The only children in this play are adults. Their motivations, their actions, their talk, their pastimes strike the audience as immature. One wonders whether adults are merely children with wrinkles. What better place to set a sad comedy dramatizing the broad streak of immaturity in the American character than West Texas, out of which historically so much was expected and so much has been achieved—materially?

The failure of success, beginning in America's small towns, is more clearly shown in the last play, *The Oldest Living Graduate* (who is also the last survivor of his class). But here neither the set nor the characters nor the shape of the action leave us with a theatrical image, a well-conceived energy source on which the audience's imagination can thrive after the house is dark. Jones seems here to be willing a trilogy rather than creating one out of inner compulsion. The Colonel, active in the first play, discussed in the second, becomes the main character here. Jones tells us in a television interview that audiences loved the old man, so he thought he ought to do more with him. He has done enough with the character, but not with the play itself, nor its relation to the first two. The only other character from an earlier play (the second) is Lu Ann's mother, Claudine, but she is a minor character.

Compared with the structure of the first two plays, so simple as to have the force of seeming inevitability, the structure of the third play is choppy. The first play is one continuous action with an intrusive intermission. The second play's three acts spring from a logic implicit in the play's conception. But *The Oldest Living Graduate* simply rambles over five scenes in two acts.

The Colonel's son, Floyd, wants to build a housing development on a lake, the only property the old man has kept under his own control because it has sentimental value for him. Even though he has already usurped control legally, the son wants the father to give the land to him willingly as an act of love. Meanwhile, to promote the development among influential people, the son tries to have graduation ceremonies for his father's old military academy held in Bradleyville where the Colonel is to be honored as the oldest living graduate. The Colonel refuses to relinquish the land (until near the end of Act II), and he refuses to be honored as the oldest graduate (partly because he is terrified to learn he is the last of his class and ashamed he had not kept up with his comrades to have mourned their passing). In the final scene, he returns home from the last meeting of the Knights of the White Magnolia (where we left him at the climax of the first play) to face death, telling his stories again, this time to Mike, the forty-nine-year-old hired hand, as the lights fade on the trilogy.

Except for the Colonel, what we see and hear is simply not very interesting. And it is only the lingering after-effect of the brilliant theatrical image of *The Last Meeting of the Knights of the White Magnolia* that seems to lend the Colonel whatever elements do command our attention.

The only genre of imaginative literature originally conceived and intended for a different medium, the printed play seems obliged to justify itself. *A Texas Trilogy* easily translates from the page to the theater of the mind and so needs no justification.

David Madden

Sources for Further Study

America. CXXXV, October 23, 1976, p. 260.

Nation. CCXXIII, October 9, 1976, p. 348.

New Republic. CLXXV, October 23, 1976, p. 20.

Newsweek. LXXXVII, May 17, 1976, p. 95.

Time. CVIII, September 27, 1976, p. 67.

THE THIRTEENTH TRIBE
The Khazar Empire and Its Heritage

Author: Arthur Koestler (1905-   )
Publisher: Random House (New York). 255 pp. $8.95
Type of work: History
Time: The Early Middle Ages
Locale: The Khazar Empire from the Black Sea to the Caspian Sea and from the Caucasus to the Volga River

An interpretation of the history of the Khazar Empire and the consequences of its fall

In *The Thirteenth Tribe: The Khazar Empire and Its Heritage,* Arthur Koestler has again, as with his book, *The Midwife Toad,* undertaken an exciting and fascinating study of a plausible but quite unsubstantiated theme. *The Thirteenth Tribe* attempts to demonstrate that most Ashkenazic Jews are descendants of the tribe of Khazars that dominated the area now known as south central Russia in the period between the seventh and the tenth centuries A.D. Thus, most Ashkenazic Jews, in Koestler's view, are not Semites, but Khazars. The author develops this thesis through his analysis of the rise and fall of the Khazar Empire and his interpretation of the Khazar heritage.

Khazaria, whose inhabitants were of Turkish origin, lay between the Black Sea and the Caspian Sea, stretching from the Caucasus on the South to Kiev on the north and from the Volga on the east to the Dnieper on the west, and it served as a buffer separating Byzantium, the barbarian tribes of the steppes (Bulgars, Magyars, and eventually Vikings or Russians) and the Muslims to the south and east. Khazaria protected Byzantium from barbarian attacks and in the seventh and eighth centuries prevented the Arab conquest and conversion of the southern steppes. Curiously, around 740, the Khazars converted *en masse* to Judaism. But what happened to the Khazars in the eleventh and twelfth centuries, after the destruction of Khazaria, remains a mystery for which Koestler claims to provide the answer. He contends that the Khazars migrated to eastern Europe, settled in Russia, Poland, Hungary, and Lithuania, and came to make up the bulk of Ashkenazic Jews.

The Khazars developed a fairly high level of civilization during the four centuries of the height of their empire. Starting as a group of fierce nomadic tribes, they settled into cities and became farmers, cattle raisers, traders, and craftsmen. They established lines of frontier fortifications that permitted for a time a stable development of the interior of Khazaria. The Khazars established hegemony over such tribes as the Bulgars, Magyars, Ghuzz, and the northwestern Slavonic tribes. Khazar armies raided Georgia to the south and the Arab Empire.

Their origin is believed to be Hun and they are spoken of as "Turks." Koestler was convinced that they were of Turkish origin and in the fifth century A.D. emerged from the Asian steppes. The earliest accounts indicate that they were under the sovereignty, with other tribes, of Attila, and, following his death, became the major power in the region, subduing such tribes as the Sabirs, the Saragurs, the Samandars, the Balanjars, and the Bulgars. By the middle of the seventh century they controlled what the Byzantines referred to as the "Kingdom of the North."

The major kingdoms of the region were Khazaria, Christian Byzantium, and the Muslim Caliphate. Alliances were made especially between Byzantium and Khazaria to prevent Arab conquest of eastern Europe. The Khazars bore the brunt of the Arab attacks and saved eastern Europe from the Arabs at about the same time that Charles Martel stopped the Arab thrust to conquer western Europe. From their efforts against the Muslims, the Khazars extended their domination into the Crimea and the Ukraine. By the early eighth century Khazaria was a powerful empire ruled by its Kagan (King) and able to muster armies of 100,000 and even 300,000, according to Arab sources.

Not only did the Khazars play the crucial role in the containment of the Arabs in the east, but they also were significantly involved in political struggles and intrigues within the Byzantine Empire, supporting some and opposing other Emperors or would-be Emperors. The Khazars also served as a conduit to spread Persian and Byzantine arts and crafts among the uncivilized tribes, and developed on their own a comparatively high level of civilization. Although their art and culture were derivative, they were of high quality, and the Khazars enjoyed the cosmopolitanism of urban living, focused first on the fortress of Balanjar, later on the city of Samandar, and finally on the city of Itil.

The Khazars were a fiercely independent tribe and Koestler argues that their conversion to Judaism was the result of that desire to remain independent from their Muslim and Christian neighbors. Khazaria, equaling the Byzantine and the Islamic empires in stature and military prowess, recognized that acceptance either of Christianity or of Islam would mean subordination to the authority either of the Byzantine Empire or the Caliph of Baghdad. In the midst of this dilemma they settled on a religion that would preserve Khazar independence—Judaism.

The choice in behalf of Judaism did not take place at once. As a cosmopolitan society, Khazaria contained Christians, Arabs, and Jews. There had, in fact, been a constant stream of Jewish refugees who had fled wave after wave of Byzantine persecution and torture in every century from the sixth through the tenth. Only in Khazaria could Jews find a refuge and the toleration that was lacking everywhere in the Christian world. They in turn, brought the culture and crafts of the Christian world to Khazaria and reinforced the atmosphere of toleration that existed there and that aroused the admiration of Arab visitors. In turn, the Jews of Khazaria apparently lived exemplary lives so that they were admirable models and served as an inducement for conversion.

The conversion apparently took place in two steps. The first was to a rudimentary Judaism primarily involving the Kagan, King Bulan, and the Court. Some generations after the initial conversion, there took place a far more widespread conversion or revival; rabbinic Judaism was adopted at this stage. Conversion, then, took the form of a progression. This was all documented in a letter written in the tenth century by a Khazar Kagan, Joseph, who described in detail his kingdom and the process of conversion.

The Khazar kingdom reached the zenith of its power and prestige in the eighth and early ninth centuries, maintaining a peace along its borders and throughout Khazaria. Symbolic of this prestige was the Byzantine Emperor, Leo the Khazar (775-780), named after his Khazar mother. However, by the ninth century, a cloud appeared on the Khazar horizon—Viking or Norse invaders, as they were known in the West, or Rus or Rhos, as they were known in the East.

The effects of the Viking raids on Khazaria were as devastating as they were in western Europe. The Vikings were savage pirates and plunderers who returned on a seasonal basis, establishing camps from which they launched their raids. Not only did they plunder, but they sold their stolen goods, so that they brought both piracy and trade to the areas that they raided. The Khazars and the Byzantines alternated in their relations with the Rus between agreements and wars. Eventually the Rus interbred with the peoples of the region, established permanent settlements, and became Russians.

Although the Rus concentrated their raids on the wealthier Byzantines for the first century of their forays, they took over some of the Khazar's vassal tribes and, therefore, somewhat reduced the size of Khazaria. In the second half of the ninth century, the Khazar city of Kiev on the Dnieper became Rus property, and Kiev became the Russian capital. Khazars remained in Kiev and helped to cosmopolitanize the Russians. The Khazars also had an influence on the Magyars in the ninth and tenth centuries, providing them with a king, Arpod, founder of the Magyar's first dynasty; and several Khazar tribes, chased out of Khazaria because of rebelliousness, also offered leadership and military competence to the Magyars as they established their kingdom to the west of Khazaria.

While the Khazars were working out their relationships with the Russians and the Magyars, the Byzantines were making treaties with the Russians and seeking to convert them to Christianity. Princess Olga of Kiev was baptized in 957, but the Russians were only converted to Greek Orthodoxy in 988 under Vladimir. In the context of improving relations between the Russians and Byzantines, Khazaria began to decline in importance and was clearly an inconvenience for Kiev and Constantinople. Throughout the tenth century, the Russians continued to encroach on Khazaria, gaining a foothold in territories previously dominated by the Khazars. Khazar control of the Slavonic tribes ended, although the heart of the Khazar Empire remained. Then, early in the eleventh century, the Byzantine-Khazar alliance was abrogated by Byzantium, the Byzantines made an alliance with the Russians, and a Byzantine-Russian army attacked and subdued Khazaria.

While the Khazars had maintained peace throughout the region, the

Byzantines and the Russians could not. The downfall of Khazaria was followed by chaos as the tribes that the Khazars had pacified now began a ceaseless warfare with one another. Branches of the tribe of the Ghuzz began moving west and pushing other tribes before them, while another branch of the Ghuzz defeated the Byzantines at the Battle of Manzikert (1071), opening Asia Minor to control by the Turks. Throughout the eastern steppes, the decline of Khajaria meant the descent of the region into instability and barbarism. In those Dark Ages, a reduced and weakened Khazaria clung to life through most of the twelfth century, after which references in historical documents to the Khazar Empire cease.

Koestler has sketched what is known of the story of the Khazars with accuracy. However, having traced the rise and fall of Khazaria, Koestler next moves to a highly speculative and questionable account of what he regards to be the Khazar heritage. For example, while the significant Jewish population in Hungary during the medieval period is believed to have been of Khazar origin, Koestler suggests without proof a similar origin for other east European Jewish populations. He contends that the Black Plague in the fourteenth century swept through the former Khazar Empire devastating all of the surrounding tribes and depopulating the steppes. This accelerated the growth of barbarism and anarchy and caused a movement of peoples throughout the area. Under these pressures, the Khazars settled in Kiev, in the Ukraine and southern Russia, and in Poland. Koestler argues that many Polish and Ukranian place names derive from "Khazar" or "Zhid" (Jew). Moreover, as many Khazars moved west, many remained behind, forming Jewish settlements in the Caucasus, the Crimea, and elsewhere.

Koestler discusses at length Jewish involvement in the early history of the Polish kingdom where Jewish Khazars were welcome. The 1264 Charter of Boleslav the Pious that received confirmation in 1334 by Casimir the Great granted the Jews autonomy over their own religious, educational, and legal matters and extended to them property and occupational rights. This pattern of grants of rights to Jews was maintained and expanded under other Polish rulers. Under such favorable conditions, the movement of Khazar Jews into Poland over the centuries was considerable. There was also a major migration of Khazar Jews into Lithuania, Hungary, and the Balkans. In fact, Koestler argues that "during the middle ages the majority of those who professed the Judaic faith were Khazars."

Koestler discusses what he believes to be other results of Khazar activities. The *shtetl*, or Jewish rural community or town, was a Khazar tradition. Moreover, some trades became a Jewish monopoly as a consequence of the Khazar heritage. Koestler speculates that gefilte fish, a Jewish delicacy, may have been a Khazar legacy. More importantly, however, Koestler contends that the number of Jews of western Europe in the thirteenth century and after that were persecuted by Christians and forced to flee to eastern Europe was too few numerically to make up the large Jewish populations of Poland, Lithuania, Russia, Hungary and other states of eastern Europe. The bulk of those populations was of Khazar origin. Thus the eastern European Jewish populations were made up of Khazars moving west and not of persecuted western European Jews moving east. Additionally, the Jewish language of Yiddish, Koestler argues, had a Khazar origin to which German, Polish, and other languages were added. Finally, Koestler lapses into the ridiculous in his speculations as he argues that the physical differences between the Sephardic Jews and the Ashkenazic Jews represent the biological distinctions between Sephardic Semites and Ashkenazic Khazars. Consequently, the traditional Semitic nose. If this sounds far-fetched, it is. Altogether, therefore, Koestler has convinced himself that the bulk of European Jews are of Khazar and not of Semitic origin.

Koestler recognizes the danger of denying the Semitic heritage of the European Jews. Since the modern State of Israel contains many European Jews, his book is tantamount to supporting the Arab argument that Israel has no right to exist. Therefore, Koestler adds a section to his book in an attempt to argue that the existence of the modern State of Israel is based on law and on the sheer presence of the Jewish people. This *de jure* and *de facto* support for Israel means, in the view of Koestler, that Israel needs no other justification. Koestler concludes that the Khazar origin of the European Jews "is irrelevant to modern Israel."

In spite, however, of this theoretical support of Israel, Koestler discloses another purpose for his book. He contends that the traditional orthodox Judaism is presently dying out among Jews everywhere, and that the most significant remaining link among Jews is emotional. The heritage and thought patterns of the European Jews—the Ghetto Jews—are breaking down in Israel and elsewhere. Although a Jew himself, Koestler produced *The Thirteenth Tribe* to help weaken that emotional link by attempting to detach the Jewish religion from the concept of a chosen people. As such, this book represents Koestler's effort to enhance Jewish assimilation and undermine the traditional belief of Jews in their unique religious heritage and mission. Koestler's motives aside, however, it is important to note in conclusion that speculation is not proof, and that far too much of this volume is speculation to merit serious consideration of Koestler's central thesis.

Saul Lerner

Sources for Further Study

Atlantic. CCXXXVIII, September, 1976, p. 97.

Saturday Review. III, August 21, 1976, p. 40.

Spectator. CCXXVI, April 10, 1976, p. 19.

Time. CVIII, August 23, 1976, p. 60.

Times Literary Supplement. June 11, 1976, p. 696.

Wall Street Journal. CLXXXVIII, August 11, 1976, p. 12.

THE TIME OF ILLUSION

Author: Jonathan Schell (1943-   )
Publisher: Alfred A. Knopf (New York). 392 pp. $10.00
Type of work: Political history
Time: 1969-1974
Locale: Washington, D.C.

A reflective account of the nation's political life during the incumbency of President Richard Nixon, from January, 1969, to August, 1974

Principal personages:
RICHARD M. NIXON, thirty-seventh President of the United States
H. R. HALDEMAN and
JOHN D. EHRLICHMAN, chief Presidential assistants
JOHN MITCHELL, major Presidential adviser and the Attorney General of the United States
HENRY KISSINGER, Presidential assistant on national security affairs and the Secretary of State of the United States
PATRICK J. BUCHANAN, Presidential political adviser and speechwriter
SPIRO T. AGNEW, Vice President of the United States

Originating as a series of articles for *New Yorker* magazine, *The Time of Illusion* represents an attempt to put Richard Nixon's years in the White House in perspective. Jonathan Schell claims that the constitutional crisis, which peaked during the Nixon Presidency, began to emerge under President John F. Kennedy. The roots of the crisis can be found in the American involvement in the war in Vietnam. American leaders had defined several war aims. In the end, only one of these aims—the protection of the credibility of the United States—endured. As the human and material costs of the war soared, the bewilderment over and opposition to it grew. Successive administrations perceived the need to resort to surreptitious and covert activities. President Lyndon B. Johnson, having his once-massive coalition of support broken over Vietnam and facing mounting opposition to his war policies, set into motion the spying on and the repression of American citizens that reached such frightful proportions under the Nixon Administration.

Schell recalls how Nixon entered office sounding the theme of unity. However, one of the basic characteristics of the new administration from the beginning was that it would *do* the exact opposite of what it was *saying*. As unity was preached, the divisions of the country were deliberately deepened. The strategy of "positive polarization" was put forward. The President had brought the country together on the illusion that the war would come to an end. Once in office, he significantly escalated it and launched major secret operations in Cambodia. As Schell discusses it, these massive secret projects acquired a domestic arm, to deal with the opposition and to close "leaks." What had begun on a minor scale under earlier administrations, assumed ever-expanding dimensions. As the "Nixon Big Charge" gathered momentum, the federal intelligence and law enforcement agencies were involved in a flurry of clandestine activities, including farflung warrantless wiretapping and domestic spying. Vice President Spiro Agnew's vituperative and strident speeches served as an outlet for the President's anger over the antiwar demonstrations.

The myriad different activities and diverse political proposals shared one marked feature, a notable gap between image and substance. The unity between word and deed, essential to make political action intelligible to outsiders, was broken, writes Schell. The White House was far more concerned about appearances than substantive results in its actions. An amazing proportion of energies was devoted to the creation and promotion of images; the entire federal government was utilized for these purposes. The President used his power to frame the issues on which he would do battle with the opposition. The way Schell sees it, Nixon used all of America as a stage. Indeed, the very language of the stage—words such as script, scenario, players—heavily permeated White House memoranda. Schell's interpretation suggests that the President's paramount concern was the preservation of presidential authority, which he perceived as being threatened across the board. The information leaks, the student demonstrations, the negative expressions of public opinion, the lack of congressional support, the bureaucratic foot-dragging on presidential directives, and the criticism by the press all added up, in the President's mind, to an insurrection which had to be put down. Governmental reorganization and concentration of power in the White House was seen as the solution. An ambitious campaign to discredit the press and television networks and an elaborate system of rigged letters and telegrams supporting the President were implemented in addition. In order to deal more effectively with the "internal threats," the White House sought to reorganize domestic intelligence. The already extensive illegal activities of the CIA and the FBI were to be supplemented by the utilization of the IRS. In Schell's view, Nixon rejected the idea of fixed constitutional forms; he acted as though it was completely up to him to decide the shape of the United States government. As a result, the fundamental balance of power between the major branches of government was about to be destroyed.

The President liked to pose as a man of peace. Yet, as the war had "come home," he became increasingly intolerant of the shaping and restraining influence of the law. When the Pentagon Papers were made public by Daniel Ellsberg, the White House set out to "destroy" him. For this purpose top presidential aides recruited E. Howard Hunt, G. Gordon Liddy, and others, who later were part of the Watergate burglary, precipitating the huge scandal that ultimately brought down the Administration. An increasing amount of both domestic and foreign White House business was conducted in secrecy. According to Schell, such widely differing activities as Henry Kissinger's secret trip to China and the scheme to destroy Ellsberg shared a certain elemental affinity, namely, the nearly fanatical concern about "leaks" that would threaten national security. In retrospect, it is truly astounding to note the extent to which major policymakers, including the President, spent their time scheming to discredit or "destroy" opponents, instead of addressing themselves to substantive policy issues. Any person, group, institution, or even country, that crossed the White House in any way, would end up on the enemies list. The degree of vindictiveness and pettiness with which such "enemies" were pursued is astonishing. As Schell recalls it, the "enemies project" permeated the conduct of business in the White House; even the social life came to be regulated by a system of punishments and rewards. The federal budget, too, became part of a "responsiveness program" to reward friends and to punish enemies. Foreign policy assumed the distinct pattern of this program, while providing in addition the stage for dramatic media events, such as Nixon's trip to China on the eve of the primaries.

As Schell develops his narrative, he reemphasizes the tendency on the part of the White House to value *images* of events more highly than substance, to be singlemindedly preoccupied with *appearances.* Regarding the 1972 elections, the President seemed to follow closely Patrick Buchanan's advice of splitting the country apart and picking up the larger half. Everything was centered on the reelection of the President. The well-coordinated effort of dividing the Democrats and playing major contenders off against one another included every underhanded technique in the book. As Schell notes, the White House made uninhibited use of federal agencies to smear the opposition and to commit a wide variety of crimes against it, as well as raise impressive sums of money for its own campaign. In the face of all the illegal activities engaged in by the White House, the President's hypocrisy could surely not have been surpassed when he called for a full return to "the law as a way of life" on the occasion of eulogizing J. Edgar Hoover. In the words of Schell, the White House instructed every spy, saboteur, con man, extortionist, forger, impostor, burglar, mugger, and bagman in its employ to work at manufacturing the appearance of public support for the President. In making his devastating observations about the nature and actions of the White House, Schell then mitigates the implications by suggesting that the President considered his political self-interest and the national interest to be identical. According to Schell's thesis, Nixon saw his own personal political survival as one with the cause of human survival.

As the election was drawing nearer, White House operations were shifted from crimes whose purpose was the discovery of national security leaks to crimes against the political opposition. The outcome is only too well known. On June 17, 1972, members of the "Gemstone" team were arrested for the burglary of the Democratic Party offices in the Watergate building, and the coverup activities, eventually ruining the Administration, began. As the constitutional crisis deepened, the White House reservoir of secrets swelled. Schell distinguishes between an "underground history" and an "aboveground history," the first superseding the second in importance. Nothing was left to chance; the convention and the election campaign were conducted according to a carefully worked-out script, attending to even the smallest details. The President wanted nothing to happen unforeseen and unauthorized by him. Schell notes Nixon's strange preoccupation with his own "history." In attempting to permit nothing to happen which was not planned and authorized, he was endeavoring to write "history" *before* the events. Nixon seemed to experience a strong anxiety that some of his actions and words might be lost. Here might well lie the answer to the puzzling question of why he installed the automatic taping system and then did not destroy the tapes when he had the opportunity, thus revealing all the damning, humiliating, and simply embarrassing information regarding himself and the Watergate coverup.

Following his reelection, Nixon went after his opposition with a vengeance. Within the executive branch, all those who had managed to retain a measure of independence had to leave. The White House wanted to be in direct charge over the federal bureaucracy. The Cabinet system was declared obsolete. Indeed, in the light of the President's systematic efforts to usurp the powers of Congress and to contain the courts, the whole system of separation of powers and checks and balances was considered outdated. What the President hoped to achieve was nothing short of revolutionary; namely, the establishment of a presidential dictatorship. Schell maintains that he did all of this because he felt the Presidency was endangered. The supreme irony was, of course, that his very efforts brought about the presidential impotence which he so dreaded.

Although Schell agrees that the Nixon Administration posed the most serious threat to liberty in the country's history, he sees it as part of a continuing systemic crisis which began under Kennedy. Despite the marked differences in the character and style of the officeholders, these men made decisions that were strikingly alike, according to Schell. As far as the crisis is concerned, Nixon seemed to pick up where Johnson left off. As noted above, Schell's thesis is that the Nixon Administration's actions, including all the aberrations, are attributable to the doctrine of credibility. In maintaining a viable strategy of deterrence in the nuclear age, it became vital for the United States to be credible; to be believed that we would do what we said we would do, regardless of the consequences. The strategy of massive retaliation required the deliberate pursuit of irrationality, an effort to convince our potential adversaries that certain actions on their part, even if these should constitute only a minor direct security threat to the United States, would lead to all-out war. "If you want peace, prepare for war," reads an old dictum. Deterrence involves both a physical and a psychological relationship. The strategy of massive retaliation, operative in the 1950's, proved deficient, precisely because we did not succeed in convincing our adversaries that we would blow up the world over a relatively minor single action. However, a series of small adverse steps could add up to a serious setback.

Illustrative of the efforts to overcome the deficiencies of massive retaliation are the strategies of limited war developed by Henry Kissinger and Maxwell Taylor. The application of this strategy of limited war required an even more concentrated and consistent demonstration of our credibility. Appearances, therefore, were everything. Kennedy apparently saw in Vietnam a test case of the American "will" to oppose Communism. Vietnam, then, acquired a certain symbolic importance that was separate from any specific tangible objective. In the late 1960's, the internal dissention grew and was seen as undermining American credibility. Opposition to the war was tantamount to an attack on the safety of the nation. By the time Nixon assumed the Presidency, the choice had boiled down to either credibility or the Republic; for everywhere the President saw signs of eroding national "will." Only Americans can defeat America, the President insisted. As he was trying to extricate the United States from Vietnam, he saw it as all the more important to uphold credibility at home. When the coverup of Watergate was gradually blown, he interpreted the whole process as an assault on the Presidency, which would fatally undermine "the structure of peace." In Schell's words, he offered the American people the spurious deal of survival at the cost of liberty. Nixon was determined to uphold American credibility at all cost; but to succeed, he had to be free of the people who kept hampering his efforts. To be free of the people, however, required the destruction of the democratic system of government, which gave the people power over the President. His ultimate, limitless justification was human survival. Could anything at all stand in the way of such a goal?

Schell manages to give all of the arbitrary, contradictory, and aberrant presidential acts a certain logic and coherence. He attributes them all to the doctrine of credibility, a doctrine that grew out of the world's still unresolved nuclear dilemma and out of the American strategy of limited war. He does not find the character of the President and those of his aides to be the basic cause, contrary to appearances and accepted interpretations concerning this period. Schell's thesis is interesting, but not entirely persuasive. The vengeful, spiteful mood of the White House, the enemies list, the illicit interference with the elective process, the Watergate coverup, cannot be explained solely in terms of protecting the office of the Presidency and American credibility. To be sure, many abuses had occurred in previous administrations committed in the name of national security. To a certain extent the Nixon Administration continued, on a larger scale, where the Johnson Administration had left off. Speculating about motives is always a risky business. However, the enormity of the aberrations and the arrogant manner of the Nixon White House must be attributed in good measure to the personalities of the principals. It is rather more comforting to assume that it was a unique phenomenon in American history.

Manfred Grote

Sources for Further Study

America. CXXXIV, May 15, 1976, p. 433.

Christian Science Monitor. LXVIII, March 9, 1976, p. 30.

Commonweal. CIII, September 10, 1976, p. 598.

New York Review of Books. XXIII, June 24, 1976, p. 21.

New York Times. January 14, 1976, p. 33.

Progressive. XL, April, 1976, p. 41.

TO JERUSALEM AND BACK
A Personal Account

Author: Saul Bellow (1915-   )
Publisher: The Viking Press (New York). 232 pp. $8.95
Type of work: Travel journal
Time: 1975-1976
Locale: Israel, primarily Jerusalem

A personal journal recording the author's impressions of the people and problems of Israel

In Saul Bellow's novel *Mr. Sammler's Planet*, published in 1970, the hero is an old man, blind in one eye, survivor of a Nazi concentration camp, a journalist and scholar. He is "attentive to everything, appalled by nothing." His detachment enables Bellow to record the social and political tensions of contemporary urban America with a curiosity and detachment that startles the reader. Sammler has seen and suffered too much to be taken in or defined by *any* experience. When Bellow has him cover the aftermath of the Six Day War for a London Polish-language newspaper, he is strangely unimpressed by the rotting corpses in the desert sun: ". . . as human affairs went, a most minor affair. In modern experience, so little." Sammler's good eye sees what his blind eye reveals. Like Oedipus at the end of Sophocles' tragedy, he is sated with reality and his detachment is really the calm of the gods. Like them, he sees all and his suffering makes him divine.

In *To Jerusalem and Back* the book's main character is Bellow himself, with the simple vision of his two eyes—the man, not the novelist. The Nobel Prize winner steps out from behind his literary creations—the Herzogs, Hendersons, Humboldts, and Sammlers who have provided the mythic embodiments of his life-affirming but morally rigorous sensibility. This book is a journal, not a novel. It purposely avoids the resolutions and hope of art. There are no larger-than-life people to shoulder the burden of experience and illuminate its humanity through comic or tragic visions. There is only Bellow, the American Jew, meeting all sorts of people, simple and prominent, and struggling to comprehend the social and historical complexity that underlies the meaning of Israel. It is the writer stripped naked with imagination curbed but his powers of observation heightened. Sammler's trip to the Sinai was based on Bellow's own experience as a correspondent at the scene. Instead of subordinating the gruesome descriptions to the theme of his fiction, Bellow produces them in the journal for their own sake, for their own inherent drama. He associates the putrefying corpses with the madness of all the conflicts in the Middle East, with their cruelty that is unique to the region. Without Sammler to filter the moment, Bellow leaves his readers with the real thing. Apprehensively but carefully, he explores all the experiences that come his way. Whereas *Mr. Sammler's Planet* is a dramatization of a certain kind of tragic memory, *To*

Jerusalem and Back plunges its readers into the puzzling and disturbing confusion of the here and now.

If this journal has any structure, it is that of a pilgrimage. But Bellow establishes very clearly that his is not a religious pilgrimage in any simple understanding of the term. When his co-passenger on the flight to Israel, a young Hasid, offers him fifteen dollars a week for life if Bellow will eat nothing but Kosher food, Bellow tactfully but firmly answers, "I can't accept such a sacrifice from you." Bellow is interested in secular "sacrifices," the passions which have made Israel a social and political reality. He finds what he is looking for in the simple flow of conversation. He talks with the "kibbutznick" seaman, John Auerbach, who survived the Warsaw ghetto, and after thirty years of hard agricultural labor, ships on oil tankers to obscure ports where his Israeli identity (he is a Wandering Israeli, not a Wandering Jew) flows into the strange ambience of "ancient mariners." He talks with the novelist Amos Oz, who observes that Israel contains as many visions of Heaven as it has immigrants; with the sixty-year-old barber of the King David Hotel who won the heart of Hubert H. Humphrey (whose signed photos adorn the barber shop wall); with Professor Sholem Kahn of the Hebrew University, who reflects on the rootlessness of modern man; and with Chaim Gouri, poet and journalist, who hopes to win over the Arabs with kindness and social services. He has a conversation with Justice Haim Cohen, who had to leave Israel to marry a divorcée because rabbinical authorities ruled that Cohen, one of the hereditary high priests, could not marry a divorced woman, and with the poet Dennis Silk, who wanders with Bellow through the alleyways of the Old City of Jerusalem.

And while steeping himself in these impressions of Israel and her people, Bellow is also reading books and articles that argue every conceivable thesis concerning Israel's role in the world and the problems attending its survival. He also meets dignitaries like the Armenian Archbishop of Jerusalem, Abba Eban; and the famous mayor of Jerusalem, Teddy Kollek. Many of his conversations with notables eventually sound like the "crisis chatter" Bellow himself condemns as characteristic of today's American society. But there is a difference. The question of survival is acutely relevant to everything that Israel does; to interpret or weigh her policies or actions is not a form of idle political theorizing; Israelis must be serious about politics. Flippancy about the future is a luxury beyond their means. They "think hard and much." Bellow says their thinking seems to make the "small slip of a country" quite large: "Some dimension of mind seems to extend into space."

Inevitably, much of Israel's thinking about the world's attitude toward her settles into a frame of mind that, at best, may be called skeptical but in truth is profoundly suspicious. The perverse logic of socialist nations condemning Israel, the only truly socialist democracy in the Middle East, only confirms Israel's exclusive trust in her own powers of self-defense. The sentimentality of many Western liberals' attitude toward the Third World offends Israel's sense of reality; Bellow himself comes down hard on the French intellectuals who turn the struggle between the Palestine Liberation Organization and Israel into an oversimplified political struggle of a victimized "socialist" people against their "colonialist" oppressor. As long as the Arabs have their oil money and the support of the Third World and the political Left—not to mention their vast superiority in population—they do not make a very convincing "victim," and they have *no* need to negotiate with Israel; that is the tough-minded appraisal of a large share of Israel's pundits. Israel must pursue a hard line. Bellow has understanding for this position; he himself becomes suspicious of Kissinger's protestations of concern for Israel's survival. But Bellow is fearful of the repercussions in America if Israel continues to hold all the territories occupied in the Six Day War. The United States is Israel's indispensable friend. As America's need for oil grows, will she continue to support Israel against the Arabs? How long will the Pentagon continue to think Israel's military strength vital to American military policy in the area? Is it conceivable that an American president, angered at the strong pressure exerted by the pro-Israel lobby in Washington, would accuse it of too interested a position and thus cast doubts on the loyalty of American Jewry? (De Gaulle gave pain to French Jews in 1967 when, in his fury that Israel went to war "without his permission," he characterized the Jews as a people "sure of itself and domineering.") It is only natural that Bellow, as an American, should be more sensitive to these possibilities than the Israelis. He seems to give some credence to the ideas of Jacob Lieb Talmon, an Israeli historian and specialist in European political history who maintains that the destruction of Israel would initiate a catastrophe that might overtake United States Jewry; at the same time Bellow wonders if Talmon is fully aware of the implications of what he is saying.

Concerned as he is about Jewish survival, in Israel and the world, Bellow's journey to Jerusalem is as much the quest of a Western humanist as it is of a Jew. Indeed, the confluence of the two identities in his own sensibility universalizes this "personal account." The Jew has always lived "on the brink of an abyss," writes A.B. Yehoshua, a young Israeli writer Bellow admires. The risk of being a Jew is great because there is something about Jewishness that has always driven others to insanity. The Jew is a witness, religiously and historically, to ethical and spiritual truths that totalitarian and dehumanized political systems must eradicate. Tyranny is a form of madness that the Jew, with his sanity, must confront again and again. All men of good will must learn the secret of the Jew's survival. Madness is growing in the world—psychological, social, and political madness. The Jew has been slightly crazed by the madness that always arises to challenge his search for normalization, for survival. Israel now bears the full brunt of a hatred so vast that there is no way to explain its origin. When the PLO says it will not recognize Israel, it means that Israel's *existence*, in the fullest sense of the word, will not be tolerated. Even the Chinese, notes Bellow, are prepared to wipe out Israel, obliterate a people they don't even know. What the world must not do is underestimate the isolation of Israel, its commitment to freedom and justice in a part of the world historically identified with repressive and autocratic societies. All the rhetoric about the Third World's suffering at the hands of colonial exploitation cannot obscure the deeply ingrained injustice of its traditions, traditions which preceded Western imperialism and have simply resurfaced in the vestments of Leftist ideology.

The Hasid we meet at the beginning of this journal has isolated himself in zealotry and deep religious faith, and he seems slightly crazed to the rest of the world. But the world, in its madness, has encouraged this solution. Bellow takes his own anxiety *and* faith back to Chicago; he brings his Jerusalem back to the West. To come from Jerusalem is never to leave it. This "personal account" has no formal ending. The Jewish experience continues to exhaust all efforts to explain it; one might as soon explain history itself.

Peter A. Brier

Sources for Further Study

Atlantic. CCXXXVIII, December, 1976, p. 113.

Commentary. LXII, November, 1976, p. 80.

New Republic. CLXXV, November 20, 1976, p. 36.

New Statesman. XCII, November 26, 1976, p. 753.

New York Times Book Review. October 17, 1976, p. 1.

Times Literary Supplement. December 3, 1976, p. 1509.

THE TRANSFORMATION OF SOUTHERN POLITICS
Social Change and Political Consequence Since 1945

Authors: Jack Bass (1934-   ) and Walter DeVries (1929-   )
Publisher: Basic Books (New York). 527 pp. $15.95
Type of work: Sociopolitical study
Time: 1945-1976
Locale: The eleven Southern states of the United States

A systematic study of social change and political patterns of development in the South since 1945

> *Principal personages:*
> JAMES EARL (JIMMY) CARTER, thirty-ninth President of the United States
> REUBIN ASKEW, Governor of Florida
> GEORGE C. WALLACE, Governor of Alabama
> DALE BUMPERS, United States Senator from Arkansas
> STROM THURMOND and
> ERNEST F. HOLLINGS, United States Senators from South Carolina
> ANDREW YOUNG, United States Representative from Georgia, 1972-1974, and ambassador to the United Nations

In this sweeping study of the formidable political change in the South, Jack Bass and Walter DeVries analyze Southern political attitudes and developments by considering each Southern state as an individual political entity and as part of a collective political group. The eleven Southern states are projected as possessing a distinctive political character and style, but the differences are comparable to those that may occur between eleven brothers and sisters coming from a single family. They are part of the South and linked by a common history. Bass and DeVries refer to such basic shared features as a plantation tradition based on slavery, a one-party system suppressing issues and removing most blacks from political participation, and the unique American experience of wartime defeat and devastation.

The Reconstruction measures imposed on the defeated Confederacy generated the solidarity reaction that gave rise to the political phenomenon of the Democratic "solid South," lasting until 1948. In the election year of 1948 the "solid South" cracked. This date may, therefore, be viewed as a turning point, the beginning of the transformation of Southern politics. As a kind of point of departure, the authors refer to the acclaimed landmark study on Southern politics by V. O. Key, which appeared in 1949, at the threshold of the new era. Key had identified and analyzed the institutional forces which suppressed the grievances of the poor and kept all power in the hands of rural conservatives. The forces discussed by Key had disintegrated with the arrival of the 1970's. During the last approximately twenty-five years the South experienced the gradual collapse of its traditional social structure, based on rigid racial segregation. Tremendous social change had been brought about by the massive movement of people from farms to cities, from agriculture to industry, and the mass migration of blacks moving out of the region and white professionals and managers moving into it. Such enormous demographic changes inevitably meant considerable political change. Among the important developments leading to the emergence of the "New South" were the acquisition of political power by blacks through the civil rights legislation and the termination of the over-representation of the rural areas through reapportionment. Coalitions of blacks and those whites who were adjusting to the changing circumstances constituted the basis for the "New South."

Bass and DeVries, who combine the resources of journalism and political science, utilize extensive opinion surveys indicating that the differences between the South and the non-South are fading. Nevertheless, some regional distinction remains. The authors note that the percentage of the black population in the South is almost three times that of the non-South; the white population is substantially more Anglo-Saxon and less East European in its ancestry; its religion is more fundamentalist Protestant; and the region's *per capita* personal income and the median level of education are lower than that of the rest of the country. The political change has been accompanied by social and economic change more rapid than in the rest of the country.

The state-by-state analysis reveals that each Southern state experienced a nearly universal political transformation in its own unique way. However, some general patterns and trends can be identified. Typically, for instance, an effective challenge by a rising Republican Party or an "anti-Establishment" force would lead to a period of upheaval and eventually to a new period of political modernization and moderation. Illustrative are the elections of Republican governors in Florida and Arkansas in 1966. Such impressive challenges brought about the revitalization of the Democratic Party and the emergence of such progressive leaders as Dale Bumpers in Arkansas and Reubin Askew in Florida. Their elections, also, reestablished Democratic dominance in their respective states.

In Georgia the anti-Establishment challenge of Lester Maddox, accompanied by a strong Republican bid for the governorship, ushered in the transition period, followed by the election of moderate Democrat Jimmy Carter for governor in 1970 and black civil rights leader Andrew Young for Congress in 1972. In this case, too, the revitalized Democratic Party restored its dominance.

In Tennessee, a Southern state where the Republican Party had been competitive for some time, the election of Republicans for governor and both United States senators provided the impetus for the Democrats to organize and recapture the governorship, as well as two congressional seats in 1974.

In North Carolina, a state which has not kept up with other Southern states in social and economic development, but stands out regarding the role of women in politics, the Republicans captured the statehouse in 1972.

Consistent with the pattern, the Democrats recaptured it in 1976.

In South Carolina, an ideological conservative Republican was able to win the governorship in 1974, because an insurgent Democrat was declared ineligible on a residency technicality. The state's United States senators—the conservative Strom Thurmond, who turned Republican in 1964, and the Democrat Ernest F. Hollings—personify in different ways the politics of accommodation for which South Carolina is known.

In Virginia, the once-dominant organization created by Harry F. Byrd, Sr., crumbled and made possible the election of a Republican governor. His son, Harry F. Byrd, Jr., lost in the Democratic primaries, but was able to prevail as an independent in the elections for the United States Senate; his possible return to the Democratic Party, which is in the process of adopting a progressive format, is unlikely to lead to his control over it.

Texas overthrew the Old Guard in 1972, when Frances Farenthold enjoyed a remarkable success in the Democratic primaries. Dolph Briscoe, "the most liberal of the conservative governors," in a state where the monied interests and politics were always closely tied, clearly plays a transitional role. The next governor is likely to project the progressive image of the "New South."

In Mississippi, the major battle ground for desegregation, the forces of modernization are also in the ascendency. The state's powerful United States senators, James O. Eastland and John Stennis, have practiced successfully the politics of accommodation. A political unknown defeated the Old Guard's candidate in the primaries for the governorship in 1975.

In Alabama, the political situation remains relatively static because of the continuing dominance of George C. Wallace. His fighting style, more than his stand on issues, has aroused admiration and strong support.

Louisiana's exotic political climate reflects its unique cultural blend. The legacy of the Longs, marked by a strong populism, stands out, as does an unparalleled record of corruption. Here the Republican Party has been unable to mount a serious challenge to the dominant, but multifactional, Democratic Party. In general, the Democrats in this state are cast in the progressive and moderate mold noticeable in the other parts of the region.

Historically, the South exerted its greatest national influence in the Congress. The operation of the one-party system allowed incumbent Southern Democrats to accumulate seniority and to rise to power as chairmen of the major committees. The South's dominance in the Congress, therefore, was disproportionately greater than its share in the membership. Since 1967, Southern power in the Congress has been waning. Moreover, as the authors have pointed out, gone are the days when civil rights served as an issue holding Southern members of Congress together. An example of this change was the support by the majority of Southern congressmen for the extension of the Voting Rights Act in 1975. The new Southern Democrats tend to vote more frequently with the party majority, rather than the old coalition of Republicans and old Southern Democrats. As the authors conclude, the emerging South in Congress is effecting a realignment, leaving Southern Republicans voting more conservatively than even the old Southern Democrats.

The rise of the Republican Party in the South began in the 1950's and peaked in 1972. A distinctive aspect has been its development from the top down, showing the greatest strength at the presidential level. However, in general, the level of Republican identification in the South has not increased since 1960. The presidential voting favorable to the Republican Party may be the result of protest and transitional confusion, rather than a genuine shift in party allegiance. Nevertheless, the authors are able to demonstrate movement in the direction of two-party competition throughout the South. Several states moved from a pure one-party category to a modified one-party category, but thus far, only Tennessee has achieved a genuine two-party status. The "Southern strategy," initiated by Barry Goldwater and carried over by Richard Nixon, prevented the Republican Party from engaging in reform. To its own misfortune, it seemed to attract the most reactionary elements. The "Southern strategy," with its deliberate appeal to racial prejudices, was shortsighted and self-defeating. It drove away the mass of black voters and all those whites who loathed an arousal of racial emotions. Although the Republican Party has lacked skillful and dynamic leadership in most of the South, the political trends continue to exert some pressure toward two-party politics, conclude Bass and DeVries.

Blacks in the South have changed their status from political object to political participant. However, the battle for "economic justice" remains to be won. The political necessity of courting growing numbers of black voters has brought about significant changes in rhetoric and attitudes of white politicians. The statistics regarding black politics in the South are impressive. Still, as the authors point out, black voter registration remains well below that for whites, and elected black officials comprise only about two percent of all elected officials in the South, while blacks constitute almost one-fifth of the voting-age population. The authors note that race remains a problem in the South. However, it is not solely a Southern problem but also a national one. It may well be, as Andrew Young has expressed it, that the changing South will give the direction to overcome racism.

Major social change was invariably imposed on the South from the outside. For this reason the "outside" was typically the enemy for traditional white Southerners, caught up in the school integration and civil rights struggles of the late 1950's and the 1960's. The struggles were intense in the states of the deep South, where resistance to the momentous Supreme Court decision of *Brown v. Board of Education of Topeka* in 1954, striking down the "separate but equal" clause for public school systems, had hardened. The first major crisis occurred in Little Rock, Arkansas, in 1957. Governor Orval Faubus mobilized the national guard in an effort to deny black students entry into a high school and openly defied President Eisenhower, ultimately compelling the latter to send federal troops into Little Rock. That same year Congress passed a civil rights act, the first of its kind since Reconstruction. Meanwhile, black leaders were involved in mobilizing the civil rights movement. Most important was the inspired and courageous leadership of Martin Luther King, Jr., who urged the assertion of black rights through nonviolent resistance. Federal troops were again required in 1962 in Oxford, Mississippi, to protect a black student who wanted to enroll in the University of Mississippi. Governor Wallace of Alabama personally tried to block the admission of two black students to the state university. More shocking, however, was the violence and the murder which the civil rights activists encountered. In the end, the political liberation of Southern blacks was achieved. The accomplishments must in good measure be credited to the presidency of Lyndon B. Johnson, who pushed through the landmark Civil Rights Act of 1964 and the Voting Rights Act of 1965. Jimmy Carter has suggested that Southerners take pride in their ability to adapt to change, and that many have accepted it with a sense of relief.

Bass and DeVries have presented an admirable assessment of Southern politics. They have conducted more than 360 interviews, including highly prominent and lesser officeholders, journalists, labor leaders, academicians, and persons from other diverse walks of life. Additional primary research contributions consist of election data analyses and surveys on perception and attitudes. A wealth of data on demographic changes and interparty competition was gathered and analyzed. This information is all contained in the form of graphs, maps, and tables in the extensive appendices. *The Transformation of Southern Politics* must be considered an important contribution to the study of contemporary politics. It is not a definitive study, but it is likely to be used as a major source by those who wish to inform themselves about an ever-fascinating region, the South today.

Manfred Grote

Sources for Further Study

America. CXXXV, November 4, 1976, p. 305.
Best Sellers. XXXVI, November, 1976, p. 268.
Book World. August 22, 1976, p. F5.
New Republic. CLXXV, September 11, 1976, p. 31.
New York Times Book Review. August 15, 1976, p. 4.
Village Voice. XXI, August 23, 1976, p. 35.

TRAVESTY

Author: John Hawkes (1925-   )
Publisher: New Directions (New York). 128 pp. $5.95
Type of work: Novel
Time: The present, with flashbacks
Locale: The interior of an automobile traveling at high speed on a deserted road in
France

*A nightmarish, erotic, and often comic monologue in which the speaker both savors
significant memories and justifies to his captives his reasons for planning their imminent
murder and his suicide*

> Principal characters:
> THE NARRATOR, an unnamed driver, designer of the crash, and the
>   only voice of the work
> HENRI, his friend, a poet
> HONORINE, his wife and Henri's mistress
> CHANTAL, their daughter and also Henri's mistress
> PASCAL, their deceased son
> MONIQUE, the narrator's former mistress

At 149 kilometers per hour and still accelerating through the curves of a
lonely road in France, the powerful beige sport touring car suddenly swerves a
bit as one of its passengers lunges at the steering wheel, trying to wrest it from
the car's driver. So begins John Hawkes's *Travesty*—quickly, nervously, a bit
violently, during the darkest quarter of a cold, wet night. But soon the auto is
back on course, the driver deftly fending off the attack and regaining complete
control. Or so he says. For as one reads on, he discovers that this well-
appointed glass-and-steel surrogate mother—the upholstery soft and comforting, the machine's heater keeping its travelers well-toasted and insulated
against the hostile natural forces—this mechanical womb, will shortly be a
tomb for its inhabitants. For though the driver says that he is in complete control, the control he possesses is that of a demented sniper behind an M-16 or a
3.5 Mannlicher, slowly but surely squeezing the trigger; this driver's target is
an old stone wall, about a meter thick, of an abandoned barn many kilometers
away.

Travesty's calculating narrator, an unnamed, middle-aged "privileged"
person, is the outgrowth of two other Hawkesian creations, two other self-
justifying confessors—Cyril of *The Blood Oranges* (1971) and Allert of *Death,
Sleep & The Traveler* (1974); and *Travesty* forms the final volume of a trilogy
concerned ultimately with probing the limits of the poetic imagination and
erotic fantasy. Like the other two narrators, this speaker talks on and on, trying
to justify his actions through much sophistical argument and simultaneously
exposing his own sexual obsessions, his self-absorption, his perversions and
madness. Meanwhile, his passengers—Henri, a poet, the narrator's supposed
friend, and sharer of his wife's bed, and Chantal, the narrator's twenty-five-

year-old daughter and lover of Henri—seem to disintegrate slowly as the time
of their "private apocalypse" draws near.

As the speaker ruminates on, gently but firmly discounting all physical, intellectual, and emotional appeals from his captives, as Chantal vomits in the
back seat and Henri begins to wheeze up front, Hawkes's *persona* coolly outlines his motives for the premeditated murder/suicide and at the same time recounts the significant experiences of his life. From the speciousness of his arguments and from his reveries, the reader pieces together a picture of a man who
is much less and much more than what he appears to be.

Albeit a simpler text in comparison with Hawkes's other novels in terms of
density of language, symbol, and time structure, the novel remains difficult because of the author's manipulation of its form, the dramatic monologue, one
used by poets from Browning to Yeats, Pound, Eliot, and Frost. In the novel
we hear only one speaker in a dramatic situation, as in "My Last Duchess,"
but the reader cannot penetrate the *persona's* glossy statements to the real
truth of the situation and the nature of the speaker as readily as he can Browning's Duke's. Hawkes's form is rather closely modeled after that of Albert
Camus' *The Fall.* Like the statements of Camus' ambiguous judge-penitent,
those of *Travesty's* narrator may or may not be true. In fact, the *persona's* comment in *The Fall*—"it's very hard to disentangle the true from the false in what
I'm saying"—is paraphrased and amended slightly by the driver of the beige
car: "The moral of it all is trust me but do not believe me." The reader must
beware, then, of lending credence too quickly or even finally to the speaker's
comments, for, in the Swiftian mode, all statements in this box are false.

Travesty, then, an uncertain reading experience, creates *angst* for its
audience through its form. For instance, one can never be sure if anyone is
really in the auto with the narrator; one must infer the presence of Henri and
Chantal, because of their violent actions and frenzied comments—so different
from the speaker's smooth, glib verbal reactions to them. Moreover, one cannot be sure that there is really any car at all, any exterior reality to the present
and past events described so hauntingly and yet so clearly; perhaps the narrator is simply dreaming, letting his suppressed memories and desires well up
and flow out. Perhaps by opening the novel the reader simply enters the dark
world of the imagination of Hawkes's *persona,* traveling with him on a psychic
journey into the depths of his mind. And, lastly, perhaps all of this is a
travesty, a distorted burlesque of supposedly enlightened twentieth century
man, of Hawkes's own creations, of Hawkes's own literary perspective. That
evidence exists which supports each of these four perspectives (real but irrational, remembered, imagined, and burlesqued) adds great ambiguity to the
work, making any final reading of it a categorical impossibility. At the same
time, that it is a frightening book, a disquieting book, cannot be denied. What
makes it so is the result of the speaker's extraordinary characterization, his
haunting and vivid descriptions of the surface textures of his past, and his

cataloging of the landscape details that seem to flash by, made visible both by the bright cone of light created by the auto's headlights and by the imaginative vision of the poet-driver.

Initially, the oily, sophisticated narrator seems to be in absolute control not only of the expensive bomb that he is accelerating toward their incomprehensible autocide but also of his emotions. For his detachment seems complete, his analytical abilities and imaginative powers superseding those of Henri, his gift for seeing likenesses in the most incongruous materials being quite precious. He considers himself above jealousy, above hatred, his code far superior to conventional morality.

But the passengers in the car and the reader know better. That the speaker is irrational, base, and immoral is quite obvious. His detailed and often inconsistent speech reveals a mythomaniacal obsession with form, with design over meaning, over morality. And although he absolutely discounts the labels "suicidal maniac" and "aesthetician of death at high speed" and denies intentional cruelty, he is continually pushing the pedal down in his drive toward their doom, continually and increasingly jabbing at Chantal and Henri with sardonic thrusts. And, finally, though he claims that his sole object is aesthetic, "a clear 'accident' in which invention quite defies interpretation" (much like the novel itself), his reveries over the joys and sorrows of his past hint that he is bent on other matters, namely punishment—of Henri for his artistic posing and, more importantly, for his intrusion into the narrator's house; of Chantal for her love of Henri, a love that the narrator himself seems to covet; and of Honorine, his wife, for her adulterous behavior. Of course, he cannot admit to any of these base but human reactions, for he considers himself above all that. In reality he is an abstracted, detached, seemingly superior but degenerate visionary, one so cut off from normal human contacts that he has had to resort to memory and especially the imagination to replace what he has lost: his essential humanity. He is a crazed man, a travesty of a sane man; a murderer, a travesty of a lover; a destroyer, a travesty of a creator.

In addition, through the narrator Hawkes seems to parody his own creations—Skipper of *Second Skin* and especially Cyril of *The Blood Oranges* and Allert of *Death, Sleep & the Traveler*—and perhaps himself as a writer addicted to formalism, one who said in 1965, "I'm a very detached writer, interested in the absolute creation of pure vision." Perhaps Hawkes is revealing in *Travesty* his own awareness of his obsession with form and pure vision and is relinquishing that obsession, for he has realized long before his narrator the dangers present in such a monomania as implied by the speaker's last statement: "there shall be no survivors. None." Perhaps Hawkes has discovered the sophistry of the driver's comments that "nothing is more important than the existence of what does not exist," that "Imagined life is more exhilarating than remembered life." Perhaps Hawkes is telling the reader that future novels will be more realistic, based more on his own remembered experiences, populated by more realistic characters in more believable situations.

That Hawkes is parodying his own creations can be seen in the split between what the narrator appears to be—one who has had a long history of lusty erotic adventures—and what he really is—one whose experiences have been largely voyeuristic, masturbatory, and perhaps sterile. Alternating with jocular responses to the protests of Henri, the speaker confesses his youthful obsession with magazines displaying dead bodies and the glossiest pornography; his own vast collection of photographs of Honorine in various phases of autoeroticism; his joy at seeing his then fifteen-year-old daughter come of age during a decadent rite after which she is crowned the Queen of Carrots; his memory of spanking his mistress, Monique (who bears much resemblance to Chantal), and then being whipped by her with her garter belt. In some of these anecdotes Hawkes reveals his great talent for creating precise, memorable, and often comic images that, put together, form an ironically sad account of the speaker's life of "dead passion." From his revery over the tatoo of a cluster of pale purple grapes on yellow stems that coils below Honorine's navel to his description of Chantal's tight, dark body, the narrator unknowingly paints a picture of lost eroticism. He has been replaced. Hinting of past and present sexual inadequacy are a very bad pun at the beginning of the work and repeated references throughout to horses, the horse being a symbol of sexual energy. The speaker recalls when a boyish jokester gave Chantal an optician's chart marked by very small letters which read "TOO MUCH SEX MAKES ONE SHORT-SIGHTED," to which the narrator adds "But do you know that I have never worn eyeglasses." Later, the speaker refers to Chantal's riding lessons and his image of Honorine as "nude beneath a severe black hunting costume for riding sidesaddle, though she has never been on a horse in all her life." As a substitute for his loss, the narrator now sits at the controls of a roaring sports car, its ruby-red engine pulling them on toward their final destruction, a fusion of death and erotic climax. Awake behind the wheel, asleep in bed, or simply detached and imagining, the speaker lifts off the page as not what he seems—cool, analytical, his instincts refined out of existence by intelligence and imagination—but rather as a pathetic and diabolical failure, both the sadness and terror of whom periodically breaks through his aloof manner.

Adding more to the disturbing nature of the novel are the narrator's comments about the rest of the characters. Even though they may or may not exist beyond the speaker's subconscious or imagination, they are either maimed or at least the opposite of what one expects. The narrator, always drawn to the incongruous, especially delights in his doctor, a man possessing an artificial leg and a constant cough, shaking hands, a great interest in pornography—a travesty of a doctor. A more significant character, Honorine, her name itself in the light of Henri's live-in liaison with her a testament to Hawkes's love of parody, is the very opposite of the conventional, respectable middle-aged aristocrat she appears to be, her tatoo an indication of her sensuality. Henri, himself a posing poet, is depicted as a rather foolish grotesque, his physical deformities resulting from brain surgery. He, too, is a travesty, a burlesque, a parody of a man of vision.

Completing this tale of discontinuity and perhaps saving it from complete obscurity are Hawkes's fine descriptions of the landscapes through which the reader travels on the road to the stone wall. They are both real and phantasmagoric, static and moving, naturalistic and surrealistic. His remarkable clarity of visual image and resonating prose rhythms are in ironical contrast to the ambiguous perspective and incongruous characters. Many precise, evocative passages such as the following are laced throughout the novel:

> Our lights will be like searchlights swiveling in unimaginable confinement, and a forlorn, artificial rose and the granite foot of one of their crucified Christs and a sudden low chimney will all approach us like a handful of thrown stones. . . . Let us hope that we are not deflected by a shard of tile or little rusted iron key or the slick, white femur of some recently slaughtered animal.

These images seem to both flash by and remain memorable, the result of the fine sense of speed that Hawkes creates, his narrator's slow, careful, and circuitous explanations nicely juxtaposed against his swift swerving into turns and flat-out acceleration of the precision automobile toward oblivion.

But the ride will not be accepted by many. As has been the fate of most of Hawkes's novels, *Travesty* will be ignored by most readers due partly to the author's refusal to represent reality realistically, partly to its difficulties of accessibility generated by the uniqueness of Hawkes's personal vision, and partly to its ambiguous design. But for those who have stamina, intelligence, and a taste not only for ambiguity but also for the positive moral vision that lies behind the apparent homage to decadence, there will be much to enjoy in this incongruous book of reveries. Unfortunately, too many readers will agree with the narrator's early statement, "But even a poet will find it difficult to share this vision on short notice."

Harold J. Joseph

Sources for Further Study

Best Sellers. XXXVI, June, 1976, p. 69.

National Review. XXVIII, April 30, 1976, p. 461.

New Republic. CLXXIV, May 8, 1976, p. 26.

New York Times Book Review. March 28, 1976, p. 23.

New Yorker. LII, April 19, 1976, p. 134.

Observer. July 18, 1976, p. 21.

TRINITY

Author: Leon Uris (1924-   )
Publisher: Doubleday and Company (New York). Illustrated. 751 pp. $10.95
Type of work: Novel
Time: The late nineteenth and early twentieth centuries
Locale: Ireland

A probing, passionate story of the political struggle in Northern Ireland

> Principal characters:
> CONOR LARKIN, a Catholic farmer turned ironmaster and revolutionary
> SEAMUS O'NEILL, the narrator and Larkin's best friend
> SIR FREDERICK WEED, a Belfast aristocrat and industrial magnate
> CAROLINE HUBBLE, Countess of Foyle, daughter of Frederick Week
> ROGER HUBBLE, Earl of Foyle, Ulster landed gentry
> SHELLEY MCLEOD, daughter of Morgan McLeod, a respected Protestant shipyard worker, and the mistress of Conor Larkin

Leon Uris came to the fore as a storyteller in the 1950's after writing such massive and well-researched works as *Battle Cry* and *Exodus*. He spent a great deal of time researching *Trinity* as well, while his wife, Jill, gathered photographs for her pictorial essay *Ireland: a Terrible Beauty,* for which Uris wrote the prose.

Trinity is the story of Conor Larkin, an Irish Catholic from a tenant farming family who becomes embroiled in the political situation of Ireland around the turn of the century. It is also a recounting of how the civil war in modern Ireland came into being, with a fairly clear explication of the motivations of each segment of the population that is involved in the war—the native Irish Catholics, the immigrant Protestant Ulstermen, and the British aristocracy.

The novel is divided into seven major parts, each introduced by a map. Although the maps are not necessary to an understanding of the action, they do lend an aura of verisimilitude to the format. Each of these major parts is divided into chapters, which are further divided into scenes. The separate scenes within the chapters are related to one another, but the chapters do not necessarily follow chronologically. Often, in fact, the locale alters considerably from chapter to chapter, and new characters appear whose relationship to the storyline is often difficult to perceive immediately.

Uris draws all of these threads of the story together and weaves them into a relentlessly powerful saga. It is a sweeping narrative, very popular in style, with enough characters to flesh out history bolstered by sufficient verifiable facts to maintain credibility, the essence of historical fiction. But it is as a fictional work that *Trinity* shines. There are times when the narrative is slow or the development of a character uneven or the dialogue improbable, but these are minor problems.

There are two structural flaws, however, that detract more seriously from the storyline. The first, fairly early in the work, is the use of the supernatural appearance of an old man to impart to the child Conor Larkin the history of the Irish struggle in general, and particularly the Larkin family's important role in it. While such background information is important to the development of the action, and while the author may find it important to clue the reader as to the significance of mysticism in Irish life, his device fails to be convincing as part of a historical novel. The reader is not overwhelmed by the magnitude of the old man's story, but puzzled by the use of the old man to tell it.

Later in the work Uris uses a nightmare to extricate himself from a predicament of his own making. The logical conclusion to the events that he has presented at one point would move Larkin out of Ireland and into a happy marriage. Uris conjures up Larkin's conscience garbed in another character to appear to him in a dream and speak to him of his Irishness. Larkin as a consequence makes a complete and total about-face to become a full-fledged revolutionary and give up all else. It is not in the least convincing.

Much of the flavor of the novel results from Uris' use of language. It is an odd mix of modern-day swearing and Gaelic lilt with just enough solid prose to keep those readers unaccustomed to Celtic phrases from losing their way. Many of the verbs are contrived from nouns—one is not placed in a casket, one rather is "casketed"—but the overall effect is usable if occasionally anachronistic.

The work seems to end abruptly, as though Uris were suddenly exhausted. Such an eventuality could be quite understandable, for in addition to presenting to his readers an enthralling story, he has also managed to provide information on any number of sidelights to the Irish lifestyle—wakes and kelp gathering, peat cutting and flax harvests, folkways and superstitions—in a dazzling array.

Lamentably, Uris' recounting of history is fairly linear, and though intrinsic to the work, is less effectively presented than the story which is woven around it. Social commentary, perhaps outright propaganda, is an integral element of this historical presentation. Each of the three factions in the political war is examined, but the native Irishmen obviously have the sympathy of the author. Uris does manage to a great degree to avoid the depiction of the Irish as the quaint folk of the popular stereotype, but he cannot resist the image of an innocent and poetical people provoked to acts of violence by their greedy and unfeeling neighbors. During one scene, as the Irish Republican Brotherhood is being resurrected, a hero of a previous rising exhorts those present to accept martyrdom as an inevitable part of being Irish, while admonishing them that no crime they commit in obtaining their goal of freedom from England could be considered as great as the crimes which will be committed by those who would prevent their success—a romantic, revolutionary version of "the end justifies the means."

Uris also paints a glorious picture of Ireland before the encroachments of the British. The Irish were simple people with a rich mythology and a lilting language that gave every man the raw material from which to create poetry. The British, however, found them to be backward rather than simple and riddled with ghosts and goblins and all manner of superstitions.

The end toward which the British aristocracy in Ireland is aiming is an economic one, cast by Uris in a thoroughly negative light which would illuminate it as colonial exploitation. Moreover, the British government is shown to be impossible to deal with and totally lacking in honor, as it uses the third segment of the population, the Protestant Ulstermen, to achieve its own ends.

The Scotsmen whose families were settled in Ireland as part of the colonization effort as well as for a reward for their part in Cromwell's revolution, are nearly two-dimensional. They are sober and industrious with no creative spark whatsoever and are equally tied out of economic necessity, along with the natives, to the British for their jobs in the shipyards or farms. Uris does paint pathetic portraits of some of these individuals, but shows almost all of them to be unable to respond to their situation rationally, for their minds are fogged by the rhetoric of their preachers.

As the Irish are portrayed as "noble savages" and the Scots-Irish as mundane, the British aristocracy is composed of greedy, grasping industrialists with the power to play both of the other segments of the population against each other in a successful effort to turn their attention toward hating each other rather than realizing that they are both being manipulated. Uris makes a strong case for this interpretation of the situation, but one cannot help but suspect that these stereotypes are more stringent than history would bear out, and that things are probably not quite so black or white.

In view of his rather simplistic view of the different classes, Uris presents those characters from each class who are prime movers in the action as atypical, if not exactly classless. Conor Larkin educates himself and goes into a trade rather than remain on the farm that he would inherit; he consequently dies in a raid rather than peacefully in his bed. The Protestant McLeod family accepts Conor almost as one of their own, seeing beyond past generations of hatred. They are ostracized by their social class and one of them is even murdered because of her intimate involvement with Conor. Lady Caroline Hubble teaches her children by example that the lower class Irish are worthy of friendship, but ruins her marriage over her son's liasion with a Catholic girl. Uris is completely pessimistic concerning the possibility of the various segments of Irish society overcoming their ingrained prejudices.

It is not precisely religious fervor that Uris sees as the moving force behind the acts of violence in Northern Ireland, but hate generated by the Protestant preachers in their flocks coupled with mindless acceptance of the position of the Church by the Catholic parishoners stemming from centuries of near-absolute control by their priests, which has been fostered by the ruling class. Upper-echelon Catholic churchmen are bought off by the British, and through the excessively hierarchical Church structure the inaction which they advocate paralyzes the peasants into a hopeless acceptance of the *status quo*. Almost all clergy in the work, Catholic and Protestant alike, are devoid of idealism.

Other than in the political arena, both Churches are also singled out for their ability to repress their parishoners' natural instincts, notably those sexual in nature, with a concomitant warping of their lives and values. The Catholic Church in the person of the parish priest ruins the marriage of Conor's parents, Tomas and Finola Larkin, by forcing Finola to forswear sexual activity once she would risk death by having any more children. Both Finola and her daughter Brigid go through agonies in having to confess that they actually enjoy sex—sinful as that enjoyment is considered to be.

The Protestant preacher does an equal amount of damage, if not more, by inciting certain female members of his flock to such a frenzy of self-righteous hate that they brutally murder Larkin's Protestant mistress.

It is significant that the primary believers in church dogma in each of these cases are women. Uris has very little of a positive nature to say concerning religious women who follow conventional morality and socially acceptable behavior. He gives, in addition, the distinct impression that sexual fulfillment should have very little if anything to do with marriage.

The heroines in the novel, one from each of the three factions, all share certain characteristics. They are, of course, all breathtakingly beautiful. Each has left her social milieu at an early age to pursue her own life and interests, with guiltless sexual gratification being a primary component thereof. Each is strong-willed if not headstrong, each thinking for herself and not in the least afraid to act upon those thoughts. None is religious. The two women who are born to the aristocracy either renounce the title or spend a great deal of time in the company of, and in sympathy with, the lower classes. All three of them find the hero, Conor Larkin, enticing, though only two are given the chance to act upon their desires (outside of the bonds of marriage, of course).

Conor Larkin is a very traditional hero. In this perspective it is not surprising that he succeeds brilliantly at everything he attempts—as master ironworker, rugby star, lover, and military strategist. There are times, however, that his up-by-the-bootstraps self-education loses credibility and the story suffers. The most notable of these instances is a courtroom scene in which Uris uses Larkin to expound upon the basis in English common law for justifying the Irish rebellion. Although such a commentary may be vital to the propaganda value of the work, the characterization of Larkin is weakened by it, for the reader is unable to believe that Conor could have such a mastery of law, given his background and experience.

Nevertheless, those who read *Trinity* are exposed to a mass of information, led through a welter of events and situations; and no reader will be left without a fuller understanding of Ireland and the struggles of its people.

Margaret S. Schoon

Sources for Further Study

Best Sellers. XXXVI, June, 1976, p. 73.

Book World. April 25, 1976, p. G7.

Booklist. LXXII, March 1, 1976, p. 960.

Critic. XXXV, Winter, 1976, p. 82.

New Statesman. XCII, October 8, 1976, p. 486.

New York Times Book Review. March 14, 1976, p. 5.

Observer. October 17, 1976, p. 33.

THE TRIUMPH OF THE NOVEL
Dickens, Dostoevsky, Faulkner

Author: Albert J. Guerard (1914-   )
Publisher: Oxford University Press (New York). 365 pp. $13.95
Type of work: Literary criticism

A detailed and stimulating consideration of three major novelists and their genre

The Triumph of the Novel is both a full, provocative study of Dickens, Dostoevsky, and Faulkner and a defense of all novels that are not primarily faithful re-creations of the world as it is. In the works of these writers Albert Guerard finds the triumph of a tradition that passes from Cervantes, Rabelais, Sterne, and Joyce to such contemporary novelists as Nabokov and García Márquez. All are fascinated by the strange and grotesque, and all "derive fictional energy from the interpenetration of the fantastic and the substantial, altogether fleshly, 'real.' " They may lack the formal control of a Henry James, but for Guerard this deficiency is far outweighed by the vitality of their creations and the effectiveness of their rhetorical experimentation.

Guerard, a professor of English at Stanford University and author of distinguished critical studies of Conrad, Hardy, and Gide, brings to this book wide and deep reading in nineteenth and twentieth century fiction, experience as a practicing novelist, and a long-standing concern with the psychology of the writer and its effect on his work. All of these factors contribute to the breadth and depth of this study, which includes extended analysis of specific texts, exploration of the minds of the novelists, and discussion of the writer's problems in shaping the reader's reaction to his material.

Three chapters are devoted to "forbidden games," psychological obsessions revealed directly or obliquely in the work of the novelists: Dickens' idealized love for his sister-in-law Mary Hogarth, who died suddenly in her late teens; Dostoevsky's "paedophilia," his preoccupation with the violation of young girls; Faulkner's misogyny and his mistrust of normal sexual relations. From the psychology of the authors, Guerard turns to aspects of their craft, analyzing Dickens' narrative voices, Dostoevsky's psychological approach to his characters, and Faulkner's experiments with language and style. He bases his generalizations about each writer on detailed discussions of a number of their works and occasional comparisons with the writing of their contemporaries, Conrad and Hardy in particular.

The final section of this study in an extended, balanced critical analysis of three novels that reveal fully the creative energy and rhetorical freedom of the fictional form Guerard is defending: Dickens' *Martin Chuzzlewit*, Dostoevsky's *The Possessed,* and Faulkner's *Absalom, Absalom!* There is, perhaps surprisingly, no general conclusion. Guerard suggests by its omission that the best argument for the greatness of this genre is the works themselves.

There are, as the author recognizes, problems inherent in the structure he has adopted here. The book does at times threaten to break apart into separate studies of the three writers and of specific works, but Guerard gives it an underlying unity through a number of recurrent themes: the interrelationship of the author's psychic state and his work, the fictional energy that arises from the free play of thought and imagination, the truth conveyed in the depiction of the "unreal." Avoiding the obvious pitfalls of dwelling on "influence" and insignificant parallels of plot and character, he illuminates the writing of each of the novelists by pointing out important similarities and differences between them—Dostoevsky's tendency to "underdramatize" scenes of violence that Dickens or Faulkner might handle melodramatically, for example.

The Triumph of the Novel is not, Guerard says, and could not be, a fully comprehensive study of the three novelists. It is rather a consideration of points that others have neglected or passed over lightly. His Dickens is "the inventive fantasist and comic entertainer," not the social critic and reformer; his Dostoevsky, "the great . . . intuitive psychologist and wayward dreamer of solitary obsessions and intense interpersonal relationships," not the "religious mystic" or "political ideologue"; his Faulkner, the "lover of the comic and grotesque, the poet intoxicated by words and rhythms," not the "sociologist of the South."

These qualities that Guerard singles out for emphasis have much to do with "paradoxical sympathies" he takes up in the second chapter of the book. What is it that makes readers respond positively to fictional characters that would repel them if they met them on the street, creations such as Daniel Quilp or Old Karamazov or Mink Snopes? Conversely, why is it so difficult to make a "good" character truly appealing? Guerard mentions Pickwick, Father Zossima, and Dilsey as notable exceptions to the general rule that the noble are much duller to read about than the wicked.

Achieving the proper balance between sympathy and moral judgment, Guerard says, is one of the fiction writer's most difficult tasks. The reader is not meant to give moral approval to characters like Jonas Chuzzlewit, Feodor Karamazov, or Jason Compson, yet he must not find them wholly distasteful either. What attracts one to these characters is their vitality, the "perfection of the portrait" that arouses "cool fascination" if not real sympathy. The technical skill of Dickens, Dostoevsky, and Faulkner makes the reader respond to their characters as "fictive creations," as works of art, not personal acquaintances. Dostoevsky's Grand Inquisitor is a particularly powerful example of a figure who must be seen to be wrong on one level yet admired and respected for the dignity and intensity with which his creator has endowed him.

Another characteristic common to these novelists, according to Guerard, is their ability to transmute their personal neuroses into art. This premise is the basis of the "forbidden games" chapters, in which the author discusses "tabooed acts and relationships, strong 'anti-social' attractions or repugnances, threatening obsessions."

Throughout Dickens' work appears the figure of an innocent, vulnerable young woman, modeled on his dead sister-in-law Mary Hogarth, who lived with him and his wife until her early death. Guerard suggests that Dickens felt for Mary a strong attraction that had to be repressed because of their relationship, and that after her death he sublimated his feelings in his portrayals of saintly young women and "asexual, heavenly" marriages. Mary is seen reflected in Rose Maylie, Florence Dombey, Agnes Wickfield, and especially vividly in Little Nell, who maintains her innocence in the face of countless threats in *The Old Curiosity Shop*. Guerard finds the greatest menace to be her grandfather, her protector except when he is obsessed by his gambling fever. Nell escapes the unstated danger of incest through her gradual fading away toward death. Guerard suggests, but does not insist upon, biographical and psychological connections here, then concludes that the strongest theme Dickens drew from Mary's death was the redemptive effect "of purity, of chastity and innocence."

Dostoevsky's "forbidden games" are related to his obsession with the welfare and especially with the sexual abuse of young girls. Guerard feels that the writer's impulse to protect may have been inextricably tied to a desire to injure the vulnerable and the weak, sometimes presented in his fiction as girls, sometimes as crippled or retarded older women—the child Liza in *The Eternal Husband*, Sonia in *Crime and Punishment*, Lizaveta in *The Brothers Karamazov*. In one of Dostoevsky's early novels, *The Insulted and the Injured*, the thirteen-year-old heroine Nellie, in part modeled on Dickens' Little Nell, is rescued from a brothel by a man whom she comes to love in a half-childish, half-adult way. Dostoevsky saves his hero from having to come to terms with his feelings for the girl by having her, like Little Nell, die.

For Faulkner the most significant "forbidden game" is the sexual relationship between adult men and women. His women are usually portrayed as destructive, overpowering, promiscuous, and in many cases symbols of moral degeneration. The female characters, especially in the early novels, suffer "appalling predicaments and punishments." The portrait of Temple Drake in *Sanctuary* reveals the author's misogyny particularly clearly.

Although Guerard considers the psychological impulses underlying the work of Dickens, Dostoevsky, and Faulkner important, he emphasizes still more strongly their artistry, their willingness to move beyond the conventional forms of language and structure. He finds in Dickens, often maligned by critics as melodramatic and sentimental, other more praiseworthy, narrative tones. Among them he singles out the "grave interior voice," seen in retrospective, meditative passages in *David Copperfield* and *Great Expectations,* the "detached contemplative voice" used to judge, condense, and create ironic perspectives in *Bleak House* and *Dombey and Son,* and the "jog trot" that creates a "cosy" relationship with the reader at the beginning of a new installment. (Guerard's enthusiasm for this third tone is distinctly less than for the first two.)

In his chapter on "The Psychology of Dostoevsky" Guerard demonstrates the "conscious understanding of unconscious processes" that led Freud to say "that everything he had discovered was already present in Dostoevsky's work." Some of Guerard's best and most useful insights come in the close studies of Dostoevskian characters that make up this chapter. His comments on the use of doubles, characters that seem to be two parts of the same personality, should enrich the reader's understanding of several of the novels.

More than a dozen of Faulkner's books are considered in the section devoted to his technique. Guerard focuses on his attempts to break away from the traditional novel forms, concentrating especially on his use of separate narratives within one work and his blending of "disparate modes, tones, and feelings." The last part of the chapter surveys the materials that Faulkner found most congenial: the history and people of Yoknapatawpha County; racial and familial tensions; hunting and drinking, especially as activities binding groups of men together; and the quest, sometimes noble, sometimes absurd, sometimes both at once. These subjects, says Guerard, are the ones that liberated Faulkner's characteristic voice and enabled it to flow freely in the long, impressionistic passages that are instantly recognizable as his and his alone.

The final three chapters of Guerard's study documents the flexibility and inclusiveness of the novel. The three works he considers in detail seem initially to have little in common. He praises *Martin Chuzzlewit* for its rich comedy and satire in its picture of London slums and Dickens' America, and for its unforgettable personages like Pecksniff and Sairey Gamp. *The Possessed* is discussed as both an ideological and a psychological novel, confused and disorderly in some respects, but ultimately a powerful character study. *Absalom, Absalom!* is for Guerard perhaps the greatest American novel, one in which the author frees the genre "from mimesis: from an obligation to be or even seem an authentic report on reality." This point brings out the essence of what Guerard has tried to communicate throughout his book—the value of the novel that ranges as far as the author's imagination can carry him, conveying its truths through eccentric characters, strange obsessions, loosely constructed plots, and linguistic experiments.

The Triumph of the Novel is an impressive work of criticism that should prove valuable to students and teachers of fiction for many years to come. It is a richly laden study and a well-written one, though it cannot be recommended as light reading. One of the book's greatest virtues may also be the greatest deterrent to potential readers. Guerard writes with ease and familiarity of almost everything his three subjects wrote, and the very number of works he discusses may be overwhelming for those who may have, at best, a passing acquaintance with *A Christmas Carol, Crime and Punishment,* and *The Sound and the Fury.* The result is likely to be a piecemeal use of the book by those interested in one of the three novelists or in a single work. Even readers who approach the volume in this way will be rewarded, however, for Guerard illuminates almost everything he takes up; but they will miss the larger dimension of the study that adds to our appreciation of the variety and vitality of the novel's form and content.

Elizabeth Johnston Lipscomb

Sources for Further Study

Kirkus Reviews. XLIV, August 1, 1976, p. 879.
Library Journal. CI, September 15, 1976, p. 1857.
New York Times Book Review. September 26, 1976, p. 27.
Publisher's Weekly. CCX, September 20, 1976, p. 22.

TURTLE DIARY

Author: Russell Hoban (1925-   )
Publisher: Random House (New York). 211 pp. $7.95
Type of work: Novel
Time: The 1970's
Locale: London and Polperro, England

A bookstore clerk and a writer of children's books kidnap sea turtles from the London Zoo in order to liberate the turtles and themselves as well

> Principal characters:
> WILLIAM G., a lonely middle-aged Londoner who clerks in a bookstore
> NEAERA H., a lonely middle-aged Londoner who writes books for children
> GEORGE FAIRBAIRN, the head keeper at the Aquarium of the London Zoo

Children, less bound by convention than their elders, are the demanding audience for which Russell Hoban has successfully written for many years. His disarmingly fresh approach to literature for adults, blended with clever imagery, is an echo from his children's works that enlivens his writing in *Turtle Diary.*

Convention and habit surround us all to varying degrees and spin a web in which we can become caught; pleasant routine often becomes a tedious rut for many. Hoban in *Turtle Diary* has presented us with the story of two such people, William G. and Neaera H., told through alternating entries from their diaries. Both are middle-aged Londoners who live very private, lonely lives. Each is drawn, separately, to the sea turtles in the Aquarium of the London Zoo. Each is greatly disturbed by the captivity of such marvelous creatures and feels the urge to liberate the turtles from their tanks. They meet when they recognize the urge mirrored in each other. Through a conspiracy with George Fairbairn, the head keeper, William and Neaera kidnap the turtles and take them back to freedom in the sea.

It is such a whimsical story that the more romantic reader would expect loud ovations for William and Neaera for their heroic deed, or at the very least a reprimand or legal suit from the Society which runs the Zoo. Neither reaction is forthcoming, however. In fact, there is no reaction from the "public" at all. Having had no crusading ecological motivation behind their action, William and Neaera are not even exceedingly self-satisfied. Taken as just the recounting of a turtle raid by two recluses, the story is somewhat pointless, perhaps even altogether peculiar.

However, the restoration of freedom to the turtles is for both William and Neaera not so much something that they want to do but something that they must do, although they do not actually articulate a reason for it even to themselves. They certainly are not acting out of sentimentality either, for both of them have lost the capability of feeling such things long ago.

The portrait of William that Hoban paints for us through his diary entries is one of a gray, drab man mired in pointless routine, moving from day to day with no hope in his future. William has a past, but he represses thoughts of it for they make him wistful at best, but more often quite depressed. While once he had a wife and two daughters and a home to take care of, since his divorce he lives by himself in a roominghouse totally out of touch with his children. Where once he was a gregarious, successful advertising executive, now he is a bookstore clerk who finds it difficult to interact with the other clerks, the customers, and other boarders at the roominghouse.

Hoban describes Neaera's life as being equally static. Her daily routine is even more private than William's, writing children's books in her apartment, speaking to very few other people, watching the movements of her pet water beetle. She tries to deny her dreadful loneliness by imagining the four walls of her apartment to be snug and cosy rather than confining, convincing herself that her corner of the world is sufficient unto itself.

Through their curiosity about the turtles, rather than any interest in each other, both William and Neaera find less and less satisfaction in their daily lives. Sea turtles in their natural environment make yearly pilgrimages through thousands of miles of ocean to lay their eggs. It is a perilous journey and they have no navigational aids save their instinct, but they make the trip anyway, swimming relentlessly until they reach their goal. It is their unthinking certainty of purpose that William envies. He realizes that time is relentlessly pushing him forward but he does not know for what purpose.

Neaera feels that a creature that has the capability to do something must not be kept from doing that something. If turtles are capable of making such a perilous swim, then they should not be confined by the four walls of their tank and prevented from fulfilling their destiny.

In short, William and Neaera recognize in the parallel of the unfulfilled destiny of the sea turtles the elements that are lacking in their own lives. It is an unconscious recognition and not exactly a welcome one. Both of them resent, in a way, such an intrusion into their privacy. It is much easier to plod through their familiar routines than to acknowledge their growing obsession much less to act upon it. And yet, both of them begin to feel within themselves potentialities for the recovery of a purpose in their lives.

Hoban is by no means overt or terribly heavyhanded with his philosophizing. His two characters, if a bit daft at times, are all too human most of the time. Having allowed their kidnaping urge to develop into a full-fledged obsession, they are both apprehensive not so much at the idea of being caught, but at the awful burden of all the real-life details to arrange. William fusses over the thought of having to drive a van during the escapade because he has never driven one before. Neither William nor Neaera ever gets around to checking on whether the tide will be in or out at the time on the day that they intend to do the job, even though it would make a crucial difference in their methodology.

Through all of this George, the head keeper, not only overlooks the thievery, but actually aids it by providing the opportunity to spirit the creatures away and even crating the turtles for pickup. William and Neaera have a ridiculously easy time of it. William does find it difficult to keep the van off the curb, but there are no problems in picking up the crates or in the drive. When they arrive at their final destination, the tide fortunately is in, so that it is just a matter of moving the crates out of the truck to the sea wall and dumping the turtles into the ocean. It is all accomplished quickly, and though the dolly makes a great amount of noise, their actions are not observed.

Although the actual liberation of the turtles is so smooth as to be nearly anticlimactic, the liberation of William and Neaera is not so easily resolved. Andre Gidé in *The Immoralist* has said that "To know how to free oneself is nothing; the arduous thing is to know what to do with one's freedom." So it is in this case. They have performed a somewhat gratifying but small task and no one has noticed save the head keeper at the zoo. George not only understands their urge to free the turtles, agreeing with it to the point of aiding and abetting the kidnaping, but he seems to have come to terms with himself on the question of the purpose of life.

Neaera, however, after the deed is done, can no longer abide her apartment; she feels restless and caged within the walls that used to form her private retreat from the world. Having done something so very uncharacteristic of herself, she can no longer be comfortable in the old routine with that somewhat altered self. She has taken a great step out of her privacy and cannot go back into it again. Neaera seeks out George in the midst of her disquiet because he emanates calm. As she realizes that her solitariness was actually desperate loneliness, she alleviates the pain that she now acknowledges by sleeping with George.

William's sexual rekindling, aided by Harriet, another clerk at the bookstore, occurs even before the turtle caper is an accomplished fact. He works out his liberation in a way different from that of Neaera. He begins by insisting that another boarder at his roominghouse, whose slovenly habits he has until now accepted with resignation, clean up after himself when using communal facilities. After several days the argument between the two men comes to blows, though not of the glorious Hollywood fight scene variety. Both men are stiff and bruised but William has manfully pressed for his rights and the slovenly ways are amended to some degree.

William's total lifestyle does not change, but his time frame does. His previous inclination was to be a spectator of his own actions, to lapse into meaningless reverie while staring at railroad tracks or children at play, to ruminate over which actors should play the scenes of his life when it is made into a film. Now he finds himself starting to live each day as it happens, real time as it were, and to relate to other people in the present tense. Other people's feelings begin to play a part in his thoughts.

Although Hoban's writing style is intense and introspective, like the characters themselves, part of the charm of the novel is that he writes with enough humor to keep the reader's perspective in focus. Two of the most clever and delightful flights of fancy involve likening the appearance of certain birds to the characteristic human types, specifically terns reflecting the postures of European philosophers as they pace up and down the beach, and oyster catchers resembling long-legged lady birdwatchers hard at work.

More than merely using such pat stereotypes, Hoban also displays for the reader numerous familiar human actions. His description, for instance, of a little boy splashing a newly acquired plastic gorilla repeatedly into a puddle of water will be familiar to anyone who has spent a few moments in the walkways just outside a zoo. Likewise, one must chuckle with recognition when William decides not to question the origins of his little aches and pains because he would rather not know about them. Hoban repeatedly makes us smile at the little human quirks so common to us all. We see our foibles reflected in his warm humor and they no longer seem to be so serious.

The work is sprinkled with more overt humor, especially the proper names that Hoban choses. He gives us such delightful nonsense as Fallopia Bothways, authoress of *Procurer to the King,* and the publishing firm of Prynword, Rush & Hope. There is also a marvelously funny scene of group pseudotherapy which mimics much of the self-important consciousness-raising that is in vogue.

Hoban has a sensitive eye and marvelous power of description that can distill the elements of a scene to its essence; his description of the steam rising from the streets on a jaunt to the zoo is a case in point. By softening his philosophizing about important questions with levity, he reminds us not to take ourselves too seriously, for we are after all only human. The contrapuntal soul-searching of William and Neaera reflects the low spots, the depressions, that most people feel at one time or another, and his affirmation that it can be a temporary state of affairs even for the hard-core recluse is a fairly restorative thought.

Hoban brings us to the end of the work with a sense of some change, even of some accomplishment, but certainly without great fanfare or glorious revelation. Which, according to Hoban, is the way life really is.

Margaret S. Schoon

Sources for Further Study

Atlantic. CCXXXVIII, August, 1976, p. 83.
Christian Science Monitor. LXVIII, April 7, 1976, p. 27.
New York Times Book Review. March 21, 1976, p. 6.
New Yorker. LII, March 22, 1976, p. 130.
Newsweek. LXXXVII, March 1, 1976, p. 76.
Saturday Review. III, May 1, 1976, p. 36.

THE TWILIGHT OF CAPITALISM

Author: Michael Harrington (1928-   )
Publisher: Simon and Schuster (New York). 341 pp. $10.95; paperback $4.95
Type of work: Economic history

A death report which seems "greatly exaggerated" when one compares the vigorous economic and social state of the capitalistic West with that of the Marxist-block countries

In the long and wonderful tradition of Lenin's *Imperialism, The Last Stage of Capitalism,* and Nkrumah's *Neo-colonialism, The Last Stage of Imperialism,* we are now treated to what might be called "Welfare Capitalism: The Last Stage of Capitalism." Or, to quote George Lichtheim, what we have here is only another pathetic addition to "the *caput mortuum* of a gigantic intellectual construction whose living essence has [already] been appropriated by the historical consciousness of the modern world." Or, to put it another way, Harrington's *tour de force* can be viewed as the last stage of moribund Marxism.

The general reader should note the almost total absence of laughter in Marxist circles; *everything* is terribly, terribly serious. Marxists take themselves and their ideas as if they were "the people," and wisdom was in danger of dying with them. They tend to engage in an enormous amount of ideological nitpicking, and become easily incensed—"morally outraged"—when others cannot understand what they are so exercised about. They tend to be "true believers," which seems to make their pronouncements occasionally perceptive, frequently obtuse, but rarely witty. They tend to be grim, econometricious prophets of doom, or hysterical celebrants of the new order. Occasionally, one may encounter a happy, vivacious Marxist landowner in Orange County; but not very often.

For one thing, anyone with a modicum of historical consciousness who reads *The Twilight of Capitalism* will tend to be outraged by the author's repeated claim that he has proved that capitalism responded inevitably to the twentieth century crises as it did. Marvelous! Dr. Pangloss—with a Marxist mentality—lives. What escapes Harrington, of course (but did not escape Voltaire's good doctor) is the self-consciousness that Harrington's own mentality inevitably produced this work. The general reader will note, from time to time, that the adoption of the Marxist paradigm saves the Marxist thinker from the sociocultural blindness which afflicts every non-Marxist; it is apparently not possible that Marxism is every bit as much a child of its times as every other explanation, although it is possible, Harrington admits, that an individual Marxist may be "stupid or inept."

The other major curiosity of the book occurs in Part II, "The Future Karl Marx, or The Secret History of the Contemporary Crisis" (a nice play on Procopius' *Secret History*), which concludes with an astounding stay of execution. After three hundred pages devoted to showing how capitalism is "outrageously unjust" and "also self-destructive," we are reminded that this has lasted more than "four centuries." But, writes Harrington,

> I do not want to suggest for a moment that the crisis of the 1970s is a final breakdown of the system, its *Götterdämmerung.* I fully expect it to recover from this cruel and unnecessary depression. The event is only a moment in a complex process of decline and fall that will certainly go on for some time to come and just as certainly will end with the collapse of the bourgeois order.

Incredible. Isn't this a little like saying that the next four hundred years will certainly see a lot of changes? Or, if the bourgeois order has already lasted for four hundred years, and it is still in surprisingly good health, shouldn't we expect it to last for another century or two? Or three? After all, its unusual adaptability—in the face of its supposedly inherent self-destructive capacity— is certainly interesting. Perhaps capitalism is inevitably adaptable. Perhaps capitalism—"welfare capitalism"—will create that long-sought, classless, utopian society. Or, perhaps it is simply stupid to try to show that either Marxism or capitalism has exclusive answers to the contemporary crisis.

Another irritation that may afflict the general reader is the gradual realization that, no matter what happens, Marxists are congenitally revisionist; thus, if events do not corroborate Marxist theories, then the theories will be revised to fit the past events. In other words, Marxists will always be right, eventually.

The benefits of inevitable revisionism should be pointed out to the uninitiated general reader. First of all, Marx left his disciples with this problem: Marxist theories *must* prove to be accurate analyses of actual events; and the master's followers were not allowed to be piecemeal Marxists, because Marx's theories involved an organic whole; in other words, the mature Marx's constructs/paradigms were absolutely right, or absolutely wrong. Very early, of course, certain individuals thought that some of Karl's ideas were very perceptive, but others were incredibly shortsighted; thus, these contemporary followers became the first revisionists. Subsequently, revisionism has become one of the great heresy-words in the Communist lexicon. Now Harrington has rescued Marx and Marxists from this albatross. Marx *himself* was a revisionist, and what is more (as "Marx was becoming a Marxist") he realized that revision of his analyses were inevitable, because future circumstances were unknown. There are distinct advantages to this sophisticated, true Marxism: all Marxists who insist upon "orthodoxy" are automatically "vulgar," "pseudo-," or "mechanistic" Marxists, and may be dismissed as "illegitimate." This takes care of Lenin, Stalin, Russia, the People's Republic of China (including, probably, Mao.) Others (like Herbert Marcuse) who have abandoned Marxism because of this "misunderstanding" may also be disfranchised by applying labels to them like "Spenglerian anarchists," leaving, of course, "revisionism" as the true Marxist way.

Given this foolishness masquerading as scholarship, why should the general reader even bother with this highly promoted work? There are at least two good reasons.

One is that Part I, "The New Karl Marx," is one of the best "secret histories" of Marxist ideologues and factions available to the general reader; and Harrington has included seven explanatory appendices, five of which help to introduce these individuals and groups to the uninitiated. Some of the argument is marvelously esoteric, and may remind us of medieval scholasticism at its worst; but this is a worthwhile experience for those who may have assumed that Marxists are all alike.

In one way, of course, they are all alike: they are all bound by Marx's initial dependency upon G. W. F. Hegel (or "Friedrich Hegel," according to Harrington's Index.) Perhaps nowhere is this hangup so obvious as it is in Chapter 6, where Harrington struggles mightily with Erich Fromm and Louis Althusser in order to correct their (and everyone else's) misunderstandings of Marx's use of Hegel. Hegel was, of course, a "spiritualist"—in other words, a philosophical idealist; reality for Hegel was ultimately an idea, a "spirit." Meanwhile, Marx had decided that reality was matter, not spirit; but Harrington, unable to avoid Marx's severe dependency upon Hegel, argues that Marx was a "spiritual materialist." What Harrington (and every other Marxist) refuses to admit is that Marx's adoption of Hegel's dialectic has forever saddled Marxism with a rigid, naïve, obsolete view of reality. Hegel, basing his theory on late eighteenth and early nineteenth century views of the human past, thought that he had discovered the universal process which explained both natural and human history—the dialectical force of Reason. Marx fell in love with this process, altered the content of the dialectic and never let it go. Thus, every attempt to explain, revise, or justify Marx has to include Hegel; and how a Marxist treats Hegel will automatically force him to change "what Marx really meant."

The other value of *The Twilight of Capitalism* is that this almost desperate attempt to resurrect the "real" Karl Marx—"the oracle in the ruins"—is a most expressive evidence of the twilight of Marxism. It is not an appeal from strength, but from weakness; it bears an emotional tone reminiscent of Machiavelli. After rehearsing the benefits of "true" Marxian analysis, Harrington asks—nay, begs his readers—to save humanity from the collectivist barbarians by making "the spirit of the new Karl Marx . . . our comrade in the struggle." This juxtaposition of Harrington and Machiavelli suggests one final dialectical irreverence: Harrington, like Machiavelli, has conned his contemporaries with an elaborate spoof. For example, Machiavelli used Cesaré Borgia as his ideal Prince, and Borgia was notoriously incompetent and unsuccessful. Now, here is Harrington, using Karl Marx, who was one of the great argumentative, dour dogmatists of the nineteenth century, as the "foe of every dogma," the "champion of human freedom." But, if Harrington has been serious from cover to cover, then he has unconsciously written a parody of Marxism; in following "the mature Marx," Harrington must inevitably contradict himself.

The alleged uniqueness of "the Marxist paradigm" will serve to illustrate this contradiction very well. First, the Marxist paradigm, "unlike the rest of the social sciences," always "looks for the class bias in the most obvious definitions of fact"—and probably finds it even if it is not there. Second, only some workers and some intellectuals "who identify with the working class can penetrate the deceptions of [capitalist] society." This is called being "rigorously scientific" and rigorously objective. Third, since men and women are both creatures and creators of their society, they are caught in the dialectic of necessity and freedom. Notice how the dialectic is assumed rather than searched for. Fourth, the paradigm assumes "the essential determinacy of the economic element in the structure of society." Fifth, "the paradigm looks for contradictions as a key element in the social dynamic"; and, of course, since "capitalist society is structurally contradictory," it is not too difficult to find the "inevitable" contradictions. Sixth, "the economic takes social form in the shape of the classes which, under capitalism, are determined in the production process." This is also a scientific and "self-critical" point. Seventh, "technology is an extremely important variable"; this is hardly unique to Marxist analysis. Eighth, "clear distinctions must be kept in mind . . . between Marxian possibilities, symptoms, and causes," even though the Marxist analyst using this Marxist paradigm will always discover the same predictable, inevitable results. Harrington tops off his argument by describing this paradigm as "distinctive," in that these eight aspects "provide a framework which is unlike that of the mainstream academic disciplines." If it is *not* unlike the mainstream frameworks, we are all in big trouble.

Keith M. Bailor

Sources for Further Study

Christian Century. XCIII, November 3, 1976, p. 965.

Harper's Magazine. CCLII, June, 1976, p. 102.

National Review. XXVIII, September 3, 1976, p. 963.

New Republic. CLXXV, August 7, 1976, p. 34.

Progressive. XL, September, 1976, p. 55.

Saturday Review. III, July 10, 1976, p. 46.

UNCLE OF EUROPE
The Social and Diplomatic Life of Edward VII

Author: Gordon Brook-Shepherd
Publisher: Harcourt Brace Jovanovich (New York). 384 pp. $12.95
Type of work: Biography
Time: 1841-1910
Locale: Great Britain, Europe

A study of the personal diplomacy of King Edward, which helped forge the Triple Entente before World War I

Principal personages:
EDWARD VII, King of Great Britain
QUEEN VICTORIA, his mother
ALBERT EDWARD, the Prince Consort, his father
WILLIAM II, Emperor of Germany, his nephew
ALICE KEPPEL, his mistress
LUIS SOVERAL, his friend

Edward was born heir to Victoria's throne, but he did not succeed her until he was fifty-nine years old. He set fashions, had a reputation for wine and women, if not song; he had a direct and personal influence on the diplomatic arrangements of his day. There are certainly a number of possibilities for a biographer or historian here: the personal, whether of the level of warmed-over gossip, or of psychological searching; the constitutional, for his reign may well have seen a turning-point in the character of the monarchy and the constitution; and the diplomatic, with tremors of the coming earthquake.

Brook-Shepherd, an English journalist with experience of Europe, and especially Austria, has chosen to focus on the social and diplomatic aspects of his subject's reign, though he could not avoid touching on the personal areas as well. His stress is on Edward's leadership of Continental society, his love for life and for people (and gift for handling the latter), and the way he turned these gifts to use in forwarding the diplomatic policies of Great Britain, policies which Brook-Shepherd sees as ones of Edward's own forming.

Not much of this is new, though Brook-Shepherd has new insights and an interesting view. One of the great preliminary difficulties, and it is one he masters as well as can be expected, is the wholly different world Edward inhabited. It really mattered that he was "Uncle of Europe" as Victoria had been grandmother and great-grandmother. There is a chart in the back of the book tracing Edward's relationships with royal families of Germany, Russia, Norway, Sweden, Denmark, Rumania, Yugoslavia, Spain, and Greece. This is not genealogical gamesmanship; some monarchs still ruled, not merely reigned, and even constitutional kings had a different position from those of today. Edward's kinship and kingship gave him leverage.

Similarly, the distinctions of class (not merely money) counted for more and counted differently. Edward could make friends with those outside the circles of club and country-house, but even for him there were some tricky places, and it is hard to imagine anyone else doing it. At its simplest and most fundamental, there is a gulf between that age and ours, created by the upheaval of World War I, which has been widened and deepened by the decades of revolution and war that have followed.

What was Edward's background? Brook-Shepherd (maybe from his Contintental experience) stresses the Germanic strains in his ancestry—not only the original Hanoverian, but the repeated German princesses, and finally, Albert Edward of Saxe-Coburg-Gotha, the Prince Consort. The German was not only by inheritance: Albert's conscientious, heavy, almost pedantic habits formed Edward's education. He resisted, crawling under desks at the age of four, and he found other escapes later, but the pattern was there. And Victoria, after Albert's death, was intent on fulfilling her beloved husband's plans.

Brook-Shepherd is perceptive about the miseducation. Edward was not, he insists, stupid or unintelligent—he may well have been unintellectual. (It is hard to think of any of the Hanoverian line as intellectual.) The stiff regime of Albert and Victoria's Germanic advisers brought resistance and rejection. And, of course, there were those nearly forty adult years in a waiting posture. The function of the heir apparent, like that of the Vice-President of the United States, is not an active one, and it is hard to imagine how it could be made so. But Victoria gave Edward no scope, no opportunity, and by negation encouraged (certainly against her intention) the pursuit of pleasure.

The education, in a sense, begins with an incognito visit to the United States. Brook-Shepherd recounts "Baron Renfrew's" tour of the United States in 1860, the year of Lincoln's election. Surely it was one of the most transparent disguises for the nineteen-year-old Prince of Wales. Through it, Americans, always excited by royalty, saw a great deal of charm, and Edward, apparently, had a good time. As one in the New York crowd said, "Come back, and we'll elect you President."

He never did go back, but there may have been the access of confidence Brook-Shepherd argues. It was the continent of Europe he traveled in the succeeding years, and came to know in his own way—theaters and spas, as well as palaces and chancelleries. In that age when royalty still counted, he knew most of the crowned heads, or their wives, as members of the family.

As in many families, the relationship was not always one of harmony and affection. The notable, and world-historical, sample is nephew William. Victoria's eldest (and some say favorite) daughter, married the heir to the Prussian kingdom, and after 1871, the German Empire. Their son, who succeeded as Emperor William II in 1889, "the Kaiser" of the twentieth century, was a storm center for his whole reign. Analysts have had a field day with his psyche—was it his withered arm that explained his militance; was his feeling for his grandmother's England love-hate? Did this, or more personal feelings, explain his attitude toward his uncle—and his uncle's to him? Brook-Shepherd, no admirer of William II, suggests jealousy, compounded by the fact that England so often treated Germany, and Edward his nephew, with a tolerant indifference which hurt worse than overt antagonism.

The story is familiar to any history student, and Brook-Shepherd neither adds much that is new, nor disputes the conventional account, so far as he touches it. Rising naval and colonial programs in Germany, added to existing military preeminence and industrial growth, challenged the British position, and forced rethinking of an uncommitted, if not isolationist, attitude. Belligerent language in the German press, and in the Kaiser's speeches, roused alarm. The division of major Continental powers into two allied and armed camps, France and Russia on the one hand, Germany, Austria-Hungary, and Italy on the other, offered danger and opportunity. Episodes—Germany's (or at least the Kaiser's) expressed sympathy for the Boers in the South African War, crises in Morocco in 1906 and 1909—both demonstrated and aggravated the situation.

Not only is it a familiar sequence, it is among the most ominous stories of the twentieth century. Edward's role, therefore, which is one of Brook-Shepherd's two themes, is fully worth studying. The thesis here is not new, though rarely put so strongly: that King Edward's personal diplomacy forged the *entente cordiale* with France, and made possible its expansion into the Triple Entente by the inclusion of Czarist Russia, which had for generations been the traditional fear of English imperialists.

Put in cautious academic language, that Edward "helped forge" or "contributed," the thesis could hardly be controverted. Put into the context of the conditions and maneuvers of the turn of the century, it is a thesis that is worth arguing and ought to be debated. What leaves a critical reader unsatisfied is that this account states it, assumes it, rather than argues it. It is one thing to follow one thread through the pattern; it is a different matter to claim it is the center and main thread of the pattern, without really showing the whole or considering alternatives.

The personal relationship of the two monarchs, uncle and nephew, is assumed to have had significant consequences. Granted that William made German policy, at least when he wanted to, and that Edward had greater impact than either his mother or his successors, still, is that the heart of the matter? Was *rapproachement* between Germany and England really prevented by William's rudeness after the Cowes regatta? Or, were relations permanently soured because Edward did not like to visit his nephew, and was bored by hours-long German military reviews?

The positive achievement is subject to the same questioning. Edward undertook a Mediterranean cruise which refreshed the ancient alliance with Portugal, built friendship with Spain, and seemed to put a wedge into the Triple Alliance with the cordiality of the Italian visit. Then he paid an official visit to

Paris, where the people forgot or forgave an enmity as old as the Hundred Years' War and as recent as Fashoda in their enthusiasm. The *entente* was the result.

Was it quite that simple? The military staff conversations, which made the *entente* a reality, are barely mentioned. Treaties, when they do play a part, are dismissed as the work of the Foreign Office—lawyers drawing up the papers once the principals have made the decisions. (In fact, one would hardly know there was a Cabinet, or a Parliament; ministers are mentioned when Edward had them to Sandringham, and that rarely.)

Let the point be labored a little. It may be that personal diplomacy weighed heavily in those prewar years; it may be that mood and style count for more than "objective conditions"; that banquets and royal progresses and appearances at the opera and the races meant more than statistics of industrial production and naval programs; that shouts of "vive le roi Edouard" move history more than general staff plans. It may very well be; but it cannot be blandly assumed. This is not so much to ask for a different book as to suggest the limits of this one.

Brook-Shepherd's other theme is Edward's "social" life, and, if less weighty in the scales of history, this topic has an interest of its own. Brook-Shepherd does not dabble in gossip, though he does not disguise Edward's long list of "loves." But Continental sophistication, after all, takes royal mistresses for granted, and Alice Keppel, the last in the list, was Edward's true friend.

What does appear clearly in the account is the world of late nineteenth and early twentieth century royal and aristocratic society—the dinners, the clubs, the hunt and the shooting (though Edward was never a good shot), the long weekends, the movement from town to country to the Continent. There are fascinating descriptions of life at Marienbad and Biarritz, the favored royal resorts—though less thorough descriptions of meals and room arrangements might have as much effect. Here character, almost more than the diplomatic life, comes through—the assurance of unquestioned position, the love of life and people, the restless interest in new scenes and persons, even—maybe the Prince Consort had some effect—a sense of duty. It is a sympathetic portrait; the flaws are there, but they are not highlighted.

Character, too, is well-handled in the case of Soveral, whose papers afford much of the detailed information, as for instance on the trip to Portugal in 1903. Mrs. Keppel and the other ladies are rather vague, and long-suffering Queen Alexandra an intermittent figure. The Kaiser is clearly and strongly drawn, but with more than a touch of acid.

The themes—monarchy, personal diplomacy, high life—all lend themselves to anecdote, and Brook-Shepherd takes full advantage, both for wit and for illumination. The tale sparkles as it moves inexorably toward the elaborate funeral procession (May 20, 1910) which was in many ways the last pageant of the old European order.

Readers who want a full and balanced account of King Edward VII and his age will turn elsewhere (probably most to Sir Philip Magnus' biography), but those who accept its limitations of theme and thesis will find much to learn and to savor in *Uncle of Europe.*

George J. Fleming

Sources for Further Study

America. CXXXIV, May 1, 1976, p. 387.
Booklist. LXXII, July 1, 1976, p. 1503.
English Historical Review. XCI, October, 1976, p. 930.
National Observer. XV, July 17, 1976, p. 17.
National Review. XVIII, May 28, 1976, p. 572.
Saturday Review. III, May 1, 1976, p. 25.

UNEQUAL JUSTICE
Lawyers and Social Change in Modern America

Author: Jerold S. Auerbach
Publisher: Oxford University Press (New York). 395 pp. $13.95; paperback $3.95
Type of work: Political history
Time: The twentieth century
Locale: The United States

A political history of the legal profession in twentieth century America using an elitist approach

"The Legal Elite" would be a more appropriate title for this study written by Jerold Auerbach—a Wellesley history professor and former Fellow in Law and History at Harvard Law School. For *Unequal Justice* is really a book about unequal lawyers, about a stratified profession rather than a differential product, and how a professional elite coped with the forces generated by the major social changes of the twentieth century, including modern corporate capitalism, immigration, war, economic depression, and political protest. The recognized maldistribution of justice in America is, in other words, treated as a fact to be explained instead of explored, and to be explained in terms of an elite structure within the legal profession.

The choice of an elitist perspective raises the issue of whether it normatively impairs Auerbach's account. For the author's part it does not, because no one can claim to be a nonpartisan observer; in writing the history of any social institution, even a "neutral" functional approach will serve "to stress (and implicitly praise) its adaption to social values without examining either the values or the implications of adapting to them." More to the point, however, is the fact that the author is seeking to sustain *generalizations* about responses to social change. Given that purpose, some conceptual framework must be selected to organize the social data in a manner permitting diachronic comparison; and the elitist perspective, for better or worse, has probably been used more than any other for such comparison. Of course one may object that the discovery of generalizations goes beyond the job of the historian, and that may well be. Still, though, the objection would merely be a reason for viewing *Unequal Justice* as a piece of social science research, not for criticizing the work *per se*.

Yet, whether considered as history or social science, the lack of a developed elaboration of the particular elitist approach employed represents a serious deficiency. We are never told if it is Mosca's organizational or Pareto's psychological or Burnham's economic or C. Wright Mills's institutional or the author's own original approach that delimits the contours of the legal elite and its struggles to remain in power. We are not told, for example, whether those who occupy elite positions do so by virtue of their exceptional organizational skills, persuasive abilities, legal talents, familial affiliations, official capacities, economic resources, or some combination thereof. True, Auerbach tells us the elite is composed primarily of white Anglo-Saxon Protestants, but this cannot constitute the distinguishing characteristic of the dominant minority within the legal profession. Not all elite lawyers are WASPs, nor are all WASP lawyers. Ethnicity is simply insufficient as the basis for elitism. Only when ethnicity correlates highly with at least one of the above elite grounds may we fruitfully use it as an indirect measure or sign of the factors underlying the observed structure of power. But even in that case ethnicity would be an imperfect indicator, and thus analysis should concentrate directly on the underlying factors whenever possible.

The author's emphasis on ethnicity is related to his research methodology, which relies heavily on the actual words of bar officials spoken during a time, pre-World War II, when it was relatively easy to create widespread support for the *status quo* by arousing passions against domestic "aliens" who could be identified by dress, speech, skin, or some other physical attribute. Dependence on this methodology has two major pitfalls that are quite relevant here: the public verbiage of elite participants may well deflect the observer (especially when it seems extraordinarily candid by contemporary standards) from seeing the real basis for the existing stratification; and when that verbiage becomes more circumspect (again, by contemporary standards), it may be interpreted as evidence of a different basis for, or even as a decline in, elitism. The extent to which Auerbach has managed to avoid these pitfalls can only be determined by a careful reading of his very readable account. Such a reading is also necessary to isolate the nature of the particular elitist approach employed— though the two tasks are more related than might appear at first. For elitist explanations depend much on what the participants are actually doing instead of on what they say, or even think, they are doing. And so the more that Auerbach's account allows us to discern the underlying pattern of elite behavior, the less has he allowed himself to be diverted by elite ideology.

Unequal Justice presents a fairly consistent description of the power struggles engaged in by lawyers at the top or trying to get there. The legal elite that reigns today is seen as having emerged at the turn of the century, when the era of genuine business competition and steadily falling prices was washed away by the first great wave of corporate mergers. It was this rise in corporate power that required and was reinforced by a new breed of lawyers, ones skilled in counseling rather than advocacy, in giving advice on how to evade Progressive regulatory legislation. The need was met through the Cravath system, which shaped the law firm to serve corporations by recruiting recent law-school graduates instead of experienced practitioners in order to create a cohesive team of complementary specialists. These were the lawyers who regularly received the highest fees and came to dominate the American Bar Association. But since the Cravath system was dependent upon the prestigious law schools for a constant supply of corporate lawyers, some of the influence that the firms enjoyed from their association with corporations naturally spilled over into academe. Yet the university law teachers—perhaps because they had less to lose and more to gain than the corporate lawyers, or because they did not fully understand that corporate needs defined their curriculum and their new status—made an attempt to bite the hand that fed them. The strategy was as straightforward as it was futile. "By claiming to speak with the authority of disinterested scientists on the reform side of public issues, they could reduce practicing lawyers to the status of special pleaders for the parochial interests of their clients." The claimed authority was of course based on a special knowledge of law. And so the challenge to the corporate attorneys was contained within the shared ideology of a professional expertise which the client, whether a private business or a public agency, was expected to follow unquestioningly.

Claims of expertise are regarded by Auerbach as being clearly an elitist trait, and the corporate lawyers and university law professors are described as constituting a single professional elite. To do so, however, mistakes ideology for reality. The facts show that the practitioners (really their clients), not the professoriat, prevailed. Before World War I the regulatory legislation was largely supported by and beneficial for the established corporations; soon after the war, a wave of merger activity occurred that is still evident in today's economy. True, the ABA and the Association of American Law Schools cooperated in the 1920's to meet the common "threat" of a dramatic surge of foreign-born lawyers entering the profession through the back door of night school. But neither this concerted response nor the shared claim of expertise justifies attributing to law teachers the elite status that is properly reserved for the practicing attorneys who served their corporate clients so well. If there was a "triumph of the new professoriat," it was confined to the campus. And the author himself later testifies to the accuracy of a one- rather than two-sided elite when he speaks of the corporate lawyers' "unchallenged professional hegemony" and of their successful assertion of their "clients' interests as professional and national interests." It was a time when a prominent New York corporate lawyer would refuse to be considered for the Supreme Court, deigning to enter public life only as one of the major parties' candidates for President. It was truly "Babbittry at the bar." As such, the early twentieth century history of the legal profession conforms roughly to Burnham's view that elites are founded on their relationship to the means of production.

Selective social mobility in the Depression decade is another topic helpful in identifying Auerbach's conception of elitist theory. The reform administration of Roosevelt provided alternative employment opportunities for lawyers during a period when solo practitioners (disproportionately consisting of highly qualified Jewish lawyers excluded from law firms) came upon especially hard times. But the New Deal regulatory legislation provided alternative opportunities for giant corporations too. Unprecedented levels of regulation provided big business with unprecedented opportunities to gain the direct access to government decision-making that would ensure the stable and predictable economic environment required for production based on modern industrial technology. Corporate use of these opportunities naturally required the services of lawyers with a new area of expertise. Accordingly, as the proliferation of alphabet agencies tapered off, those lawyers who had been most responsible for framing and applying the new regulations began departing from government to join old corporate law firms in New York and form new ones in Washington.

Much is made, by the author, of the resulting change in the composition of the legal elite, specifically the admission of non-WASPs (principally Jewish lawyers) into the preserve of the WASPs. The assimilation of what he calls a "new elite" is seen as a timely move on the part of the "old" elite to maintain traditional professional values. But his earlier emphasis on the bar's publicly advocated discrimination diverts him from focusing on the broader picture he himself now presents. Ethnic outsiders were accepted not because they challenged professional values and so had to be co-opted, but because they possessed the administrative law expertise needed by the legal elite's clients. In other words, some lawyers were indeed given a new deal, but the game stayed the same and the same dealer still dealt. Whether what transpired comes closer to Mosca's "molecular rejuvenation of the elite" or Pareto's "circulation of elites" cannot be explored here. In either case, however, the process perpetuated the legal elite in a manner most compatible with economic factors, not ethnic. And the maldistribution of justice persisted.

In the light of the rather limited nature of the changes effected even in a decade of depression and reform, it is fitting to turn to Auerbach's proposal for contemporary change and consider the prospects for realizing equal justice. Equal justice is interpreted by him as equal access to legal services in the form of neighborhood law firms, which are to be made possible by substantial federal subsidies (supplemented by an excess profits tax on corporate law firms) after having first established public regulation of the legal profession. Impressed by the apparent accomplishments of the federal legal services program of the 1960's before its demise, Auerbach is in essence recommending its legislative revival together with government legislation that would this time prevent the ABA from compromising its potential effectiveness before it is even passed. And an extra tax on the legal elite is thrown in to help redistribute professional wealth. How a program more threatening to elite interests than its shortlived progenitor is supposed to fare any better is nowhere explained. Possibly the corporate lawyers are expected to respond to the "authority of disinterested scientists on the reform side of public issues"—except today it will be legal historians instead of law teachers who will offer counsel on the public interest. If this is the expectation, it is more than vaguely reminiscent of Mills's belief that the power elite could and should be guided by the "free intellect." And, like Mills, it seeks fundamental change through the replacement of one elite by another.

In any event, having adopted an elitist perspective for his history, the author has ultimately become entrapped by the logic of his own analysis. Having convincingly documented the tenacious persistence of a legal elite through three quarters of a century fraught with social disruptions, he can hardly avoid the conclusion that any foreseeable changes in the distribution of justice will have to rely on reforms that accept the continued existence of some legal elite, either corporate or government or academic. Starting with an elitist approach he must follow it where it has led all the classical elite theorists, to an implicit affirmation that the future must resemble the past, that elitism is inescapable.

Yet Auerbach's failure to consider alternatives absent from the past he so ably relates appears to spring from a source deeper than his adoption of an elitist perspective. The ideology of change through law that permeates the thinking of those being observed is uncritically accepted by the observer. For it is only by accepting what Stuart Scheingold calls the "myth of rights"—all desirable rights are in the American Constitution, legal reasoning can apply them to today, and what judges decide, politicians do—that access to the services of lawyers becomes so important that its denial is viewed as tantamount to unequal justice. In effect the author thereby "stresses and implicitly praises" the legal institutions in much the same way as might a functionalist. A critical analysis, in contrast, would note the crucial role played by the courts in the application of laws and regulations and then ask how the unequal distribution of legal services can be changed within a system of law characterized by legal services that are distributed unequally. Critical analysis would conclude that equality of traditional legal aid is too narrow a conception of equal justice, that litigation directed toward political mobilization might benefit disadvantaged groups more than litigation proceeding from the myth of rights, and that ways should be found and promoted to minimize the importance of the distribution of legal expertise in the first place.

The need for alternative change strategies is plainly indicated, albeit indirectly, by the facts recounted in *Unequal Justice*. Jerold Auerbach therefore deserves our thanks for having written a political history of the legal profession that lets us see the real story behind the superficial one of ethnicity and elitism. Change toward equal justice, like any political change, requires such looks at the past. After all, only by knowing our history do we know what not to repeat.

E. Gene DeFelice

Sources for Further Study

America. CXXXIV, May 1, 1976, p. 393.
Booklist. LXXII, April 15, 1976, p. 1146.
Commentary. LXII, August, 1976, p. 65.
Current History. LXXI, July, 1976, p. 29.
Harvard Law Review. XC, November, 1976, p. 283.
Progressive. XL, September, 1976, p. 58.

THE UNSEEN REVOLUTION
How Pension Fund Socialism Came to America

Author: Peter F. Drucker (1909-   )
Publisher: Harper & Row Publishers (New York). 214 pp. $8.95
Type of work: Current affairs
Time: The present
Locale: The United States

A penetrating and provocative analysis of an emerging economic institution in the United States and the impact of this phenomenon on American society and the world

Unlike many books where the title poses a question, Peter F. Drucker answers his question in the first ten pages. Having the suspense out of the way, he then proceeds to analyze and study the ramifications of the institutional changes and the accompanying series of events facing this country and many countries in the near future. In this way, Drucker is able to impress upon the reader the significance that "pension fund socialism" has for the future rather than focusing on the new idea that he brings forth.

It is certain that this work will be a topic of discussion and controversy in many circles simply because Peter Drucker has a sizeable following among people in management and business who will read *The Unseen Revolution: How Pension Fund Socialism Came to America* if for no other reason than to read the fifteenth book published by the venerable author. Written in the same vivid and clear writing style, Drucker brings together many of the insights and views expressed in his earlier works. In fact, many portions of this work have appeared in *The Public Interest,* a previous work by Drucker. However, this book will leave its impressions primarily because the author is dealing with a societal problem rather than the changing role of management, which has been a constant theme of interest for business people who have read Drucker's work for other reasons. Drucker has been attempting to determine the changing role of business enterprise and professional management in society but with ramifications that are much more profound. He is a political philosopher who deserves attention from a much wider audience. In this work he unfolds an important episode in his evolving philosophy and brings out worthwhile intellectual substance that a wide-ranging audience can appreciate.

What Drucker defines as pension fund socialism is the result of a change in the structure of the pension fund system in America. He points to a subtle but significant event in 1950 when Charles Wilson, the President of General Motors Corporation, decided to establish a pension fund program for the employees of General Motors that would be vested in equity or common stock holdings of many corporations. Although this decision was not innovative and had precedents, Drucker recognizes that this decision by a major corporation under pressures to the contrary led the way to a major change in the structure of the pension fund system. Drucker points out that what appeared to be a subtle point now has a major impact on the structure as well as the future of the American system. The important difference is that through pension funds, American workers now own, technically, a substantial portion of the American productive system. By 1985, approximately fifty percent of equity capital will be owned by American workers via pension funds. Ironically, Drucker points out that this institution has resulted in a basic structural change in the American system and that change is, according to Drucker's interpretation, that the American system has evolved into the only true socialist system where the means of production are "owned" by the workers and the primary unit of value becomes labor. Chastising other economic systems that lay claim to being socialism as mere forms of "government capitalism," Drucker does not belabor this point with persuasion or argument, but focuses on the implications of pension fund socialism and points to the most difficult questions that society must address. Drucker has a special talent for bringing in provocative insights and startling conclusions as brief but ratiocinative inferences.

Associated with this new institution that Drucker calls pension fund socialism is a phenomenon of demographics. Drucker reflects on the fact that America will experience an era that no other civilization has experienced, an era where the population will be predominantly aged. Drucker enumerates some of the implications an older population will have on the structure of society but focuses on the implications to the economic system and the funding of pension funds and other welfare programs. A basic problem that Drucker examines is the funding of social security and industry-wide pension programs when the work-age population is diminishing in proportion to the retired population.

Drucker attacks three ailing institutions and points out the serious problems that will plague our generation as a consequence of their deficiencies. These institutions are the social security system, industry-wide pension programs, and government pension programs. Arguing that social security is a welfare system and not a retirement program, the author focuses on the contemporary problem of funding the social security system. In stressing the problems plaguing government pension programs and industry-wide programs, Drucker establishes a firm foundation for the pension fund system advocated in his concept of pension fund socialism. The dangers of these other, inept systems, as he vividly shows, is the gross underfunding of these other institutions.

Probably the most fascinating aspect of Drucker's new book is the speculation for the future of social security and the pension programs of governments and industry-wide programs. Drucker has an inclination toward programs such as TIAA-CREF, the pension program in which many college professors, including Drucker himself, participate. Many of his suggested remedies reflect features of the TIAA-CREF program and the references to that program at times overshadow the primary thrust of the book. But the vital questions are the most difficult and they are usually left unanswered. This is not a special case. Other questions such as how to encourage the young productive workers to increase their holdings in pension funds at an age when the advantages of compounding are most apparent but the demands for present consumption are greatest, remain only questions.

Probably the most fascinating element of this work is its timeliness and appropriateness for the American public. The issue of social security and its promise for a future is a burning one. The author stresses the desires of most Americans for security in retirement and hits hard on the underlying problems of the present system from a historical as well as an economic perspective. Making the point that social security is a welfare system and not a retirement pension system is sufficient but not profound. The alternatives as well as the problems of funding social security take on new meanings with the background developed by Peter Drucker.

Pointing to the ills of social security and governmental pension programs as well as certain industry-wide pension programs, Drucker focuses on the myopic power struggles and political irresponsibility as irreconcilable defects that will lead to impending disaster for those involved if fundamental changes do not occur. Such rhetoric has a fascination and also a purpose in pointing to the fundamental structural differences that have such profound consequences but usually escape public attention. As an example, Drucker attacks the system of public or governmental pension programs for being grossly underfunded. He argues that this is the consequence of the popular political approach of offering something apparently for nothing.

The author calls attention to the role of professional management in society. Probably the most difficult questions and the most complicated aspects of the basic societal problems addressed have to do with the more subtle aspects of organization. If these aspects were not addressed, the entire work would be an intellectual disappointment. Calling attention to the changing demographic profile of the country and an era of increasing numbers of retirees and a diminishing work-age population, stressing that pension fund programs in governments have pension liabilities that are insufficiently funded, and pointing out that many industry-wide pension programs are grossly underfunded or even corrupt is of little consequence. To reflect on the ramifications for the coming generation is of questionable advantage. To point out the basic structural problems is of basic consequence. The subtleties of organizational defects are the most difficult to analyze. Drucker relies on sentiment and illusion to make his points come across in an interesting and nontechnical fashion. He points to attitudes and purpose in the management of the pension funds as basic forces that will affect our destiny. A philosophy is evoked, dealing with the complex relationship between the worker, the growth of capital, and economic prosperity. These relationships that intrigue the economist and the manager have not promoted popular speculation and review by the general public in the past decade. Drucker is a master at bringing out complex insights and tying current events to economic progress in a historical, evolving format.

Addressing such questions as, Can labor unions survive? or Which is the greater evil, inflation or unemployment? and yielding nonconventional responses, Drucker's study makes for interesting as well as provocative reading. But to deal with concepts such as "affluence," "equality," and "growth management" provides a playground to interest a wide and diverse audience. The book is of interest not only to the student of business, but to the student of government, history, and philosophy as well. An attempt to understand the changing role of important economic institutions, *The Unseen Revolution* is credibly presented in this philosophic treatise by a renowned expert in management circles.

Jonathan M. Furdek

Sources for Further Study

Choice. XIII, November, 1976, p. 1178.
Christian Century. XCIII, November 3, 1976, p. 965.
Economist. CCLXI, November 20, 1976, p. 142.
Library Journal. CI, September 1, 1976, p. 1768.
New Yorker. LII, September 6, 1976, p. 94.

THE USES OF ENCHANTMENT

Author: Bruno Bettelheim (1903-   )
Publisher: Random House (New York). 327 pp. $12.50; paperback $3.95
Type of work: Psychology

An analysis of the psychological benefits of fairy tales for children

In *The Uses of Enchantment,* Bruno Bettelheim delivers a compelling argument for radical change in parents' thinking about what their children should and should not read. This century, particularly in America, has seen a move away from fantasy and toward true-to-life experiences. Social comment, documentaries, starless movies are all the rage. Such insistence on the factual, the real, has similarly affected children through educators and parents. Even Santa Claus may have slipped in popularity. Bettelheim claims that schoolbooks teach skills rather than meaning, give information rather than delight. "The worst feature," he says, "of these children's books is that they cheat the child of what he ought to gain from the experience of literature: access to deeper meaning, and that which is meaningful to him at his stage of development." And what is meaningful to the adult may not necessarily be meaningful to the child. Bettelheim is careful to point out that such "true" stories have their place, but that they are somewhat barren and do not encourage the active play of the child's imagination.

Cycles are common, and it seems we have come full circle once again with the publication of this book. Whereas society has been pronouncing fairy tales to be unhealthy fare, Bettelheim claims otherwise. The violence of fairy tales, the devouring wolves, the wicked stepmothers, the poisoned apples, the powerful giants are, in fact, beneficial to the young child and serve a function which more realistic literature cannot. Bettleheim convincingly sums up just what children's literature should do for children. He believes that it must develop and enrich both the intellect and the imagination, and, at the same time, speak to the child's unconscious fears, anxieties, and troubles. In short, appropriate literature addresses itself to "all aspects of [the child's] personality—and this without ever belittling . . . the seriousness of the child's predicaments. . . ." This, admittedly, is a tall order, but one which Bettelheim believes can be supplied by the folk/fairy tale. Even Victorian parents, the masters of sober morality and strict propriety, saw no harm in enriching their children's lives with the reading of fairy tales. Bettelheim, throughout the book, quotes the great and near-great, such as Dickens, Chesterton, C. S. Lewis, and Tolkien, to lend credence to his own belief in the appropriateness of such literature. He seems to be saying that what has been good for children for centuries should not be suddenly condemned in this modern age. In fact, with the pervasive, deadening effects of television on children, fairy tales may be more necessary than ever. Such unillustrated books encourage the child to develop his own mental picture of the dark forests, the moat and castle, and the wicked leers of evil queens.

Before beginning a more detailed analysis of the structure and meaning of fairy tales, Bettelheim carefully outlines, summarizes, and defends his thesis in the Introduction. This is probably a good thing for readers, serving as it does to clarify and buttress the ambitious scope of the book. The Introduction also gives readers unfamiliar with Bettelheim's reputation an opportunity to learn how the idea was conceived and executed and what Bettelheim's own experience has been, as a child psychologist, with the uses of fairy tales. As a therapist working with disturbed children, Bettelheim wondered why "children—normal and abnormal alike, and at all levels of intelligence—find fairy tales more satisfying than all other children's stories." Working with a grant from the Spencer Foundation, he proceeded to answer that question; hence this book.

Bettelheim applies a Freudian model to interpret the separate elements of fairy tales which help the child deal with life in the present, and with the mixture of good and bad feelings the child may have about himself. Such psychoanalytic jargon sometimes makes it heavy going for the average reader, but Bettelheim is ever careful to define his terms and to supply specific examples. Words such as "integration," "Oedipal conflicts," "transformation," and "autonomy" regularly crop up, but always with a specific fairy tale which illustrates the point. For example, when the knight in shining armor rescues the damsel in distress from the flaming jaws of the dragon, a resolution of an Oedipal conflict occurs. A young boy, listening to such a tale, could legitimately play out his fantasy of having Mother (the damsel) all to himself by slaying the dragon (Daddy). On the unconscious level the child has wished to be rid of Daddy, but at the same time felt guilt because he loves Daddy too and recognizes that without Daddy the family would be left alone and unprotected. The child, identifying with the knight or hero, is able to emerge triumphant without bringing harm to those he loves. Bettelheim is careful to stress that the child knows the story is not real, nor could the child understand such repressed and unsavory urges as wooing and winning his own mother. It would be wrong and would seriously undermine the magical quality of the story for the parent conscientiously to explain the Freudian meaning of the story. Stressing that children need the magic, Bettelheim says, "In trying to get a child to accept scientifically correct explanations, parents all too frequently discount scientific findings of how a child's mind works." So important is the exposure to such magic in early childhood that Bettelheim claims children deprived of fantasy may later attempt to make up for lost time. Perhaps we are seeing now, and saw in the 1960's, the effects of such fantasy deprivation. Bettelheim claims that such children, having had no magic, are incapable of coping with adulthood. They must seek out gurus, astrology, drugs, "black magic," or the occult to recapture somehow what they missed. He adds that such people were "prematurely pressed to view reality in an adult way."

Having made an effective case for the return to the reading of fairy tales,

Bettelheim is quick to anticipate reader queries on why this and only this special form of fanciful literature will do the job, psychologically speaking. What of fable, myth, or allegory, which likewise spring from the imagination and meet the criterion of good literature by delighting and instructing? He spends much time distinguishing between the fairy tale and myth and lauding the superiority of the fairy tale. The primary function of fairy tales is not, as with religion, myths, and fables, to teach "correct ways of behaving in this world." He adds, "The fairy tale is therapeutic because the patient finds his *own* solutions, through contemplating what the story seems to imply about him and his inner conflicts at this moment in his life." The heroes in myths are impossible to emulate because they are either superhuman or divine. Fables are likewise difficult for the child to appreciate because they "demand and threaten—they are moralistic." Fairy tale characters are part of this world, and therefore the child enters the realm of the possible. He sees the third or weakest child succeed, Jack slay the giant, Cinderella overcome her early suffering. The child begins to see that some day in the future he may be all that he wants to be. He learns too that good and evil exist side by side, that success does not always come on the first try, and that one's animal and human nature can become integrated. Fairy tales also affirm that we do not "subjugate animal nature to one ego or superego." Instead, "each element must be given its due." However, the child does not confuse the difference between fantasy and reality. As Bettelheim puts it, "The child who is familiar with fairy tales understands that these speak to him in the language of symbols and not that of everyday reality." Bettelheim also believes that when parents read to a child, they give "the child the feeling that since his inner experiences have been accepted by the parent as real and important, he—by implication—is real and important."

The organization and scope of *The Uses of Enchantment* pose the biggest obstacles to enjoyment of the book. Although the Introduction helps the reader exceedingly by telling him where he is going, he may nevertheless be hard pressed to persevere, to assimilate, and to retain such a vast body of material. The opening chapters of the book are difficult to follow at times because Bettelheim, using some psychological catch phrase, then dips into several tales to pull out elements which support and illustrate that phrase. Under the section headed "Transformations: The Fantasy of the Wicked Stepmother" he discusses "Little Red Riding Hood," "Hans, My Hedgehog," "The Seven Ravens," and "The Three Wishes." In such sections, he must recap the plot, analyze the meaning, and supply comparable illustrations of real-life dilemmas. Problems arise, too, in the sheer conscientiousness of Bettelheim's work. It seems that in covering so many stories, many of which are not at all familiar to the reader, he defeats his purpose, which is to influence broad public opinion in favor of fairy tales. In Part Two, he leaves off the subject headings which force him to combine bits and pieces from various stories, and instead gives a thorough treatment of seven very well-known fairy tales, including such standards as "Hansel and Gretel," "Jack and the Beanstalk," "Goldilocks and the Three Bears," and "The Sleeping Beauty." This arrangement is more successful because it encourages the parent to pick up the book on a sudden whim and read about the effect a particular story might have on his child. After all, very few people would think to wonder about such things as "Vicarious Satisfaction versus Conscious Recognition," a heading which appears in Part I. They simply want to know what is going on in Susie's head when she listens wide-eyed to "The Sleeping Beauty." Certainly, some people will read the book from beginning to end, but most parents are more likely to consider *The Uses of Enchantment* as a reference book.

Bettelheim has performed a long-delayed but necessary task by reinstating the fairy tale to its deserved position in children's literature. He has convincingly reassured parents that fairy tales, far from unnerving and harming their children, do, in fact, enrich their lives and bring greater mental and emotional health. The only flaw, if indeed it can be called that, is his scientist's zeal for thoroughness, his wish to tell us perhaps more than we ever wanted to know about his theories. However, given the recent unhappy status of such tales, it is probably vital that he leave no happy-ever-after unfulfilled.

Suzanne Britt Jordan

Sources for Further Study

Atlantic. CCXXXVII, June, 1976, p. 103.

Christian Century. XCIII, June 23, 1976, p. 603.

Harper's Magazine. CCLII, June, 1976, p. 94.

New Statesman. XCII, November 26, 1976, p. 765.

New York Review of Books. XXIII, July 15, 1976, p. 10.

North American Review. CCLXI, Gall, 1976, p. 89.

Time. CVII, May 3, 1976, p. 71.

Times Literary Supplement. October 1, 1976, p. 1245.

V WAS FOR VICTORY
Politics and American Culture During World War II

Author: John Morton Blum (1921-   )
Publisher: Harcourt Brace Jovanovich (New York). 372 pp. $12.95
Type of work: History
Time: 1941-1945
Locale: The United States

A study of selected facets of American politics and culture during World War II

World War II has long been a forgotten episode in America's domestic history. Scholars have carefully chronicled the exploits of the millions who marched off to battle and have examined the war years in search of the diplomatic antecedents of the subsequent Cold War. But what of those who remained behind manning the home front? John Morton Blum attempts to tell their story in *V Was for Victory.*

More precisely, Blum seeks to tell parts of their story. As he himself makes clear at the outset, this book is not a history of the home front *per se* but rather a collection of essays on selected facets of American politics and culture during the war years. It is a strangely discursive work, unified by the theme of World War II as a profoundly conservative experience for the American people. The desire for military victory overwhelmed all other goals and destroyed any hope that the war would be waged as a glorious crusade for a better world of international tranquillity and domestic justice. As Blum observes, "wartime needs reinforced institutional patterns of prewar society, and in so doing stamped postwar conditions." The message resonates through chapters treating such widely diverse topics as government propaganda, popular perceptions of the enemy and of the American G. I., the wartime experiences of various minority groups, presidential and congressional politics, and business-government relations.

This volume is both rewarding and disappointing. Fortunately, its virtues are many. Blum writes well, and the general reader especially will be pleased to find a work of genuine scholarship which does not bore. The prose is always straightforward and clear; the tone of the book is almost conversational and quite engaging. Scholars will marvel at the range Blum exhibits as he moves deftly from a discussion of wartime magazine advertisements to an analysis of the cultural significance of Norman Mailer's *The Naked and the Dead,* from a study of the maneuverings of the big-city bosses at the 1944 Democratic convention to a brilliant examination of the impact of Keynesian economics on businessmen and politicians alike. Equally admirable, Blum knows when to pull up short. Franklin D. Roosevelt clearly mystifies him: "He was now bold, now cautious, now exuberant, now moody, now generous, now cruel. He never let his right hand know, he once told a friend, what his left hand was doing." Those who had hoped to have the chameleon-like F.D.R. exposed at last will be disappointed, but one cannot help but appreciate Blum's candor as he throws up both hands and admits his inability to penetrate the magic and mystery of that man in the White House.

The author handles complicated issues with subtlety and an appreciation of paradox. In examining the treatment accorded Japanese-Americans, he demonstrates how white racism and the political vulnerability of the minuscule Japanese-American community resulted in policies laced with hatred and distrust. These policies, in turn, bred the very alienation on the part of those victimized that officials had suspected at the outset; it was a classic example of the self-fulfilling prophecy at work. As Blum makes clear, the situation was far different for Italian-Americans, who were white and who did have considerable political clout, especially in the Northeast, and who were therefore able to protect themselves from the worst ravages of official prejudice.

Blum also has a keen eye for the fascinating figure and the interesting anecdote. The successful struggle of Philip K. Wrigley to have his product, chewing gum, considered an essential war material so as to guarantee continued access to rationed sugar, is little short of hilarious. Wrigley's public relations machine strove mightily to portray thirst, nicotine, and Adolf Hitler as an evil Nazi triumvirate best fought in American war plants with heavy barrages of Wrigley's Spearmint.

More significantly, the author focuses on the rapid rise of businessmen like Andrew J. Higgens and Henry J. Kaiser. These men combined the traditional hustle of the self-made entrepreneur with a shrewd ability to take full advantage of the government's wartime largess. Constantly on the phone—Kaiser's long-distance telephone bill during the war hovered at around $250,000 a year—cultivating contacts such as former New Dealer Thomas G. Corcoran, Kaiser parlayed government aid into a true industrial empire. Such was the triumph of "free enterprise" during the war. As Blum points out, the wartime expansion of the federal government seemed only to foster the further growth of big business, big agriculture, and big labor. The resulting "confirmation of size" that occured during the war years sounded the death knell for whatever quixotic hopes remained among the neo-Brandeisians left over from the 1930's that American democracy could somehow be made safe for the little man.

Despite the frequency of such interesting insights, however, readers will also find much in this volume to trouble them. Blum's eclectic approach raises serious questions regarding the book's balance and proportion. Not all of his topics are equally interesting and informative, and the section on the government's wartime propaganda effort is far too prolix. At the same time, other topics that lie particularly in the nexus between politics and culture which so interests Blum, are given scant attention. For example, the impact of rationing and price administration is never adequately analyzed. These experiences would have provided interesting windows through which to view the interaction of such variables as military necessity, partisan opportunism, political tradition, and cultural attitudes.

A further complaint arises out of Blum's admirable attempt to put some issues into comparative perspective. His comparisons of the ways in which Americans and Russians perceived their respective fighting men and of the treatment accorded alien minorities in wartime Britain and the United States are interesting but never arresting. Considering Blum's major theme, one wishes that he had chosen to compare more extensively the American and English experiences. In Britain, a different store of political experience and cultural tradition, when mixed in the crucible of war, yielded not conservatism but rather a Labor government and the institutionalization of a cradle-to-grave welfare state. War obviously was not a universally conservative phenomenon, and a deeper plumbing of the English experience might have helped to explain more precisely why the American situation turned out as Blum argues it did.

But perhaps the war was not quite as conservative an experience as Blum implies. Simply put, this book is a liberal's history, for Blum is unable to transcend the largely political categories of traditional liberal scholarship. What seems to bother him most about the wartime experience is that it failed to give birth to a liberal super-New Deal (or even to continue the reformist thrust of the Depression). He errs, however, in making this his overriding criterion of change, and as a result he misses much of the socioeconomic change that the war did indeed set in motion or significantly accelerate. For example, the war fostered the economic growth in the South and West which underlies our more recent discovery of the rise of the "Sun Belt." World War II was also the only time during the twentieth century when America underwent a significant redistribution of wealth and income. Similarly, other historians have viewed the war as a watershed in the bettering of the objective economic conditions of American women. Historian Richard Dalfiume, for one, has found that it was the seeds sown during World War II that ultimately blossomed into the civil rights revolution of the 1950's and 1960's. And what of the contribution of the G. I. Bill, in terms of educational benefits and housing opportunities, to the creation of that postwar middle class which has become, for better or worse, a decisive political and cultural force in modern American life? It is this pattern of change which Blum's liberal ideological blinders prevent him from exploring or appreciating fully.

The liberal bias intrudes in other annoying, but ultimately less important, ways as well. One result is that Blum adopts a noticeably condescending tone when describing those who were not Eastern-liberal-Establishment types. Conservatives are too often described simply as pinched, vindictive, venomous, sanctimonious, or malicious men. Was there truly no nobility on the other side, or venality among Blum's favorites? His vision of the forces of good and evil is a consummation devoutly to be wished, for it would greatly simplify politics, and life as well; reality, alas, is not always so easily described. Blum's ideological orientation also causes him to focus especially on the attractive, "liberal" might-have-been's of wartime politics—Henry A. Wallace and Wendell Willkie. But if the war did indeed represent the triumph at least of political conservatism, as the author convincingly argues, one wonders whether less attractive figures, such as conservative Jesse Jones, would not have been more rewarding character studies.

In sum, *V Was for Victory* is a tantalizingly mixed bag. Blum's many strong qualities as a historian shine through and illuminate his topics with occasional brilliance. His version of history is a dynamic one which moves to an ideological conclusion. He refuses to become mired in the morass of moral ambiguity. While this sort of scholarship entails a certain sacrifice of complexity, it flows from a long and rich tradition, and it deserves a respectful reading by laymen and scholars alike.

Robert M. Collins

Sources for Further Study

America. CXXXV, November 13, 1976, p. 328.
Best Sellers. XXXVI, September, 1976, p. 202.
Christian Science Monitor. LXVIII, August 18, 1976, p. 27.
Kirkus Reviews. XLIV, March 15, 1976, p. 354.
Newsweek. LXXXVII, June 7, 1976, p. 88.
Saturday Review. III, July 10, 1976, p. 54.

THE VIEW FROM HIGHWAY 1
Essays on Television

Author: Michael J. Arlen (1930-   )
Publisher: Farrar, Straus and Giroux (New York). 293 pp. $8.95
Type of work: Essays

> *One of the few truly perceptive television critics of our time looks carefully at the medium and writes about it as if it really mattered*

If a reasonably intelligent person were to read carefully through the latest "Fall Preview" of *TV Guide,* by far the most popular magazine in America, he would probably have a difficult time taking seriously most of the new offerings. Redd Foxx describes his new variety program, for only one example, with the following: " 'I'm going to do anything that can possibly be different from what's been done before,' he says. 'I'll be doing skits, bits, obnoxious things. I might play "Romeo and Juliet" with a gorilla.' " "The show will be aimed at adults," *TV Guide* replies glibly. Michael J. Arlen, acutely aware of the difficulties of dealing with such deliberate nonsense, nevertheless takes television, its form and content, seriously. In a collection of twenty-one critical essays published originally in the *New Yorker* between September, 1974, and December, 1975, Arlen uncovers the significance of television, the meanings that lie deep beyond the meretricious, banal, and outright sappy shimmering and flickering surfaces that play on the millions of Zeniths and Sonys throughout the land. In doing so, he performs a great service to those who wish to understand the cultural and sociological and even psychological effects of the medium that enthralls or deadens but nonetheless captures anywhere from one-quarter to one-third of the nation on any viewing night.

In his truly fine introduction to the collection, Arlen synthesizes the overriding themes of the rest of the essays and indicates very forcefully his point of view. Here he contradicts the defenses and counterattacks created by television producers and executive directors to fend off the too-few critical assaults on the medium. Against the networks' allegation that television is a neutral and passive communications link that portrays life realistically and gives the people what they want, Arlen asserts that to many of its viewers television is really an active, shaping authority. The networks obviously have great power, and by the very forms and processes of television production, they shape and limit what we hear, see, and understand of the world. Between sixty-five and seventy million people get their daily information about the world, country, and local area solely through television news. Also, news programming consists essentially of selecting stories, framing them, and then editing and transmitting what the audience sees and hears. Because of these two facts, television can neither reject its own role as active authority nor depict an ultimately objective reality to its audience as it claims. In brief, "The television set transmits *its* version of our Yeas and *its* version of their rebuttal: our Nays ...

television does have a role and . . . it is virtually impossible for this role to be matter-of-fact or neutral." And to counter the assertion that television simply gives its audience what it desires, Arlen offers the theory that "if a reader cannot, in advance, conceive of *Moby Dick* on his own, how should he ask the culture somehow to provide such a work?"

What Arlen presents in his collection, in short, is a thinking person's guide to comprehending the significance of a medium that most thinking people allege they do not want to waste their time with, yet often escape to for entertainment, news, or sports. *The View from Highway 1*, immensely readable and sensible, provides those viewers with an insightful analysis of materials too fleeting to promote easy investigation. Arlen's task is one of clarification: making coherent sense out of Tom Snyder's hostile but ultimately aloof interviewing techniques, ferreting out the truth beneath the surfaces of such insanities as the commercials which blare "Ring around the collar," probing the truly serious failings of network news. Nicholas Johnson, former head of the Federal Communications Commission, said in 1969, "Television is one of the most powerful forces man has ever unleashed upon himself. The quality of human life may depend enormously upon our contributions to comprehend and control that force." Michael J. Arlen, through *The View from Highway 1* and an earlier collection of critical essays entitled *Living-Room War* (1967), makes his contribution to the effort formalized by Johnson.

One of the most striking qualities of television programming is its remarkable variety. On any given night, a person near a major metropolitan area can choose between the serious and the ridiculous, programs of quality and of very bad taste, anything from *I Love Lucy* reruns and *The Gong Show* to live baseball coverage, William F. Buckley's *The Firing Line,* the sweathogs of *Welcome Back, Kotter,* or *Upstairs, Downstairs.* Arlen's book treats that variety of programming and diversity of quality in his text. Investigated both in depth and in passing, the programs used to initiate the author's arguments include *All in the Family, Kojak, Bozo's Circus,* and *Saturday Night;* dozens of others are discussed as well.

It is evident that Arlen has spent many hours watching his object of criticism, attempting to penetrate its facial ways and means. But while starting out most of his essays with a concrete example from a particular show, he rarely holds his concern with the immediate object at hand; instead, he moves on to more important matters, namely the ideas under the surface, the true realities of the television program that are missed by even the most perceptive, habitual viewer. For example, when analyzing the reasons behind the enormous popularity of such Norman Lear productions as *All in the Family, Maude,* and *Sanford and Son,* Arlen sees through their surfaces—the jokey topicality, unfunny lines made palatable by studio-audience laughter, and rather routine grimaces—to its heart, "the constant and steady presence of anger." What is most significant about the violence is that it is vague, directionless, purposeless, much like the ambivalent consciousness of those who are informed primarily by the media. Arlen's ultimate conclusion is that Lear's comedies are successful largely because he has tapped into an audience whose perceptions and responses have been conditioned by television; viewers

> who, as informed adults and media children, discuss, with all the appearance of passion and involvement, events that have occurred in places we have no knowledge of and had no previous interest in, and with implications we have rarely examined, or tried to connect backward or forward to other events.

In short, the rap is on television's effects in general, not on those of *All in the Family* in particular.

Throughout the book, Arlen uses concrete examples from television programming as springboards leading into truly intelligent assertions about the media's overall influence and nature. From an analysis of the tone of Howard Cosell, of ABC's *Monday Night Football,* and of Tom Snyder of *Tomorrow,* the author finds that the most disquieting thing about them is not their hostility, which is but a pretense, but a meaningless neutrality, a quality of disconnection and aloofness from their subject matter that is eminently more disconcerting. The mediators do not really care; the informing center is empty. This fact troubles Arlen not because he is worried about Cosell or Snyder but because the "disconnection" that they exemplify is already part of our fragmented reality and because mediators in particular and television in general are nurturing it.

Other concerns of Arlen's essays are children's television (appropriately titled "Kidvid"), PBS programming, American television's avoidance of real death, insensitive interviewing, the absence of true adventure narrative, television's treatment of women and violence, and modern comedy. Well-documented, loaded with concrete examples, full of historical background, and consistently reflecting startling insights, these essays are comprehensive and worthy of the reader's time. Interesting too are Arlen's interspersed parodies that, although exaggerated, ring sadly true.

But the most significant of the essays are those concerned with television news, especially those programs of the past dealing with the American presence in Southeast Asia. Through unified, logical argument, Arlen in six different essays articulates the faults of television news coverage. Consistently making reasonable concessions to the opposition (the author frequently praises particular reporters and the information-spreading ability of television—in less than one and one-half hours after the event, ninety percent of all Americans learned of President Kennedy's assassination), Arlen persuades his audience that the fragmented, distorted, and trivialized pictures that are seen of the world through the networks' lenses are largely unreal, leading audiences adrift, leaving them detached, misinformed. He alleges that television coverage of Vietnam never really told the full story, that initially it mouthed the official statements of the governments, and that it continued throughout to present only a fragmented picture of the Vietnam reality. Instead of a unified and coherent view of our involvement there and our subsequent understanding of what we were doing, why, and at what cost, we received images of artillery fire and F-4's, of starving children and roads clogged with refugees, of air bursts of bombs and smoke swirls in the far-off wooded areas and mountains—these images repeated over and over until they became iconic but ultimately meaningless. In so doing, Arlen alleges, "American network news did [not] do much beyond contribute to the unreality, and thus the dysfunction of American life. . . . Television has dealt us a cheap hand."

On the whole, Arlen is an extremely persuasive writer, largely because of his reasonableness, his avoidance of unqualified assertions, and his considerable knowledge of media, the history of entertainment, and literature. It is rather refreshing to read the work of a critic who bases his investigation first on close scrutiny of his object and then writes about it not out of any desire to grind axes but out of a thrust toward opening up our eyes to the shortcomings of, and therefore the possibilities of improving, the medium. He is clarifying for us a fact of our lives that we usually disregard. Second, his prose is lean, readable, nicely balanced, rather classical in its construction but modern in its rhythms. Though lacking the spontaneity of the essays of *Living-Room War*, those of *The View from Highway 1* are still energetic and forceful in syntax and diction.

Michael J. Arlen, simply stated, is America's best television critic. One will find, however, that his works are not simply reviews of individual programs; most of those, except for *Saturday Night, Upstairs, Downstairs* and a few others, are so deliberately banal that he refuses to waste much space on extensive analysis of them. Instead, he devotes his energies to the realities beyond their simplistic surfaces and the effects of their forms on all of us. If Marshall McLuhan's enlightened "global village" is to become a reality through the unifying force of television, then the discontinuity, superficiality, and mindlessness currently being foisted on us all by the controllers of the medium will have to stop. Arlen's *The View from Highway 1* makes us aware that television is doing more to us than we know and that it can be changed for our benefit.

Harold J. Joseph

Sources for Further Study

America. CXXXV, November 6, 1976, p. 308.
Book World. November 21, 1976, p. E4.
Kirkus Reviews. XLIV, August 19, 1976, p. 930.
New York Times Book Review. October 10, 1976, p. 7.
New Yorker. LII, December 13, 1976, p. 163.

VIPER JAZZ

Author: James Tate (1943-   )
Publisher: Wesleyan University Press (Middletown, Connecticut). 80 pp. $3.45 (paper-
back)
Type of work: Poetry

A transitional volume by one of our most adventurous young poets

In this sixth major collection of poems, James Tate fulfills the promise of his
earlier work to become to the contemporary poem what Donald Barthelme is
to short fiction: the master of the conversationally miraculous *non sequitur*.
Throughout his work, Tate's amazingly consistent *persona* has shocked us with
its untimeliness, delighted us with its wit, surprised us with its unexpectedness.
We know that to adhere to the tenet of unpredictability largely for its own sake
is to fall into the trap through the back door, to become predictable. This had
become a problem in some of Tate's earlier books (especially *The Oblivion Ha-
Ha* and *Absences*) where many of the pieces give off the air of being slapped
together from as many ephemeral trains of thought as could be maintained in
one sitting. Tate had abandoned the finished, linear polish of his excellent first
book, *The Lost Pilot*, in order to write a more ambitious and, as is often the
case, a more failure-prone type of poem which, in the light of *Viper Jazz*, can
now be viewed as necessarily transitional. The longer of these "middle" poems
border on being nearly unreadable as their lack of tension both in their
content and in their physical appearance, plus a lack of object-relationships
which can invite scrutiny, reduce the works to pretentious, discursive
disjointedness.

Viper Jazz is the product of the honed method, the intermarriage of the first
artifacts and the middle meanderings to produce poems which are more legitimately imaginative than surrealistic, and which seem to have been reworked
to the point beyond which they could not be any more spontaneous. If their
lengths appear standardized, it is due to the greater demands an artificer has
made upon his material, forcing the winding content into a tensely submissive
posture where, conversely, the same content has much greater room within
which to exert itself. Not one poem in this collection has grown out of control;
this is a noteworthy accomplishment for any poet and a major one for Tate.
The prosily discursive body is attenuated—at moments where the process of
roving, ironic attentions has not simply petered out, leaving a word glut in its
trail, but rather at points of sharp, unnerving closure. The *persona* emerges as
a misanthropic reveler, far more bitter and now more adept than in the earlier
poems, where irony is mostly served by the literal awareness of clichés, a
device that tires as the clichés mount up. Now Tate plays upon more sophisticated methods, all of which use the background *pastiche* of the poem as an
alien springboard against which actual things and feelings come into
contradistinction.

In "The Television Was Reminded of the Story," for example, the speaker uses for his setting a "town of stove-pipe hats," as good a description as any for the nondescript nature of the place and its events. The poem ends with these lines:

> A sign said YIELD
> and a woman ran through the streets
> actually crying.

The reader responds with shock at this portrayal of the woman's tears of fear, depression, or despair; the image of the running woman is enlarged out of the real world by its incongruous introduction into a world of a different sort, one that is deceptively presented as a mundane, uninteresting place. Actual emotion is both exalted and demeaned, anything but weighed for its own value, as in another poem, "Hooked on a Star," which begins:

> I like everything about you
> though you are just a piece of plastic.
> I know that and it doesn't influence me.
> I still love you.

These humorous but chilling lines show us the familiar speech of the verbs "to like" and "to love," suddenly so strange, so out of context. Often, poems that hinge on the same key words or devices are paired on facing or consecutive pages, so that "A Voyage from Stockholm," with its last line "and in the distance the distance," is echoed in the ending of the next poem "The Hairy Cup of Coffee:" "he deliberately pinpricked/my pinprick." Repetition links the close of a previous poem, "Cruisin' Even," ("the speakable sadness of a dried-up port") with the next title, "Eavesdropper Without a Port, Becoming Small." One feels the obvious connective effect of this permutation within verbal limits, but it also heightens the new intangibility of the commonplace, the sudden added import or, other times, lost meaning of a recurring item. All of this blurring of linguistic existence reaches fruition early in the book in a poem called "The Door," where the same sound is stripped of its meaning in the alternate, nonexistent spellings "dore" and "doar" until the utterance of "dour" infuses this short poem with an entirely different purpose: to unveil the negative core at the heart of our speech. The speaker's final assertion, "I'm waking up," resounds as both the excuse for the dream-like elision of spelling and, taken as the familiar cliché, the realization that our ever spoken "door" moves toward "dour," the mind seeking the lowest point for rest.

The overt humor of these poems surprise the reader when viewed against the overall backdrop of a more committed antihumanism. Tate's *persona* is funnier than ever before in such lines as the bizarre couplet, "the ghost of baloney through violent will/ toothless wrenching baloney now you are still," or "And by rubbing granite cliffs together/ morning becomes Thor Heyerdahl/ on his way to work." Other examples abound, but these two, along with the title "Blonde Bombshell Unnerves Squirts," bring laughs with the hit-or-miss abandon of someone who has forsaken the caution and restraint implied by poetic activity. In previous books, Tate has always exercised his license to say anything; now, where that license is willfully curtailed, the attempts at humor are more successful, as are also the moments of sincerity and poignancy.

Viper Jazz is exemplary of a recent type of poetry which Donald Hall sketches well in his introduction to the second edition of his anthology *Contemporary American Poetry*. Hall calls this poetry "subjective without being confessional," and "expressionist," for its relationship to paintings in which the emphasis is on building and sustaining an emotional complex which has, as its verbal components, words and images chosen for their functional values above the literal level. In further describing how the poet may be deciding between two opposite words for the same slot in a poem, thereby illustrating the arbitrariness of choice once outside the limits of actuality, Hall seems to be describing the artistic problem indigenous to Tate's book. It is the purely imaginative act which must solve the problem; all of the available choices do not yield equal satisfaction, so a good poet seems to be one who works with preternatural guidance, what is usually called "instinct." No rational process, for example, can account for the second image in the lines, "I picture myself as a hummingbird/ or as a nail robbing a grave." Yet the image is exact and its meaning clear in an irrational fashion; we "feel" rather than "know" how the speaker pictures himself.

The poem "Come the Thaw" begins with a similar tactic:

> There is a conspiracy
> for and against you,
> a nebulous precision
> like the feel of suicide,
> words refused by worlds.

The idea of a "nebulous precision" cannot have an automatic word/idea appeal to the intellect because of the conflicting definitions of the two words, but from "nebulous" we do feel a sinister vagueness and in "precision" we assume the mechanical ability to invade the particular, so the phrase does not cancel itself out but rather threatens with both implications. "Like the feel of suicide" sharpens the *angst* of the previous line and definitely characterizes the "nebulous precision" as an element of mortality, so removed that one's own self could be inducing the fatality. This more specific reference to suicide is qualified in the next "poeticized" line, where the act of a world refusing words reinstates experience as a function of emotional projection and not intellectual simulation. Tate is at his most stimulating when juggling passages that radiate in such oblique directions with his disarmingly straightforward moments of comedic recklessness.

Viper Jazz does, however, have its erratic parts, instances where poetic tactics are only half thought-out or pursued to ends which never rise above being trite, cute, or clever. In a late poem in the book, the closing distich, "No part of this flower may be reproduced/ without permission in writing from the Creator," has simply fallen away from the spirit of creativity and emulates a type of verbal artifact that is part of the ready-made, popular culture. In some ways, this same criticism holds true for the book as a whole. Tate has pushed the kind of poem he writes to a much higher level of competence; indeed, this probably is his finest collection. However, there is a strong feeling that the poet has matured into this work through the simple process of aging and revising, rather than challenging his previously established poetic precepts. One sees in *Viper Jazz* two one-line poems and at least two other pieces that appear to be prose-poems; where Tate may appear to be experimenting with the limits of his art, he is actually "experimenting" with the new freedoms of "publishability." How much of a formal factor this stylishness will become seems to be predetermined by the cloying visibility these works demand without deserving; they are obviously separate from the rest of the book in spirit and quality. James Tate's sixth book is an oddity, that well-written, often easy but occasionally ambitious work that creates as much of a need for new rigors as it satisfies. The field may not be exhausted, but it has been explored to its boundaries. *Viper Jazz*, itself the culmination of transitional works, is perhaps most important for the further work it foreshadows.

Harrison Fisher

Sources for Further Study

Booklist. LXXIII, November 15, 1976, p. 451.
Christian Science Monitor. LXVIII, October 28, 1976, p. 27.
Kirkus Reviews. XLIV, September 15, 1976, p. 10.
Library Journal. CI, August, 1976, p. 1640.
New York Times Book Review. November 21, 1976, p. 65.

A VOICE FROM THE CHORUS

Author: Abram Tertz (Andrei Sinyavsky)
Translated from the Russian by Kyril Fitzlyon and Max Hayward
Publisher: Farrar, Straus and Giroux (New York). 328 pp. $10.00
Type of work: Letters
Time: 1966-1971
Locale: The U.S.S.R.

> *A collection of excerpts from letters, musing about religion, art, literature, and folk-lore, set against a prison camp background*

The tradition of prison literature is a long and honorable one, and *A Voice from the Chorus* is a worthy addition. Andrei Sinyavsky, a young teacher and literary critic, had his writings smuggled out of the Soviet Union and published in the West under the pseudonym "Abram Tertz." (The name is that of the "hero" of an underworld ballad.) The works were in no ordinary sense politically subversive. They rather represented, both in critical writing and practice, a reaction against "Socialist Realism" which in some eyes may have been even more dangerous. After successfully publishing in the West from 1959, Sinyavsky was discovered and arrested. With another author similarly charged, he was brought to trial in February, 1966. Despite protests from the Western world, and murmurs and disillusion within the Soviet Union, he was sentenced to seven years in "corrective labor camps." Released in June of 1971, he later moved to Paris.

A Voice from the Chorus is not a narrative of prison experience; it is not really a narrative at all. Nor is it an analysis of that experience, nor an attack on the system. Comparison with *The Gulag Archipelago*, for example, would be irrelevant. During his six years in Dubrovlag, Sinyavsky wrote long letters to his wife—two a month were all the rules permitted, and these, of course, went through censors. She kept the letters, and the book is a series of extracts, often only a sentence or two, rarely more than a page, from the letters. What we have then, is a book of *pensées*. Although the prison experience adds interest, and may have sharpened or deepened the author's thoughts, it is the explicit theme only rarely, and then the concern is usually with human conditions and reactions, rather than political or sociological observations.

In counterpoint to the author's soliloquy throughout are snatches of conversation from the other prisoners—the "chorus" of the title. The sections are rarely connected—they are fragments, hardly ever more than a sentence in length—though often they are unified by a common note or theme. Most of the speakers are evidently ill-educated or uneducated, many are recognizably "ordinary criminals," not political prisoners like Sinyavsky. According to the Introduction, the Russian of these passages is full of dialect, argot, and slang; and the vernacular is part of the message. Probably with wisdom, the translator has not attempted to convey this flavor in English, though there is a suggestion that one passage is full of malapropisms. The subjects of these chorus passages are frequently neither fixed nor clear, as snatches of overheard conversation hardly ever can be. The meditations and musings Sinyavsky himself sets down range widely, as is to be expected from a series of letters. The weather recurs, not merely as the staple concern it is with most people, but as a subject of reflection. Camp routine and depictions of relations among prisoners are there, but they are not of primary interest.

What interests Sinyavsky is art, and above all, literature. For the non-Russian, the references to Russian literature, which of course dominate, may fascinate, but not always satisfy—like the allusions in Russian novels to folk songs unheard of in the West. However, so much of the concern in these brief passages is with art and literature in general, not with specific criticism, that the difficulty is not great. What may seen remarkable to the reader is Sinyavsky's familiarity with a wide variety of English literature. In fact, when the Tertz pieces first appeared, it was argued that they could not have been written inside the Soviet Union, so wide and sophisticated was the literary knowledge they displayed. One might expect familiarity with Shakespeare, and *Hamlet* is indeed the subject of numerous reflections by foreign authors; but the discussions of Swift and Defoe, the judgment that *Robinson Crusoe*, is the "most useful, exhilarating, and benign novel," strike the reader as particularly well-informed remarks.

At one point during his imprisonment, the author's wife had written him of reading to their small son Kipling's story of the baby elephant who is almost victim to the crocodile, and the boy was in tears. The mother reassured him; he had heard the story before, and knew it came out right, but, said the boy through his tears, suppose this time he doesn't make it? Sinyavsky takes the reaction and pursues an idea: this is the fascination of literature, that we can be enthralled even when we know the ending. This is why fairy tales should never be interrupted. This is why the "Great Drama" was not just a single occurrence, but is reenacted through the cycle of liturgical feasts.

The passage also points out several other of Sinyavsky's consistent interests. Religion is an abiding concern, surprising perhaps in one reared in the modern Soviet Union, but not surprising at all in a Russian. Himself a Russian Orthodox Christian, the author discusses the tremendous importance of verbal differences in religious quarrels, as illustrated by the Old Believers' insistence on retaining precise words in the Creed. There is the suggestion, elsewhere, that Catholicism is the religion of the Father, Protestantism of the Son, but Orthodoxy of the Holy Spirit. He does not pursue the comparison, but discusses (in one of the longer passages) the influence of the Spirit on Russia and the Russian character. Still another passage, this one from an article on early Russian church architecture, puts emphasis upon the Russian idea of the protective mantle of the Virgin.

Here again, no thorough investigation or amplification appears. Sinyavsky is not a theologian or even a spiritual writer, but a man writing his wife thoughts stimulated by something he has read, yesterday or ten years ago, or heard, or somehow else brought to mind. Here, too, however, the thought and insight can cast sparks. If primarily this is the result of a thoughtful and original mind, it is also a well-stocked mind. It is the very depth and range of Sinyavsky's interests and knowledge that make sharper the contrast with his "Chorus." Some of their remarks reflect sheer ignorance, whether of science or language; but nevertheless, the chorus often echoes a certain "folk-wisdom," or "street knowledge," and reflects a wide range of experience. Though all Sinyavsky does is to quote these bits and pieces, the arrangement somehow unmistakably conveys his compassion and his respect for the choristers as people. Their frequently disconnected observations cover crime and punishment, women and sex, money, and the other things that interest single men in barracks. Comments on the prison itself, or on the guards and other attendants, are rare. (The censorship may account for that.) Here, somehow again by arrangement, the atmosphere of the labor camp is conveyed, rather than in any extended discussion by Sinyavsky himself.

Yet the camp is the persistent setting and environment of the book—always there, whether mentioned or not. One feels, not so much the mention of forbidden zones, which does occur, but the pressure of enforced living with all these others, when solitude is plainly a necessity (occasional, but still a necessity) for a man like Sinyavsky. One feels, though direct expression is rare, his longing for wife and son. Yet complaint and self-pity are almost totally absent, and their very absence may make the horror of the camps and the system more real.

Perhaps what gives prison literature its special character is the separation from the rest of society; perhaps, as Dr. Johnson said of the prospect of hanging, it concentrates the mind. What gives this prison book its further character is the knowledge on our part that the crime for which Sinyavsky was sentenced—whatever the legal jargon—was his refusal to submit his *mind*, to stop thinking and writing, and the further crime that the world knew it. Perhaps, through the censorship, the "chorus" says something about both the pressures of the society and the resistance. Perhaps, as Hayward suggests in the Introduction, when Sinyavsky describes the code of honor among thieves, and their high respect for it, he is saying something about Soviet society. Such thoughts are bound to occur. It is a further consideration that the trial and imprisonment took place, not under Stalin, but years after his death. Systems and ideas have a way of outliving individual leaders.

The book itself is hard to assess as a whole, because it is a collection; some items in the collection are wonderful, while some inevitably produce a desire for further elaboration, or for more careful argument. But these weaknesses are offset by the virtues of brevity and multiplicity. The book's organization and unity stem not from a scheme, but from the presentation of a single personality. There are books whose importance lies in their ideas, and others whose great value is that they put the reader in touch with a person. There are certainly ideas in *A Voice from the Chorus,* but it is our insight into one man's mind which is truly exceptional. In the presence of the author's courage and serenity one is both fascinated and impressed.

George J. Fleming

Sources for Further Study

America. CXXXV, October 16, 1976, p. 237.

Commentary. LXII, November, 1976, p. 66.

Commonweal. CIII, December 3, 1976, p. 788.

Nation. CCXXIII, September 4, 1976, p. 185.

New Leader. LIX, September 13, 1976, p. 16.

New Republic. CLXXV, September 25, 1976, p. 41.

New Yorker. LII, October 11, 1976, p. 165.

Saturday Review. III, July 24, 1976, p. 27.

THE WATCHES OF THE NIGHT

Author: Harry M. Caudill (1922-   )
Publisher: Little, Brown and Company (Boston). 275 pp. $8.95
Type of work: Current affairs
Time: 1963-1976
Locale: The Cumberland Plateau, rural southern and eastern Kentucky

A record of the Kentucky Cumberland Plateau showing the lasting poverty existing among the people, the despoliation of the land by strip mining, and the corruption of a government where coal is the primary resource

Harry M. Caudill established himself as a regional writer of rural Kentucky in 1963 with his book *Night Comes to the Cumberlands,* an account of the eastern and southern section of Kentucky where coal is king. The primary focus of his novels and books is the despoliation, poverty, and government corruption in the Cumberlands. *Darkness at Dawn: Appalachia and the Future,* also published in 1976, details the genealogical heritage of Kentucky's British descendants, describing the culture and tradition of the people. Caudill, a native Kentuckian, rehashes a similar subject, the coal industry that carelessly rapes the environment. The book that established his reputation, *Night Comes to the Cumberlands,* described the poverty and deprivation in this Kentucky plateau region which is rich in coal. *The Watches of the Night* is a sequel to *Night Comes to the Cumberlands*; it updates that book and shows the continued bleakness of lives and politics of the Cumberland Plateau.

The mid- to late-1960's was doubtless the time for public awareness, good works, and crusades on poverty. It became almost faddish during this time to protest to "gain insight" into the disadvantaged, and so in the mid- to late-1960's, Kentucky, perhaps the heart of American poverty, was invaded with "hordes of pampered young people" who wanted to "view and interview living and suffering poverty." Television documentaries, college study groups, VISTA volunteers, and other public awareness groups came to Kentucky to see, to study, and to attempt to correct the poverty that Caudill portrayed in his 1963 book.

VISTA, one of President John F. Kennedy's creations in his war on poverty, sent people to "help the inhabitants rise up and cast off the shackles of want." When VISTA workers saw at firsthand that local politicians were allied to coal interests, they sought immediate reform. The results of their efforts to bring the poor to an awareness of their plight, of political and industrial outrages, merely destroyed their effectiveness. Kentucky politicians called their national legislators and demanded that the volunteers be recalled. They railed against the volunteers, calling them "radical" and "disruptive," and VISTA died by 1967. In recalling these events and others like them, Caudill in turn rails against the government, saying that "The federal echelon is only the upper structure of a system built on precincts, counties, cities and towns, and to war on the base will shatter the security on top."

Caudill is constantly critical of the government because so often, as he sees it, when help groups came to the Cumberlands and touched on the corruption of politicians, the poverty, and the health hazards in the mines, federal subsidies for the organizations dried up or new directives were issued for the group.

After VISTA came Appalachian Volunteers, a group of college students helping with housing and education. Following publication of a brochure on "Appalachian's 40 Thieves" its federal funding was dropped and the organization fell apart.

Today Caudill points out that Appalachia is perhaps in worse shape than it was thirteen years ago before all the help groups were sent by the government. President Johnson and his Great Society's war on poverty made a "welfare reservation" out of much of the Cumberland area. Strip mining has ruined much of the fertile land and made silt and mud flats out of lakes created by the Army Corps of Engineers for flood control and recreation. In addition, the forests and the soil, once depleted in productivity but now replenished, lie unused and wasted, for the majority living in the Cumberland Plateau either worship the king coal or the welfare check. And as Caudill repeatedly demonstrates, such worship begins with the small businessmen who increase prices as soon as the miners get raises, and extends to the local, state, and federal government because coal is the number-one industry in the state.

With the increased need for coal, Caudill says, comes the continued despoliation of the land. Strip mining has left the land raped and has created soil erosion which destroys property. Coal mining in Kentucky has "vastly hastened the erosive processes that are relentlessly leveling the Appalachians." Roads have been and continue to be torn up by the oversized Mack trucks that create huge potholes and destroy paving. Laws fail to be enforced to meet the requirements for truck size and weight. Yet taxes on trucks and coal are kept low because coal is Kentucky's only major industry. Any fines levied at coal trucks or at unsafe mining conditions would bring the coal entrepreneurs down the throats of legislators who seek reelection and therefore need the support and funding of big industry. But Caudill never presents the coal industry's perspective; his presentation is onesided.

With the land exhausted agriculturally in the 1960's and with the mechanization of coal mining, the plateau people remained unemployed and found the government ready and willing to care for them via the all-too-easily obtained welfare check. Today, Caudill states, much of the farmland is replenished, but welfare has destroyed individual motivation; hence, those who have received relief for years prefer the free ticket. Worse, welfare has become an inherited trait passed along from one generation to the next. Welfare, Caudill says in recalling Franklin D. Roosevelt's warning to the nation in the 1930's, should be temporary because "continued dependence upon relief in any form slowly but surely reduces the recipient to habitual dependency, passivity and political impotence." Reared in the Cumberland region where he has chosen to remain, Caudill has observed this dependency spread over the region, from relative to relative, from father to son. But here again Caudill is too harsh; he simplifies the welfare problems.

What makes the picture Caudill paints even more bleak is that he sees no positive alternatives; he has no answers. In suggesting alternatives he also sees pitfalls. One alternative is the nationalization of coal, but Caudill, who distrusts government, feels that such a process would not work. Perhaps an honest politician is needed who, seeing the deplorable condition of Appalachia, could stand up and say no to the coal tyrant. But Caudill is so cynical he feels no honest politician exists. He believes that even the few courageous and ethical politicians cannot offer lasting help because there are simply too few politicians who are anti-coal and pro-Appalachia. With all his research, with the years he has lived in the Cumberland region, Caudill still has no definitive answer, yet he expects others from afar to provide solutions.

Caudill is biased, and he lets his bias show. He condemns the coal industry and the politicians who allow coal to control the Cumberland Plateau at the expense of the land and the people. He condemns welfarism for creating a society that is dependent on the monthly government check. His prejudices show in his constant repetitions, which often annoy the reader. But Caudill repeats not only to stress points, but also to express his anger.

His indignant verbal attacks may tend, as Caudill hopes, to incite the reader concerning the ruination of the environment by industry with the approval of the government. But his rather tedious and sometimes technical style may undermine his exhortations. The book is not light reading; it often deadens rather than inspires. Then too, the author displays a limited vocabulary and tends to repeat coined phrases.

The book is divided into six chapters and, in the longest, entitled "The Mad Reign of King Coal," Caudill lays blame on every government organization that came to Kentucky. The Army Corps of Engineers, the Tennessee Valley Authority, the United Mine Workers of America, the Appalachian Regional Council, the local, state, and federal government are attacked for their combined and conscious rape of the Cumberland Plateau in Kentucky.

The Army Corps of Engineers, for example, acquired land for flood control and recreational purposes from poor Kentuckians, often for less than its appraised value. People who sold their land had difficulty buying at the same price because talk of the reservoir inflated land prices along the other nearby creeks. Many were forced to move out of the mountains which had been their home for generations into trailer parks. Lakes, financed with government money, were eventually sacrificed to the coal industry because, as erosion from nearby strip mining continued, the lakes became mud flats.

The author condemns the coal industry, too, for trying to keep the union out, an effort that kept wages low and people in poverty. The pro-United Mine

Workers of America cause was effectively destroyed when the 1963 government-funded Work Experience program drove union picketers from the demonstration line to menial janitorial jobs for which they received $1.25 per hour. But $1.25 was better than no pay on the picket line. Without the union, miners received no retirement pensions, no compensation, no hospitalization. Critical of an industry which would offer its employees no benefits, Caudill points out that "This failure to meet . . . the financial burdens emanating from the industrial carnage cast thousands of dependent people onto the public assistance rolls and the demoralizing influence of 'welfare as a way of life.'" But, as Caudill consistently points out, coal takes supremacy over people in the Cumberland Plateau.

Today new government policies have provided some benefits to coal miners whose health has been impaired by years underground. But when the state and government started new policies in an effort to provide health needs to the people, they were also abused. The new policies, according to Caudill, failed to help the people or the region. Many policies, such as the "black lung bonanza," merely milked the United States Treasury since many who never worked in a mine sought and obtained compensation, while others who spent the majority of their lives in the mines were refused because some doctors attributed their lung problems to cigarette smoking.

Besides Caudill's bias, he also tends to make broad generalizations that stereotype miners in particular and Southerners in general. In discussing the wealth of the coal interests and in detailing how growth led to wealth for many mine operators, Caudill says, "Small southern towns esteem wealth almost to the exclusion of other values."

Caudill is obsessed with the influence coal interests have on political officials. He believes, and presents a fairly convincing case, that

> the small-bore officials who run the states are the most greedy and least scrupulous, and the coal royalists learned early in their corporate history how relatively paltry sums, if well placed, could bring the passage of helpful laws, the veto of harmful ones and, in a pinch, the nullifying of judicial opinions. After that lesson was learned the "coal interests" had hosts of eager friends, and state legislators, governors, congressmen and senators vociferously served their cause.

But this is too sweeping a judgment.

The Watches of the Night will definitely create interest in the environmental destruction occuring in Appalachia, in the corruption of the government on every level, and in the condition of the people who have lived in the area in poverty for generations. Biased as Caudill is, the book should still be read by those whose concern for the environment, for the poor, and for an ethical government remains genuine.

Janet H. Hobbs

Sources for Further Study

Booklist. LXXIII, September 1, 1976, p. 8.

Library Journal. CI, November 15, 1976, p. 2386.

National Observer. XV, October 30, 1976, p. 21.

New Yorker. LII, November 1, 1976, p. 165.

Newsweek. LXXXVIII, October 18, 1976, p. 105.

Time. CVIII, November 1, 1976, p. 88.

WHAT SHALL WE WEAR TO THIS PARTY?
The Man in the Gray Flannel Suit Twenty Years Before & After

Author: Sloan Wilson (1920-   )
Publisher: Arbor House (New York). 442 pp. $12.95
Type of work: Autobiography
Time: 1920-1975
Locale: The East Coast

An autobiography which interprets an entire American generation through the experiences of the author, who was himself for a time one of the men in gray flannel suits

> *Principal personages:*
> SLOAN WILSON, author of *The Man in the Gray Flannel Suit*
> ELISE PICKHARDT WILSON, his first wife
> BETTY JOAN STEPHENS, his second wife
> RUTH DANENHOWER WILSON, his mother
> RICHARD SIMON, of Simon and Schuster, the author's friend and publisher
> JESSICA WILSON, the author's child by his second wife

In 1955 Sloan Wilson captured the imagination of the middle class of the 1950's, particularly readers of his own generation, in a novel which achieved great popularity and gave a phrase to the American language. That novel, *The Man in the Gray Flannel Suit,* was a fictional study of men who adopted a kind of uniform, the suit of gray flannel, which identified them as belonging to the post-World War II generation of men, mostly in business careers, who were typical of the times in their outlook on life and in their goals. Sloan Wilson, himself of that group of men, has utilized his own life to interpret a half century of life for himself and for his generation.

Looking backward as he began to think and write about his life, Wilson discovered that the great event of his lifetime was World War II, in which he served as an officer in the U.S. Coast Guard for four years. He found that the war had affected his whole generation, burning itself into their memories. As he began to write his autobiography he discovered that his war experience threatened to usurp his whole remembrance. Indeed, three of the nine chapters of his autobiography are used to relate Wilson's experience in that war, although only four of his fifty-five years were spent in the Coast Guard. At least three points emerge for Wilson about that experience. For one, he and his generation (of which more than ten million men and women served their country in uniform) were not militarists, although they accepted the war between the Axis powers and the Allied nations as a genuine moral struggle between good and evil. Second, he and others of his generation saw the war as a personal test which they had to pass in order to keep their self-respect. They had to determine whether they were competent to learn the skills for survival in war, and they believed they had to find out if they had the courage to face military action or discover their own cowardice. Third, Wilson and others of his generation tried to get ahead in the military service, as they were later to strive to get ahead in civilian life. For them earning a commission, being promoted in rank, and gaining positions of military command were important aspects of their brief military careers. Wilson shows how he was typical of those people, achieving a commission in the Coast Guard, and later rising in rank and responsibility to command ships—first a converted trawler, the *Nogak,* on patrol off Greenland, and later a supply ship and a gasoline tanker in the Pacific Theater of Operations.

Upon his release from the service at the end of World War II, Wilson, like so many men of his generation, returned to his interrupted college career; he went back to Harvard to complete the requirements for his baccalaureate degree. Then, having aspired to become a writer since boyhood, he began to write. Soon he had published some poetry, four prose pieces in the *New Yorker,* and a full-length novel, *Voyage to Somewhere,* all written in the coalbin of the apartment house where he lived, a coalbin he had cleaned out, whitewashed, and converted to a study by adding a table, a chair, and a light on a long extension cord. His success, plus some family connections, led to his becoming a manuscript reader for Houghton Mifflin, and from that work he moved to journalism, taking a job as a reporter for the Providence *Journal.* Partly he took the job to earn a living, but more importantly to learn how to write, remembering that his father, a professor of journalism who had helped start the school of journalism at New York University, had often commented before his death that anyone who aspired to be a writer should work two years for a good newspaper.

Wilson's entry into the world of the gray flannel suit in 1947 came when he left newspaper work: he had a chance to go to work for *Time* in New York City. Although he disliked the magazine, the temptation of a job which paid five thousand dollars a year was enough, for by then he had a wife and two children to support. When he went to New York, he learned a lesson about clothing and also acquired, unknowingly, the title for the present volume. His wife Elise asked him, in reference to an invitation to a cocktail party to meet some of the *Time* staff members the evening before his interview, "What shall we wear to this party?" Within days Wilson learned that in the world of corporate life his blue serge Coast Guard officer's uniform, devoid of its original brass buttons, was altogether inappropriate for the officers of *Time.* He was advised pointedly to go to Brooks Brothers to buy a gray flannel suit, with the admonition that such things were important in his new situation.

Fate and a letter of recommendation from one of his Harvard professors to Roy Larsen, president of Time, Inc., kept Wilson from a career as a writer for *Time.* Within two days Wilson found himself working as a reporter, writer, and public-relations man for the National Citizens Committee for Public Schools, of which Roy Larsen was a key member. In the five years he worked at this job, Wilson was to learn much about himself and the other men of his generation, especially those who entered corporate careers, and finding, too, the material which would make him famous as the author of *The Man in the Gray Flannel Suit.* He learned that corporate life had its hard work and its serious responsibilities. He also learned that such a life meant commuting from New Canaan, Connecticut, every day to work in New York City. And he learned that life meant working hard to fulfill ambitions. But most of all he learned that life involved tension and worry, worry especially about the money needed to buy bigger houses in better neighborhoods, boats, and automobiles; the money to pay bills for growing families as children were born; and the money to entertain other people. It was from this kind of life that Wilson recoiled, wanting to escape to his career as a novelist. But any escape to novel writing meant that he needed a cash advance from a publisher on which to live and provide for his family during the months it takes to write a good novel. Richard L. Simon, president of Simon and Schuster, was the man who appeared to give Wilson the cash advance he needed.

Throughout his writing career, Wilson has found that writing fiction does not come easily, that a writer has periods when material seems to flow freely from his mind to his typewriter, but that there can also be long periods when a man seems to have written himself out, when no ideas come to him, when it appears that his career has come to an end. Those times are crises in a writer's life, crises which carry a whole train of problems. In Wilson's case the problems centered about marriage and alcohol, as well as money. His first marriage ended in divorce, and alcoholism was a problem for many years. But success, too, creates problems. When *The Man in the Gray Flannel Suit* was published in 1955 he became famous and, he thought, wealthy. The sales of his book were high, with editions published in translation throughout the world. Movie rights, too, seemed to be worth a great deal of money. But the wealth proved illusory in more ways than one. A wife and a growing family required a great deal of money to be supported in the way they and their upper-middle-class society expected. In addition, the Internal Revenue Service became a constant threat. Wilson discovered that large amounts of his earnings had to be kept in reserve to satisfy the demands of income taxes, and that what he owed the government in income taxes was subject to revision over a period of years because of his status as a writer. A crucial result of these findings was that he felt constantly under pressure to write to make more money, since the money to answer his needs seemed always to be out of his reach. Even tax-sheltered investments worked out by his lawyers were no answer to his financial problems, for the tax-shelters themselves took the money from immediate use.

At the age of thirty-eight, with two bestselling novels behind him, Wilson found himself beset by personal problems in marriage. His first marriage, contracted before World War II while he was still an undergraduate at Harvard, had become an unhappy one. As the years had passed both husband and wife had changed. Unable to reconcile their differences, they had become embittered and, eventually, they were divorced. Wilson also found that the popularity of his novels was both a blessing and a curse. His popularity made him suspect in the literary world. He found that book reviewers accused him of being simpleminded, of pandering to the public taste, and of being a salesman of soap opera. As a serious writer Wilson was hurt by such reactions to his work from the literary world; he wanted to be a success financially, but he also needed, for his self-respect and inner integrity, to know that he was something more than a man with a golden typewriter—that he was a serious writer trying to do his best.

Following his divorce came a lonely period in which Wilson found himself too depressed to write, and he became an admitted alcoholic. Love and remarriage were a partial rescue. Later, the arrival of a child by his second wife and the use of lithium to control his drinking enabled him, as he sees it, to return to successful writing in a serious way. He views his autobiography as proof of that return.

As one reads Wilson's autobiography it becomes apparent that both boats and women have been of great importance to him and that they have been intertwined elements in his life. He has been happiest when with boats and with women's love. Indeed, he writes that as an adolescent he made a conscious decision to turn to sailing as his way of proving the physical prowess he thought necessary to attract young women to him. That decision led, at least, to a long series of boats. Fortunately for him as a youngster, his parents were enthusiastic for yachts of all sizes and had the financial means to provide their son with the money to have boats and care for them. He sailed and raced in a series of craft including a catboat, a Star-class boat, and an inland scow. Later his family owned a forty-three-foot schooner, graduating finally to a sixty-foot ketch. In the fateful summer of 1939, when World War II began in Europe, Sloan Wilson captained a crew of fifteen Harvard undergraduates who paid for the privilege of a cruise aboard the family's boat, the *Aigrette*, to Cuba and along the Atlantic coast. Wilson's father had bought the eighty-seven-foot vessel, a schooner, just for the cruise. Later in life, after wartime service aboard ships, Sloan Wilson sought happiness on another series of boats of varying sizes and kinds, from an old Friendship sloop he owned for a time to a powerboat designed after a World War I submarine chaser. On the latter Wilson, his second wife, and their small daughter Jessica spent five years, from 1966 to 1971. What he regards as his two best books, *Away from It All* and *All the Best People*, were written in its aftercabin.

One of the most interesting (and, in a way, amusing) parts of Wilson's autobiography is its Epilogue, a series of nineteen items he terms "Things I Have Learned in a Half Century of Living." Partly tongue-in-cheek, partly with seriousness, he lists an incongruous batch of items. Of people, he suggests that one should beware of persons who are always well-dressed, that it is impossible to treat a child or a woman too well, and that friends are more dangerous than strangers. Of women he particularly notes that a beautiful woman is by definition a woman who loves him, and that it is impossible for a woman to treat him too well. On rearing children, he says that he has found the most difficult part is teaching them to ride bicycles, and that one way to teach them the hard truths about alcohol is to drink too much. His final word is that with his wife and children he has found the only real meaning in life, that without them he would have only despair.

Gordon W. Clarke

Sources for Further Study

Atlantic. CCXXXVIII, July, 1976, p. 92.
Kirkus Reviews. LXIV, April 15, 1976, p. 523.
Library Journal. CI, June 15, 1976, p. 1415.
New Leader. LIX, November 8, 1976, p. 20.
New York Times Book Review. May 16, 1976, p. 7.
Publisher's Weekly. CCIX, April 12, 1976, p. 62.
Saturday Review. III, July 24, 1976, p. 27.

WHY NOT THE BEST?

Author: Jimmy Carter (1924-   )
Publisher: Broadman Press (Nashville, Tennessee). 154 pp. $4.95; paperback (Bantam)
    $1.95
Type of work: Autobiography
Time: The twentieth century
Locale: The United States, especially the rural South

A study in perseverance for a goal-oriented, hero-worshiping youth who aspires to become the President of the United States and along the way acquires the diversified expertise of a peanut farmer, a nuclear submarine naval officer, a nuclear physicist, and a Southern Baptist lay minister

> *Principal personages:*
> JIMMY CARTER, President of the United States
> ROSALYNN CARTER, his wife
> EARL AND LILLIAN CARTER, his parents

Jimmy Carter seems to have written *Why Not the Best?* in an attempt to convince us that he is actually the person that we want to believe in for the salvation of us all. This thought glimmers to the surface through the simple, unpolished writing style (by literary standards at least) that Carter uses. However, upon closer scrutiny, it becomes apparent that the author really believes in the image that he presents, and that he wants nothing more than to show the reader, as well as the American public, the light. As a philosophical mirror to the man, Carter's work offers a window through which we can see the man and his beliefs at face value.

All politicians must have a campaign biography, especially in this advanced age of political commercialism, and, in this case, Carter has chosen to write his own life story. He takes us from his childhood and youth in Plains, Georgia, through his stint in the Navy's nuclear submarine program, and back to Plains in an attempt to return to his roots to establish a political base. He then recounts all his handshaking, footsore treks across his home state on his way to the State House, his hopes and aspirations for the Presidency, and his solutions for all of our collective ills. It is a revealing journey.

In the beginning of his autobiography, Carter attempts to establish the tone of the journey he intends to take us on when he asks, Why can't our government by the people, for the people, and of the people be "honest, decent, open, fair . . . compassionate . . . and competent?" An honorable question indeed; however, in order to understand the man who asks the question, we must first return to his home, back to his life as a child. The young Carter is presented as a hero-worshiper, a God-fearing boy, a youth with the thirst for knowledge of a Lincoln, the intelligence of a Kennedy, and the audacity of a Roosevelt or a Truman. Carter's proselytizing of the American work ethic is quite convincing throughout the book, and his parallels are neither unintentional nor inaccurate. They serve to show that the boy James Earl Carter could strive, aspire, and ultimately achieve. As we can see from a historical retrospect, it has proven true; he has completed the cycle through to the White House.

In his early days as a farmboy in Georgia, Jimmy Carter was a student, a farmer's helper, and a churchgoer. He alternately admired and feared his father, Earl, as a figurehead, and, more importantly, as a man. Earl Carter was respected in his community by divergent sectors: the white suburban farmer, affluent, as far as the times would allow; and, the poor, black sharecropper. "Mr. Earl" was to both groups a father-figure as well as a mentor; he was stern but compassionate. It was from his father that young Jimmy began to develop his aspirations; from him that he acquired the tenacity to survive, the will to achieve, and the perseverance necessary to acquire the knowledge to make it all work. However, it was not until much later in his life that he would find the precise words to describe his philosophy, in that particular phrase that was to become the catchword of the 1976 presidential campaign: "Why not the best?"

Despite a strict upbringing, Carter's early years were not rebellious. He describes himself in his youth as diligent, a young schoolboy memorizing Bible passages to satisfy his thirst for knowledge of God and His creation. He tells the familiar story of passing into manhood, leaving behind the trappings of his youth and gradually gaining the wisdom that comes with increasing age. It is a Huck Finn journey of trial and tribulation leading through difficult decisions and malcontent among relatives.

If there is one feeling, one recurring theme in this autobiography, it is guarded altruism, which steadied his aspirations, tempered his dreams, organized his thoughts and actions, and, ultimately, carried him through to his final goal of the Presidency. Stemming from this reform-oriented altruism was his stern insistence on tackling the inequities of the system; his consistent attempts to bring into the open the activities of the behind-closed-doors decision-makers; and his desire to streamline the governmental bureaucracy.

This idealism first manifested itself in Carter's tackling of the Certified Seed Organization in his home state. After becoming president of this organization, he rectified the inequities of the system, eliminated much unnecessary red tape for the small farmer, and set that government of agrarians on an equitable footing for all. For his efforts, he became a hero much like those he had admired as a child, and he proved to himself that he had the ability to move organizations, to change policies, and to represent the common man for the good of all. The stage was thus set for Carter's role as spokesman for the common people. Grassroots politicking became standard procedure—his "see what I can do for you" approach, which would soon win him a seat in the Georgia State Senate. In all his campaigns, Carter would attempt to replace political catchwords, promises, and polemics with his frank, comfortable, believable offer of honesty, fairness, and straightforwardness in government.

His years in the Senate were formative ones. Having made a campaign promise of "reading every bill before voting on it," Carter made good his word; he admits that he regretted making the promise, but that he never broke it during his four years in the Senate. It was also during these four years that an important idea took shape: If the elimination of the "many niches in which special interests could hide" worked on a State Senate level, then why not strive for the best and take on the entire state of Georgia? So, in spite of the overwhelming popularity of former Governor Carl Sanders in the 1970 election, and despite the urging of his closest friends and advisers not to run for the governor's seat but to aim for the lieutenant governorship, Carter took on the fight for the State House. The decision was typical, in keeping with the self-disciplined philosophy of striving for the best, no matter what the outcome. Starting in the fall of 1966, Jimmy Carter spent four long, grueling years making ". . . about 1,800 speeches . . . and personally shaking hands with more than 600,000 people in Georgia."

It was during this campaign that an important test of Carter's philosophical standards took place. An Atlanta-based newspaper had published a seething condemnation of the "ignorant and bigoted redneck peanut farmer from Plains" and endorsed Sanders as the best, the only, candidate for Governor. Carter responded with a letter to the editor of the paper; that letter not only went unpublished, it went unacknowledged as well. At this point, Carter decided to utilize his time during the annual convention of the Georgia Press Association to read his unpublished rebuttal. Carter states in his book that this was a "mistaken and counterproductive action" on his part, but he felt that not to respond strongly to the attack would be to compromise himself. Therefore, despite the urging of his associates against his decision, Carter took on the entire fourth estate in Georgia; he simply could not stand by and let others railroad him into oblivion without the opportunity to defend himself. But, although this grandstanding did hurt him temporarily, in the long run it did not affect the outcome of the race. It did, however, have a definite effect later in the Democratic primary: in part because of the editorial, in part because of his blazing response, Carter lost a sizable portion of the black vote, as well as the financial support of many Atlantans. However, the general election went well, and a last minute campaign to get out and meet the people paid off for Carter; he won handily. Regarding Carter's term as Governor, there are two very divergent stories. Carter's version, of course, is one of streamlining, eliminating red tape, and returning the government to the people. The opposing version, heard often enough that it becomes important in any assessment of this book, was espoused most vociferously by former Lieutenant Governor Lester Maddox, and was echoed elsewhere throughout the State. It contends that Carter did nothing during his one-term office, that there was no such thing as zero-based budgeting in Georgia, that if anything, there was more red tape and more bureaucratic forms and figureheads than before. If one is to believe in the basic themes of *Why Not the Best?* such conflicting reports bear further investigation.

What emerges most strongly from this personal history is Jimmy Carter's belief that we *can* have a government that is all-inclusively honest, decent, open, fair, compassionate, and competent— but only if we are willing to work for it. We must be willing to entrust a "new guard" of politician who is dedicated to striving for the good of all the people. According to Carter, the old concept that the people are in their homes and all's right with Washington can no longer be tolerated; politics must be brought out from under its cloak of secrecy, out from behind its closed and sometimes locked doors. We can no longer accept the chasm that exists between our elected leaders and ourselves. Confidence can, and must, be restored through trustworthiness. We must appoint chairmanships and diplomatic posts on the basis of merit, not reward. And, no matter how deeply ingrained in Americans' minds is the notion that the government is hopelessly big, illogical, and inefficient, the "new guard" of leaders must effectively demonstrate that the system can still be made to serve those for whose benefit it was originally established.

Carter has successfully argued his point, and his book turns out to be a completely convincing piece of campaign literature. But, although *Why Not The Best?* is definitely a sales pitch, it is very readable. It offers enough insight into its author to hold the reader's interest throughout all the tales and anecdotes that make up the man's background. What starts out to be a "vote-for-me" advertisement, ends up to be an enjoyable journey through one man's origins and personal philosophy.

John J. Concialdi

Sources for Further Study

Best Sellers. XXXVI, July, 1976, p. 133.
National Review. XXVII, October 29, 1976, p. 1193.
New Republic. CLXXV, September 11, 1975, p. 27.
New York Review of Books. XXIII, August 5, 1976, p. 22.
New York Times Book Review. June 6, 1976, p. 4.

THE WILD BOY OF AVEYRON

Author: Harlan Lane
Publisher: Harvard University Press (Cambridge, Massachusetts). 351 pp. $15.00
Type of work: Experimental psychology
Time: 1800 to 1860's
Locale: Aveyron and Paris, France

A historical description of the attempt to return a wild boy to society, and a meditation on its significance for later generations

> *Principal personages:*
> VICTOR, the wild boy of Aveyron
> DR. ITARD, his principal teacher
> ABBE BONNATERRE, his first custodian
> ABBE SICARD, a teacher of deaf-mutes
> DR. PINEL, the founder of psychotherapy
> DR. SEGUIN, a pupil of Itard who later had great success in teaching the deaf

Harlan Lane's *The Wild Boy of Aveyron* is, essentially, two books in one. It is a narrative of the discovery, capture, and subsequent treatment of a twelve-year-old child who, having been abandoned by his parents, lived in the forest from his fifth to his twelfth year. It is also a meditation upon the meaning of the narrative, as it traces some developments in educational theory and methods, in the treatment of deaf-mutes, and in philosophical conceptions about man's nature that arose from the diagnosis and treatment of this unusual child. The two sections of the book are, unfortunately, sometimes intermingled so that the reader is often frustrated by shifts in time and perspective. However, the book as a whole is fascinating; it is useful in its resurrection of reports and letters connected with the capture of the wild child, and, above all, historically imaginative in seeing future benefits from the probings of scientists, philosophers, and medical men of the early nineteenth century who came in contact with this child.

The narrative is likely to interest the common reader most; it is a compelling story dominated by the struggle of the child to return to society, and it is told with sympathy and no little drama. Lane begins the book by introducing us to the two main characters, the wild boy and Dr. Itard. They are not to meet until a year after the child's capture, and they could not have been more different. The child was left to the mercies of the forest and grew up with only animals for his companions; he was an outcast whose condition is almost impossible to imagine today. Itard, however, was the son of a loving father and rose rapidly in the flux of revolutionary France. He was a social man who was blessed with opportunities and benefactors. There is little doubt, however, that although Itard had great affection for the child and worked with him closely for more than four years, he must have seen the child as a challenge and another opportunity to advance and to make a name and a career for himself.

After this brief and dramatic introduction, the focus shifts to the capture and description of the child.

The child was seen a number of times in the area of Aveyron during an extremely cold winter, and he was finally captured by some hunters. The boy ran very fast on all fours; he ate only nuts, vegetables, and potatoes, and he managed to survive in the most severe winter in memory virtually without clothing. He was a phenomenon, an event, and word of his capture spread rapidly. He was an important discovery not only as an object of revolutionary charity but also because it was felt that the wild child would supply data that would help settle the debate over man's nature. Was he a noble savage? Did he possess innate ideas? Was he a statue that could be made to speak and reason once he entered society and received the blessings of civilization? The first step was to assign the child to a competent observer. He was placed in the care of the Abbe Bonnaterre, and he was brought to Paris where he contracted smallpox as his first benefit from civilization. Bonnaterre treated the boy very kindly and left a lengthy description of his condition soon after he was dragged from the forest. Lane has managed to find this document, and it is reprinted here for the first time in English. The most significant aspects of the report concern the boy's deprivation of speech and his lack of any signs of affection: "he loves no one; he is attached to no one. . . ." But in spite of these central deficiencies, Bonnaterre ends the report full of hope for the future: "Go forth, poor youth, on this unhappy earth, go forth and lose in your relations with men your primitiveness and simplicity!"

The great hopes that Bonnaterre and others had for the wild child were, however, soon dashed. The distinguished teacher of the deaf, Abbe Sicard, reached a diagnosis of idiocy after failing to train the boy. Pinel, called by Lane the founder of psychotherapy, compared the boy to other idiots he had examined and was certain that the wild child was uneducable. At this point Dr. Itard and the wild child were united. Itard felt that the boy appeared to be an idiot because he had been so completely isolated from society rather than that he had been abandoned because he was an idiot. Itard was a follower of Condillac, who did not believe in innate ideas but felt that man needed language, which the boy obviously lacked, in order to rise above an animal level. Itard, then, attempted to supply the missing piece; he tried to refine, train, and return the boy to the human community where he would acquire language, reason, humanity. Condillac's statue was to come alive.

Itard first created a pleasant environment for the boy to woo him from the forest that he continually gazed at and tried to escape to. He tried to awaken some of the dormant senses of the boy; his dominant sense before his training was smell. The boy's affections were increased, and he became devoted to his governess. Needs were created, and soon he could not do without cooked food, baths, walks in the company of others, and milk. He even learned to say the word "lait" to request the milk he received every day. Itard, after some failures with toys and sweets, used "primary reinforcers" and managed to improve the boy's concentration and his ability to perform simple tasks. Most notably, Itard taught the pupil, rather than a body of knowledge, a principle that was adopted by future educators. Itard's efforts were often failures, although the boy did make remarkable progress under his tutelage. The boy even acquired a name, Victor, and enlarged his social contacts. Finally, after the intense and innovative efforts of Itard, the boy was still unable to speak more than a few words, and his education was abandoned. The now partially socialized wild child was left in the care of his governess, and he died at the age of thirty-seven.

Two questions remain. First, why was Victor unable to speak more than a few words? Second, what benefits accrued because of the imaginative and innovative treatment he received? The first question is difficult to answer. Some have embraced the early diagnosis that Victor was an idiot and, therefore, unable to respond to even careful and thoughtful treatment. Others have seen the signs of mental retardation or autism. Lane makes a case for environmental factors; he feels that Victor lost the crucial skill of imitation in the forest, and he cites the example of a California girl who was isolated in a room from age four to fourteen and made very slow progress in speaking, as proof of his claim. It is difficult not to agree with Lane. Victor was capable of mastering a few skills, and he could "match to sample," but he apparently could not recapture the language skill that is acquired by imitation. Aristotle suggests that man learns his earliest lesson by imitation, and he takes delight in such learning. Victor had lost the will to learn except to fulfill immediate needs.

The second question is easier to answer. The special measures taken to educate Victor profoundly affected the treatment of the deaf and influenced educational theory and practice in such later developments as the Montessori Method. Lane gives the most emphasis to Victor's legacy to the deaf, and, although it seems more lengthy and recondite then necessary, it is certainly of interest.

Itard turned to educating deaf-mutes after his experience with Victor. He felt, at first, that his patients should learn to communicate by using oral language rather than sign, ironically the method he had used with the wild child. Later he was led, by his failures, to teach sign language alone for many of his patients and also to use it as a supplement for those who were trained to use oral language. This seemed to be the most useful and productive method since those with residual hearing could use both sign and oral language, and those with a severe loss of hearing could use sign language alone. Some felt that sign was the "natural" language of the deaf, and Lane feels that Victor might have achieved much more if he had been trained to use sign language. In spite of successes in using sign language for the deaf, oral training became the dominant means of instruction in France and later in America when Gallaudet visited France and brought back their methods. The controversy between oral and sign instruction has yet to be reconciled. We can only note that Itard, through his efforts with Victor, extended the interest in teaching the deaf and aided their attempts to break the shell of silence.

Near the end of his life, Itard was persuaded to supervise the instruction of an idiot by his friend and pupil, Seguin. At this time, idiots were believed to be uneducable. Seguin followed Itard in training and developing the senses, in providing a "favorable" environment for his patients, in adapting instructional devices to his pupils' needs, and in returning the idiots to society. Seguin also had the advantage of studying Itard's failures, and he succeeded in releasing many of his patients from their supposedly incurable affliction. The work of Itard and Seguin later came to the attention of Maria Montessori, and she saw in their methods an instructional program for ordinary as well as retarded children. Lane summarizes the Montessori Method in clear and accurate terms that also show its relationship to Itard and Seguin.

> All of these principles imply the next, which Montessori calls the "biological concept of liberty in pedagogy": the child must be free to act spontaneously and to interact with the prepared environment. The entire program is concerned with the individual child; the spontaneity, the needs, the observation, the freedom are always those of the individual. Finally, the modus operandi of the method is sensory training.

The Montessori Method was, of course, adapted and included in the educational reforms of the last fifty years, and it can be found in our kindergartens, elementary schools, and high schools.

There is an archetypal dimension to this story. A half human-half animal child emerges from the forest and brings enlightenment to others while he remains, in part, a creature of the wild. He is a nature spirit who shows others how to alter their "natural" deficiencies, and he is also the sensorily deprived child who shows how education must be "biological." This depth of reference is one of Lane's major achievements in the book. If we now look closely at current instructional materials, attitudes toward children, and the treatment of deaf-mutes and the mentally ill, we cannot help but see behind our up-to-date views the tortured face of the wild boy of Aveyron.

James Sullivan

Sources for Further Study

Atlantic. CCXXXVIII, August, 1976, p. 87.

Book World. May 2, 1976, p. L8.

Contemporary Psychology. XXI, August, 1976, p. 601.

Human Behavior. V, July, 1976, p. 74.

New York Review of Books. XXIII, September 16, 1976, p. 10.

New Yorker. LII, June 28, 1976, p. 90.

Science. CXCIV, October 15, 1976, p. 311.

WILL YOU PLEASE BE QUIET, PLEASE?

Author: Raymond Carver (1938-   )
Publisher: McGraw-Hill Book Company (New York). 249 pp. $8.95
Type of work: Short stories

A collection of short stories which dissect the vacuities of contemporary American life

It is difficult for an established writer to convince a publisher to take a chance on issuing a collection of short stories. Thus, when a relatively new and unknown author comes out with such a book, the reader may rest assured that the book must succeed on its own merits. Raymond Carver, whose stories heretofore have appeared largely in the smaller literary magazines (though some have appeared in *Esquire* and *Harper's*), specializes in very short, delicate vignettes of the commonplace. Although some of these stories have been previously anthologized in *Best American Short Stories: 1967, Short Stories from the Literary Magazines,* and *Best Little Magazine Fiction* of 1970 and 1971, they are now made available as a group to a wider reading public for the first time through the present publication. These stories are not the type to be readily understood or appreciated by a popular audience, but the more discerning reader will find a rare treat in the subtle, enigmatic portraits of modern life.

Carver does not condescend to entice readers with shocking or startling attention-getting openings. Rather, the stories almost invariably begin with flat understatement, and progress through to their subtle, inconclusive endings, leaving the reader barely aware that something of significance has happened. A closer reading, however, yields wry insights, judgments that are usually beyond the command of the characters in the stories themselves.

Carver's short stories are masterpieces of concision and understatement. Attempts at analysis cannot do justice to the delicate spell woven by these glimpses of domestic tranquility marred by the occasional unexpected happening. The title of the book itself, which is also the title of the longest story in the collection, illustrates Carver's basic appeal. An expression of exasperation, of a breakdown in communication familiar to all of us, it is spoken by a harried husband after spending the night trying to deal with his wife's admitted infidelity of four years previous. His suspicions had smoldered all these years until he finally wheedled an admission from her. His reaction to the news is more of a shock to him than the fact of her unfaithfulness, and wandering about in a kind of daze, he is finally mugged at the waterfront. On his return home in the morning, his problem is still unresolved; his wife's attempts to discuss it elicits from him on the phrase, "Will you please be quiet, please?" as he tries to sleep. As in real life, there is no neat, pat solution to his dilemma; the story ends with his marveling at the "impossible changes he felt moving over him." Will he be able to live with his new burden, or will his relationship with his wife radically change? Many readers will wonder what occurs at the conclusion of this and several other stories in this collection, for everything, including the endings, is underplayed.

If there is a unifying theme running throughout all the stories, it is that life continues and our task is simply to endure. Crises are not disposed of with finality, never to arise again. At best one can only hope, with the hero of the title story, that such an "impossible" change may come over him and he will be able to come to terms with reality. Throughout, one is left with the feeling expressed by another of Carver's characters from the story, "Sixty Acres": "Yet he could not understand why he felt something crucial had happened, a failure. But nothing had happened." Paradoxically, something has happened, but these forlorn protagonists cannot grasp its significance.

Ranging from the two-page description of relatives commenting on the appearance of the newborn child in "The Father," to the title story of twenty-four pages, the twenty-two stories comprising this volume are very short, usually less than ten pages. Sometimes exciting things almost happen, or are alluded to, but these are not the substance of Carver's tales. Instead, he concentrates on the commonplace. In "Put Yourself in My Shoes," he ironically plays with this concept of the writer ignoring sensational stories to concentrate on the minor domestic quarrels of everyday life. The title of the story is a double pun, referring both to the author living other people's lives in his writing, and to the writer in the story living in another person's house. In this story, Myers, who has quit his job to be a writer, is vacuuming rugs at home when he is invited by his wife to an office party, an invitation he declines. He learns about the firing and subsequent suicide of one of his former coworkers. Later, visiting the couple whose home he and his wife had sublet, he hears the host tell of a boy who threw a can of soup at his estranged father, giving him a concussion. Later, the host and his wife relate an incident which they experienced in which a well-dressed woman returned their wallet which she had found. She indicated that there had been no money in it when she found it, but while speaking with them she suffered a heart attack. As they looked in her purse for identification they discovered the missing money still in the clip in which they had kept it. These are the usual subject matter for commercial short story writers, and the host is trying to be helpful in recounting them to Myers. But they are not grist for Carver's mill. His story concerns the gradually emerging suppressed anger of the host at Myers and his wife for their misuse of the host's home and furnishings while they had occupied it. Typically, the story ends with the host no longer able to restrain his seething rage, shouting at Myers and his wife, asking for an explanation while Myers and his wife scurry off.

One of the charms of these stories is the recognition of ourselves and ordinary people we know among Carver's antiheroes. Sometimes the things that happen are extraordinary, but the character sketches are unmistakable, such as the boy who fakes illness to stay home from school, and then after a hasty recovery, goes fishing; or the husband and wife who surreptitiously spend their evenings spying on their neighbor who, in turn, sneaks outdoors and watches his own wife as she undresses; or the postman, bothered by the lifestyle of the hippies who have just moved in, constantly dropping hints of where they can find a job in town. Although most of the settings are in Carver's own Northwest, the people are recognizable middle-class Americans as apotheosized by innumerable Norman Rockwell magazine illustrations.

The incidents recounted herein, too, are largely those of typical, dull, everyday life. Cumulatively, the stories leave a sense of the pointless routine of most of our lives, although often the characters themselves do not realize or understand their plight. What they cannot articulate is conveyed by the author's subtle understatement. In "The Student's Wife," after spending a sleepless night punctuated by the demands of her husband and children, the wife's feelings are exquisitely conveyed in the line, "Not in pictures she had seen nor in any book she had read had she learned a sunrise was so terrible as this." In "The Neighbors," a husband and wife who have been vicariously sampling their more affluent neighbors' lifestyle while taking care of their apartment for them do not understand their own motivation or feelings. After locking themselves out of the apartment, they stand bewildered. As Carver sums up, "They stayed there. They held each other. They leaned into the door as if against a wind, and braced themselves." How much self-realization is ever reached by these cultural victims is wisely left up in the air.

There are some stories which will frustrate the reader. As in Chaucer's tale of Sir Thopas, many things almost happen, but do not, and it is the reader who is the ultimate butt of the joke. In "Are You a Doctor?" a mysterious telephone call appears to be leading to a romantic interlude between the married doctor and the mother who apparently dialed the wrong number. What actually transpires conforms more to true life experiences than what we are led to believe in most fiction. "Night School" concerns a man picked up in a bar by two women who are looking for a car to drive to the home of their adult education instructor. He walks with them to his house ostensibly to borrow his parents' car, but instead of asking for the keys, he simply goes to bed, abandoning the girls outside. "Jerry and Molly and Sam" is a genuine shaggy dog story of a man who originally takes his children's pet to a strange neighborhood and abandons it. Later, suffering pangs of conscience, he goes to retrieve the dog. After circling around the vicinity where he left the animal and asking people whether they have noticed a strange dog wandering about, he sees it—briefly—before it disappears forever.

Stylistically, Carver's prose matches his subject matter. Without a superfluous detail the scene is set in a deceptively simple fashion. Carver's lean, spare style wastes no time with indulgent commentary or needless purple patches, nor does it condescend to call attention to or summarize the underlying verities; elucidation would destroy the atmosphere created and lose the subtle essence of the stories. Even those tales which are presented from the protagonist's point of view do not betray the author's presence. Carver's fictional narrators are as oblivious to their predicaments as the rest of his characters. It is as if the narrator is a camera, simply recording apparently commonplace occurrences. The technique is dramatic. Most of the action is carried by the dialogue of the principles, with the author's narration intruding only to fill in the necessary details, and occasionally summing up the situation in an enigmatic, striking phrase or two. Economy of language is total.

When finished with this book, the reader may be hard pressed to recall very many outstanding or sensational incidents having occurred. Beyond a few family quarrels and one mugging, no real violence takes place at all. However, some rather bizarre incidents abound. A vacuum cleaner salesman walks off with the homeowner's mail; a husband and wife vicariously sample their neighbors' food and clothing; a husband sends his wife to sell their old car and to an almost certain assignation with the prospective buyer. Yet, none of these incidents causes the expected blow-up. The changes which overcome these people are usually intuitive and the reader must exercise his imagination.

In any event, the perceptive reader will come away from this book with a deeper insight into the lives of the characters, and ultimately a greater appreciation of the quiet desperation of the lives most people lead. Carver's journey is into the soul of *ennui,* and he has succeeded in vividly creating a small segment of twentieth century American existence.

Roger A. Geimer

Sources for Further Study

Choice. XIII, July/August, 1976, p. 659.
Christian Science Monitor. LXVIII, April 1, 1976, p. 31.
Hudson Review. XIX, Summer, 1976, p. 270.
New York Review of Books. XXIII, April 1, 1976, p. 34.
New York Times Book Review. March 7, 1976, p. 4.
Newsweek. LXXXVII, April 26, 1976, p. 97.

THE WIND WILL NOT SUBSIDE
Years in Revolutionary China—1964-1969

Authors: David Milton (1923-   ) and Nancy Dall Milton (1929-   )
Publisher: Pantheon Books (New York). Illustrated. 397 pp. $15.00
Type of work: History
Time: 1964-1969
Locale: China

An account of the Cultural Revolution, based on the authors' experiences and observations in revolutionary China from 1964 to 1969

Principal personages:
> MAO TSE-TUNG, chairman of the Chinese Communist Party and its preeminent theoretician until his death in 1976
> CHOU EN-LAI, a prominent Chinese Communist Party leader and the premier of the People's Republic of China until his death in 1976
> LIN PIAO, a prominent Chinese Communist Party leader and the defense minister until his death in 1971
> CHIANG CH'ING, wife of Mao and a leader of the radical faction of the Chinese Communist Party
> CH'EN PO-TA, a prominent Chinese Communist Party leader and editor of the Party journal *Red Flag*
> LIU SHAO-CH'I, chairman of the People's Republic of China and a major representative of the "revisionist" line in opposition to Mao

The Wind Will Not Subside constitutes an admirable effort to shed light on the period of astounding revolutionary turmoil in China known as the Great Proletarian Cultural Revolution. Americans David and Nancy Milton were in China during this period as teachers at the Peking First Foreign Languages Institute. The Institute functions directly under the Foreign Ministry, and their presence there afforded the Miltons an excellent opportunity to observe at firsthand aspects of the monumental struggle between two divergent ideological lines within the Chinese Communist Party. It should be noted that the Miltons consider themselves friends of the Chinese revolution and admirers of its late leader, Mao Tse-tung. This orientation gives a sympathetic aura to their account. They begin with an interesting description of their arrival in China, together with their three sons, and their general circumstances at the Foreign Languages Institute. The attendance of a reception and lunch given by Mao in honor of Anna Louise Strong, a respected senior member of the foreign community in Peking, was one of the highlights of their stay preceding the complex revolutionary activities to follow.

The Cultural Revolution commenced in May, 1966, when classes were abruptly stopped before the term was up. The Miltons present an engrossing account of the unfolding of this rather confusing, yet tremendously significant, period of post-1949 Chinese politics. The seriousness and absorption of the students in the political debates about the proper "line," as described by the Miltons, is amazing. The students had been encouraged to make trouble and to generate mass attacks on the established Communist Party cadres by Mao and his propagandists. The youth of China responded enthusiastically to the venerated Mao's bidding. Red Guard organizations mushroomed and were exhorted to spread the revolutionary fever across the nation. Free transportation was provided for the roaming students; in fact, the entire railroad system was placed at their disposal. Eventually, the First Foreign Languages Institute came to be the locale of some of the fiercest contests carried out during the Cultural Revolution. For the Institute's close relationship to the Foreign Ministry gave many of its students and teachers direct access to some of the major contestants struggling for power.

The Cultural Revolution had a distinctly dual character. As the Miltons suggest, it was both a power struggle and an effort to combat revisionism, "the bourgeois-reactionary line." Chaotic as it seemed at times, it was coordinated at the top by Mao, his skillful and loyal ally Chou En-lai, and Lin Piao, who at the time was Mao's declared successor. At first it seemed that Mao allowed the Red Guards a rather free reign and intended to let the Cultural Revolution find its own direction and momentum. Only gradually the Maoist forces created a network to oppose the regular Communist Party apparatus. The basic objective was to test the Party cadres for their Maoist purity and to either reform or purge them, if they did not follow the correct line. Despite Mao's preaching about trusting the masses and respecting their initiatives, the movement was directed by elites under Mao. As the Cultural Revolution gained momentum, individual major adversaries were identified. The most prominent victim was Liu Shao-ch'i, the formal chief of state, who was deprived of his high party and state offices. In order to achieve his objectives and to dispute established authority, Mao, in turn, had to put together a leadership group of undisputed authority. The thirteen-member Cultural Group appointed by him served his needs and constituted a kind of storm center in the intensifying factionalism and chaos.

In general, the ideology and the institutions of the Cultural Revolution were directed toward eliminating the inequalities between city and countryside, industry and agriculture, and mental and manual labor. As such, it was a continuation of the basic revolutionary goal of egalitarianism and the achievement of true Communism. From the Maoist point of view, political leadership had to be purified, so that the fundamental transformation of Chinese society could continue and the true aims of the Chinese revolution be fulfilled. To bring about the purification, the process of revolution itself had to be intensified from the Cultural Revolution. In affirming the creative potential of the masses, in emphasizing mass participation over elite prerogatives, and in insisting on decentralization of power and resources, the Cultural Revolution reaffirmed the basic vision and the significant features of the legacy of Yenan.

Mao, in talking with André Malraux in 1966, said that humanity left to its own devices would not necessarily reestablish capitalism, but it would reestablish inequality. He saw the forces forging new classes as being extremely powerful, and he perceived revisionism as causing the death of the revolution. He insisted that revolution could not simply mean the stabilization of victory; it had to be a continuing process.

In a detached, abstract sense, it may be said that there never has been a revolution prior to the Chinese one that continued to place the same high ideal and practical value on egalitarianism and mass participation, once the mobilization and the destructive phase of the revolution were completed. Other revolutions, as they became institutionalized, would typically sacrifice egalitarianism and mass participation to such goals as national power or modernization. With the Cultural Revolution Mao seemed to fight a historical pattern. The Cultural Revolution amounted to a campaign against a new privileged class. Indeed, it was an attack not merely against the members of that class, but against the very legitimacy of the institutions and organizations from which privilege in Communist China arose. The Red Guards and the other rebel groups could be seen as counterinstitutions capable of both limiting the drift toward hierarchy and privilege and reasserting the revolutionary goals of egalitarianism and mass participation. In this context the cult of Mao became a practical, effective weapon in the assault on the Communist Party and the government. Mao's thought was raised to a new high, higher than that of Marx, Engels, and Lenin and, thus, higher than the Chinese Communist Party and any ideology upon which the Party might base its claim of legitimacy in opposition to Mao. Mao's line was the only correct course. Mao had retained his intense radicalism, and was perhaps the only revolutionary leader in history who retained his radical purity after the achievement of power.

However, as the Miltons note, factionalism and anarchism threatened to get out of hand, and even the indispensable Chou came under severe attack. At this stage Mao came unmistakably down on the side of Chou and the elements of moderation. The Cultural Revolution had escalated beyond the educational and propaganda institutions; it extended into the economic enterprises, the countryside, government and party offices. The new rebel groups were largely drawn from the working population and became significantly broader mass organizations than the student Red Guards. A new formula for the seizure of power from below was promulgated. It involved the three-way alliance of revolutionary cadres of the Party, representatives of the Peoples Liberation Army, and representatives of mass organizations. As the Miltons describe it, the three-way alliance turned into a three-way power struggle.

In the summer of 1967 a state of semi-anarchy prevailed in much of the nation, with administration having virtually ceased. The Peking Red Guards had split into two basic rival factions, referred to in typical Chinese fashion as the Heaven and the Earth factions. As the rift between the two groups widened, every student was forced to support one or the other. In their fight for leadership control the groups engaged each other in battles and resorted to medieval siege tactics. Similar conflicts and leadership struggles occurred in other areas of the country. After one year, Mao's experiment with permanent revolution had revealed its limitations, and he had to concede that the ultra-left offensive had been effectively contained by the moderates. He relented and focused his attention on the rebuilding of the Party and the preparation of the Ninth Party Congress. According to the Miltons' account, Mao was disappointed by the student "path breakers." In the end, he relied on the workers to get the students to end their direct revolutionary involvement and to resume their normal activities at their respective institutions.

By September, 1968, a surge toward conclusion and consolidation of the Cultural Revolution ensued. The whole society had been exposed to merciless inspection and criticism. The initial enthusiastic and purposeful mood of the people had yielded to one that was grim and resentful. It was time to call a halt. Mao had already noted that one Cultural Revolution might not be enough. Before this one was over, at least for the time being, one final, elemental struggle among the top leaders occurred. The fundamental issue, according to the Miltons, was which of the two superpowers—the United States or the Soviet Union—China should choose. Mao and his earlier chief supporter and presumed heir, Lin Piao, parted ways over the development of a new world view and general foreign policy orientation. When Lin Piao and others opted for the Soviet Union, they became counterrevolutionaries in the eyes of Mao. For the whole purpose of the Cultural Revolution had been to smash revisionism, the very consequence of Soviet influence over Chinese affairs. In shaping China's destiny, Mao wanted to be completely free of Soviet influence. Ultimately, only Lin's violent death in 1971 could resolve this conflict. With the exit of Lin Piao and Ch'en Po-ta, the stage was set for Richard Nixon and Henry Kissinger.

The Miltons may well be correct in their assumption that Mao's solutions for China have applicability beyond that country in the so-called Third World, perhaps even in Western industrialized societies attempting the seemingly impossible task of "democratizing bureaucracy." Of course, only time will tell how successful Mao's way is. The authors' account suffers somewhat from their strong pro-Mao sentiment. Their biases are especially apparent in their earlier chapters, incorporating uncritically and approvingly cited Maoist propaganda rhetoric and gratuitous references to United States imperialism. Nevertheless, the Miltons' account of the Cultural Revolution is well-written and extremely interesting. They are able to provide authoritative and fascinating detail about this complicated and, to the average Westerner, highly confusing period. This alone makes their work a welcome and valuable study of contemporary China.

Manfred Grote

Sources for Further Study

America. CXXXIV, May 1, 1976, p. 397.

Best Sellers. XXXVI, July, 1976, p. 127.

New York Times Book Review. May 9, 1976, p. 6.

New Yorker. LII, June 7, 1976, p. 138.

Time. CVII, April 19, 1976, p. 94.

Virginia Quarterly Review. LII, Summer, 1976, p. 86.

THE WINTHROP COVENANT

Author: Louis Auchincloss (1917-   )
Publisher: Houghton Mifflin Company (Boston). 246 pp. $8.95
Type of work: Novel
Time: 1630-1973
Locale: Massachusetts, principally Boston; New York City; Paris

A searching examination of the Puritan ethic and its influence upon various members of a prominent American family

> *Principal characters:*
> JOHN WINTHROP, Governor of the Massachusetts Bay Colony
> ANNE HUTCHINSON, a dissenter
> WILLIAM HUTCHINSON, her husband
> WAIT STILL WINTHROP, a judge in the Salem witch trials
> THEODOSIUS LEIGH, a Boston minister
> FRANCIS BAYARD, Patroon of Bayardwick on the Hudson
> REBECCA, his wife
> PHILIPPE GEYELIN, the tutor to their children
> SAMUEL SHAW RUSSELL, a diplomat
> WINTHROP WARD, a lawyer
> JULES BLEECHER, a journalist
> ADAM WINTHROP, President of the Patroons' Club in New York
> ADA GUEST, a novelist
> DANNY BUCK, chaplain of Farmingdale School
> TITUS LARSEN, presiding officer of the school
> NATICA SELIGMANN, the victim of a matchmaker
> ERNEST SELIGMANN, her husband
> JOHN WINTHROP GARDINER, a career man in the Central Intelligence Agency

Puritanism, that development of Calvinist doctrine which inspired the early settlers of New England, has left an indelible mark on American culture. It has been, perhaps more than any other single factor, responsible for those strange contradictions in our behavior that have come to be called hypocrisy, and we hold to many of its principles even as we struggle to escape its influence. A majority of the faults we decry today   intolerance, bigotry, prudery, inhibition, repression, censorship—have been identified by social critics with this integral part of our national heritage.

For the individual Puritan, life was no easy matter. The two basic doctrines were original sin and predestination. This meant, first, that the individual's waking hours must be dedicated to acts of atonement for not being born in a state of grace; and second, that whether the individual would be saved or damned had been decided long before he was born. Thus he lived in fear, hoping for salvation and at the same time convinced that in spite of his best efforts he was most unlikely to be numbered among the fortunate few. He was informed that a life dedicated to good works would not redeem him if his damnation had been foreordained. This led to an odd combination of fatalism and

fanaticism: obviously, if the individual's ultimate fate had been predetermined, it mattered little what sort of life he led. But there was always the secret hope that a godly existence might nonetheless weight the scales in his
favor. It is easy in this context to feel a certain pity for such people; but they
exhibited little of it themselves, particularly toward those whose behavior was,
or might conceivably be, indicative of sin as they defined it. And their definition of sin was very broad indeed. Fantacism always begets ignorance and ex-
tremism, and the extremes to which Puritanism could go are best memo-
rialized by the Salem witch trials.

However repellent inflexible dedication and stern discipline may be to the
more tolerant among us, it is obvious that they strengthen any movement
which employs them. That Puritanism has declined is due, in the final analysis,
less to its narrow structure than to its rejection of human warmth. A smile was
the mark of frivolity under most circumstances; laughter was a serious impro-
priety; an outward display of affection was the sign of unchastity, the worst of
all sins. A sober simplicity was cultivated to the point of ugliness, and time not
spent in honest labor was reserved for prayer and meditation. This was not
entirely true of everyone, for human nature will not be denied altogether; but
it can be suppressed, and was, to the greatest extent possible. There is a
marked contrast between Puritan austerity and the feeling of joyful happiness
that permeates the four Gospels, as there is between a narrowly restricted kind
of salvation and the message preached by Jesus. But Puritanism leaned more
heavily on the Old Testament than the New, and God was characterized always by vengeance rather than love. A cold, bleak, aggressively intolerant
faith, Puritanism often crushed the human spirit it professed to save.

Paradoxically enough, the Puritans were responsible for a number of our
cherished freedoms and for many of the principles that have made Americans
a sturdy and self-reliant people. It is to them that we owe the concepts of religious freedom, separation of Church and state, and the right to dissent—although, like most dissenters, they were harshly repressive toward anyone who
disagreed with them. Much of the English Bill of Rights, adopted in the late
seventeenth century and later incorporated into our own Constitution and Bill
of Rights, originated with the Puritans. Their conviction that they had nothing
to fear but God made them formidable adversaries; their self-discipline made
them well-adapted to survive in hostile environments, enforced as it was by
ideals of sobriety, honesty, and industry. These characteristics played an important role in America's phenomenal growth as an industrial nation in the
nineteenth and early twentieth centuries, when the expression "Yankee ingenuity" became a byword. Puritanism was thus an important factor in the rise
of American capitalism, and this explains in part why so many empire builders
of that era were both pious and ruthless. Their contradictory behavior is recon-
cilable in terms of the Puritan ethic; it was a code to which most of the self-
made men subscribed, whether consciously or otherwise.

conservative religious sects, its presence as an active force in our contemporary society is for the most part greatly diluted, and manifested in less obvious ways. Its most notable survival, the Puritan conscience, remains as a social impulse: that overwhelming sense of guilt, which is played upon so skillfully by the unscrupulous among us and has made us the most generous, and at times the most hated, people on earth.

In *The Winthrop Covenant,* a novel made up of nine loosely related short stories, Louis Auchincloss explores the Puritan ethic and the ways in which it has manifested itself through members—both real and fictional—of one prominent American family. He spans three and a half centuries, beginning with an example of Puritanism in its early and perhaps most admirable form; he then follows its general decline and metamorphosis, and ends with a tale that displays its ultimate perversion. The structural device and theme will not be new to his readers, but the stories, as might be expected, are superbly crafted and rich in psychological insight.

The first episode concerns itself with dissent among the dissenters: the Massachusetts Bay Colony, barely established, finds its precarious stability threatened by the radical notions of Anne Hutchinson. Deceptive in its simplicity, this story is actually a complex and subtle study of diverse personalities. We identify emotionally with the garrulous Anne, a living spark amid austerity, but she is also clearly a troublemaker. We identify objectively with Governor John Winthrop, who cannot risk the survival of his colony by tolerating divisive activity within it, although we know such behavior would not be permitted in any case. We sympathize most clearly with William Hutchinson, a decent and kindly man who understands nothing of the forces around him and, baffled, follows his wife into exile. The author's skill is demonstrated most effectively here by his deft characterization of Winthrop, who appears only briefly but nonetheless dominates the entire story as an entity of great power in whom irresistible force and immovable object are combined.

The legacy of John Winthrop takes various forms in his descendants. It appears as the Puritan conscience in grandson Wait Still Winthrop, a judge at the Salem witch trials, who is tormented on his deathbed by the possibility that he was not a righteous instrument of God but a murderer instead. A further extension of conscience is seen in Rebecca Bayard, obsessed by the need to atone for ancestral guilt at Salem, who not only ruins her own life and those of her children but indirectly causes the death of an innocent man. More positive aspects of the legacy are revealed in Samuel Shaw Russell, who demonstrates that his Puritan standards need not render a person cold or intolerant even though they enable him to remain incorruptible. Danny Buck, the kindly and pious chaplain of a private school, is unaware of his own unworthy resentments until they are revealed and thus purged in a journal he has been asked to keep.

In other stories, the Winthrop legacy takes on more sinister overtones. Here Puritanism continues to produce the ruthless, exclusionary life and the sense of mission, but piety has been replaced by practicality. *The Arbiter* is a comedy of ironies, in which an urbane and wealthy clubman, arbiter of artistic taste and literary style, shapes the writing of his friend, a female novelist. She is stifled and dominated by the standards he imposes, while he serves as material for various unflattering characterizations in her novels. A more tragic example, and the most memorable story in this collection, bears an ironic title: *In the Beauty of the Lilies Christ Was Born Across the Sea.* Set in the New York of 1860, it portrays obsession with propriety in its most chilling and virulent form. Lawyer Winthrop Ward learns that the wife of his partner and cousin is apparently being seduced by another man, and he cannot rest until he has brought about the interloper's destruction. We learn that we will go to any lengths in the name of standards which he forces upon others—and that he also harbors a secret desire for the woman he insists on protecting. This character study is not only an absorbing view of authoritarian prudery in a Victorian world; it also portrays graphically the means by which aristocracy protects itself from intrusion by outsiders.

The final degeneration of Winthrop's legacy, as Auchincloss sees it, is told in two brief stories. One deals with an empty marriage dominated by self-assured older relatives; the other is a bitter appraisal in which the old ruthless sense of mission is seen as no longer restrained by any moral influence whatever. John Winthrop Gardiner, career man in the CIA, has destroyed his own family and made everyone he knows a stepping stone to power; the reader is left to shudder over what Gardiner will do with that power once it lies within his grasp.

Auchincloss has been criticized for writing only of the people he knows best, the American aristocracy of position and inherited wealth; but he is perhaps the only writer who sees them so clearly as a group of human beings rather than as a social aberration. Most writers who deal with such people tend to present them as caricatures, but Auchincloss understands them and allows us to see them clearly from the inside. The present novel has also been criticized on the premise that Puritanism is not hereditary and therefore cannot be handed down from one generation to another; but such critics do not understand the tenacity of family tradition, particularly as it exists in aristocracies.

Louis Auchincloss writes quietly, in a low key, and tells his stories in a leisurely fashion without sacrificing economy or excellence. His style is solid rather than spectacular and his social criticism reasoned rather than shrill. For these qualities he has been called old-fashioned; but the charge is warranted only in the sense that genuine craftsmanship is increasingly rare, in writing as in other things. *The Winthrop Covenant* is a thoughtful and perceptive view of an ethic that shaped America. The *Winthrop Covenant* is a thoughtful and perceptive view of an ethic that shaped America. It may be that we have outgrown that ethic, but we would be less than honest with ourselves if we ignored it. This book is a good way to renew the acquaintance.

John W. Evans

Sources for Further Study

Atlantic. CCXXXVII, April, 1976, p. 112.
Book World. March 21, 1976, p. 1.
Critic. XXXV, Fall, 1976, p. 96.
National Observer. XV, May 15, 1976, p. 21.
New York Times. March 22, 1976, p. 23.
Publisher's Weekly. CIX, January 26, 1976, p. 280.

THE WOMAN SAID YES
Encounters with Life and Death

Author: Jessamyn West (1907-   )
Publisher: Harcourt Brace Jovanovich (New York). 180 pp. $7.95
Type of work: Memoirs
Time: The twentieth century
Locale: Pennsylvania and California

A two-part memoir of the author's impressions of her mother and sister

Principal personages:
JESSAMYN WEST, the author
GRACE, her mother
CARMEN, her sister

Jessamyn West's *The Woman Said Yes* is an autobiographical work which is actually a dual biography. While West is a main personage of the book, the substance of the work is dedicated to an anecdotal memoir of her mother Grace and her sister Carmen, two very courageous women. West makes it clear from the outset that this is a woman's book. She therefore necessarily pares down the facts about the men in their lives, even to the extent that she refuses to tell the reader the names of her two brothers, with an admonishment not to worry about such things as this is a book about the women in her family. With the ground rules laid, the work is then divided into two separate stories, one about a woman who survived a crisis and one about a woman who did not.

The title of the book is explained by West as a suitable epithet for her mother Grace who repeatedly said "yes" to life and living, stalwartly refusing to be rattled by it. The central problem of the first half of this work, which reads like a novel, was Jessamyn's near-fatal case of tuberculosis. After spending nearly two years in a tubercular clinic, West is brought home "to die" within the more soothing confines of her parents' home. For the average woman in her early twenties, married and almost finished with her doctoral studies, this would be a catastrophic experience, and, indeed, it was for West. Her mother, however, refused to accept the mournful prediction of the doctors and proceeded to direct her attentions to proving them wrong, as much because of her own natural tenacity as to save her daughter, the author would have us believe.

The way in which Grace accomplished this feat (West modestly refusing to take any of the credit herself) is rather unimportant in itself. The primary reason why she recounts this time of her life is to show what a remarkable, indefatigable woman her mother was. It is the method of her healing, rather than the individual incidents, which show Grace's courage and guile.

Anyone who finds solace in reading stories of great courage and victory over insurmountable odds will not find the usual material here; the book is much more the story of a plain country woman who lived in a world of dreams and who, because of her own strength of character, was able to make many of her dreams come true. She was, it could be said, a perfect example of "the power of positive thinking." Though by West's description Grace was a homely, unattractive woman, her wit and imagination made her a sought-after belle. She picked out a handsome man with great potential, and after pursuing him in a rather shameless fashion during the early twentieth century, asked him to marry her.

The love between Grace and her husband Eldo was exceedingly strong. There was nothing which she would not do for him, nor he for her. It was such a strong love that, in a sense, there was no need of anyone else in their relationship; although they loved their four children, West quotes Robert Louis Stevenson's line "the children of lovers are orphans," to express the type of lives they had. Because of her parents' love and her mother's frailty, West has some unusual memories of children. Whenever Grace was not ill, she was usually helping her husband in some way. Thus, her four children instinctively learned that if they were to survive to adulthood, they would have to fend for themselves. By West's own admission they were the worst wrinkled, least clean children in their school because their mother never noticed whether they were dressed properly. Despite the fact that Grace was in no way the traditional loving, domestic mother, her children still respected and loved her deeply. If she were not around to tend to the daily crises, at least they felt that she could be depended upon in a major one. This is perhaps why West was able to come through her ordeal of tuberculosis when she grew to adulthood. All of Grace's children *knew* that their mother, if called upon, would be capable of superhuman strength—fighting off a mountain lion or stopping a freight train. This dichotomy between seeming incompetence in day-to-day motherhood and supernatural powers at her disposal was another manifestation of Grace's daydreams.

Grace's imagination was obviously of the romantic type. Jessamyn became privy to some of her mother's dreams because of her prolonged illness and the resultant constant hours of being alone with her. The reader is therefore shown some insight into the *alter ego* of an ordinary woman. Not concerned with keeping up appearances or achieving great financial success in life, Grace was instead a constant dreamer who apparently found solace in imagining herself an Indian princess of the nineteenth century, or at the very least the heroine of a gothic novel. It is somehow incongruous to imagine such a down-to-earth woman obsessed with daydreams, but again, this was the dichotomy in her personality which made her unique.

A curious factor in West's writing is her rambling, almost "folksy" style of narration. She constantly interrupts herself with anecdotes, so that occasionally, as in the case of listening to a garrulous maiden aunt, the reader finds himself faced with a conclusion that does not seem to match the original story. This fault most assuredly is due to the author's Pennsylvania upbringing rather than her doctoral studies in Medieval English literature. There are definite strains of the same type of characters here who sprang from the pages of West's most well-known work, *Friendly Persuasion.* These are the warm, uncomplicated people who seem to confine themselves to small towns and rustic settings in literature, rather than the sophisticated, cynical antiheroes and antiheroines of the modern urban novel.

Because of her dependence upon the homespun aspects of the lives of her characters, the cynical reader might find the material lacking depth. Even the major crises of the characters' lives seem rather superficial due to the airiness of the narration. Indeed, while West explains that each day when she had tuberculosis she cried when she awakened, saddened by the knowledge that she had yet another day to endure, it is difficult to feel great emotional attachment to the problem. The admission of a desire for death seems out of place amidst a stream of whimsical anecdotes. This is a major flaw of the book, but is something which was unavoidable when dealing with a character like Grace. Additionally, West's writing style simply does not lend itself well to tragedy— her inbred optimism and enthusiasm, due in part to Grace's, show through at every turn.

West comes across better in her narration of the story of her sister Carmen. Less rambling and staccato than the first segment of the book, Carmen's story is nonetheless another manifestation of the author's philosophy of life. Carmen's portion of *The Woman Said Yes* concerns her unsuccessful fight with cancer. Again in a relaxed anecdotal style West recounts the long and painful dying days of a woman who was vibrant and full of life to the end. In pain much of the time, Carmen was still able to enrich the lives of those around her. West obviously admired and even envied her sister in much the same way that she loved her mother, and she never loses an opportunity to let the reader know this. Unfortunately, the best passages of this book, both in Part One and Part Two, deal with stories about other things. The first pages of Carmen's story are far more interesting than the latter pages simply because they concern Jessamyn West herself. For several pages the author describes her four-month stay in England in the late 1950's when she was hired to write a screenplay for the remake of the movie *Dark Victory.* The significance of this story of a beautiful young woman dying in the prime of life is not lost to the author or the reader, but, not dwelling on parallels, West gives some interesting insights into English as opposed to American life and manners. One wishes that the author had spent more time discussing her life in London, but then *The Woman Said Yes* is the story of Grace and Carmen, not Jessamyn.

The intrinsic flaw of this book is that its primary theme, acceptance of death, seldom makes good reading. The television dramas so popular now about dying athletes, cancer-ridden children, and yet another remake of *Dark Victory* may be inspiring as dramatizations, but as works of literature these stories are rarely more than tear-producing bedtable reading. In fact, it is often rather tedious to endure stories here about Carmen's preoccupation with things like what underwear she should wear to the mortuary. It may be something that people with terminal cancer worry about, but as an example of Carmen's great courage, it comes across rather badly, as do some of the other anecdotes in her story.

What is good about the book is West's insight into the characters she deals with. Though occasionally making sweeping generalizations, as in the case of recounting a story about the cleaning lady's husband LeRoy, when West asks the absurd question "do all sexually aggressive men have an *o* in their names?" She does, however, manage to raise some provoking questions about the nature of sickness and healing. She also shows that even a catastrophic condition in one's life can be endured, or even overcome, if one keeps one's wits and sense of humor. What makes the subjects here extraordinary was their ability to come to grips with ordinary human problems. Without breakdowns or self-pity they were able to survive.

West has an easy style and gives her readers pleasurable moments in this as in many of her other stories, but the final impression of this work is that the author was writing a testimonial to her mother and sister more for herself than for a reading public.

Patricia King Hanson

Sources for Further Study

Booklist. LXXII, May 1, 1976, p. 1236.

Christian Century. XCIII, September 15, 1976, p. 791.

Critic. XXXV, Winter, 1976, p. 80.

New York Times Book Review. May 2, 1976, p. 4.

Publisher's Weekly. CCIX, February 16, 1976, p. 4.

Time. CVII, May 24, 1976, p. 90.

THE WOMAN WARRIOR
Memoirs of a Girlhood Among Ghosts

Author: Maxine Hong Kingston
Publisher: Alfred A. Knopf (New York). 209 pp. $7.95
Type of work: Memoir
Time: 1940's to the present
Locale: A Chinese community in Stockton, California

Recollections of a girl growing up in America and haunted by the ghosts of the tiny peasant village in China from which her parents emigrated

> *Principal personages:*
> MAXINE, a Chinese-American girl
> BRAVE ORCHID, her Chinese mother
> MOON ORCHID, sister of Brave Orchid
> FA MU LAN, a legendary woman warrior

An invisible world surrounded children born to Chinese immigrants in the United States. Growing up American, they struggled to ascertain what things in them were Chinese. How could they separate those things from "what is peculiar to childhood, to poverty, insanities, one family, your mother who marked your growing with stories"? How did Fa Mu Lan, the legendary woman warrior, compare with goddesses of the silver screen? How did a young girl growing up among American teenage mores relate to her ancestor, the outcast "No Name Woman"? In *The Woman Warrior,* Maxine Hong Kingston recalls a girlhood spent in her parents' laundry in a California city, in American and Chinese schools, and in the enchanting fables and fantasies of her ancient heritage.

Written from a feminist perspective, *The Woman Warrior* is the story of a girl's awakening as a strong individual, in the face of misogynistic Chinese folk traditions. The tensions among these traditions, paradoxical myths of female heroism, and everyday postwar America are the background of this sensitive memoir.

Especially haunting is the tale of "No Name Woman," Maxine's great-aunt, who drowned herself and her newborn baby in a well. The woman's husband had gone to America, and she had been forced by a man of the village to lie with him. She gave birth to his child in a pigsty, as was the custom of country women in old China; they believed the gods, who did not snatch piglets, would be fooled. The true punishment for No Name Woman was not the raid of her home by outraged villagers, nor her suicide. The true punishment, Maxine decides, was silence. The family deliberately forgot her. But fifty years later, the nameless woman still haunts Maxine.

Nevertheless, ancient Chinese legends taught that a girl failed if she grew up merely to be a wife or a slave instead of a swordswoman. Fa Mu Lan, the girl who took her father's place in battle, inspired Maxine. She tells the story of the woman warrior as if it were part of her own girlhood—as indeed it was. An elderly couple tutored Fa Mu Lan for fifteen years, training her to survive barehanded among tigers, as well as to understand the ways of dragons. She learned to make her mind as large as the universe, to allow room for paradoxes. Her parents carved on her back oaths and the names of persons who had wronged her family. Then, assembling a joyous army, she rode to battle. Fa Mu Lan's army did not rape. They took food only when there was plenty for all. Wherever they went, they brought order.

Like Joan of Arc, this Chinese woman dressed as a man, for it was the custom to execute women who disguised themselves as soldiers or students, "no matter how bravely they fought or how high they scored on the examinations." To accept this paradox, Maxine must expand her mind, as Fa Mu Lan did.

Kingston's woman warrior is unique. Unlike the virginal Joan of Arc, Fa Mu Lan has a husband, who visits her in battle. She carries his child, gives birth on the battlefield, and then sends the baby home to her family. After many hardships, the army reaches the cruel emperor, beheads him, cleans out the palace, and inaugurates "the peasant who would begin the new order." Her public duties finished, Fa Mu Lan returns to her family and her traditional female role.

After living this tale, Maxine reflects that her drab American life is a disappointment. In school, she is awkward and shy. At home, she balks at the old prejudices, casually repeated by her loving family: "It is more profitable to raise geese than daughters." Kingston skillfully juxtaposes the family's poverty and prejudices against the girl's dreams and the stories told by her mother, Brave Orchid.

These unresolved tensions have created ambivalent feelings in the author, as she readily admits. Fantasies of revenge for ancient wrongs contrast with her own experience that fighting and killing are "not . . . glorious but slum grubby." Yet she aspires to be like the warrior so that her family will accept her female strength. They say, "When fishing for treasures in the flood, be careful not to pull in girls," because that is what Chinese say about daughters. She believes they love her, but she had to get out of "hating range" in order to become strong. Later, wrapped in successes as an American woman, Maxine still resists the restrictive roles thrust on females, while envying other women, who are "loved enough to be supported." Even as an adult, she recognizes that China still "wraps double binds around my feet."

With women throughout the world seeking their own identity and learning independence, Kingston's timely memoir is a scrapbook of experiences that are universal and yet particular: The Chinese word for the female *I* is "slave." The dream of having one's own room appears in Communist photographs of "a contented woman sitting on her bunk sewing. Above her head is her one box on a shelf. The words stenciled on the box mean 'Fragile,' but literally say

'Use a little heart.' The woman looks very pleased. The Revolution put an end to prostitution by giving women what they wanted: a job and a room of their own."

Her mother, Brave Orchid, while training as a midwife in China, had had an opportunity to live out this daydream of women—a room of one's own, "even a section of a room, that only gets messed up when she messes it up herself." Kingston's portrait of Brave Orchid is memorable as a real-life counterpart of the woman warrior. We see only sketches of her father, as in the photographs he sent from America: with friends at Coney Island ("He's the one in the middle with his arms about the necks of his buddies.") In another snapshot, he is glimpsed smiling in front of a pile of clean laundry. "In the spring he wears a new straw hat, cocked at a Fred Astaire angle."

Assimilation into an alien culture seemed unimportant to Brave Orchid, secure in her own identity. As a mature woman, she had studied exorcism, midwifery, and modern medicine. A brilliant scholar and a dragoness, she once fought off a Sitting Ghost, a great furry creature that saps the energy of its victims. All night, Brave Orchid insulted the ghost and then chanted her lessons for the following day's classes. The next morning, she and the other women, chanting and singing, smoked out the creature and killed it.

Brave Orchid told her daughters that children with birth defects were often left to die—as were girl babies sometimes. Maxine, trying to make her life "American-normal," pushes the deformed into her dreams, "which are in Chinese, the language of impossible stories."

In an eerie blend of the real and the surreal, Kingston recreates the steamy laundry where the family worked from 6:30 in the morning till midnight, while the children slept on shelves among the clean clothes. To fool the gods, Brave Orchid calls Maxine "Little Dog"; both mother and daughter are dragons. When the temperature reaches 111 degrees, Maxine's parents tell ghost stories to "get some good chills up our backs."

A child of World War II, Maxine also heard her mother "talk-story" about bomber planes. Shiny silver machines haunt her dreams, and she comes of age in an America of machines and ghosts—Taxi Ghosts, Bus Ghosts, Police Ghosts, Fire Ghosts, Meter Reader Ghosts, Five-and-Dime Ghosts, the fearsome Garbage Ghost. The family laundry ultimately falls prey to Urban Renewal Ghosts.

The clash of ancient ways with Americanized Chinese is vividly depicted in the story of Moon Orchid, sister of Brave Orchid. After staying behind in China for thirty years, Moon Orchid timidly comes to America to claim her husband, a successful brain surgeon who had sent her money and supported their daughter, "even though she's only a girl." But he had taken a new wife. Brave Orchid goads her to find her errant husband and "demand your rights as First Wife." In an awkward confrontation on the street, he confesses, "It's as if I had turned into a different person. The new life around me was so complete; it pulled me away. You became people in a book I had read a long time ago." Moon Orchid retreats into a paranoid fantasy. After trying to chant away her sister's fears, Brave Orchid finally recognizes Moon Orchid's incurable madness and commits her to a mental asylum, where she dies happy. Resolving fiercely that they would never allow men to be unfaithful to them, Brave Orchid's daughters vow "to major in science or mathematics."

Learning was to become Maxine's escape route to independence, but her early school experiences humiliated the little girl, who failed kindergarten and got "a zero IQ" in first grade. Suffering from an intense shyness, she at first refused to speak in school. From men teachers in the Chinese school, held each afternoon until 7:30 p.m., Maxine learned to chant. Later she developed an American-feminine speaking personality. But her traumatic early years marked her childhood. In an agonizingly vivid scene, Maxine torments another girl who remains silent even in Chinese school. Maxine corners her after school in the girls' lavatory and brutally ridicules the girl, pulls some of her hair out, and defies her to say a word. Finally, Maxine cries too.

> "Now look what you've done." I scolded. "You're going to pay for this. . . . You don't see I'm trying to help you out, do you? Do you want to be like this, dumb (do you know what dumb means?), your whole life? Don't you ever want to be a cheerleader? Or a pompon girl? What are you going to do for a living? Yeah, you're going to have to work because you can't be a housewife. Somebody has to marry you before you can be a housewife. . . . You think somebody is going to take care of you all your stupid life?"

As Kingston traces her own maturing from "bad girl" (telling people she wants to be a lumberjack) to independent woman, she portrays the painful period of rebellion which forced her to leave her beloved family in order to find herself. Maxine feared being sent to China, where girls could be sold. (No one had told her parents that the Communists had outlawed girl slavery and girl infanticide.) To make herself unsellable, Maxine decides to be the crazy woman in her house. But such behavior had its perils. The old Chinese, her father warned, smeared honey on bad daughters-in-law and tied them naked on top of anthills. When a retarded boy courts Maxine, her parents appear to encourage the match. She rebels: "They say I'm smart now . . . I'm going to get scholarships, and I'm going away. And at college I'll have the people I like for friends. I don't care if they were our enemies in China four thousand years ago. So get that ape out of here. . . . And I don't want to listen to any more of your stories; they have no logic. They scramble me up." But later she reflects, "Be careful what you say. It comes true. It comes true. I had to leave home in order to see the world logically, logic the new way of seeing."

The pain and triumph of this girl, the captive of two cultures, is echoed in the tale of Ts'ai Yen, an ancient poetess, who was kidnaped and raped by barbarians. Hearing the flute music of her captors, she began singing to her babies, songs about China and her family there. The words seemed Chinese, with barbarian phrases, but the savages understood their sadness and anger. Later

Ts'ai Yen was ransomed and married well. But she carried back with her the savage songs, which translated well.

This delicate and moving memoir is proof that Maxine Hong Kingston has translated with sensitivity and wit the syllables of pain and growth and beauty.

Roberta Madden

Sources for Further Study

Booklist. LXXIII, November 1, 1976, p. 385.

Harper's Magazine. CCLIII, October, 1976, p. 100.

National Observer. XV, October 9, 1976, p. 25.

New Yorker. LII, November 15, 1976, p. 213.

Newsweek. LXXXVIII, October 11, 1976, p. 108.

Time. CVIII, December 6, 1976, p. 91.

WOMEN OF THE SHADOWS

Author: Ann Cornelisen (1926-   )
Publisher: Little, Brown and Company (Boston). 228 pp. $8.95
Type of work: Popular sociology
Time: Post-World War II to the present
Locale: Southern Italy, primarily Lucania

A sociological study of the oppressed peasant class in a southern Italian village

Principal personages:
PEPPINA,
NINETTA,
TERESA,
MARIA,
PINUCCIA, and
CETTINA, peasant women from a small village in southern Italy

Ann Cornelisen brilliantly portrays the frustrated, dehumanizing struggle of poor families whose lives take on the desolation and alienation of their surroundings. They suit each other—the bleak land and the dour people who have no joy in life, only an eternal struggle which they cannot quite win. The cruel world defeats them as they have been defeated for centuries, young and old alike, driven, plodding slowly, heavily, stopping occasionally to shift their load. Cornelisen captures the wretched isolation of these people with her lifelike descriptions and penetrating insight into their actions and motivations. Having lived for twenty years among them, she writes with unquestionable authority and profound respect for a subject to which she has devoted, in large part, her career.

Cornelisen is a magnificent stylist. She writes clearly and, as a scientist, she is very mindful of the objective truth. At the same time, she cannot help reflecting more subjective, personal observations in her study. As she examines the slow repetition of day after day, year after year that she spent in the southern villages, she evokes the villagers' sense of inner isolation, one which she believes she has never entirely lost. She has adopted a part of their feelings and attitudes in her involvement with them, but she must forcibly distance herself from their emotions in order to become an effective observer and reporter.

The "women of the shadows" are the painfully human women of tremendous strength around whom life in the southern Italian villages is centered. The social structure of most poor, relatively isolated Western communities, where the Catholic Church either dominates or is an outright state religion, is matriarchal. It is a system felt by everyone that functions every day, but it is not codified and does not have to be recognized. Men make no large decisions, and day-to-day existence is left to the women, who unconsciously take over all the practical aspects of life. Although men boast with aggressive pride about their power over women, it is really the women who consolidate their hold over husbands and sons with tremendous control.

The lives of the women and men described by Cornelisen are peculiarly separate. Even when they work together in the fields, they share little. What they do share is a wordless, clinging grief at the illnesses and deaths that strike their families. They never seem more helpless or closer to each other than when they stand looking down at a mute, feverish child in a hospital bed. As their lives have been arranged for centuries, peasants have only one responsibility—the family. And it is the women who earn the most dependable source of cash. They work in the fields, teach the children, manage expenses, and most of all, create security. In terms of religious teaching, women can identify immediately with Mary, the all-suffering Mother, and perhaps take consolation in her importance to all men. Much as the Vatican may condemn it, in the South, Christ is on the altar, but the people pray to and worship the Virgin Mary.

The women Cornelisen discusses are not lovable or even objects of our admiration. Instead, they are blunt, often crude, and at times unable to control their savage tempers. They have a certain wit and resourcefulness and a ferocious courage. Sometimes they are compassionate with one another, but always with a warning not to trust entirely the outsider who may betray them later.

When Cornelisen examines the lives of individual women, she is splendidly candid and provides fascinating, intimate detail. She uses detail to enhance her pictures of real people, who seem so lifelike that the reader would immediately recognize any of her characters on the street. Peppina, for example, is a short, lumpy woman dressed in hand-me-downs, who lived in the apartment across from the author. She was preoccupied with callers, never for herself, for she rarely had any, but always listened for the sound of footsteps leading to the doors of others. Her continual loneliness is depicted in Cornelisen's picture of her listening at the door for footsteps, realizing the visitor is not for her, then ducking back into her apartment to close the door silently. The added touch of poignancy to this picture is that Peppina, unlike many, would never eavesdrop at conversations.

One of the major commandments of the women of the shadows is that there is no escape from work. They earn livings working in the fields or working in the homes of others as maidservants. The working conditions are usually oppressive and very exploitative. Especially when working as maids, they are frequently underpaid and rarely paid on time, but they must accept the abuse for fear of not being hired again; they feel that should they complain, the homeowners would blacklist them for future employment. Cornelisen relates case after case of this miserable exploitation of the peasants by more "civilized" city-dwellers.

Some of the family scenes described in the study are grotesque and revolting. Vicious fights and brutal treatment among family members do not seem to alarm the participants very much. Indeed, the people almost seem to cherish catastrophes—that is, those that happen to someone else. Their own problems are so overwhelming that they welcome the calamities of others as a kind of purgative. Gossip becomes a major factor in the villagers' lives, and though they can barely write their names, they have an uncanny aptitude for remembering to the minutest detail events that cause misery for themselves and others. The womens' voices in particular are shrill and can be heard through the town like the siren's wail. Rivals may attack each other with kicks and slaps and bites that send them to the ground in savage combat. At times, people seem to border on madness. They describe seeing demons; they imagine strange, elaborate schemes against them; they brood excessively and curse the inevitable gloom that envelops their existence.

In the peasant villages, there are no spinsters. The people cannot afford such whims, and the convents, the only refuge from suitors repulsive to women but acceptable to their families, are becoming less and less appealing. Husbands are as obligatory for women as wives are utilitarian for men. Physical charms may attract some suitors, or better prospects for the future may make others appear more acceptable, but the strength of youth has its own value that transcends beauty or money; other considerations seem minimal by comparison. To the southern Italian peasant woman, women's liberation is a phrase without meaning, and marriage remains a duty as holy as any of the Commandments.

The living conditions in the village mirror the pain on the people's faces. In a one-room apartment, nothing is private. The street becomes a second room, so that the neighbors know when sheets need mending again and how ragged underwear is and when husbands and wives and children fight. One woman tells of having borne nine children in that one room; only three lived. She describes her father, brothers, husband, and husband's brothers all sitting outside, drinking wine and waiting while the women ministered to her in the agony of childbirth. She believed that if she made a sound, she would disgrace herself, so that she and the others stifled her moans as best they could. She believes that she will die in the same way. Hers is a strange dignity shared by others of her class. Outsiders may report that peasant women feel less pain and suffer less than "other women," but the insensitive outsider does not understand the peasant woman's strict code of behavior and the sense of shame she would bring on herself should she display weakness. She feels and remembers every searing pain that more pampered, more complaining women do, but she will not exhibit that pain to others.

Cornelisen lists herself as one of those thousand idealists who believed in and worked for reform in southern Italy. She believed that should the wasteland be reclaimed, the peasants would be released from a strangling feudal system and have their own land. But the issues, she has come to understand, are much more complicated. Ignorance and political corruption have acted to defeat the good intentions of reformers, and such failure leaves a bitter aftertaste. At present, social scientists, anthropologists, and psychologists are attempting to alter patterns within the community. Cornelisen believes that their efforts are mostly futile. According to her, they use empty jargon in order to deny the people their one irreducible quality—their humanity. The peasant's infinite variety—his courage, his poverty, his ignorance, his pettiness, his shams, his dignity—must be understood, not just tabulated, before change can be brought about. In the end, Cornelisen believes that it is the women whose confidence must be won, in order to break the spell of bondage and frustration.

Ann Cornelisen is a reformer and a humanitarian, two concepts which unfortunately do not always find acceptance. During two decades, the author spoke to the women of the south, watched them, and listened to them. She has a feeling for them that goes much deeper than that of the team of men and women who visit briefly only to distribute questionnaires and correlate principles. She knows the deep-rooted mistrust the people have of outsiders, and the difficulty involved in trying to win them over to change. In the end, her mood is realistic in the sense that she deludes us with no great expectations about the prospect for reform. Only hard work, she believes, can achieve the "miracle" these people desperately need.

Gloria Sybil Gross

Sources for Further Study

Contemporary Review. CCXXIX, October, 1976, p. 213.
Human Behavior. V, July, 1976, p. 75.
National Observer. XV, April 17, 1976, p. 19.
New Statesman. XCII, August 20, 1976, p. 244.
New Yorker. LII, April 12, 1976, p. 139.
Saturday Review. III, March 20, 1976, p. 25.

A WORLD OF LIGHT
Portraits and Celebrations

Author: May Sarton (1912-   )
Publisher: W. W. Norton and Company (New York). 254 pp. $8.95
Type of work: Autobiography
Time: 1937-1959
Locale: Europe and America

A collection of vivid portraits of the author's friends and family, tied together by Sarton's reflections and unifying vision of life

Principal personages:
> MAY SARTON
> GEORGE AND MABEL SARTON
> CÉLINE DANGOTTE LIMBOSCH
> EDITH FORBES KENNEDY
> GRACE ELIOT DUDLEY
> ALICE AND HANIEL LONG
> MARC TURIAN
> ALBERT QUIGLEY
> S. S. KOTELIANSKY
> ELIZABETH BOWEN
> LOUISE BOGAN
> JEAN DOMINIQUE

In *Plant Dreaming Deep* (1967), May Sarton remarks that, like Yeats, she wants her works, (a formidable collection of poetry, novels, articles, and autobiography, published at a rate of almost one volume per year since 1937) "to be seen as a whole . . . a vision of life, which, though unfashionable all the way, has validity." Her works before and since that time seem to fulfill that criterion through recurring themes that bind them together. That her vision of life was "unfashionable" is easily attributed to the fashionable despair and skepticism about the nature of man, of his relationship with nature, with others, with himself, and the ultimate fate of the civilization that he had created—ideas prevalent in major writers following World War I and World War II. With these attitudes, nearly every one of Sarton's books has taken issue.

Conscious as she is of the dual heritage of Europe and America, Sarton finds her roots in humanism and romanticism, pointing the way back to an older tradition. For her, the "true tradition" of American Romanticism is that of Emerson, Thoreau, and Whitman—a tradition which, while acknowledging the imperfection of man and this world, still emphasizes the potentials and joys of man's journey to self-awareness, the significance of the individual, the importance and complexity of man's relationships with nature and with other men, and the final importance of the truth of the human heart. The need for a greater, more intense life achieved only with some struggle and pain, a desire for an order and harmony between past and present, between the inner and outer world, and a celebration of the basic human values—all these themes mark May Sarton's best works. *A World of Light: Portraits and Celebrations,* Sarton's fourth autobiographical work, both reiterates these unifying themes and helps the reader understand how and why they became the basis of the author's vision of life and of her work.

In her Preface, Sarton poses the question of how a person grows and changes, in part "through the influence of friends," and thus states one focus of her book: the complex interweavings of human relationships. Likewise, she acknowledges the artistic challenge of trying to capture "the essence of a person and our relationship" made all the more difficult by her awareness of the past as an ever-shifting flux. This interpretation of past and present becomes another important theme of the book. In spite of the flux, Sarton affirms the daily presence of each of the friends (now all dead but one) in her daily life: "We become what we have loved." The persons developed here have imagination, dedication, warmth, and intensity, qualities shared by Sarton and apparent in all her work. The effort "to capture the essence" is more successful in some portraits than in others, yet the reader will find in the wealth and range of characters and relationships ones that echo the fabric of his own life. To some degree, also, because of the ages and backgrounds of the persons included, the book is partially a history of an age, of changing times, and of the effect of history upon individuals and entire classes.

As a record of the changing forces of history, *A World of Light* is fascinating in its wealth of detail and anecdote. Mabel Elwes Sarton, for instance, discovers her illegitimacy, a fact that leads her to break off her relationship with George Sarton and contributes to a nervous breakdown; even after her recovery and their reconcilement, she is painfully aware that his family looks down on her as a "poor match." Both reactions are remnants of a society that no longer exists. The married Sartons escape with almost nothing in front of the advancing German army, and their reestablishment in America represents the displacement of many previously well-to-do European immigrants during those chaotic times. The gradual decay and final sale of Céline's estate, *Pignon Rouge* (the first place May Sarton had found roots and thought of as "home"), and Céline's removal to an apartment in the city, is the history of a whole class whose fortunes were irrevocably changed by the war. Likewise, Elizabeth Bowen's aunt's old estate is described as becoming a ruin with the gardeners and servants no longer available. "Bowen's Court" in Ireland after the war, was also sold and later torn down by the new owners.

The process of modernization and the irretrievable loss of old values is presented most poignantly in the portrait of Marc Turian, the Swiss *vigneron,* whose winery and land had been owned by his family for generations. Being pushed out of the market after the war by cheaper wines, Marc joined a cooperative to try to compete, but finally returned to his own independent operation, regaining his sense of pride, independence, and family heritage, but at the risk of losing his vineyards. Sarton herself often gives vent to this sense of loss, of growing chaos, of a modern world losing its grip on what is humanly important. Yet, more importantly, she also finds certain places and persons that contain a sense of "vertical past" fused with the present in which stable humanistic values are preserved and celebrated. Marc Turian, doomed to be a species that will ultimately lose to the conglomerates, will endure forever, not just for the writer, but for the reader, both as an individual and as a symbol of values to cherish.

The changeless "black and white" values of Céline and "Kot," different though they may be, both convey a sense of stability in the midst of a changing world. So does the ritualistic ceremony of having tea with "Kot." This same sense of stasis is found in the depiction of Grace Eliot Dudley and her home, *Le Petit Bois*. Returning to the house several years after Grace's death, Sarton finds the house still "full of peace, of Grace's own presence, all alive and still, all in depth . . . a healing balm." Even places touched by loved ones, like the memory, preserve some things from change. The seasonal "ceremonies" of the Longs in their Santa Fe garden likewise are linked to a sense of the changeless. Descendants of the original Indians of the area still celebrate seasonal rites, fused long ago with the seasonal rites of the Roman Catholic Church. In this portrait, Sarton's gift of "catching the essence" is especially remarkable in the evocation and celebration of the harmony of past and present, of pagan and Christian, of place and person. Indeed, she remarks that it was this quality of Santa Fe that gave her a sense of "coming home" to America.

Another homecoming to basic values, to a sense of past and present and to lasting values is presented in the portrait of Quig. There she finds the same sense of harmony with the historical past of New England evident in his sense of values, his personal relationships, his art—harmonies that are never lost, even when Quig dies. Even friendships that are broken are evaluated in terms of harmony with the "vertical past" and do not vanish from our lives, as seen in the portrait of Elizabeth Bowen. Sarton cites Bowen's Anglo-Irish background as one influence that makes her "unknowable" in the final essence. The presence of the past is never absent from Bowen's ancient Irish estate, yet her mixed heritage makes her simultaneously an intruder among the Irish and a foreigner among the English. Even after the breakdown of their once close friendship, never completely understood by Sarton, she asserts the presence of Bowen in her daily life. Like Céline, whose imperfections she came to understand, Sarton affirms that, in the perpetually shifting sea of time, friendship remains: "When one has completely had an experience, there is no grief when it ends"—whether the end is death, abandonment, or breakdown.

The importance and intricacies of multiple human relationships are seen not only in the relationship of Sarton herself to each of the major persons presented in the "portraits," but in each person's relationship with other individuals developed in the portraits: no one stands alone. The portrait of Grace Eliot Dudley, for instance, introduces the Maillet family, who risked their lives

saving an unknown American pilot from the collaborators; an old peasant
shares his evening meals of two baked potatoes with Grace and May; when
Grace is dying, she remembers the villagers by having May purchase pots of
basil for each home on St. Basil's day; the villagers come to bring gifts of
produce and flowers to the sick woman, and form the best funeral procession
they can, full of love, for the once-foreigner who came to be part of their lives.

Parent-child relationships are also treated with sensitivity and awareness.
Sarton writes, as she has often done before in autobiography and poetry, of the
richness of the gifts she received from her own parents. As an older woman,
she can analyze the estrangement of Céline and her daughters, realizing that
Céline's own obsessive and demanding love was itself the cause. Only after the
home was sold and the children freed from her web, could they begin to give
Céline the love she had always desired. In contrast, Edith Forbes Kennedy is
presented as a woman who sacrificed much of her own true talent with no
regret, writing stories for *True Confessions* at night to support her sons, freeing
them "for what they wanted in life," helping without ever being possessive.
Sarton suggests an analogy in her own mother's sacrifice of her artistic talents
to earn money to protect her husband and nourish her daughter.

The book presents, too, a multiplicity of male-female relationships. Sarton
begins with the relationship between her parents, in which her father, excellent
and disciplined scholar though he was, seldom took time to spend with his
family except for tea. She discovers a man of "epistolary friends" beyond
counting, and a man who, having been protected by his wife for years, spent
the days of Mabel's final painful illness tenderly caring for her every need. The
memoirs of this loving and harmoniously balanced marriage are followed by
the contrast of that of Céline and Raymond, when Sarton as an adult observes
their marriage finally turning into a hell, a situation unknowingly engineered
by Céline herself through her overabundant, possessive love, which emascu-
lated Raymond as an artist and as a person. In Céline's case, Sarton attributes
this failure to the lack of self-confidence and self-knowledge, which kept
Céline from the growth and change necessary for a mature relationship. Elizabeth Bowen's marriage she admires, and sees as essentially a good one, because Bowen, in spite of extramarital affairs, was able to keep her own and her
husband's personal dignity intact, never hurting him, always retaining a
healthy sense of humor and one of decorum.

The two best marriages depicted in the book, the Longs' and the Quigleys',
share certain qualities that make Sarton wonder, at one point, whether good
marriages are not more rare than good poems. These marriages possess a sense
of stability and love, of tolerance, humor, and "imaginative concern" between
husband and wife, that allows each partner the total freedom of being himself
without apology, and creates a pattern of living intensely for the moment:
"ceremony, laughter, tenderness," as Sarton sums it up. Again, in Marc
Turian's life, richly endowed with feminine influences—his aunt, his cousin,

his wife—imagination, independence of spirit, and a flair for living contribute
to his happy marriage. In each of these three marriages, a sense of order and
harmony, not always obvious on the surface, is apparent. Other types of male-
female relationships are also depicted. Of Sarton's own relationships with
men, there are only a few references to affairs that ended unhappily. But in her
more platonic relationships with married men already mentioned, there is evidence of deep and abiding friendships which can nourish each party without
the presence of sex. The portrait of Koteliansky, with his sensitivity to others,
intense loyalty to his friends, and moral commitment to art, vividly illustrates
how the young can benefit from the kindness and wisdom of their elders.
Among the younger women to whom "Kot" imparted lasting values were
Katherine Mansfield and May Sarton, who were able to find in his criticism of
their works a faith in their ability to become truly good writers.

Relationships between two men, such as that between Quig and Alec
James, and between two women, are equally seen as contributing to the wealth
and richness of human life. Each of the women Sarton depicts contributes
something to her knowledge of life, or others, and finally, of herself. Céline
gave her the theater; Edith Forbes Kennedy taught her "to *think* clearly and
hard about *feeling*"; Grace Eliot Dudley showed her the value of living deeply
and calmly in the moment. Elizabeth Bowen gave her moments of love and
friendship and insight into the handling of multiple relationships; Louise
Bogan, a sense of the importance of the intense inner life, of meetings as occasions, of what poetry really was, and of what it was like to live always on the
brink of total breakdown. The most complex woman-woman relationship handled in the book is found in the final portrait of Jean Dominique, a Belgian
poetess, who, as Marie Closet, taught Sarton for a year when Sarton was
twelve. Sarton renewed the relationship at twenty-six, when her volume of
poetry was published; Jean Dominique was sixty-five at that time, living with
two of her oldest friends, Blanchette and Gaspari, for the rest of their lives. For
Sarton, the following years became an "uninterrupted communion." It is also
through her coming to understand the relationships among the three friends
that she came to recognize the complexity of true friendship, that it is "an
exacting exercise of the heart, a creation, a poem," that "harmonized and
consoled" all who contacted it. Surely this statement concentrates one of the
major thrusts of *A World of Light*. From Jean Dominique, too, Sarton learned
a second supreme lesson: "she who taught us so much taught us finally to die."
The value of memory, the strength to face despair, the ability still to find
something to celebrate, to create anew from loss, to see life and death finally as
an unending song—no better summations of the major themes of this book or
of Sarton's works could be made than this single portrait. The triumphant end
of Jean Dominique's journey to death marks a triumphant conclusion to this
book.

It is a tribute to Sarton's artistry that each person painted here is treated equally; she does not give in to the temptation to ignore the public "unknowns" in favor of lengthy, sensationalized treatments of public figures. The regularity of her presentation is also fitting to her theme: loved and loving friends are the greatest riches life can bestow, a gift that death cannot take from us. The material included, of course, is not all new: the portraits of Quigley and Koteliansky seem little changed from her earlier autobiography; the portraits of George Sarton, Marc Turian, and Alice and Haniel Long are reprints. Yet the bringing together of these people in conjunction with new material not only allows the reader to find them all in one volume; it allows a clearer sense of Sarton's development as an artist and a clearer view of the major themes that link *A World of Light* with the rest of her work. *A World of Light* is a successful celebration of life and of friendship and love, of homes and nature, of human nature itself—imperfect, inconsistently admirable, but, on the whole, inspiring in creative potential and filled with love, generosity, humor, and courage. As Sarton remarks of one of her friends, reading this book is often an "experience . . . rich, deep, sustaining, and wholly beneficent."

Ann E. Reynolds

Sources for Further Study

Booklist. LIII, September 15, 1976, p. 111.
Kirkus Reviews. XLIV, August 1, 1976, p. 893.
Library Journal. CI, September 1, 1976, p. 1769.
New York Times Book Review. October 3, 1976, p. 6.

WORLD OF OUR FATHERS

Author: Irving Howe (1920-   )
Publisher: Harcourt Brace Jovanovich (New York). 714 pp. $14.95
Type of work: Social and cultural history
Time: Chiefly 1880-1920; also 1920-1976
Locale: New York City and other American cities; Eastern Europe

A definitive social and cultural history of the origins and consequences of the great wave of migration of East-European Jews to major American cities, particularly New York City, during four decades beginning in the 1880's

From 1880, when there were approximately 80,000 Jews in New York, until 1912, when the Jewish population in that city rose to over a million, a great wave of migration from the ghettos and other restricted Jewish zones of Eastern Europe spilled over to the shores of the metropolis. In *World of Our Fathers,* a National Book Award-winning social and cultural history treating the origins and consequences of this migration, Irving Howe describes in meticulous detail and with dramatic flair the lives of immigrant Jews centered mostly in New York City. Other scholarly but less ambitious histories have investigated the impact of Jewish migration upon smaller communities—notably Edwin Wolf II and Maxwell Whiteman's *The History of the Jews of Philadelphia: From Colonial Times to the Age of Jackson* and Selig Adler and Thomas E. Connolly's *From Ararat to Suburbia: The History of the Jewish Community of Buffalo.* And other scholars have edited anthologies or collected pictorial records concerning the immigrant Jews of New York City, among them Milton Hindus' *The Old East Side;* Allon Schoener's *Portal to America: The Lower East Side 1870-1925;* and Abraham Shulman's *The New Country: Jewish Immigrants in America.* Still other writers have treated in affectionate, mostly impressionistic terms parts of the same subject, for example Harry Golden in *Greatest Jewish City in the World.* Vastly more informative than these works, *World of Our Fathers* is the definitive history of the East-European Jewish experience in New York City and, by extension, the story of two million people from this migration wave who eventually settled throughout America.

Without question, the story needed to be told. Published in the year when Alex Haley's *Roots* and Lucille Clifton's slighter memoir *Generations* also appeared, *World of Our Fathers* treats the similar theme of investigating the origins and recording the early hardships of a minority people in America. Based in part upon an exhaustive research into documentary materials, Howe's book is more than a detailed history; it is also a living record, informed by the commentaries of a great many Jews who experienced the shock of passage, the struggles of settling in the strange new land. From their diaries, letters, and autobiographies, the author allows the witnesses to tell the stories of their own sufferings and triumphs. Altogether, the book is a powerful social document, a model of historical research humanized by a sense of social and cultural values.

Howe, who has published literary studies on Thomas Hardy, William Faulkner, and Sherwood Anderson, as well as a great many shorter monographs on other writers, brings to his task a full appreciation of the complex psychological forces that operate upon individuals. Moreover, his interest in social upheavals—the forces that work upon masses of people—is evidenced in such works as *The American Communist Party: A Critical History* and *The U. A. W. and Walter Reuther*. *World of Our Fathers* shows both concerns, a psychological curiosity about the ways in which ordinary people in a hostile environment fail, prosper, or simply survive; and a social curiosity about the organization of people who strive together or clash as they interact to achieve their goals. Because the first subject holds greater interest for most readers, the early sections of the book concerning the immigrant experience are likely to be favored. However, the author's particular contribution as a social historian may be measured as well in the sections dealing with "Jewish Labor, Jewish Socialism," and "Breakup of the Left." Also, Howe is unusually well-qualified to assess the cultural impact of literature, journalism, drama, and popular entertainment upon Jewish life in America. His extensive discussion of "The Culture of Yiddish"—treating such topics as "The Yiddish Word," "The Yiddish Theatre," "The Scholar-Intellectuals," and "The Yiddish Press"—increases significantly our knowledge about a great heritage, now all but lost to the descendants of immigrant stock.

It is, after all, to these descendants that the book is chiefly addressed. More than a historian intent upon recapturing an era of lost time, Howe is a philosopher who asks questions pertinent to contemporary readers. These questions, implicit in his study, are: What are the special qualities that distinguished East-European Jewish migration from that of other national, religious, or ethnic groups? And what permanent contributions to American culture were left behind by these immigrants?

To answer the first question, Howe examines the special conditions under which the predominantly Russian and Polish Jewish immigrants left their *shtetls* and ghettos during the decade of the 1880's and thereafter to seek a better life in a golden land, the *goldeneh medina* rumored to offer freedom, opportunity, and fortune. Like many other peoples, they had been the victims of oppression, both religious and social, in their native lands; they were mostly poor, undernourished, and uneducated; they were generally from the lower classes; and they were ignorant of the language, customs, and institutions of the country for which they ventured everything. Unlike other national, racial, or ethnic groups, however, they had to overcome unique disadvantages before they could assimilate into American mainstream life. Almost all the first-generation European Jews were deeply pious, committed to an orthodox faith altogether opposed in spirit to the hedonism, materialism, and worldly vanity they encountered in the New World. "Goodbye God, we are sailing to America" was a popular quip bitter in its ironic truth. More than suffering from spiritual estrangement, the immigrants were also psychologically disoriented. Ill-prepared to earn a living in America, most had to scrounge for work in the most humiliating occupations—as peddlars, sweat-shop seamstresses, piece-work tailors. Because in Europe they had not been allowed to till the soil or own land or property, had been excluded from the professional classes, and generally had been prohibited from joining the craft guilds, they were forced to crowd together in urban centers competing for the same meager jobs. Under such conditions, their lives were often burdened by agonizing toil, to which was added the torments of spiritual and psychological guilt. Nevertheless, the immigrants managed to survive, indeed to pass on to their children a legacy of courage, a burning desire to succeed: to become true Americans.

One reason why the first-generation immigrant Jews overcame their harsh environment, Howe believes, is that they shared a messianic vision. Trusting that their suffering would eventually end, if not in their own lifetimes then in their children's, they were sustained by an emotional fervor for redemption. "The emotionality of the Jews," Howe writes, "often regarded with distaste by sophisticated gentiles and embarrassment by emancipated Jews, was a sign not merely that they had behind them a long history of tumult and woe; it was the psychic shadow of a great idea—the idea of messianism as sacred burden—which must surely be at the heart of any attempt to explain Jewish survival, if indeed it can be explained at all."

Assuming that this analysis is correct—that because of their messianic fervor the Eastern European Jewish immigrants were unique among the many troubled peoples who boarded ships for America during the 1880's and the three decades following—the question follows: What permanent contribution to American culture did they leave behind? In the great social melting pot of all classes and conditions of people, they certainly assimilated to the common ore, becoming less recognizably Jewish and more American. Howe traces their progress, if this word is appropriate, toward cultural assimilation. Divided into four main sections, *World of Our Fathers* shows the stages of this progress: "Toward America," which discusses the origins of the great migration from Eastern Europe, the arrivals of the Jews in New York and other large cities, and their orientation to the new life; "The East Side," which discusses in depth the problems of psychological and spiritual displacement suffered by most immigrants, the means of employment open to them, and the many avenues to economic, social, and cultural assimilation upon which they traveled; "The Culture of Yiddish," which treats the high-water mark of their unique experience, as expressed in the popular arts, the theater, literature, journalism, and other manifestations of the intellectual life; and finally, "Dispersion," which shows the "journeys outward" of assimilated Jews, their increasing self-confidence and success in all aspects of society, their metamorphosis into totally established Americans.

To Howe, the progress of these immigrant Jews was unquestionably upward—toward acceptance, security, and finally a measure of opulence and
power. Yet the question remains: Along the way to progress, what losses did
the Jews suffer as well? A historian sensitive to moral issues, Howe does not
neglect to treat this question. His answer, implicit throughout the book, is that
the losses were grave, no matter how inevitable. Nearly lost to the descendants
of these immigrants was the great culture of Yiddish, together with the social
values of "Yiddishkeit." Howe makes clear to the reader the high level of
achievements in literature and the theater that has been attained by those to
whom Yiddish was a language of extraordinary suppleness, range, discrimination, and vigor. Now the Yiddish culture is virtually dead, except in isolated
pockets of New York and a few other major cities; the press is feeble, the stage
empty, the poets stilled.

In addition to cultural loss, Howe shows how the progress toward assimilation accelerated among the Jewish immigrant families a loss of stability. As
traditional strong family ties, in which the father was the dominating figure,
began to fall apart, the children often suffered anxiety and stress. Once the
fixed center of Jewish life, the family structure remained merely an emotional,
not a spiritual prop to support the members. Children became breadwinners,
educated themselves to fit into American life, and in the process of securing
their economic independence often turned their backs upon parents, relatives,
and the community. In a brilliant elegiac chapter, "Fathers and Sons," Howe
describes the emotional losses from such dislocations. "The sons knew how
great, how oppressive, was their debt and how little they could show by way of
gratitude," he writes;

> The distance between generations came to be like a chasm of silence which neither affec-
> tion nor good will could bridge. Inner shame, outer irritation, a rare coming together in
> grief—life ripped people apart, and when fathers and sons could manage a little ob-
> jectivity, they might acknowledge that finally no one was to blame.

Yet the tone of *World of Our Fathers* is not generally elegiac, nor is it senti-
mentally nostalgic. In spite of their cultural and social losses resulting from the
melting process, the younger generations of Jews have created a new American
destiny for themselves, one glittering with the outward show of success. Jewish
actors, comedians, composers, movie stars, Hollywood producers, writers, and
artists have left their permanent imprint upon gentile America. Jewish men
and women in business, the professions, the unions, the helping services, and
politics and public life have moved to the highest positions of responsibility in
their communities and the nation. But much the same could be said of the
generations of other ethnic, racial, or national groups. From the point of view
of worldly success, however, the record of the children of Jewish immigrants
compares favorably with that of the descendants of the Irish, Italians, Germans, or any other immigrant stock. To Howe, the permanent contribution of

the Eastern European Jews, one which remains unique and valuable, is the product of their messianic fervor. By now, more than halfway through the twentieth century, he believes that messianism has lost virtually all of its religious significance. Yet he writes:

> A good portion of what was best in Jewish life, as also what was worst, derives from . . . secularized messianism as it passed on from generation to generation, sometimes all but snuffed out and at other times suddenly flaring up violently.

Howe never quite defines "secularized messianism," but the shape of his idea is firm enough. Rooted in the "intense moral seriousness of Jewish life," involving both "a streak of madness" and a rage for purity, this fervor operates to achieve what is difficult, to strive for excellence, to advance everywhere the human potential. Howe believes that the special messianism has not died with new generations of Jews. It survives in "such distinctive traits of the modern Jewish spirit at its best as an eager restlessness, a moral anxiety, an openness to novelty, a hunger for dialectic, a refusal of contentment, an ironic criticism of all fixed opinions." Inasmuch as these qualities of spirit appear among many American gentiles as well, one could argue that the particular contribution of the Eastern European Jews endures as a permanent heritage for the country they adopted with so much hope, so much love. "Let us now praise obscure men," says Howe—the fathers whose world has passed into historical memory but whose dream has become ours also.

Leslie B. Mittleman

Sources for Further Study

Atlantic. CCXXXVII, April, 1976, p. 114.

Commentary. LXI, April, 1976, p. 83.

Commonweal. CIII, May 21, 1976, p. 340.

National Observer. XV, March 6, 1976, p. 19.

Virginia Quarterly Review. LII, Summer, 1976, p. 74.

Wall Street Journal. CLXXXVII, March 15, 1976, p. 12.

Western Humanities Review. XXX, Summer, 1976, p. 249.

WORLD OF WONDERS

Author: Robertson Davies (1913-   )
Publisher: The Viking Press (New York). 358 pp. $8.95
Type of work: Novel
Time: The present
Locale: Sorgenfrei, Switzerland; London, England

A psychological study of the world's "greatest magician" and the formative influences of his life as narrated by him to a group making a film on the life of the French magician, Robert Houdin

> Principal characters:
> DUNSTAN RAMSAY, an elderly Canadian schoolteacher acting as historian for a film company
> MAGNUS EISENGRIM (NEE PAUL DEMPSTER), boyhood companion of Ramsay, now a world-renowned magician playing the role of Robert Houdin in a B.B.C. film
> JURGEN LIND, Swedish director of the film
> DR. LISELOTTE (LIESL) NAEGELI, lover of Ramsay and Eisengrim
> HARRY KINGHOVEN, a cameraman
> ROLAND INGESTREE, executive producer of the film

This, the third and concluding book of Davies' trilogy (*Fifth Business,* 1970, *The Manticore,* 1972) is one of those rare works which does not require a knowledge of the first two books for its appreciation. In fact, new readers coming upon Davies' characters for the first time in *World of Wonders* have an added thrill of discovery as the author ties together the threads of the apparently disparate lives and careers of many of the characters.

The underlying premise of the three books is an incident which altered the lives of all those involved in it: a young boy threw a snowball with a stone embedded in it at his playmate; his companion ducked and the snowball struck the pregnant wife of the Baptist minister, causing her to give birth eighty days early and ultimately causing her to go mad. *Fifth Business,* the first novel in the trilogy consists of a lengthy letter written by Dunstan Ramsay, the boy who averted the snowball and is now an elderly Canadian schoolmaster, detailing his lifelong remorse over the incident, and introducing the mysterious circumstances of the death of Percy Boyd (Boy) Staunton, the snowball thrower, with the same stone in his mouth, decades later. *The Manticore* presents a psychological study of Boy Staunton's son who has become a drunken lawyer. *World of Wonders* traces how Paul Dempster, the unborn child, grew to become Magnus Eisengrim, a world-renowned magician who is now called upon to portray the life of the legendary French magician, Robert Houdin, for a B. B. C. film.

As in his previous books, Davies is more interested in ideas than in the simple narration of plot. This novel presents a story within a story, the framework of which is related by Ramsay. While working on the film, the various principals gather to listen to Magnus Eisengrim relate how he became the world's greatest magician to provide a kind of "subtext" for the proposed film of Houdin. This subtext idea permeates the entire novel under various guises. Underlying all is the question of what is the truth. The narrator, Dunstan Ramsay, a historian, sees truth in the documentary records left behind by a society. To Jurgen Lind, the Swedish film director, it is an era's "music, the way its clothes ought to be worn, the demeanour of its people, and its quality of life and spirit." Lind's cameraman, Harry Kinghoven, sees reality as something he can manipulate by camera angles and the intensity and shading of light. Eisengrim the magician is primarily concerned with illusions created by attention to details. Author Davies' narrative technique lets his characters dole out bits and pieces of truth as they see fit; but the interruptions and differing interpretations of others bring the reader to realize that objective truth is ultimately attainable only through looking at the same details through every possible point of view, or as Liesl says, from God's point of view.

Within this frame story, Magnus Eisengrim takes over and relates his life's experiences which led to his present position. But the same problem the filmmakers have found with Houdin's autobiography arises with Eisengrim's relation. As an autobiography is self-serving, it is often used to hide the inner person, sometimes unwittingly. Eisengrim's narration is an exciting tale beginning in Canada where, as a boy of ten, he was sodomized and kidnaped by a second-rate village fair carnival magician named Willard. As the magician's assistant he was forced to hide in the inner workings of a mechanical man and work the mechanism to trick the fairgoers. To keep up the illusion of the creature being entirely mechanical, he was required to spend long hours alone in the dark cramped quarters. It is here that he learned his magician's tricks, practicing in the dark between shows. Since Eisengrim repeatedly insists that Willard was not very skilled and that he made no effort to add to his repertoire beyond perfecting his pocket-picking technique, it is questionable exactly how Magnus could have developed beyond a limited point in these endeavors. Yet, in his very full later life, there is little indication that he even spent much time practicing his old tricks, much less learning new ones.

Davies' recounting of the life of the Wanless's World of Wonders carnival troupe rings a responsive chord for anyone who has witnessed a traveling carnival. His tale combines the exotic intimate details of the life of these freakish vagabonds and misfits with the familiar mundane petty jealousies and quarrels which afflict all coworkers in what is finally an extremely boring job. From Eisengrim's description of the Fat Woman pathetically reciting biblical verses to the audience to counter the double-meaning jokes of Charlie, the barker, to the digressions in his tale, and arguments among the film crew, there is an undercurrent running throughout the novel questioning the nature and extensiveness of evil in our life. Ramsay (who comes closest to being the author's mouthpiece) says, "I have been wondering if humour isn't one of the most brilliant inventions of the Devil. . . . It diminishes the horrors of the past, and it veils the horrors of the present, and therefore it prevents us from seeing straight, and perhaps from learning things we ought to know." One illustration of the nature of evil explored is Eisengrim's admission of his sadistic pleasure in taking over the magician's role when Willard degenerated to a helpless, fawning morphine addict, and was exhibited as a Wild Man or a geek in the side show.

Following his experiences in carnivals and the vaudeville circuit, Eisengrim next became an actor in London, serving as a double for Sir John Tresize, an elderly actor of the old school still trying with some success to keep romance alive in the theater despite the changing tastes of the times. Again, the plot serves Davies' thematic analysis of the truth of one's existence. Here, Eisengrim admits to his role of losing his own identity by "getting inside" Sir John, aping his every gesture. Eisengrim is used as Sir John's double to perform acrobatic feats which would be beyond Sir John's ability. Through these experiences Eisengrim learns the theatrical side of his magician's trade. It is at this time too, that he meets the youthful Roland Ingestree, one of his present auditors who is currently the executive producer of the film being made. Eisengrim and Ingestree have widely divergent opinions stemming from their experiences with Sir John. Here we see that Eisengrim's interpretation of reality is not the only one possible.

The final segment of Eisengrim's apprenticeship is his being hired to fix a priceless collection of mechanical toys which had been destroyed by the grotesque, monkeyish Liesl Naegeli. Liesl, a withdrawn, almost autistic child because of her hideous appearance, is reached and befriended by Eisengrim, and when she inherits her father's wealth, she joins him in setting up a magic show.

After the film company disperses, Ramsay brings up the question of who killed Boy Staunton, and all the events of the three books are finally drawn together in this mystery-like final section. For the reader who has not read the earlier two novels, the mystery does not receive enough emphasis to make it a major concern; but the solution marvelously draws together all the philosophical concerns of appearance and reality and our varying viewpoints regarding it.

Davies' style has been compared to that of Dickens, but with an added depth of psychological insight. Indeed, his romantic plot and Dickensian characters on the carnival circuit are most impressive, but the main characters tend to be one-dimensional, serving as mouthpieces for the author's ideas. Ultimately, it is the author's skillful interweaving of bits of life to come up with the complete fabric of truth that is most satisfying.

Roger A. Geimer

Sources for Further Study

America. CXXXIV, June 5, 1976, p. 503.

Book World. May 30, 1976, p. F7.

New Leader. LIX, March 29, 1976, p. 16.

New York Times. March 4, 1976, p. 29.

Publisher's Weekly. CCIX, February 23, 1976, p. 116.

Times Literary Supplement. May 14, 1976, p. 588.

THE WORM OF CONSCIOUSNESS AND OTHER ESSAYS

Author: Nicola Chiaromonte (1901-1972)
Edited by Miriam Chiaromonte and with a Preface by Mary McCarthy
Publisher: Harcourt Brace Jovanovich (New York). 270 pp. $10.00
Type of work: Essays

    Collected essays dealing primarily with Chiaromonte's political and theatrical criticism

In his lifetime, Nicola Chiaromonte published only two books—*La Situazione Drammatica,* a collection of his writings on the theater, and *The Paradox of History.* Both works received only scant attention in England and the United States. *The Worm of Consciousness,* a posthumous collection of essays, should finally attract the serious attention that Chiaromonte merits. It is the ultimate product of a mind that was intimately associated with the conflicting philosophies of the twentieth century.

After completing his education at the University of Rome, Chiaromonte fled the Fascists and went into self-imposed exile in Paris in 1934. In 1936 he was in Spain fighting for the Spanish Republic, flying with André Malraux's Republican squadron. When the Germans invaded France he fled to Algeria, where he became friends with Camus. In 1941 he arrived in New York and became part of the circle of intellectuals who wrote for Dwight Macdonald's *Politics.* Chiaromonte, who by this time had experienced some of the traumas of European liberalism, added a certain philosophical dimension to this group which was trying to maintain a radical outlook while abandoning Marxism. His literary acquaintances in New York also included Mary McCarthy, Meyer Schapiro, and James T. Farrell. After barely eking out his living writing essays for such journals as *Atlantic Monthly, The New Republic, Partisan Review,* and *Politics,* he returned to Italy in 1947 and became drama critic for the liberal weekly *Il Mondo.* Between 1956 and 1968 he edited the monthly *Tempo Presente* with Ignazio Silone.

Chiaromonte avoided the mainstreams of Italian intellectual life and was consequently fated to isolation in his lifetime. Much of his problem and yet something of an asset, as revealed in *The Worm of Consciousness,* was his refusal to be labeled intellectually. He was neither Marxist nor anti-Communist, neither existential nor New Leftist. Fashions and schools all repelled him, thus he was not widely acclaimed by any group. He died in 1972, relatively unknown outside Italy.

The Worm of Consciousness is an impressive collection of writings representative of the author's interests—the interaction of political authority and modern freedom, the role of the intellectual and the influence of mass culture on the humanist tradition. Included also are statements on Dante, Pirandello, the practice of criticism, and the political theater. The book is enriched by the inclusion of several memoirs which blend a mixture of personal modesty with an assurance that the path of history threads through the author's experience—a kind of reflection possible only in an age of mass communication in which the humblest person can find himself caught up in world history.

Chiaronmonte's essays constitute a testament to the impact of the philosophies and events of this century upon an alert and incisive mind. He might occasionally be wrong, but he is never deluded. In her preface to this collection, Mary McCarthy adroitly points out that Chiaromonte's ideas do not fit into an established category; "he was neither on the left nor on the right. Nor did it follow that he was in the middle; he was alone." Though his thought remains faithful in its way to philosophical anarchism, he had no belief in political "effectiveness." His experiences in the Spanish Civil War had cured him, personally, of any hope for the application of force to the realm of ethics and ideals. He was immune to those fevers of twentieth century politics which have made so many intellectuals discover that there is always something they value just a little more than freedom.

The political essays embody a rational effort to identify those currents of thought and feeling that have enabled totalitarianism to flourish in our time. The Western intellectual, according to Chiaromonte, is unaware of the greatest threat to freedom—the advanced regimentation of collective life. This is an inevitable consequence of the "uncontrolled and uncontrollable authority" bred by the egalitarianism peculiar to industrial society. The author considered freedom the only guarantee of human dignity, and a free man was a man who could think for himself. Chiaromonte makes an emphatic rejection of the claim that in order to understand anything you must first believe in a larger theory which explains everything. Such theories, he explains, descend like opaque curtains between ourselves and our real situation. They violate what he calls "the sacred boundary that separates ideas from facts."

Chiaromonte is perhaps at his best in his attacks on the Marxists. "What I demand," he states, "is the right to regard as false—or, rather as equivocal— such notions as that of the class struggle without being accused of being a tool of capitalism." His criticisms of metaphysical history and historicist politics reaffirm the reasoning intellect with its processes of clarifying facts, constructing hypotheses, and confirming or refusing them. "Genuine conviction," according to Chiaromonte, "is based on direct, natural evidence, on primary facts of inner and outer experience." This is the author's "dearest wisdom . . . to trust the event for suggesting what our response to it shall be."

In establishing his codes of intelligent behavior—his perception of the interaction between freedom of thought and participation in the community— Chiaromonte promulgated the classical view of the intellectual as developing his ideas in isolation and later relating to his fellow citizens the truths he discovered. This notion that truth and its followers existed on the periphery of society is, of course, an axiom of the humanist tradition which existed until the advent of Karl Marx. Marx contended that truth was historical, a theoretical prelude to actions, and was therefore attainable only from within the ranks of the working classes who were alone exempt from false consciousness. The intellectual had to belong to the masses. This, for Chiaromonte, was the unfortunate relationship of the intellectual to modern society. An irony that both Marx and Chiaromonte failed to note, however, is the tendency of intellectuals in Western society to form their own stratum. But this tendency lends greater urgency, perhaps, to Chiaromonte's call for pure independence of thought. Ultimately, it is a matter of choice. Either free intellectualism is possible or it is not.

Chiaromonte's criticism of the Marxists consists of his repudiation of their determination. He rejects achievement based on necessity. He believes in free human spirit and it makes no difference whether the attacks come from the right or the left. He would resist.

For most readers in this country, the essays on drama are probably the most difficult to accept because Chiaromonte views the theater as requiring a certain positive intellectual response from an audience, whereas in America many theatergoers are content to be passive and ready for stimulation. Chiaromonte begins with a discussion of Pirandello's notion of *L'umorism*: "A writer is humorous when his attitude is one of reflection, judgment, and humanity, in other words, when the writer is a living presence in his work." A distinctive feature of the humorous writer is the rejection of the mask of objectivity. The humorist is responsible for the world he creates. This interpretation of Pirandello's technique is viewed by a number of critics as an aesthetic jab at the theaters of Brecht and Artaud. It actually opens something of a sustained moral criticism of any number of major playwrights as well as directors whom Chiaromonte holds to be contemptuous of the true end of the theater—contemplated action or thought embodied in a dramatic event. He feels that modern man is not interested in drama in the true sense but is instead concerned with action or potential action which pertains to a succession of images, movements, gestures, and words that arouse overwhelming emotions and active participation. It corresponds, says the writer, to a ritual action, "a dance or collective frenzy, in which we participate with limbs and nerves but not mind."

Chiaromonte's dramatic criticism, like his political writing, comes finally to a principled defense of humanism and reaches its peak in a direct attack on Brecht. He calls Brecht's thought Marxist in form while in substance it matches the opinions of the conservative and the philistine; it is typical of those two groups, he says, that both are interested only in situations in which they can act. "This is the reason why the conservative and the philistine really dislike either the serious theater or any form of unbiased thought or free art."

Everywhere one looks in Chiaromonte one finds the mind, but only in his drama criticism does the reader encounter inflexibility and censoriousness. For the author, the theater was the one last refuge of metaphysical decorum, of reason unhamped by reality. He could make demands of the theater that he was not foolish enough to require of the real world. A significant part of what has been sensationalist and irrational in contemporary theater can be understood in the terms Chiaromonte discusses. His ideas may be dismissed by some as merely traditionalist in nature, although, in an irrational world, traditionalism takes on a revolutionary import.

One might have wished for more literary criticism than *The Worm of Consciousness* gives us. The discussion of Dante introduces Chiaromonte's critical method, and the short essay on Moravia is a testament to the author's faith in the ability of art to shed light upon experience. His pieces on Pirandello and Artaud are sensitive, but his attitude toward the theater was not the same as his attitutde toward poetry and fiction. Nevertheless, his concerns as a literary critic are apparent, and again his favorite themes are reason, clarity, lucidity, and the need for a truthful relation to things.

The true nature of all authentic poetry, states Chiaromonte, is a mastery of the senses and feelings "by the mind and techne alone"—together with an immediate and substantial contact of mind with the nature of things. He expects of literature a logical cogency and architectural pattern in its rendering of experience. He seeks the very linkage of consciousness to its world. This is a major reason for his admiration for Alberto Moravia's novel *The Empty Canvas*, which attempts to capture the initial intersection of consciousness with the objects around it—those swift and abrupt moments when objects come alive to become vehicles for human awareness. Chiaromonte's intellectual view of literature is not as pronounced in these essays as in his criticisms of the theater, and the reader may come away disappointed at not having more examples of the author's literary criticism for study in this collection.

On the whole, *The Worm of Consciousness* is an impressive collection of essays. The selections are characterized by plainness and economy of style—qualities notably missing from much modern critical writing. A certain self-discipline is also evident in Chiaromonte's style, making each essay a slow, steady journey with each step slowly building on the preceding one. The guide is reason. Thus, his well-reasoned essays serve as touchstones—simple, concise and intelligent examples of what modern political and critical writing should be.

It is a characteristic of our society, perhaps, that Chiaromonte's death in 1972 should have prompted an awakening of interest in his writings. The young generation that will discover his thought in *The Worm of Consciousness* may well demonstrate a greater affinity for his ideas than did his own generation, which was uncomfortable with him because he could not be neatly classified or assigned to a dominant belief.

Stephen Hanson

Sources for Further Study

Booklist. LXXII, April 15, 1976, p. 1144.

Choice. XIII, July, 1976, p. 65.

Dissent. XXIII, Fall, 1976, p. 443.

New York Times Book Review. July 11, 1976, p. 25.

New Yorker. LII, September 20, 1976, p. 147.

AUTHOR INDEX

I

II

AUTHOR INDEX

III